Communications
in Computer and Information Science   1174

Commenced Publication in 2007
Founding and Former Series Editors:
Phoebe Chen, Alfredo Cuzzocrea, Xiaoyong Du, Orhun Kara, Ting Liu,
Krishna M. Sivalingam, Dominik Ślęzak, Takashi Washio, Xiaokang Yang,
and Junsong Yuan

More information about this series at http://www.springer.com/series/7899

Mohammed I. Khalaf · Dhiya Al-Jumeily ·
Alexei Lisitsa (Eds.)

Applied Computing to Support Industry

Innovation and Technology

First International Conference, ACRIT 2019
Ramadi, Iraq, September 15–16, 2019
Revised Selected Papers

 Springer

Editors
Mohammed I. Khalaf
Al Maaref University College
Ramadi, Iraq

Dhiya Al-Jumeily 🆔
Liverpool John Moores University
Liverpool, UK

Alexei Lisitsa 🆔
University of Liverpool
Liverpool, UK

ISSN 1865-0929   ISSN 1865-0937 (electronic)
Communications in Computer and Information Science
ISBN 978-3-030-38751-8   ISBN 978-3-030-38752-5 (eBook)
https://doi.org/10.1007/978-3-030-38752-5

This Springer imprint is published by the registered company Springer Nature Switzerland AG
The registered company address is: Gewerbestrasse 11, 6330 Cham, Switzerland

Preface

The First International Conference on Applied Computing Research to Support Industry: Innovation and Technology (ACRIT 2019), was hosted and organized by the Al-Maarif University College, Ramadi, Iraq, during September 15–16, 2019. ACRIT is an international conference focused on the latest topics related to Computer Science, Computer Networks and Security, Data Science, Artificial Intelligence (AI), and Machine Learning.

Recent years have witnessed a dramatic increase in applied computing for solving real-world problems due to the significant improvement and advancements in information technologies. A variety of applications, such as AI systems, robotics, sensors technology, communication networks, and the Internet of Things (IoT), have helped industry to solve a number of real-world problems. There is a large number of applications proved the practical potential of several domains as significant, and their popularity is rising. For most of the scientists and engineers introducing applied computing into practice looking at the growing number of new approaches, and understanding their theoretical principles and potential for value creation has become an increasingly difficult task.

The main aims of this conference is to gather state-of-art solutions to provide a robust system with the ability to operate in dynamic and changing environments, including methods for industry and real-world problems. All of the submitted manuscripts addressed either a theoretical or practical perspective that related to an aspect of the conference, as well as contributions presenting relevant applications. However, the theme for this conference was "Applied Computing Research to Support Industry." Papers focusing on this theme were solicited, addressing applications in science and technology.

ACRIT 2019 received 159 submission from 21 countries around the world. All manuscripts underwent through a rigorous peer-review process and each paper received a minimum of three peer reviewers. Based on the review reports, the Program Committee decided to select and accept only 39 papers among 159 long and short papers, which were arranged into 4 tracks, resulting in a strong program with an acceptance rate of less than 25%, to be included in this volume of proceedings published by Springer: Communications in Computer and Information Science (CCIS). The selected papers were distributed into main tracks including: Theory, Method and Tools; Computer Security and Cryptography; Computer Network and Communication; and Application Fields in Information Science and Technology.

We would like to thank the Program Committee, locally and internationally, and the reviewers for their collective time and effort in reviewing and soliciting the papers. Special thanks go to Alfred Hofmann, Vice-President Publishing, Amin Mobasheri and Alla Serikova, Computer Science Editor, Saravanan Gnanaprakasam, Project Manager, for their continuous support in publishing the proceedings. Finally, we also owe a great debt to all the researchers who submitted high-quality papers to our conference: ACRIT 2019.

December 2019

Mohammed I. Khalaf
Dhiya Al-Jumeily
Alexei Lisitsa

Organization

General Chair

Mohammed Abdulhakim
  Al-Saadi
University of Malaya, Malaysia

Conference Co-chairs

Hoshang Kolivand
Liverpool John Moores University, UK

Malik Ghazi Qasaimeh
Princess Sumaya University for Technology, Jordan

Technical Program Committee

Mohammed I. Khalaf
Al-Maarif University College, Iraq

Mahmood Al-Saadi
Al-Maarif University College, Iraq

Thar Baker
Liverpool John Moores University, UK

Li Zhang
Northumbria University, UK

International Steering Committee Chairs

Abir Hussain
Liverpool John Moores University, UK

Hissam Tawfik
Leeds Beckett University, UK

Publication Chairs

Jade Hind
Liverpool John Moores University, UK

Ahmed Jasim Mohammed
University of Anbar, Iraq

Keynote Speakers

Abir Hussain
Liverpool John Moores University, UK

Alexei Lisitsa
The University of Liverpool, UK

Jamila Mustafina
Kazan Federal University, Russia

Hilal A. Fadhil
Al-Farabi University, Iraq

Steering Committee

Mohannad Abdulsttar Hameed
Al-Maarif University College, Iraq

Mohamed Bahjat Naeem
Al-Maarif University College, Iraq

Basim Al-Khashab
University of Mosul, Iraq

Mohammad Abdulrahman
  Rajab
Al-Maarif University College, Iraq

Jwan K. Alwan	University of Information Technology and Communication, Iraq
Ali Al-Nooh	University of Mosul, Iraq
Ahmed Jasim Mohammed	University of Anbar, Iraq
Mohammed Khaild Al-Omar	Al-Maarif University College, Iraq
Azmi Shawkat Abdulbaqi	University of Anbar, Iraq
Mohammed A. Abdulhameed	Imam Azam College, Iraq
Omer Abdulrahman Dawood	University of Anbar, Iraq
Mohammed Basil Abdulkarim	Al-Maarif University College, Iraq
Idress Mohammed Husien	University of Kirkuk, Iraq
Essa Ibrahim Al-Juborie	University of Kirkuk, Iraq
Akeel Thulnoon Abdulraheem	University of Anbar, Iraq
Khudair Abd Thamer	Al-Maarif University College, Iraq
Mustafa Salam Kadhm	Imam Ja'afar Al-Sadiq University, Iraq
Hussam Jasim Mohammed	University of Anbar, Iraq
Hazem Hakoush Maarj	Al-Maarif University College, Iraq
Balasem Al-Janabi	University of Technology, Iraq
Dhafar Hamed Abd	Al-Maarif University College, Iraq
Shihab Hamad Khaleefah	Al-Maarif University College, Iraq
Mohammed Esmat Sino	Al-Maarif University College, Iraq
Areej Adnan Abed	Al-Maarif University College, Iraq
Aymen Jalil Abdulelah	Maarif University College, Iraq
Ahmed Hashim Mohammed	Al-Mustansiriyah University, Iraq
Qahtan Majeed Yas	University of Diyala, Iraq
Khattab M. Ali Alheeti	University of Anbar, Iraq

International Scientific Committee

Salama A. Mostafa Alabdullah	University Tun Hussein Onn, Malaysia
Ala Al Kafri	Liverpool John Moors University, UK
Rozaida Ghazali	Universiti Tun Hussein Onn, Malaysia
Ibrahim Idowu	Liverpool John Moors University, UK
Hoshang Kolivand	Liverpool John Moores University, UK
Abir Hussain	Liverpool John Moores University, UK
Dhiya Aljumeily	Liverpool John Moores University, UK
Alexei Lisitsa	The University of Liverpool, UK
Thar Baker	Liverpool John Moores University, UK
Suparawadee Trongtortam	Naresuan University, Thailand
Amando P. Singun Jr.	Higher College of Technology in Muscat, Oman
Sud Sudirman	Liverpool John Moors University, UK
Malik Ghazi Qasaimeh	Princess Sumaya University for Technology, Jordan
Shumoos T. Al-Fahdawi	University of Bradford, UK
Pimsara Yaklai	Naresuan University, Thailand
Li Zhang	Northumbria University, UK
Casimiro A. Curbelo Montañez	Liverpool John Moors University, UK

Jamila Mustafina	Institute at Kazan Federal University, Kazan, Russia
Mohammed A. Jadoo	University of Technology Sydney, Australia
Aine MacDermott	Liverpool John Moores University, UK
Chitinout Wattana	Naresuan University, Thailand
Saleh Mustafa Abu-Soud	Princess Sumaya University for Technology, Jordan
Alaa Al-Waisy	University of Bradford, UK
Omar Sami Thiab	Warsaw University of Technology, Poland
Bilal Hamid Abduljabbar	University of Southern Queensland, Australia
Phillip Kendrick	Liverpool John Moors University, UK
Andi Besse Firdausiah Mansur	King Abdulaziz University, Saudi Arabia
Moamin A. Mohmoud	University Tenga National, Uniten, Malaysia
Ali Al-Atababy	University of Liverpool, UK
Syed Zahurul Islam	Olympia University College, Malaysia
Jade Hind	Liverpool John Moores University, UK
Bal Singh	Leeds Beckett University, UK
Wachira Punpairoj	Naresuan University, Thailand
Ahmad Hoirul Basori	King Abdulaziz University, Saudi Arabia
Rawaa Al-Jumeily	Belvedere British School, UAE
Aida Mustapha	Universiti Tun Hussein Onn, Malaysia
Abayomi Otebolaku	University of Sheffield, UK
Kevin Kam Fung Yuen	Singapore University of Social Sciences, Singapore
Mutinta Ngululu Mwansa	Liverpool John Moores University, UK
David Tully	Liverpool John Moores University, UK
Mohammad Alauthman	Zarqa University, Jordan
William Hurts	Liverpool John Moores University, UK
Attakrai Punpukdee	Naresuan University, Thailand
Pual Fargus	Liverpool John Moores University, UK
Mohamed Alloghani	Abu Dhabi Health Service Company (SEHA), UAE
Udomlak Srichuachom	Naresuan University, Thailand
John Henry	Manchester Metropolitan University, UK
Shamaila Iram	University of Huddersfield, UK
Shan Luo	University of Liverpool, UK
Omar Al-Dhaibani	Liverpool John Moors University, UK

Additional Reviewers

Mohammed Majeed Alkhabet	Susan A. Zwyea
Mohammad Khamees Khaleel	Amando P. Singun, Jr.
Murtadha Mohammed Al-Hetee	Abd Alaesawi
Sin Ying Tan	Hiba B. Alwan
Dheyaa Ibrahim Ahmed	Duraid Yehya Mohammed
Osama Awad	Atheer Bassel Abdulkareem
Manal Obaid Hamzah	Ali Fawzi Najm Al-Shammari
Nur Haryani Zakaria	Zinah Abdulridha Abutiheen

Ayad Hazim Al-Adhami

Belal Al-Khateeb

Hussein Ibrahim Hussein Sarhan

Nadia Mahmoud Jebril

Sarmad N. Mohammed

Khalid Shaker Alhity

Bashar Sami Bashar

Jun Qi

Mohammed Zeki Al-Faiz

Ahmed Ali

Ahmed Hameed

Khudhair Abbas Mohammed

Mustafa Maad Hamdi

Mohammed Abdallazez M.

Lafta Ali Alkhazraji

Ayad Hameed Mousa

Bassam Shaker

Ismail Taha Darej

Mohammed Subhi Hadi

Sana Ahmed Kadhim

Ahmed Jamal Ibrahim

Ahmad Bader

Ahmed Ghanim Wadday

Shafivulla Sayyed

Mohanad Hazim Nsaif

Qasim Arain

Mazin S. Al-Hakeem

Ahmed Abbas Jasim Al-Hchaimi

Al-Mutazbellah Itaiwi

Wafaa M. Salih

Karrar Muttair K.

Ragad M. Tawafak

Sinan Q. Salih

Naeem Howrie

Ijaz Khan

Muntaser Abdul-Wahed Salman

Mutinta Ngululu Mwansa

Zaid Jassim

Athraa Jani

Saif Saad Hameed

Mostafa Abdul-ghafoor Mohammed

Ihab Abdulrahman Satam

Anas M. Mzahm

Ahmad Saeed Mohammad

Hassaan Thabet

Ahmed H. Mohammed

Nada Ismail Najim

Mustafa Majeed Abd Zaid

Huthiafa Q. Qadori

Omar Al-Okashi

Mohammed W. Al-Neama

Yasir Amer Abbas

Ali Hussein Ali Alnooh

Noor Haitham Saleem Al-Ani

Abdul Mateen Ahmed

Ahmed Lateef Khalaf

Nawaf Barnouti

Omar Salim Abdullah

Sundos Alazawi

Bashar M. Nema

Sinan Al-Dabbagh

Sara Haleem Al-Sharaa

Intisar Al-Mejibli

Sadeem Al-Chalabi

Basim M. Mahmood Khashab

Osamah Ibrahim Khalaf

Marwa Adeeb Al-Jawaherry

Hamza Saad

Hassan Hadi Saleh

Asmaa Yaseen Hamo Al-Hamdani

Reem Majid Shukr

Israa A. Mishkhal

Akhilesh Kumar Sharma

Omar Ibrahim Obaid

Ahmed Abdullah

Raid Daoud

Ruqayah R. Al-Dahhan

Mazin Abed Mohammed

Sachi Mohanty

Imran Memon

Official Sponsor

Al-Maarif University College was the main sponsor for the conference and supported ACRIT 2019 financially. We would like to thank Al-Maarif University College for all the effort that made ACRIT 2019 successful.

Technical Sponsor

Applied Computing Research (ACR) Lab was the main technical sponsor of ACRIT 2019.

Contents

Computer Security and Cryptography

Computer Network and Communication

Real World Application in Information Science and Technology

Theory Methods and Tools to Support Computer Science

Lung Boundary Detection and Classification in Chest X-Rays Images Based on Neural Network

Yousif A. Hamad[1,3(✉)] [iD], Konstantin Simonov[2,3] [iD],
and Mohammad B. Naeem[2,3] [iD]

[1] Siberian Federal University, Academician Kirensky, 1st Building,
Krasnoyarsk, Krasnoyarsk Krai 660074, Russian Federation
y.albayati8@gmail.com

[2] Institute of Computational Modeling of the Siberian Branch
of the Russian Academy of Sciences, Akademgorodok Krasnoyarsk,
Krasnoyarsk Krai 660036, Russian Federation
simonovkv50@gmail.com, alnaeem2004@gmail.com

[3] Department of Computer Science, Al-Maarif University College,
Ramadi, Anbar 31001, Iraq

Abstract. The isolation of different structures is often performed on chest radiography (CXR) and the classification of abnormalities is an initial step in detection systems as computer-aided diagnosis (CAD). The shape and size of lungs may hold clues to serious diseases such as pneumothorax, pneumoconiosis and even emphysema. More than 500,000 people die in the United States every year due to heart and lung failure, often being tested for the normal CXR film. With an increasing number of patients, the doctors must over-work, hence they cannot provide the advice and take care of their patients correctly. In this case, the computer system that supports image classification and boundary CXR detection is needed. This paper presents our automated approach for lung boundary detection and CXR classification in conventional poster anterior chest radiographs. We first extract the lung region, size measurements, and shape irregularities using segmentation techniques that are used in image processing on chest radiographs. For the CXR image, we extract 18 various features using the gray level co-occurrence matrix (GLCM) which enables the CXR to be classified as normal or abnormal using the probabilistic neural network (PNN) classifier. We measure the performance of our system using two data sets: the Montgomery County (MC) x-ray dataset and the Shenzhen X-ray dataset. The proposed methodology has competitive results with relatively shorter training time and higher accuracy.

Keywords: Chest X-ray imaging · Balance Contrast Enhancement Technique · Lung boundary detection · Gray level co-occurrence matrix · Probabilistic neural network · Classification

1   Introduction

Chest radiography or chest X-ray (CXR) is still the most commonly used imaging modality for diagnosing various pulmonary diseases and the most widely used diagnostic imaging in the world due to its low radiation, free of side-effects, economic feasibility, and moderate sensitivity. Many people die annually due to chest diseases such as lung infections, pulmonary disease, and lung cancer. For most diseases, many drugs are effective only in the early stages and without symptoms of the disease. An examination can help in early diagnosis, and chest radiography is the most common method of popular imaging for the above reasons [1].

The important steps in the automatic analysis of chest x-ray images in the chest are to accurately detect the lung boundaries and classify them to normal and abnormal. It is an early diagnostic tool commonly used in clinical settings to monitor defects in the heart, including the lungs, heart, bleeding, fusion, breast surgery, pleural effusion, edema, cardiac hypertrophy, and hypertrophy [2]. In some diagnostic cases, the information is based on images directly related to the border and easy without further analysis. For example, the availability of irregular shape, volume measurements, total lung volume [3] evidence of serious diseases such as heart enlargement [4] pneumonia, pneumonia, or emphysema [5].

There have been many studies on the discovery of lung abnormalities in the past. Computer-assisted diagnosis (CAD) has become part of routine clinical work in many countries. The discovery of chest x-ray lung areas is an important component, especially in determining whether the lung is normal or abnormal [6]. The detection of lung fields is usually the first important step in the computerized analysis of chest radiography. Once you know the limits of the lung fields, further assessment of the condition of the lungs can be made [7].

Neural networks are a relatively modern programming methodology for computers. They are excellent in performing many tasks that cannot be performed by artificial intelligence and machine learning such as pattern recognition. Programs that use Artificial Neural networks (ANN) can achieve self-learning and will be able to cope with changing circumstances [8]. ANN is a methodology for processing information with key ideas inspired by the mechanism of human minds to process information. In other words, ANN is inspired by human neurotransmitters.

Neural network applications in computer diagnostics are the main direction of computing Intelligence in medical imaging [9]. Their penetration and participation in almost all-inclusive. Health problems due to the fact that: (1) neural networks have the adaptive nature of learning input Information, using the appropriate learning algorithm, can improve itself depending on the variety and Change the input content, (2) neural networks have the ability to improve the relationship between; Input and output through distributed computing, training and processing, leading to the reliable solutions required Specifications; (3) The medical diagnosis is based on a visual examination and provides most of the medical imaging. An important tool to facilitate this verification and visualization. In the training process, the connection line tables are frequently corrected so that the network can resolve the current problem. Gained deep neural networks or automated learning in general, popular in recent years due to outstanding performance in several difficult images analysis problems, such as image classification and detecting objects and the segmentation of semantics [10]. In particular, the radiologist can help reduce the workload. There are several suggested classification methods to resolve this issue. At present, there are common ways to solve image classification problems, such as K-Mean, K-NN, deep neural network and vector support machine (SVM). The convolutional neural network (CNN) is one of the deep learning models that has received considerable attention from researchers in recent years. It is frequently used in image classification, image recognition, language translation, medical diagnoses, and many other fields, etc. [11].

In the proposed method, the first stage presents contrast enhancement of CXR using the Balance Contrast Enhancement Technique (BCET), and segmentation techniques that are used in image processing on chest radiographs to identify the lungs region, size measurements, and shape irregularities. And the second stage is to extract features from chest x-ray images using the gray level co-occurrence matrix (GLCM). In the end, a classification of the normal and abnormal CXR is conducted by using PNN. When tested on a public database of chest x-ray images, the proposed method achieved comparable and higher accuracy on most of the structures than the state-of-the-art segmentation methods.

The rest of the paper is organized as follows. In Sect. 2 the related work is analyzed. Section 3 provides details of materials and methods for lung boundaries detection and classification of CXR images to normal and abnormal. In Sect. 4, the experimental study is described and the main results obtained are presented. The conclusions are given in Sect. 5.

2 Related Works

The advent of digital chest radiography CXR and digital image processing have given new impetus to computer diagnostics and diagnostics. However, despite its presence in medical practice, the CXR standard is a very complex visualization tool. A deep learning neural network methodology used to help clinicians identify stenosis of the lumbar spine through semantic segmentation and identification of scans of magnetic resonance imaging (MRI) of the lumbar spine [12]. And the work in [13] addresses to automatic tomography of the lumbar MRI to determine the border between the anterior arch and the posterior arch of the lumbar spine. This is necessary to effectively identify the occurrence of stenosis of the lumbar spine as the main cause of chronic lower back pain. And a separate training group is created for each region, and the final rating is by voting and weighted integration. Image processing techniques are used on chest radiographs to determine lung area, size measurements, and shape irregularities using segmentation methods [14]. Besides, they use the difference between the corresponding regions in the left and right fields of the lungs as markers

To classify images of TB, it is proposed to classify images of TB using the Multi-Layer Perceptron (MLP) neural network activated by Support Vector Machine (SVM) and the results are compared with the state-of-the-art approach, Back Propagation Neural Network (BPNN) [15]. Ways to detect natural and pathological forms of tuberculosis should increase the classification accuracy, to a large extent both on the image and at the level of the object. Chest x-ray using an anatomical atlas with undiluted registration in [16] suggested methods for detecting lung boundaries that are superior to current indicators, as well as improving modern standard estimates of abnormal lung forms. Computer diagnostics are used to detect pulmonary tuberculosis during a chest x-ray, lung proliferation, as well as texture and shape. Features of extraction, classification using vector support machines to achieve high accuracy [17]. A hierarchical graph of directional gradients [17] using the edge map, to automate the examination of pulmonary anomalies. To distinguish normal and abnormal CXR images using the corresponding chest edge, first translate the area of interest (ROI). In [18] the subsystems of textual, focal, and shape distortions are combined into one system to deal with heterogeneity. An abnormal expression in different population groups. Performance on tuberculosis screening and TB database is open using both External and radiological reference standards [18]. In [19] this work is a way to classify CXRs into two parts: TB and non-TB. Depending on the ways the shape is selected, the structure is considered an advantage, then combed and categorized by classification such as SVM and CNN.

3 The Proposed System

As mentioned above, the purpose of this work is to develop methods of segmentation and classification of x-ray chest, which can determine the limits of lung regions and abnormalities in the form of X-rays. During the design of our method, there was a set of design objectives kept in our mind. These set of design objectives include:

- Extracting the minimal set of features that distinguish between normal and abnormal X-ray images.
- Achieving high accuracy of segmentation lung boundaries and classification.
- Minimizing the time required for the process of segmentation and classification.

The main purpose of the proposed method to lung boundary detection automatically and classification from the chest X-ray images. The extracted information from the segmented image is useful in computer vision applications and to identify constituent parts in the image. The PNN workbook showed good accuracy, very short training time, resistance to weight changes and small retraining time. The results-based performance will be analyzed at the end of the development phase. The final output of the proposed method is lung boundary detection and either normal or abnormal chest X-ray image. A detailed block diagram of the proposed method is shown in Fig. 1.

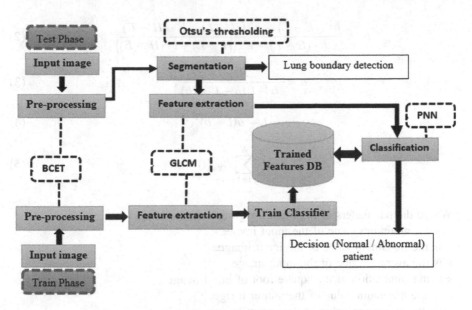

Fig. 1. A detailed block diagram for the proposed method.

3.1 Preprocessing

The primary task of pretreatment is to improve the quality of X-ray images of the chest and to make them suitable for further processing by human or computer vision. Pre-processing helps to improve certain parameters of chest x-ray images such as improving the signal-to-noise ratio and enhancing the visual appearance of the chest x-ray images, removing the irrelevant noise and undesired parts in the background. To improve the contrast for highlighting the area of interest the researchers proposed to use Balance Contrast Enhancement Technique (BCET). Typically, during medical image processing, the contrast enhancement is required for the area of interest. The work of Kumbhara, Patila, and Rudrakshi ware used in [20] to harmonize the limited variance restriction (CLAHE) to improve the performance of medical images for appropriate diagnosis. Unsharp masking is another interesting approach to image enhancement. It aims to enhance the edges and details, but the usage of a high-pass filter also makes the method extremely sensitive to noise [20].

The images can be extended or contrasted without changing the (I_{Old}) image graph pattern. The solution depends on the equivalent function obtained from the input image. The general form of an equivalent function is defined as follows:

$$I_{New} = a \cdot (I_{old} - b)^2 + c . \tag{1}$$

Transactions A, B, and C are derived from the input value, the minimum image output value (I_{New}), the maximum image output value, and the average image output value

$$b = \frac{h^2 \cdot (E - L) - s \cdot (H - L) + l^2 \cdot (H - E)}{2 \cdot [h \cdot (E - L) - e \cdot (H - L) + l \cdot (H - E)]}, \tag{2}$$

$$a = \frac{H - L}{(h - l)(h + l - 2b)}, \tag{3}$$

$$c = L - a(l - b)^2, \tag{4}$$

$$s = \frac{1}{N} \sum_{i=1}^{N} I_{Old}^2(i). \tag{5}$$

Where the parameters of the input image and output images as:

l is the minimum value of the input image.

h is the maximum value of the input image.

e is the average value of the input image.

s is the summation of the square root of input image.

L is the minimum value of the output image.

H is the maximum value of the output image.

3.2 Segmentation

In medical CXR images, lung regions are segmented. The higher segmentation accuracy in medical image analysis identifies the disease more precisely. There are two approaches in segmentation they are discontinuity and similarity-based approaches. Discontinuity based approach is used for identifying isolated points, lines and edges in an image (ex-identifying lung boundary in CXR). Similarity-based approach is the grouping of similar intensity values in an image. The operation in this approach is clustering, thresholding, region splitting, and merging. The lung segmentation based on geometric features like object edge, circularity and image size has long been introduced to isolate the lung region from other anatomies inside the CXR image. Segmenting the lung with edge detection is fundamental and essential in the pre-processing step because edges represent important contour features within the corresponding image [21].

3.3 Otsu's Thresholding Method

The Otsu thresholding is one of the similarities-based approaches, which is simpler to divide the image into two regions. Let's assume that the image has a dark object toward the light background or vice versa. The intensity values in the image are mainly concentrated near two regions, whereas the dark areas consist of low-intensity values or photoreceptors of higher intensity values. In the case of CXR, the dark object means the lungs and others are its backgrounds. After lung segmentation, the lung boundary detected using canny edge detection filters. An example shown in the Fig. 2, Obtained segmented chest x-ray image will be helpful in the medical diagnosis. Additional, our segmentation method allows getting the size of the left lung, right lung, and all lung.

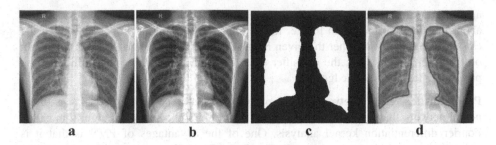

Fig. 2. (a) Is the source CXR image of a patient, (b) result after pre-processing, (c) result of modified segmentation and (d) lung boundary detection.

3.4   Feature Extraction

The GLCM is a robust way of statistical image analysis. It's used to evaluation of images features regarding second-order statistics, by looking at the link between two neighboring pixels in one offset as the second-order texture. GLCM Texture Measurement is a method of analyzing image texture. This is a powerful way to calculate the properties of the first and second-order of an image. In addition, the GLCM matrix represents a schedule of occurrence of different combinations of gray levels in an image. The accuracy of the classification depends on the quality of the extracted features. The gray level co-occurrence matrix is a robust way of statistical image analysis. It is used for the evaluation of images features regarding second-order statistics. GLCM is defined as a two-dimensional matrix of joint probabilities between pairs of pixels over an image (I) as the distribution of co-occurring values at a given offset (dx, dy) for an image with size N × M:

$$C_{dx,dy}(i,j) = \sum_{p=1}^{N} \sum_{q=1}^{M} \begin{cases} 1, & if\ I(p,q) = i\ and\ I(p+dx,\ q+dy) = j \\ 0, & otherwise \end{cases} \quad (6)$$

Features were chosen after Gómez et al. [22]: Energy (F8), Contrast (F2), Correlation (F3), Autocorrelation (F1), Entropy (F9), Homogeneity (F10), Dissimilarity (F7), Cluster Shade (F6), Cluster Prominence (F5), Maximum Probability (F12), Sum Of Square (F13), Inverse Difference Moment (F21), Sum Average (F14), Sum Variance (F16), Sum Entropy (F15), Difference Variance (F17), Difference Entropy (F18) and Information Measure Of Correlation (F19).

In our work, we have tried different dataset values in computing the GLCM matrix. In order to obtain better classification results, GLCM matrixes were generated for different offsets (from 2 to 4 pixels) and angles (0°, 45°, 90°, and 135°).

3.5   Classification

Neural networks are a relatively modern programming methodology for computers. Probabilistic neural network (PNN) is effective machine learning technique for classification and regression. In this stage of the test phase. Given a grey level image, after applying the feature extraction steps, the PNN classifier is used to make a decision about the status of the given image. It is a binary classification process in which the classifier determines whether the given image is a normal or abnormal CXR image. In order to perform its role, the classifier uses the extracted features in addition to the previously learned knowledge.

Probabilistic Neural Network: A probabilistic neural network (PNN) is a direct neural network that depends on a Bayesian algorithm and a statistical algorithm called Fourier differentiation kernel analysis. One of the advantages of PNN is that it is insensitive to emissions. As shown in Fig. 3, the PNN file consists of four layers: the input layer, hidden layer, template layer/composite layer, output layer. We used this algorithm to distinguish a normal image from a stego [23]. The workbook is used to detect abnormal x-rays. To do this, we use PNN, which classifies vectors as calculated as normal or abnormal, regardless of whether the x-ray image on the chest is affected with TB or not.

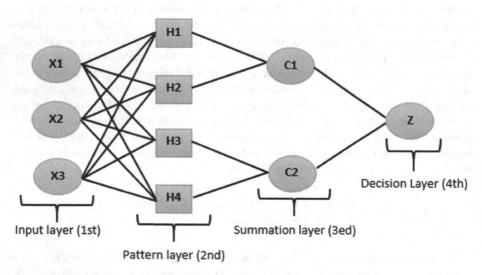

Fig. 3. The structure of a typical probabilistic neural network.

4 Experiments

In this work, we used two datasets, the Montgomery County chest X-ray set (MC) and Shenzhen chest X-ray set [24] to assess the proposed lung boundary detection and classification method. The MC group was assembled in collaboration with the Department of Health and Human Services of Montgomery County, Maryland, and USA. The group contains 138 X-ray images of a screening program for tuberculosis in the Montgomery district, of which 80 are normal and 58 with manifestations of tuberculosis (TB). And the Shenzhen dataset was collected in collaboration with Shenzhen No.3 People's Hospital, Guangdong Medical College, and Shenzhen, China.

The chest X-rays are from outpatient clinics and were captured as part of the daily hospital routine within a 1-month period, using a Philips DR Digital Diagnose system. The set contains 662 frontal chest X-rays, of which 326 are normal cases and 336 are cases with manifestations of TB. The X-rays are provided in PNG and DICOM format. The size of the X-rays is either 4,020 × 4,892 or 4,892 × 4,020 pixels for Montgomery County chest X-ray set and 3K × 3K pixels for Shenzhen chest X-ray set. The proposed system was implemented under a MATLAB2016 platform, windows7 OS, and Intel core i5-2400@1.6 GHZ CPU.

For lung boundary detection we compute the figure of merit (FOM), Jaccard similarity coefficient Ω, sensitivity and accuracy and compared with the works in [2, 6, 12, 15], and [20], our method outperforms all the other methods. Besides, our qualitative results are shown in Fig. 4.

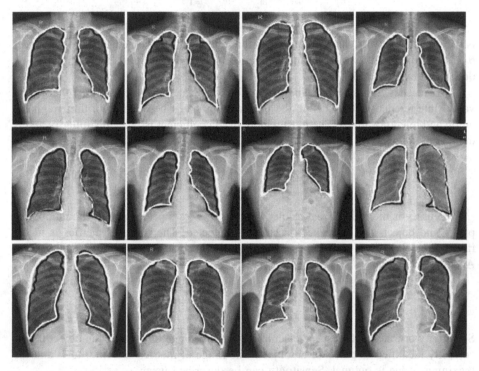

Fig. 4. Lung boundary detection results of our method on the used dataset. The green contour indicates the ground truth while the red contour is generated by using our method. We get a high-quality lung region annotation that is comparable to manually labeled ground truth. (Color figure online)

To assess the reliability and correctness of detection of the lung border obtained by the proposed method, the following parameters were used: Pratt's Merit Index (*FOM*),

Jaccard similarity coefficient Ω, sensitivity, and accuracy. These parameters are mainly based on the values of TP, TN, FP, FN, and RECnt, where TP is the number of correctly selected pixels as tumor lines, TN is the number of pixels correctly detected as background, FP is the number of fake pixels defined as lung borders, and FN - The number of pixels erroneously identified as background. It represents the number of link edges (RE_{Cnt}) the edge of the number of pixels of a reference map created by an expert.

Pratt's Merit Index (PMI) is another useful measure for evaluating the performance of edge detectors. This measure uses the distance between all pairs of corresponding points to determine the difference between the flaps. The PMI, which evaluates contour similarity, is defined as:

$$PMI = \frac{1}{\max(RE_{Cnt}, AE_{Cnt})} \cdot \sum_{i=1}^{AE_{Cnt}} \frac{1}{1 + \alpha \cdot d_i^2} \tag{7}$$

where RE_{Cnt} and AE_{Cnt} are two ideal numbers (ref) and the actual point of the edge, di is the distance between the edge of the pixel and the nearest pixel edge of the reference, α is the experiment with constant calibration ($\alpha = 1/9$ was used, the optimal value developed by Pratt [25]).

PMI reaches a maximum value of one for identical, and gives contrast the lowest value. Interference metrics define the overlapping space between algorithm fragmentation and reference limits. The most widely used coefficient is Jaccard similarity and is defined as follows:

$$\Omega = \frac{Tp}{TP + FP + FN} \tag{8}$$

Accuracy is the ratio of real results. Accuracy gives a percentage of the number of pixels and objects that have been accurately detected. The range of metrics is in the range from 0 to 1. If the accuracy value is 1, the result will be the same record. Accuracy is defined as:

$$Accuracy = \frac{TP + TN}{TP + TN + FP + FN} \tag{9}$$

Sensitivity or true positive speed calculates the percentage of pixels in an object that is correctly identified as pixels of an object. The range of metrics is from 0 to 1, and the maximum value is optimal. Sensitivity can be described using:

$$Sensivity = \frac{TP}{TP + FN} \tag{10}$$

Table 1 demonstrates several techniques for the formation of a lung boundary detection for the model images shown in Fig. 4.

Table 1. Quantitative of lung boundary detection of the proposed method.

patients	Ω	FOM	Sensitivity	Accuracy
Patient 1	0,9662	0,9725	0,9533	0,9600
Patient 2	0,9736	0,9717	0,9488	0,9592
Patient 3	0,9365	0,9287	0,9312	0,9730
Patient 4	0,9554	0,9296	0,9224	0,9429
Patient 5	0,9547	0,9621	0,9507	0,9661
Patient 6	0,9436	0,9339	0,9187	0,9320
Patient 7	0,9677	0,9646	0,9600	0,9466
Patient 8	0,9569	0,9556	0,9743	0,9712
Patient 9	0,9752	0,9654	0,9604	0,9549
Patient 10	0,9652	0,9403	0,9560	0,9427
Patient 11	0,9584	0,9369	0,9699	0,9568
Patient 12	0,9636	0,9702	0,9560	0,9702

Two different experiments have been conducted to evaluate the performance of the classifiers. The first one used dataset 1 features while the second one used dataset 2 features. The results are shown in Table 2 and Fig. 5.

Table 2. The results of the proposed system using PNN classifier based on dataset 1 and dataset 2.

The sets	No. of images in the tests	Dataset 1		No. of images in the tests	Dataset 2	
		Ratio of correctly classified images	Ratio of incorrectly classified images		Ratio of correctly classified images	Ratio of incorrectly classified images
Normal images	75	95.94%	4.06%	99	96.89%	3.11%
Abnormal images	50	94.98%	5.02%	99	95.77%	4.23%
Total	125	95.93%	4.11%	198	96.73%	3.15%

From Table 2 we conclude that the dataset 2 get a better result than the dataset 1. Where the accuracy of dataset 2 is 96.73%, but the accuracy of dataset 1 is 95.93%. Where the ratio of correctly classified images from normal chest x-ray image increased from 95.94% in dataset 1 to 96.89% in dataset 2, and the ratio of correctly classified images from an abnormal chest x-ray images increased from 94.98% in dataset 1 to 95.77% in dataset 2. While the ratio of incorrectly classified images from normal chest x-ray images decreased from 4.06% in dataset 1 to 3.11% in dataset 2, and the ratio of incorrectly classified images from an abnormal chest x-ray images decreased from 5.02% in dataset 1 to 4.23% in dataset 2. We note the dataset 2 give the high ability to the PNN to detecting normal or abnormal chest x-ray image.

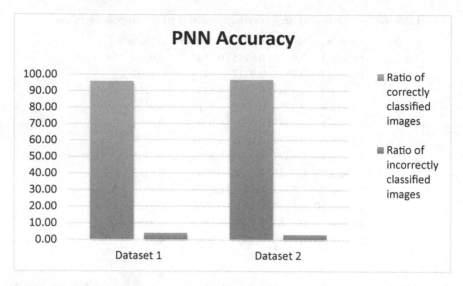

Fig. 5. The accuracy of the proposed system using PNN classifier

5   Conclusion

In this study, we developed a methodology that allowed us to create an automated system for detecting the boundaries of lung and classifying CXR images. The proposed methodology consists of three main stages. Initially, CXR image enhancement is performed by reducing noise and adjusting the contrast. The lung areas are then detected. After that, we calculate the CXR extraction feature set after optimization as input for a PNN workbook, which classifies the selected input image as normal or abnormal. The proposed method of rapid detection and accuracy of the lung area is consistent with other methods according to the similarity of Jaccard and Dyce. The average values for these indicators are 0.915 and 0.955 in contrast. A PNN-based workbook shows good results with moderate detection accuracy on CXR images. Thus, a correct estimate of an average of 94.98–95.77% depends on the data set. Images classified incorrectly with pathology are about 4–5%, which is not enough for full automation. However, a system based on the proposed methods can be used as an auxiliary component for medical professionals.

References

1. Ahmad, W.S.H.M.W., Zaki, W.M.D.W., Fauzi, M.F.A., Tan, W.H.: Classification of infection and fluid regions in chest x-ray images. In: 2016 International Conference on Digital Image Computing: Techniques and Applications (DICTA) (2016)
2. Candemir, S., et al.: Lung segmentation in chest radiographs using anatomical atlases with nonrigid registration. IEEE Trans. Med. Imaging **33**, 577–590 (2014)

3. Carrascal, F.M., Carreira, J.M., Souto, M., Tahoces, P.G., Gómez, L., Vidal, J.J.: Automatic calculation of total lung capacity from automatically traced lung boundaries in postero-anterior and lateral digital chest radiographs. Med. Phys. **25**, 1118–1131 (1998)
4. Meyers, P.H., Nice, C.M., Becker, H.C., Nettleton, W.J., Sweeney, J.W., Meckstroth, G.R.: Automated computer analysis of radiographic images. Radiology **83**, 1029–1034 (1964)
5. Coppini, G., Miniati, M., Monti, S., Paterni, M., Favilla, R., Ferdeghini, E.M.: A computer-aided diagnosis approach for emphysema recognition in chest radiography. Med. Eng. Phys. **35**, 63–73 (2013)
6. Li, X., Chen, L., Chen, J.: A visual saliency-based method for automatic lung regions extraction in chest radiographs. In: 2017 14th International Computer Conference on Wavelet Active Media Technology and Information Processing (ICCWAMTIP) (2017)
7. Iakovidis, D.K.: Versatile approximation of the lung field boundaries in chest radiographs in the presence of bacterial pulmonary infections. In: 2008 8th IEEE International Conference on BioInformatics and BioEngineering (2008)
8. Gurney, K.: An Introduction to Neural Networks. CRC Press, Boca Raton (2014)
9. Anwar, S.M., Majid, M., Qayyum, A., Awais, M., Alnowami, M., Khan, M.K.: Medical image analysis using convolutional neural networks: a review. J. Med. Syst. **42**, 226 (2018)
10. Wang, C.: Segmentation of multiple structures in chest radiographs using multi-task fully convolutional networks. In: Sharma, P., Bianchi, F.M. (eds.) SCIA 2017. LNCS, vol. 10270, pp. 282–289. Springer, Cham (2017). https://doi.org/10.1007/978-3-319-59129-2_24
11. Kieu, P.N., Tran, H.S., Le, T.H., Le, T., Nguyen, T.T.: Applying multi-CNNs model for detecting abnormal problem on chest x-ray images. In: 2018 10th International Conference on Knowledge and Systems Engineering (KSE) (2018)
12. Al-Kafri, A.S., et al.: Boundary delineation of MRI images for lumbar spinal stenosis detection through semantic segmentation using deep neural networks. IEEE Access **7**, 43487–43501 (2019)
13. Kafri, A.S.A., et al.: Segmentation of lumbar spine MRI images for stenosis detection using patch-based pixel classification neural network. In: 2018 IEEE Congress on Evolutionary Computation (CEC) (2018)
14. Jaeger, S., Karargyris, A., Antani, S., Thoma, G.: Detecting tuberculosis in radiographs using combined lung masks. In: 2012 Annual International Conference of the IEEE Engineering in Medicine and Biology Society (2012)
15. Priya, E., Srinivasan, S.: Automated object and image level classification of TB images using support vector neural network classifier. Biocybern. Biomed. Eng. **36**, 670–678 (2016)
16. Candemir, S., Antani, S.: A review on lung boundary detection in chest x-rays. Int. J. Comput. Assist. Radiol. Surg. **14**, 563–576 (2019)
17. Santosh, K.C., Vajda, S., Antani, S., Thoma, G.R.: Edge map analysis in chest x-rays for automatic pulmonary abnormality screening. Int. J. Comput. Assist. Radiol. Surg. **11**, 1637–1646 (2016)
18. Hogeweg, L., et al.: Automatic detection of tuberculosis in chest radiographs using a combination of textural, focal, and shape abnormality analysis. IEEE Trans. Med. Imaging **34**, 2429–2442 (2015)
19. Vajda, S., et al.: Feature selection for automatic tuberculosis screening in frontal chest radiographs. J. Med. Syst. **42**, 146 (2018)
20. Kumbhar, U., Patil, V., Rudrakshi, S.: Enhancement of medical images using image processing in MATLAB. Int. J. Eng. Res. Technol. **2**, 2359–2364 (2013)
21. Saad, M.N., Muda, Z., Ashaari, N.S., Hamid, H.A.: Image segmentation for lung region in chest x-ray images using edge detection and morphology. In: 2014 IEEE International Conference on Control System, Computing and Engineering, ICCSCE 2014 (2014)

22. Gómez, W., Pereira, W.C.A., Infantosi, A.F.C.: Analysis of co-occurrence texture statistics as a function of gray-level quantization for classifying breast ultrasound. IEEE Trans. Med. Imaging **31**, 1889–1899 (2012)
23. Nandhagopal, N., Gandhi, K.R., Sivasubramanian, R.: Probabilistic neural network based brain tumor detection and classification system. Res. J. Appl. Sci. Eng. Technol. **10**, 1347–1357 (2015)
24. Jaeger, S., Candemir, S., Antani, S., Wáng, Y.X.J., Lu, P.X., Thoma, G.: Two public chest x-ray datasets for computer-aided screening of pulmonary diseases. Quant. Imaging Med. Surg. **4**(6), 475 (2014)
25. Abdou, I., Pratt, W.: Quantitative design and evaluation of enhancement/thresholding edge detectors. Proc. IEEE **67**, 753–763 (1979)

Detection of Copy-Move Forgery in Digital Image Based on SIFT Features and Automatic Matching Thresholds

Muthana S. Mahdi$^{(\boxtimes)}$ (iD) and Saad N. Alsaad (iD)

Department of Computer Science, Mustansiriyah University, Baghdad, Iraq
muthanasalih007@gmail.com,
dr.alsaadcs@uomustansiriyah.edu.iq

Abstract. Today the technology age is characterized by the spread of the digital images. It's the most common form of information transmission whether through the internet or newspaper. This huge use of images technology has been accompanied by an evolution in editing tools which makes modifying and editing an image very simple. This paper proposes an effective and fast method for copy-move forgery detection. The paper adopts a SIFT technique for features extraction and wavelet technique to estimate the matching threshold. The low-frequency components are used to compute a dynamic threshold rather than a fixed threshold. Also, a method to remove false positive areas is proposed in order to produce the best possible results. The method can detect accurately and quickly the forgery even after more complex transformations. The experimental results refer that the proposed method can also detect forgery against post-processing operation and multiple copies.

Keywords: Copy-move · Image forgery · Image forgery detection · Features extraction · Digital forensics · Multimedia security

1 Introduction

In general, images are considered effective tools for human communication comparing with texts. The visual system can obtain pictorial information extremely faster than any other type of information. This information forms approximately 75% of information perceived by a visual system [1]. Nowadays different applications like newspapers, social media applications, Journals, courtrooms, and others are dealing daily with thousands of digital images. These images can be easily forged without leaving any obvious signs, due to the advancement of the digital image processing software and editing tools. Sometimes it is very difficult to know if the digital image is forged or not by the naked eyes. In many cases, the purpose of this tampering is to deliberately influence the attention of the recipient, so, it has become very important to confirm the reliability and authenticity of the images [2].

© Springer Nature Switzerland AG 2020
M. I. Khalaf et al. (Eds.): ACRIT 2019, CCIS 1174, pp. 17–31, 2020.
https://doi.org/10.1007/978-3-030-38752-5_2

1.1 Copy Move Forgery

There are many types of image forgery, but the most popular type is Copy-Move forgery (CMF) or cloning, easy to implement and difficult to detect. This type of forger copies part or parts of an image and paste to it again. The copied regions can be in any position or can have any shape, including rotation, translation, scaling, and combining of many types.

This kind of forgery is more difficult to detect than other kinds because the usual methods of detecting incompatibilities that use statistical measures to compare different parts of the image are useless for CMF detection [3]. The task of forgery detecting is becoming more difficult when the forgery image subjects to additional several possible operations of post-processing (image blurring, color reduction, noise addition, etc.) to making the forged image look more realistic.

Figure 1 shows an Iranian modify photograph released in July 2008, showing four missiles rising into the air instead of three through a test firing in an Iranian desert. Ironically, many western media, including the Los-Angeles Time and New York Times published that fake image as an authentic one [4]. The figure shows a simple example of CMF, where one of the missiles was copied and pasted only without any complex transformations.

Fig. 1. An example of copy-move forgery, the original image at the left and the tampered image at the right [5]

1.2 Copy-Move Forgery Detection

Many methods of copy-move forgery detection (CMFD) are available. But most of these methods are not robust against more complex transformations, post-processing attacks, and time-consuming. Generally, they can be classified into two main criteria: Block-based and Key-Point-based methods [6].

Copy-Move forgery detection can be performed either using one of these methods or a combination of both (as hybrid approach). In General, Keypoint-based methods work well in terms of robustness, memory usage, and computation time compared to block generation methods, but at the same time, they produce a false positive in flat regions [7].

The main steps in the detection of copy-move forgery are pre-processing, features extraction, matching, and post-processing. Figure 2 represents a general framework for detection of copy-move forgery [8].

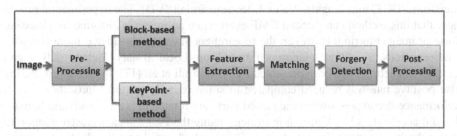

Fig. 2. General framework for copy-move forgery detection [9]

Pre-processing: This process is applied in both block-based and keypoint-based techniques. It depends on the application itself. Different preprocessing functions are applied such as convert the color image into a grayscale, dimension reduction, image resizing, and image filtering [10].

Feature Extraction: This process to extract or find the important features of the input image. The goal of feature extraction is to compute the specific representation of the data that can highlight the relevant information. Features must have two basic requirements: The redundancy in the original image should be avoided and dimensionality of data should be reduced [11].

Matching: In CMF, different parts are copied and moved to the same image, so there is a strong correlation between these parts. This can be used as evidence to detect the forgery. But the main challenge is to find effective features and matching algorithms to find the associated regions. The feature matching is performed to find a high similarity or matching between feature descriptors. If the similarity between feature descriptors is found then it's interpreted as an indicator for duplicated regions [12]. Many methods can be used to identify these similarities. The common methods either sort the feature vectors lexicographically and calculate the Euclidean distance between the adjacent stored vectors, or building the k-dimension tree (k is the number of dimensions) contain all the feature vectors and finding the k-Nearest Neighbors for each feature. However, the incorrect matches in some areas of the image can be appearing when the image contains a similar texture such as the sea or the sky, therefore, these erroneous matches should be deleted [13].

Post-processing: It helps to show the forgery regions with a certain color or shape and reduce the false matches [14].

2 Related Works

The distinguishing feature of the copy-move forgery is the copied region and pasted region are the same. So, one of the ways to detect forgery is an exhaustive search. However, this method is not possible because of its computational complexity. In recent years, many schemes have been proposed to detect a CMF [15].

Zhao and Guo [16] proposed a method to detect a CMF based on Discrete Cosine Transform (DCT) and Singular Value Decomposition (SVD). The experimental results show that this method can detect a CMF even when an image is distorted by Gaussian Noise or image blurring. However, the researchers have not considered more complex transformations. A different approach based on Local Binary Pattern (LBP) and neighbor clustering have been presented by Al-Sawadi et al. [17]. In this approach, the false positive rate was reduced compared to some recently related approaches, but its performance decomposes when the pasted parts are rotated or scaled. Fadl and Semary [18] did accelerate a block matching strategy using the Fast k-means cluster method to cluster the blocks into different classes. This method can detect the duplicated areas, reduced the time of processing, and has good accuracy except its weak against complex transformations. Lee et al. [19] divided the image into overlapping blocks and applied the histogram of orientated gradients of each block. Although this approach is capable of detecting multiple examples of CMF, it is weak with rotation and scaling over large areas. The algorithm that was developed by Khan and Kulkarni [20] of CMFD based on discrete wavelet transform (DWT) has been improved by Haimour et al. [21]. The khan algorithm works by applying a DWT first to the input image to obtain a lower representation of dimensions. Afterward, the compressed image is split into overlapping blocks using the phase correlation as a similarity criterion. These blocks are then sorted to determine the duplicated blocks. In the improved method, a set of enhancements have been applied to reduce the time complexity. The improved method can accurately and quickly detect the duplicated regions. In addition, the processing time was reduced compared with khan algorithm. However, this method insensitive to the image blur and complex transformations. Parihar et al. [22] used the localized angular phase (LAP) to extract features from each block. This method works well with a translation, image blur, and change the illumination. But they are not robust against some kinds of scaling and rotation. Almost all of the above methods are block-based which trying to find effective and strong representation for each block. Moreover, they are expected to be insensitive to common complex transformations.

Unlike block-based methods, key-point-based methods depend on the identification of high-entropy image areas which are robust against many geometric transformations such as scaling and rotation. Chen [23] proposed a method by extracting Harris corner points as key-points and using step sector statistics to represent the small circle image area around each Harris point. Singh et al. [24] employed DCT and scale invariant feature transform (SIFT) to extract the features from the image and then matching those features to detect the forgery in the image and also perform the localization of the forged regions. Recently, a different keypoint-based method using a speeded up robust features (SURF) and adaptive overlapped segmentation has been presented by Sreelakshmy et al. [25]. Yang et al. [26] presented a CMFD strategy using a strategy of keypoints distribution to keypoints selection. This strategy can detect duplicate areas. But it requires an additional cost of computational. The major drawback of most keypoint-based methods is producing false matches as false positives in flat regions [7]. Table 1 illustrates a comparison between different types of CMFD techniques.

Table 1. Comparison of different Copy-Move forgery detection techniques

Method used	Paper serial	Strength points	Weak points
DCT and SVD	[16]	Robust against noise and blurring	Not tested for more complex transformations
LBP and neighborhood clustering	[17]	The false positive rate was reduced	Not robust to rotation and scaling
Block matching strategy using the Fast k-means clustering	[18]	Reduced time complexity	Weakness against complex transformations
Block matching using the histogram of orientated gradients	[19]	Able to deal with translation, image blur, color reduction, and brightness change	Weakness against rotation and scaling over large areas
Block matching based on DWT	[20]	Reduced the dimension	Fails in case of scaling, rotation, and image blur
Block matching based on DWT improved	[21]	Processing time was reduced	Fails in case of scaling, rotation, and image blur
Block matching based on LAP	[22]	Works well with a translation, image blur, and change the illumination	Not robust against some kinds of scaling and rotation.
Harris corner keypoints and step sector statistics	[23]	Robust to several transformations	Produces false matches in flat regions
DCT and SIFT	[24]	Invariant to rotation and scaling	Relatively large time complexity
SURF and adaptive segmentation	[25]	Fast and robust to rotation and scaling	Produces a false positive in flat regions
The strategy of keypoints distribution based on SIFT	[26]	Able to detect the duplicate areas, invariant to rotation and scaling	Requires additional cost of computational

In this paper, an effective and robust detection algorithm has been developed based on SIFT features and automatic thresholds. In addition, processing to solve the false matches problem is implemented. The series of experiments conducted on realistic images of forgery showed effective detection of multiple CMF even with complex transformations (i.e. translation, rotation, scaling, and combination) and post-processing attacks (such as image blur, brightness change, and noise addition).

3   Proposed Method

The CMF in digital images can be done in one region or more. The task of detection methods is to determine whether the image contains duplicated areas or not. Since the size and shape of the duplicated areas are unknown, it's definitely computationally impossible attempt to compare pixels by pixels. In order to make a forgery detection algorithm efficient and has less computational complexity, the robust features are used.

This scheme is pictorially shown in Fig. 3. First, the input image is converted to grayscale. The SIFT algorithm is applied to extract keypoints features and their descriptors. Afterward, the ratio of the low-frequency components is computed to estimate threshold values using the wavelet technique. Then, the k-nearest neighbors of each keypoint are found and the matched keypoints which satisfy the conditions are determined. Finally, removing the false positive regions is applied. The proposed method is summarized in the Algorithm 3.1.

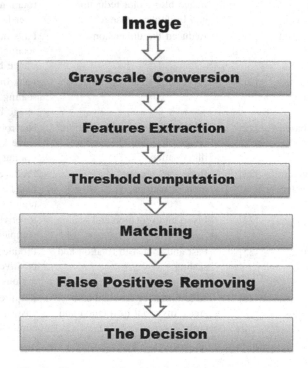

Fig. 3. The general framework of the proposed method

Algorithm 3.1 (forgery detection)

Input: Image.

Output: Decision (forged or authentic image).

Begin

    Step1: Convert the image to grayscale. // *Grayscale conversion.*

    Step2: Extract keypoints features and their descriptors using a SIFT technique. // *Features extraction.*

    Step3: Compute automatic thresholds based on low-frequency components. // *Threshold computation.*

    Step4: Euclidean distance between all key-points is computed, k-nearest neighbors of each key point are determined, and matched key points are found. // *Matching.*

    Step5: Remove the false positives. // *False positives removing.*

    Step6: Determine the image is forged or authentic. // *Decision.*

End

3.1 *Grayscale Conversion* (Preprocessing)

In order to obtain a better representation, the color image is converted to grayscale as a pre-processing step.

3.2 Features Extraction

There are a lot of key-points in each image, which can be extracted to provide a description of the image. With the implementation of the SIFT technique, a large number of the featured keypoints can be withdrawn which are invariant to different factors such as scaling or rotation and robust to change in illumination and noise. Thus, these features are considered to be very distinctive. So, the chance of finding a matching between one feature and the database of features is very probable. These characteristics are well-suited for detecting a forgery in images. In fact, the copied part has the same appearance as the original part, so keypoints extracted in that area will be exactly the same as the original. Therefore the matching of SIFT features can be used to detect the copied part. So, in this phase, the SIFT algorithm is used to extract the important keypoints of the image. Each keypoint consist of two parts: a location vector and a descriptor vector. The descriptor vector of each keypoint consists of 128 dimensions. The number of keypoints extracted is not fixed. It depends on the image itself. The details of the SIFT algorithm are illustrated in [27].

3.3 Threshold Computation

The threshold between feature vectors is one of the most important parameters to detect the CMF. This threshold depends on the image itself and varies from one image to another based on characteristics of the image (e.g. color distribution, texture, and edges).

It is worthy to mention that an image with large smooth flat regions such as sky or sea, it has large low-frequency components. Thus key-points descriptors in these regions will be similar each together because they have similar characteristics. This leads to increases the false matches (false positive) whenever the matching threshold increases.

Conversely, when the image does not contains large smooth flat regions. This leads to the emergence of some false negatives whenever the matching threshold decreases.

In both cases, the static threshold leads to increasing the regions of false positives and false negatives. So, in this phase, the automatic thresholds are used.

In order to give more precision to detect the correct matches only, the mini distance threshold has been added. Each two matched key-points have the distance between them less than the determined mini distance threshold will be rejected. Because the key-points close to each other have similar descriptors. This similarity increases as the closer between these key-points increase especially when the image contains large flat regions.

The method to estimate the automatic threshold of the matching and mini-distance has been proposed based on the ratio of low-frequency components of each image. The main steps of this method are illustrated in the Algorithm 3.2.

Algorithm 3.2 (Automatic Threshold Estimation)

Input: Image.

Output: The matching threshold and mini distance threshold.

> Begin
>> **Step1:** *DWT is applied to the input image and this process is repeated until level 4.*
>> **Step2:** *Sum of low-frequency (LF) components is computed.*
>> **Step3:** *Sum of high-frequency (HF) components is computed.*
>> **Step4:** *The low-frequency ratio (LFR) in the image is computed.*
>>> $LFR = LF / (LF + HF) * 100.$
>> **Step5:** *The matching threshold and mini distance threshold are determined based on the ratio of low-frequency components.*
>>> *If LFR >= 40 then matching threshold = 0.4 && mini distance = 50.*
>>> *If LFR < 40 then matching threshold = 0.5 && mini distance = 10.*
> End

3.4 Matching

The simplest method to match key-points is to set a constant threshold for Euclidean distance between the descriptors. However, because of the high dimensionality of the feature space, this method obtains a low accuracy because some descriptors are much more discriminative than others. Thus many features will not have any correct match.

A more effective procedure can be obtained using the ratio between the distances of the first nearest neighbor to the second nearest neighbor, then comparing it with the threshold (i.e. the so-called G-Nearest Neighbor (GNN) test). To declare the match, this percentage must be less than the determined threshold.

It is Must be noted, that in the high dimensional feature space such as SIFT features. The similar features show low Euclidean distances with each other. The idea of the GNN test is that percentage between the distance of the matching candidate and the distance of the second nearest neighbor is low in case of matching and is very high in case of two random features.

This technique works well when the area is copied one time, but not if copied several times. This is the main drawback in this procedure. To deal with this case, a matching procedure that is a generalization of the third neighbor is used to be able to deal with multiple copies. This means the two keypoints are considered matched now only if the following constraint is satisfied:

$$\frac{d1}{d3} < T \tag{1}$$

Where:

- d1 is the Euclidean distance between the key-point descriptor and the G-nearest neighbors (GNN).
- d3 is the Euclidean distance between the key-point descriptor and the G+2 nearest neighbors (G+2NN).
- T is the selected matching threshold.
- G is 1, 2...15.

To giving more accuracy to the matching process, the mini distance condition has been added. The distance between the locations of each two matching keypoints must be greater than the mini distance threshold, as follows:

$$\text{The distance between keypoint location \& GNN location} > \text{mini distance} \tag{2}$$

Where:

– GNN is G-nearest neighbors.
– G is 1, 2...15.

Finally, by iterating this GNN and mini distance strategy on all keypoints, the set of matched keypoints can be obtained. This allows identifying the duplicated areas, therefore detecting if the image has tampered or not.

Already in this phase, the draft idea of the image authenticity is provided. But can be happened that the images legitimately contain regions with a very similar texture, that might give false matches (false positives). The following phase of the proposed algorithm removes this possibility.

3.5 False Positives Removing

An image can contain regions with a very similar texture. This leads to show false matches (false positives) in some area of the image. A method to remove the false matches from the image is proposed by rejecting all key-points in matches list that own neighbor less than N (the default value of N is 2).

The idea of this method can be summarized as follows: In general, the copied region has a very similarity with the original, this leads to emergence the many matched key-points between them, due the Euclidean distances are low between them. Therefore, any key-point in the matches list will have many neighbors because these key-points describe a specific region, so their locations are close to each other, thus can be considered robust key-points.

On the other hand, in the case of false matches (false positives). These keypoints will be scattered in different regions of the image since they consist of the chaos of background. This means, their locations are not close to each other, thus they will not have multiple neighbors in the matches list.

So, the number of neighbors of each key-point in the matches list can be computed. Then, each key-point which has neighbors less than N value will be removed. Algorithm 3.3 illustrates the main steps of this phase.

Algorithm 3.3: (False Positives Removing).

Input: Candidate matches.

Output: Matched key-point.

Begin

    Step1: *The Euclidean distance is computed between locations of each keypoint with others.*

    Step2: *The first k-nearest neighbors of each keypoint are determined, (K= N+1, because the first distance is zero).*

    Step3: *The Threshold of a neighbor distance (TND) is determined based on the size of the inputting image.*

    Step4: *The coordinate of the keypoints are saved which satisfy:*

        The Euclidean distances between keypoint location and each one of the k-nearest neighbors < TND

End

3.6   The Decision (Forged or Authentic Image)

The final phase of the proposed algorithm shows the final result of the input image. In case no matched key-points, the input image will be shown as an authentic image. Conversely, in case a matched keypoints exist, the input image will be shown as a forged image, the matched key-points will be shown, and the regions which have been tampered are identified.

4   Results and Discussions

The proposed algorithm has been implemented using Windows 7 and Matlab R2016a. VLFeat library (written in C++ language) is exploited, to increase the implementation speed of the SIFT algorithm.

The testing and analysis process has been performed using 300 images determined from two different datasets: "MICC" [28] and "CoMoFoD" [29] as well as some other images.

The datasets MICC-F220 and MICC-F8_Multi have been used and some selected images from datasets CoMoFoD and MICC-F600. Some original and tampered images used in the testing process illustrated in the Figs. 4 and 5 respectively.

Fig. 4. The detection results for some tampering images under different complex transformations.

In the figure above, the proposed algorithm took about 0.8 s, 5 s, 0.6 s, and 4 s respectively to determine the tampered areas. The size of these images is 800 * 532 pixels, 1440 * 957 pixels, 737 * 492 pixels, and 1280 * 958 pixels respectively from left to right. Note that the processing time increases as the image size increases.

The collection of tested images consists of two parts: The first one consists of 131 original images without any kind of tamper. The second part consists of 169 forged images containing tampering with complex transformations (translation, rotation, scaling, and combination) and common post-processing operations (brightness change, image blur, and noise addition). The tamper region size covers at least 3% of the entire image. This collection is composed of images that have different size (The smallest size is 512 * 512 pixels and the largest size is 3264 * 2448 pixels), divided between the JPEG and PNG images format. Table 2 illustrates the number of images tested upon each dataset.

| Original image | Tampered image | Tampered image with brightness increase |

| Tampered image with brightness decrease | Tampered image with noise addition | Tampered image with blurring |

Fig. 5. The detection results for some tampering images under post-processing attacks.

Table 2. The number of images used in the testing

Dataset name	Number of images
MICC-F220	220
MICC-F8_Multi	8
MICC-F600	10
CoMoFoD	42
Other	20
Total number	300

The number of original images that are exactly detected as original was 128 from 131. The number of forged images that are detected as forged was 165 from 169. The processing time average for all tested images was 3.41 s. Table 3 presents the final results of testing.

Table 3. Final results of the test.

TP	TN	FP	FN
165	128	3	4

Where TP (true positive) is the number of forged images that are detected as forged, TN (true negative) is the number of original images that are detected as original, FP (false positive) is the number of original images that are detected as forged, FN (false negative) is the number of forged images that are detected as original.

To evaluate the performance of a CMFD algorithm, TP Rate, TN Rate, FP Rate, FN Rate, and accuracy criteria are used. Table 4 presents the final rates of evaluation.

Table 4. The total rate of the testing

TP Rate	TN Rate	FP Rate	FN Rate	Accuracy
$\frac{TP}{TP+FN} = 0.97633$	$\frac{TN}{TN+FP} = 0.97709$	$\frac{FP}{FP+TN} = 0.02290$	$\frac{FN}{FN+TP} = 0.02366$	$\frac{TP+TN}{TP+FN+TN+FP} = 0.97666$

Figure 6 shows the processing speed comparison of ten images between the proposed algorithm and the algorithm of Haimour et al. [21] which worked an improvement of the Khan and Kulkarni algorithm [20]. The figure refers that the processing time for the proposed algorithm is much speedier.

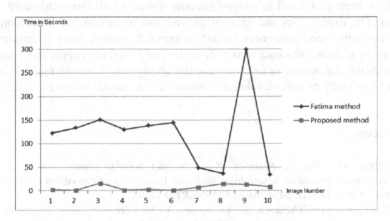

Fig. 6. The comparison of the processing time between the proposed method and Fatima's method

To assess the accuracy of the proposed algorithm, it has been compared with three algorithms mentioned in the related works. Figure 7 illustrates the overall accuracy of these forgery detection algorithms.

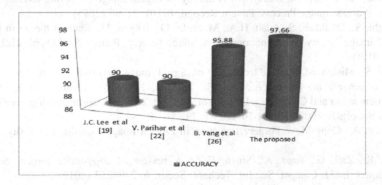

Fig. 7. The comparison process between the proposed method and other related works

These algorithms were implemented and applied to the same set of forgery images. The proposed algorithm indicates that it is the highest accuracy.

5 Conclusions

The detection of forgery in the digital image is an interesting research topic in forensic science. The specific type of image tampering (copy-move forgery) can be considered one of the emerging problems in the field of digital image forensics. There is a large number of published papers on copy-move detection can be found in the literature. The number of these papers is increasing. However, most of these algorithms are time-consuming. In this paper, an effective algorithm is proposed for Copy-Move forgery detection using key-points methods and automatic matching thresholds. Many experiments have been performed to suggest suitable values of all thresholds used in the algorithm. The experiments and analysis proved this algorithm has lower computational complexity, good robustness towards common post-processing operations, can detect forgery regions and locate accurately and rapidly even after apply more complex transformations (e.g. scaling or rotation), and the ability to handle with multiple copies. Therefore this study presents a valuable contribution to digital image forensics.

References

1. Sivakumar, M., Roy, P., Harmsen, K., Saha, S.: Satellite remote sensing and GIS applications in agricultural meteorology. In: Paper Presented at: Proceedings of the Training Workshop in Dehradun, India. AGM-8, WMO/TD (2004)
2. Zandi, M., Mahmoudi-Aznaveh, A., Talebpour, A.: Iterative copy-move forgery detection based on a new interest point detector. IEEE Trans. Inf. Forensics Secur. **11**(11), 2499–2512 (2016)
3. Walia, S., Kumar, K.: Digital image forgery detection: a systematic scrutiny. Aust. J. Forensic Sci. **51**, 1–39 (2018)
4. Shivakumar, B., Baboo, S.S.: Automated forensic method for copy-move forgery detection based on Harris interest points and SIFT descriptors. Int. J. Comput. Appl. **27**(3), 9–17 (2011)
5. Parashar, N., Tiwari, N., Dubey, D.: A survey of digital image tampering techniques. Int. J. Sig. Process. Image Process. Pattern Recogn. **8**(10), 91–96 (2015)
6. Sadeghi, S., Dadkhah, S., Jalab, H.A., Mazzola, G., Uliyan, D.: State of the art in passive digital image forgery detection: copy-move image forgery. Pattern Anal. Appl. **21**(2), 291–306 (2018)
7. Panda, S., Mishra, M.: Passive techniques of digital image forgery detection: developments and challenges. In: Kalam, A., Das, S., Sharma, K. (eds.) Advances in Electronics, Communication and Computing. LNEE, vol. 443, pp. 281–290. Springer, Singapore (2018). https://doi.org/10.1007/978-981-10-4765-7_29
8. Khayeat, A.: Copy-Move Forgery Detection in Digital Images. Cardiff University, Cardiff (2017)
9. Kaur, R., Zail, G., Kaur, A., Singh, G.Z.: A review of copy-move forgery detection techniques. Int. J. Comput. Sci. Inf. Technol. Secur. **6**, 249–253 (2016)

10. Dixit, A., Gupta, R.: Copy-move image forgery detection using frequency-based techniques: a review. Int. J. Sig. Process. Image Process. Pattern Recogn. **9**(3), 71–88 (2016)
11. Asghar, K., Habib, Z., Hussain, M.: Copy-move and splicing image forgery detection and localization techniques: a review. Aust. J. Forensic Sci. **49**(3), 281–307 (2017)
12. Qureshi, M.A., Deriche, M.: A bibliography of pixel-based blind image forgery detection techniques. Sig. Process. Image Commun. **39**, 46–74 (2015)
13. Li, Y.: Image copy-move forgery detection based on polar cosine transform and approximate nearest neighbor searching. Forensic Sci. Int. **224**(1–3), 59–67 (2013)
14. Warif, N.B.A., Wahab, A.W.A., Idris, M.Y.I., et al.: Copy-move forgery detection: survey, challenges and future directions. J. Netw. Comput. Appl. **75**, 259–278 (2016)
15. Bayram, S., Sencar, H.T., Memon, N.: A survey of copy-move forgery detection techniques. In: Paper Presented at: IEEE Western New York Image Processing Workshop (2008)
16. Zhao, J., Guo, J.: Passive forensics for copy-move image forgery using a method based on DCT and SVD. Forensic Sci. Int. **233**(1–3), 158–166 (2013)
17. AlSawadi, M., Muhammad, G., Hussain, M., Bebis, G.: Copy-move image forgery detection using local binary pattern and neighborhood clustering. In: Paper Presented at: 2013 European Modelling Symposium (2013)
18. Fadl, S.M., Semary, N.A.: A proposed accelerated image copy-move forgery detection. In: Paper Presented at: 2014 IEEE Visual Communications and Image Processing Conference (2014)
19. Lee, J.-C., Chang, C.-P., Chen, W.-K.: Detection of copy–move image forgery using histogram of orientated gradients. Inf. Sci. **321**, 250–262 (2015)
20. Khan, S., Kulkarni, A.: Robust method for detection of copy-move forgery in digital images. In: Paper Presented at: 2010 International Conference on Signal and Image Processing (2010)
21. Haimour, F.O., Khraiwesh, M.A., Mahmoud, K.W.: An improved method for detecting copy-move forgery in digital images, Zarqa University (2015)
22. Parihar, V., Mehtre, B.M.: Copy move forgery detection using key-points structure, Sardar Patel University of Police, Security and Criminal (2016)
23. Chen, L., Lu, W., Ni, J., Sun, W., Huang, J.: Region duplication detection based on Harris corner points and step sector statistics. J. Vis. Commun. Image Represent. **24**(3), 244–254 (2013)
24. Singh, R., Oberoi, A., Goel, N.: Copy move forgery detection on digital images. Int. J. Comput. Appl. **98**(9), 17–22 (2014)
25. Sreelakshmy, I, Anver, J.: An improved method for copy-move forgery detection in digital forensic. In: Paper Presented at: 2016 Online International Conference on Green Engineering and Technologies (IC-GET) (2016)
26. Yang, B., Sun, X., Guo, H., Xia, Z., Chen, X.: A copy-move forgery detection method based on CMFD-SIFT. Multimed. Tools Appl. **77**(1), 837–855 (2018)
27. Lowe, D.G.: Distinctive image features from scale-invariant keypoints. Int. J. Comput. Vis. **60**(2), 91–110 (2004)
28. Amerini, I., Ballan, L., Caldelli, R., Del Bimbo, A., Serra, G.: A sift-based forensic method for copy–move attack detection and transformation recovery. IEEE Trans. Inf. Forensics Secur. **6**(3), 1099–1110 (2011)
29. Tralic, D., Zupancic, I., Grgic, S., Grgic, M.: CoMoFoD—New database for copy-move forgery detection. In: Paper Presented at: Proceedings ELMAR-2013 (2013)

An Effective Protein Multiple Structure Alignment Using Parallel Computing

Mohammed W. Al-Neama[1(✉)] 🆔, Salwa M. Ali[2] 🆔,
Fahad Layth Malallah[3] 🆔, and Mustafa Ghanem Saeed[4] 🆔

[1] Education College for Girls, Mosul University, Mosul, Iraq
mwneama@uomosul.edu.iq
[2] Faculty of Science and Arts-Unaiza, Qassim University, Qassim, Saudi Arabia
s.mussa@qu.edu.sa
[3] Computer and Information, Electronics Engineering College,
Ninevah University, Mosul, Iraq
fahad.malallah@uoninevah.edu.iq
[4] Computer Science Department, College of Science, Cihan University-Slemani,
Slemani, Iraq
mustafa.saeed@sulicihan.edu.krd

Abstract. Multiple spatial alignments of protein structures are an important tool of structural biology. Analysis of protein structures allows us to establish their homology; i.e., the origin from a common ancestor. The rapid growth in the number of known protein structures determines the requirements for the speed of the spatial alignment algorithms. This paper proposes a strategy for using parallel computations to efficiently construct multiple spatial equalizations using multi-core cluster system. The developed algorithm is based on the well-proven sequential method of spatial alignment of Multiple Alignments with Translations and Twists (MATT). Results show that the best speedup (38.44) and the least difference between the experimental and theoretical efficiency (0.01) was obtained. The speedup and efficiency based on (128) nodes have been evaluated using LinkSCEEM-2 systems at Bibliotheca Alexandrina, Egypt.

Keywords: Bioinformatics · Parallel algorithm · Proteins structural alignments · MATT

1 Introduction

Proteins are the basis of the structure's organism and all its life reactions. Any change in these proteins leads to a change in life processes occurring in the body. Proteins are irregular polymers, i.e. molecules whose functions are substantially determined by the number, composition, and order of the monomers contained in them. In the early 50s of the last century, it was shown that the protein chain has a unique sequence of links - amino acid residues ("residue" is what remains of a free amino acid after its incorporation into a protein chain). This chain has a chemically regular backbone ("main chain"), from which various side groups of amino acids produce. Proteins fit into complex asymmetrical three-dimensional (tertiary) structures [1].

© Springer Nature Switzerland AG 2020
M. I. Khalaf et al. (Eds.): ACRIT 2019, CCIS 1174, pp. 32–43, 2020.
https://doi.org/10.1007/978-3-030-38752-5_3

Spatial alignment allows us to study the relationship between the structure and functions of proteins. Spatial alignment is a method of establishing organization similarity, as well as evolutionary relationships between two or more protein structures, based on a comparison of their tertiary structures. The goal of spatial alignment is the best geometric matching of the elements of the tertiary structure [2].

Figure 1 shows an example of the alignment of a pair of human thioredoxins proteins (structure number in PDB: 3TRX) and Drosophila (1XWC). The figure shows that significant parts of the structures of these proteins, which correspond to a fragment of ancestral styling (the so-called three-layer sandwich), after applying geometric transformations (translations and rotations of whole structures) that are combined with a high degree of similarity. This suggests the general origin of these proteins in evolution, and also makes it possible to compare the mechanisms of their action [3].

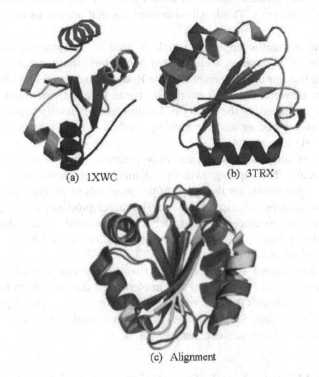

(a) 1XWC   (b) 3TRX

(c) Alignment

Fig. 1. Alignment of the Drosophila thioredoxins proteins of (a) Drosophila melanogaster (1XWC), (b) human (3TRX), and (c) The red ribbon in the alignment represents the human protein, the yellow – Drosophila [3]. (Color figure online)

Systematic bioinformatics analysis of the alignments of families of related proteins allows us to find the necessary structural changes to construct new proteins with desired properties. In addition, the similarity of tertiary structures can be used to predict the functions of poorly understood proteins. Due to the structural alignment, evolutionarily equivalent amino acid residues can be determined if the aligned proteins to be have a common ancestor [4].

Furthermore, if similar proteins have conserved regions in which the structure remains almost unchanged, this may indicate a functional or structural significance of this region. Multiple structural leveling programs are usually based on the methods of pair-wise spatial alignment. Even simplified versions of spatial alignment algorithms are Non-Polynomial-complex [5].

The methods of pair-wise spatial alignment can be divided into three classes:

First, Methods based on aligned fragments pairs (AFP) of structure [6, 7]. These methods use short fragments from both protein structures, which are producing some transformations on them and assemble them into a geometrically acceptable structure. Second, Methods that consider pairwise distances separately within each structure in order to look for the greatest number of amino acid residues having similar pairwise distances in both structures. Third, All other methods that are not included in the first two points.

The classical geometric approach which is used to measure the quality of the structural alignment of proteins, includes two parameters: the number of amino acid residues that are used in the alignment and the Root-Mean-Square Deviation (RMSD) of the distances between atoms. It should be borne in mind that today there is no universal metric for assessing the quality of leveling and often only expert judgment is decisive in choosing one or another leveling method. MATT [8] is a well-proven method of multiple alignments.

The quality of alignment is not the only criterion for choosing a program of multiple alignments. The rapid growth in the number of known protein structures determines the requirements for the speed of the programs of multiple alignments and the number of sequences processed by them. This paper proposes a strategy for using parallel computations to efficiently construct multiple spatial equalizations by using multi-core cluster system. The developed algorithm is based on the well-proven sequential method of spatial alignment of MATT.

This paper is organized as follows: the *next section* presents a brief of the MATT. Then Sect. 3 demonstrates parallelized and implemented this algorithm by the cluster system. In Sect. 4, evaluates the performance of the proposed parallel implementations with discussion. After that, Sect. 5 shows the computational experiment. The conclusion is presented at the end of the paper in Sect. 6.

2   Multiple Alignment with Translation and Twists

MATT is an algorithm based on the method of aligned pairs of structure sections (AFP) [8]. A distinctive feature of MATT is the weakening of the stiffness of the main protein chain. This weakening allows the protein structure to bend and rotate to achieve the desired alignment.

MATT performs better on standard test data sets [9] and [10] compared to well-known multiple leveling programs. As input, MATT uses files in the Protein Data Bank (PDB) format [3], which is describing the proteins to be aligned. The result of the equivalent multiple at the output of MATT is also saved in a PDB file. The block diagram of the algorithm is shown in Fig. 2. A set of g structures is given to the MATT program input. Initially, each structure forms a separate group [8].

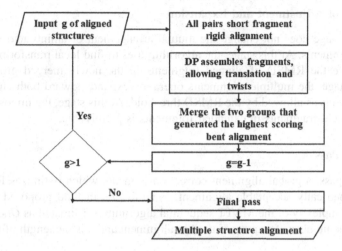

Fig. 2. MATT algorithm diagram [8].

The iterative part of the program consists of $g - 1$ iterations. At each iteration, two groups of aligned structures merge into one, forming a new alignment. In the iterative part of MATT, geometrically unacceptable changes in the structure are appeared. After the completion of the iterative part, the global alignment is corrected, which results in a geometrically acceptable structure. In the iterative part of the MATT sequential program, there are four main stages:

2.1 Pairs of Fragments

The actions of the first stage are similar to those performed by many methods based on AFP. MATT considers fragments of 5 to 9 contiguous amino acid residues. A couple of fragments will be considered 2 fragments of the same length. The alignment score of a pair of fragments, one from each group, is calculated based on the transformations performed on all the structures of the group. For each pair of fragments, an alignment score is calculated.

2.2 Assembly with Turns and Shifts

The main innovation of MATT is the way of assembling short fragments into a global alignment. MATT uses dynamic programming to produce longer aligned groups of fragments at each iteration. The alignment quality assessment is based on the sum of the alignment estimates of each aligned fragment for geometric transformations of the main chain of one protein to another.

MATT finds a pair of groups with a better quality rating and assembles them into new multiple alignments, and then combines the two groups. If exactly one group remains, the algorithm moves to the final stage, otherwise, the re-aligning and extending are phases performed and the transition to the next iteration is performed.

2.3 Stage of Adjustment and Expansion

Adjustment stage does not change the mutual arrangement of amino acid residues in multiple alignments. At this stage, the algorithm tries to find local transformations that would reduce the RMSD of aligned fragments in the newly merged group. In the expansion stage, the multiple alignments operation expands toward both ends of each of the fragments as allowed by the RMSD threshold. At this stage, the imposition of up to 5 amino acid fragments in extended fragments is permissible.

2.4 Final Pass

In the final pass, a global alignment correction is made, which optimizes RMSD and builds geometrically acceptable alignment. For this, the method proposed by [11] is used. The complexity of the MATT sequential algorithm is estimated as $O(k^2 n^3 log(n))$, where k is the number of sequences used in alignment and n is the length of the longest sequence.

3 Parallel Multiple Alignment Algorithm

There is a motive to choose the best techniques of parallel programming to get the advantages of performance for the protein pairwise alignment process. Some of the parallel algorithms solve it by Central Processing Unit (CPU) while others use Graphic Processing Unit (GPU). Both of them are significantly different which makes them suitable to perform different instructions and provide particular benefits for specific problems [12]. A sequential computer has one CPU, (i.e. independent device hosting one node). Nowadays, multi-core computers, clusters, and grids systems have turned out to be accessible and became dominant [13].

As well as, the multicore computer has few cores, which implies that it cannot efficiently process several operations [14]. Conversely, a GPU has hundreds of cores that are designed to process a gigantic amount of time-consuming operations Single Instruction Multiple Data (SIMD) [12].

Along these lines, it is important to utilize high-performance technologies to open the capability of such frameworks. In the interim, parallel programming libraries, for example, OpenMP and Message Passing Interface (MPI) [15] made it feasible for software engineers to exploit the incredible computational ability of multicore and cluster systems for broadly useful utilization [16]. Numerous methods have been a handle to effectively process the structural alignment. Different techniques that can deal with long sequences and produce exact alignment are generally moderate. the motivation of this paper is to give an effective technique that joins the speed and the capacity to align protein Structure.

Based on MATT'S sequential algorithm, a strategy for using parallel computing to effectively construct multiple structural protein alignments using a cluster computer has been proposed and implemented. There are four main stages in the MATT program: data entry, preliminary processing of all possible pairs, iterative part, final pass. In this case, most of the computations are performed at the stage of preprocessing of various pairs, when various alignments of pairs of initial structures are considered and in the iterative part of the algorithm, when the algorithm selects the best pairs for alignment.

The initial construction of pairwise alignments is considered the most computationally demanding step of the algorithm. These alignments are done between all input structures and further iterative progression of the multiple alignments within each available node after distributing the overall workload using the proposed scheduling technique. The computations are stored in the Random Access Memory (RAM) and distributed (by using MPI library) across all allocated nodes to use the available resources efficiently. Then, each node applies its multithreading approach on the concluding refinement step, which was accelerated by introducing the OpenMP support (i.e., the shared-memory multitasking). Figure 3 illustrates the flowchart of parallel MATT.

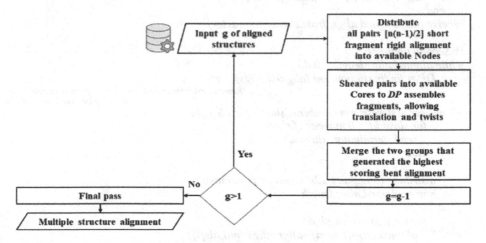

Fig. 3. The flowchart of parallel MATT.

In MATT, the *function Align* () is responsible for handling all sorts of pairs and the iterative part of the algorithm. The profiling of the original version of the program showed that the *Align* () function at the preprocessing stage of pairs and in the iterative part uses the same *AlignAlignments()* function for alignment, the computations of which take the main program runtime.

For parallelization of computations based on the MATT algorithm, the collective decision method is used. The master process at the first stage of the algorithm receives all pairs of structures, serializes and distributes them evenly among all the available processes. Next, the *Align_Alignments* function is executed by all processes (including the master process). The master process collects and desterilizes data.

At each iteration of the second stage, alignment is selected with the best estimate among the already aligned structures, serialization and uniform distribution of n structures and better alignment among all available processes. Next, the *AlignAlignments* function is executed by all processes (including the master process), data is collected and deserialized in the master process.

Figure 4 presents the pseudo-code of the first and second stages of the parallel algorithm.

| Input | : g of aligned structures |
| Output | : Multiple structures alignment |

Function master (alignments)

/* First stage */
alig.pairs = generate (aligs) /* n(n-1)/2 all kinds of pairs */
distribute (alig.pairs, als, toslaves, frommaster)
                                              /*▷ Distributing alig.pairs over P nodes*/
    for i = 0 to als.length do
    | aligned.aligs [i] = align.aligs (als [i])
    end
receive (als, aligned.aligs, from.slaves, to.master)

/* Second phase */
while aligned.aligs.length> 0 do
    DP = findbestalignment (aligned.aligs)
                        /*Remove everything that contains ma from both sets*/
                                        /*▷ sheard DP over C cores*/
    number.of.slaves= min (number.of.slaves, aligs.length)
        for slave.id = 0 number.of.slaves do
            send (terminator, slave.id)
        end

    distribute (alig.pairs, als, toslaves, frommaster)
    naa = aligned.aligs.length

        for i = 0 to als.length do
            aligned.aligs[naa+i]=align.aligs (ma,als[i])
        end

    receive (als, aligned.aligs+naa, fromslaves, tomaster)
end
return aligs [0]

Fig. 4. Pseudo-code of the 1st and 2nd stages of the parallel implementation of the MATT algorithm for the master process.

Parallelization of MATT'S computations was done using distributed memory by MPI technology [15]. MPI is an application programming interface (API) for transmitting information that allows exchanging messages among parallel processes that perform the same task.

For the analysis of the time-consuming sequential MATT code, the gperf tools profiler was used [17]. The comparison of the results of the sequential version and the parallel implementation of the MATT program was carried out using the standard Linux.

4 Performance Evaluation

The study of the developed algorithm is carried out according to the classical defini-
tions of acceleration and efficiency. The Speed-up (S_p) of a parallel algorithm is the
ratio of the Time (T_1) of a sequential program to the time (T_p) of a parallel program on
n processors [18].

$$S_p = \frac{T_1}{T_p} \tag{1}$$

Let n be the number of chains, the alignment time of one pair is constant and equal
to t_o, τ_s is the program operation time in the non-parallelizable part, the overhead of
sending one pair is constant and equal to τ_m.

Then the running time of the sequential version of MATT will be:

$$T_1 = \tau_s + \frac{n(n-1)}{2}t_o + \sum_{k=1}^{n-1} kt_o$$

$$\because \sum_{k=1}^{n-1} kt_o = \left(\frac{n(n-1)}{2}\right)t_o$$

$$\therefore T_1 = \tau_s + t_o\left(\frac{n(n-1)}{2} + \frac{n(n-1)}{2}\right)$$

This is implying to:

$$T_1 = \tau_s + t_o n(n-1) \tag{2}$$

The running time of the parallel algorithm on p processors given by:

$$T_p = \tau_s + \frac{n(n-1)}{2}\left(\frac{t_o}{p} + \tau_m\right) + \sum_{k=p}^{n-1} k\left(\frac{t_o}{p} + \tau_m\right) + \sum_{k=1}^{p-1} k\tau_m + (p-1)t_o$$

and after simplicity:

$$T_p = \tau_s + \frac{t_o}{p}n(n-1) + \frac{t_o}{2}(p-1) + \tau_m n(n-1) \tag{3}$$

Substitute Eqs. (2) and (3) in Eq. (1)

$$S_p = \frac{\tau_s + t_o n(n-1)}{\tau_s + \frac{t_o}{p}n(n-1) + \frac{t_o}{2}(p-1) + \tau_m n(n-1)} \tag{4}$$

The efficiency (E) of the parallel algorithm determines how to increase the size of the task while increasing the number of processors to maintain constant efficiency. The efficiency (E) of some parallel systems is a polynomial in the dimension of the processor: $O(p^x)$, where $x \geq 1$. It is clear that if $x = 1$, then the scalable parallel algorithm is linear. It is given by:

$$E_p = \frac{S_p}{p} \tag{5}$$

From Eq. (4), let $\tau_s = 0$ and $\tau_m = \alpha t_o (\alpha > 0)^1$, this is implied to:

$$S_p = \frac{t_o n(n-1)}{\frac{t_o}{p} n(n-1) + \frac{t_o}{2}(p-1) + \alpha t_o n(n-1)}$$

$$= \frac{2pn(n-1)}{2n(n-1) + p(p-1) + 2p\alpha n(n-1)}$$

$$S_p = \frac{2pn(n-1)}{2n(n-1)(1+\alpha p) + p(p-1)} \tag{6}$$

Substitution Eq. (5) in Eq. (6):

$$E_p = \frac{2n(n-1)}{2n(n-1)(1+\alpha p) + p(p-1)}$$

Then, efficiency becomes as follows:

$$E_p = \frac{1}{1 + \alpha p + \frac{p(p-1)}{2n(n-1)}} \tag{7}$$

The low degree of p in the efficiency (E) indicates high scalability. If an exponential (or any other rapidly growing function) dependence takes place, then that is mean weakly scalable systems. Algorithms with an efficiency of the order are considered close to a linearly scalable algorithm. Equation (7) can be used to assess the scalability of a parallel algorithm, as well as to select the required number of computational nodes to solve a problem with a given efficiency with a known amount of dataset.

5   Computational Experiments

The proposed parallel algorithm was conducted on the cluster of multicore system, which is part of the supercomputer complex of LinkSCEEM-2 systems at Bibliotheca Alexandrina, Egypt, in which it has 128 nodes and 64 GB memory: each node contains two Intel quad core Xeon 2.83 GHz processors (64-bittechnology), 80 GByte hard disk, 8 GByte RAM, and a dual port in fin band (10 Gbps), a Giga Ethernet Network port: the operating system is 64-bit Linux.

To check the program operation correctness, PDB files obtained at the output of the original sequential program and parallel program were compared. A benchmark dataset of protein structures was constructed taken as input. A total of 500 randomly selected domains from Structural Classification of Proteins (SCOP) (19), by taking into account the number of structures in each SCOP fold and the size of structures (50–500) residues. The structures in SCOP contain up to 386 different folds, covering 370 of the 449 folds and 41 of the 46 folds with >50 and >1000 structures respectively. As noted previous, the coefficient α in Eq. (7) depends on both: the length of the sequence and the parameters of a particular computing system. For the cluster system, $\alpha = 0.0003$ was found with a sequence length.

To confirm that the parallel algorithm is more efficient than a sequential algorithm, the parallel efficiency based on the maximum number of available cores has been evaluated. Table 1 illustrates the parallel runtime (in seconds) of the proposed parallel algorithm of MATT and the speedup compared to the runtime of the sequential program of MATT, as well as the experimental (E_e) and theoretical (E_t) efficiency and the difference between them. It shows that the greater of the number of available nodes, the more acceleration of proposed algorithm computation, and the difference between the experimental and theoretical efficiency is the least.

Table 1. Results of the parallel program launches on the cluster system.

No. of P	Runtime (sec.)	S_p	Experimental E_e	Theoretical E_t	$|E_e - E_t|$
1	215607.00	1.00	1		
4	90416.42	2.38	0.78	0.97	0.19
8	44019.68	4.90	0.71	0.90	0.19
16	23580.35	9.14	0.58	0.69	0.11
32	13748.90	15.68	0.51	0.57	0.06
64	8722.26	24.72	0.43	0.47	0.04
128	5609.17	**38.44**	0.36	0.37	0.01

As can be seen in Fig. 5, the behaviors of the theoretical and experimental curves coincide, which confirms the validity of the proposed efficiency estimate, and the maximum achieved speedups when comparing the sequential and parallel program at 128 nodes.

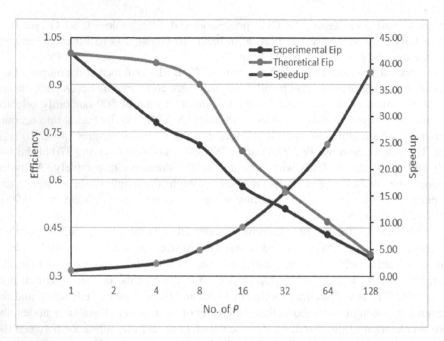

Fig. 5. Shows the comparisons of performance between experimental and theoretical efficiencies (in master axis), and speedup comparisons between sequential and parallel program of MATT.

6 Conclusion

This study introduces a parallel algorithm for 3D- alignment of multiple protein structures, based on the MATT program. It handles the problem of creating a parallel tool for multi-cores cluster system that produces the alignment of multiple sequences in a short runtime using low storage space. The proposed algorithm has achieved a significant enhancement to the overall performance. Implementations were integrated with MPI and OpenMP primitives and conducted on Bibliotheca Alexandria cluster system using 128 nodes (8 cores). The resulted protein structures at the output of the implementation's algorithm exactly coincide with the structures, which are obtained by the original sequential algorithm. In this case, the parallel implementation can significantly reduce the time spent on finding alignment of multiple protein structures.

Results show that the best speedup is scored to be (38.44) and the least difference between the experimental and theoretical efficiency (0.01), in which it was obtained by using 128 nodes. This consequence leads that, if more nodes are available, better execution will be obtained, and a higher speedup will be achieved.

A theoretical assessment of the effectiveness of the developed parallel algorithm is given. The proposed assessment is confirmed by experimental results. Evaluating efficiency allows to determine the optimal number of computational nodes for solving a problem with a given amount of input data.

Further improvement of the parallel algorithm will be aimed at removing the limitations of the existing implementation on the number of structures being processed.

Currently, the number of processed structures is determined by the amount of RAM in the computational node on which the master process is performed. The experiment performed using the computational nodes of the cluster system with a large RAM allows the processing of a significant number (thousands) of structures in a reasonable time.

Acknowledgment. Authors would like to thank Bibliotheca Alexandria, Egypt, for granting the access for running their computations on its platform.

References

1. Ramasarma, T., Vaigundan, D.: Hydrogen bond-linked pathways of peptide units and polar groups of amino acid residues suitable for electron transfer in cytochrome c proteins. Mol. Cell. Biochem. **453**(1–2), 197–203 (2019)
2. Suplatov, D., Voevodin, V., Švedas, V.: Robust enzyme design: bioinformatics tools for improved protein stability. Biotechnol. J. **10**(3), 344–355 (2014)
3. PDB File Format. http://www.rcsb.org/pdb/static.do?p=file_formats/pdb/index.html
4. Suplatov, D.A., Kopylov, K.E., Popova, N.N., Voevodin, V.V., Švedas, V.K.: Mustguseal: a server for multiple structure-guided sequence alignment of protein families. Bioinformatics **34**(9), 1583–1585 (2017)
5. de la Higuera, C., Casacuberta, F.: Topology of strings: median string is NP-complete. Theoret. Comput. Sci. **230**(1–2), 39–48 (2000)
6. Fesko, K., Suplatov, D., Švedas, V.: Bioinformatics analysis of the fold type I PLP-dependent enzymes reveals determinants of reaction specificity in l-threonine aldolase from Aeromonas jandaei. FEBS Open Bio **8**(6), 1013–1028 (2018)
7. Xu, R., et al.: Identification of DNA-binding proteins by incorporating evolutionary information into pseudo amino acid composition via the top-n-gram approach. J. Bimol. Struct. Dyn. **33**(8), 1720–1730 (2014)
8. Menke, M., Berger, B., Cowen, L.: Matt: local flexibility aids protein multiple structure alignment. PLoS Comput. Biol. **4**(1), e10 (2008)
9. Mizuguchi, K., Deane, C.M., Blundell, T.L., Overington, J.P.: HOMSTRAD: a database of protein structure alignments for homologous families. Protein Sci. **7**(11), 2469–2471 (1998)
10. Van Walle, I., Lasters, I., Wyns, L.: SABmark—a benchmark for sequence alignment that covers the entire known fold space. Bioinformatics **21**(7), 1267–1268 (2004)
11. DeBlasio, D., Kececioglu, J.: Parameter advising for multiple sequence alignment. BMC Bioinform. **16**(2), A3 (2015)
12. Nobile, M.S., Cazzaniga, P., Tangherloni, A., Besozzi, D.: Graphics processing units in bioinformatics, computational biology and systems biology. Brief. Bioinform. **18**(5), 870–885 (2016)
13. Schmidt, B.: Bioinformatics: High Performance Parallel Computer Architectures. CRC Press, Boca Raton (2011)
14. Mohammed, N.M., Ebeid, H.M., Mostafa, M.G., Gadallah, M.E.: Parallel protein structure alignment: a comparative study of two parallel programming paradigms. Int. J. Comput. Appl. **150**(7), 43–48 (2016)
15. Mpi-forum.org.: MPI Forum (2019). https://www.mpi-forum.org/. Accessed 24 July 2019
16. Wang, K., Zhang, Q., Tian, S.Q., Luo, C., Zhang, M., Jiang, B.: Parallel optimization of accelerator toolbox by OpenMP and MPI (2016)
17. GitHub: GitHub Forum (2019). https://github.com/gperftools/gperftools
18. Farber, R.: Parallel Programming with OpenACC. Newnes, London (2016)

SMARF: Smart Farming Framework Based on Big Data, IoT and Deep Learning Model for Plant Disease Detection and Prevention

Ahmad Hoirul Basori[1(✉)] 📧, Andi Besse Firdausiah Mansur[1] 📧,
and Hendra Yufit Riskiawan[2] 📧

[1] Faculty of Computing and Information Technology Rabigh,
King Abdulaziz University, Rabigh 21911, Makkah, Saudi Arabia
{abasori,abmansur}@kau.edu.sa
[2] Information Technology Department, Politeknik Negeri Jember,
PO BOX 164 Mastrip, Jember, Indonesia
yufit@polije.ac.id

Abstract. Plant disease can become a serious threat toward food production and security since the demand for food increased significantly over the year. The big data and deep learning have been discussed and explored highly in recent years due to its capability to detect certain features in smart ways. Whilst, crop disease that attack leaves can be cured if farmer detects the early symptoms and avoid the spreading of the disease. This paper presents the capability of big data and deep learning to give predictive analytic toward the plant crop disease. Some features such as leaves, weather, soil and other landscapes condition are taken as an input for the system. Smart farming will utilize IoT technology on capturing the data and localize the position of the infected plant. The combination of computer vision and GPS technology will be able to pinpoint the disease location in efficient ways. The experimental result has shown that deep learning is superior compare to logistic regression with 72% accuracy of identification of an infected leaf. Of course, this result can be augmented further by involving the extra of the leaf. Overall, the Smart Farming framework is able to give a better solution for plant disease spreading prevention by early detection and localization of the disease. A farmer might get advantage by this notification, especially for wide-scale farming. The future work might involve real-time data from the drone or CCTV camera in the real farming field.

Keywords: Plant disease · Big data · Disease localization · IoT

1 Introduction

Smart farming has been initiated for the past few years. More machine and sensor have been involved in the process of farming plant or processing. It concerned high-end technology that can be controlled and supervised easily by a human through data-driven of the farming plant. Farmer is currently moved toward sensor and wireless control of IoT technology to observe their farming plant from anywhere and anytime, this kind of trend known as smart farming [1].

© Springer Nature Switzerland AG 2020
M. I. Khalaf et al. (Eds.): ACRIT 2019, CCIS 1174, pp. 44–56, 2020.
https://doi.org/10.1007/978-3-030-38752-5_4

Furthermore, the researcher focused on augmenting the meticulousness of agriculture that will stimulate smart farming to do a more advanced task that covers context-awareness in the daily situation [2]. It covers the real-time response toward an event that occurs unexpectedly such as disaster due to weather or another natural disaster. It should able to trigger the warning alert for the disease or disaster that will occur in the upcoming future. The artificial intelligence may help a farmer to predict and anticipate based on the availability of data that previously-stored and processed for a certain purpose. Even though the human has used advanced technology to boost food production to keep up of demand for around seven billion people on the earth. This still barely enough if facing climate factor such as natural disaster or plant disease [3]. This paper consists of several sections which are started by the introduction of the research followed by related works. Afterwards, the proposed framework is discussed and continued by deep learning analysis for the crop disease. Finally, it is closed by a conclusion.

2 Related Works

Therefore the involvement of Artificial intelligent and big data analysis is very important to make prediction and estimation with several factors such as plant growth timeline, disaster, plant disease, water supply, etc. Plant disease detection and diagnosis through computer vision and image processing are very crucial for the early prevention toward spreading of plant disease [4, 5]. Mohanty et al. Did a comparison among two convolutional neural networks (CNN) to identify 26 diseases on a plant based on leave images database of fourteen different plants.

The convolutional neural network in deep learning also used widely to do automatic recognition for plant-based on their leaves features [6]. The other researcher present more powerful network based on the leaves vein pattern to identify the plant [7, 8]. While Big data also play an important role to give deep learning algorithm a better training data set and made them smarter to identify any plant disease spreading in the future [9, 10]. The previous work can be summarized as described in Table 1.

Table 1. Research comparison of Big data and deep learning utilization for farming.

Authors	Research finding
Wolfert et al. [2]	Utilizing the internet as a collaborative platform in providing healthy food
Mohanty et al. [4]	They used a deep learning algorithm to identify plant disease based on an image of the leaves
Konstantinos [5]	Using deep learning detect and analyze the plant disease in agriculture
Pantazy et al. [12]	They are using Local Binary Patterns (LBPs) to extract the features and classify based on One-class classification. Their method is applied for crop disease identification automatically
Singh and Misra [13]	They proposed an approach based on image segmentation for classification and identification of plant disease

(*continued*)

Table 1. (*continued*)

Authors	Research finding
Bhange and Hingoliwala [14]	The proposed Smart Farming for pomegranate disease based on image processing. Its initiated by resizing the image and all its features such as colour, shape are used for clustering and classification input using K-means and SVM to determine either the plant infected or not
Proposed framework	A combination of Big data, IoT technology and deep learning that can help the farmer to study the behaviour of plant disease from previous data and collect data simultaneously through IoT and identify the plant disease by analyzing through a deep learning algorithm. The synergy between these three main elements will help farmers to produce better plan and prevention toward plant disease spreading and boost the productivity of the plant

3 Proposed Framework

The proposed framework is suggesting the combination of big data and deep learning algorithm for analyzing the data from the farm. The artificial neural network consists of several components such as activation function, weights, cost function, learning algorithm. Basically, a neural network mainly consists of input, hidden layers, and output. The complex network comprised of input, three hidden layers and output. The more hidden layer means greater processed are conducted and of course more computational cost. Additionally, deep learning as a special form of machine learning used a convolutional neural network that consists of more complicated layers of a network as shown in Fig. 1.

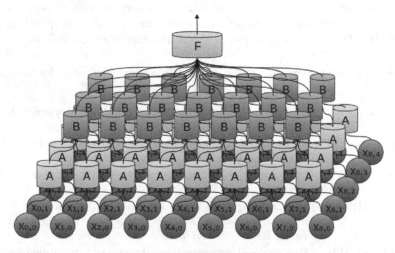

Fig. 1. Convolutional network [8]

Whilst in the Fig. 2, the CNN is described by numerous convolution tagged by pooling process that will continue until the feature map size lessens to one.

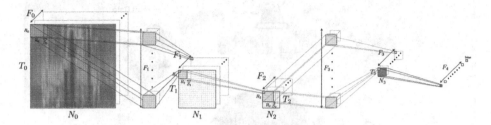

Fig. 2. Typical convolutional neural network architecture

The discrete convolution of functions f and g is labelled as Eq. 1:

$$(f * g)(x) = \sum_t f(t)g(x+t) \tag{1}$$

Whilst two dimensional signal (images) can be computed as two-dimensional convolutions.

$$(K * I)(i, j) = \sum_{m,n} K(m,n)I(i+n, j+m) \tag{2}$$

K: convolution kernel for images

Based on the initial observation, it is found that smart farming requires an integration framework since planting the seed process until the crop period. At the beginning of the planting process, some variable such as temperature, humidity, soil water composure, fertilizer composition, air quality, wind and other climate factor affect the seed plant. All these elements can be captured through the planted sensor, while the picture and video can be detected through the installed camera in the field. The plant leaves, a stem will be monitored and all data will be sent through the server for further analysis. The data will be processed to identify the plant disease in the early stage, so the farmer may take action immediately.

The tag of location also plays an important role to notify the exact location of detected plant disease, so the farmer will not find any difficulty to check the infected plant. All the collected data will be sent through a data network. This monitoring process from seed plantation till crop will be continued and make synergy among each part to achieve optimum harvest. The data analysis will act as an observatory and decision support to a farmer to take immediate action toward a certain plant that got infected by disease or destroyed by climate factors as early as possible to maintain the finest harvest (refer to Fig. 3 for SMARF architecture).

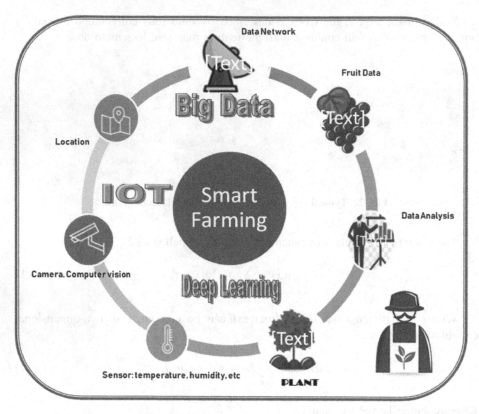

Fig. 3. SMARF: smart farming architecture.

4 Deep Learning Analysis on the Plant Crop Disease

In order to prove our hypothesis regarding the machine learning process to identify the crop disease, there are several steps of image processing that need to be performed before determining whether the crop infected or not. We did use deep learning in this case convolutional neural network (CNN) to identify the crop disease. CNN is given by Eqs. 1 and 2 in Sect. 2. In order to prove our hypothesis of a smart framework, the collection of image dataset of crop disease from Sharma [11] is analyzed and evaluated. Figure 4 is representing the original image of a leaf with crop disease then it will be processed further by image segmentation using mean shift. The mean shift responsible for finding the maxima of density function or also known as mode-seeking approach (refer to Fig. 5).

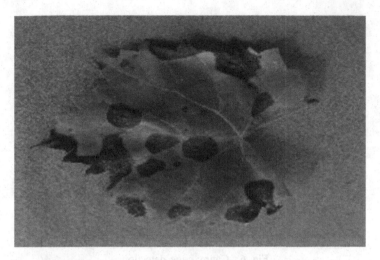

Fig. 4. The original sample of leaf image with crop disease

Fig. 5. Mean shift segmentation

This image segmentation will localize the image based on their density and it will be useful for further processes such as edge detection and contour observation. Figure 6 is the result of canny edge detection of the leaf image, it will show the boundary of the leaf. It will give a clear picture of object shape by removing the noise and give a black and white pattern. Edge detection is capable to detect discontinuity of brightness in the image. The shape of the object will be revealed and it will help us to identify the object properties.

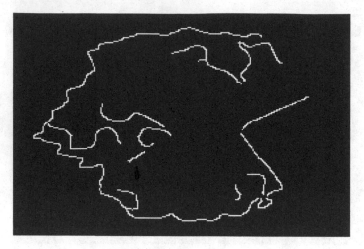

Fig. 6. Canny edge detection

The further process is contour segmentation, its different with edge detection because contour may contain hierarchy that may be valuable for an object inside object localization (Fig. 7). Contour segmentation focused on the edges with the same colour or intensity value that grouped together around the boundary. It is stored as a hierarchy to be used further.

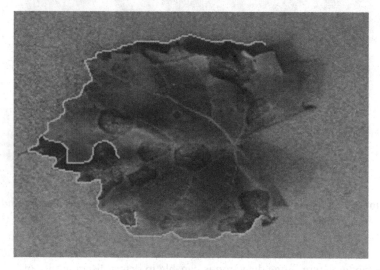

Fig. 7. Contour edge detection of the crop disease

Figure 8 represents the region of interest (ROI), it focused on an area that will be processed with various filtering techniques or other operation. The process is started by initiating the mask in a binary form where the mask size must have had the same size as the image that will be processed. The ROI pixels will be created with 1 value for all the ROI while other pixels will be adjusted to 0.

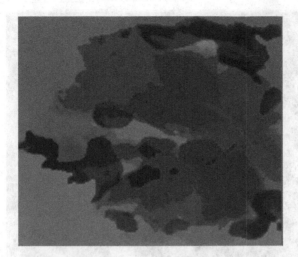

Fig. 8. Region of Interest (ROI) of the crop disease

Fig. 9. HLS of the crop disease

Figure 9 represents the high-level synthesis (HLS) of the image that potential for features extraction. HLS will be useful for graphic acceleration since the image processing process required a high amount of resources for the graphic card and processors.

While Fig. 10 is masked out of the crop disease that clearly reveals some region which is identified as a region of disease. The masking process is a non-destructive procedure to highlight certain region with a particular purpose, as mentioned before to identify the region of the disease.

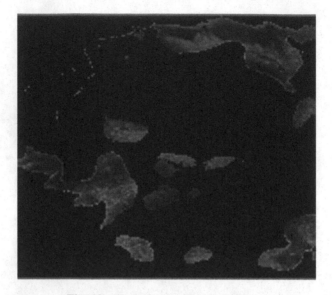

Fig. 10. Masked out of the crop disease

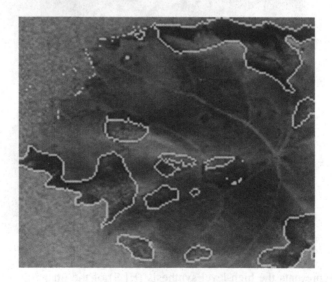

Fig. 11. Contour Masked of the crop disease

Figure 11 is a sample of contour masked for the infected leaf. Contour masked focused on enhancing the detected region by giving a clear boundary around. The combination of contour and masked out will bring a good combination to augment the identified region.

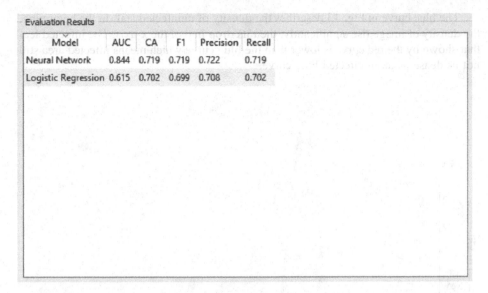

Model	AUC	CA	F1	Precision	Recall
Neural Network	0.844	0.719	0.719	0.722	0.719
Logistic Regression	0.615	0.702	0.699	0.708	0.702

Fig. 12. Test and score result for deep learning neural network and logistic regression

Figure 12 shows the evaluation result which demonstrates the superiority of deep learning neural network compares with logistic regression with accuracy 72%. While Figs. 13, 14 and 15 show the density of each feature: feature 1 (are of the leaf), feature 2 (the percentage % of the infected leaf and feature 3 is the perimeter of the leaf.

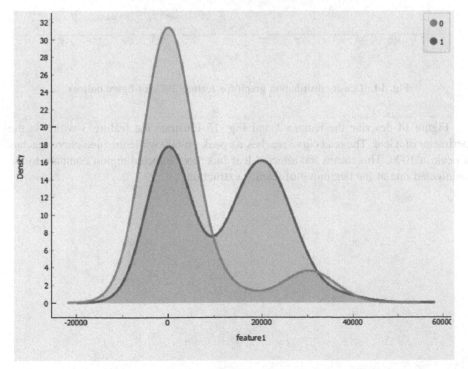

Fig. 13. Density distribution graph for feature 1 (Color figure online)

The blue curve in Fig. 13 describes the density of uninfected leaf. In the beginning, the density of image rise significantly, then its drop in 0 of the x-axis. The infected leaf that shown by the red curve is lower than the blue curve which means infected area still not as dense as an uninfected blue curve.

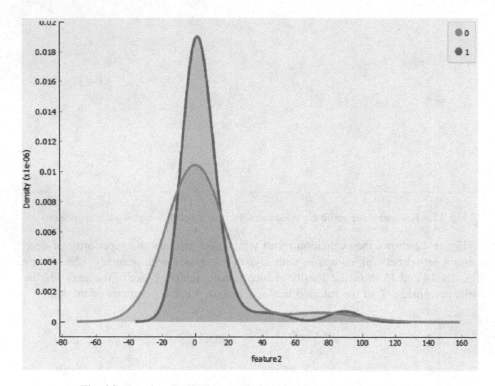

Fig. 14. Density distribution graph for feature 2 (Color figure online)

Figure 14 describe the feature 2 and Fig. 15 illustrate the feature 3 which is the perimeter of a leaf. The read curve reaches its peak on 600 while the blue curve reaches a peak in 1000. This means the infected leaf has more infected region compare to the uninfected one at the beginning of feature extraction.

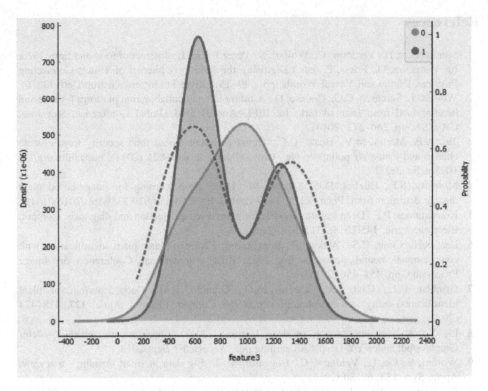

Fig. 15. Density distribution graph for feature 3 (Color figure online)

5 Conclusion

The proposed framework that presented in this paper is a result of an observation of the previous system. It offered an integration of Big data analytics, IoT technology for data communication and deep learning algorithm for further analysis. This synergy of three main elements is very crucial for preliminary plant disease detection so the farmer can take necessary action to keep harvest optimum and reduce plant disease as low as possible. The further analysis with deep learning and logistic regression has shown that deep learning neural network was able to perform good identification of the infected leaf with 72% accuracy, this result still able to be enhanced further by giving more features to be analyzed. This result is a little bit better than logistic regression. The experimental result and evaluation have shown the prospective of smart farming to boost up the crop harvest. Early identification of crop leaf disease may prevent the spreading of disease and make the handling easier.

Acknowledgements. This work was supported by the Deanship of Scientific Research (DSR), King Abdulaziz University, Jeddah Saudi Arabia and Information Technology Department, Politeknik Negeri Jember. The authors, therefore, gratefully acknowledge the DSR technical and financial support.

References

1. Sundmaeker, H., Verdouw, C., Wolfert, S., Pérez Freire, L.: Internet of food and farm 2020. In: Vermesan, O., Friess, P. (eds.) Digitising the Industry - Internet of Things Connecting Physical, Digital and Virtual Worlds, pp. 129–151. River Publishers, Gistrup/Delft (2016)
2. Wolfert, J., Sørensen, C.G., Goense, D.: A future internet collaboration platform for safe and healthy food from farm to fork. In: IEEE Annual SRII Global Conference, San Jose, CA USA, pp. 266–273 (2014)
3. Tai, A.P., Martin, M.V., Heald, C.L.: Threat to future global food security from climate change and ozone air pollution. Nat. Clim. Change **4**, 817–821 (2014). https://doi.org/10.1038/nclimate2317
4. Mohanty, S.P., Hughes, D.P., Salathé, M.: Using deep learning for image-based plant disease detection front. Plant Sci. **7**, 1419 (2016). https://doi.org/10.3389/fpls.2016.01419
5. Konstantinos, P.F.: Deep learning models for plant disease detection and diagnosis. Comput. Electron. Agric. **145**(2018), 311–318 (2018)
6. Lee, S.H., Chan, C.S., Wilkin, P., Remagnino, P.: Deep-plant: plant identification with convolutional neural networks. In: 2015 IEEE International Conference on Image Processing, pp. 452–456 (2015)
7. Grinblat, G.L., Uzal, L.C., Larese, M.G., Granitto, P.M.: Deep learning for plant identification using vein morphological patterns. Comput. Electron. Agric. **127**, 418–424 (2016)
8. Li, Y.: A brief introduction to deep learning (2018). https://www.cs.tau.ac.il/~dcor/Graphics/pdf.slides/YY-Deep%20Learning.pdf. Accessed 1 Sept 2018
9. Wolfert, S., Ge, L., Verdouw, C., Bogaardt, M.-J.: Big data in smart farming - a review. Agric. Syst. **153**, 69–80 (2017)
10. Epelbaum, T.: Deep Learning: Technical Introduction (2017). https://arxiv.org/pdf/1709.01412. Accessed 5 Sept 2018
11. Sharma, S.R.: Plant Disease Dataset (2018). https://www.kaggle.com/saroz014/plantdisease/metadata. Accessed Apr 2019
12. Pantazi, X.E., Moshou, D., Tamouridou, A.A.: Automated leaf disease detection in different crop species through image features analysis and One Class Classifiers. Comput. Electron. Agric. **156**, 96–104 (2019)
13. Singh, V., Misra, A.K.: Detection of plant leaf diseases using image segmentation and soft computing techniques. Inf. Process. Agric. **4**(1), 41–49 (2017)
14. Bhange, M., Hingoliwala, H.A.: Smart farming: pomegranate disease detection using image processing. Proc. Comput. Sci. **58**, 280–288 (2015)

VIKOR Algorithm Based on Cuckoo Search for Multi-document Text Summarization

Zuhair Hussein Ali(✉) ⓘ, Ameen A. Noorⓘ,
and Muntaha Abood Jassimⓘ

Department of Computer Science, College of Education,
AL-Mustansiriyh University, Baghdad, Iraq
{zuhair72h,a.ameen63,
Muntaha.abood}@uomustansiriyah.edu.iq

Abstract. Due to the huge amount of documents on the internet and the redundancy contained in each document makes it difficult for the user to get useful information. Automatic text summarization is a solution to such problems of information overload. Text summarization is the process of generating a single document summary from a set of documents or from a single document. This paper proposes a method based on the VIseKriterijumska Optimizacija I Kompromisno Resenje (VIKOR) algorithm. In the first stage based on extracting six features for each sentence in the document collection, the next cuckoo search algorithm was applied to compute weights for these extracted features. Finally, the VIKOR algorithm used to rank the sentences. The sentences with a high score and less redundancy selected to be included in the final summary. The proposed model is evaluated by using the dataset supplied by the Text Analysis Conference (TAC-2011) for English documents. The performance of the proposed model is evaluated using the Recall-Oriented Understudy for Gisting Evaluation (ROUGE) metric. The obtained results support the effectiveness of the proposed model.

Keywords: Text summarization · VIKOR · Cuckoo search · Feature weight

1 Introduction

Based on the excessive use of the Internet and the World Wide Web, the availability of text data grows exponentially, which increases the attention of researchers in this area. The huge amount of documents makes it difficult for the user to get useful information [1]. To manage such an issue of data over-burden, Automatic Text Summarization (ATS) has been utilized as an answer. ATS is the way toward creating a single document summary from a set of documents or from a single document without losing its main ideas [2]. This process helps users to the general review of all related documents and interesting issues with understanding the main content of the summarized documents; this process also helps to reduce the time needed to get these briefs. Rely on the amount of document to be summarized ATS can be classified as a Single Document summarization (SDS) or Multi-Document summarization (MDS). In SDS only one document can be summarized into a shorter one, whereas in MDS a set of related

© Springer Nature Switzerland AG 2020
M. I. Khalaf et al. (Eds.): ACRIT 2019, CCIS 1174, pp. 57–67, 2020.
https://doi.org/10.1007/978-3-030-38752-5_5

documents with the same topic is summarized into one shorter summary [3]. Summarization methods, also, can be classified as abstractive summarization and extractive summarization. Abstractive summarization depends on Natural Language Processing (NLP) strategies, which request a deep understanding of NLP techniques to analyze the sentences and paragraphs of the document since some changes have to be done to the selected sentences. Whereas in the extractive summarization, no change applies to the sentences which are selected to be included in the final summary [4]. Thus abstractive summarization seems to be more difficult and time-consuming than extractive summarization [5]. Also, summarization can be categorized as query summarization and generic summarization. In the query-based summarization, a summary was generated according to the user query, where the documents searched to match with the user query [6]. While generic summarization creates a summary that includes the main content of the documents. One of the most challenges for the generic summarization is that no topic or query available for the summarization process [7].

In this paper a model for extracting generic MDS for English text is proposed that is based on extracting six features for each sentence in the documents, then a Cuckoo Search Algorithm (CSA) is used for assigning a weight for each feature. The weights of the selected features are used as input to the VIKOR algorithm. The VIKOR uses both: the selected features and their calculated weights to rank the sentences. The Text Analysis Conference (TAC-2011) dataset was used to assess the summarized results. Also, ROUGE package used to evaluate the proposed model. The reminder of this paper is organized as follows. In Sect. 2, we illustrate the related works for text summarization, while Sect. 3 presents the feature extraction. The proposed model discusses in Sect. 4, whereas the removing redundancy presented in Sect. 5. The experimental results discuss s in Sect. 6. The conclusion presented in Sect. 7.

2 Related Works

There are many approaches to deal with extractive text summarization. Some of these approaches are considered in this section.

In [8] in 2011 the authors proposed an approach for MDS for Arabic and English documents. The approach based on the K-means clustering technique. The main idea of this approach based on treating all documents to summarize as a single bag of sentences, where the sentences are clustered using a single cluster, the sentences then ranked according to the similarity to the centroid of the cluster. The summary is created by choosing sentences in that ranked order. The selection process was repeated until reaching the expected limit. The TAC-2011 dataset was used in this approach. The results were embedded in the TAC-2011 dataset for both Arabic and English documents. In [9] in 2012 the authors suggested a method based on selecting five features. These features are sentenced position, sentence length, numerical information, thematic words, and title feature. The genetic algorithm was used to train the dataset and assign a weight to each feature. Their results showed that the importance of these features is in the following order title feature, sentence position, thematic words, sentence length, and numerical information. In [10] in 2015, a set of features were extracted for each sentence; this set was used as input to a model consist of three functions: Cellular

Learning Automata (CLA), Particle Swarm Optimization (PSO), and fuzzy logic. The CLA was used to calculate the similarity between sentences to reduce the redundancy. While the PSO was used to set a weight for each feature, then the fuzzy logic was used to give scores to the sentences, these scored sentences were arranged in descending order, and the sentence with the higher score was selected to be included in the created summary. In [11] in 2018 the authors proposed a method based on calculating sentence score using two methods. For the first method set of the text feature calculated for each sentence in the document, then a weight assigns for these features, then linearly combining these features scores with the weights to produce final sentence score. Method two scores the sentences by simply averaging the scores of each text feature. The two-score method used to rank all sentences, then the collaborative ranking has been adopted to choose the most important sentences. All these methods that based on scoring the sentences depending on features value suffer from the problem that some features may have more effect than other features, therefore sentence that with higher values of these features have more chance to be included in the final summary. Our proposed model overcomes this problem by giving each feature an equal chance using the VIKOR algorithm. VIKOR algorithm computes the feature value according to the highest value of that feature. This technique helps to give importance to all set of selected features.

3   Features Extraction

In the beginning, a preprocessing applied to every document in the dataset. The pre-processing consists of sentence segmentation, tokenization, stop word removal and stemming, porter stemmer algorithm applied in this paper [12]. After that six features extracted from each sentence as in [13]. These features are as follows.

A-Sentence Position (SP): higher score will be given to the first sentence; the score decreases according to the sentence position in the document. This feature can be computed according to Eq. (1).

$$F1(Si) = \frac{N - i + 1}{N} \tag{1}$$

Where i is the position of the sentence (s) in a document of N sentences

B-Sentence length (SL): This feature is computed by dividing the sentence length by the length of the longest sentence in the document as in Eq. (2).

$$F2(Si) = \frac{L(Si)}{Lmax} \tag{2}$$

Where L(si) is the length of the sentence is and Lmax is the length of the longest sentence in the document.

C-Numerical data (ND): has important information to be included in the summary. This feature is calculated by dividing the number of numerical data in the sentence by the sentence length as in Eq. (3).

$$F3(Si) = \frac{Num(Si)}{L(Si)}$$ (3)

Where Num(si) is the number of numerical data in the sentence (si)

D-Thematic Words (TW): terms that appear most frequently than other terms in the document. TW can be calculated as in Eq. (4).

$$F4(si) = \frac{TW(Si)}{TWmax}$$ (4)

TW is the number of thematic words in the sentence.

TWmax maximum thematic words in the sentences.

E-Title Feature (TF): This feature computed by finding the overlap between the title sentence and every sentence in the document as in Eq. (5).

$$F5(si) = \frac{No.of\ TF}{L(Title)}$$ (5)

Where TF is the words that exist in both: Si and Title

F-Proper Noun (PN): based on computing the number of PN in every sentence as in Eq. (6).

$$F6(Si) = \frac{PN(Si)}{L(Si)}$$ (6)

Where PN is the number of proper nouns in a sentence si.

4   The Proposed Model

They are many stages in the proposed model, that include computing feature weights, applying the VECOR algorithm to rank the extracted sentences and finally remove redundancy. Figure 1 shows the main stages of the proposed model.

4.1   Cuckoo Search Algorithm

CSA is an optimization algorithm developed by Yang and Deb in 2009. The basic idea is inspired by some cuckoos placing their eggs in the nests of other birds. Some host birds can discover the egg is not their own, it will either build a new nest and abandon its nest or thrown out these eggs away elsewhere [14].

CS is seeming to be more successful than other nature-motivated algorithms. PSO, differential evolution (DE) and Simulated annealing (SA) can be considered as special

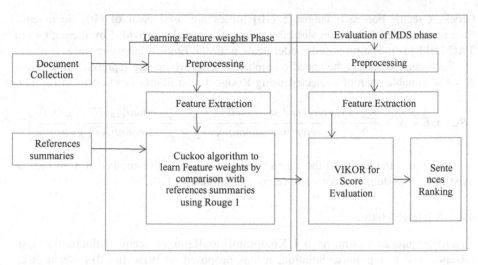

Fig. 1. Block diagram of proposed model.

cases of CS algorithm, hence it is no surprise why the CS algorithm outperforms them [15]. The CS algorithm is faster than DE to reach an optimal solution [16]. Also, the CS algorithm accounted for as being more computationally productive than the PSO [17]. For these reasons, CS was chosen in the proposed model.

4.2 CS Encoding

This section is similar to [9, 18] but CS used to compute features weights instead of PSO and genetic algorithm. Concerning to six features in the proposed model each solution can be represented as six bits. Each bit corresponding to one feature value. The bit value can be either one or zero, one means the corresponding features will be selected zero means the corresponding features will be ignored. Figure 2 shows the structure of the features representation.

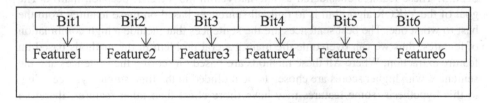

Fig. 2. Feature structure representation

4.3 The Training Procedure

TAC-2011 data set used to train the proposed model. TAC-2011 which consists of a document set written in seven languages (English, Arabic, Hebrew, French, Hindi,

Greek, Czech). For each language (10) topics are used each of (10) documents. Summarization of (10) pre-evaluated documents were also provided by the authors of TAC-2011 [19]. The proposed model deals with the English language only.

Each cuckoo selects the specific number of eggs where egg represents a solution. A set of suitable solutions selected using Rouge-1 as a fitness function as in Eq. (7).

$$ROUGE - N = \frac{\sum_S (s \in reference\ summaries) \sum_{n-grame S} count_{match}(N - gram)}{\sum_S (s \in reference\ summaries) \sum_{n-grame S} count(N - gram)} \quad (7)$$

Where n is the length of the n-gram and count $_{match}$ is the number of n-grams that exist in both system summary and reference summaries [20].

4.4 VIKOR Method

VIseKriterijumska Optimizacija I Kompromisno Resenje means Multicriteria Optimization and Compromise Solution, it was proposed in 1979. In 2011 Jahan et al. proposed a modification to original VIKOR. This modified version of the VIKOR method covers all kinds of criteria with an emphasize on a compromise solution. VIKOR technique can be considered as a Compromise Ranking Method, it is based on ranking and choosing a suitable alternative from a set of alternatives. Each alternative is evaluated according to each criterion function, then choose the alternative that closeness to the ideal solution. The weight of each criterion is required for the evaluation process [21].

4.5 VIKOR as Summary Generator

In this paper VIKOR employed in MDS to propose a mathematical model for ranking sentences and choose the most suitable ones. The VIKOR method was introduced for the multi-criteria optimization problem, Where many criteria can help the decision-makers to get a final solution. The compromise solution is a possible solution which is the closest to the ideal solution. The proposed model based on this idea where each sentence in the document collection represented as a set of features as described in Sect. 5. These features considered as alternatives in the VIKOR decision matrix. The goal of the VIKOR algorithm is to rank all sentences based on these features from the best to worst one. The best sentences are the sentences that include a high combination of features, thus we can overcome the main general problem in the methods based on feature extraction. Where All these methods are based on scoring the sentences and the sentences with higher scores are chosen to be included in the final summary. According to this hypothesis, some features may have more effect than other features, therefore sentences that with higher values of these features have more chance to be included in the final summary. To create a decision matrix for VIKOR six features and M sentences are used as shown in Table 1.

At the end of the training procedure, a set of good solutions is created. The average of these solutions is computed by summing every bit with its corresponding bits in other solutions then dividing them by the total number of solutions.

Table 1. Decision matrix for TOPSIS method

	F1	F2	F3	F4	F5	F6
S_1	$X_{1,1}$	$X_{1,2}$	$X_{1,3}$	.		.
S_2	$X_{2,1}$	$X_{2,2}$	$X_{2,3}$	.	.	$X_{2,6}$
.	.	.	.	.	.	.
S_M	$X_{M,1}$	$X_{M,2}$	$X_{M,3}$	.	.	$X_{M,6}$

Algorithm 1 shows the main steps of the VIKOR algorithm.

Algorithm 1: VIKOR algorithm
Input: Decision matrix
Output: sentences in descending order

Step1: use CSA to compute feature weight W

Step2: Normalized a decision matrix by $F_{i,j} = \dfrac{x_{i,j}}{\sqrt{\sum_{i=1}^{n}(x_{i,j})^2}}$

Step3: Determine the best f_j^* And the worst f_j^-
Where $f_j^* = \max_i f_{ij}, f_j^- = \min_i f_{ij}$
Step4: Calculation of utility measure (S) and regret measure (R):
Where $S_i = \sum_{j=1}^{n} w_j \frac{(f_j^* - f_{ij})}{(f_j^* - f_j^-)}$ and $R_i = \max_j (S_{ij})$
Step5: Compute of VIKOR index (Q_i)by
$$Q_i = \frac{v(S_i - S^-)}{(S^* - S^-)} + \frac{(1-v)(R_i - R^*)}{(R^* - R^-)}$$
Here v=0.5
Step6: sort all sentences based on the results of step5 in descending order

---

5 Remove Redundancy

This stage is very necessary for MDS. There are many documents with the same topic, some sentences may be repeated in more than one document. A technique is required to remove the redundant sentences from the generated summary, which allows the final summary to include the most important ideas for the summarized documents. The cosine similarity as explained in Eq. (8) is used to compute the similarity between two sentences and exclude the sentence from a final summary when the similarity between them is more than a specified threshold [22].

$$Similarity(A, B) = \frac{\sum_{i=1}^{z} AiBi}{\sqrt{\sum_{i=1}^{z}(Ai)^{2*}}\sqrt{\sum_{i=1}^{z}(Bi)^2}} \qquad (8)$$

The Following Algorithm 2 illustrates reducing redundancy and generating a summary in the proposed MDS model.

Algorithm 2: Remove Redundancy
input 1- set of ranked sentences in descending order from VIKOR algorithm called scored_sent
2- Max summary size called Max_size
output generated summary called summary
Step1: let summary =[]
Size=0   No_of_sen=0
Step2 : from Scored_sent select Si with highest score
Step3 :Flag=false
for j from 1 to No_of_sen
compare Si with Sj{Sj sentence from summary} according to Eq.(8)
If (Similarity(Si,Sj) >threshold) then flag=true
Step4:if (flag) delete Si go to step2
Else Put Si in the summary
Size=size+count_words (Si)
NO_of_sen=No_of_sen+1
Step5: if size<max_size goto step2
Else end

6   Experimental Results

There are two main purposes of the proposed model for MDS. The first purpose is to compute the weight of the features that indicate the importance of these features. Figure 3 shows the weights of each feature in the proposed model. The results show the order of effective features weights are as follows TF, SP, PN, TW, SL, and ND.

The second purpose of the proposed model is to evaluate the generated summarize using Rouge-1 and Rouge-2 to compute the effectiveness of the proposed model. The results of the proposed model were compared with the results of the Ref. [8] That included as peer summaries in the TAC-2011 data set. Figures 4 and 5 shows the results of the proposed model and Rf. [8] using ROUGE-1 and ROUGE-2 respectively.

As it's clear the results of the proposed method are better than the results of the peer summaries and that because of two reasons. Firstly the good performance of the VIKOR algorithm to rank all sentences in good form, which overcame the problem of sentence ranking in other methods. The second reason the effect of the selected features which improves the performance of a VIKOR method. One of the most important points of the proposed model is the lack of need for the decision-maker to put criteria weights where the weights computed automatically.

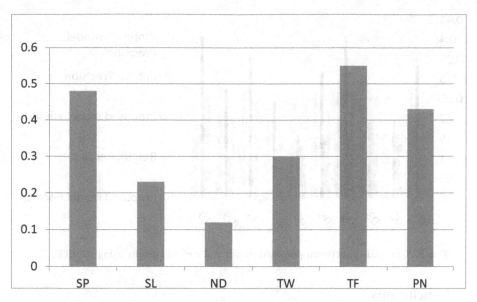

Fig. 3. Features weights

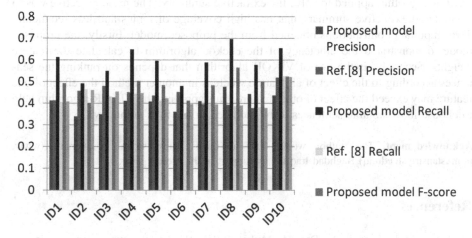

Fig. 4. Comparison between the proposed model and Ref. [8] results using ROUGE-1

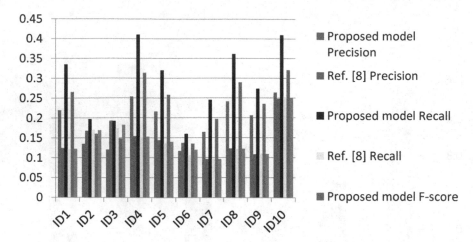

Fig. 5. Comparison between proposed model and Ref. [8] results using ROUGE-2.

7 Conclusions

The need for effective MDS methods to extract important information from a document collection becomes of necessity. In this article, a new model based on CS and the VIKOR algorithm applied to solve the extractive summary. The basic objective was to generate an extractive summary that has high coverage of topics and less redundant. Two important contributions obtained from the proposed model. Firstly, the proposed model demonstrated the efficiency of the cuckoo algorithm to calculate the feature weights. Secondly, is the use of VIKOR algorithm that depends on ranking the sentences according to the effect of all feature whereas in another method the effect of one feature may exceed the effect of other feature, thus applying the VIKOR algorithm help to choose most suitable sentences to be included in the final summary.

Acknowledgment. The author would like to thank Mustansiriyah University (www. uomustansiriyah.edu.iq) Baghdad-Iraq for its support in the present work.

References

1. Pattanaik, A., Sagnika, S., Das, M., Mishra, B.S.P.: Extractive summary: an optimization approach using bat algorithm. In: Hu, Y.-C., Tiwari, S., Mishra, K., Trivedi, M. (eds.) Ambient Communications and Computer Systems. AISC, vol. 904, pp. 175–186. Springer, Singapore (2019). https://doi.org/10.1007/978-981-13-5934-7_16
2. Kumar, R., Chandrakal, D.: A survey on text summarization using optimization algorithm. ELK Asia Pac. J. 2(1), 1–10 (2016)
3. Huang, L., He, Y., Wei, F., Li, W.: Modeling document summarization as multi-objective optimization. In: Intelligent Information Technology and Security Informatics (IITSI), pp. 382–386 (2010)

4. Song, W., Choi, L.C., Park, S.C., Ding, X.: Fuzzy evolutionary optimization modeling and its applications to unsupervised categorization and extractive summarization. Expert Syst. Appl. **38**(8), 9112–9121 (2011)
5. Babar, S.A., Patil, P.D.: Improving performance of text summarization. Proc. Comput. Sci. **46**, 354–363 (2015). ICICT 2014
6. García-Hernández, R.A., Ledeneva, Y.: Single extractive text summarization based on a genetic algorithm. In: Carrasco-Ochoa, J.A., Martínez-Trinidad, J.F., Rodríguez, J.S., di Baja, G.S. (eds.) MCPR 2013. LNCS, vol. 7914, pp. 374–383. Springer, Heidelberg (2013). https://doi.org/10.1007/978-3-642-38989-4_38
7. Alguliev, R., Isazade, N., Abdi, A., Idris, N.: A model for text summarization. Int. J. Intell. Inf. Technol. **13**(1), 67–85 (2017)
8. El-Haj, M.: Multi-document arabic text summarization. Albert Sloman Library, Essex University. Thesis (Ph.D.), School of Computer Science and Electronic Engineering – University of Essex (2012)
9. Abuobieda, A., Salim, N., Albaham, A., Osman, A.H.: Text summarization features selection method using pseudo genetic-based model. In: Conference on Information Retrieval & Knowledge Management, CAMP, pp. 193–197 (2012)
10. Ghalehtaki, R., Khotanlou, H., Esmaeilpour, M.: A combinational method of fuzzy, particle swarm optimization and cellular learning automata for text summarization. In: IEEE Conference, vol. 15, no. 1 (2014)
11. Verma, P., Om, H.: Collaborative ranking-based text summarization using a metaheuristic approach. In: Abraham, A., Dutta, P., Mandal, J., Bhattacharya, A., Dutta, S. (eds.) Emerging Technologies in Data Mining and Information Security. Advances in Intelligent Systems and Computing, vol. 814, pp. 417–426. Springer, Singapore (2019). https://doi.org/10.1007/978-981-13-1501-5_36
12. Porte, M.R.: An algorithm for suffix stripping. Program **14**(3), 130–137 (1980)
13. John, A.: Multi-document summarization system: using fuzzy logic and genetic algorithm. Int. J. Adv. Res. Eng. Technol. **7**(1), 30–40 (2016)
14. Yang, X., Deb, S.: Engineering optimization by Cuckoo search. Int. J. Math. Modell. Numer. Opt. **1**(4), 330–343 (2010)
15. Yang, X.: Nature-Inspired Optimization Algorithms, 1st edn. Elsevier, London (2014)
16. Solihin, M., Zanil, M.: Performance comparison of Cuckoo search and differential evolution algorithm for constrained optimization. In: International Engineering Research and Innovation Symposium (IRIS), vol. 160, no. 1, pp. 1–7 (2016)
17. Adnan, M., Razzaque, M.: A comparative study of particle swarm optimization and Cuckoo search techniques through problem-specific distance function. In: 2013 International Conference on Information and Communication Technology (ICoICT), Bandung, Indonesia (2013)
18. Binwahlan, M.S., Salim, N., Suanmali, L.: Swarm based text summarization. In: International Association of Computer Science and Information Technology-Spring Conference, IACSITSC 2009. IEEE (2009)
19. Giannakopoulos, G., El-Haj, M., Favre, B., Litvak, M., Steinberger, J., Varma, V.: TAC 2011 MultiLing pilot overview. In: Text Analysis Conference (TAC) 2011, MultiLing Summarisation Pilot, TAC, Maryland, USA (2011)
20. Lin, C.-Y: ROUGE: a package for automatic evaluation summaries. In: Proceedings of the Workshop on Text Summarization Branches Out, Barcelona, Spain, 25–26 July, pp. 74–81 (2004)
21. Wei, J., Lin, X.: The multiple attribute decision- making VIKOR method and its application. In: 4th International Conference on Wireless Communication Networking and Mobile Computing (2008)
22. Lin, Y., Jiang, J., Lee, S.: A similarity measure for text classification and clustering. IEEE Trans. Knowl. Data Eng. **26**(7), 1575–1590 (2014)

A Classification Approach
for Crime Prediction

Nur Ain Syahira Zaidi, Aida Mustapha$^{(\boxtimes)}$ ⓘ, Salama A. Mostafa ⓘ,
and Muhammad Nazim Razali ⓘ

Faculty of Computer Science and Information Technology,
Universiti Tun Hussein Onn Malaysia, 86400 Parit Raja,
Batu Pahat, Johor, Malaysia
syahieraa97@gmail.com, {aidam, salama}@uthm.edu.my,
nazim.uthm@gmail.com

Abstract. Crime is a universal social issue that affects a society's nature of life
and economic growth. With ever-increasing crime rates, law enforcement
agencies have begun to show interest in data mining approaches to analyze
crime patterns in an effort to protect their communities. Existing work in crime
prediction is carried out by clustering the attributes into a set of crime categories.
This paper is taking the classification approach to predict crime category by
building and comparing the performance of two classifiers; Random Forest and
Support Vector Machine. The classification model is built using the UCI Crime
and Communities dataset that consists of demographic information and other
attributes. The results have shown that Random Forest has outperformed the
Support Vector Machine in classifying the crimes with an accuracy of 99.9%
due to the mixed nature of numerical and categorical features in the datasets.

Keywords: Crime prediction · Classification · Random Forest · Support
Vector Machine (SVM)

1 Introduction

Crime is a harmful act against the public and one of the dangerous factors for any
country. Crimes have several types such as murder, robbery, sexual harassment, rape or
kidnapping. There are a few factors that can attract convicts to commit a crime such as
social and lifestyle pressure, poverty rate, an education level [1], and individual history.
The results from the previous year have shown that the number of criminal records has
steadily increased across the globe whether in urban or rural areas. According to
records, crimes such as burglary and incendiary have been reduced while crimes such
as murder, sexual abuse, and gang rape have increased [2].

Crime data analysis can now help law enforcement officials to solve crime cases
with the use of Intelligent Computing approaches, in particular, data mining to predict
the crime events. Crime prediction is widely used to analyse the trend and the factors
related to crime events. Crime prediction is the activity in which to predict future crime
behaviours based on the previous year of crime dataset. Predictions of crime activities
give a positive impact on the police department in tracking and improving the

M. I. Khalaf et al. (Eds.): ACRIT 2019, CCIS 1174, pp. 68–78, 2020.
https://doi.org/10.1007/978-3-030-38752-5_6

preventive measure to control the crimes in the future. Generally, data mining is divided into two categories with respect to the data to be mined, which are descriptive mining such as the clustering approaches and predictive mining such as using the classification approaches [3]. Each of the techniques has its own advantages and method to predict large dataset. Classification is a method that typically has strong modelling interactions, which can classify the item of datasets based on the characteristics of the items [4].

This research aims at classifying the category of crimes in distinct countries of the USA on the basis of features linked to community and society [5]. For the classification approach, we propose to use two classification algorithms, which are the Random Forest and Support Vector Machine (SVM) algorithms. At the end of this research, we will analyse which algorithm produces the highest accuracy and efficiency in predicting the crime. The rest of the paper is organized as follows. Section 2 reviews all works related to crime. Section 3 presents the CRISP-DM methodology used to conduct data mining tasks together with the dataset and the evaluation metrics. Section 4 provides the experimental outcomes, Sect. 5 discusses the results and lastly, Sect. 6 concludes with some guidance for future work.

2 Related Work

Iqbal et al. [5] performed an experimental study in classifying crimes. They applied two different classification algorithms, which are Decision Tree and Naïve Bayesian to predict the Crime Category for the different state in the USA. They used a nominal attribute to differentiate the value of 'Low', 'Medium', and 'High' for crime category based on the resulting confusion matrix. The results from both algorithms were evaluated by using four performance measurements named Accuracy, Precision and Recall, and F-Measure. From the experiments, the accuracy using 10-fold cross-validation for Decision Tree and Naïve Bayesian showed that Decision Tree performed better than the Naïve Bayesian.

Chandrasekar et al. [6] performed an experiment of crime prediction and classification in San Francisco City. The experiments were conducted by using San Francisco Classification dataset and improved by additional demographic data to predict which category of crime that is most likely occur based on time, place and demographics of the place. At first, they applied two algorithms such as Naïve Bayes and Random Forest model as the initial understanding quality of feature set. Then they continued with two other algorithms, which are Gradient Boosted Decision Trees (GBDT) and Support Vector Machines (SVM) to perform collapsed classes by splitting into two crime classes which are Blue Collar/White Collar Crime and Violent/Non-Violent Crimes. The experiment is measured by precision and recall for Blue Collar/White Collar Crime and Violent/Non-Violent Crimes in each algorithm. The results produced the highest precision and recall when using GBDT and SVM.

Yadav et al. [7] proposed four algorithms that are Association Mining, Clustering, Naïve Bayes Classification Techniques, Correlation, and Regression. The experiments were conducted on the dataset by using WEKA Tool and R Tool. The research aimed to provide a comprehensive summary of theory and research on crime prevention in society and to predict the crime and its pattern by implementing different data analysis algorithms. They used supervised, semi-supervised and unsupervised learning techniques in crime records to discover knowledge and to improve the predictive accuracy of the crime.

Most recent work in crime prediction, [8] highlighted the usage of data mining technique, which is decision tree (DT) for effective investigation of recidivism or a person's relapse into criminal behaviours, especially in domestic violence. They predicted whether the offender is going to recommit domestic violence (DV) connected offense for a period of 24 months. They used the DT induction to minimize the size and complexity of DTs trained while to retain a high degree of predictive precision. Different approaches have been used to deal with class imbalance, which is the majority class under-sampling and the minority over-sampling class to minimize and balance the dataset. They evaluated the accuracy of the training of DTs by measuring the area under the receiver operator characteristic curve (AUC-ROC) generated when plotting the True Positive Rate (TPR) against the False Positive Rate (FPR). In addition, the research also used the F-measure to average both types of errors; false positive and false negative.

3 Methodology

In predicting the crime category of the Crime and Communities dataset, this research employs the Cross-Industry Process for Data Mining (CRISP-DM) methodology that allows repetitive phases until a satisfactory result is obtained [9]. The CRISP-DM methodology offers a structured strategy and summary of the life-cycle of a data mining project. As shown in Fig. 1, the life-cycle of a data mining project is split into six phases but for this study, we only use four phases from the original phases, which includes data understanding, data preparation, modelling, and evaluation. The arrows indicate the dependencies between each phase and it expects the result of each phase that indicates from the relevant task of the next stage to be carried out [9].

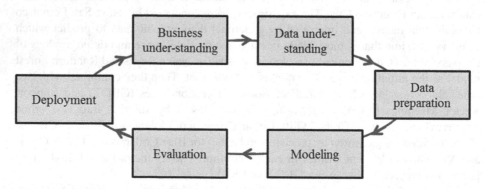

Fig. 1. Flow diagram of the CRISP-DM methodology [9].

Based on Fig. 1, the experiments in this paper adopts the classification approach in the modeling stage of CRISP-DM, where two classification algorithms will be used; Random Forest and Support Vector Machine (SVM). The detailed steps in the modelling stage are shown in Fig. 2.

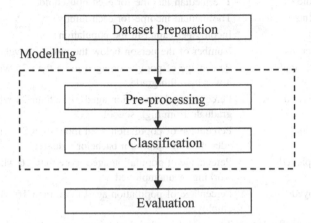

Fig. 2. Steps in the modelling stage of CRISP-DM.

The experiment is carried out using the Waikato Environment for Knowledge Analysis (WEKA) tool. WEKA is a system written in Java and distributed under the General Public License (GNU) [10]. WEKA provides with a variety of algorithms and data mining tasks with more specific that can easily use to the dataset. WEKA also provides a collection of techniques for data analysis and predictive modelling which ease to use over its graphical user interfaces. For this research, the data was validated with 10-fold cross-validation method to train the crime classification models. Cross-validation is a resampling procedure that is used to assess machine learning models on a restricted data sample. In k-folds cross-validation, the specific value for k is chosen and use in place of k in the model reference, which $k = 10$ becoming 10-fold cross-validation [11, 15].

3.1 Dataset

For this research, the dataset was retrieved from socioeconomic data from 1990 US Census, law enforcement data from the 1990 US LEMAS survey, and crime data from the 1995 FBI UCR [5] and it was available through a UCI Machine Learning Repository Dataset website. The dataset includes a total of 147 characteristics and 2,216 cases. This dataset is titled as crime and communities. The data that provided is in numeric and un-normalized. Each instance of data belongs to different states of the USA and each of the states is represented by the number of country code respectively to USA state. This dataset was used by previous researchers to predict the crime category for different states of the USA. The excerpt of the dataset is shown in Table 1.

Table 1. Features from the UCI Crime and Communities dataset

No	Features name	Description
1	States	States in the US
2	Population	Community population in each state
3	MedIncome	The median income for each household
4	MedFamInc	The median income for each family
5	PerCapInc	Income per capita in the population
6	NumUnderPov	Number of the person below the poverty level
7	PctLess9thGrade	Percentage of population aged more than 25 with education lower than 9th-grade
8	PctNotHSGrad	Percentage of population aged more than 25 who do not graduate from high school
9	PctBSorMore	Percentage of population aged more than 25 with tertiary education of minimum bachelor's degree
10	PctUnemployed	Percentage of population aged more than 16 who are already working or unemployed
11	PctEmployed	Percentage of population aged more than 16 who are employed
12	ViolentCrimesPerPop	Total number of violent crimes for each population of size 100,000 person
13	Crime Category	Crime categories – Low, Medium, High

3.2 Pre-processing

Before implementing the dataset into machine learning algorithms, pre-processing is discharged in order to improve the data quality. The dataset consists of total 2,216 instances which consist of several missing values. A few techniques were used for the pre-processing phase, which are data cleaning, integration, reduction, and transformation [5]. In preparing for the classification experiment, we performed feature selection, removal of missing values, and introduced a new attribute, which is the class attribute. The detailed activities are explained as follows.

- Feature selection is completed by selecting the most effective attributes in a dataset. Only twelve attributes were selected to be used in this experiment including ViolentCrimesPerPop, PctEmployed, PctUnemployed, PctBSorMor, Population, PctNotHSGrad, PctLess9thGrade, NumUnderPov, MedFamInc, PerCapInc, MedIncome, and States. The attributes are selected and choose based on previous research and to which attribute have less missing value.
- Removing missing value in row. The dataset contains one missing value in the instance for the attribute of state. To improve the dataset, the instance was reduced one row and the total instances that will be used in the experiment are 2,215. For 'Violent Crimes Per Pop' attribute, there are some missing values and to improve this dataset, the data is handled by computing the overall mean of the data in the attribute.

- A new attribute called 'Crime Category' was added to the set of attributes in the dataset. The values of this category are based on the percentage of 'ViolentCrimesPerPop' attribute. The Crime Category attribute is manually added for the 2,215 instances in order to improve the classification accuracy. This process is known as discretization, which is important in the classification experiment whereby the classes should be nominal rather than continuous values. These 'Crime Category' attribute is divided into three nominal classes which are Low, Medium and High. Each of the classes is evaluated using separation of percentage 'ViolentCrimesPerPop' attribute. If the percentage is lower than 25% then, it is Low. If the percentage is equal or larger than 25% and less than 40% then, it is Medium. If the percentage is larger than 40% then, it is High.

3.3 Classification Algorithms

This section explains the algorithms that will be used for this research study which is Random Forest and Support Vector Machine (SVM). Random Forest is a supervised classifier that combines a mixture of tree predictors. Every tree depends on the values of a random vector selected separately and each node is divided using the highest partition between all variables [11]. This factor makes Random Forest achieve high accuracy.

A random forests classifier [6] aggregates a family of classifiers of $h(x|\theta_1)$, $h(x|\theta_2)$, ... $h(x|\theta_k)$. Each member of the family, $h(x|\theta)$, is a classification tree and k is the number of trees chosen from a model random vector and each θ_k is a randomly choose from the parameter vector. If $D(x, y)$ denotes the training dataset, each classification tree in the ensemble is built using a different subset $D\theta_k(x, y) \subset D(x, y)$ of the training dataset. Thus, $h(x|\theta_k)$ is the kth classification tree which uses a subset of features $x\theta_k \subset x$ to build a classification models. Each tree then works like regular decision trees of it partitions the data based on the value of the feature, until the data is fully partitioned, or the maximum allowed depth is reached. The final output y is obtained by aggregating the results as shown in Eq. 1, where I denote the indicator function.

$$y = argmax_{p\in\{h(x_1)...h(x_k)\}}\left\{\sum_{j=1}^{k}(I(h(x|\theta_j) = p))\right\} \qquad (1)$$

Support Vector Machine (SVM) is an example of supervised classification techniques [12]. It is a new and promising algorithm to be used in data mining techniques. SVM aims to choose the best classification function to form parallel hyperplanes of separation (H1 and H2) that can maximize the margin between the two datasets [13]. The margin is basically the distance between the left hyperplane and right hyperplane. The bigger the margins, the lesser the generalization error of the SVM classifier.

The classical for binary class classification SVM by finding the maximum margin of the hyperplane splitting points for $x_i = 1$ against $x_i = -1$ and the linear separable training dataset between to hyperplanes is $\frac{2}{|w|}$. This means to increase to maximize the margin, we must minimize the weight vector $|w|$. Equation 2 shows the positive class hyperplane with positive x values and Eq. 3 shows the negative class hyperplane with negative x values, where w is a weight vector, x is input vector, and b is the bias.

$$w . x_i + b = 1 \tag{2}$$

$$w . x_i + b = -1 \tag{3}$$

Next, Eq. 4 shows the equation to maximize the margin between two hyperplanes or class, which represent the minimum magnitude of vector w.

$$\min|w| = y_i(w . x_i + b) \geq 1; \quad i = 1; \ldots, N \tag{4}$$

3.4 Evaluation Metrics

The Accuracy, Precision, Recall and F-Measure are used to measure and compare the performance of both algorithms; Random Forest and Support Vector Machines (SVM).

- Accuracy: Percentages (%) of the total sample numbers that are appropriately classified to the total number of the sample. The formula for calculating the accuracy is shown in Eq. 5.

$$\text{Accuracy (A)} = \frac{(TP + TN)}{(TP + TN + FP + FN)} \tag{5}$$

  where TP, TN, FP and FN are true positive, true negative, false positive and false negative.

- Precision: Percentages (%) of items selected that is right and calculated as in Eq. 6.

$$\text{Precision (P)} = \frac{TP}{(TP + FP)} \tag{6}$$

  where TP and FP represent as true positives and false positives respectively.

- Recall Percentages (%) of selected correct items and the calculation for it as in Eq. 7.

$$\text{Recall (R)} = \frac{TP}{(TP + FN)} \tag{7}$$

  where TP and FN represent true positives and false negatives, respectively.

- F-Measure: The balance of precision and recall. The calculation for F-Measure as in Eq. 8.

$$F - \text{Measure} = \frac{2 * (\text{Recall} * \text{Precision})}{(\text{Recall} + \text{Precision})} \tag{8}$$

Following [14], the performance of the classification methods will be compared by Accuracy, Precision, Recall and F-Measure. The methodology of this research is adopted from An Experiment Study of Classification Algorithms for Crime Prediction (2013).

4   Experimental Results

The objective of the experiment is to compare the accuracy of the crime prediction performance using the Random Forest and Support Vector Machine (SVM) algorithms in WEKA. The results of this research will separate into four evaluations, which are Accuracy, Precision, and Recall and F-Measure that are used to predict the crime dataset. This experiment is validated using 10-fold cross-validation method. The results from two classification algorithms of this experiment evaluated according to four performance measures which are defined in Table 2.

Table 2. 10-fold cross validation and accuracy results for Random Forest and SVM

Algorithm	Accuracy (%)	Error (%)	Precision (%)	Recall (%)	F-Measure (%)
Random Forest	99.8645	0.1355	0.999	0.999	0.999
SVM	97.1996	2.8004	0.973	0.972	0.970

From the results that collected in Table 2, it showed that Random Forest is the most efficient and the best classifier with 99.8645% of accuracy compared to Support Vector Machine (SVM) with 97.1996% for classifying the crime dataset. Figure 3 shows the comparison of Accuracy, Precision, Recall and F-Measure for two algorithms. The value of Accuracy, Precision, Recall and F-Measure for Random Forest are almost the same while the Accuracy, Precision, Recall and F-Measure for SVM are almost the same.

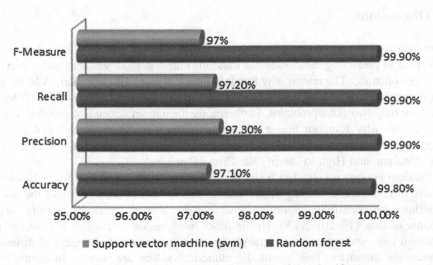

Fig. 3. Performance measures the results of the classifiers.

Tables 3 and 4 illustrate the confusion matrix for each class of Random Forest and SVM respectively. For the confusion matrix of Random Forest, it contains 1,937 items that classified into the class Low which 1,936 out of 1,937 are correctly classified. For class Medium, there are 191 items classified with 190 items are correctly classified. For class High, there are 86 items classified and 86 items are correctly classified.

Table 3. Confusion matrix of Random Forest.

Category	Low	Medium	High	Total
Low	1936	1	0	1937
Medium	1	190	0	191
High	0	1	85	86

Table 4. Confusion matrix of SVM.

Category	Low	Medium	High	Total
Low	1936	1	0	1937
Medium	28	163	0	191
High	0	33	53	86

The confusion matrix for SVM of each class is explained similarly to the confusion matrix of Random Forest. For class Low, there are 1,937 items are classified with 1,936 items are correctly classified. For class Medium, there are 191 items are classified and only 163 items are correctly classified while others are wrongly classified. For class High, there are 86 items are classified and only 53 items out of items are correctly classified while others are wrongly classified [16, 17].

5   Discussions

From the experimental results, it is clear that Random Forest and SVM have both well performed in predicting the classes but Random Forest is more efficient and achieved better performance. The reason why Random Forest is more efficient than SVM in this experiment is that Random Forest is suitable for multiclass problems while SVM is suited for only two-class problems. Furthermore, the dataset dependent problem is the other reason why Random Forest performed better than SVM. Recall that in this experiment, one column was added in categorical features with three values named Low, Medium, and High to classify the Crime Category.

Random Forests are also much simpler to train as they can work very well with a mixture of numerical and categorical features. The Random Forest is one of the finest algorithms for classifying algorithms that can be able to precisely classify large amounts of data [18–20]. SVM, on the other hand, needs to convert the dataset in numerical form and maximize the margin because it relies on the concept of distance between the instances. This means the numerical values are needed to ensure the separation of hyper-plane is efficient. SVM generally performs better on linear dependencies. These results will be the benchmark for future classification experiments using the same dataset as this dataset has only used previously in clustering tasks.

6 Conclusions and Future Work

In conclusion, this paper presented a comparison of two classification algorithms for crime prediction, which are Random Forest and Support Vector Machine (SVM) in classifying the crime. The results from the experiment validated using the 10-fold cross-validation showed that the Random Forest classification algorithm produced better accuracy as compared to SVM.

In the future, this research is hoped to explore more factors contributing to crime inclination with other types of algorithms. In addition, we will look into another method for handling the data for training and testing data to improve the performance of classifiers. Finally, we will explore more classification algorithms specific using this dataset since previous works mainly involved clustering experiments.

Acknowledgement. This research is supported by Universiti Tun Hussein Onn Malaysia.

References

1. Bennett, P.: The heterogeneous effects of education on crime: evidence from Danish administrative twin data. Labour Econ. **52**, 160–177 (2018)
2. Sathyadevan, S., Gangadharan, S.: Crime analysis and prediction using data mining. In: 2014 First International Conference on Networks & Soft Computing (ICNSC), pp. 406–412. IEEE, August 2014
3. Malathi, A., Baboo, S.S.: An enhanced algorithm to predict a future crime using data mining (2011)
4. Mostafa, S.A., et al.: Examining multiple feature evaluation and classification methods for improving the diagnosis of Parkinson's disease. Cogn. Syst. Res. **54**, 90–99 (2019)
5. Iqbal, R., Murad, M.A.A., Mustapha, A., Panahy, P.H.S., Khanahmadliravi, N.: An experimental study of classification algorithms for crime prediction. Indian J. Sci. Technol. **6** (3), 4219–4225 (2013)
6. Chandrasekar, A., Raj, A.S., Kumar, P.: Crime Prediction and Classification in San Francisco City (2015). http://cs229.stanford.edu/proj2015/228_report.pdf
7. Yadav, S., Timbadia, M., Yadav, A., Vishwakarma, R., Yadav, N.: Crime pattern detection, analysis & prediction. In: 2017 International conference of Electronics, Communication and Aerospace Technology (ICECA), vol. 1, pp. 225–230. IEEE, April 2017
8. Wijenayake, S., Graham, T., Christen, P.: A decision tree approach to predicting recidivism in domestic violence. arXiv preprint arXiv:1803.09862 (2018)
9. Wirth, R., Hipp, J.: CRISP-DM: towards a standard process model for data mining. In: Proceedings of the 4th International Conference on the Practical Applications of Knowledge Discovery and Data Mining, pp. 29–39. Citeseer, April 2000
10. Kalmegh, S.: Analysis of Weka data mining algorithm REPTree, simple cart and RandomTree for classification of Indian news. Int. J. Innov. Sci. Eng. Technol. **2**(2), 438–446 (2015)

11. Kalmegh, S.R.: Comparative analysis of WEKA data mining algorithm RandomForest, RandomTree and LADTree for classification of indigenous news data. Int. J. Emerg. Technol. Adv. Eng. **5**(1), 507–517 (2015)

12. Mostafa, S.A., Mustapha, A., Khaleefah, S.H., Ahmad, M.S., Mohammed, M.A.: Evaluating the performance of three classification methods in diagnosis of Parkinson's disease. In: Ghazali, R., Deris, M., Nawi, N., Abawajy, J. (eds.) SCDM 2018. AISC, vol. 700, pp. 43–52. Springer, Cham (2018). https://doi.org/10.1007/978-3-319-72550-5_5

13. Mostafa, S.A., Mustapha, A., Mohammed, M.A., Ahmad, M.S., Mahmoud, M.A.: A fuzzy logic control in adjustable autonomy of a multi-agent system for an automated elderly movement monitoring application. Int. J. Med. Inform. **112**, 173–184 (2018)

14. Gupta, A., Mohammad, A., Syed, A., Halgamuge, M.N.: A comparative study of classification algorithms using data mining: crime and accidents in Denver City the USA. Education **7**(7), 374–381 (2016)

15. Arunkumar, N., Mohammed, M.A., Mostafa, S.A., Ibrahim, D.A., Rodrigues, J.J., de Albuquerque, V.H.C.: Fully automatic model-based segmentation and classification approach for MRI brain tumor using artificial neural networks. Concurr. Comput. Pract. Exp. e4962 (2018)

16. Hassan, M.H., Mostafa, S.A., Mustapha, A., Wahab, M.H.A., Nor, D.M.: A survey of multi-agent system approach in risk assessment. In: 2018 International Symposium on Agent, Multi-Agent Systems and Robotics (ISAMSR), pp. 1–6. IEEE, August 2018

17. Khaleefah, S.H., Mostafa, S.A., Mustapha, A., Darman, R.: A general framework of multi-agent features extraction operators for deformed images identification. In: 2018 International Symposium on Agent, Multi-Agent Systems and Robotics (ISAMSR), pp. 1–5. IEEE, August 2018

18. Rodriguez, J.D., Perez, A., Lozano, J.A.: Sensitivity analysis of k-fold cross validation in prediction error estimation. IEEE Trans. Pattern Anal. Mach. Intell. **32**(3), 569–575 (2010)

19. Khalaf, B.A., Mostafa, S.A., Mustapha, A., Mohammed, M.A., Abduallah, W.M.: Comprehensive review of artificial intelligence and statistical approaches in distributed denial of service attack and defense methods. IEEE Access **7**, 51691–51713 (2019)

20. Al Amrani, Y., Lazaar, M., El Kadiri, K.E.: Random forest and support vector machine based hybrid approach to sentiment analysis. Proc. Comput. Sci. **127**, 511–520 (2018)

Classifying Political Arabic Articles Using Support Vector Machine with Different Feature Extraction

Dhafar Hamed Abd[1,2]([✉]) [iD], Ahmed T. Sadiq[1]([✉]) [iD],
and Ayad R. Abbas[1]([✉]) [iD]

[1] Department of Computer Science, University of Technology, Baghdad, Iraq
Dhafar.dhafar@gmail.com, Drahmaed_tark@yahoo.com,
ayad_cs@yahoo.com
[2] Department of Computer Science, Al-Maarif University College, Alanbar, Iraq

Abstract. In the recent years, the number of web logs, and the amount of opinionated data on the World Wide Web, have been grown substantially. The ability to determine the political orientation of an article automatically can be beneficial in many areas from academia to security. However, the sentiment classification of web log posts (political web log posts in particular), is apparently more complex than the sentiment classification of conventional text. In this paper, a supervised machine learning with two feature extraction techniques Term Frequency (TF) and Term Frequency-Inverse Document Frequency (TF-IDF) are used for the classification process. For investigation, SVM with four kernels for supervised machine learning have been employed. Subsequent to testing, the results reveal that the linear with TF achieved the results in accuracy of 91.935% also with TF-IDF achieved the 95.161%. The linear kernel was deemed the most suitable for our model.

Keywords: Term frequency · Term Frequency-Inverse Document Frequency · Support Vector Machine (SVM) · Arabic Article · Political and machine learning

1 Introduction

Sentiment classification is defined as the ability to decide whether a passage of text is positive, negative or nature, with regards to a specific subject matter [1, 2] in more precise words, It is the ability to grade a passage in keeping with its overall sentiment $p \in \{-1, 1\}$, in which -1 signifies an unfavourable depiction, while 1 signifies a favourable depiction [3]. This type of classification facilitates the separation of a compilation of opinions into two conflicting divisions. The application of sentiment classification, to the extensive amount of opinions in the mounting number of on-line documents, has proven to be very advantageous. The predicting and labelling of a web log post can enhance the web logging process, by organizing the available information for users. Thus, the users can share and discus their opinions smoothly in weblogs [4].

© Springer Nature Switzerland AG 2020
M. I. Khalaf et al. (Eds.): ACRIT 2019, CCIS 1174, pp. 79–94, 2020.
https://doi.org/10.1007/978-3-030-38752-5_7

This paper investigates two issues: the general classification of political regimes, and the manner in which the Arabic data set ought to be classified. With regards to the latter issue, the labelling of political regimes cannot proceed without a comprehensible definition of these regimes.

Political web logs are a recent development in the field of sentiment classification studies. The objective of our undertaking is to assess the viability of the current available technology for sentiment classification [5]. We focused to establish machine learning techniques, especially using support vector machines [6]. A number of studies has been carried out that explore sentiment analysis, which deal with different levels of the analysed texts, including word, sentence, and document level. Word level sentiment analysis explore the orientation of the words in the text. While, sentence level express a single opinion and attempt to describe its orientation. The proposed method of the current study is concentrate on sentiment analysis for document level opinion mining.

This study examines the application of sentiment classification for a wide group of opinions available in web logs, focusing specially on political web logs. It is common that political web logs are opinionated and loaded with sentiment. Predicting a political web post's sentiment (include predicting whether the source of the post is a reform, revolutionary or conservative blogger), can potentially be more complex than predicting the sentiment of conventional text (such as those related to products or movie reviews). In general, non-professionals are considered the most contributors to web logs and most the writings assumed to be in conversational document mode [7, 8].

The reminder of this paper is organized as follows. Related works discusses in Sect. 2. Section 3 illustrates the model architecture. The evaluation matric introduces in Sect. 4, followed by the presentation of our approach experimental results in Sect. 5. Finally, Sect. 6 discuss our conclusions and future works.

2 Related Works

Previous investigations in this area can be categorized according to the technique employed, to realize sentiment classification. The knowledge-based approach relies mainly on linguistic models to gather information on the sentiment of a passage. In order to investigate more about the knowledge-based approach, statistical and machine learning were used in our experiment.

Several survey papers, regarding sentiment classification, are documented in literature review to this subject [9–11]. Forwarded a categorization process for sentiment classification techniques. In their initial step, the approaches were separated into two categories. They were either learning-based or lexicon-based approaches. The learning-based techniques were then split into two groups, one representing supervised knowledge, and the other unsupervised techniques.

Zhou et al. [12] suggested the existence of a third category: semi-supervised learning. The development of an extensive labelled dataset calls for a substantial amount of time and expenditure. As such, the application of unsupervised learning [13], or semi-supervised learning [14] techniques, should be considered viable alternatives.

Nasukawa and Yi [15] took a unique route towards the realization sentiment classification. They opted to consider a topic an item holding a variety of components or characteristics, and strived to detect the sentences with opinions related to the topic's characteristics. Sentiment analysis entails the recognition of the polarity and potency of the expressions, with regards to their association to the topic. Subsequent to the selection of a specific topic of interest, Tetsuya and Jeonghee Yi proceeded to manually define a sentiment lexicon for classification. Their approach proved to be functional during efforts aimed at assessing customer satisfaction, regarding a specific manufactured item. The availability of online product web logs provides consumers with the opportunity to assess the quality of manufactured items. This situation is deemed beneficial to both manufacturers and consumers.

The successful application of standard machine learning procedures, to a movie review database, is credited to Lee, Pang and Vaithyanathan [16]. This landmark achievement was made possible through the application of Naïve Bayes, Maximum Entropy and Support Vector Machines. Their representation of the reviews came in eight distinct layouts, with the most uncomplicated depicted as a unigram representation. The precision of their most effective representation (the unigram feature set representation), and their most applicable machine learning induction process (the support vector machines), delivered an accuracy level of 82.9%. Their Naïve Bayes classifier, with a unigram feature set representation, provided an accuracy level of 81.0%. From here, this team went on to develop a system that takes the nature of a review into consideration. They put forward that the objective sentences in a review depict the movie's story line, while the subjective sentences define the opinion of the reviewer with regards to the story. They successfully generated extracts from the reviews holding the most opinionated sentences. Their approach led to the creation of extracts 60% the size of the initial review, with a degree of accuracy superior, or at the least equivalent, to that of the whole text [17].

Both, Hearst [18] and Sack [19] are used cognitive linguistics models for the sentiment classification of whole documents. Huettner and Subasic [20], Das and Chen [21], as well as Tong [22], are among the researchers who delved into the manual or semi-manual crafting of a discriminate word lexicon, for the categorization of the sentiment of a passage.

Hatzivassiloglou and McKeown [23], and Turney and Littman [24] discussed the classification of the orientation of words, instead of a whole passage. They relied on the semantic orientation of distinct words or phrases, to establish the semantic orientation of the holding passage. Their approach entailed the pre-selection of a compilation of seed words, or the application of linguistic heuristics, for sentiment classification of the passage.

3   Methodology

The classification of political regimes is generally considered difficult and time-consuming procedure. Thus, this paper proposed a new solution that can facilitate the classification of political articles. The proposed approach aimed to determine the efficiency of established sentiment classification techniques, with regards to our innovative compilation of political web posts. We intended the employment of machine learning techniques, involving support vector machines, and assessed their applicability to our area of interest.

The development of our model begins with the gathering of data from various websites (blogs, newspapers and social networks) for the generation of raw data. Figure 1 portrays the phases involved in the development of this model.

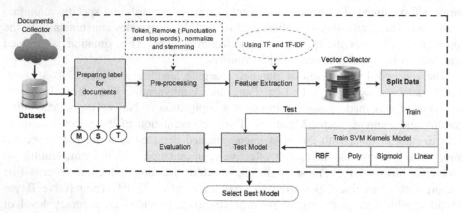

Fig. 1. Portrays the phases involved in the development of this model.

3.1 Dataset Collection

The general idea of political regimes database is presented in this section. Raw data were gathered from website blogs and newspapers. Our dataset comes with three labels in total of 206 documents as illustrated in Table 1. The labels were converted from Arabic to English in order to render it more concise.

Table 1. Illustrated our dataset.

Document number	Label of document by Arabic	Encode label
80	تيار اصلاحي (Reform Party)	S
58	تيار محافظ (Conservative Party)	M
68	تيار ثوري (Revolutionary Party)	T

3.2 Preparing Label

The label indicates the specific category or the data class. Although the labelling process is considered simple and straightforward, it is still an essential part of data pre-processing in Machine learning. The training sets of our model is based on historical data with pre-identified target features (values). Mapping is an essential part for the identification of target features through algorithms. The labelling process needs to be conducted precisely, as any error or imprecision can render the quality of the dataset, and the general performance of the predictive model.

3.3   Pre-processing

Pre-processing is considered such an effective technique to ensure the validity of the collected data. For the purpose of assessing contemporary technology relevant to this domain, we generated three separate compilations of classifiers. Each compilation facilitated the assessment of one known feature of a particular technology, relevant to sentiment classification.

The initial pre-processing step involves the breaking up of sentence chains, into words known as tokens. During this process, certain sentence elements (such as punctuation marks or English words) are removed to trim down the data corpus.

Normalization. This procedure is employed to normalise the data's array of independent variables and attributes. This procedure is usually executed during the data pre-processing process. Normalization involves three steps [25], beginning with the removal of a diacritics from an Arabic word, and culminating in the conversion of an alphabetic word into another. An example of this process is displayed in Fig. 2.

Fig. 2. The diacritics have to eliminate

Remove (——) from Arabic writing (الاصـــلاح, "reform") to realize (الاصلاح, "reform"), then convert the alphabetic word into another, as depicted in Table 2. When normalization complete, we can remove less than three alphabetic words.

Table 2. The third normalization of words

Original	Become	Example	
اآأإ	ا	الأصلاح "reform"	الاصلاح "reform"
ى	ي	قوى "strong"	قوي "strong"
ؤ	ء	اداؤه "performance"	اداءه "performance"
ئ	ء	يتلائم "fits"	يتلاءم "fits"
ة	ه	ثورية "Revolutionary"	ثوريه "Revolutionary"

Stop Words. The Arabic stop word can be filtered from a document by removing the token, and matching the word with the stop words listed in the catalogue. The catalogue is divided into two sections: The first section is a built-in NLTK library [26], and the second section register the words that are inconsequential to the sentence.

Stemming. The most crucial procedure in pre-processing step for sentiment analysis is stemming [27]. Generally, stemming serves to condense a word into stem mode, and diminish the data corpus. Arabic stemming can be applied through two different procedures [28] Among these procedures is light stemming, which was employed for this investigation [29].

3.4   Feature Extraction

Term frequency (**TF**) indicates the rate of recurrence in a particular document. Since the length of documents varies from one to another, it is common for a particular term to be repeated more often in longer than in shorter documents. To realize normalization, the term frequency is usually divided by the document through the following equation:

$$TF = \frac{n}{\sum Tn} \tag{1}$$

In which n represents the recurrence of a term in the sentence, while Tn represents the overall count of terms in the document.

TF-IDF: This scheme computes the products of term frequency (TF) and inverse document frequency (IDF) [30]. IDF Inverse document frequency refers to the procedure for gauging the importance of a term. During calculations for TF, all terms are regarded similarly significant. However, terms such as 'في', 'الى' and 'على' while occurring frequently, are of little significance. Thus, frequent terms need to be weighed down, while the uncommon ones need to be scaled up. The following Eq. (2) serves to realize an ideal outcome:

$$IDF = \log\left(\frac{N}{df}\right) \tag{2}$$

In which N represents the overall document count, and df represents the number of documents with the particular term. TF-IDF is a sophisticated scheme capable of discerning words in the document as well as in the corpus. The equation for computing TF-IDE is expressed as follows:

$$TF - IDF = TF * IDF \tag{3}$$

This scheme diminishes the weight of features in documents, prior to feature selection to reduce the vector size. Subsequently, the features are subjected to machine learning techniques [31, 32].

3.5   Split Dataset

During this phase, we split our data into training and testing sets. As exhibited in Table 3, the 70% split for training amounted to 144 documents, while the 30% split for testing amounted to 62 documents.

Table 3. Split data for training and testing

Documents label	Training for number of documents	Testing for number of documents
S	55	25
M	43	15
T	46	22
Total	**144**	**62**

4 Model Description

Support Vector Machines (SVMs) is among the most frequently utilized classifiers. The fundamental concept of SVM is the use of hyperplanes for the separation of dissimilar classes. While SVM is highly acclaimed for its precision when dealing with linearly separable data, its performance falls short when it comes to non-linearly separable data. The solution to this problem lies in the use of kernel functions, to shift the data to a broader dimensional space. With this move, the data can now be linearly separated.

The main idea of SVM is to select an appropriate kernel function, as well as adjusting of kernel parameters. In terms of calculations, seeking for the most appropriate decision plane is an optimization issue. An appropriate decision plane would serve to facilitate the generation of linear decisions by the kernel function, through a nonlinear transformation as shown in Eq. (4).

$$f(x) = w^T x_i + b$$
$$f(x) = \sum_{i=0}^{N} \lambda_i y_i \left(w_i^T x + b \right) \tag{4}$$

w^T represents the vector weight, $f(x)$ represents the feature sets of both classes, λ_i represents the dual function returned subsequent to training, x represents the training data set, y represents the classes (output) and b bias represents omega 0.

4.1 Kernel Function

Support vector machines perform well in linearly separable situations. However, there are situations in which linear separation is not feasible. In the face of non-linear situations, the performance of support vector machines leaves much to be desired. To overcome this dilemma, the kernel method was conceived as shown in Eq. (5). This method allows the use of a linear classifier to manage non-linear situations.

Other than their usefulness for non-linear issues, kernels also come with the advantage of tuneable parameters. A well-known kernel strategy involves utilizing a radial basis function (RBF) kernel and maximizing its sigma parameter together with the C parameter. While the RBF kernel is frequently employed for fitting data due to its flexibility, other prominent kernels, including the polynomial and sigmoid kernels, are also applied and maximized in a like manner.

Other than the kernel and SVM parameters, the data too is a significant classification factor. The SVM algorithm is dependent on the data values, for the plotting of training examples in a high dimensional space. While the conversion to the high dimensional space is the function of the kernel as, the effortlessness of separation is highly reliant on the accessibility of the feature set. There are several kernel listed in Eqs. (6–9) [33, 34].

$$f(x) = \sum_{i=0}^{N} \lambda_i y_i \left(w_i^T x + b \right) K \left(x_i, x_j \right) \tag{5}$$

Linear kernel:

$$K(x_i, x_j) = (x_i . x_j) \tag{6}$$

Polynomial kernel:

$$K(x_i, x_j) = (x_i . x_j + c)^d \tag{7}$$

where d is the degree of kernel
  RBF Kernel:

$$K(x_i, x_j) = e^{(-\gamma \|x_i - x_j\|^2)} \tag{8}$$

Sigmoid kernel:
We can use Sigmoid as the proxy for neural networks. Equation is

$$K(x_i, x_j) = \tanh(\alpha x^T . y + c) \tag{9}$$

SVM provides training sets of documents as input and output, input belongs to TF or TF-IDF feature extraction attributes $(x_1, x_2, x_3, \ldots, x_n)$ and the output result for the documents (classes) $(y_1, y_2, y_3, \ldots, y_m)$ where $x_i \in inputfeatures$ and $y_i \in \{class\}$, then become (x_n, y_m). There are a set of weight w_i to estimate the accurate value of (y) is described in Algorithm 1 [35].

Algorithm 1: Support Vector Machine

1 **Input:**
2 S = {$(x_i, y_i) | x_i \in$ R^n,$y_i \in$ m, $i \in$ {1,2,...,N}} – the set of N training samples and class;
3 Z = {z_i| $z_i \in$ R^m,$i \in$ {1,2,...,t}} – the set of t test samples;
4 **Initialization:**
5   Y $\leftarrow \emptyset$
6   **Computation:**
7   **for** $z_i \in$ Z **do**
8   K $\leftarrow$ the kernel functions according to S;
9     $y \leftarrow$ the class predicted by applying K on z_i;
10    $Y \leftarrow Y \cup \{y\}$;
11   **Output:**
12    $Y = \{y_i | y_i \in$ N $i \in$ {1,2,...,t}} - the set of predicted class for the test samples in Z.

---

5   Evaluation Metric

We nominated to apply a comparable validation procedure for every classifier percentage. A dataset with roughly similar sizes and class distributions was considered. The classifier is trained for every fold, using the percentage for class. In this segment, we provide a clarification based on the performance measurement for the machine learning classification problem, whereby the output can comprise two, or more than two classes. The three classes (M, S and T) in our investigation, and the 9 different combinations of predicted and actual values, are shown in Table 4.

Table 4. Exhibited Confusion matrix

		Predicted label		
		M	S	T
True label	M	MM	MS	MT
	S	SM	SS	ST
	T	TM	TS	TT

A confusion matrix is a highly proficient procedure for measuring accuracy, recall, precision and F1-Score [36, 37].

Based on the confusion matrix, several measurements can be accessed to test the model's level of accuracy. This level of accuracy can be ascertained through the formula shown below (Formula 10).

$$AC = \frac{MM + SS + TT}{(MM + MS + MT) + (SM + SS + ST) + (TM + TS + TT)} \tag{10}$$

The main objective of Eq. 11 is to determine the classification correctness for 'recall'.

$$Recall(M) = \frac{MM}{(MM + MS + MT)}$$

$$Recall(S) = \frac{SS}{(SM + SS + ST)} \tag{11}$$

$$Recall(T) = \frac{TT}{(TM + TS + TT)}$$

'Precision', which was incorrectly classified, can be determined through the equation shown below (Eq. 12).

$$Precision(M) = \frac{MM}{(MM + SM + TM)}$$

$$Precision(S) = \frac{SS}{SS + MS + TS)} \tag{12}$$

$$Precision(T) = \frac{TT}{(TT + MT + ST)}$$

The 'F1-score' can now be ascertained by way of the equation below (Eq. 13).

$$\text{F1-Score} = 2 * \frac{Recall * Precesion}{Recall + Precesion} \tag{13}$$

It is common practice to employ the confusion matrix for the evaluation of accuracy. In this situation, the confusion matrix relies principally on the selection of datasets. Our application of the contingency table is mainly for the enhancement of accuracy and performance.

6   Experimental Results

Experiments were conducted, to assess the performance of the recommended procedure, for the optimization of SVM parameters. During training, a category sample was classified in a separate class from the remaining samples. Unknown samples were classified under the category of those with the greatest possible classification function value.

While the performance of SVMs in linearly separable situations has been deemed effective, the same cannot be said for its performance in non-linearly separable situations. The introduction of kernels has proven to be an appropriate response to this problem. In a situation where the data are non-linearly separable, SVM employs kernel functions to map the data into a higher dimensional space, where linear separation of the data becomes possible. SVM and kernel parameters were applied to realize the results exhibited in Table 5. Python programming was used for the testing process.

Table 5. Parameters of SVM

Parameters	Value	Details
C	1.0	Penalty parameter
Coef0	0.0	Independent term in kernel function. It is only significant in poly kernel and sigmoid kernel
Degree	3	Degree of poly kernel
Gamma	1/features	Kernel coefficient for (RBF, poly and sigmoid)
Max iteration	−1	No limit
Tol	0.001	Tolerance for stopping criterion
Cache size	200	Cache of kernel size in MB
Decision function shape	OVO	Decision function which has shape (samples, classes * (classes - 1)/2) [38]

As shown above in Table 3 in Sect. 3.5, our data comprising 206 documents were split into two sets: one for training, and the other for testing. Table 6 offers an example of how a confusion matrix can contribute towards the enhancement of accuracy.

Table 6. Confusion matrix of RBF Kernel using TF

		Predicted label		
		M	S	T
True label	M	6	9	0
	S	0	25	0
	T	0	5	17

Table 7 provides the number of correct predictions and the values for all the kernels in TF. We carried out two separate tests, one for the application of TF, and the other for the application of TF-IDF. The table below portrays the test for the application of TF with four distinct SVM kernels.

Table 7. TF with different kernels

Kernel	Label	Precision	Recall	F1-score	No. of correct predict	Avg. Accuracy
RBF	M	1	0.40	0.57	6	77.419%
	S	0.64	1	0.78	25	
	T	1	0.77	0.87	17	
poly	M	0	0	0	0	40.322%
	S	0.40	1	0.57	25	
	T	0	0	0	0	
sigmoid	M	0	0	0	0	43.548%
	S	0.42	1	0.59	25	
	T	1	0.09	0.17	2	
linear	M	0.78	0.93	0.85	14	**91.935%**
	S	0.95	0.84	0.89	21	
	T	1	1	1	22	

As shown in the above table, the linear kernel achieved a higher level of accuracy (91.935%) while RBF kernel achieved (77.419%), Sigmoid kernel (43.548%), and finally poly kernel (40.322%). The training and testing curve are displayed in Fig. 3.

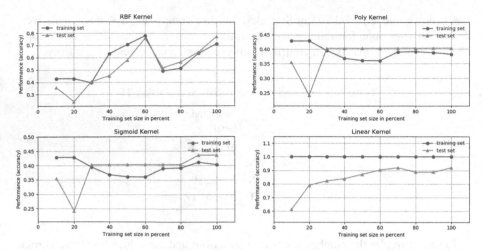

Fig. 3. Dataset training and testing

As revealed in Fig. 3, the linear kernel is produced better outcomes as it comes with a space between training and testing. Through previous experiments and studies, it has been shown, when the start of being high-value training will be in the best. Also observed the testing begins a high value and the end is the same it, that's mean is the best case (Table 8).

Table 8. TF-IDF with different kernels

Kernel	Label	Precision	Recall	F1-score	No. of correct predict	Avg. Accuracy
RBF	M	0	0	0	0	40.322%
	S	0.40	1	0.57	25	
	T	0	0	0	0	
poly	M	0	0	0	0	40.322%
	S	0.40	1	0.57	25	
	T	0	0	0	0	
sigmoid	M	0	0	0	0	40.322%
	S	0.40	1	0.57	25	
	T	0	0	0	0	
linear	M	0.93	0.93	0.93	14	**95.161%**
	S	0.92	0.96	0.94	24	
	T	1	0.95	0.98	21	

Also, linear kernel achieved a higher level of accuracy (95.161%) than other kernels. The training and testing curve are displayed in Fig. 4.

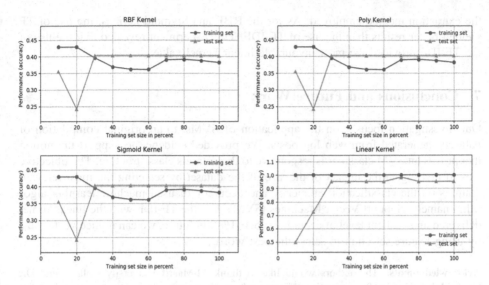

Fig. 4. Kernel model accuracy

As Fig. 4 show the linear kernel is also favourable as it comes with a space between training and testing. Figure 5 illustrate the model accuracy in our empirical study.

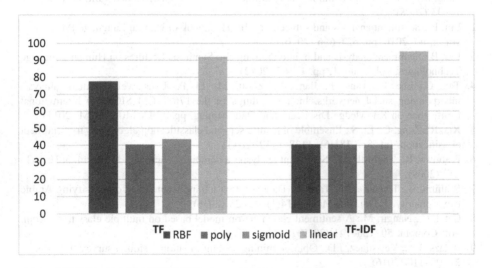

Fig. 5. Model accuracy

TF was used for the extraction of the features, which were then applied to four types of kernels. This test revealed the linear kernel to be of the highest value. The linear value for data extraction through TF-IDF was observed to be above those of the other kernels. It is notable that the value for poly kernel remained unchanged no matter the extraction method employed. As for the RBF and Sigmoid kernels, the use of TF yielded better results than the use of TF-IDF. This experiment revealed that the use of the TF-IDF provided the most favourable linear kernel value.

7 Conclusions and Future Work

Our investigation focused on the application of SVMs, to an original compilation of datasets, generated from web log posts. We provided evidence to support the notion that proves an SVM classifier is responsive to the datasets class structure. The objective was to investigate the impact of the size of the dataset by selecting the most relevant features on the classification efficiency and accuracy of used machine learning algorithm namely; Support Vector Machines (SVM). Use the TF-IDF with the linear kernel delivered an excellent level of accuracy (95.161%). In future, we can reduce vector size by using feature selection to select the best words.

Acknowledgments. The authors would like to thank Al-Maarif University College and Dr. Falah Mubark Bardan for supporting this research.

References

1. Pang, B., Lee, L.: Opinion mining and sentiment analysis. Found. Trends® Inf. Retr. 2(1–2), 1–135 (2008)
2. Liu, B.: Sentiment analysis and subjectivity. In: Handbook of Natural Language Processing, vol. 2, no. 2010, pp. 627–666 (2010)
3. Liu, B.: Sentiment analysis and opinion mining. In: Synthesis Lectures on Human Language Technologies, vol. 5, no. 1, pp. 1–167 (2012)
4. Tan, C., Lee, L., Tang, J., Jiang, L., Zhou, M., Li, P.: User-level sentiment analysis incorporating social networks. In: Proceedings of the 17th ACM SIGKDD International Conference on Knowledge Discovery and Data Mining, pp. 1397–1405. ACM (2011)
5. Xia, R., Zong, C., Li, S.: Ensemble of feature sets and classification algorithms for sentiment classification. Inf. Sci. 181(6), 1138–1152 (2011)
6. Prabowo, R., Thelwall, M.: Sentiment analysis: a combined approach. J. Inform. 3(2), 143–157 (2009)
7. Brahimi, B., Touahria, M., Tari, A.: Data and text mining techniques for classifying Arabic tweet polarity. J. Dig. Inf. Manag. 14(1), 15–25 (2016)
8. Catal, C., Nangir, M.: A sentiment classification model based on multiple classifiers. Appl. Soft Comput. 50, 135–141 (2017)
9. Balazs, J.A., Velásquez, J.D.: Opinion mining and information fusion: a survey. Inf. Fusion 27, 95–110 (2016)
10. Medhat, W., Hassan, A., Korashy, H.: Sentiment analysis algorithms and applications: a survey. Ain Shams Eng. J. 5(4), 1093–1113 (2014)
11. Ravi, K., Ravi, V.: A survey on opinion mining and sentiment analysis: tasks, approaches and applications. Knowl.-Based Syst. 89, 14–46 (2015)
12. Zhou, S., Chen, Q., Wang, X.: Fuzzy deep belief networks for semi-supervised sentiment classification. Neurocomputing 131, 312–322 (2014)

13. Turney, P.D.: Thumbs up or thumbs down?: semantic orientation applied to unsupervised classification of reviews. In: Proceedings of the 40th Annual Meeting on Association for Computational Linguistics, pp. 417–424. Association for Computational Linguistics (2002)
14. Sindhwani, V., Melville, P.: Document-word co-regularization for semi-supervised sentiment analysis. In: 2008 Eighth IEEE International Conference on Data Mining, pp. 1025–1030. IEEE (2008)
15. Nasukawa, T., Yi, J.: Sentiment analysis: capturing favorability using natural language processing. In: Proceedings of the 2nd International Conference on Knowledge Capture, pp. 70–77. ACM (2003)
16. Pang, B., Lee, L., Vaithyanathan, S.: Thumbs up?: sentiment classification using machine learning techniques. In: Proceedings of the ACL-02 Conference on Empirical Methods in Natural Language Processing, vol. 10, pp. 79–86. Association for Computational Linguistics (2002)
17. Pang, B., Lee, L.: A sentimental education: sentiment analysis using subjectivity summarization based on minimum cuts. In: Proceedings of the 42nd annual meeting on Association for Computational Linguistics, p. 271. Association for Computational Linguistics (2004)
18. Hearst, M.A.: Direction-based text interpretation as an information access refinement. In: Text-Based Intelligent Systems: Current Research and Practice in Information Extraction and Retrieval, pp. 257–274 (1992)
19. Sack, W.: On the computation of point of view. In: AAAI, p. 1488 (1994)
20. Huettner, A., Subasic, P.: Fuzzy typing for document management. In: ACL 2000 Companion Volume: Tutorial Abstracts and Demonstration Notes, pp. 26–27 (2000)
21. Das, S., Chen, M.: Yahoo! for Amazon: extracting market sentiment from stock message boards. In: Proceedings of the Asia Pacific Finance Association Annual Conference (APFA), Bangkok, Thailand, vol. 35, p. 43 (2001)
22. Wang, Z., Tong, V.J.C., Ruan, P., Li, F.: Lexicon knowledge extraction with sentiment polarity computation. In: 2016 IEEE 16th International Conference on Data Mining Workshops (ICDMW), pp. 978–983. IEEE (2016)
23. Hatzivassiloglou, V., McKeown, K.R.: Predicting the semantic orientation of adjectives. In: Proceedings of the 35th Annual Meeting of the Association for Computational Linguistics and Eighth Conference of the European Chapter of the Association for Computational Linguistics, pp. 174–181. Association for Computational Linguistics (1997)
24. Turney, P.D., Littman, M.L.: Unsupervised learning of semantic orientation from a hundred-billion-word corpus. arXiv preprint cs/0212012 (2002)
25. Oussous, A., Lahcen, A.A., Belfkih, S.: Impact of text pre-processing and ensemble learning on Arabic sentiment analysis. In: Proceedings of the 2nd International Conference on Networking, Information Systems & Security, p. 65. ACM (2019)
26. Hardeniya, N., Perkins, J., Chopra, D., Joshi, N., Mathur, I.: Natural Language Processing: Python and NLTK. Packt Publishing Ltd., Birmingham (2016)
27. Mustafa, M., Eldeen, A.S., Bani-Ahmad, S., Elfaki, A.O.: A comparative survey on arabic stemming: approaches and challenges. Intell. Inf. Manag. 9(02), 39 (2017)
28. Abooraig, R., Al-Zu'bi, S., Kanan, T., Hawashin, B., Al Ayoub, M., Hmeidi, I.: Automatic categorization of Arabic articles based on their political orientation. Digit. Investig. 25, 24–41 (2018)
29. Taghva, K., Elkhoury, R., Coombs, J.: Arabic stemming without a root dictionary. In: International Conference on Information Technology: Coding and Computing (ITCC 2005)-Volume II, vol. 1, pp. 152–157. IEEE (2005)

30. Aggarwal, C.C., Zhai, C.: A survey of text classification algorithms. In: Aggarwal, C., Zhai, C. (eds.) Mining Text Data, pp. 163–222. Springer, Boston (2012). https://doi.org/10.1007/978-1-4614-3223-4_6

31. Alowaidi, S., Saleh, M., Abulnaja, O.: Semantic sentiment analysis of arabic texts. Int. J. Adv. Comput. Sci. Appl. **8**(2), 256–262 (2017)

32. Abd, D.H., Sadiq, A.T., Abbas, A.R.: A new framework for automatic extraction polarity and target of articles (2019)

33. Deng, N., Tian, Y.: Support Vector Machines: A New Method in Data Mining. Science Press, Beijing (2004)

34. Al-Mejibli, I.S., Abd, D.H., Alwan, J.K., Rabash, A.J.: Performance evaluation of kernels in support vector machine. In: 2018 1st Annual International Conference on Information and Sciences (AiCIS), pp. 96–101. IEEE (2018)

35. Khalaf, M., et al.: An application of using support vector machine based on classification technique for predicting medical data sets. In: Huang, D.-S., Jo, K.-H., Huang, Z.-K. (eds.) ICIC 2019. LNCS, vol. 11644, pp. 580–591. Springer, Cham (2019). https://doi.org/10.1007/978-3-030-26969-2_55

36. Khalaf, M., et al.: Recurrent neural network architectures for analysing biomedical data sets. In: 2017 10th International Conference on Developments in eSystems Engineering (DeSE), pp. 232–237. IEEE (2017)

37. Abd, D.H., Alwan, J.K., Ibrahim, M., Naeem, M.B.: The utilisation of machine learning approaches for medical data classification and personal care system management for sickle cell disease. In: Annual Conference on New Trends in Information & Communications Technology 2017 (2017)

38. Mayoraz, E., Alpaydin, E.: Support vector machines for multi-class classification. In: Mira, J., Sánchez-Andrés, Juan V. (eds.) IWANN 1999. LNCS, vol. 1607, pp. 833–842. Springer, Heidelberg (1999). https://doi.org/10.1007/BFb0100551

Mitigate the Reverberant Effects on Speaker Recognition via Multi-training

Duraid Y. Mohammed[1]([⊠]) [iD], Khamis A. Al-Karawi[2] [iD],
Idress Mohammed Husien[3] [iD], and Marwah Abdullah Ghulam[4]

[1] School of Education for Women, Al-Iraqia University, Baghdad, Iraq
`duraidyehya19@gmail.com`
[2] University of Diyala, Diyala, Iraq
`alkasi_68@yahoo.com`
[3] School of Computer Science, Kirkuk University, Kirkuk, Iraq
`husienidress@gmail.com`
[4] Ministry of Higher Education and Scientific, Baghdad, Iraq

Abstract. Speaker recognition techniques have been developed into a relatively mature status over the past few decades through continuous research and development work. Existing methods typically use robust features extracted from clean speech signals, and therefore in idealized conditions can achieve very high recognition accuracy. For critical applications, such as security forensics robustness and reliability of the system is crucial. The reverberation condition can be represented by two main parameters namely Reverberation Time (RT) and Direct to Reverberation Ratio (DRR) (which represent the distance of the microphone to the source). This paper presents an efficient method to mitigating or at least alleviates the impacts of reverberation upon speaker verification. Multi-condition training approaches are investigated to alleviate such detrimental effects. Three multi-condition training methods are then investigated to mitigate such detrimental effects. The first uses matched train/test speaker models based on estimated reverberation time (RT) values. The second utilizes two-condition training where clean and reverberant models are used. Lastly, a four-condition training setup is proposed and conducted to improve the system performance. The utilized data set building, for SV experiments, training, and speech test material are obtained from the University of Salford Anechoic chamber database (SALU-AC). Experimental results show the first and the last types of multi-condition training providing significant gains in performance relative to the baseline.

Keywords: GMM · MFCC · Speaker recognition · Reverberate · Robustness

1 Introduction

Robustness of automatic speaker recognition (ASR) is crucial for real-world applications. In everyday acoustic conditions, additive noise, room reverberation, and channel/handset variations combine to pose significant challenges to such systems. Much research has been dedicated to dealing with individual challenges. Channel variability and/or train-test mismatch have been viewed as serious harmful factors for

© Springer Nature Switzerland AG 2020
M. I. Khalaf et al. (Eds.): ACRIT 2019, CCIS 1174, pp. 95–109, 2020.
https://doi.org/10.1007/978-3-030-38752-5_8

automatic speech and speaker recognition technologies. Many approaches have been suggested to address these limitations. In the feature domain, for instance, methods such as cepstral mean subtraction (CMS) [1], relative spectral (RASTA) processing [2], and feature mapping [3] have been utilized to minimize additive and convolutional channel distortions. While a lot of attention has been given to channel variability, limited work has been done to address the issue of room acoustics in far-field ASV, particularly regarding room reverberation. It is known that in far-field speech applications, the signal captured by the microphone is comprised of the direct path signal, plus numerous reflections off the walls, floor, and ceiling. Reverberation causes colouration of the speech signal, plus temporal smearing, which severely degrades the performance of several automated speech technologies, particularly ASV [4, 5]. To overcome these detrimental effects, different approaches have been proposed.

As examples for speaker verification and identification, microphone arrays [6], score normalization [7], feature normalization [4], and alternative feature representations [8–10] have been proposed. By far the most popular method of combating room reverberation, however, has been multi-condition training, where speaker models are developed for different reverberation levels and the best model is found during verification via a reverberation time (RT) estimator [7, 11, 12]. Moreover, in these previous studies, synthetic room impulse responses (RIRs) and traditional features (mel-frequency cepstral coefficients, MFCC) have been commonly explored (e.g., [12]). Speakers can be modelled in multiple noisy environments to reduce the mismatch between training and test conditions [13].

Speech enhancement approaches, such as spectral subtraction, have been explored for noise-robust speaker recognition [14]. The aim of this paper is three-fold. First, we discover the improvements achieved with four multi-condition training models to combat the impacts of reverberation on automatic speaker verification (ASV) performance. More exactly, we investigate the broadly of the utilized technique of train-test reverberation level matching. Also, another two approaches such as the utilize of clean and reverberant speech models in two condition training, and secondly, the utilize of clean, low, medium, and high reverberation level speaker models in four condition training.

The remainder of this paper structured as follows. In Sect. 2 the bookshelf software with the current algorithm is illustrated. Then we explain the general experiments setup in Sect. 3, while Sect. 4 demonstrates experiments results. Finally, the conclusions are presented in Sect. 5.

2   Background

2.1   MSR Toolbox for a Speaker Recognition System

Microsoft Speaker recognition (MSR) identity toolbox was Microsoft Speaker recognition (MSR) identity toolbox was developed by Microsoft research as a Matlab toolbox to help with speaker-recognition research [15–18]. This toolbox contains a collection of MATLAB tools and routines that can be used for research and development in speaker recognition. It provides researchers with a test bed for developing new front-end and back-end techniques, allowing replicable evaluation of new advancements.

It will also help new comers in the field by lowering the "barrier to entry", enabling them to quickly build baseline systems for their experiments. Although the focus of this toolbox is on speaker recognition, it can also be used for other speech related applications such as language, dialect and accent identification. The Identity Toolbox provides tools that implement both the conventional GMM-UBM and state-of-the-art i-vector based speaker recognition strategies. A speaker recognition system includes two primary components: a front-end and a back-end [19]. The front-end transforms acoustic waveforms into more compact and less redundant representations called acoustic features. Cepstral features are most often used for speaker recognition. It is practical to only retain the high signal-to-noise ratio (SNR) regions of the waveform; therefore there is also a need for a speech activity detector (SAD) in the front-end. After dropping the low SNR frames, acoustic features are further post-processed to remove the linear channel effects. Cepstral mean and variance normalization (CMVN) is commonly used for the post-processing. This toolbox provides support for the normalization techniques, although no tool for feature extraction or SAD is provided. The Auditory Toolbox [15] and VOICEBOX which are both written in MATLAB can be used for feature extraction and SAD purposes. Figure 1 shows the framework of the MSR toolbox.

2.2   The Inclusion of Reverberant Cases in the Training

The aim of speaker identification (SI) is to define which voice sample from a set of known voice samples greatest matches the features of an unknown input voice sample [20]. While the speaker verification (SV) aims the decision to accept or reject the speaker. SI is a two-phase technique involving training and testing. In the training phase, which, is shown in Fig. 2, speaker dependent feature vectors are extracted from a training speech signal, and a speaker model is built on each speaker's feature set. In the testing stage shown in Fig. 3, feature vectors are extracted from a test signal (unknown speaker) and are scored against all S speaker models and the most likely speaker identity decided. The set of training signals leads to a set of speaker models for each uttered, and test signals are scored utilizing the models.

To evaluate the effect of room reverberation on the accuracy of the speaker, recognition approaches which include reducing the mismatch between the reference model and the test material for the target speaker such that they have the same reverberation characteristics. Multi utterances for each speaker were used in this work from the different environment to increase the matching between training and testing sets. A set of speaker models (one for each utterance) now for each speaker. Figure 4 illustrates the training stage using a multi-speaker utterances approach. During training, obtain UBM of speaker models for clean speech and speech corrupted by reverberation from different utterances. Figure 5 illustrates the test stage for multiple utterances. Extracted feature vectors are scored against all the S-N speaker models. This experiment conducted in four stages, in the first stage, a baseline for our system was created, and Fig. 1 shows GMM-UBM baseline which have applied in this work. This baseline

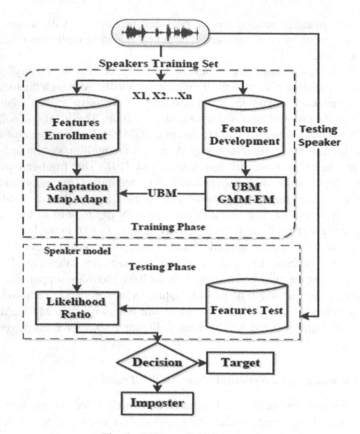

Fig. 1. MSR toolbox framework

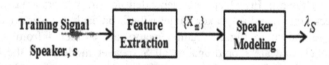

Fig. 2. Training phase

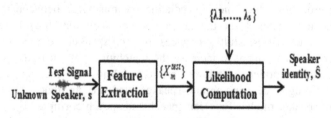

Fig. 3. Testing phase

module is generated based on the MFCC features, computed via a set of 26 triangular (Mel. Gaussian mixture model (GMM) parameters were acquired through the well-known expectation-maximization (EM) algorithm. In our experiments, a 64-component diagonal covariance matrices GMM was used.

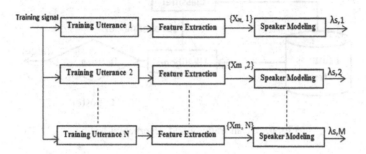

Fig. 4. Block diagram of multiple utterance training model

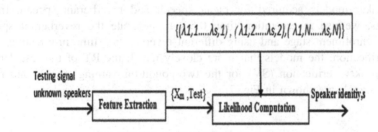

Fig. 5. Testing stage using multiple speaker models for each speaker

We establish this value to strike an excellent stability between model complexity and system performance on our dataset. Through training stage, speaker models have acquired through Maximum a Posteriori (MAP) adaptation. Scoring and decision are then achieved depending on log-likelihood thresholding. We first establish baseline results for an SV system, which uses clean training signals and reverberant test signals. Figure 6 shows the system, which is using clean training signals and reverberant test signals. Two factors, reverberation time and direct to reverberation ratio, appear to degrade SV accuracy levels reliable with how increases in these factors can increase the degradation.

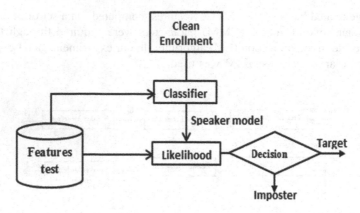

Fig. 6. Clean training and reverberant testing

2.3   Two-Condition Training: Clean and Reverberant Models

To address the impact of reverberation on the SV tested two-condition training system where speaker models acquired for clean speech and reverberant speech. In our experiments, we use reverberation time 0.5 s to generate the reverberant speaker models for enrollment stage and using different reverberation time in a testing stage. During verification, the models that more closely match the RT of the test data are utilized. Speaker verification (SV) for the two-condition training signals and reverberant test signals are shown in Fig. 7.

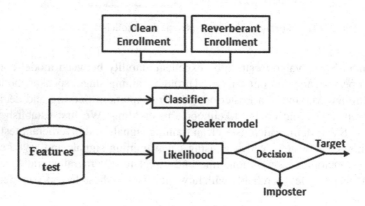

Fig. 7. Two-condition multi-condition training

2.4   Four-Condition Training

A four-condition training system utilized where speaker models of clean speech, speech corrupted by low reverberation time (0.5 s), medium reverberation time (1 s), and high reverberation time levels (2 s) are used as well as using different reverberation time value in the testing stage. During verification, the models that more closely match the RT of the test data are used. Speaker verification (SV) for the four-condition training signals and reverberant test signals are shown in Fig. 8.

2.5   Train and Testing Matching

The last step is the multi-condition training system represents reverberation time matching between training and testing conditions. This setup is represented by Fig. 9. Through the training stage, UBM models are acquired under various reverberation time conditions. The enrolment involved of the similar reverberation time environments utilized before for modelling. Through verification, the models that more closely match the RT of the test data are utilized.

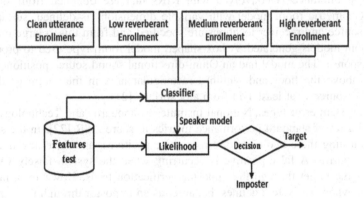

Fig. 8. Four-condition training

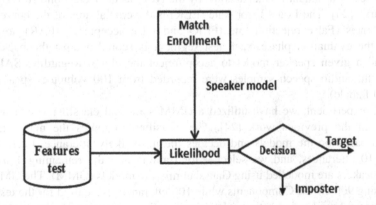

Fig. 9. Training and testing matching

3 Experiments Setup

Regarding data set building, for SV experiments, training, and speech test material are obtained from the University of Salford Anechoic chamber database (SALU-AC). We used an anechoic database because the study of speech needs the availability of a recording condition with very low background noise and reflected sound.

The dimensions of this chamber are (5.4 * 4.1 * 3.3 m), and the background noise level is (−12.4 dB). While the Cut-off frequency 100 Hz. On the other hand, commercial software CATT-Acoustic is employed to generate synthetic 100 impulse responses. The experiments have been carried out in ten rooms, all with different dimensions and acoustic properties to investigate the effect of direct to reverberation ratio and reverberation time on system accuracy. 5-different room was used to generate room impulse response.

Each test utterance is convolved with RIRs that are obtained from simulation software. Geometric room model with variable dimensions is defined, surface properties and source and receiver locations are specified and from this, a large number of realistic room models generated. A box-shaped model room type used to produce the impulse response. The model had an Omni-directional sound source positioned on the stage 2 m above the floor and within a rectangular area in the centre of the stage ensuring the source is at least 1 m from any surface [21].

For the system error types, National Institute of Standards and Technology (NIST) has created a set of standard performance metrics to score ASR [22]. In the statistical hypothesis testing there two sorts of errors, false positives, and false negatives, often called false alarms. A false positive is occurring when the system falsely verifies an impostor as the target through the impostor verification trials. However, a false negative occurs when the system defines the target as an impostor through the verification target trials.

A very informative method of presenting the system performance is a linear plot of bit error rates on a standard scale, denoted by the NIST as the Detection Error Trade-off (DET) curve [23]. The Equal Error Rate (EER) is the crucial area of the curve where the error rates (False rejection rate (FRR) and false acceptance (FAR) are equal. Through the evaluation phase, each test segment is scored against the background model and a given speaker model to accept/reject the claim. Regarding SALU-AC database, the audio speech samples were recorded from 100 volunteer speakers (50 males, 50 female).

In this experiment, we have utilized a GMM statistical classifier which we have described in the previous work [24]. The classifier computes the maximum log-likelihood based on the models and decides the most likely utterance. Each speaker provides 10 utterances, and we select 9 for training and the remaining 1 used for testing. Speakers are modelled using Gaussian mixture models (GMM). The GMM was trained using 900 GMM Components while 100 utterances were used for the test trials. Simple energy-based voice activity detection applied to remove the large chunks of silence in the excerpt. Then the speech is sampled at 16 kHz. The aim of these experiments are not testing speaker recognition against talker, but the real purpose is to test speaker recognition against reverberation condition, for this reason, limited speech samples have been used.

4 Experimental Results and Discussion

Figure 10 depicts the box plot obtained depending on the percentage EER with the baseline, matching, two-condition training and four-condition training setups, respectively. The box plots are used to show overall patterns of response to a group. In addition, they provide a useful way to visualise the range and other characteristics of responses in a large group. This simplest possible box plot displays the full range of variation (from min to max), and it corresponds to the standard deviation according to the percentage of the Error Equal Rate (EER) for each scenario performance with the different reverberation time (RT). The diagram below shows a variety of different box plot shapes and positions. In this Figure, the matching training and four-condition training appear to have approximately close centres, which exceed those of the baseline and the two-condition training. The baseline seems to have larger variability than the other three scenarios. Depending on the lower max, the box plot indicated that the training\testing matching scenario and four-condition training scenario produce the best performance compared with the other scenarios. Furthermore, for more investigation, the discussion of the results begins with the summary of the EER for each scenario (Table 1 Summarize the EER with different RT).

The evidence from this study suggests that the EER of the training/testing matching scenario for all reverberation time levels is better than the other scenarios". "The percentage EER obtained from all scenarios is depicted in Fig. 11. The x-axis represents the degree of reverberation time in seconds, while the y-axis represents the recognition accuracy of the system based on the equal error rate. The finding highlights that increasing the reverberation time value caused significant performance degradation in the case of the baseline system, consisting of clean training and reverberant testing. "For example, the percentage EER for a baseline is 0.42% with RT = 0.33 s. This percentage increased to just 2.44% when the reverberation time increased to 0.53 s. Moreover, the EER rose to 19.32% at RT = 2 s. However, in the second scenario train/test matching, an inverse relationship was found. The system accuracy shows more reverberation robustness when reverberant speech samples are used in the enrolment stage compared with using clean speech samples for enrolling; especially with (RT < 1.2 s) the EER remained below 0.98% and increased to 3.22% at RT = 2 s.

These amounts are considered a significant relative reduction in EER percentage. However, the performance of the other types of training condition was less than training/testing matching. Regarding two training conditions, there is a clear degradation in system performance when the reverberation time increased, especially over 0.62 s. Despite the poor performance relative to other types of training, the RT-matched setup clearly improved performance, and a relative reduction could be seen in the percentage EER at different levels of reverberation time. Furthermore, the detection error trade-off curves plotted in Figs. 12, 13, 14 and 15 clearly show DET curves, the false negative (rejection) rate and false positive (acceptance) rate for the training/testing matching are better with different reverberation time values". It can be seen that the accuracy of the false positive rate (FPR) for the training/testing matching and four-condition training (the red and blue line) shows significant improvement compared to the baseline result.

The conclusion that can be drawn from the present study is that using reverberant training can improve the performance of the system and can to some extent mitigate the degradation. Therefore, if acoustic conditions can be somehow estimated and suitably included in the pre-training of the models, the robustness of the system can be improved.

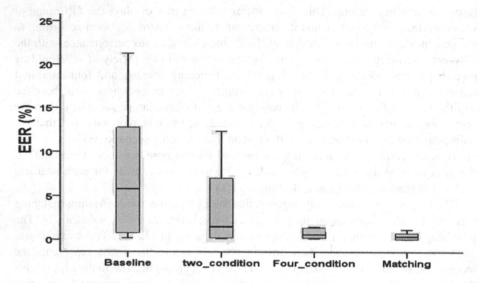

Fig. 10. Box plots of EER using different RT for each scenario

Table 1. Summary of the Equal Error Rates with different RT tests

Testing RT	EER %			
	Training RT			
	Baseline	Matching	Two condition	Four condition
Clean	0	0	0.16	0.15
0.23	0.24	0.22	0.23	0
0.33	0.42	0.51	0.52	0.07
0.53	2.44	0.14	0.13	0.12
0.62	4.55	0.74	0.71	0.31
0.84	6.98	2.26	0.81	0.44
1	9.88	4.34	0.52	0.49
1.2	12.93	7	1.48	0.76
1.5	15.44	9.44	1.39	1.17
2	19.32	12.33	7.44	3.11

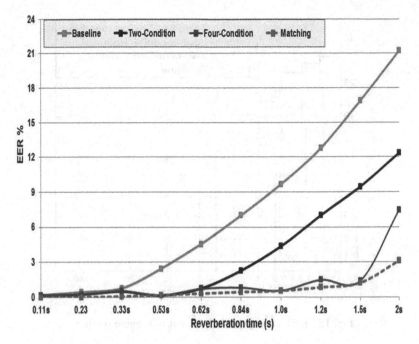

Fig. 11. System performance using multi-training conditions

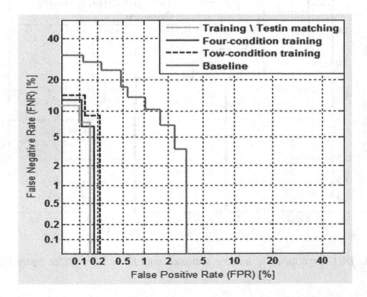

Fig. 12. DET curve with RT = 0.53 s (Color figure online)

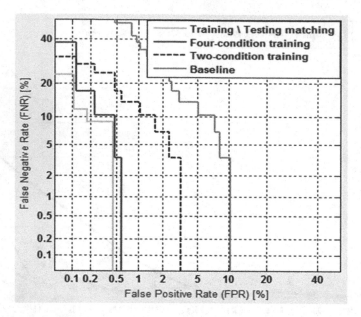

Fig. 13. DET curve with RT = 1 s (Color figure online)

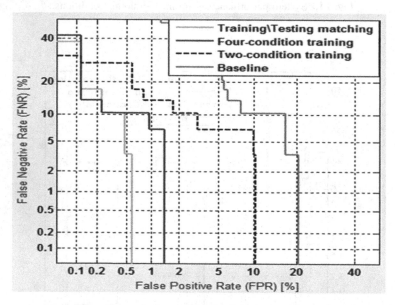

Fig. 14. DET curve for multi training scenarios with RT = 1.2 s (Color figure online)

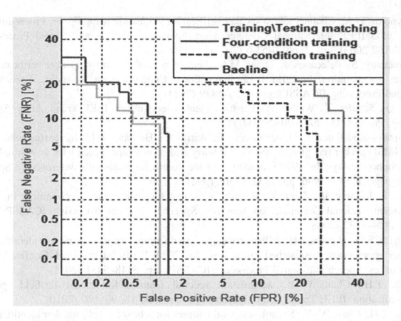

Fig. 15. DET curve for multi training scenarios with RT = 1.2 s (Color figure online)

5 Conclusion Remarks

The work in this paper improves the robustness of speaker recognition using speech signals corrupted by the reverberation time in the training stage. Three scenarios have been considered in this work: The first scenario used clean speech samples in the enrolment phase and the second included reverberant samples in the enrolment phase. Thus, the potentials and limitations of including reverberant samples in the training phase to improve system robustness are identified. The third scenario is using two and four condition training to mitigate the effects of reverberation on the system performance. The best results occur when the reverberation characteristics of training and test speech are as close as possible, but an exact match is not necessarily needed. "These findings suggest that in general, the inclusion of environmental conditions in the training stage can to some extent mitigate the performance degradation; therefore, if acoustic conditions can be somehow estimated and suitably included in the pre-training of the models, the robustness of the system can be improved.

References

1. Furui, S.: Cepstral analysis technique for automatic speaker verification. IEEE Trans. Acoust. Speech Signal Process. **29**, 254–272 (1981)
2. Hermansky, H., Morgan, N.: RASTA processing of speech. IEEE Trans. Speech Audio Process. **2**, 578–589 (1994)

3. Reynolds, D.A.: Channel robust speaker verification via feature mapping. In: Proceedings of the 2003 IEEE International Conference on Acoustics, Speech, and Signal Processing, (ICASSP 2003), vol. 2, pp. II-53-6 (2003)
4. Ganapathy, S., Pelecanos, J., Omar, M.K.: Feature normalization for speaker verification in room reverberation. In: 2011 IEEE International Conference on Acoustics, Speech and Signal Processing (ICASSP), pp. 4836–4839 (2011)
5. Jin, Q., Schultz, T., Waibel, A.: Far-field speaker recognition. IEEE Trans. Audio Speech Lang. Process. **15**, 2023–2032 (2007)
6. González-Rodríguez, J., Ortega-García, J., Martín, C., Hernández, L.: Increasing robustness in GMM speaker recognition systems for noisy and reverberant speech with low complexity microphone arrays. In: 1996 Proceedings of the Fourth International Conference on Spoken Language, ICSLP 1996, pp. 1333–1336 (1996)
7. Peer, I., Rafaely, B., Zigel, Y.: Reverberation matching for speaker recognition. In: 2008 IEEE International Conference on Acoustics, Speech and Signal Processing, ICASSP 2008, pp. 4829–4832 (2008)
8. Sadjadi, S.O., Hansen, J.H.: Hilbert envelope based features for robust speaker identification under reverberant mismatched conditions. In: 2011 IEEE International Conference on Acoustics, Speech and Signal Processing (ICASSP), pp. 5448–5451 (2011)
9. Falk, T.H., Chan, W.-Y.: Modulation spectral features for robust far-field speaker identification. IEEE Trans. Audio Speech Lang. Process. **18**, 90–100 (2010)
10. Falk, T.H., Chan, W.-Y.: Spectro-temporal features for robust far-field speaker identification. In: INTERSPEECH, pp. 634–637 (2008)
11. Gammal, J.S., Goubran, R.A.: Combating reverberation in speaker verification. In: 2005 Proceedings of the IEEE Instrumentation and Measurement Technology Conference, IMTC 2005, pp. 687–690 (2005)
12. Zhao, X., Wang, Y., Wang, D.: Robust speaker identification in noisy and reverberant conditions (2014)
13. Ming, J., Hazen, T.J., Glass, J.R., Reynolds, D.A.: Robust speaker recognition in noisy conditions. IEEE Trans. Audio Speech Lang. Process. **15**, 1711–1723 (2007)
14. Wang, N., Ching, P., Zheng, N., Lee, T.: Robust speaker recognition using denoised vocal source and vocal tract features. IEEE Trans. Audio Speech Lang. Process. **19**, 196–205 (2011)
15. Sadjadi, S.O., Slaney, M., Heck, L.: MSR identity toolbox v1. 0: a MATLAB toolbox for speaker-recognition research. Speech and Language Processing Technical Committee Newsletter (2013)
16. Kinnunen, T., Koh, C., Wang, L., Li, H., Chng, E.: Temporal discrete cosine transform: towards longer term temporal features for speaker verification. In: Proceedings Fifth International Symposium on Chinese Spoken Language Processing (ISCSLP 2006), Singapore, pp. 547–558 (2006)
17. Turk, U., Schiel, F.: Speaker verification based on the German VeriDat database. In: Eighth European Conference on Speech Communication and Technology (2003)
18. Larcher, A., Bonastre, J.-F., Fauve, B.G., Lee, K.-A., Lévy, C., Li, H., et al.: ALIZE 3.0-open source toolkit for state-of-the-art speaker recognition. In: INTERSPEECH, pp. 2768–2772 (2013)
19. Campbell, J.P.: Speaker recognition: a tutorial. Proc. IEEE **85**, 1437–1462 (1997)
20. Rose, R.C., Reynolds, D.A.: Text-independent speaker identification using automatic acoustic segmentation. In: 1990 International Conference on Acoustics, Speech, and Signal Processing, ICASSP 1990, pp. 293–296 (1990)
21. International Standard: 3382. Acoustics–measurement of the reverberation time of rooms with reference to other acoustical parameters. International Standards Organization (1997)

22. Doddington, G.R., Przybocki, M.A., Martin, A.F., Reynolds, D.A.: The NIST speaker recognition evaluation–overview, methodology, systems, results, perspective. Speech Commun. **31**, 225–254 (2000)
23. Chen, Y.-W., Lin, C.-J.: Combining SVMs with various feature selection strategies. In: Guyon, I., Nikravesh, M., Gunn, S., Zadeh, L.A. (eds.) Feature Extraction. STUDFUZZ, vol. 207, pp. 315–324. Springer, Heidelberg (2006). https://doi.org/10.1007/978-3-540-35488-8_13
24. El Bachir, T., Benabbou, A., Harti, M.: Design of an automatic speaker recognition system based on adapted MFCC and GMM methods for Arabic speech. Int. J. Comput. Sci. Netw. Secur. **10** (2010)

Dynamic Power Systems Phasor Estimation Using Kalman Filter Algorithms

Omar Sami Thiab[1,2]([✉]) [iD], Łukasz Nogal[2] [iD],
and Ryszard Kowalik[2] [iD]

[1] General Middle Region Power Transmission Company, Ministry of Electricity,
Baghdad 10064, Iraq
thiabo@ee.pw.edu.pl
[2] Institute of Electrical Power Engineering (IEn-PW),
Warsaw University of Technology, 00-661 Warsaw, Poland
{Lukasz.Nogal, Ryszard.Kowalik}@ien.pw.edu.pl

Abstract. In the electrical power system, the accuracy of phasor estimation represents essential and critical issue due to the dependability of many fields on the characteristic of the estimated signals. Therefore, several algorithms have been suggested to estimate the main aspects of these signals. This paper presents a comparative evaluation of dynamic phasor estimation algorithms, namely the linear Kalman and extended Kalman filter. Many tests have been made on the dynamic filters were developed in the Simulink environment of MATLAB, The tests include amplitude step, phase step, frequency step, total vector error and computation time. Test and simulation results are provided to highlight each algorithm suitability and limitations to estimate the phasor of the power system.

Keywords: Kalman Filters · Phasor estimation · Protection Relays · WAMS · Discrete Fourier Transformation

1 Introduction

Wide-area electrical disturbances in the interconnected stressed power systems that operated outside the design limits have shown that protective relay systems are very often involved in major system perturbations. Sometimes, the relay systems prevent further propagation and sometimes share in the spread of the disturbances [1–3]. Protective devices are responsible for protecting equipment and the surrounding systems from major failures and damages. Protective devices set for working at conditions beyond the normal and steady state to avoid serious outages and damage. Many protection aspects are affected by wide-area disturbances such as the design of the protection scheme, the relay setting, and coordination under stressed system conditions, the performance of algorithms, and hidden failures [4–6].

The input signals of relays practically contain noise, decaying DC offset, undesired harmonics, and power system frequency deviation. These unknown disturbances on the input signal can reduce the validity of estimations [7, 8]. Discrete Fourier transform (DFT) may introduce errors into phasor and frequency estimations under dynamic conditions, such as power oscillations. A dynamic phasor and frequency estimator is

© Springer Nature Switzerland AG 2020
M. I. Khalaf et al. (Eds.): ACRIT 2019, CCIS 1174, pp. 110–122, 2020.
https://doi.org/10.1007/978-3-030-38752-5_9

proposed to improve accuracy by considering the dynamic characteristics of power systems expressed as Taylor derivatives [9]. The increase in the number of variables and equation represents one of the disadvantages of dynamic estimators. Several literatures discussed new algorithms of dynamic phasor estimation to eliminate the errors due to different kinds of disturbances [10–13].

In this paper, the concepts of dynamic estimations using linear Kalman filter and Extended Kalman filter are be presented in Sects. 2 and 3 respectively as the most popular algorithms for dynamic estimations. Results of Dynamic Phasor Estimation Simulation Tests and discussions are presented in Sect. 4. Finally, the conclusion performed in Sect. 5.

2 Dynamic Phasor Estimation Using Linear Kalman Filter

Kalman filter is a method that estimates optimal state variables recursively and instantaneously. To analyze the dynamic system, state space model is needed; the state value at each sample is calculated with respect to its value at previous sample. The main advantage of estimation algorithms that based on Kalman is the ability for tracking instantaneously. Considering a discrete-time state-space representation of a linear system:

$$\hat{X}_k = A_k X_{k-1} + W_K \tag{1}$$

Where $\hat{X}_k$ represents the predicted new state, X_{k-1} is the previous estimated state, A_k represents the state transition matrix at time k, and W_K is the state noise transition matrix. One way to finding A_k is by evaluate Taylor series as presented previously. The predicted process covariance matrix $\hat{P}_k$ also can be calculated by the previous covariance P_{k-1} and covariance noise Q_K as:

$$\hat{P}_k = A_k P_{k-1} A_k^T + Q_K \tag{2}$$

The measurement equation that will be used to represent the Kalman gain will be represented as:

$$\hat{Y}_k = B_k X_{mk} + R_K \tag{3}$$

Where $\hat{Y}_k$ represents the measured new input, X_{mk} is the measured state, B_k represents the state transition matrix at time k, and R_K is the state noise transition matrix during measurement. The Kalman filter Gain is calculated from the predicted and measured states with process covariance $\hat{P}_k$ and measurement covariance matrix R as shown below:

$$KG_k = \hat{P}_k H \left(H_k \hat{P}_k H_k^T + R \right)^{-1} \tag{4}$$

The updating process will be done using Kalman Gain to the predicted state and predicted covariance which will be the final output of current iteration and will be used to predict the next states. Equations (5) and (6) below will show the updating processes [14].

$$X_k = \hat{X}_k + KG(\hat{Y}_k - H_k\hat{X}_k) \tag{5}$$

$$P_k = (I - KG\,H_k)\hat{P}_k \tag{6}$$

Figure 1 below shows a flowchart of Kalman Filtering process Algorithm.

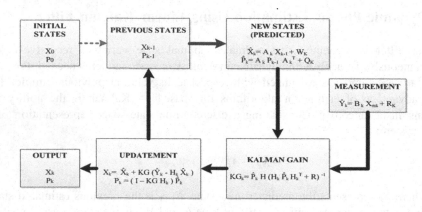

Fig. 1. Kalman filter algorithm

The phasor representation in polar form at Eqs. (1) and (2) can be re-written as:

$$z_{ab}(k) = z_a(k) + j\,z_b(k) \tag{7}$$

$$z_{ab}(k) = A(k)e^{j(\omega k\Delta t + \varphi)} \tag{8}$$

To estimate the amplitude A and the phase angle φ, state variables at time instant k will be [15]:

$$x_1(k) = z_a(k) = A(k)cos(\omega k\Delta t + \varphi(k)) \tag{9}$$

$$x_2(k) = z_b(k) = A(k)sin(\omega k\Delta t + \varphi(k)) \tag{10}$$

For the next instant $(k + 1)$, the state variables equation expressed as follows:

$$x_1(k+1) = A(k+1)\cos(\omega k\Delta t + \omega\Delta t + \varphi(k+1)) \tag{11}$$

$$x_2(k+1) = A(k+1)\sin(\omega k\Delta t + \omega\Delta t + \varphi(k+1)) \tag{12}$$

By assuming $A(k+1) = A(k) = A$ and $\varphi(k+1) = \varphi(k) = \varphi$, the state variable equations will be equal to:

$$x_1(k+1) = x_1(k)\cos(\omega \Delta t) - x_2(k)\sin(\omega \Delta t) \tag{13}$$

$$x_2(k+1) = x_1(k)\sin(\omega \Delta t) + x_2(k)\cos(\omega \Delta t) \tag{14}$$

The state variable equation can be written in the form of a matrix as follow:

$$\begin{bmatrix} x_1(k+1) \\ x_2(k+1) \end{bmatrix} = \begin{bmatrix} \cos(\omega \Delta t) & -\sin(\omega \Delta t) \\ \sin(\omega \Delta t) & \cos(\omega \Delta t) \end{bmatrix} \begin{bmatrix} x_1(k) \\ x_2(k) \end{bmatrix} \tag{15}$$

The measurement equation will be:

$$z_{ab}(k) = \begin{bmatrix} 1 & 0 \end{bmatrix} \begin{bmatrix} y_1(k) \\ y_2(k) \end{bmatrix} \tag{16}$$

The estimated phasor amplitude and angle will be calculated by:

$$A = \sqrt{x_1^2 + x_2^2} \tag{17}$$

$$\varphi(k) = \tan^{-1}\frac{x_2}{x_1} \tag{18}$$

There are two choices to implement the linear Kalman filter using Matlab; either using command function named "Kalman" or by using Simulink block named "Kalman Filter" in control system toolbox library which is used in this paper as shown in Fig. 2 below.

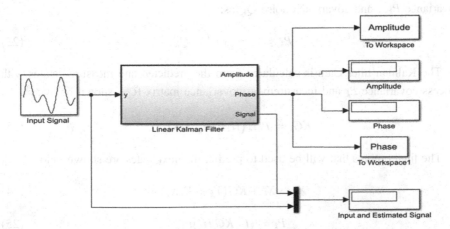

Fig. 2. MATLAB design for phasor estimation using linear Kalman filter

The Kalman Filter block contains the parameters of state equation, measurement equation, process covariance matrix, measurement covariance matrix, and initial states. The filter parameters are chosen upon the system nominal frequency and the sampling rate that already used on analog to digital conversion.

3 Dynamic Phasor Estimation Using Extended Kalman Filter

In a case that the model is non-linear like in practical power system, the model can be linearized in order to estimate the state variables, which known as Extended Kalman Filter. Considering the system model:

$$\hat{X}_k = F_k(X_{k-1}) + W_K \tag{19}$$

The measurement is:

$$\hat{Y}_k = H_k(X_{mk}) + R_K \tag{20}$$

The function F_k will be used to calculate the predicted state from the previous estimate. Similarly, the function H_k will be used to compute the predicted measurement from the predicted state. However, these functions will be applied to covariance by using a matrix of partial derivatives (the Jacobian) as below:

$$
\begin{aligned}
F_k &= \frac{\partial f_{k-1}}{\partial x_{k-1}} \hat{x}_{k-1} \\
H_k &= \frac{\partial g_k}{\partial x_k} \hat{x}_{k-1}
\end{aligned}
\tag{21}
$$

The predicted process covariance matrix $\hat{P}_k$ also can be calculated by the previous covariance P_{k-1} and covariance noise Q_K as:

$$\hat{P}_k = F_k P_{k-1} F_k^T + Q_K \tag{22}$$

The Kalman filter Gain is calculated from the predicted and measured states with process covariance $\hat{P}_k$ and measurement covariance matrix R as shown below:

$$KG_k = \hat{P}_k H \left(H_k \hat{P}_k H_k^T + R \right)^{-1} \tag{23}$$

The final outputs that will be used to predict the next states are shown below [16]:

$$X_k = \hat{X}_k + KG\left(\hat{Y}_k - H_k \hat{X}_k\right) \tag{24}$$

$$P_k = (I - KG H_k)\hat{P}_k \tag{25}$$

The estimation of phasor parameters using the extended Kalman filter EKF is based on the fact that the phasor is rotated between two samples by the amount of $(2\pi T_s f)$ [17]. The frequency deviation is related linearly to the average rate of change of the phase angle as below.

$$\frac{\partial \phi}{\partial t} = \Delta f \tag{26}$$

By representing the system frequency during frequency deviation $f_0 + \Delta f$ as third state x_3, the nonlinear model of the signal can be written as:

$$
\begin{aligned}
x_1(k+1) &= x_1(k)\cos(2\pi T_s x_3(k)) - x_2(k)\sin(2\pi T_s x_3(k)) \\
x_2(k+1) &= x_1(k)\sin(2\pi T_s x_3(k)) + x_2(k)\cos(2\pi T_s x_3(k)) \\
x_3(k+1) &= x_3(k)
\end{aligned}
\tag{27}
$$

The state variable equation can be written in the form of a matrix as follow:

$$
\begin{bmatrix} x_1(k+1) \\ x_2(k+1) \\ x_3(k+1) \end{bmatrix} =
\begin{bmatrix}
\cos(2\pi T s x_3(k)) & -\sin(2\pi T s x_3(k)) & 0 \\
\sin(2\pi T s x_3(k)) & \cos(2\pi T s x_3(k)) & 0 \\
0 & 0 & 1
\end{bmatrix}
\begin{bmatrix} x_1(k) \\ x_2(k) \\ x_3(k) \end{bmatrix}
\tag{28}
$$

The measurement equation will be:

$$
z(k) = \begin{bmatrix} \cos(2\pi T s x_3(k)) & -\sin(2\pi T s x_3(k)) & H_3(k) \end{bmatrix}
\begin{bmatrix} y_1(k) \\ y_2(k) \\ y_3(k) \end{bmatrix}
\tag{29}
$$

Where the $H_3(k)$ will be equal to:

$$H_3(k) = 2\pi T_s(-x_1(k)\sin(2\pi x_3 T_s(k)) - x_2(k)\cos(2\pi x_3 T_s(k)) \tag{30}$$

To implement the Extended Kalman filter using Matlab, there are two choices; either using command function named "extendedKalmanFilter", or by using Simulink block named "Extended Kalman Filter" in control system toolbox library which is used in this paper as shown in Fig. 3 below.

The Extended Kalman Filter block estimates the states of a discrete-time nonlinear system using the first-order discrete-time extended Kalman filter algorithm. The nonlinear state transition function 'myStateTransitionFcn(x)' and the nonlinear measurement functions 'myMeasurementFcn(y)' for the system will be used by the Extended Kalman filter block to produce the state estimation, while the Jacobian of state transition function will be calculated using 'stateTransitionJacobianFcn' function. The filter parameters are chosen upon the system nominal frequency and the sampling rate that already used on analog to digital conversion.

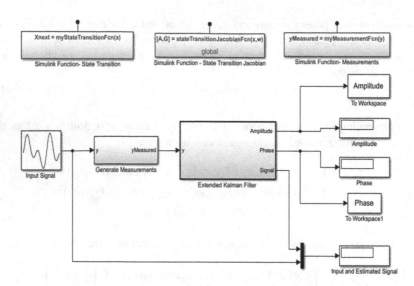

Fig. 3. MATLAB design for phasor estimation using extended Kalman filter

4 Results of Dynamic Phasor Estimation Simulation Tests

The dynamic phasor estimation algorithms that are presented in this paper will be tested during several oscillations conditions to evaluate the performances of these algorithms.

4.1 Magnitude and Phase Estimation

The test signal that is used to examine the algorithms is shown in Fig. 4 below.

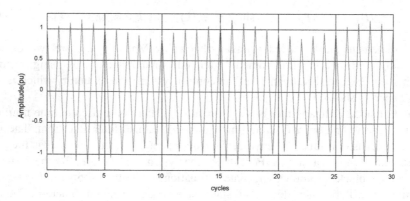

Fig. 4. Input signal

The test signal will be in oscillating condition around the fundamental frequency (± 0.15) with sampling rate 1000 Hz (20 sample per cycle for 50 Hz signal) as shown in Equation below.

$$S(t) = a(t)\cos(2\pi f_1 t + \varphi(t)) \tag{31}$$

Where

$$a(t) = a_0 + a_1 \cos(2\pi f_a t)$$
$$\varphi(t) = \varphi_0 + \varphi_1 \cos(2\pi f_a t)$$
$$a_0 = \varphi_0 = 1, a_1 = \varphi_1 = 0.15$$

Figures 5 and 6 below show the Amplitude of phasor estimations; the dashed lines represent the real amplitude while the solid lines show the estimated ones using different algorithms.

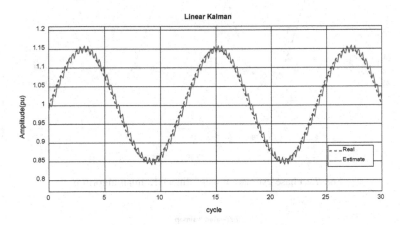

Fig. 5. Amplitude estimation using linear Kalman algorithm

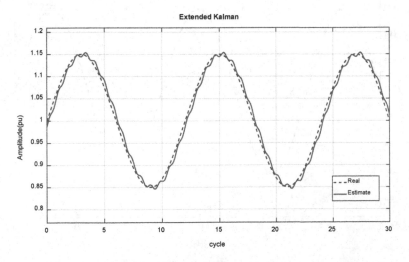

Fig. 6. Amplitude estimation using extended Kalman algorithm

Figures 7 and 8 below show the estimated phase angle; the dashed lines represent the real phase angle while the solid lines show the estimated ones using different algorithms.

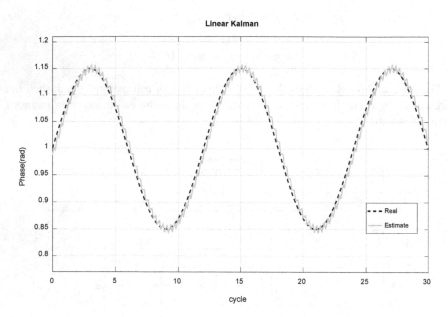

Fig. 7. Phase estimation using linear Kalman algorithm

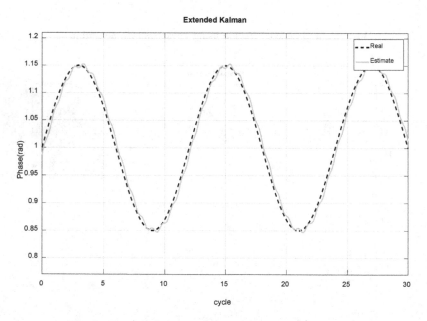

Fig. 8. Phase estimation using extended Kalman algorithm

A slight distortion appears at the estimated amplitude in Fig. 5 and estimated phase in Fig. 7 using the linear Kalman algorithm. This distortion is reduced using Extended Kalman methods as shown in Figs. 6 and 8.

4.2   Total Vector Error

According to IEEE C37.118-2005 standard, total vector error (TVE) compares both the magnitude and phase of the phasor estimate with the theoretical phasor signal for the same instant of time to detect errors in estimation [18].

$$\text{TVE} = \sqrt{\frac{(X'r(n) - Xr(n))^2 + (X'i(n) - Xi(n))^2}{(Xr(n))^2 + (Xi(n))^2}} \tag{32}$$

Where the Xr and Xi are the real and imaginary components of the input signal respectively. While $X'r$ and $X'i$ represent the estimated components. Figures 9 and 10 below present the TVE values for the first ten cycles derived from the estimations of the presented algorithms for the test signal that presented in previous section.

The Kalman filter based algorithm show less vector error during linear Kalman which reduced more during extended Kalman algorithm.

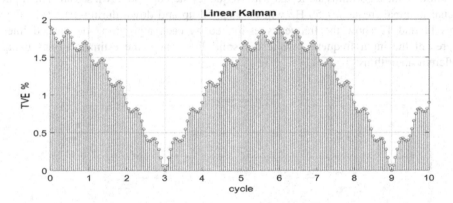

Fig. 9. Total vector error (TVE) for linear Kalman estimation

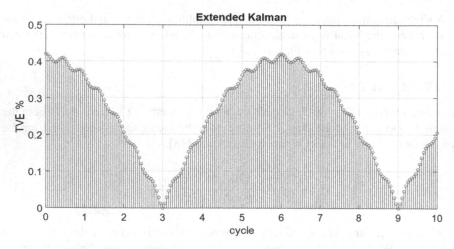

Fig. 10. Total vector error (TVE) for extended Kalman estimation

4.3 Frequency Step up and Down

To evaluate the performance of the presented algorithms during frequency deviation conditions, the algorithms are tested with frequency step up and down signal. The input signal nominal frequency 50 Hz will be stepped up and down during 10 s test. Figures 11 and 12 show the frequency estimated by each algorithm, the dashed lines represent the input frequency while the solid lines show the estimated ones using different algorithms.

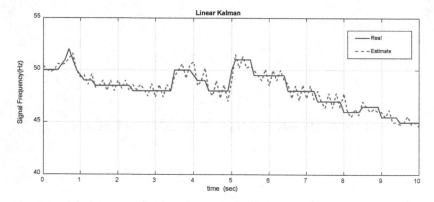

Fig. 11. Estimated frequency using linear Kalman algorithm

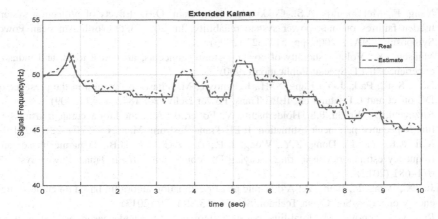

Fig. 12. Estimated frequency using extended Kalman algorithm

Results show that the longest transient period and high overshoot value appear at Linear Kalman algorithm, while the Extended Kalman based algorithms appears with less settling times and overshoot.

5 Conclusions

This paper dealt with a comparative evaluation of the Linear Kalman and Extended Kalman phasor estimators intended for power quality monitoring, controlling and protection. The dynamic estimation algorithms are evaluated in terms of step change tests in amplitude and phase, total vector errors (TVE), as well as frequency change test. In simulation tests, it has been shown that the Extended Kalman estimator out-performs the linear Kalman filter one during different kinds of tests. As future work it is needed to investigate how to reduce the overshoot of the dynamic estimation algorithm during transient. In addition, it is interesting to apply the presented algorithms for power system protection applications.

References

1. Novosel, D., Begovic, M.M., Madani, V.: Shedding light on blackouts. IEEE Power Energy Mag. **2**, 32–43 (2004)
2. Vaiman, M., Bell, K., Chen, Y., Chowdhury, B., Dobson, I., Hines, P., et al.: Risk assessment of cascading outages: methodologies and challenges. IEEE Trans. Power Syst. **27**, 631 (2012)
3. Chen, J., Thorp, J.S., Dobson, I.: Cascading dynamics and mitigation assessment in power system disturbances via a hidden failure model. Int. J. Electr. Power Energy Syst. **27**, 318–326 (2005)
4. Bae, K., Thorp, J.S.: A stochastic study of hidden failures in power system protection. Decis. Support Syst. **24**, 259–268 (1999)

5. Yang, F., Meliopoulos, A.S., Cokkinides, G.J., Dam, Q.B.: Effects of protection system hidden failures on bulk power system reliability. In: 2006 38th North American Power Symposium, NAPS 2006, pp. 517–523 (2006)
6. Mansour, Y.: Voltage stability of power systems: concepts, analytical tools, and industry experience. IEEE Special Publication (1990)
7. Nam, S.-R., Park, J.-Y., Kang, S.-H., Kezunovic, M.: Phasor estimation in the presence of DC offset and CT saturation. IEEE Trans. Power Deliv. 24, 1842–1849 (2009)
8. Ritzmann, D., Wright, P.S., Holderbaum, W., Potter, B.: A method for accurate transmission line impedance parameter estimation. IEEE Trans. Instrum. Meas. 65, 2204–2213 (2016)
9. Mai, R.K., Fu, L., Dong, Z.Y., Wong, K.P., Bo, Z.Q., Xu, H.B.: Dynamic phasor and frequency estimators considering decaying DC components. IEEE Trans. Power Syst. 27, 671–681 (2012)
10. Jin, X., Wang, F., Wang, Z.: A dynamic phasor estimation algorithm based on angle-shifted energy operator. Sci. China Technol. Sci. 56, 1322–1329 (2013)
11. Ren, J., Kezunovic, M.: Real-time power system frequency and phasors estimation using recursive wavelet transform. IEEE Trans. Power Deliv. 26, 1392–1402 (2011)
12. Platas-Garza, M.A., Platas-Garza, J., de la O Serna, J.A.: Dynamic phasor and frequency estimates through maximally flat differentiators. IEEE Trans. Instrum. Meas. 59, 1803–1811 (2010)
13. UmaMageswari, A., Ignatious, J.J., Vinodha, R.: A comparitive study of Kalman filter, extended Kalman filter and unscented Kalman filter for harmonic analysis of the non-stationary signals. Int. J. Sci. Eng. Res. 3(7), 1–9 (2012)
14. Chui, C.K., Chen, G.: Kalman Filtering. Springer, Heidelberg (2017). https://doi.org/10.1007/978-3-319-47612-4
15. Ma, H., Girgis, A.A.: Identification and tracking of harmonic sources in a power system using a Kalman filter. IEEE Trans. Power Deliv. 11, 1659–1665 (1996)
16. Haykin, S.: Kalman Filtering and Neural Networks, vol. 47. Wiley, Hoboken (2004)
17. Routray, A., Pradhan, A.K., Rao, K.P.: A novel Kalman filter for frequency estimation of distorted signals in power systems. IEEE Trans. Instrum. Meas. 51, 469–479 (2002)
18. IEEE Standard for Synchrophasors for Power Systems. IEEE Std C37.118-2005 (Revision of IEEE Std 1344-1995), pp. 0_1–57 (2006)

SCEHMA: Speech Corpus of English, Hindi, Marathi and Arabic Language for Advance Speech Recognition Development

Santosh Gaikwad[1](✉) , Bharti Gawali[2] , and Mohammad Basil[3]

[1] Department of Computer Science, Model Degree College, Ghansawangi, Jalna, M.S., India
santosh.gaikwadcsit@gmail.com
[2] Department of Computer Science and Information Technology, Dr. Babasaheb Ambedkar Marathwada University, Aurangabad, M.S., India
bharti_rokade@yahoo.co.in
[3] Department of Computer Science, AlMaarif University College, Ramadi, Iraq
f_com22@yahoo.com

Abstract. The database is an essential key element for speech recognition research. This research describes the development of the SCEHMA speech database dedicated to advance speech recognition applications in Hindi, English, Marathi and Arabic languages. The SCEHMA corpus is a collection of isolated word and continuous sentences of speech. For the application domain of agriculture, polyclinic and general-purpose speech recognition in Marathi language 28420 isolated words and 17470 sentences are collected from 300 male and 200 female subjects of 22–30 age groups. The corpus consists of 900 sentences in the Hindi language for accent recognition domain collected from 18 male and 12 female of 18–30 age groups. The English speech corpus was collected from 22–30 age groups of 750 isolated words and 750 sentences from 12 male and 3 female of age group 22–30 for the general domain. The Arabic speech corpus contains 4520 words and 40 sentences from 12 male and 9 female of 18–30 age groups for recognition domain. To achieve a high quality of speech corpus, the recording took place in 10 by 10 office room without a noisy sound environment. The speech utterances were recorded in 16 kHz in three recordings medium, a headset, desktop mounted microphone and Mobile phone. The data was recorded in the morning, and evening session in the room temperature and normal humidity. Speaker was asked to sit in front of the microphone with a distance of about 12–15 cm. The database is collected as per LDCIL protocol and the corpus is transcript through Google Unicode editor. Praat is used for corpus labeling and annotation. The total size of the SCEHMA corpus is 33690 isolated words and 19160 continuous sentences. The corpus will be made available to the scientific community for agricultural, polyclinic, medical, accent recognition, age group identification, gender recognition, and general-purpose recognition system after the transcription and annotation.

Keywords: LDCIL · SCEHMA · Polyclinic inquiry system · Accent recognition · General-purpose recognition system

© Springer Nature Switzerland AG 2020
M. I. Khalaf et al. (Eds.): ACRIT 2019, CCIS 1174, pp. 123–135, 2020.
https://doi.org/10.1007/978-3-030-38752-5_10

1   Introduction

The oldest way of communication and information exchange between human beings is speech. The man-machine interface has always shown a testing range in Natural language processing and in speech recognition research. Around 6900 languages are used for correspondence throughout the world [1]. Stream investigation underlines the inconveniences in overseeing assortment usually shown in speech and languages. These are creating interests in making machines that can recognize speech as information in everyday language. In a split second, 22 power languages are used for correspondence as a piece of India. In such a far-reaching multilingual society, speech and language developments accept a basic part in enabling information access to the overall population using a speech-based control structure and are continuous towards application [2].

English is now the most widely used language in the world. It is spoken in many countries. It is the first language of the United Kingdom, the United States, and Canada. There are about 375 million native speakers and 220 million more people speak it as a second language and there are as many as a billion people who are learning it. It has 20 vowels and 25 consonant phonemes [3]. Hindi is an Indo-Aryan language. Hindi is a direct descendant of Sanskrit through Prakrit. It is a very expressive language. More than 180 million people in India regard Hindi as their mother tongue. Another 300 million use it as a second language. It has 10 vowels and 28 consonants phonemes [4]. Marathi is also an Indo-Aryan language, talked in the western and central region of India. The Marathi language utilizes Devanagari, a character-based script. Marathi discourse is phonetic in nature. There are 90 million of familiar speakers all over the world [5, 6]. There are 12 vowels and 36 consonants in Marathi dialect. It is an official language in Maharashtra [7]. Arabic is a Semitic language, and it is one of the oldest languages in the world. It is the fifth widely used language nowadays. In the Arab Countries, 420 million speakers (native and non-native) use Arabic as the first language [8].

The motivation behind this research is to create and test the Speech Corpus of English Hindi, Marathi and Arabic language (SCHMA) for the development of advanced speech recognition system. The different speech recognition techniques are implemented on SCEHMA to develop IVRS for polyclinic and agricultural-based application. Speech recognition for digit, character, and accent identification is also explained with the same database. The productive experiment for Marathi Speech Activated Calculator (MSAC) and Marathi speech Activated Electrical Equipment (MSAEE) is also explained in this research.

This paper is structured as follows: Sect. 2 depicts the SCEHMA speech corpus development. Section 3 is explaining methods used on SCEHMA corpus. Section 4 illustrates execution assessment of SCEHMA corpus for various applications. Section 5 describes standardization for SCEHMA corpus development. Section 6 is highlighting the conclusion followed by references.

2 SCEHMA Corpus Development

The fundamental step of automatic speech recognition is the selection of vocabulary sentences, words to be recorded by local speakers of the language [5]. For the collection of vocabulary word the elementary school reading material and everyday life, correspondence words are utilized as a source. As a whole SCEHMA corpus is the collection of 33690 isolated words and 19160 sentences of Marathi, Hindi, English and Arabic languages. The word from the primary textbook discovered as syntactically rich. Detail representation of the size of the SCEHMA corpus is described in Table 1.

Table 1. Size of the schma corpus

Sr.No	Language	Isolated word	Sentences
1	Marathi	28420	17470
2	Hindi	0	900
3	English	750	750
4	Arabic	4520	40
Total size of database		33690	19160

2.1 Acquisition Setup

To achieve high audio quality, the recording took place in the 10×10 office room without noisy sound and effect of an echo. The Sampling frequency for all recordings was 16000 Hz in the Room temperature and normal humidity. The speaker was asked to sit in front of the microphone with the Distance of about 12–15 cm. The speech data are collected with the help of Computerized speech laboratory (CSL) using the single-channel as well as Normal computer system. CSL is a complete hardware and software system with specifications and performance [9, 10]. The duration of Speech Corpus is explained in Table 2.

Table 2. Duration of speech corpus

Language	Isolated database (Hh: mm)	Sentence database (Hh: mm)	Average duration of each isolated utterance (Sec)	Average duration of each Sentences utterance (Sec)
Marathi	17:36	20:29	2.20	4.10
Hindi	0:0	1:05	0.0	4.23
English	0:57	1.23	2.7	4.50
Arabic	3:1	0.58	2.4	4.50

3   Speech Recognition Techniques Applied on SCEHMA Corpus

3.1   Mel Frequency Cepstral Coefficients

Mel Frequency Cepstral Coefficients (MFCC) technique is the robust and dynamic technique for speech feature extraction. For each tone of speech sample subjective pitch is measured with respective actual frequency scale known as Mel scale. The value of Mel scale is varies as per the frequency.

The Mel-frequency scale is linear frequency spacing below 1000 Hz and a logarithmic spacing above 1000 Hz. For the reference point, the pitch of a 1 kHz tone, 40 dB above the perceptual hearing threshold, is defined as 1000 Mels. The following formula is used to compute the Mels for a particular frequency [9]. The calculation of the MFCC features is explained in Eq. 1.

$$Mel(f) = 2595 \times \log_{10}((1 + f)/700) \tag{1}$$

Currently researcher were used the MFCC and its derivative for applied applications.

For this research MFCC used with 12, 13, 26 and 39 variations as original feature and derivative of it.

3.2   Dynamic Time Warping

Dynamic time warping (DTW) is a well-known technique to search out a best alignment between two given (time-dependent) speech sequences under certain restrictions. It is used to measuring similarity between two sequences based on time or speed. Naturally, the sequences are warped in a nonlinear fashion to match each other. Originally, DTW has been used to compare different speech patterns in automatic speech recognition. In speech recognition, DTW has been successfully applied to automatically manage with time deformations and different speeds associated with time-dependent data [10].

3.3   Linear Discriminate Analysis (LDA)

Linear Discriminate Analysis (LDA) is commonly used technique for data classification and dimensionality reduction. It easily handles the case where within-class frequencies are unequal and their performance is been examined on randomly generated test data. The extracted LDA features are the combination of projection matrix, eigenvalues, mean square representation error, bias and mean of training data [11].

3.4   Principal Component Analysis

Principal Components Analysis (PCA) is a method of identifying patterns in data. It highlights and expresses similarities and differences of data. The PCA Extracted feature is the combination of 30 features which is the combinations of projection feature, in class variation, mean and eigenvalues of the speech signal [12].

3.5 Linear Predictive Coding (LPC)

LPC is based on the source-filter model of speech signal. In this research we used the LPC for feature extraction. The predictor coefficient is transformed to a more robust set of parameters known as Cepstral coefficients. Predictor coefficients are estimated for every frame. LPC Feature contains the pitch, gain and duration coefficient parameters of energy [13].

3.6 Word Error Rate (WER)

Word error rate is a common technique for the performance evaluation of speech recognition. The performance is calculated as distance matrix and Number of Token passed. Word error rate is computed as given in Eq. 2.

$$WER = \frac{S+D+I}{N} \tag{2}$$

Where S is the number of substitutions, D is the number of the deletions, the variable I is the number of the insertions, N is the number of words in the reference.

3.7 Real Time Factor (RTF)

The real time factor (RTF) is a common metric for computing the speed of an automatic speech recognition system. It takes time P to process an input of duration I, the real time factor is calculated using Eq. 3.

$$RTF = \frac{P}{I} \tag{3}$$

The performance of the system is not only depending on accuracy but also highly dependent of RTF value. The performance is described in Eq. 4.

$$Performance = Accuracy * RTF \tag{4}$$

The accuracy of a speech recognition system, on the other hand, is measured with the word error rate.

4 Various Application of SCEHMA Corpus

The following are the various applications which are developed to evaluate the execution of SCEHMA corpus.

4.1   Interactive Voice Response System

The motivation behind an IVRS is mostly to make the initial process of answering and routing a call more efficiently. Currently, IVRS utilized as a part of managing an account, telephonic industries, government organizations, and online booking framework and government information sources. This is an Interactive Voice Response System, which enables the farmers to obtain the solution for their queries.

The performance of an ASR significantly depends on the quality of speech data used to train the system. With quality, we created Marathi isolated and sentence database from 10 male and 10 female speakers. The size of the Marathi IVRS corpus was 3000 isolated words and 2000 sentences. The background noise also differs depending upon the location of the caller so, that the data was preprocessed when it passed to test the system.

The execution of the framework is calculated by Word Error Rate (WER). In this experiment, MFCC is implemented for feature extraction and Euclidian distance is used for classification. The performance of IVRS based recognition system is shown in Table 3. The IVRS framework is examined on the premises of gender. The overall recognition rate of the framework comes to be 91%. This IVRS system as is directly beneficial to farmers for their daily queries regarding the routine farm work.

Table 3. The performance of IVRS based recognition system

Sr.No	Gender	Sentence passed	Sentence recognize	Accuracy
1	Male	50	46	92
2	Female	100	90	90

4.2   Polyclinic Inquiry System

The polyclinic inquiry system is an IVRS for Multi-specialist hospital. The database of the Polyclinic inquiry system created using doctor name, appointments and queries of patients. The database was collected from 20 Male and 10 Females. The Vocabulary size of the database is 4000 isolated word and 3000 continuous sentences. This system was implemented using MFCC and Euclidian distance. The performance of the system is evaluated on the basis of Word Error Rate. The system required approximately 4 min fifty five second for training and one minute for testing. Tables 4 and 5 show the performance of system on the basis of gender and age group parameter respectively. The overall accuracy of the system is 88%.

Table 4. Response of system on the basic Classification of Gender

Sr.No	Gender	Sentence passed	Sentence recognize	Accuracy
1	Male	130	112	92
2	Female	100	90	90

Table 5. Response of system on the basic classification of age group

Sr.No	Age group	Sentence passed	Sentence recognize	Accuracy
1	20–25	200	176	87
2	25–30	100	90	90
3	35–40	50	46	92

4.3   Accent Identification System

In Speech processing, improvement of recognition is very important, where accent plays an important role. To lead towards speech recognition, accent recognition experiment was also implied on the SCEHMA database. The database for accent includes Marathi and Arabic accented English as well as Marwadi, Urdu & Marathi accented Hindi. The vocabulary of recording is taken from daily routine word and sentences as well as from famous Hindi Novel Godan and Gaban.

The Marathi accent database was collected from 50 male and 50 female speakers of 18–30 age groups. The size of the Marathi accent database was 5,000 isolated words. The Hindi accent database was collected from 18 male and 12 female speakers. The aggregate size of Hindi accent database was 900 continuous sentences of 18–30 age groups. The Arabic accented database was made from 20 male and 10 female. The total size of this database is 2000 isolated word.

For the recognition of accent MFCC, DTW, and LPC features are used and evaluated. The acoustic features like energy, formant frequency and pitch was also considered for analyzing the recognition performance and it is observed through the results of experimentation that MFCC, DTW and LPC coefficients along with acoustic features results in effective recognition of accents.

4.4   General Speech Recognition Systems

This experiment is focused on digit, character and continuous speech recognition. The digit and character recognition experiment was evaluated in Marathi, English and Arabic language. The characters vocabulary is designed as a vowel, consonant of each language. The vocabulary for continuous speech experiment was taken from daily routine sentences.

The database for the Marathi language experiment was collected from 10 male and 10 female subjects. The size of vocabulary is 2000 word. An Arabic language database was created from 12 male and 9 female speakers. The size of vocabulary was 4520 words. The English language database was recorded from 12 male and 3 female speakers. The size of vocabulary was 750 words. The database of the continuous speech experiment was collected from 10 male and 10 female speakers. The vocabulary size was 5000. The performance of digit and character recognition was done using MFCC and DTW techniques. Table 6 describes the comparative performance of digit recognition for Marathi, English and Arabic language. The performance of character recognition shows in Table 7. The continuous speech system is tested using MFCC, and fusion of MFCC with PCA, LDA, and DWT. The overall performance of a continuous speech recognition system is described in Table 8.

Table 6. Comparative analysis of digit recognition

Language technique	Marathi (%)	Arabic (%)	English (%)
MFCC	90	91	85
DTW	90	89	88.70

Table 7. Comparative analysis of digit recognition

Language technique	Marathi (%)	Arabic (%)	English (%)
MFCC	91	80	89
DTW	83	74.28	85

Table 8. Comparative analysis of digit recognition

Sr. No	Name of technique	Accuracy
1	MFCC	77.21
2	MFCC+PCA	86.20
3	MFCC+LDA	89.24
4	MFCC+DWT	90.21
5	MFCC+PCA+DWT	92.90
6	MFCC+LDA+DWT	95.06
1	MFCC	77.21

4.5   Speech Based Interface System

Marathi Speech Activated Talking Calculator (MSAC) and Marathi speech Activated Electrical Equipment (MSAEE) are the two interfaces developed using Marathi Speech. For MSAC experiment, the database was created using calculator operation, number, interface command and activation interfaces. The vocabulary size of MSAC experiment was 300 words. For MSAEE experiment database was recorded as the name, operation and control commands of equipment. The vocabulary size of MSAEE experiment was 50 words. The designed working diagram of MSAC system is described in the Fig. 1. The Fig. 2 is explaining the functional diagram of MSAEE system.

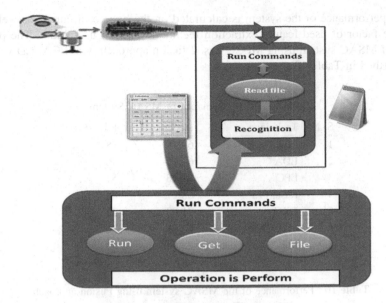

Fig. 1. Working of MSAC system

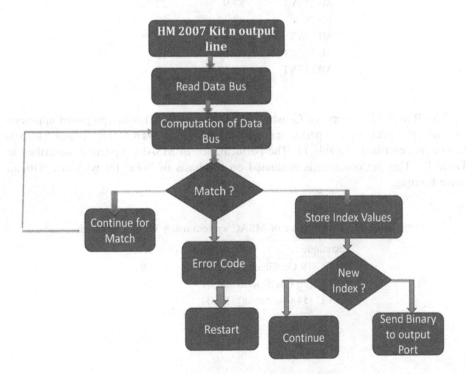

Fig. 2. Working of MSAEE system

The performance of the system is calculated on the basis of accuracy as well as a real time factor of used feature extraction techniques shown in Table 9. The performance of MSAC system using MFCC based fusion approach with PCA, LDA, DWT are described in Table 10.

Table 9. The performance of MSAC System

Sr.No	Technique	Accuracy (%)	RTF (%)
1	PCA	62.19	38
2	LDA	67.17	46
3	LPC	61.23	51
4	Rasta-PLP	68.27	48
5	DWT	71.02	32
6	MFCC (13 feature)	75.78	26
7	MFCC (39 Feature)	78.03	38

Table 10. Performance of the MSAC system using Fusion approach

Fusion approach	Accuracy (%)	RTF
MFLDA	87.9	22
MFPCA	87.12	20
MFDWT	86.17	6
MFPDWT	89.09	12
MFLDWT	90.12	10

The Wavelet Decomposed Cepstral coefficient (WDCC) is the proposed approach for feature extraction. The performance of MSAC using WDCC 18, 36 and 54 coefficients is described in Table 11. The performance of MSAEE system is described in Table 12. This performance is evaluated on the basis of WER for with and without noise training.

Table 11. Performance of MSAC system using WDCC approach

Technique	Accuracy (%)	RTF
WDCC(18 Coefficient)	94.03	9
WDCC (36 Coefficient)	95.01	20
WDCC (54 Coefficient)	98.04	27

Table 12. Performance of MSAEE system with and without noise training

Training word (In English)	Without noise training		With noise training	
	WER (%)	Accuracy (100-WER) (%)	WER (%)	Accuracy (100-WER) (%)
Bulb On	1.22	98.78	10.17	88.73
Bulb Off	1.27	98.73	10.23	88.77
Start	1.13	98.87	10.09	88.91
Off	1.08	98.92	10.13	88.87
One	1.04	98.96	10.09	88.91
Two	1.04	98.96	10.74	88.26
Three	1.08	98.92	10.09	88.91
Four	1.04	98.96	10.13	88.87
Total		**98.88**	**88.77**	

5 Standardization of SCEHMA Corpus

For database standardization we focused on the, transcription, labeling and annotation of speech corpus.

5.1 Corpus Transcription

The corpus is transcript through a Google Unicode editor. For marinating the dictionary of the word, we used the CMU lexicon tool and the alphabet symbol. The alphabet is a phonetic transcription code developed by Advanced Research. ARPAbet has been used in several speech synthesizers, including basic speech processing research. It is also used in the CMU Pronouncing Dictionary for speech transcription. The corpus transcribed on the basis of ARPAbet symbol.

5.2 Labeling and Annotation

The formula was used for the nomenclature and labeling of the database is explained in Eq. 5.

$$Labeled = \sum_{i=1}^{n} LAK \tag{5}$$

Where L is used for language, A is used for number of speaker and k is used for utterances index.

Praat is used for labeling, segmentation and corpus annotation. It is a product of the Phonetic Sciences department of the University of Amsterdam [14–16] and hence oriented for acoustic-phonetic studies by phoneticians. It has multiple functionalities that include speech analysis/synthesis and manipulation, labeling and segmentation, listening experiments. The graphical representation labeling of Marathi continuous speech using Praat Tool described in Fig. 3.

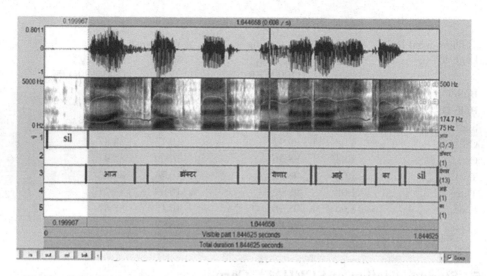

Fig. 3. Graphical interface for speech, labeling of Marathi continuous speech recognition

5.3 Preprocessing and Normalization

This experiment used the Praat and Matlab tool for preprocessing. The data point was taken from 20 ms clips of utterances and was averaged over a window of 2.5 s to form feature. Various preprocessing techniques were attempted to include sliding windows, hamming window, voice –unvoiced detection and zero padding from data point.

5.4 Corpus Availability

This research is developed by SCMRL research laboratory, after completion of all segmentation, labeling and annotation, the SCEHMA database will be made available online to the research community through the prior request permission of the institution. The release will include the speech files (Wav and NIST Format) and transcript file.

6 Conclusion

This paper is discussed optimal design and development of SCEHMA speech corpus for English, Hindi, Marathi and Arabic Language. The standard methodology of database creation presented will serve as catalyst for the creation of more dynamic speech databases for other Indian languages. The research is also contributing towards the transcription, labeling, and annotation of the speech corpus. Transcription is the great interest for researchers working in same domains. The work is extended towards the performance evaluation of the SCEHMA corpus for the farmer IVRS system, Polyclinic Inquiry system, accent identification experiment, digit recognition, general purpose speech recognition system and character recognition. This database is also tested in real time productive MSAC & MSAEE speech interface systems. The release of this database will be helpful for the speech community within India and abroad towards development of speech system in Indian and Arabic languages. The corpus is useful for the research to develop the agricultural, medical and language identification application in Marathi, Hindi, English and Arabic Language.

References

1. Schultz, T., Weibel, A.: Language independent and language adaptive acoustic modeling for speech recognition. Speech Commun. **35**(1–2), 31–51 (2001)
2. Murthy, H.A., et al.: Building unit selection speech synthesis in Indian languages: an initiative by an Indian consortium. In: Proceedings of COCOSDA, Kathmandu, Nepal (2010)
3. English Language [Online]. http://en.wikipedia.org/wiki/English_language. Accessed Dec 2018
4. Hindi Language [Online]. http://en.wikipedia.org/wiki/Hindustani_phonology. Accessed Dec 2018
5. Singh, S.P., et al.: Building large vocabulary speech recognition systems for Indian languages. In: International Conference on Natural Language Processing, pp. 245–254 (2004)
6. Marathi CIIL corpus [source]. http://tdil.mit.gov.in/corpora/achcorpora
7. Gaikwad, S., Gawali, B., Mehrotra, S.: Creation of Marathi speech corpus for automatic speech recognition. In: International Conference Oriental COCOSDA held Jointly with the 2013 Conference on Asian Spoken Language Research and Evaluation (O-COCOSDA/CASLRE) (2013)
8. Al-Zabibi, M.: An acoustic–phonetic approach in automatic Arabic speech recognition. The British Library in Association with UMI (1990)
9. Gaikwad, S.K., Gawali, B., Yannawar, P.: A review on speech recognition technique. Int. J. Comput. Appl. **10**, 16–24 (2010)
10. Godin, C., Lockwood, P.: DTW schemes for continuous speech recognition: a unified view. Comput. Speech Lang. **3**(2), 169–198 (1989)
11. Yuliani, A.R., Sustika, R., Yuwana, R.S., Pardede, H.F.: Feature transformations for robust speech recognition in reverberant conditions. In: 2017 International Conference on Computer Control Informatics and its Applications (IC3INA), pp. 57–62 (2017)
12. Prasetio, M.D., Hayashida, T., Nishizaki, I., Sekizaki, S.: Structural optimization of deep belief network theorem for classification in speech recognition. In: 2017 IEEE 10th International Workshop on Computational Intelligence and Applications (IWCIA), pp. 121–128 (2017)
13. Khara, S., Singh, S., Vir, D.: A comparative study of the techniques for feature extraction and classification in stuttering. In: 2018 Second International Conference on Inventive Communication and Computational Technologies (ICICCT), pp. 887–893 (2018)
14. Gawali, B.W., Gaikwad, S., Yannawar, P., Mehrotra, S.C.: Marathi isolated word recognition system uses MFCC and DTW features. ACEE Int. J. Inf. Technol. **1**(1), 21–24 (2011)
15. Praat Tutorial [Online]. http://www.stanford.edu/dept/linguistics/corpora/material/PRAAT_workshop_manual_v421.pdf
16. Praat Tutorial [online] source. http://www.fon.hum.uva.nl/praat

Evaluation of Local Texture Descriptors for Eyebrow-Based Continuous Mobile User Authentication

Ahmad Saeed Mohammad[1]([⊠]) [iD], Ajita Rattani[2] [iD],
and Reza Derakhshani[3] [iD]

[1] Department of Computer Engineering, College of Engineering,
Mustansiriyah University, Baghdad, Iraq
ahmad.saeed@uomustansiriyah.edu.iq
[2] Department of Electrical Engineering and Computer Science,
Wichita State University, Wichita, KS, USA
ajita.rattani@wichita.edu
[3] Department of Computer Science and Electrical Engineering,
University of Missouri-Kansas City, Kansas City, MO, USA
derakhshanir@umkc.edu

Abstract. Mobile user authentication plays an important role in securing physical and logical access, especially to globally ubiquitous smart phones. Several studies have evaluated face, ocular and finger modalities for mobile user authentication. Human eyebrow is among the less explored traits for mobile biometric use cases where device front facing cameras can easily scan them. A handful of studies suggest the potential of human eyebrows for person authentication. Using Histogram of Oriented Gradients (HOG) based texture descriptors, we show equal error rates as low as 15.32% and areas under ROC curve as high as 0.92 on publicly available VISOB dataset when fusing left and right eyebrow units.

Keywords: Biometric · Computer vision · Local texture descriptors · Mobile authentication · Ocular recognition · Eyebrows · Continuous user authentication

1 Introduction

Eyebrow is a novel biometric trait within the largely popular facial region of interest [10, 16]. Eyebrows have been considered as one of the important soft biometric traits similar but arguably accurate when compared to other soft traits such as ethnicity, gender, and age. As such, it may aid and enhancement primary biometric traits like iris and face [17, 18, 30–32]. Similar to other ocular and periocular modalities [14, 24, 25], the performance of eyebrow recognition maybe impacted by dim-light conditions, eyeglasses, frame shadow, and eyeglasses occlusion which effects the major portion of ocular region [19, 20].

The mobile technology involving sensor, memory, and storage has undergone dramatic and continuous evolution. This rapid evolution has facilitated biometric modalities such as face, ocular region, and fingerprint to be acquired using the already

© Springer Nature Switzerland AG 2020
M. I. Khalaf et al. (Eds.): ACRIT 2019, CCIS 1174, pp. 136–147, 2020.
https://doi.org/10.1007/978-3-030-38752-5_11

installed camera and processed for mobile user authentication [26–29]. In order to improve user experience, researchers are investigating continuous user authentication by reducing the requirements on the primary biometric modality for mobile use cases, thus reducing the need for frequent re-authentication through the usually more demanding primary hard biometrics [4]. In this regard, the eyebrows, representing $\frac{1}{6}$ of face size, and other auxiliary modalities such as teeth imagery and voice have been used to assist the authentication process [8, 21].

The aim of this paper is to *evaluate local texture descriptors for eyebrow-based mobile user authentication*. To this aim, ten local descriptors, and their fusion, were evaluated when extracted from region of interest (ROI) consisting of the left and right eyebrow units cropped from ocular images in publicly available VISOB dataset [33]. The ROC curves of our experimental results suggest a minimum Equal Error Rate (EER) of 15.32% and a maximum Area Under Curve (AUC) of 0.92 from the fusion of Histogram of Oriented Gradients (HOG) descriptors from left and right eyebrow units.

The rest of this paper is organized as following: Sect. 2 discusses previous work on eyebrow recognition. Section 3 lays out the proposed methodology. Experimental evaluations are discussed in Sect. 4. Conclusions are drawn in Sect. 5.

2 Previous Work

Juefei-Xu et al. [5] investigated eyebrows as a stand-alone biometric for person authentication. They used Local Binary Pattern (LBP) as feature representation with three different transforms, namely, Walsh-Hadamard, Discrete Cosine, and Fourier transform. The best reported results show false acceptance rate (FAR) between 0.033 to 0.082 for the eyebrow verification rate of 0.1%. Also, the RANK1 identification was reported to be between 0.195 to 0.053.

Le et al. [11] implemented an Active Shape Model using $2D$ profiles for eyebrow segmentation. Singular value decomposition (SVD) was applied to the segmented eyebrows. The reported results show 76% and 85% of identification accuracy on the AR and MBGC datasets, respectively.

Jun-Bin et al. [6] proposed an approach based on the Support Vector Machine (SVM) with Radial Basis Function (RBF) kernel along with wavelet transform. The best reported results were 29.58% of FAR, and 8.22% of False Rejection Rate (FRR) on in-house eyebrow database of 100 subjects.

Li et al. [12] implemented a fast template matching approach to locate the eyebrow region in an ocular image, then the Fourier spectrum distance was applied to infer the identity. The reported results show 80%–94% of identification accuracy on the color FERET database.

Li et al. [13] applied a Hidden Markov Models (HMM) on a manually selected polygon around the eye for eyebrow recognition. The highest accuracy obtained was 92.6% on eyebrow recognition on a small-scale dataset of 54 frontal eyebrows from 27 subjects.

Yong et al. [36] proposed an approach based on Sparsity Preserving Projection (SPP) by computing the sparse weight matrix using the projection matrix, and recognizing identity based on the lower-dimensional data. Their results show 92.5%, and

80.63% accuracy on open and closed eye images, respectively. The database used consists of 32 subjects with 10 images per subject.

Yujian et al. [37] applied a Discrete Fourier Transformation on eyebrow images from a database of 32 subjects. The authors concluded that the eyebrow is a promising trait and the reported accuracy varies between 81.25% and 93.75%.

Guo et al. [3] applied distribution-based descriptors, namely Gradient Orientation (GO) Histogram, LBP, and SIFT descriptor on a small-scale database consisting of 30 subjects. The reported accuracies were 77.5% and 80% for right and left eyebrow units, respectively.

Mohammad et al. [21] implemented a deep learning based convolutional neural network (CNN) for continuous mobile user authentication using eyebrows and eyeglasses. The best reported results showed 99.96% accuracy on fusion of right and left eyebrow units. Table 1 shows the summary for the previous work mentioned above.

Table 1. Summary of previous eyebrow-based user authentication methods.

Ref	Method	Database	Subjects	Images	Accuracy
[5]	LBP, Walsh-Hadamard, Discrete Cosine, and Fourier transform	FRGC	4003	16,012	FAR = 8.2%
[11]	Active Shape Model	MBGC + AR	574 + 126	2341 + 4000	85–76%
[6]	Support Vector Machine with wavelet transform	In house	100	2000	FAR = 29.58%
[12]	Fourier Spectrum Distance	FERET	989	1978	80%–94%
[13]	Hidden Markov Models	In house	27	58	92.6%
[36]	Sparsity Preserving Projection	In house	32	320	80.63%–92.5%
[37]	Fourier Transformation	In house	32	192	81.25%
[3]	LBP and SIFT with Gradient Orientation Histogram	In house	30	210	77.5%–80%
[21]	Convolutional Neural Network (Heavy computational method)	VISOB + FERET	550 + 989	135K	99.96%

3   Proposed Work

Figure 1 shows the steps involved in our proposed scheme for eyebrow-based continuous mobile user authentication. These steps are ROI extraction, feature descriptor extraction, matching score computation and fusion of left and right eyebrow units.

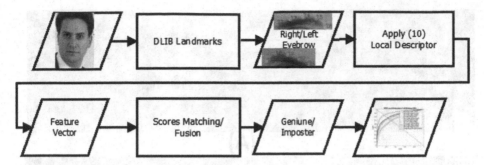

Fig. 1. The block diagram of our proposed approach for eyebrow-based short-term mobile user authentication.

3.1 Region of Interest Extraction

As the first step the ROI consisting of eyebrows from right and left ocular units are cropped from VISOB dataset using Dlib landmark library [9].

Figure 2 shows the steps involved in ROI extraction which include extracting 68 landmark points using Dlib and cropping the eyebrow using geometrical operations.

3.2 Feature Descriptor Extraction

Local descriptors, namely, Rotated Local Binary Pattern (RLBP), Completed Local Binary Pattern (CLBP), Local Ternary Pattern (LTP), Local Oriented Statistical Information Booster (LOSIB), Locally Uniform Comparison Image Descriptor (LUCID), Local Phase Quantization (LPQ), Local Binary Pattern (LBP), Binarized Statistical Image Feature (BSIF), Pattern of Oriented Edge Magnitudes (POEM), and Histogram of Oriented Gradients (HOG) were used for feature extraction from left and right ROIs at four different scales as follows:

Figure 3 shows the visualization of LBP feature descriptors. Texture based descriptors such as RLBP [15], CLBP [3], LTP [34], and LBP were applied to the extracted ROIs to compute the texture of hair strands in the eyebrow region. These descriptors were obtained by tiling the ROI into small cells of the size 16×16 pels, followed by comparing the neighbor pixel values with the center pixel of the tile and replacing them with the resultant 0 or 1 (for RLBP, CLBP, and LBP), or -1, 0, and 1 (for LTP). Consequently the histogram of each cell was computed, the histograms were normalized and concatenated to form the ROI feature vector [22].

LOSIB features are based on the statistical information of ROI. This descriptor is based on computing the differences in mean along a particular orientation to enhance the capability of LBP descriptor [2].

LUCID descriptor compute the alteration distances of RGB values inside a small region in ROI [38].

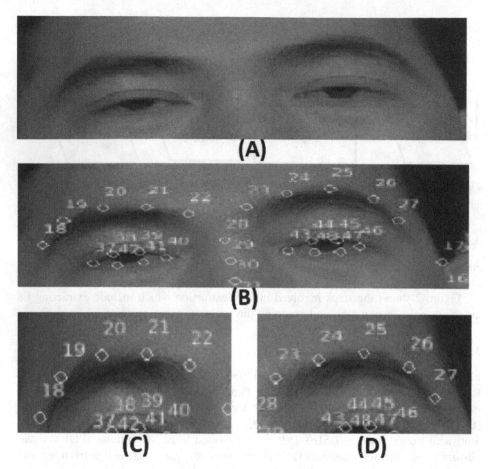

Fig. 2. Region of Interest (ROI): (A) original ocular region, (B) ocular region after applying Dlib, (C) right eyebrow, and (D) left eyebrow unit.

LPQ is a robust descriptor for blurred images based on computing the phase information for each cell or tile in an ROI window. A histogram is generated to form the feature vector. This descriptor is invariant to illumination changes [23].

BSIF extracts ROI features based on statistics of natural images rather than heuristic code construction. This descriptor is obtained by projecting local image patches into a subspace to compute the binary code of each pixel [7].

POEM is a multi-resolution descriptor which provides valuable information about the ROI. This descriptor is obtained by computing the histogram of divided cells inside the ROI and then concatenating these histograms to provide the self-similarity oriented magnitude structure [35].

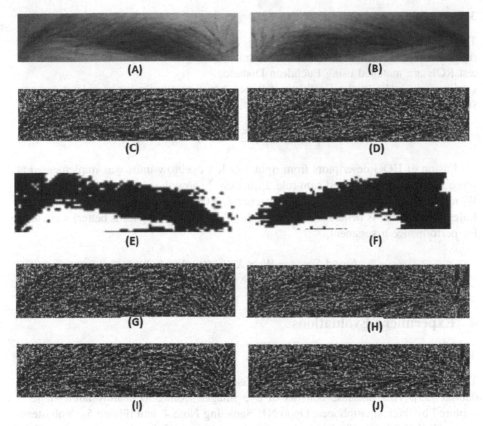

Fig. 3. Visualization of LBP feature descriptors: (A, B) original ROI, (C, D) RLBP, (E, F) CLBP, (G, H) LTP, (I, J) LBP, for right and left eyebrow units, respectively.

HOG is obtain by tiling an ROI into small cells, and then computing the histogram of edge orientation along each pixel in the cell. The final feature vector is obtained by combining the resulting histograms [1]. Figure 4 visualizes HOG descriptors.

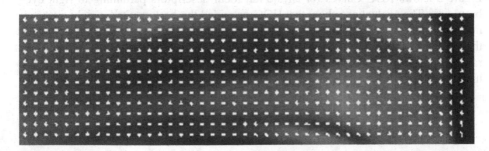

Fig. 4. Visualization of Histogram of Oriented Gradients (HOG) obtained for left and right eyebrow ROIs.

3.3   Matching and Fusion

The final step consists of feature matching, score computation and fusion of left and right unit scores for final decision. The extracted features from pair of enrollment and test ROIs are matched using Euclidean Distance.

Equation 1 shows the Euclidean distance between enrollment sample p and test sample q

$$\sqrt{||p||2 + ||q||2 - 2 \times p \times q} \tag{1}$$

Fusion of HOG descriptors from right and left eyebrow units was implemented at score level using a weighted sum rule. Equation 2 show the weighted sum rule where W_i represents the wight assigned to matcher i. ROC Curves along their Equal Error Rates (EER, lower is better) and Areas Under Curve (AUC, higher is better) were used for performance assessment.

$$Fused\ Score = W_i \times X_i + \ldots + W_m \times X_m \tag{2}$$

4   Experiment Evaluations

4.1   Dataset

The proposed approach was evaluated on Visible Ocular Biometric Database (VISOB) dataset [33]. This database consists of eye images from 550 healthy adult subjects captured by three smartphones: Oppo N1, Samsung Note 4, and iPhone 5s. Volunteers were asked to take "selfies" using front facing cameras of the phones in two sessions that were about 10 to 15 min apart. The distance between the camera and volunteers face was 8 to 12 inches. For each session, the images were taken in three lighting conditions: bright light, office light and dim light.

4.2   Results

Figure 5 shows ROC Curves for all the ten local descriptors pertaining to right eyebrow unit. The evaluations show that HOG provided the best results for right eyebrow unit with the lowest EER of 19.4%. Figure 6 shows AUC and EER comparison for these local descriptors. It can be seen that AUC ranges from 0.74 to 0.88, and the EER ranges from 32.7% to 19.4% for all the descriptors. HOG descriptor obtained the highest AUC of 0.88, while CLBP obtained the lowest AUC of 0.75.

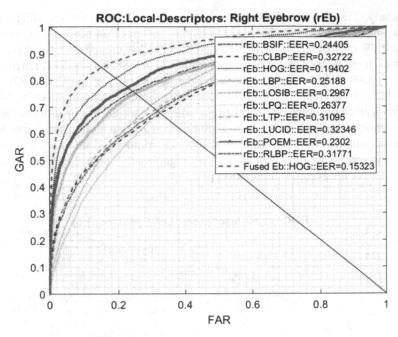

Fig. 5. ROC of ten local descriptors for ROI consisting of right eyebrow and the fusion of the best descriptor (HOG) for ROI consisting of left and right eyebrow units.

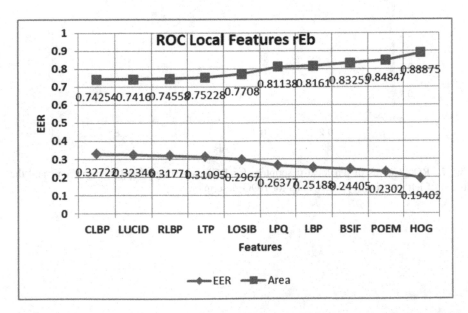

Fig. 6. EER and AUC values for these ten descriptors for ROI consisting of right eyebrow unit.

Similarly, Fig. 7 shows ROC curves of ten local descriptors pertaining to left eyebrow units. It can be seen that again HOG out-performed all other descriptors with the least EER of 19.4%. Figure 8 shows AUC and EER comparison for these local descriptors. It can be seen that AUC ranges from 0.74 to 0.88, and the EER ranges from 32.7% to 19.4%. HOG descriptors obtained the best result with AUC of 0.87, while CLBP obtained the least AUC of 0.74. Our experimental results may not readily be compared with those obtained on existing studies due to the use of different performance evaluation methods and metrics. Further, when assessing our results, one should take into account that they are based on shallow descriptors and thus they may not be directly comparable to those obtained using significantly more complex and data-intensive CNNs for eyebrow recognition [21].

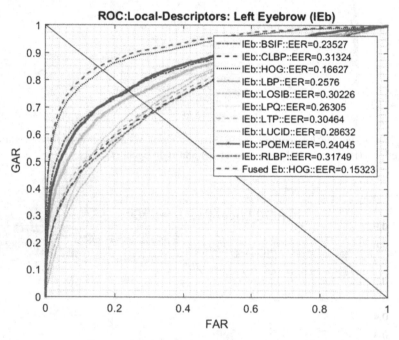

Fig. 7. ROC Curves of ten local descriptors for ROI consisting of left eyebrow unit and the fusion of left and right eyebrow units for HOG descriptor.

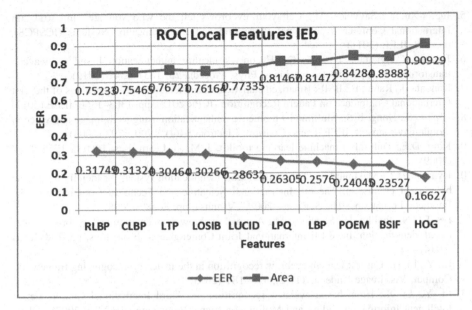

Fig. 8. EER and AUC values for the ten descriptors for ROI consisting of left eyebrow unit.

5   Conclusions

This paper evaluates various state-of-the-art local texture descriptors for eyebrow based mobile user authentication. Thorough experimental evaluation on VISOB dataset suggests that grid-based local HOG descriptors yield EER compared to other local descriptors such as LBP, LOSIB, LUCID, BSIF, and POEM for both the left and right eyebrow units. These evaluations suggest the better potential of HOG descriptor in capturing edge information and the gradient structure of eyebrow hair strands as a discriminatory feature vector. The performance was further improved by fusion of left and right eyebrow units. This suggest the presence of complimentary information in the left and right eyebrow units that can be fused to further enhance the authentication accuracy. As a part of future work, our experiment maybe be extended to other datasets with confounding factors such as presence of sunglasses and makeup.

References

1. Dalal, N., Triggs, B.: Histograms of oriented gradients for human detection (2005)
2. García-Olalla, O., Alegre, E., Ferna´ndez-Robles, L., González-Castro, V.: Local oriented statistics information booster (LOSIB) for texture classification. In: 2014 22nd International Conference on Pattern Recognition, pp. 1114–1119. IEEE (2014)
3. Guo, Z., Zhang, L., Zhang, D.: A completed modeling of local binary pattern operator for texture classification. IEEE Trans. Image Process. **19**(6), 1657–1663 (2010)
4. He, D.: An efficient remote user authentication and key agreement protocol for mobile client–server environment from pairings. Ad Hoc Netw. **10**(6), 1009–1016 (2012)

5. Juefei-Xu, F., Savvides, M.: Can your eyebrows tell me who you are? In: 2011 5th International Conference on Signal Processing and Communication Systems (ICSPCS), pp. 1–8. IEEE (2011)
6. Jun-bin, C., Haitao, Y., Lili, D.: Eyebrows identity authentication based on wavelet transform and support vector machines. Phys. Procedia **25**, 1337–1341 (2012)
7. Kannala, J., Rahtu, E.: BSIF: Binarized statistical image features. In: Proceedings of the 21st International Conference on Pattern Recognition (ICPR 2012), pp. 1363–1366. IEEE (2012)
8. Kim, D.S., Hong, K.S.: Multimodal biometric authentication using teeth image and voice in mobile environment. IEEE Trans. Consum. Electron. **54**(4), 1790–1797 (2008)
9. King, D.E.: Dlib-ml: a machine learning toolkit. J. Mach. Learn. Res. **10**(Jul), 1755–1758 (2009)
10. Kyazimov, T., Makhmudova, S.J.: Information identification system for identifying people by portrait photos. In: The 6th International Scientific and Technical Conference of the Internet—Formation—The Science—2008," Vinnitsa, pp. 86–89 (2008)
11. Le, T.H.N., Prabhu, U., Savvides, M.: A novel eyebrow segmentation and eyebrow shape-based identification. In: IEEE International Joint Conference on Biometrics, pp. 1–8. IEEE (2014)
12. Li, Y., Li, H., Cai, Z.: Human eyebrow recognition in the matching-recognizing framework. Comput. Vis. Image Underst. **117**(2), 170–181 (2013)
13. Li, Y., Li, X.: Hmm based eyebrow recognition. In: Third International Conference on Intelligent Information Hiding and Multimedia Signal Processing (IIH-MSP 2007), vol. 1, pp. 135–138. IEEE (2007)
14. Marsico, M.D., Nappi, M., Riccio, D., Wechsler, H.: Mobile iris challenge evaluation (MICHE)-I, biometric iris dataset and protocols. Pattern Recogn. Lett. **57**, 17–23 (2015)
15. Mehta, R., Egiazarian, K.O.: Rotated local binary pattern (RLBP)-rotation invariant texture descriptor. In: ICPRAM, pp. 497–502 (2013)
16. Mohammad, A.S., Rattani, A., Derakhshani, R.: Short-term user authentication using eyebrows biometric for smartphone devices. In: IEEE Computer Science and Electronic Engineering Conference, pp. 1–6 (2018)
17. Mohammad, A.S., Al-Ani, J.A.: Towards ethnicity detection using learning based classifiers. In: 2017 9th Computer Science and Electronic Engineering (CEEC), pp. 219–224. IEEE (2017)
18. Mohammad, A.S., Al-Ani, J.A.: Convolutional neural network for ethnicity classification using ocular region in mobile environment. In: 2018 10th Computer Science and Electronic Engineering (CEEC), pp. 293–298. IEEE (2018)
19. Mohammad, A.S., Rattani, A., Derakhshani, R.: Eyeglasses detection based on learning and non-learning based classification schemes. In: 2017 IEEE International Symposium on Technologies for Homeland Security (HST). pp. 1–5. IEEE (2017)
20. Mohammad, A.S., Rattani, A., Derakhshani, R.: Comparison of squeezed convolutional neural network models for eyeglasses detection in mobile environment. J. Comput. Sci. Coll. **33**(5), 136–144 (2018)
21. Mohammad, A.S., Rattani, A., Derakhshani, R.: Eyebrows and eyeglasses as soft biometrics using deep learning. IET Biometrics **8**, 378–390 (2019)
22. Ojala, T., Pietikäinen, M., Mäenpää, T.: Multiresolution gray-scale and rotation invariant texture classification with local binary patterns. IEEE Trans. Pattern Anal. Mach. Intell. **24** (7), 971–987 (2002)
23. Ojansivu, V., Heikkilä, J.: Blur insensitive texture classification using local phase quantization. In: Elmoataz, A., Lezoray, O., Nouboud, F., Mammass, D. (eds.) ICISP 2008. LNCS, vol. 5099, pp. 236–243. Springer, Heidelberg (2008). https://doi.org/10.1007/978-3-540-69905-7_27

24. Park, U., Ross, A., Jain, A.K.: Periocular biometrics in the visible spectrum: a feasibility study. In: 2009 IEEE 3rd International Conference on Biometrics: Theory, Applications, and Systems, pp. 1–6. IEEE (2009)
25. Rattani, A., Derakhshani, R.: Ocular biometrics in the visible spectrum: a survey. Image and Vis. Comput. **59**, 1–16 (2017)
26. Rattani, A., Derakhshani, R.: On fine-tuning convolutional neural networks for smartphone based ocular recognition. In: IEEE International Joint Conference on Biometrics (IJCB), pp. 762–767, October 2017
27. Rattani, A., Derakhshani, R.: Online co-training in mobile ocular biometric recognition. In: IEEE International Symposium on Technologies for Homeland Security (HST), pp. 1–5, April 2017
28. Rattani, A., Derakhshani, R.: A survey of mobile face biometrics. Comput. Electr. Eng. **72**, 39–52 (2018)
29. Rattani, A., Derakhshani, R., Ross, A.: Selfie Biometrics: Advances and Challenges, 1st edn. Springer, Cham (2019). https://doi.org/10.1007/978-3-030-26972-2
30. Rattani, A., Reddy, N., Derakhshani, R.: Convolutional neural network for age classification from smart-phone based ocular images. In: 2017 IEEE International Joint Conference on Biometrics (IJCB), pp. 756–761, October 2017
31. Rattani, A., Reddy, N., Derakhshani, R.: Gender prediction from mobile ocular images: a feasibility study. In: IEEE Symposium on Technologies for Homeland Security, Waltham, MA, pp. 1–6 (2017)
32. Rattani, A., Reddy, N., Derakhshani, R.: Convolutional neural networks for gender prediction from smartphone-based ocular images. IET Biometrics **7**, 423–430 (2018)
33. Rattani, A., Derakhshani, R., Saripalle, S.K., Gottemukkula, V.: ICIP 2016 competition on mobile ocular biometric recognition. In: 2016 IEEE International Conference on Image Processing (ICIP), pp. 320–324. IEEE (2016)
34. Ren, J., Jiang, X., Yuan, J.: Relaxed local ternary pattern for face recognition. In: 2013 IEEE International Conference on Image Processing, pp. 3680–3684. IEEE (2013)
35. Vu, N.S., Caplier, A.: Face recognition with patterns of oriented edge magnitudes. In: Daniilidis, K., Maragos, P., Paragios, N. (eds.) ECCV 2010. LNCS, vol. 6311, pp. 313–326. Springer, Heidelberg (2010). https://doi.org/10.1007/978-3-642-15549-9_23
36. Yang, X., Xu, X., Liu, C.: Eyebrow recognition based on sparsity preserving projections. In: IEEE Conference Anthology, pp. 1–4. IEEE (2013)
37. Yujian, L., Cuihua, F.: Eyebrow recognition: a new biometric technique. In: Proceedings of the 9th IASTED International Conference on Signal and Image Processing, pp. 506–510 (2007)
38. Ziegler, A., Christiansen, E., Kriegman, D., Belongie, S.J.: Locally uniform comparison image descriptor. In: Advances in Neural Information Processing Systems, pp. 1–9 (2012)

Deep Learning Approach Based Dominant Age Group Based Classification for Social Network

Mohammad Basil[3] ⒾD, Santosh Gaikwad[1](✉) ⒾD,
and Alaa Sabeeh Salim[2] ⒾD

[1] Department of Computer Techniques Engineering,
AI Maarif University College, Ramadi, Iraq
santoh.gaikwadcsit@gmail.com
[2] Department of Computer Science, Model Degree College,
Ghansawangi, Jalna, M.S., India
alaasabeeh@gmail.com
[3] Al-qadisiyah Education Directorate,
Um aikhail, Street 20, Al- Qadisiyah City, Iraq
dr.mohd.alnaqeeb@gmail.com

Abstract. In the current era of technology, the social network is the most important tool of data science. Social network have a largest dataset of people profile, comments and their day to events with photographs. Some people hide the personal data such as age, gender and other demographics. The sentimental analysis is used for the business, political reviews and social opinion about the events. For the sentimental analysis and opinion mining the age and gender are the dominant features. The social nature of the people has been changed as per the age group and gender. This research provides the one of the most relevant parameter of user profile in account creation strategy such as age group. The behavior of the same age group persons are similar and the behavior is homogeneous if discussion of the same topic. The dataset for this experiment has been collected from the Facebook, Twitter. The dataset was 20,000 sample sentences. The experiment was tested over the collected sample sentence dataset. The detail analysis has been done with use of punctuation, number of character, topic used in the sentence. The above characteristics are used for the age group classification. This dataset has been tested deep convolution neural network algorithm for classification of age group as a two class such as teenager and adult age group. Deep Convolution Neural Network (DCNN) had the best performance, reaching a precision of 0.89 in the validation tests. For the validation of the performance of proposed model for age group classification enhanced Sentiment Metric (eSM) is used. In the performance validation, subjective tests are performed and the eSM with the proposed model reached a Root Mean Square Error and a Pearson Correlation Coefficient of 0.32 and 0.89, respectively outclassing the eSM metric.

Keywords: Sentiment analysis · Social network · Facebook · LinkedIn ·
DCNN · Text mining · eSM

© Springer Nature Switzerland AG 2020
M. I. Khalaf et al. (Eds.): ACRIT 2019, CCIS 1174, pp. 148–156, 2020.
https://doi.org/10.1007/978-3-030-38752-5_12

1 Introduction

In the current trends of technology the internet become the necessary part of human life. Using the internet human being is done the e-commerce business, reading daily news and entertainment. The human spends their more than 5 h per day on the internet. Social media acts as a dominant of human life in day to day activity. On the social media the persons posted their views and opinion in the comment form. On the basis of person opinion and comments the online business and marketing is dependent. The provided comment is analyzed and improvement has been done using the outcome from analysis of service provider.

The Facebook and Twitter based comments has been analyzed and update has been done in the product and its marketing. The comment is the key part for the service provider. The customer satisfaction rate for the service provider is based on social media comment and review analysis [1]. The sentimental comments have been depending on the age of the customer. The recognition of sentimental behavior and age of the customer from the posted comments on social media is the challenging task.

This sentimental analysis were applied over the healthcare, ecommerce business, marketing, online purchase, online advertisement and pathology services. The tool for the sentimental analysis was developed using the internet and without internet as per the requirement of the service provider [2–5]. This sentimental analysis area is helpful for the psychotherapist and psychology counselor. The age and gender is directly affecting the result of sentiment analysis. The age group is the dominant parameter for the sentimental analysis [6, 7].

The research based on age group and stress recognition for web service provider has been done and it is useful for web based services [8]. This unit represents the relationship of age group and sentiment analysis strategy. The behavior is the different in different age group person [9, 10]. The security of the private information is not been proved by teen agers so, the maximum review and post are available from this age group [11]. Twitter has the property to alter the posted information or delete the post from anyone account if it is created impact towards the society [12]. There is need of the age group based sentimental analysis using the social media in the accurate manner for Facebook and Twitter.

This paper is structured as follows: Sect. 2 depicts the sentimental analysis. Section 3 is explaining deep learning for sentimental analysis. Section 4 illustrates experimental analysis. Section 5 describes conclusion followed by references.

2 Sentiment Analysis

In the data sharing the text and media such as audio, video acts as an important role. The online comments affect the social behavior. The sentiment of social media comments directly shakes the business of services of provider [13]. The researchers were done the reliable and realistic comment analysis.

The sentiment is the pattern of representation of behavior and mood for the customer. The comments are the key pattern for sentimental analysis. The feedback analysis was done using the sentimental analysis results [14]. The review based online product selling were great impact of the customer sentiment regarding the service and product.

The gender and age group of the customer varies the performance of the sentimental analysis. The product based review need the sentiment analysis for the service improvement in online social media [15]. The sentimental domain was extracted from the comments of Facebook and Twitter. The detail domain structure and flow diagram of the sentimental analysis is shown in Fig. 1. For the deep learning approach the decision tree is the important task. For this experiment the age and gender are the dominant tree point. The layer is created using the age group and gender. The two class classification and decision tree classification has been done in this experiment.

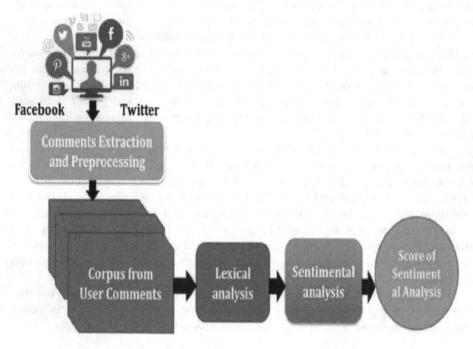

Fig. 1. Domain structure and flow diagram of sentimental analysis

The proposed decision tree for the experiment was shown in the Fig. 2. It described the working structure of the model. This proposed model was applied over the Facebook and Twitter Dataset. For the dominant age group classification this dataset is classified over the two classes teenage and adult.

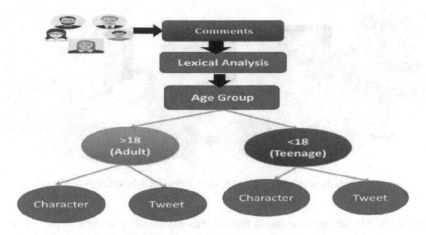

Fig. 2. Representation of proposed decision tree for the classification

3 Deep Learning Approach for Sentiment Analysis

The deep learning is the advance feature of the convolution Neural network (CNN). For the experiment of the large amount of data classification has been done [16]. The CNN based classification was calculated high precision based result. The decision tree is also the approximation and tested pattern for the experiment. The use of deep learning for the research has been increasing day by days. The application of the deep learning is proved the robust and dynamic in the field of image, text and data information extraction [16, 17]. The Deep Leaning algorithm allows computational models that are composed of multiple processing layers to learn representations of data with multiple levels of abstraction. Recently, Deep Learning methods have started to be also applied to text classification [18, 19], and the algorithms have obtained excellent results for classifying text models [20, 21]. Deep Learning are usually interpreted in terms of the universal approximation theorem [22] or probabilistic inference [23]; the approximation theorem defines a class of universal approximates, which refers to the ability of neural networks of direct feeding with a single occult layer, of finite size, to approximate continuous functions. The probabilistic interpretation derives from the machine learning, which includes inference as well as optimization concepts such as training and tests, related to adaptation and generalization. The DCNN can perform classification tasks, and it is composed of multiple layers, each one computes convolution transforms [24–27]. The illustration of the CNN architecture is shown in Fig. 3.

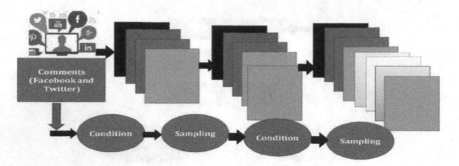

Fig. 3. Extraction of age feature using DCNN structure.

In the DCNN the age calculation feature was extracted by several steps. The detail steps were given in Fig. 3. We were train the deep model of CNN for a multiclasses age estimation task. The leaned structure is used to predict the age given a testing image.

4   Experimental Analysis

For this experiment the dataset has been collected from facebook and twitter online websites. The dataset has 20000 comments and twits. The experiment has been carried out over the dataset.

Table 1. Classification of age group multilayer perception.

Age group	Metric	Precision
Teen ager	0.819	0.832
Adults	0.890	0.899

Table 2. Classification of age group multilayer perception.

Gender	Metric	Precision
Teen ager	0.867	0.856
Adults	0.890	0.879

The graphical representation of the age group in two classes means two dataset such as Facebook and Twitter for the three features of CNN is shown in Fig. 4.

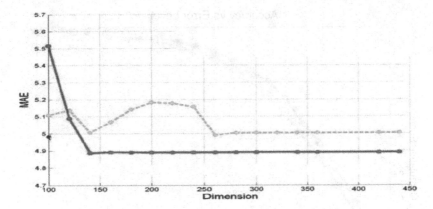

Fig. 4. Results of deep learning based age estimation

The pattern of deep learning for the gender and age group is shown in the Fig. 5.

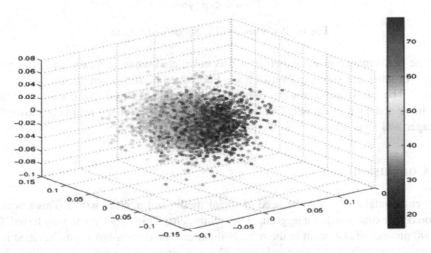

Fig. 5. Visualization of deep learning pattern

The performance and error rate for this experiment is shown in the Fig. 6.

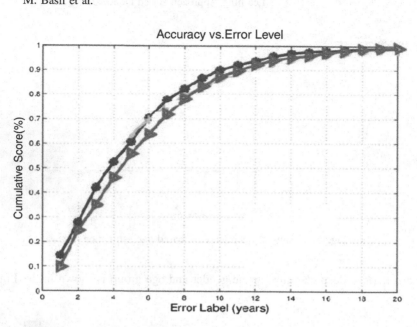

Fig. 6. Performance of the proposed system

The performance of the experiment was calculated using accuracy and error rate. The Error label was showing the two lines. Each one line shows the one dataset for the testing. The classifications were done using two class based classification means Facebook and Twitter dataset. The two class classification for the results is shown for teenager and adult class.

5 Conclusion

The sentimental analysis is the need of social media and internet world. This research devoted to extraction for age group from comment. This experiment was tested for 20,000 number of statement in the reliable manner. The dataset has been classified into the age group such as teenager and adult. The experiment was carried out for two class based classification such as teenage and adult class. The dataset is trained using two classes such as Facebook and Twitter. The experimental data is been collected from user profile and detailed information available on the online mode. The data is collected from Facebook and Twitter. This experiment is tested on the gender based classification also. Form this results, it is observed that Deep Convolution Neural Network (DCNN) is the best performance, reaching a precision of 0.89 in the validation tests. Furthermore, in order to validate the usefulness of the proposed model for classifying age groups, it is implemented into the enhanced Sentiment Metric (eSM). In the performance validation, subjective tests are performed and the eSM with the proposed model reached a Root Mean Square Error and a Pearson Correlation Coefficient of 0.32 and 0.89, respectively, outperforming the eSM metric when the age group information is not available.

References

1. Goldsmith, R.E.: Explaining and predicting consumer intention to purchase over the Internet: an exploratory study. J. Mark. Theory. Pract. **10**(2), 22–28 (2002)
2. Guimaraes, R.G., Rodrıguez, D.Z., Rosa, R.L., Bressan, G.: Recommendation system using sentiment analysis considering the polarity of the adverb. In: 2016 IEEE International Symposium on Consumer Electronics (ISCE), Sao Paulo, Brazil, September 2016, pp. 71–72 (2016)
3. Peersman, C., Daelemans, W., Van Vaerenbergh, L.: Predicting age and gender in online social networks. In: Proceedings of the 3rd International Workshop on Search and Mining User-generated Contents. Glasgow, Scotland, UK, October 2011, pp. 37–44. ACM (2011)
4. Van de Loo, J., De Pauw, G., Daelemans, W.: Text-based age and gender prediction for online safety monitoring. Comput. Linguist. Netherlands **5**(1), 46–60 (2016)
5. Filho, R.M., Almeida, J.M., Pappa, G.L.: Twitter population sample bias and its impact on predictive outcomes: a case study on elections. In: IEEE/ACM International Conference on Advances in Social Networks Analysis and Mining, Paris, France, August 2015, pp. 1254–1261. ACM (2015)
6. Nguyen, D.-P., Gravel, R., Trieschnigg, R., Meder, T.: How old do you think i am? a study of language and age in Twitter. In: Seventh International AAAI Conference on Weblogs and Social Media, Palo Alto, CA, USA, July 2013, pp. 439–448. AAAI Press (2013)
7. Sloan, L., Morgan, J., Burnap, P., Williams, M.: Who tweets? deriving the demographic characteristics of age, occupation and social class from Twitter user meta-data. PloS one, 10 (3), 1–20 (2015)
8. Schler, J., Koppel, M., Argamon, S., Pennebaker, J.W.: Effects of age and gender on blogging. In: AAAI Spring Symposium: Computational Approaches to Analyzing Weblogs, Stanford, CA, March 2006, pp. 199–205 (2006)
9. Sawyer, S.M., et al.: Adolescence: a foundation for future health. Lancet **379**(9826), 1630–1640 (2012)
10. Jang, J.Y., Han, K., Shih, P.C., Lee, D.: Generation like: comparative characteristics in Instagram. In: Proceedings of the 33rd Annual ACM Conference on Human Factors in Computing Systems, Seoul, Republic of Korea, April 2015, pp. 4039–4042. ACM (2015)
11. Utz, S., Kramer, N.C.: The privacy paradox on social network sites revisited: the role of individual characteristics and group norms. J. Psychosoc. Res. Cyberspace **3**(2), 73–79 (2009)
12. Nguyen, D.-P., et al.: Why gender and age prediction from tweets is hard: Lessons from a crowdsourcing experiment. In: Proceedings of the 25th International Conference on Computational Linguistics, Dublin, Ireland, August 2014, pp. 1950–1961 (2014)
13. Filho, J.A.B.L., Pasti, R., de Castro, L.N.: Gender classification of twitter data based on textual meta-attributes extraction. New Advances in Information Systems and Technologies. AISC, vol. 444, pp. 1025–1034. Springer, Cham (2016). https://doi.org/10.1007/978-3-319-31232-3_97
14. Pennebaker, J.W., Stone, L.D.: Words of wisdom: language use over the life span. J. Pers. Soc. Psychol. **85**(2), 291 (2003)
15. Schwartz, H.A., at al.: Personality, gender, and age in the language of social media: the open-vocabulary approach. PloS one, 8(9), 73–79 (2013)
16. Neviarouskaya, A., Aono, M.: Sentiment word relations with affect, judgment, and appreciation. IEEE Trans. Affect. Comput. **4**(4), 425–438 (2013)

17. Goodfellow, I.J., Bulatov, Y., Ibarz, J., Arnoud, S., Shet, V.: Multidigitnnumber recognition from street view imagery using deep convolutional neural networks. Comput. Vis. Pattern Recogn. **6**(2), 1–13 (2015)
18. Shin, H.-C., Orton, M.R., Collins, D.J., Doran, S.J., Leach, M.O.: Stacked auto encoders for unsupervised feature learning and multiple organ detection in a pilot study using 4D patient data. IEEE Trans. Pattern Anal. Mach. Intell. **35**(8), 1930–1943 (2013)
19. Chen, T., Xu, R., He, Y., Wang, X.: Improving sentiment analysis via sentence type classification using BiLSTM-CRF and CNN. Expert Syst. Appl. **72**, 221–230 (2017)
20. Kim, Y.: Convolutional neural networks for sentence classification, nCoRR, abs/1408.5882, September 2014. http://arxiv.org/abs/1408.5882
21. Socher, R., et al.: Recursive deep models for semantic compositionality over a sentiment treebank. In: Proceedings of the 2013 Conference on Empirical Methods in Natural Language Processing. Seattle, WA, October 2013, pp. 1631–1642. Association for Computational Linguistics (2013)
22. Zheng, X., Chen, H., Xu, T.: Deep Learning for Chinese Word Segmentation and POS tagging, Seattle, Washington, USA, June 2013, pp. 647–657. ACL (2013)
23. Glorot, X., Bordes, A., Bengio, Y.: Domain adaptation for large-scale sentiment classification: a deep learning approach. In: Proceedings of the Twenty-eight International Conference on Machine Learning, Washington, USA, July 2011, pp. 513–520 (2011)
24. Zhang, X., Zhao, J., LeCun, Y.: Character-level convolutional networks for text classification. In: Proceedings of the 28th International Conference on Neural Information Processing Systems. Montreal, Canada, April 2015, pp. 649–657. MIT Press (2015)
25. Hornik, K., Stinchcombe, M., White, H.: Multilayer feed forward networks are universal approximates. Neural Netw. **2**(5), 359–366 (1989)
26. Murphy, K.P.: Machine Learning: A Probabilistic Perspective. MIT Press, Cambridge (2013)
27. Cun, Y.L., et al.: Advances in neural information processing systems. In: Touretzky, D.S. (ed.) San Francisco, Morgan Kaufmann Publishers Inc. (1990)

A Novel Detection System for Human Retina Based on Fuzzification Neural Network

Khattab M. Ali Alheeti[1]([✉]) [iD], Azmi Shawkat Abdulbaqi[2] [iD],
Hadeel M. Saleh[3] [iD], and Muzhir Shaban Al-Ani[4] [iD]

[1] Department of Computer Networking System, College of Computer Sciences
and Information Technology, University of Anbar, PO Box 55, Ramadi, Iraq
co.khattab.alheeti@uoanbar.edu.iq
[2] Department of Computer Sciences, College of Computer Sciences
and Information Technology, University of Anbar, Ramadi, Iraq
Azmi_msc@yahoo.com
[3] College of Education for Women, University of Anbar, Ramadi, Iraq
Hadealms89@gmail.com
[4] College of Science and Technology, Department of Information Technology,
University of Human Development, Sulaymaniyah, Iraq
muzhir.al-ani@uhd.edu.iq

Abstract. Automated methods are based on human biometrics for the purpose of verifying a person's identity based on the physiological or behavioural features of humans. Biometrics traits include facial, iris, retina, fingerprint, and tongue. Preserving biometrics is very important because it is one of the means of preserving the information of others. One of the most important biometrics, most accurate, and powerful methods of identity verification is human retina. The unique retina features per person can be displayed as a compact binary form. For the purpose of confirming an individual's identity, the unique retinal features of the individual can be easily compared with the reference template. In this paper, a novel detection system is proposed for retinal images utilising the fuzzification model that integrated with deep learning neural networks. In addition, identification system based on human retina is considered the most protect scheme of modern applications. The novelty in this paper is integrated between fuzzy set and deep learning neural networks. Practically, this is first time to integrate between fuzzification model and artificial neural network. The obtained experimental results of the proposed identification system demonstrate that the suggested approach possess outstanding detection rate with decline error rate as well as reducing the number of false alarms.

Keywords: Human retina · Deep learning · Biometric · Detection · Artificial intelligent

1 Introduction

Practically, biometrics are utilized in automatic identification and detection systems for organizations that required high-security systems. These biometrics are composed of speech recognition, fingerprint, face recognition, iris, and retina. In addition, human

© Springer Nature Switzerland AG 2020
M. I. Khalaf et al. (Eds.): ACRIT 2019, CCIS 1174, pp. 157–170, 2020.
https://doi.org/10.1007/978-3-030-38752-5_13

biometric recognition schemes become a real demand for enhancing the protection technique in various modern applications. Despite the accuracy of these systems and its biometrics-based, they can easily forgery all these devices for some unknown reasons. However, human retina can be utilized in a biometric system, due to it contains a blood vessel pattern that is unique at anyone. In addition, the vascular pattern in human retina traditionally employed is the almost strong and stabilized source of biometric technique. In more detail, it is hard to forge it due to it is found at the ends of the humans' eyes and not accessible directly. It is found at the back of the eye area whereas the coloured region between the pupils and sclera is namely iris. Therefore, retina recognition basis is the vascular pattern at human retina [1].

Modern recognition systems use a retina pattern for uniqueness and identification. The iris and retina anatomy are shown in Fig. 1. In the automatic identification systems, the retinal images are used to improve current security that suffered from various threats. In more detail, retina images are obtained by using a digital camera consisting of a low energy microscope and utilized by specialists' retinal eye. However, the acquisition process of the retinal images is not as easy as other biometrics, such as fingerprints, and faces [2]. These systems are suitable for military zones and high-security places because of their high stability and reliability.

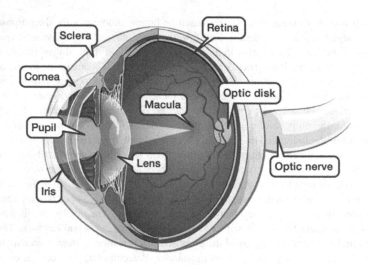

Fig. 1. Iris and retina anatomy [3].

The retina consists of various layers of palpable tissue and a massive count of photoreceptors (cells) whose volume is to change light spar to neural impulses. These inducements accordingly go to the cerebrum along the optic nerve, where they are changed over to photos. Two distinctive sorts of photoreceptors survive interior the retina: the rods and the cones. Whereas cones (6-million for every eye) assist us to see unique hues, the rods (125 million for each eye) stimulate night and fringe vision. It is the engaging form of the vein representation in the retina that designs the creation for retinal recognition and has been utilized for biometric identification [3].

Retinal recognition of an individual is finished by securing an interior self-perception. However, it does not generally utilize in business applications. Whereas considered much invasive and costly, retinal recognition is as yet the most strong and stable method for biometric identification. Although the advantages of retinal recognition at present bypassed the barrier, it's across the board utilize is kept down by open acceptance. The retina is actually a thin layer of cells located on the other side of the eyeball of vertebrates. It is the part of the eye which varies over light from nervous signals [4].

The contributions in this paper are summarized below:

- A novel intelligent identification system is proposed that employed at more sensitive organizations, such as military applications.
- Integrating fuzzy set with deep learning network to enhance detection rate and reducing false alarms.

The proposed system in this paper that based human retina is provided a higher level of protection because it's inherent strongest against various communication threats. The detection system is based on the DRIVE dataset that employed at training and testing phases of the intelligent detection system [5]. In more detail, the fuzzification model is integrated with deep learning neural networks that utilized in design new detection systems to secure sensitive information. However, it has the ability to avoid unauthorized access. The novelty of our work is integrated between fuzzy set and deep learning neural networks. Practically, this is the first time to integrate between fuzzification model and neural network [5].

The research is presented as follows. Section 2 reviews the recent studies that have a direct relation to our research. Section 3 describes the basic structure of deep neural network which based on retina recognition system. Section 4 presents the experimental results obtained for the detection system. Section 5, discussion our results as well as compares it with current researches while Sect. 6, presents the conclusion and future directions.

2 Literature Review

Many available methods are there in the literature in biometric attributes based on establishing network security that acquired from an individual user [6]. In this section, some of the biometric techniques are discussed.

Abdul Rahman and et al. have been suggested a new design for safe access to organizations via computers from a remote location. They utilized, for authentication, a biometrics module and method of password on a top" secure socket layer (SSL). Furthermore, they also presented three layers of communication network security levels and a mechanism for accesses also to a secure file building on custom security privileges for different users.

Chung and et al. proposed a technique of generating a secret key based on the biometrics of the protection technique. However, data security identifiers are user-provided by the authority on a digital signature data structure called a biometric certificate. There are numerous applications such as automatic selection and user authentication with message encryption which contains the biometric key from the biometric data [7].

Dutta and et al. suggested a new method for network security providing utilising a biometric and cryptography. The author suggested biometric encryption and decryption technique based on the fingerprint. In addition, the create a unique key is the use of a part of the fingerprints of both sender and receiver nodes. This random key is generated as a random sequence where it is utilized as an asymmetric key on encryption sides and decryption sides. The unique generated key is sent by the sender to the recipient after it is placed in a watermark with an encrypted message in the sender's fingerprint. The computational requirements and network security advantages were clarified. The major feature of the suggested scheme is that it does not have to be searched from security and database is preserved [8].

In [9], the security of network issues is evaluated for internet networks. The integration of biometric information in a series of documents highlights a new problem. Biometric authentication systems are frequently used in network applications to maintain overall network security, authentication chain integrity, counterfeit resistance methods, network protocols. However, it has been proven through many features. This study presents a mid-layer architecture of an interoperable consisting of a set of generic interfaces and protocol descriptions. This approach provides a future introduction to new units and applications with minimal development work.

Suggest fingerprint-based a modern security method and designed by Suriza and et al. in [10]. In order to ensure more security of the system, there is a unique and well-protected ID number or password that is presented as authentication to the user in the traditional system. The system based on biometrics presents a different and best strategy for user authentication. To understanding biometrics authentication comprehensively, it can be defined as an automated method in which confirmed identity by testing a behavioral characteristic or testing a unique physiological characteristic. It includes a fingerprint, iris or signature because the physiological characteristics of individuals have constant physical properties that do not change over time.

Kwanghyuk and et al. have presented a recognition iris algorithm based on (Independents Components Analysis) ICA for feature extraction. Current conventional methods are heavily based on one Gabors Waveletse to take then parameters for fixed bases, such as frequency, spatial location, and orientation. The ICA is applied to produce optimal source vectors for extracting efficient merit vectors problem of which express iris signals. However, it is basis vector is translated into both space and frequency such as Gabor wavelets. As merit vector, the ICA coefficients the expansion are utilized. Then, encoded all iris merit vector into the iris code [11].

The intelligent integration process between a fuzzy set and deep learning neural network is distinguished from work from others. In more detail, the proposed security system in this research will identify from others by enhancing the detecting rate, reducing error rate, declining false alarms and increasing efficiency of the neural network.

3 Biometric Human Retina

The retina is the biometric feature that is more trustworthy one because of its innate properties and minimum potential of swindle. In addition, a person's retinas scarcely change throughout their lifetime and also it is settled and could not be tampered. For this reason, it is considered an optimal choice in a select robustness security system for sensitive organizations.

A restricted number of the merit vector is another benefit of the retina. The retina feature is the faster identification and authentication from another biometrics. The identification and recognition systems that are based on the retina have the distinction and particular constancy because retina's vessels patterns are unrivaled and stationary. Although with this suitable assign, previously retina has not been used frequently because of technological restriction and its costly devices. Currently, modern applications have established a trade-off between flexibility and security. Unfortunately, this aspect of flexibility for wireless applications made keeps on security and privacy is the trickiest [12]. In this case, we are trying to find a strong security system, such as the human retina. Moreover, it has the ability to face various threats that have a direct and negative impact on sensitive information, control data and cooperative awareness messages.

The retina coating the internal part at the end of the eye and it has "0.5 mm" thick. The optical nerve with about "2 × 1.5 mm" towards is placed internally the major portion of the retina. Blood vessels compose a linked pattern such as an arbor as root above the exterior of the retina. These vessels compose a singular pattern for each person which could be utilized for identification [13].

Basically, there are two phases in biometric systems. There are enrolment phase and an authentication phase. In addition, the modules consisting of a sensor utilised biometric techniques such as video and audio to extract data. The merit extraction module is used in obtaining a template that is extracted from the merits of the biometric data. Each merit is signed with an identity of an individual person. The matching module is employed in the stage of authentication, where the template data is compared with data that gained from the user and that it estimates the likeness between these data. These likeness elements are processed in a decision-making module used for individual identification [24]. The retina recognition system is composed of three stages which are image acquisition phase, pre-processing phase and image detection phase as shown in Fig. 2.

The vascular pattern can be considered as the base of retinal recognition, which proves the uniqueness of several human beings. It is necessary to properly extract the entire blood vessel structure from the insertion of an image on the retina. The first phase of the proposed program is pre-processing in any vascular pattern extraction system using a Gabor wavelet and a method of the multilayered threshold. The pre-processing is also performed to eliminate the noise and additional area of the input image fundus. In the proposed detection system, the selection of fixed range value with Gabor Wavelet was experimentally modified and utilized 100 in orientation [14]. When the maximum wavelet response per pixel is selected, 18 different response results are obtained from these wavelets. The enhances of blood vessels are based on promoting

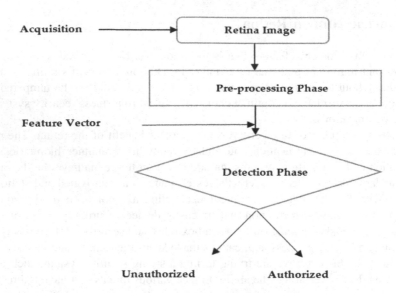

Fig. 2. A block diagram of the retina identification system.

the wavelet transformation by providing high responses to the vascular regions but the thick vessels still have a high wavelet response compared to thin vessels. Therefore, it is difficult to get a single optimum value of the threshold for an accurate blood vessel to extract without all supervised algorithm [15].

4   The Methodology of the Proposed Detection System

In this paper, a novel detection system is proposed to improve the security of the proposed system using human retina images. To improve the detection rate of the security system, the fuzzification model is integrated with a deep learning neural network. The flowchart of the proposed system is shown in Fig. 3.

In this paper, we do not have a contribution to the enrollment module, blood vessel enhancing, blood segmentation, feature extraction. The main point of this paper is the integrated fuzzification model with a neural network to enhance the detection rate. In other words, the numeric values of segmented retinal are utilised in this proposal. The stages below explain methodology process of the proposed system.

- Generating of blood vessels in the retina of the eye: in this phase, a blood vessel is generated from the DRIVE database. However, line tracking and histogram green are extracted from the original image of the database. The sample of these segmented is shown in Fig. 4.
- Input feature vectors: the input features of the security system are extracted from the segmented retinal that generated from the previous stage. These segments are converted into numeric values to modulation with random values of neural network weights. To reduce the number of input feature vectors, segmented and averaged are

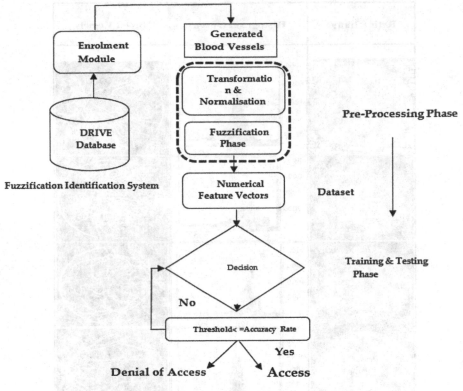

Fig. 3. Flowchart of the proposed systems.

applied to the scaled image. In other words, the system can assign one average pixel per segment of a pattern. However, this process is heavily based on Eq. 1 mentioned below:

$$av_k = \sum_{i=1}^{N} \sum_{j=1}^{M} x(i, j)/(N + M) \qquad (1)$$

where the average of each segment is measured based on Eq. 1. The output of this step is establishing a feature vector that considered as input features for the proposed security system.

- Normalization dataset: to increase the efficacy of deep learning neural, normalization is applied to numerical features that are extracted from segments of retina images. These values are converted into new numerical values between one and zero-based on Eq. 2:

$$X = \frac{x - min}{max - min} \qquad (2)$$

Normalizing on the dataset plays an important role to enhance detection rate as well as reducing the number of false alarms of the proposed system [16].

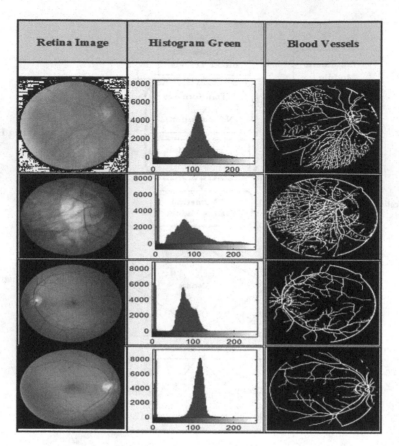

Fig. 4. Extracting histogram green and blood vessels from DRIVE database. (Color figure online)

- Fuzzification dataset: many scientific research approve a vital role of fuzzification model with classification problems. In other words, the behaviour of features extracted from retina images segments has a direct impact on the proposed system performance. In this case, when the boundary between classes of the dataset does not sufficiently clear that had a direct and negative impact on the performance of the identification system. In addition, this ambiguates between behaviours of a dataset will increase the number of false alarms as well as reducing accuracy rate of the proposed system. The researchers are considered that fuzzification is a suitable scheme for classification problems via establishing clear border between various classes of dataset [17].

$$f(x, a, b, c) = max\left(min\left(\frac{x - a}{b - a}, \frac{c - x}{c - b}\right), 0\right) \tag{3}$$

where the fuzzy domain is represented by a, b and c values whereas x is normal value. This process will play important in resolve confusion between classes of features by generating five values for each variable of a dataset. However, Eq. 3 will be applied to all input numerical value of the proposed identification system. The fuzzification model will generate five values for the fuzzy domain that had a range of intervals is [0, 1].

- Deep learning neural network: deep learning neural networking is applied in this paper for the identification of retina images. The proposed system is composed of five layers which are the input layer, three hidden layers, and the output layer. The sigmoid activation function is employed at the neurons of hidden and output layers. The input layer consists of 200 neurons, hidden layers are composed of different number of neurons depend on error-trial principle in selecting the best number of neurons at each layer. Whereas, the output layer consists of one neuron which is authorized or unauthorized. Figure 5 shows basic structure of deep neural network.

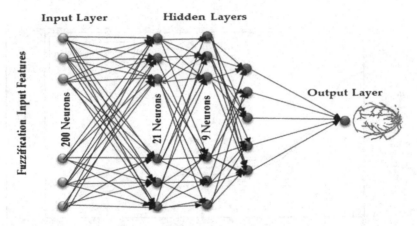

Fig. 5. Basic structure of deep neural network.

The learning parameter α that utilized in this paper for all experiments is $1*10{-}5$. Moreover, learning will continuously adjust to obtaining the best training rate. The configuration parameters of deep learning network are shown in Table 1. The simulation environment of the identification system is designed on an Intel Core i5 processor "2.23 GHZ" and 8 GB RAM memory.

Table 1. Neural network parameters.

Parameter	Value
Train parameter epochs	458
Train parameter ln.	$1*10^{-5}$
Train parameter goal	0
Train parameter minimum gradient	$1*10^{-14}$

5 Experimental Results and Discussion

The proposed system in this paper is heavily based on the features of human retina images. However, the vascular segmentation of retina images is utilized in informed input feature vectors for the proposed system. However, these observations with a fuzzification – deep learning model are applied for the classification of human retina images. In this paper, a deep learning neural network is applied for detection of retina images. The utilised intended artificial neural network includes input layer, multi-hidden layers, and the output layer. However, each neuron at the output layer is associated with specific classification kind which is access or denial of access.

This simulation system of the proposed classification is composed of two main phases which are training and testing. The training phase of fuzzification – a neural network is shown in Figs. 6 and 7.

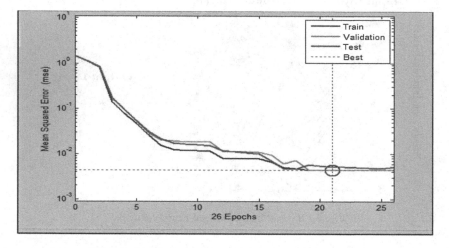

Fig. 6. Validation training of deep learning network.

According to Figs. 6 and 7, we can easily observe that training of the classification system is performed with 26 epochs with an accuracy rate of 98.26%. After that, the training of the proposed intelligent system has been done. Therefore, the network that trained and saved at the training phase will utilise at testing phase to evaluate performance of the classification system.

The trail – error principle is employed in determining the number of neurons at each hidden layer that was shown in Fig. 8.

In order to measure the validity of the proposed system, some performance metrics are utilized, such as True Positive (TP), True Negative (TN), False Positive (FP), False Negative (FN), accuracy rate and error rate. Here, the training phase is finished, and the result is a trained intelligent classification system that will be tested in the next phase.

In order to test the performance of the proposed system at the testing phase, the intelligent classification system will evaluate with fuzzification dataset. Firstly, the fuzzy – deep learning network is evaluating with DRIVE dataset that describes human

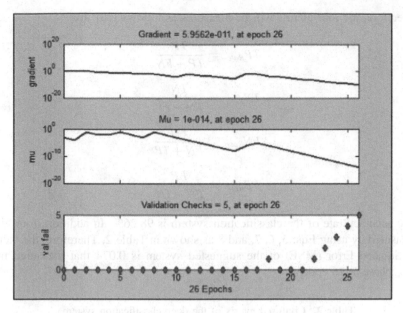

Fig. 7. Controlling parameters for classification system.

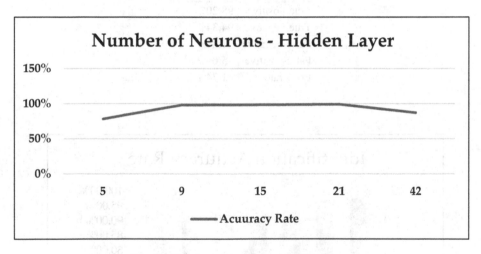

Fig. 8. Number of neurons at hidden layers.

retina images [18]. The accuracy of classification rate, error rate, and four alarms are utilized as performance metrics to evaluate the deep classification model which suggested in this research. The classification accuracy can be calculated as follows [19]:

$$Accuracy\ Classification = \frac{Number\ of\ correctly\ idenified\ patterns}{Total\ number\ of\ patterns} \tag{4}$$

Therefore, the four alarms will be measures as follows [20]: Let

$$TP_{Rate} = \frac{TP}{TP+FN} \tag{5}$$

$$TN_{Rate} = \frac{TN}{TN+FP} \tag{6}$$

$$FN_{Rate} = \frac{FN}{FN+TP} \tag{7}$$

$$FP_{Rate} = \frac{FP}{FP+TN} \tag{8}$$

The accuracy rate of the classification system is 98.26%. In addition, four alarms are measured by using Eqs. 5, 6, 7, and 8 as shown in Table 2. Therefore, the value of Mean Squared Error (MSE) of the suggested system is 0.074 that measured in the training phase at 26 epochs.

Table 2. Confused matrix of the deep classification system.

Alarm type	Accuracy
True positive	98.20%
True negative	94.34%
False-negative	1.8%
False-positive	5.66%
Error rate	1.74%

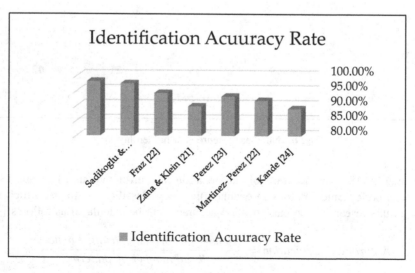

Fig. 9. Comparative results.

To measure the efficiency of the proposed system, it will be compared with other systems at the same research scope shown in Fig. 9.

According to Fig. 9, we can easily notice that the fuzzification deep learning network proposed in this paper is more efficient and effective than others. The fuzzification mode plays import role in improving detection rate and reducing amount of error rate.

6 Conclusion and Future Works

In this paper, a new detection system is proposed to enhance the identification rate of the security system based on retina images. However, the novelty in this paper is integrated between fuzzy set and deep learning neural networks. Practically, this is first time to integrate between fuzzification model and artificial neural network. In addition, it is devoted to the synthesis of deep learning neural networks based on extracting feature vectors. As we know, security system that based on retina images is one of the most secure schemes for detection of an identity. The proposed system is composed of two main stages wish are pre-processing and classification phase. However, the pre-processing phase is applied to convert DRIVE retina images to blood vessels and generate numerical input features from these segments. These feature vectors are considered input features for fuzzification neural network. Hence, this network is employed to classify retina images. Our experimental results of the proposed identification system demonstrate that the suggested approach possesses outstanding detection rate with decline error rate as well as reducing the number of false alarms. High deep classification rates are obtained through measurements: true positive is 98.20% and true negative is 94.34%.

In the future, we are trying to apply other technique in design detection systems, such as fuzzy Petri net, support factor machine, and genetic algorithm.

References

1. Schmidt-Erfur, U., et al.: Artificial intelligence in retina. Prog. Retinal Eye Res. **67**, 1–29 (2018)
2. Cao, C., et al.: Deep learning and its applications in biomedicine. Genomics Proteomics Bioinf. **16**, 17–32 (2018)
3. Kermany, S.D., et al.: Identifying medical diagnoses and treatable diseases by image-based deep learning. Cell **172**, 1122–1131 (2018). https://doi.org/10.1016/j.cell.2018.02.010
4. ter Haar Romeny, B.M.: Vision for vision – deep learning in retinal image analysis. In: Signal Processing algorithms, architectures, arrangements, and applications, SPA 2018, September 19–21, 2018, Pozna, Poland, The Institute of Electrical and Electronics Engineers Inc. (2018)
5. Xiao, X., et al.: Weighted Res-UNet for high-quality retina vessel segmentation (2018). http://dx.doi.org/10.1109/ITME.2018.00080
6. Jin, Q., et al.: DUNet: a deformable network for retinal vessel segmentation. J. Latex Class Files **14**(8) (2015)
7. Mahapatra, D., et al.: Retinal vasculature segmentation using local saliency maps and generative adversarial networks for image super-resolution. arXiv:1710.04783v3 (2018)

8. Fang, S., et al.: Image saliency analysis based on retina simulation. In: IEEE 3rd International Conference on Multimedia Big Data (BigMM), pp. 142–145 (2017)
9. Triwijoyo, B.K., et al.: Retina disease classification based on colour fundus images using convolutional neural networks. In: 2017 International Conference on Innovative and Creative Information Technology (ICITech), pp. 1–4 (2017)
10. Raja, B.K., et al.: Multi-patch deep sparse histograms for iris recognition in visible spectrum using collaborative subspace for robust verification. Pattern Recogn. Lett. **91**, 27–36 (2017)
11. Zago, G., Andreão, R.V., Dorizzi, B., Salles, E.O.T.: Retinal image quality assessment using deep learning. Comput. Biol. Med. **103**, 64–70 (2017)
12. Wang, Y., et al.: Responsive neural activities in the primary visual cortex of retina-degenerated rats. Neuroscience **383**, 84–97 (2018)
13. Sadikoglu, F., Uzelaltinbulat, S.: Biometric retina identification based on neural network. Procedia Comput. Sci. **102**, 26–33 (2016)
14. Güleryüz, M.Ş., Ulusoy, I.: Retinal vessel segmentation using convolutional neural networks. In: 26th Signal Processing and Communications Applications Conference (SIU), pp. 1–4. IEEE (2018)
15. Rong, Y., et al.: Surrogate-assisted retinal OCT image classification based on convolutional neural networks. IEEE J. Biomed. Health Inform. **23**(1), 253–263 (2019)
16. Lyu, X.Z., et al.: Deep tessellated retinal image detection using convolutional neural networks. In: 2017 39th Annual International Conference of the IEEE Engineering in Medicine and Biology Society (EMBC), pp. 676–680. IEEE institute (2017)
17. Chaudhuri, S., Chatterjee, S., Katz, N., Nelson, M., Goldbaum, M.: Detection of blood vessels in retinal images using two-dimensional matched filters. IEEE Trans. Med. Imaging **8**(3), 263–269 (1989)
18. https://www.isi.uu.nl/Research/Databases/DRIVE/. Accessed 15 Feb 2019
19. Alheeti, K.M., Gruebler, A., McDonald-Maier, K.D.: An intrusion detection system against malicious attacks on the communication network of driverless cars. In: 2015 12th Annual IEEE Consumer Communications and Networking Conference (CCNC), January 9 2015, pp. 916–921. IEEE (2015)
20. Alheeti, K.M., Gruebler, A., McDonald-Maier, K.D.: An intrusion detection system against black hole attacks on the communication network of self-driving cars. In: 2015 Sixth International Conference on Emerging Security Technologies (EST), September 3 2015, pp. 86–91. IEEE (2015)
21. Zana, F., Klein, J.C.: Segmentation of vessel-like patterns using mathematical morphology and curvature evaluation. IEEE Trans. Image Process. **10**(7), 1010–1019 (2001)
22. Fraz, M.M., et al.: An approach to localize the retinal blood vessels using bit planes and center line detection. Comput. Methods Programs Biomed. **108**(2), 600–616 (2012)
23. Ibrahim, D.: A dan Z ye Matlab ile çalhmmak (2004)
24. Abdulbaqi, A.S., et al.: Biometrics detection and recognition based-on geometrical features extraction. In: International Conference on Advance of Sustainable Engineering and its Application (ICASEA), pp 59–63. Wasit University, Iraq (2018)

A Novel Car-Pooling Optimization Method Using Ant Colony Optimization Based on Network Analysis (Case Study: Tehran)

Mojtaba Davoodi$^{(\boxtimes)}$ (iD) and Saeed Hasani (iD)

Faculty of Geodesy and Geomatics, K. N. Toosi University of Technology, Tehran, Iran
Mojtaba.Davoodi@ut.ac.ir, Hasanisaeed91@gmail.com

Abstract. The dramatic increment in the number of cars in cities makes numerous challenges including either air or noise pollution and traffic congestion. Outweighing these problems needs essential planning in urban management such as using new procedures in transportation systems. Sharing vehicles is one of the most useful methods which some countries have been experiencing it. In this issue, 2 or 3 people share a car, and it decreases running vehicles, and the urban traffic will be declined. This article uses a novel method to share cars based on Ant Colony Optimization Algorithm. The proposed model tries to find the best matching of passengers in cars so that the maximum of shared cars is found. Consequently, some vehicles will be switched off, and this helps to decrease the traffic. The results depict the proposed method turns off 41.8% of cars; besides, 27.8% of them carry 2, 3 or 4 passengers.

Keywords: Car sharing · Urban traffic management · Route finding · Ant Colony Optimization Algorithm

1 Introduction

Either traffic or air pollution is one of the most critical problems in megacities, which cars are the main reason for them. Traffic management is the first step in solving traffic congestion and mentioned pollutions. Transportation experts have introduced "Shared Economy" to overcome these problems [1]. This concept is sharing the assets of individuals between themselves, in such a way that each person provides their needs through the temporary possession of the assets of others.

Car sharing is one of the issues in the shared economy. In Car-sharing more than one person can use a car simultaneously which is one of the most useful methods to decrease the number of moving vehicles in the cities. The merits of car sharing are the elimination of tampering, saving fuel consumption, reducing traffic jams, lowering vehicle lateral costs, reducing driving stress, and declining the need for parking. This trick saves the costs of both the car owner and passengers.

Therefore, we are going to represent a novel method to optimize the ride-sharing problem in this paper and propose a model to maximize the number of people who use shared vehicles. Accordingly, we used the Ant Colony Optimization algorithm to solve

© Springer Nature Switzerland AG 2020
M. I. Khalaf et al. (Eds.): ACRIT 2019, CCIS 1174, pp. 171–184, 2020.
https://doi.org/10.1007/978-3-030-38752-5_14

the problem, which is one of the most common metaheuristic algorithms due to the big answer set of this problem. Because there are plenty of probable answers for the problem (thousands of possible arrangement of passengers in various cars). In addition, we used the Origin-Destination cost matrix in "Network Analyst" toolbox in ArcGIS software to help the ACO to calculate the cost of travel between points in the street network of the study area.

The structure of this paper includes:

- Literature Review: A review of previous researches related to car-sharing
- Proposed Model: Explanation of the way we used the algorithms, data, etc.
- Results: The maps, tables, charts represented results of the proposed model
- Conclusion: A short analysis of the results of the paper and solutions.

2   Literature Review

Fahnenschreiber et al. developed a hybrid method to combine ridesharing services and public transportation systems such as subways. In this research, dynamic ridesharing services that re-route according to the requests of passengers are combined with different trains time table to promote the performance of ridesharing platform. The experiments, compared to unimodal train connections, a significant improvement of the results are obtained [2]. Wei solved routing for the taxi-pooling problem by using Ant Colony Optimization (ACO) algorithm. Three main aims are considered in this article: (1) minimizing the cost of passengers, (2) maximizing the benefit of drivers and (3) maximizing the load rate. The simulated results show that the developed model can effectively solve the taxi-pooling routing problem with the above three objectives [3].

Nourinejad and Roorda evaluated the performance of Agent-based modeling (ABM) for dynamic ridesharing problem. In this research, a vicinity approach supports potential matching choice sets for either drivers or passengers. The results demonstrate higher user cost savings and vehicle kilometers traveled (VKT) savings when allowing multi-passenger rides. Besides, short term revenue is maximized by a commission rate of roughly 50% [4]. Huang et al. solved the carpooling problem by using Tabu Search algorithm. In this paper, a new model is proposed, which involves several origins and one destination. This work is carried out by considering environmental pollution, parking problems, traffic jams, and low utilization of resources. A Tabu search algorithm is used to solve the problem and it aims at a wide range of passenger distribution and routing problems. To evaluate the performance of the method, real data are used, and the empirical results prove the effectiveness of the developed algorithm [5].

Rayle et al. carried out a study about ridesharing and compare taxis, transit, and ride-sourcing services in San Francisco, USA. They accomplished a survey of ride-sourcing (Uber/Lyft/Sidecar) users. The results illustrate that ride-sourcing wait times are shorter and more reliable than taxis [6]. Zhan et al. used an Artificial Bee Colony algorithm for optimization the dynamic taxi-sharing problem. The model proposes a mobile application platform which maximizes the total benefits of the taxi sharing network considering time, cost, and capacity constraints. Dividing the problem into several small continuous static sub-problems based on a specific time interval is the strategy of authors to solve it. The developed model is compared with the greedy randomized adaptive search procedure (GRASP) with path relinking proposed by Santos and Xavier [7] and the results depict that the performance of the proposed ABC model is better than the GRASP model and the average saving ratio can reach 26% at the cost of only 16% extra travel time [8].

Stiglic et al. examined promoting urban mobility by mixing ride-sharing and public transportation that provide speedy, secure, and affordable transfer to and from transportation stations in urban areas. Although the computational actions note that joining ride-sharing and public transit can magnificently improve urban mobility, driver enthusiasm to serve more than one passenger is essential for success [9]. Simonetto et al. presented a novel, computationally economical, a dynamic algorithm to simulate real-time city-scale ridesharing via linear assignment problems. The algorithm is based on a linear assignment problem and a federated optimization architecture. Besides, it provides great computational performance and quality of service. Real-time ridesharing is determined to give explicit profits even with partial adoption. In multi-company scenarios, uninterested consequences could arise in terms of the higher number of transports [10].

Huang et al. applied an ant path-oriented carpooling allocation approach to optimize the carpool service obstacle with time windows. In this research, three methods were investigated: (1) assignment-based ant colony optimization, (2) genetic algorithm, and (3) simulated annealing. These methods are compared with path-based and assignment-based representations by examining two objective functions: (1) The principal objective that maximizes the whole number of paired passengers and seat usage rates (SURs), and (2) a secondary one that declines passengers' distances [11].

3   Proposed Model

In this paper, firstly, the required data are generated. These data include the urban road network as a platform for calculations, passengers, and cars information. The traveler's information includes the origin of the travel, the travel destination, and the travel request time. The simulation environment in this article is the urban road network, and passengers, cars, and control center (which performs calculations) is considered as agents that interact with each other and make decisions.

The main part of the problem is finding the best matching of travelers in cars. The method of making the answer in this study is that a matrix which is constructed according to the number of cars, and each row contains the number of different passengers indicating the arrangement of passenger's origins and destinations. The order of the origin and destination of passengers is determined "randomly" in each row for each car. Several rows (cars with passenger's arrangement) create a matrix. The fitness function for each row (car) is the total distances between passengers, and this total travel length is calculated for all (rows) cars. The scheme of a car is illustrated in Fig. 1. The red ones demonstrate "origin" points, and the green ones indicate "destination" spot.

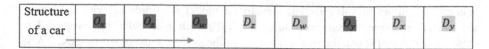

Fig. 1. The structure of a car including origins and destinations of passengers (Color figure online)

All car arrangements are put together, and it creates an answer. The final scheme of an answer is shown below. Although, some cars may transport only 1 passenger, others may take 2 or 3 passengers. Indeed, it is not mandatory to fill each car with 4 passengers. Besides, some cars do not take any passengers, and they will be turned off. Certainly, it is the main goal of the article to reduce the number of moving cars to take their passengers by other vehicles.

Figure 2 depicts an example of random composition of cars and passengers; therefore, we have some cars with 4 passengers, some vehicles with 3 travelers, some cars with 2 passengers, others take only one passenger, and finally some cars have no passenger, and they will not move (such as 5th Car); hence, the number of moving vehicles decreases, and it is going to overcome the traffic problem.

1st Car	O_x	O_z	O_w	D_z	D_w	O_y	D_x	D_y
2nd Car	O_p	O_h	D_p	D_h				
3rd Car	O_i	O_f	D_f	O_m	D_i	D_m		
4th Car	O_l	D_l						
5th Car	-	-	-	-	-	-	-	-
...								
(n-1)th Car	O_o	O_g	D_o	O_q	D_q	D_g		
nth Car	O_t	D_t	O_b	O_g	O_k	D_b	D_b	D_k

Fig. 2. The final structure of an answer

3.1   OD Matrix

At this step, the origin-destination cost matrix must be created between all these points (origins and destinations of passengers). The OD matrix determines the network traveling cost [12]. For example, the route from one city to another may have a cost of 45 km. The cost of the network can be anything but generally, it is the distance or time.

A network data set must have at least one cost attribute for using in network analysis, because network analytics always optimize the cost. The concept of OD Matrix is depicted in Fig. 3:

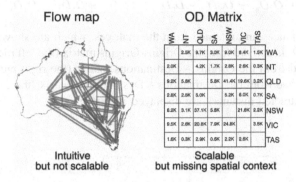

	WA	NT	QLD	SA	NSW	VIC	TAS	
		2.5K	9.7K	3.0K	9.0K	8.4K	1.5K	WA
	2.0K		4.2K	1.7K	2.8K	2.6K	0.3K	NT
	9.2K	5.8K		5.8K	41.4K	19.6K	3.2K	QLD
	2.8K	2.5K	5.0K		5.2K	6.0K	0.7K	SA
	8.2K	3.1K	37.1K	5.8K		21.8K	2.2K	NSW
	9.5K	2.6K	20.8K	7.9K	24.8K		3.5K	VIC
	1.6K	0.3K	2.9K	0.5K	2.2K	2.6K		TAS

Flow map — Intuitive but not scalable

OD Matrix — Scalable but missing spatial context

Fig. 3. An example of network cost and OD matrix

In this study, three OD matrices are required that is generated and computed in the following way:

1. OD matrix for travel cost between the origins of all passengers. (Origins-Origins)
2. OD matrix for travel cost between the destinations of all passengers. (Destinations - Destinations)
3. OD matrix for travel cost between the origins and destinations of all passengers. (Origins - Destinations).

These OD Matrices are produced by Network Analyst toolbox in ArcGIS®. This toolbox represents some Network Analysis like OD Matrix, Service Area, Route Finding, etc. We need OD matrix between all origins because when a car starts the shared travel, it goes after the second (even third or fourth) passenger, so it will be needed to calculate the distance between the origins of passengers. In the same way, OD matrices of Destinations – Destinations, and Origins – Destinations will be created. The structure of these matrices is illustrated in Fig. 4.

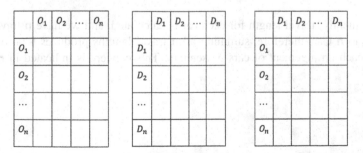

Fig. 4. The structure of Origins - Origins, Destinations – Destinations, and Origins – Destinations matrices

We use these matrices to calculate the travel length between passengers in each car. For instance, the distances between the origins and destinations of the first car (first row in Fig. 2.) are calculated in this way:

$$O_xO_z + O_zO_w + O_wD_z + D_zD_w + D_wO_y + O_yD_x + D_xD_y = L_1 \qquad (1)$$

All these distances are obtained from the matrices, which are shown in Fig. 4. As an example, O_xO_z is derived from the Origins-Origins matrix (the left picture in Fig. 4), O_wD_z is obtained from the Origins – Destinations matrix (the right picture in Fig. 4), and D_xD_y is derived from the Destinations – Destinations matrix (the central picture in Fig. 4). All 7 extracted distances are displayed in Fig. 5.

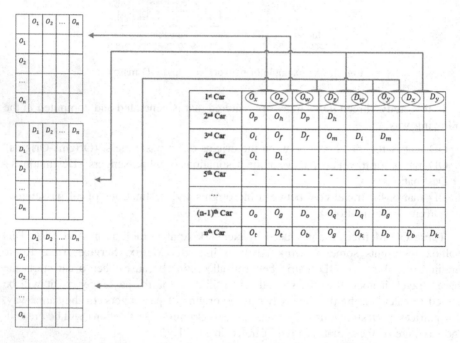

Fig. 5. The way that the travel length of each car is calculated.

Consequently, travel length for each car is calculated, and we have **n** travel length according to **n** Car; therefore, summing all **n** travel lengths produces total travel distance for each arrangement of cars-passengers. This concept is indicated in Fig. 6.

Car number	Passengers' arrangement								Car travel length
1st Car	O_x	O_z	O_w	D_z	D_w	O_y	D_x	D_y	L_1
2nd Car	O_p	O_h	D_p	D_h					L_2
3rd Car	O_t	O_f	D_f	O_m	D_i	D_m			L_3
4th Car	O_l	D_l							L_4
5th Car	-	-	-	-	-	-	-	-	$L_5 = 0$
...									...
(n-1)th Car	O_o	O_g	D_o	O_q	D_q	D_g			L_{n-1}
nth Car	O_t	D_t	O_b	O_g	O_k	D_b	D_b	D_k	L_n
							Total Travel Distance		D

Fig. 6. Total travel distance for each arrangement of cars-passenger

In fact, total travel length is calculated by:

$$D = L1 + L2 + L3 + L4 + L5 + \ldots + L(n-1) + Ln \qquad (2)$$

3.2 Ant Colony Optimization

In this step, Ant Colony Optimization is used to gain the most suitable solution. "ACO is a meta-heuristic technique which applies artificial ants to obtain answers of combinatorial optimization obstacles. ACO is based on the postures of actual ants investigating a path between their colony and a source of food" [13]. This idea is indicated in Fig. 7.

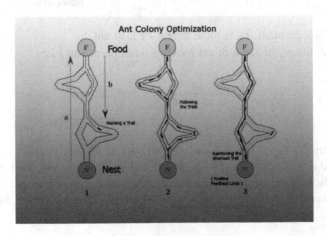

Fig. 7. Behaviour of ants in reality

In the real world, ants search for food around their colony and release a chemical substance named "Pheromone" as they move. Pheromone invites additional ants; therefore, while a significant source of food is discovered, the ants obey the first ant who observed the food and more ants interest to the food; hence, more ants track that path [14].

This style can be simulated in computational obstacles. At the first stage, several primary answers can be created; thus, in an iteration, a positive score is added to immeasurable answers. This process will be continued until the best answer will be found.

Indeed, there is a vital step in this process called "pheromone update". In every iteration, a positive score will be added to all answers; therefore, better answers receive more pheromone than others. Consequently, the good answers will be enhanced, and at the end of the iteration, the best answer will be distinguished. However, the pheromones are temporary, and they will eliminate smoothly. In reality, the phenomenon evaporates, and in the algorithm, it is a parameter called "evaporation rate".

It is irrefutable that there is a huge similarity between route-finding problem and ant's movements; so the Ant Colony Optimization algorithm is very useful in routing. A route includes some nodes (like i, j ...) and edges. In simple ACO the value of an edge corresponds with its length. The pheromones are considered for each edge as a value. Several routes between origin and destination will be considered and be evaluated. Better solutions attract more pheromones in pheromone update process so that at the end of the iteration the best route attracts most pheromone and introduced as the best solution between two points. Thus, the shortest path between two points will be found. Pheromone update equation is:

$$\tau_{ij} \leftarrow (1 - \rho)\tau_{ij} + \sum_{k=1}^{m} \Delta\tau_{ij}^{k} \tag{3}$$

Where ρ is evaporation rate, m is number of ants and:

$$\Delta\tau_{ij}^{k} = \begin{cases} \frac{Q}{L_k} & \text{if ant } k \text{ used edge } (i, j) \text{ in its route} \\ 0 & \text{otherwise} \end{cases} \tag{4}$$

Where Q is a constant, L_k is route length of k-th ant.
The probability p_{ij}^{k} of the k-th ant moving from point i to j is:

$$p_{ij}^{k} = \begin{cases} \frac{\tau_{ij}^{\alpha}.\tau_{ij}^{\beta}}{\Sigma_{l \in allowed_k} \tau_{ij}^{\alpha}.\eta_{il}^{\beta}} & \text{if } j \in allowed_k \\ 0 & \text{otherwise,} \end{cases} \tag{5}$$

Where $allowed_k$ is the list of nodes not yet visited by k-th ant.

Not only the ACO can evaluate the routes between points and determine the best path, but it also can be performed on the structure of our problem and find the best matching of passengers similarly. In fact, in the proposed model, each answer that is created by random passengers (shown in Fig. 2) is imported into ACO. In each iteration, answers are created and evaluated by ACO. Those answers who have better fitness function (less total distance) get more pheromone, and it helps to converge the algorithm to the best answer.

The fitness function uses the OD matrices to calculate the travel cost of each car (length of travels), and it will be done for all cars. Accordingly, the travel cost of all cars will be calculated, and the total length of an answer will be determined. This process continues until the ACO converges, and the best arrangement of shared passengers is specified. This is the final answer.

Although the fitness function calculates the distances between the origin and destination of passengers and evaluates the total distance that a car will travel, the request time of passengers are considered when a row is being created. If the request time of earlier passengers does not match with the last passenger in a car, the row will be deleted, and another random combination of passengers in a car will be produced again.

100 answers are created based on the structure which is illustrated in Fig. 2 as "initial population", and each answer is equal to an ant that evaluates the total length of the vehicle which contains some passengers. Consequently, in each answer, the ant starts to move from the first point in the first car and move along the arrays. While the ant crosses the points that are determined in the whole answer, it drops "pheromone" on routes between those origins and destinations. Consequently, after the first run in the algorithm, all answers get pheromones, and they are evaluated. The concept of action of ants is displayed in Fig. 8:

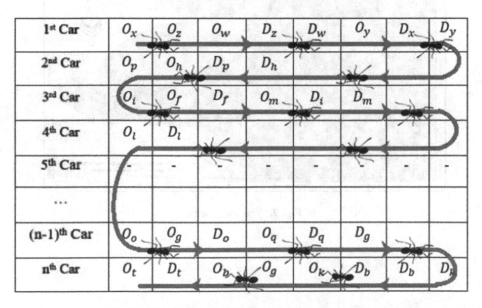

Fig. 8. The movement of ants to evaluate the answers

After the first stage, the ants do not move randomly, and they consider the amount of pheromones on the answers; thus, they choose answers based on "Roulette Wheel" rule [15]. In this step, each ant chooses its next movement based on the amount of the pheromone and does not act randomly. Therefore, all answers are evaluated again, and the best answer in each step will be determined. Moreover, this process will continue until the difference between the amount of fitness function of the best answer in two last iterations does not change considerably. Of Course, the evaporation rate parameter is set to 0.15, and in each step, it is applied for all answers.

4 Results

Evaluating the proposed model is done by implementing on a real network. The street network of region 1, 3, 4, 6, 7 and 8 of Tehran city (the capital of Iran) are selected as a case study (Fig. 9). The random origins and destinations of passengers are illustrated in Figs. 10 and 11.

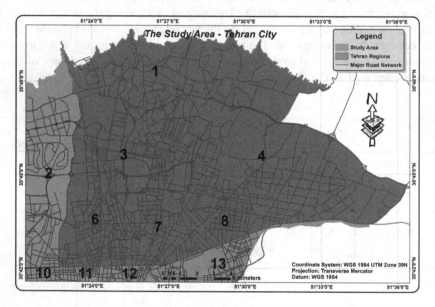

Fig. 9. The study area

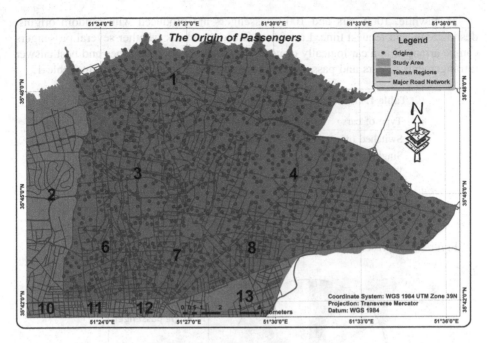

Fig. 10. The origin point of passengers

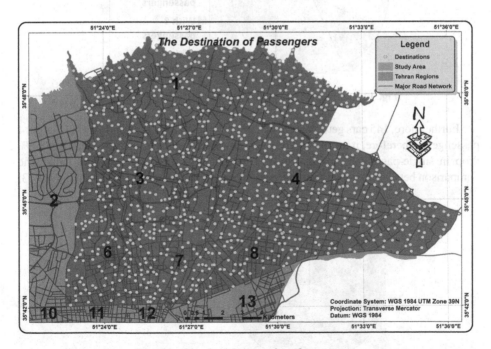

Fig. 11. The destination point of passengers

Meanwhile, 1000 cars and 1000 passengers are produced with random origins, destinations, and request time. Last factor is used to check whether several passengers can be arranged in a car logically or not. ACO is processed 100 times and best answer (arrangements of cars and passengers) is found. The results are shown in Table 1.

Table 1. Percentage of cars with different number of passengers.

Type of cars	Number	Percentage	Number of passengers
Switched off	569	56.9%	0 (0%)
Single passenger	112	11.2%	112 (11.2%)
With 2 passenger	145	14.5%	290 (29%)
With 3 passenger	98	9.8%	294 (29.4%)
With 4 passenger	76	7.6%	304 (30.4%)

Figure 12 represents these statistics in a better way:

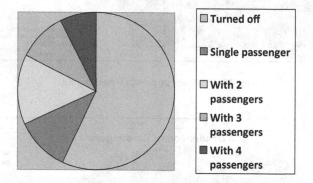

Fig. 12. Percentage of cars with different type of passengers

Furthermore, 145 cars get 2 passengers, 98 cars get 3 passengers, and 76 vehicles get 4 passengers. Therefore, it means 888 passengers shared vehicles, and it is equal to 88.8% drop in single-passenger cars that have a tremendous influence on traffic jams. The comparison between cars carrying one passenger and shared cars is illustrated in Fig. 13:

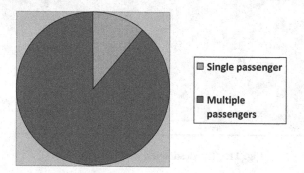

Fig. 13. Single passenger trips vs. shared trips

5   Conclusion

Results show that 569 of 1000 cars do not move in the network in comparison to the single-ride scenario when each car carries one passenger. In the shared-travel scenario, 56.9% of cars are turned off, and this greatly helps our environment and decreases either air pollution or traffic.

Therefore, results depict the performance of car-sharing methods in reducing urban traffic. Besides, the proposed model and the ACO algorithm find better solutions rather than previous researches. Indeed, it is the effect of using OD matrices, which help the ACO to achieve better answers and decrease the number of moving cars.

We wholeheartedly believe that car-sharing is one of the most effective human policies that we can use it, and the governments should expand these programs. Because it has no additional cost for the society, and the only thing we need is a web-mobile application to gather the users to use this platform and decrease the traffic jams in cities.

References

1. Böckmann, M.: The shared economy: it is time to start caring about sharing; value creating factors in the shared economy. Univ. Twente Fac. Manag. Gov. **350** (2013)
2. Fahnenschreiber, S., Gündling, F., Keyhani, M.H., Schnee, M.: A multi-modal routing approach combining dynamic ride-sharing and public transport. Transp. Res. Procedia **13**, 176–183 (2016)
3. Wei, X., Dai, J., Sun, B.: Routing for taxi-pooling problem based on ant colony optimization algorithm. Rev. Fac. Ing. U. C. **31**(7), 234–246 (2016)
4. Nourinejad, M., Roorda, M.J.: Agent based model for dynamic ridesharing. Transp. Res. Part C Emerg. Technol. **64**, 117–132 (2016)
5. Huang, C., Zhang, D., Si, Y.W., Leung, S.C.: Tabu search for the real-world carpooling problem. J. Comb. Optim. **32**(2), 492–512 (2016)
6. Rayle, L., Dai, D., Chan, N., Cervero, R., Shaheen, S.: Just a better taxi? A survey-based comparison of taxis, transit, and ridesourcing services in San Francisco. Transp. Policy **45**, 168–178 (2016)
7. Santos, D.O., Xavier, E.C.: Taxi and ride sharing: A dynamic dial-a-ride problem with money as an incentive. Expert Syst. Appl. **42**(19), 6728–6737 (2015)
8. Zhan, X., Szeto, W.Y., Sam, S.: An artificial bee colony algorithm for the dynamic taxi sharing problem (No. 19-03116) (2019)
9. Stiglic, M., Agatz, N., Savelsbergh, M., Gradisar, M.: Enhancing urban mobility: integrating ride-sharing and public transit. Comput. Oper. Res. **90**, 12–21 (2018)
10. Simonetto, A., Monteil, J., Gambella, C.: Real-time city-scale ridesharing via linear assignment problems. Transp. Res. Part C Emerg. Technol. **101**, 208–232 (2019)
11. Huang, S.C., Jiau, M.K., Liu, Y.P.: An ant path-oriented carpooling allocation approach to optimize the carpool service problem with time windows. IEEE Syst. J. **13**(1), 994–1005 (2018)
12. Van Zuylen, H.J., Willumsen, L.G.: The most likely trip matrix estimated from traffic counts. Transp. Res. Part B Methodol. **14**(3), 281–293 (1980)

13. Davoodi, M., Mesgari, M.S.: GIS-based route finding using ant colony optimization and urban traffic data from different sources. Int. Arch. Photogrammetry Remote Sens. Spat. Inf. Sci. **1**, 129–133 (2015)
14. Claes, R., Holvoet, T.: Ant colony optimization applied to route planning using link travel time predictions. In: 2011 IEEE International Symposium on Parallel and Distributed Processing Workshops and Phd Forum, pp. 358–365 (2011)
15. Lipowski, A., Lipowska, D.: Roulette-wheel selection via stochastic acceptance. Phys. Stat. Mech. Appl. **391**(6), 2193–2196 (2012)

A Trusted MANET Routing Algorithm Based on Fuzzy Logic

Qahtan M. Yas[1]($\boxtimes$) (iD) and Mohammed Khalaf[2] (iD)

[1] Department of Computer Science, University of Diyala, Baqubah, Iraq
yahoophd@gmail.com
[2] Department of Computer Science, Al-Maarif University College, Ramadi, Iraq
M.i.khalaf@acritt.org.uk

Abstract. MANET wireless network changes network topology continuously and dynamically due to the absence of infrastructure and central control. Typically, this network used for areas where unavailable basic communications services such as battlefield, emergency relief, and virtual classes. However, ad hoc networks exposed to different attacks as in malicious or selfish nodes that impede packets delivery. A new algorithm proposed of the MANET using a fuzzy logic system to solve malicious nodes problem. The routing algorithm relies on two main principles as trust level and shortest path (hops count). The finding obtained from three key parameters as high packet delivery fraction with low end-to-end delay and normalized routing load in this study. These results calculated based on the comparison between the FLTS algorithm with AODV protocol and without a drop.

Keywords: MANET · Trusted routing · Fuzzy logic · Trust · Hop count

1 Introduction

The wireless network of MANET could be working without any infrastructure where the nodes arbitrarily moving based on the dynamic network topology [1–3]. In such networks often relies upon multi hops with path trustworthy to serve communication between various nodes or devices within a single network. These nodes working according to the principle of routing to delivery and forwarding of packets to the rest of the nodes in the network. Routing is a procedure or a function to deliver the messages from the source to the desired destination within telecommunication networks to achieve a significant contribution to the design of the network architecture [4].

Generally, the routing protocols in MANET classified in reactive (demand-driven) and proactive (table-driven). A proactive routing protocol exchange topology information for nodes during selecting its route any time when requested such as DSDV (Destination Sequenced Distance Vector protocol) [5]. Whereas, in reactive routing protocols [4, 6, 7] the nodes only search on the route when is needed such as AODV protocol (Ad hoc On-demand Distance Vector). The wireless network topology of MANET changes over time because consists of nodes that able to mobility continuously. Therefore, it is often vulnerable to various harmful attacks. Given the nature of MANET may be malicious nodes have able to easily join to the network and then do all

© Springer Nature Switzerland AG 2020
M. I. Khalaf et al. (Eds.): ACRIT 2019, CCIS 1174, pp. 185–200, 2020.
https://doi.org/10.1007/978-3-030-38752-5_15

types misbehaviour. In this study, we attempt to address this problem with trusted routing [8]. In trusted routing, the nodes adapt a trust level for the route to face various potential threats. The routing algorithm takes a trust level of the path into consideration when making a routing decision. Thereby, the nodes avoid the routes not trusted and take the trust path.

Machine learning techniques presented various solutions for many studies such as management field, industry sector, and communication network [9]. Besides, many researchers used artificial intelligence algorithms, which adapted to solve specific issues in the MANET. Recently, many studies applied the fuzzy logic system with MANET and the various communication systems [10–12]. However, it is a sophisticated manner to decision making according to the multiple criteria [13, 14]. In this study, a new routing algorithm proposed based on the fuzzy logic approach called FLATS algorithm. The routing algorithm relies on the trust level and hops count for nodes represented in the routing metrics. This paper aims to implement a routing algorithm by selection the shortest path according to the trust level and hop count in the network.

The paper organized under different sections as follows. The introduction presented in Sect. 1. While Sect. 2, discussed some works related to our research. Section 3 describe the proposed fuzzy logic algorithm and clarified the parameters are used. Section 4, simulation setup. Section 5, analyzed and discussed the results. Finally, the conclusion performed in Sect. 6.

2 Related Work

Many researchers have already recognized the need to use trusted routing algorithm in MANET. Jassim et al. [15] proposed a new protocol called R-AODV (reliant ad hoc on-demand distance vector routing) to enhance a security aspect of the AODV protocol. This work presented a novel idea based on modifying the trust mechanism for the model of direct recommendations to the integration with the AODV protocol by selection the shortest path and trustworthy. Harris et al. [16], proposed a new trust mechanism called Trust-AODV to increase the security of the AODV protocol. This study improved the performance of the secure protocol based on the ant algorithm. Xia et al. [17], proposed an AOMDV routing protocol (ad-hoc on-demand multipath distance vector) to select trustworthy paths and prevent harmful attacks. This study created a protocol based on multiple trustworthy paths to select a single path led to the desired destination. Currently, many studies adopted a fuzzy logic system to solve essential problems in MANET. Chaudhary et al. [18], developed a new system to discover infiltration according to the fuzzy logic approach. This work assigned the reasons for dropping of the packets due to malicious attacks in the MANET and prevent of protection for the mobile nodes. Anuradha and Mala [19] proposed routing protocol to detection and congestion for a cross-layer using Fuzzy logic. Therefore, according to the fuzzy interference rules, the proposed protocol determines the appropriate path for sending messages successfully. Robinson et al. [20] a new methodology proposed based on the fuzzy logic-based collaborative watchdog approach to increase the trust value and reduce the time of detection misbehave of the nodes. This approach provided a secure efficient routing through discovering the black holes attacks.

3 Proposed FLTS Algorithm

We proposed a novel algorithm adapted fuzzy rules compared with AODV protocol with and without a drop to achieve study objective. This algorithm relies on the trusted rout and selects the shortest path with minimum hop accounts. It included two inputs as fuzzification and one output defuzzification according to the fuzzy rules. Further details in the next section.

3.1 FLTS Algorithm Architecture

The fuzzy logic system in MANET used as a controller unit by various researchers to solve different problems. Besides, the controller mechanism of the fuzzy logic implemented in many sectors of pure science and engineering recently. Therefore, fuzzy control rules should be used to discover and identify the relationships between the parameters of the system based on smart agencies [21]. Figure 1 illustrates components of a fuzzy logic control system.

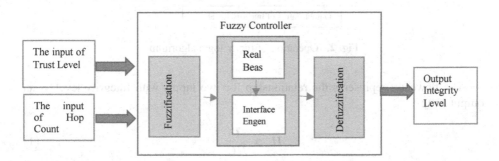

Fig. 1. Fuzzy logic control system

In this study, applied fuzzy logic rules for data represented in the mathematical forms. For instance, the statement consist of the (trust level and hop counts) used to select the shortest path in the network and so on. However, the fuzzy logic system explains some blurry statements as such, so that logical meaning follows for each case.

3.2 FLTS Algorithm Implementation

The fuzzy system constructed from two inputs membership function as fuzzification which denoting to the crisp set and the output variable as defuzzification [22, 23]. In this study, fuzzy logic adapts with an on-demand routing protocol to select the shortest path according to trust level and hop count. The main objective of the study to select the trusted path based on the rules of fuzzy logic by two inputs represented as trust level (T) and hop count (Hc) with optimal integrity level (IL) as output. Figure 2 shows the operation steps for FLTS algorithm implementation.

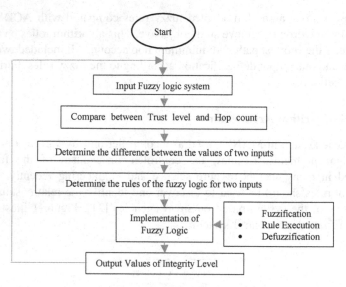

Fig. 2. Operation of fuzzy logic algorithm

The flowchart represents the relationship for two inputs with Integrity level as an output [10]:

$$IL \propto \frac{T}{HC} \tag{1}$$

Therefore, when updating the inputs of membership function lead to the change in the output of the integrity level according to the fuzzy logic system.

The first variable represents the trust level (T). The fuzzy set included three items (Low, Moderate, and High), which represented in the values (0, 50, 100). The membership function of the fuzzy set for the input variable (T) represented in Equation:

$$T = \{Low, Moderate, High\} \tag{2}$$

The membership function of the input (T) illustrated in Fig. 3.

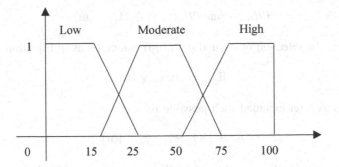

Fig. 3. Membership function of fuzzy input for trust level variable (T)

The second input represents the hop count (HC). The fuzzy set is consist of three elements as (short, medium, and long) which represented in values as in (0, 40, 80). The membership functions in the fuzzy set for the input variable (HC) represented in Equation:

$$HC = \{Short, Medium, Long\} \tag{3}$$

The membership function of the input (HC) illustrated in Fig. 4.

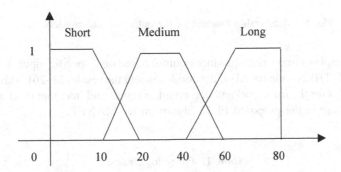

Fig. 4. Membership function of fuzzy input for hop counts level variable (HC)

The linguistic variables distributed in three main variables namely, a trust value, hop counts, and integrity level as a fuzzification inference engine. The fuzzification parameters included three variables as a low, moderate, and high for the trust level of the nodes, other variables as a short, medium, and long for the hop count level for every path. While, the integrity level represented the outcome during delivery of the data packets, which distributed into five variables; Poor, Few, Normal, Good, and V.Good. The outcome as a defuzzification for crisp logic of output variables, which computed as in Eq. 4.

$$PIL_x = \min PIL_{xy} \quad y \in (1, \ldots, m) \tag{4}$$

Therefore, the selection of desired path (dp) computed as in Equation:

$$IL_{dp} = \max_{x \in A} IL_x \tag{5}$$

Where A as a set included each possible routes:

$$A = \{R1, R2, \ldots\ldots, Rn\} \tag{6}$$

A membership function for the output (IL) represented in Fig. 5.

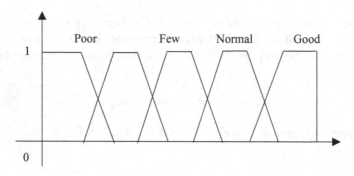

Fig. 5. Membership function of the output of integrity level (IL)

The principle of fuzzy rules produces output based on a specific input. It is a simple term with (IF-THEN) rule based on the condition and the result [24–26]. Table 1 shows the fuzzy rules for the trust level and hop count as inputs and integrate level as output to evaluate a route in the proposed FLTS algorithm for MANET.

Table 1. Fuzzy logic rules.

Input variable (T)	Input variable (HC)	Output variable (IL)
Low	Short	Normal
Low	Medium	Few
Low	Long	Poor
Moderate	Short	Good
Moderate	Medium	Normal
Moderate	Long	Few
High	Short	Very Good
High	Medium	Good
High	Long	Normal

3.3 Trust Model

In MANET many trust models adapted to establish proper relationships between network nodes. A simple trust model adopted in this study. This model takes a minimum trust value (min_t) in the tth path to avoid the high computations and overhead to the network [27, 28]. The discovery operation of the route leads to the trusted path created from the first hop. While the nodes determined the routing options based on the trust level and hop count, and selected the next hop to select the shortest paths and trustworthy.

3.4 Shortest Model

Mobil ad hoc network used the shortest path to delivery of packets during selection their route in the network. Given for many security issues facing MANET that need solutions to enhance the work in these networks. However, often the opted shortest paths to the destination in the network may not prove to be consistently the best. In this situation, the paths may be crowded or maybe consist of malicious or selfish nodes that negatively affected the networks. Typically, AODV routing included information as hop count, sequence numbers, and the source and destination IDs according to their routing table [27].

Practically, the path discovery mechanism for the proposed FLTS algorithm relies on the trust level (trusted path) and hop count (shortest path). Therefore, the RREQ and RREP messages, which generated or forwarded within the network from the source and destination also depend on the same measures.

4 Fuzzy-Rout Discovery

FLTS algorithm selected the desired Path (dp) based on the shortest path and trustworthy for all routers in the network. Therefore, the routing table maintains on the routing information for each node in the path is selected. Table 2, includes a list of data as inputs for each node as follows:

Table 2. Routing table inputs

Routing table inputs	
(DIA)	Destination IP address
(DSN)	Destination sequence number
(IL)	Integrity level
(HC)	Hop count
(MT)	Min trust
(NH)	Next hop
(LT)	Lifetime

4.1   Fuzzy-Route Request (F-RREQ)

Firstly, the initial message sent from the source node (S) and delivery to the destination node (G) during the discovery of the route, and then verify this route. While, if the source node (S) lost its correct path then it can discover its route by sending a message of the route request (RREQ) over the neighbour nodes to reach the desired destination. The request message (RREQ) included each destination information as (sequence number, IP address, integrity Level, hop count and lifetime). Recently, this information was sent by the source node in the RREQ message, which included the last sequence number for a destination copied from the routing table. On the other hand, the sequence number of the flag should be set as an integrity level to be equal to the integrity level of the source node when the sequence number was unknown. Therefore, the hop count should be equal to zero.

Finally, the data packet is delivered to the destination node (G) by the neighbour node and the trust value is added to it. Figures 6 and 7 shows the operation and components of F-RREQ message format.

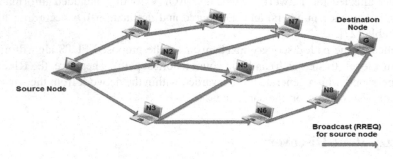

Fig. 6. Illustrated broadcast (RREQ) message for source node

Type |J|R|D|U| Received Hop Count
RREQ ID
Destination IP address
Destination Squance Number
Originator Ip Address
Minimum Trust

Fig. 7. Fuzzy - route request message

4.2 Fuzzy-Route Reply Massage

Initially, the destination node generated a reply message (RREP) to be broadcasted for the neighbouring or intermediate node until delivered to the source node. After creation the RREP message by the destination node, and copy the IP address, sequence number and integrity level from RREQ message to be put it them in the RREP message or packed them in the RREP message. In contrast, the sequence number of the destination node should be updated to the maximum before create an RREP message. In this case, when the intermediate node received the reply message, then its value increased by one value per node by the number of hops when forwarding the message through a reverse path. Therefore, the sequence number of the reply message (RREP) should be compared with the sequence number of the destination node and not be less than its value as in the routing table. In contrast, the minimum value is determined integrity level of the reply message (RREP) compared to the current nodes integrity level.

Finally, when decreasing the RREP message value the integrity level updated at the route. Figures 8 and 9 illustrates the establishment of an RREP message and components of F-RREP message format in the network.

Fig. 8. Illustrated route established (RRER) for receiver node

Type |R|A| Received |Prefix Sz| Hop counts
Destination IP address
Destination Squance Number
Originator Ip Address
Lifetime
Minimum Trust

Fig. 9. Fuzzy - route reply message

4.3   Maintenance of the Route

The AODV protocol nodes used "hello message" considered the first local broadcast of the packet in the network to notify all mobile to maintain the local connectivity within its area [29, 30]. The nodes keep "hello messages" that related to the active route. The protocol nodes received a "hello messages" from the neighbour previous nodes, after that, the neighbour nodes do not receive any packets such (hello messages or otherwise) for more than allowed_hello_loss* hello_interval milliseconds. Therefore, this node is considered to have lost its connection with neighbour nodes. It creates an error message (RERR) to be sent to the rest of the neighbouring nodes. In contrast, the node of the source tries to check routes again to select an alternative path to reach the desired destination node and get started maintenance of the local route.

5   Simulation Setup

The object-oriented simulator (NS2) used a C++ language and an OTcl interpreter, which serve a high duty to the front-end. NS2 simulator included hierarchy class deriving of C++ language with other hierarchy class implemented in the interpreter of the OTcl. [31, 32]. In the NS2 environment implemented a new routing algorithm called FLTS compared with AODV protocol to get the results. Figure 10 shows the NS2 architecture.

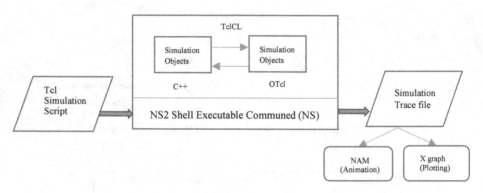

Fig. 10. NS-2 architecture

The simulation is performed using the NS2 simulator. Table 2 included each parameter used to simulate the Max Speed scenario (Table 3).

Table 3. Simulation parameters for max speed scenario

Parameter	Value
MAC protocol	IEEE 802.11 with distributed coordination function (DCF)
Max speed	15, 20, 25, 30, 35, 40, 45, to 50 m/s
Area size	750 m × 750 m
Pause time	10\Sec
Nodes	80
Simulation period	900\Sec
Type of traffic	CBR (constant bit rate)
Mobility model	Randomly points
Packet size	512 bytes
Number of connection	5
Data rate	4 pkts/sec

Three parameters of the performance matrix evaluated based packet delivery fraction (PDF), end-to-end delay (E2E), and normalized routing load (NRL) as following:

1 **Packet Delivery Fraction (PDF):** is the ratio of the number of data packets received successfully at the destinations, which generated from constant bit rate (CBR) source.
2 **Average End-to-End Delay (E2E):** is the average of the time assigned to generate the data packets delivered from the source to the destination in the MANET.
3 **Normalized Routing Load (NRL):** It understood as the ratio of all routing control packets transmitted per nodes, which receive data packets at the destination nodes within the network.

6 Discussion Results

The Max Speed scenario included various vectors to implement the network. This scenario used 80 nodes distribute in the area (750 m × 750 m) to connect the number of the node equal to 5. Simultaneously, moving nodes speed in this area ranged from (15, 20, 25, 30, 35, 40, 45, to 50 m/sec), while the pause time at (0) for testing the network. The experiments tested three basic performance measures as packet delivery fraction (PDF) to calculate the delivery rate of packets, end-to-end delay (E2E) to calculate the delay rate, and normalized routing load (NRL) to calculate the proportion of packets that have been delivered to the destination node.

6.1 Packet Delivery Fraction (PDF)

In this scenario, a new FLTS algorithm is compared with an AODV protocol with and without a drop based on the results. The result shows a calculation of the ratio of packet delivery fraction according to the movement of nodes in the network. In this experiment, the packet delivery fraction is high due to the nodes in the often tend to move slowly towards the centre of the network, when the maximum speed of nodes is low, while the ratio of load density of the centre of the network does not change frequently. Therefore, the AODV without drop is mostly stable for a long time, where its value reached to 98.704. Its performance is better when the maximum speed is low. At the same time, the AODV with a dropped packet obtained the lowest ratio of the packet delivery fraction and its value reached at 21.7887. As for the FLTS with a drop, the packet delivery fraction is slightly higher and its value reached at 32.6725. Therefore, the FLTS with drop shows a better performance than the AODV with a drop in the terms of the packet delivery fraction (Fig. 11).

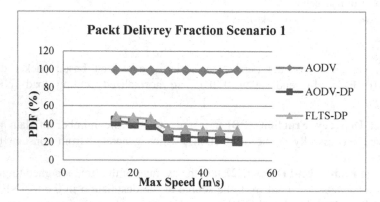

Fig. 11. Packet delivery fraction for scenario 1

6.2   Average End-to-End Delay (E2E)

This result also compared the performance of the new algorithm of FLTS to the AODV protocol without and with drop packet. Figure 12 shows the network almost continuous motion due to movement speed of nodes leads to unstable of the network that impacts on the protocol performance. Therefore, the AODV without drop records a high average end-to-end delay at value 0.0593. Meanwhile, the AODV with drop also records a slightly high average end-to-end delay with at value 0.0352. The expected result for the FLTS with drop recorded a high ratio of the average end-to-end delay at value 0.0452. While the experimental results in this scenario show, the FLTS has a high delay due to the unstable network. Therefore, FLTS presents an excellent performance to achieve the average end-to-end delay ratio. Thereby, FLTS with drop has better performance than the AODV with a drop in the E2E delay ratio.

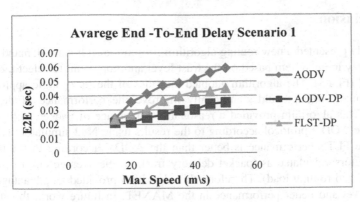

Fig. 12. Average end-to-end delay scenario 1

6.3 Normalized Routing Load (NRL)

Similarly, this result presents also a new algorithm of FLTS performance compared to the AODV protocol without and with drop packet. Figure 13 illustrates the max speed of nodes within the network that affected the performance of the protocol due to unstable of the network. The AODV without drop has a reasonable rate of normalized routing load and its value at 3.5215. Meanwhile, the AODV with drop record a high-normalized routing load at value 6.5128. Whereas, the FLTS with drop its value reached to 4.7894. This experiment shows the normalized routing load ratio for the FLTS with drop has a slightly higher compared to the AODV without a drop. Therefore, FLTS recorded the lowest ratio of normalized routing load compared to the AODV with a drop.

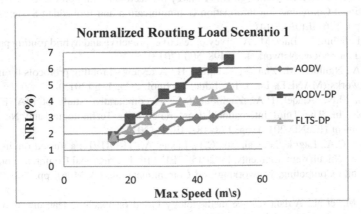

Fig. 13. Normalized routing load scenario 1

7   Conclusion

In this study presented a new routing algorithm for mobile ad hoc on-demand protocol using a fuzzy logic system based on the trust level and hop count to select the shortest path called (FLTS). The algorithm adopted the rules of the fuzzy logic approach as a simple manner, which could significantly improve the performance of the ad hoc networks. This algorithm provided a reasonable percentage of packets delivery compared to the AODV protocol according to the results using NS2 simulator. The results showed the FLTS performance is better than the AODV according to the three significant vectors calculated as (packet delivery fraction, the average end-to-end delay, and normalized routing load). Therefore, this algorithm provided an advantage, a high integrity level and better performance in the MANET. In future work, this algorithm can be applied with other protocols of the mobile ad hoc network.

Acknowledgement. The author would like to thank the University of Diyala\Scientific Research Center (SRC) for supporting this major research project and also to some friends who gave me advice during working this research.

References

1. Computing, M.: An overview of MANET: applications, attacks and challenges abstract. Int. J. Comp. Sci. Mobile Comput. 3(1), 408–417 (2014)
2. Kaid, A., Ali, S., Kulkarni, U.V.: Characteristics, applications and challenges in mobile ad-hoc networks (MANET): overview. Wirel. Netw. 3(12), 6–12 (2015)
3. Eldein, D., Ahmed, M., Khalifa, O.O.: An overview of MANETs: applications, characteristics, challenges and recent issues. IJEAT 3, 128–133 (2017)
4. Patel, D.N., Patel, S.B., Hemangi, R.: A survey of reactive routing protocols in MANET. In: International Conference on Information Communication and Embedded Systems (ICICES 2014), pp. 1–6. IEEE (2014)
5. Kaur, H., Sahni, V., Bala, M.: A survey of reactive, proactive and hybrid routing protocols in MANET: a review. Network 4(3), 498–500 (2013)
6. Hinds, A., Ngulube, M., Zhu, S., Al-aqrabi, H.: A review of routing protocols for mobile ad-hoc networks (MANET). Int. J. Inf. Educ. Technol. 3(1), 1–5 (2013)
7. Alslaim, M.N., Alaqel, H.A., Zaghloul, S.S.: A comparative study of MANET routing protocols. In: The Third International Conference on e-Technologies and Networks for Development (ICeND 2014), pp. 178–182. IEEE (2014)
8. Kerrache, C.A., Lagraa, N., Calafate, C.T., Lakas, A.: TROUVE : a trusted routing protocol for urban vehicular environments. In: 2015 IEEE 11th International Conference on Wireless and Mobile Computing, Networking and Communications (WiMob), pp. 260–267. IEEE (2015)
9. Khalaf, M., et al.: A data science methodology based on machine learning algorithms for flood severity prediction. In 2018 IEEE Congress on Evolutionary Computation (CEC), pp. 1–8. IEEE (2015)
10. Yas, Q.M., Khalaf, M.: Reactive routing algorithm based trustworthy with less hop counts for mobile ad-hoc networks using fuzzy logic system. J. Southwest Jiaotong Univ. 54(3), 1–11 (2019)

11. Inaba, T., Sakamoto, S., Kulla, E., Caballe, S.: An integrated system for wireless cellular and ad-hoc networks using fuzzy logic. In: 2014 International Conference on Intelligent Networking and Collaborative Systems, pp. 157–162. IEEE (2014)
12. Balan, E.V., Priyan, M.K., Gokulnath, C., Devi, G.U.: Fuzzy based intrusion detection systems in MANET. Procedia Comput. Sci. 50, 109–114 (2015)
13. Yas, Q.M., Zadain, A.A., Zaidan, B.B., Lakulu, M.B., Rahmatullah, B.: Towards on develop a framework for the evaluation and benchmarking of skin detectors based on artificial intelligent models using multi-criteria decision-making techniques. Int. J. Pattern Recogn. Artif. Intell. 31(03), 1759002 (2017)
14. Yas, Q.M., Zaidan, A.A., Zaidan, B.B., Rahmatullah, B., Karim, H.A.: Comprehensive insights into evaluation and benchmarking of real-time skin detectors: review, open issues & challenges, and recommended solutions. Measurement 114, 243–260 (2017)
15. Jassim, H.S., Yussof, S., Kiong, T.S., Koh, S.P., Ismail, R.: A routing protocol based on trusted and shortest path selection for mobile ad hoc network. In: 2009 IEEE 9th Malaysia International Conference on Communications (MICC), pp. 547–554. IEEE (2009)
16. Vlpduhpduh, K., et al.: Performance analysis of optimized trust AODV using ant algorithm. In: 2014 IEEE International Conference on Communications (ICC), pp. 1843–1848. IEEE (2014)
17. Xia, H., Jia, Z., Ju, L., Li, X., Sha, E.H.: Impact of trust model on on-demand multi-path routing in mobile ad hoc networks. Comput. Commun. 36(9), 1078–1093 (2013)
18. Chaudhary, A., Kumar, A., Tiwari, V.N.: A reliable solution against packet dropping attack due to malicious nodes using fuzzy logic in MANETs. In: 2014 International Conference on Reliability Optimization and Information Technology (ICROIT), pp. 178–181. IEEE (2014). C. Science, E. Communication, and C. Science
19. Anuradha, M., Mala, G.S.A.: Cross-layer based congestion detection and routing protocol using fuzzy logic for MANET. Wirel. Netw. 23(5), 1373–1385 (2016)
20. Robinson, Y.H., Rajaram, M., Julie, E.G., Balaji, S.: Detection of black holes in MANET using collaborative watchdog with fuzzy logic. World Acad. Sci. Eng. Technol. Int. J. Comput. Electr. Autom. Control Inf. Eng. 10(3), 622–628 (2016)
21. Kumar, K.V., Sankar, T.J., Prabhakaran, M., Srinivasan, V.: Fuzzy logic based efficient multipath routing for mobile adhoc networks. Appl. Math. Inf. Sci. 11(2), 449–455 (2017)
22. Sarkar, A.: Application of fuzzy logic in transport. Int. J. Soft Comput. 3(2), 1–21 (2012)
23. Ghasemnezhad, S., Ghaffari, A.: Fuzzy logic based reliable and real-time routing protocol for mobile ad hoc networks. Wirel. Pers. Commun. 98(1), 593–611 (2017)
24. Sambariya, D.K., Prasad, R.: A novel fuzzy rule matrix design for fuzzy logic-based power system stabilizer. Electr. Power Compon. Syst. 45(1), 34–48 (2016)
25. Chettibi, S., Chikhi, S.: Dynamic fuzzy logic and reinforcement learning for adaptive energy-efficient routing in mobile ad-hoc networks. Appl. Soft Comput. 38, 321–328 (2016)
26. Pouyan, A.A., Tabari, M.Y.: FPN-SAODV: using fuzzy petri nets for securing AODV routing protocol in mobile ad hoc network. Int. J. Commun Syst 30(1), 1–14 (2015)
27. Jia, X.L.Z., Zhang, P.Z.R.: Trust-based on-demand multipath routing in mobile ad hoc networks. IET Inf. Secur. 4(4), 212–232 (2010)
28. Xia, H., Jia, Z., Li, X., Ju, L., Sha, E.H.: Ad hoc networks trust prediction and trust-based source routing in mobile ad hoc networks. Ad Hoc Netw. 11(7), 2096–2114 (2013)
29. Keerthi, T.D.S., Venkataram, P.: AODV route maintenance using honeypots in MANETs. In: 2015 World Congress on Internet Security (WorldCIS), pp. 105–112 (2015)
30. Kumar, R.S.: A review and design study of cross-layer scheme based algorithm to reduce the link break in MANETs. In: 2013 International Conference on Pattern Recognition, Informatics and Mobile Engineering, pp. 139–143. IEEE (2013)

31. Patel, R., Patel, N., Kamboj, P.: A comparative study and simulation of AODV MANET routing protocol in NS2 & NS3. In: 2014 International Conference on Computing for Sustainable Global Development (INDIACom), pp. 889–894. IEEE (2014)
32. Bouras, C., Charalambides, S., Drakoulelis, M., Kioumourtzis, G.: Simulation modelling practice and theory a tool for automating network simulation and processing tracing data files. Stimul. Model. Pract. Theory 1–21 (2012)

Minimum Array Elements and Snapshots for Performance Analysis Based on Direction Of Arrival (DOA) Estimation Methods

Bashar S. Bashar[✉] [iD] and Marwa M. Ismail[iD]

Computer Engineering Techniques, Al-Nisour University College, Baghdad, Iraq
{Bashar.s.eng, Marwa.m.eng}@nuc.edu.iq

Abstract. The minimum array elements and snapshots for performance analysis of several Direction of Arrival (DOA) estimation methods are presented in this paper. The DOA algorithm's effectiveness is evaluated by its ability to resolve several spaced signals. Previous studies have been concerned with determining the impacts of the design parameter on the results of the DOA techniques. These studies concentrate on the impact of no more than two sources that impinge on an antenna array. In the true globe, there are several multipath and Angles of Arrivals (AOA) that interfere with the initial signal. The receiver site must, therefore, be able to calculate the AOA and decipher the presented transmitters with their angular locations. This research takes into account the impacts of interference and multipath. The emphasis was placed upon the study of the minimum number of snapshots and array elements needed to solve multiple interfering signals for a range of different DOA procedures. The result shows that over other algorithms the MUSIC algorithm has the best result.

Keywords: Direction of arrival · Adaptive antennas · Uniform linear array · Correlation matrix · MUSIC · Root-MUSIC

1 Introduction

Adaptive antenna arrays provide advanced performance in various fields compared to traditional antennas, it has a crucial role in improving various forms of wireless communication technology extending from mobile wireless systems to (PSC) services to radar systems [1–3]. An adaptive antenna array is an array of antenna elements connected to a digital signal processor to send and receive adaptively, i.e. adaptively changing patterns according to the environment [4, 5]. The main lobe is steered toward the strongest signal component, the side lobes are steered in the direction of the multipath components, and the nulls are steered in the direction of the interference [6, 7] as shown in Fig. 1.

The adaptive antenna array is based upon estimating the angle of arrival of impinging sources and calculate the optimum weight needed to maximize certain criteria. These weights are updated automatically according to the changing environments [8].

© Springer Nature Switzerland AG 2020
M. I. Khalaf et al. (Eds.): ACRIT 2019, CCIS 1174, pp. 201–212, 2020.
https://doi.org/10.1007/978-3-030-38752-5_16

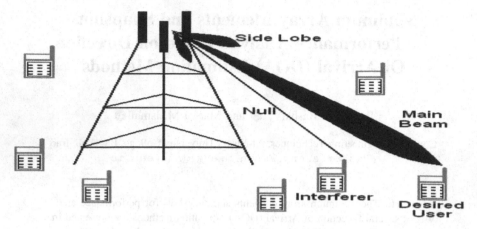

Fig. 1. Adaptive antenna concept [9]

In the propagation path, the received signals are corrupted by Additive White Gaussian Noise (AWGN), and they are received by the recipient with many other signals. These multipath signals affected the accuracy of the detection and reduced the resolution of the DOA estimation [10]. Therefore, it is necessary to estimate the direction of the sources accurately and this information can be used to combine or eliminate signals to increase fidelity and reduce interference.

Direction-Of-Arrival (DOA) estimation algorithms as it named aims to find the direction of arrival of multiple sources impinging on an antenna array, there is an urgent need to study AOA estimation algorithms to its fundamental role in identifying and tracking sources in military and civilian applications.

The resolution and accuracy of DOA estimation methods can be influenced by several factors such as the number of array elements, the number of the effecting sources, angle differences and the number of snapshots, SNR, antenna array geometry. Etc. In this paper, the emphasis was placed on studying the resolution capability of a variety of DOA estimation methods by specifying the minimum number of antenna array elements, and snapshots needed to distinguish eight closely spaced sources in noisy environments. This study aims to analyze the performance of these algorithms and gives a detailed study of their behavior in terms of:-

- Test the ability of the algorithms to accurately tracking and identifying the various signal sources in the real world, where there are several multi-paths, interferes, and angles of arrivals.
- Analyze the effect of the number of antenna elements and snapshots on the performance of each algorithm, and which one has a significant impact on the accuracy of the algorithm.
- Identify the best algorithm that achieves the best performance after changing the resolution capabilities under the conditions assumed in this paper.
- Identify the number of antenna elements and snapshots required to separate eight sources with closely separation angles.

The paper is structured as follows. In Sect. 2, a brief description of the research background is given, in Sect. 3, the model description is presented, in Sect. 4, the current algorithms used in the methodology are presented. Whereas the simulation result and discussion are presented in Sect. 5. Finally, the conclusion and future work are represented in the last section.

2 Literature Review

An analytical Study between three different DOA methods is investigated by Khedekar [11]. ESPRIT, MUSIC, and Mechanical rotation of the antenna array are analyzed and compared for a three-dimensional approach. The result showed that the mechanical rotation of the antenna array provides combined features of ESPRIT and MUSIC. It gives robustness and accuracy.

Three famous Eigen structure algorithms [MUSIC, ESPRIT, and MLE] are compared and analyzed by Ihedrane [12]. The performance of these algorithms is based on Uniform Linear Array (ULA) structure. It has been observed that the MUSIC algorithm is more stable and accurate compared to the ESPRIT and MLE algorithms, and it has the highest efficiency with an error not exceeding 0.8%.

A study analyzing the system's performance factors is established by Kwizera [13], the emphasis was placed on studying the DOA for uniform linear array and non-uniform linear array based on a music algorithm, the performance factors that affect the resolution and accuracy of the system are analyzed and tested using Matlab. The result shows that the direction of arrival estimation based on combined MUSIC method for two decomposed non-uniform linear array is the best array arrangement due to its accuracy, efficiency, and degree of freedom compared to ULA.

Several directions of arrival estimation methods are studied and presented by Ganage [14], a comparative performance regarding Signal-to-Noise Ratio (SNR), resolution, separation angle and the number of snapshots are simulated and tested for a uniform linear array. It starts with conventional methods of MVDR algorithm along with MUSIC, root-MUSIC, ESPRIT...etc., the results show that SNR, antenna elements, number of snapshots. The separation angle between the signals and the coherent nature of signals can affect the direction of arrival algorithms outcomes, and it is found that the MUSIC algorithm has a relatively better resolution than the other algorithms.

3 Signal Model for Uniform Linear Array (ULA)

ULA consisting of an array of M antenna elements with element spacing d = λ/2 and M potential weight, receiving D narrowband signals from D directions with uncorrelated AWGN as shown In Fig. 2.

Array output is given by the following Eq. (15):-

$$y(k) = \bar{w}^T \bar{x}(k) \tag{1}$$

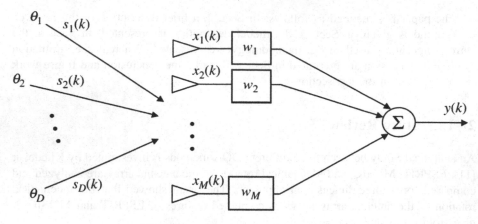

Fig. 2. M-antenna array with D-signals

Where:-

$$\bar{x}(k) = \bar{A}.\bar{s}(k) + \bar{n}(k) \tag{2}$$

And

$\bar{w} = [w_1 \quad w_2 \quad w_M]^T$ denotes the array weights.

$\bar{s}(k) = [s_1(k) \quad s_2(k) \quad s_3(k)]^T$ denotes vector of incident signals at time k.

$\bar{n}(k) = [n_1(k) \quad n_2(k) \quad n_3(k)]^T$ denotes the noise vector at each array element.

$\bar{A}(k) = [\bar{a}(\theta_1) \quad \bar{a}(\theta_2) \quad \bar{a}(\theta_D)]$ denotes M*D matrix of steering vectors $\bar{a}(\theta_j)$.

It is observed that the signals are uncorrelated and monochromatic and the number of the arriving signals D < M, the arriving signals are time-varying and thus the calculations are based on time snapshots of the incoming signals, various time samples of the incoming signal plus noises were collected. The ergodic process was assumed, and the correlation matrices were estimated via time averaging. In this case, the correlation matrix is defined by [16]:-

$$\hat{R}_{xx} \approx \bar{A}\hat{R}_{ss}\bar{A}^H + \bar{A}\hat{R}_{sn} + \hat{R}_{ns}\bar{A}^H + \hat{R}_{nn} \tag{3}$$

$$\hat{R}_{ss} = \frac{1}{k}\sum_{k=1}^{k} \bar{s}(k)\bar{s}^H(k) \tag{4}$$

$$\hat{R}_{sn} = \frac{1}{k}\sum_{k=1}^{k} \bar{s}(k)\bar{n}^H(k) \tag{5}$$

$$\hat{R}_{ns} = \frac{1}{k}\sum_{k=1}^{k} \bar{n}(k)\bar{s}^H(k) \tag{6}$$

$$\hat{R}_{nn} = \frac{1}{k} \sum_{k=1}^{k} \bar{n}(k)\bar{n}^{H}(k) \tag{7}$$

Angle Of Arrival (AOA) estimation techniques provide a function that is an indication of the AOA based upon the maximum versus the angle. This function is called the pseudospectrum ($P(\theta)$) and the units of it can be in watts or in energy. Some of the most popular pseudospectrum are summarized in the next section.

4 AOA Estimation Algorithms

The direction of arrival algorithms indicates the angles at which electromagnetic waves reach a series of antennas [13]. There is a variety of DOA algorithms, some of them are listed below:-

4.1 Bartlett AOA Estimate

That is known as the Conventional beamforming, it is a beamforming technique that is based on electronic steering of the antenna array in a specified direction and measures its output power, thus when the steered direction synchronizes with the direction of arrival of the signal, the maximum output power is obtained [15].

If the antenna array elements are uniformly weighted, Bartlett AOA estimation method can be defined as:

$$P_{B}(\theta) = \bar{a}^{H}(\theta).\bar{R}_{xx}.\bar{a}(\theta) \tag{8}$$

4.2 The Linear Prediction AOA Estimate

This algorithm aims to reduce the prediction error between the actual output and the output of the (mth) sensor, where $\bar{u}_m$ is the (mth) column of the (M × M) identity matrix [17].

The center element of the antenna array is selected and the linear composition of the remaining antenna elements gives better performance because the other antenna elements are equally spaced around the phase center of the antenna array.

The linear prediction pseudospectrum is given by [18]:-

$$P_{LP_m}(\theta) = \frac{\bar{u}_m^T \bar{R}_{xx}^{-1} \bar{u}_m}{\left| \bar{u}_m^T \bar{R}_{xx}^{-1} \bar{a}(\theta) \right|^2} \tag{9}$$

4.3   Maximum Entropy AOA Estimate

It is similar to the linear prediction method. The goal of the Maximum entropy is finding a pseudospectrum, that would maximize the Entropy function subjecting to constraints. pseudospectrum is given by:-

$$P_{ME_j}(\theta) = \frac{1}{\bar{a}^H(\theta)\bar{C}_j\bar{C}_j^H\bar{a}(\theta)} \tag{10}$$

Where $\bar{C}_j$ is the Cartesian basis vector which is the jth column of the inverse array correlation matrix $\bar{R}_{xx}^{-1}$.

4.4   Pisarenko Harmonic Decomposition (PHD) AOA Estimate

The PHD method minimizes the mean-squared error of the antenna array output under the condition that the norm of the weight vector must equal unity. The eigenvector that minimizes the Mean-Squared Error (MSE) corresponds to the smallest eigenvalue of the cross-correlation of the output antenna array [11]. PhD pseudospectrum is given by

$$P_{PHD}(\theta) = \frac{1}{|\bar{a}^H(\theta)\bar{e}_1|^2} \tag{11}$$

4.5   MUSIC AOA Estimate

The MUSIC algorithm is a part of the most prevalent methods for high resolution and reliability [19]. It gives an unbiased estimate of the angles of arrival, the number of signals, and the intensity of the incoming waveforms.

First, the array correlation matrix was calculated (assuming uncorrelated noise and equal variance) as given by Eq. 3. Next, the eigenvalues and eigenvectors are calculated for $\bar{R}_{xx}$ [20]. The MUSIC pseudospectrum is given by:-

$$P_{MU}(\theta) = \frac{1}{|\bar{a}^H(\theta)\bar{E}_N\bar{E}_N^H\bar{a}(\theta)|} \tag{12}$$

4.6   Root-MUSIC AOA Estimate

The advantage of this algorithm resides in the calculation of the direction of arrival by finding the roots of the polynomial. Which replaces the search for maxima necessary for music [21]. The denominator expression of Eq. 14 can be simplified by defining the Hermitian matrix

$$\bar{C} = \bar{E}_N\bar{E}_N^H \tag{13}$$

The Root-MUSIC expression can be expressed as:-

$$P_{RMU}(\theta) = \frac{1}{|\bar{a}^H(\theta)\bar{C}\bar{a}(\theta)|} \tag{14}$$

The denominator in Eq. (14) can be written as:-

$$\bar{a}^H(\theta)\,\bar{C}\bar{a}(\theta) = \sum_{l=-M+1}^{M+1} c_l e^{jkdsin\theta} \tag{15}$$

Where c_l represents the sum of the diagonal elements of the Hermitian matrix $\bar{C}$:-

$$c_l = \sum_{n-m=l} C_{mn} \tag{16}$$

Equation (15) can be simplified to a polynomial form with c_l coefficients:-

$$D(z) = \sum_{l=-M+1}^{M+1} c_l z^l \tag{17}$$

Where $z = e^{jkdsin\theta}$

Equation (18) is used to calculate the AOA of the incoming sources as given by the following equation [22]:

$$\theta_i = -\sin^{-1}\left(\frac{1}{kd} arg(z_i)\right) \tag{18}$$

Where z_i denotes the i closest root to the unit circle.

4.7 Experimental Results and Discussion

In this section, the resolution capability of each algorithm is tested. The minimum number of antenna elements and snapshots needed to separate 8 signals with an angular distance of ($4°$, $8°$, $12°$ and $16°$) is determined. The simulation is performed by taking 8 signal sources affecting a uniform linear array of identical antenna elements with a spacing equal to half the wavelength of the signal, at first 9 antenna elements with 100 snapshots are selected, and the number of antenna array elements and snapshots is changed until the minimum number that satisfies the resolution of eight sources is obtained. The simulations are performed using Matlab R2016b. The signals are assumed to be binary Walshlike signals of amplitude 1 with finite samples, and the noise is a random process generated using a Matlab function. In the next section, the simulations performed are presented. The response of each algorithm for two values of the snapshots and the number of antenna elements [Before/After Resolution] is presented.

Figure 3 represents the Bartlett AOA algorithm, the resolution is limited by the array half-power beamwidth, with 9 antenna elements and 100 snapshots, no signals are resolvable. An increase in AOA resolution demands a larger antenna array. 55 elements with 1000 snapshots are needed in order to resolve 8 sources.

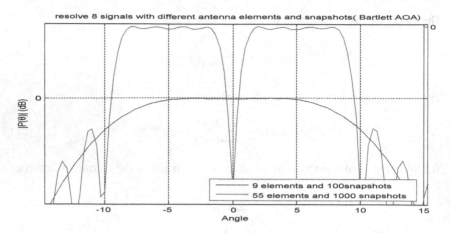

Fig. 3. The Bartlett AOA spectrum

For larger arrays, the resolution is equal to $1/M$, thus when two sources are separated by an angle greater than the antenna array resolution, they can be detected but bias is produced. This bias causes the peaks to deviate from the actual angle of arrival. This bias decreases as the length of the antenna array increases as shown in Fig. 3.

The advantage of the Bartlett algorithms is that this algorithm is a nonparametric solution and thus one does not need to have prior knowledge of the particular statistical characteristics. The linear predictive algorithm provides not only the angle of arrival information details, but also it is an indication of the signal strength as shown in Fig. 4.

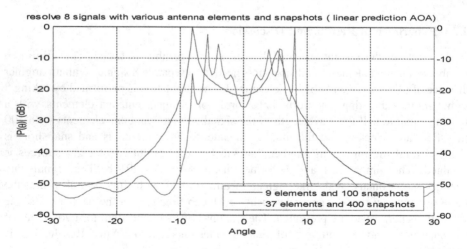

Fig. 4. The linear predictive AOA spectrum

The linear predictive algorithm provides better performance compared to the Bartlett AOA algorithm, 2 sources are resolved before resolution and after resolution

37 elements and 400 snapshots are needed to resolve 8 signals. The performance efficacy is dependent on the array element selected (the center element is selected in this case) and the subsequent vector.

The maximum entropy method needs 36 elements and 300 snapshots to resolve 8 sources as shown in Fig. 5, the choice of $\bar{C}_j$ can greatly affect the resolution achieved. The center columns produce better performance according to the conditions assumed in this paper and in the maximum entropy algorithm, when the middle column of $\bar{R}_{xx}^{-1}$ is selected, it will perform similar to the linear predictive method.

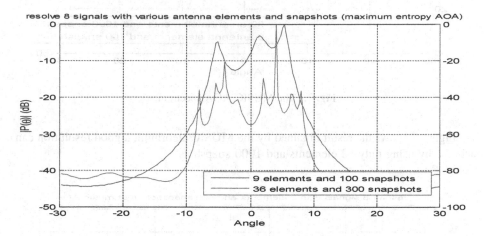

Fig. 5. The maximum entropy AOA spectrum

The Pisarenko method has the best resolution over the earlier methods as shown in Fig. 6, only 34 elements and 800 snapshots are needed to separate 8 signals. The PHD algorithm doesn't combine all noise eigenvectors, it only uses the first noise eigenvector. The Pisarenko peak is not an indication of the signal amplitude as in the linear prediction method.

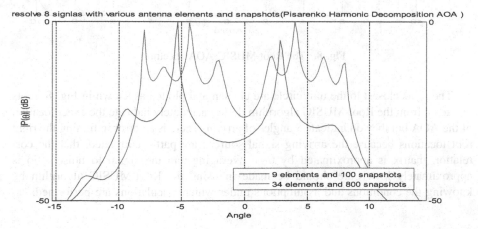

Fig. 6. The Pisarenko AOA spectrum

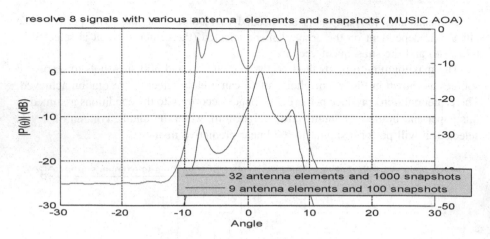

Fig. 7. The MUSIC AOA spectrum

Figure 7 shows the result obtained by the MUSIC algorithm, a good resolution can achieve by using only 32 elements and 1000 snapshots.

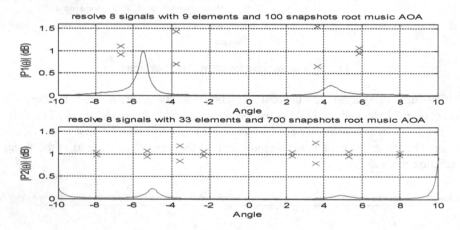

Fig. 8. The Root-MUSIC AOA spectrum

The roots closest to the unit circle are chosen and plotted as shown in Fig. 8, roots extracted from the Root-MUSIC algorithm do not accurately indicate the exact location of the AOA but they do indicate 8 angles of arrival. There is an error in finding the right root locations because the arriving signal sources are partly correlated, that the correlation matrix is approximated by time averaging and the signal to noise ratio is approximately low. Care should be made in using the Root-MUSIC algorithm by knowing the conditions and assumptions under which calculations are performed.

The following table shows a summary of the simulation results (Table 1).

Table 1. Summary of the results

Angle Of Arrival (AOA) estimation methods	Before resolution		After resolution	
Name	No. of antenna elements	No. of snapshots	No. of antenna elements	No. of snapshots
The Bartlett AOA method	9	100	55	1000
The linear predictive AOA method	9	100	37	400
The maximum entropy AOA method	9	100	36	300
The Pisarenko AOA method	9	100	34	800
The MUSIC AOA method	9	100	32	1000
The Root-MUSIC AOA method	9	100	33	700

5   Conclusion

In this paper, the performance analysis and resolution capability of several directions of arrival methods have been discussed. The performance resolution of the AOA methods has been presented by searching the minimum antenna elements and snapshots needed to detect eight closely spaced signals. The results showed that the linear predictive and the maximum entropy algorithms have similar performance when selected the center column, it was shown that the number of snapshots is less effected on detecting the sources than the antenna array elements, the outcomes of the simulation results show that the MUSIC algorithm is the best one and at the same time requires fewer array elements to separate eight closely spaced signals. As future work, further investigations, including different methods with different stimulation parameters are needed to be performed with additional statistical analysis of the results.

References

1. Ganage, D., Ravinder, Y.: Wavelet-based denoising of direction of arrival estimation signals in smart antenna. In: 2018 IEEE Global Conference on Wireless Computing and Networking (GCWCN). IEEE (2018)
2. Boustani, B., Baghdad, A., Sahel, A., Badri, A.: Performance analysis of direction of arrival algorithms for smart antenna. Int. J. Electr. Comput. Eng. 9, 2088–8708 (2019)
3. Zheng-yan, J., Hui, C., Jia-jia, Z.: Improved SVD algorithm for DOA estimation of coherent signal sources. In: 2017 36th Chinese Control Conference (CCC). IEEE (2017)
4. Ali, E., Ismail, M., Nordin, R., Abdulah, N.F.: Beamforming techniques for massive MIMO systems in 5G: overview, classification, and trends for future research. Front. Inf. Technol. Electron. Eng. 18(6), 753–772 (2017)

5. Sundaresan, K., Sivakumar, R.: Cooperating with smartness: using heterogeneous smart antennas in multihop wireless networks. IEEE Trans. Mobile Comput. **10**(12), 1666–1680 (2011)
6. Sharma, R., Senapati, A., Roy, J.S.: Beamforming of smart antenna in cellular network using leaky LMS algorithm. In: 2018 Emerging Trends in Electronic Devices and Computational Techniques (EDCT). IEEE (2018)
7. Samantaray, B., Das, K.K., Roy, J.S.: Beamforming in smart antenna using some variants of least mean square algorithm. In: 2nd National Conference on Mechatronics, Computing and Signal Processing, MCSP-2017, Centurion University of Technology & Management, Bhubaneswar (2017)
8. Sharma, A., Mathur, S.: Performance analysis of adaptive array signal processing algorithms. IETE Tech. Rev. **33**(5), 472–491 (2016)
9. Senapati, A., Roy, J.S.: Performances of some combined algorithms for adaptive beamforming in smart antenna using linear array. Asian J. Appl. Sci. **4**(03), 720 (2016). ISSN 2321–089
10. Wang, Y., Yang, X., Xie, J., Wang, L., Ng, B.W.-H.: Sparsity-inducing DOA estimation of coherent signals under the coexistence of mutual coupling and nonuniform noise. IEEE Access **7**, 40271–40278 (2019)
11. Khedekar, S., Mukhopadhyay, M.: Analysis of estimation of direction of arrival by comparative study. Mater. Today Proc. **5**(1), 1696–1703 (2018)
12. Ihedrane, M.A., Seddik, B.: Direction of arrival estimation using MUSIC, ESPRIT and maximum-likelihood algorithms for antenna arrays. Walailak J. Sci. Technol. (WJST). **13**(6), 491–502 (2015)
13. Kwizera, E., Mwangi, E., Konditi, D.B.: Performance evaluation of direction of arrival estimation using uniform and non-uniform linear arrays. J. Sustain. Res. Eng. **3**(2), 29–36 (2017)
14. Ganage, D., Ravinder, Y.: Parametric study of various direction of arrival estimation techniques. In: Singh, D., Raman, B., Luhach, A.K., Lingras, P. (eds.) Advanced Informatics for Computing Research. CCIS, vol. 712, pp. 175–184. Springer, Singapore (2017). https://doi.org/10.1007/978-981-10-5780-9_16
15. El Ouargui, I., Safi, S., Frikel, M.: Minimum array elements for resolution of several direction of arrival estimation methods in various noise-level environments. J. Telecommun. Inf. Technol. **2**, 87–94 (2018)
16. Gross, F.: Smart antennas for wireless communications with MATLAB. McGraw Hills, New York (2005)
17. Mondal, D.K.: Studies of different direction of arrival (DOA) estimation algorithm for smart antenna in wireless communication. SKFGI Mankundu Hoogly WB India IJECT **4**, 43–47 (2013)
18. Khmou, Y., Safi, S., Frikel, M.: Comparative study between several direction of arrival estimation methods. J. Telecommun. Inf. Technol. **1**, 43 (2014)
19. Shahid, M.U., Nauman, M., Haider, D., Imran, Y.: Comparative analysis between direction of arrival algorithms. In: 2017 International Conference on Infocom Technologies and Unmanned Systems (Trends and Future Directions) (ICTUS). IEEE (2017)
20. Mane, M.S.V., Bombale, L.: Angle of arrival estimation for smart antenna using variations in music algorithms. Asian J. Converg. Technol. (AJCT) **3**(III), 43 (2017)
21. Osman, L., Sfar, I., Gharsallah, A.: Comparative study of high-resolution direction-of-arrival estimation algorithms for array antenna system. Int. J. Res. Rev. Wirel. Commun. (IJRRWC) **2**(1), 74 (2012)
22. Bakhar, M., Hunagund, D.P.: Eigen structure based direction of arrival estimation algorithms for smart antenna systems. IJCSNS Int. J. Comput. Sci. Netw. Secur. **9**(11), 96–100 (2009)

Experimenting Two Machine Learning Methods in Classifying River Water Quality

Siti Nur Mahfuzah Mohd Nafi[1] (ID), Aida Mustapha[1(✉)] (ID),
Salama A. Mostafa[1] (ID), Shihab Hamad Khaleefah[2] (ID),
and Muhammad Nazim Razali[1] (ID)

[1] Faculty of Computer Science and Information Technology, Universiti Tun Hussein Onn Malaysia, 86400 Parit Raja, Batu Pahat, Johor, Malaysia
mahfuzahmohdnafie@gmail.com, nazim.uthm@gmail.com,
{aidam, salama}@uthm.edu.my
[2] Faculty of Computer Science, Al Maarif University College, 31001 Anbar, Iraq
shi90hab@gmail.com

Abstract. Water is very important to human life. It is a vital aspect of human and ecosystem survival and health. As it affects human lives individually, the quality of water is a universal concern across the globe. When the quality of water deteriorates, the problem of water scarcity will follow. Water quality is highly dependent on various factors such as the increase of population, the rapid development of economic expansion, as well as environmental pollution. The objective of this study is to build a classification model for water quality. Two classification models are built by the WEKA data mining tool, which are the Random Forest algorithm and Random Tree algorithm. The performance of the model is measured based on accuracy, precision, and recall. The results showed that Random Forest gives a higher performance across all three evaluation metrics as compared to Random Tree algorithm. The results are hoped to assist the classification of water quality categories in different states and river locations across the world.

Keywords: River water quality · Classification · Random forest · Random tree

1 Introduction

Water is a vital aspect for the survival and health of human and its entire ecosystem. Due to its fundamental needs among human lives, it is important to ensure high-quality water supply in addition to avoid water scarcity. Water scarcity is a direct consequence of quality deterioration. In safeguarding water quality, may factors must be monitored and analysed, such as the increase of population, the rapid development of economic expansion, as well as environmental pollution. Therefore, the study of analysing and forecasting the quality of water in of high importance in order to prevent or a least minimize water quality deteriorations [1].

© Springer Nature Switzerland AG 2020
M. I. Khalaf et al. (Eds.): ACRIT 2019, CCIS 1174, pp. 213–222, 2020.
https://doi.org/10.1007/978-3-030-38752-5_17

Classification of water quality can be performed by data mining techniques that have been proven in their ability for simulating and modelling various physical phenomena in assessing the quality of water [2]. Data mining is a process used to extract usable data. Data mining is the one application in multiple fields, for example, research. As an application of data mining, the researcher can use data mining as a method because it can help to predict data appropriately. This paper is set to build a classification model for water quality based on real-life water river data from India using a data mining approach [3].

Data mining, or widely known as the Knowledge Discovery in Data (KDD) [4, 5], is becoming a research area with increasing importance due to its inherent ability to automatically discover important information in the form of patterns from a large data repository. Data mining is capitalizing in sophisticated mathematical algorithms to perform data segmentation and to predict the probability of future events. Data mining models are deployed to analyse large databases in order to find novel and useful patterns using various machine learning algorithms. They also provide capabilities to predict the outcome of future observation.

The rest of the paper is prepared as follows: Sect. 2 describes the related work on classification models. Section 3 presented the CRISP-DM methodology used to perform the data mining task along with the description of the dataset and the evaluation metrics used for evaluation. Section 4 presents the results and finally, Sect. 5 concludes with some direction for future work.

2   Related Work

The definition of a river is a natural water string and water bar [6]. Besides that, the river is also one of the natural resources exposed to pollution. Wastewater from industrial activity is potentially a source of contaminants that reduces water quality and river capacity [7]. As a nation with the highest use of water and freshwater resources in Malaysia, rivers are of major importance to the development of Malaysia that contributes up to 98% of the total water consumption [8].

There are many previous types of research that discussed the classification of water quality parameters such as using the Artificial Neural Networks (ANN) using worldwide water data sources. The works used combined Genetic Algorithms (GA) and ANN for classification and forecasting of water quality in rivers. One example if the classification of Johor river water using the ANN models developed from its quality parameters [9]. The research proposed the method to predict the water quality in terms of electrical conductivity and turbidity as well as total dissolved solids in the Johor river. The parameters of water quality in the research was extracted based on thirty samples collected from the rivers within the duration of 1998 until 2002. The proposed ANN model requires no prior knowledge of the natural physical process of these water quality parameters [10]. The ANN classification model showed reliable and robustness performance in predicting the dissolved, electrical conductivity and turbidity parameters with different data inputs patterns that used in training the model.

Research by [27] has also proposed the approach of combining ANN and GA for classification of river water quality. This is carried out by adding the Principle

Component Analysis (PCA) to the ANN and GA. Similar approach has also been followed by [10] and [11] in the form of a hybrid intelligent algorithm designed to predict river water quality. The dataset consists of 23 water quality index factors that were then compressed into only 15 aggregative indices. The results showed that PCA performed highly in terms of training speed among the follow-up algorithms, hence able to reduce data dimensionality. Then, the BPNN of the parameter will optimize by GA. Based on the combination of two methods, which are ANN and GA, their work was able to predict water quality with a considerable high accuracy which is very important to support real-time early warning systems [12]. The performance of the combined model showed it more suitable for predicting water quality. It also compared BPNN classification accuracy without using GA and the results showed that without GA, the solution cannot be searched therefore the accuracy of the prediction model declined. Using BBPN model to study classification and prediction of water can overcome good advantage due to its high training speed and good classification accuracy.

3   Proposed System

This study will use the Cross-Industry Standard Process for Data Mining (CRISP-DM) to develop the research project. The CRISP-DM is an industry-standard process out predictive analytics. Although CRISP-DM has some limitations, it is one of the most widely used methodologies in data mining and business analytics industry. CRISP-DM methodology increases the likelihood of success in the business analytics or data mining project. Therefore, CRISP-DM is a suitable methodology for this subject.

CRISP-DM methodology is formed based on structured phases in order to ensure the reliability and reproducibility of a project [13]. Hence, if anything happens during one of the phases of the project development, the respective phase can be done repeatedly until the condition is satisfied without affecting the current phase which is ongoing. There are six phases involved in this methodology, which are model understanding, data understanding, data preparation, modelling, evaluation and deployment. However, those six phases are not dependent on each other as described in Fig. 1. The sequence of the six phases is not as rigid as it is schematized. CRISP-DM methodology has also been well documented.

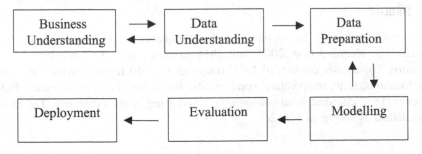

Fig. 1. The overall process of the CRISP-DM methodology

All the stages in the CRISP-DM methodology are organized, structured and well defined in order to ensure the planning for an entire project is understood by all parties involved and is easy to be revised. All CRISP-DM phases were used for this study except for the deployment phase, which will be discussed in future works.

- **Business Understanding:** The primary phase focused on understanding from a business perspective of the project goals and requirements. After retrieving the dataset of water quality that contains a class of water, this defined the research goal which is to predict the water quality.
- **Data Understanding:** The phase of data understanding started with the acquisition of dataset through initial data collection as well as the analysis of each type of variables used for attributes was carried out.
- **Data preparation:** This phase included activities froth initial raw data to build the final dataset. The variables or attributes in the dataset must be identified and prepared to generate the models used in the next phase. This classification model was created for the dataset that contains a class of water attributes.
- **Modelling:** In this phase, two classification models have been chosen and applied, which are Random forest and Random Tree Based on previous studies, these to classifiers never been used for this dataset. Thus, this can produce new findings predictive models of water quality performance.
- **Evaluation:** The phase in important to measure the performance of classification models constructed during the modelling stage. Apart from assessing the performance of the models, evaluation is also important to assess whether the data models have solved the issues raised during the business understanding phase. In this paper, the generated classification models were evaluated using Accuracy, Precision and Recall.
- **Development:** This phase can be as simple as the company-wide carried out the implementation of the data mining process.

The classification experiment will carry out using WEKA tools. WEKA is a system written in Java and distributed under the General Public Licence (GNU) [14]. WEKA provides with a variety of algorithms and data mining tasks with more specific that can easily use to the dataset. WEKA also provides a collection of techniques for data analysis and predictive modelling which ease to use over its graphical user interfaces [15].

3.1 Dataset

This research focuses on the classification of water quality in a certain location in India. The data was recorded from 2003 until 2014 extracted from UCI machine learning repository. The dataset consists of 1,992 instances with 10 features, which are station code, locations, state, temperature, conductivity, biochemical oxygen demand (BOD), nitratenan, fecal coliform, total coliform, year and 1 target class category. The excerpt of the dataset is shown in Fig. 2.

STATE	Temp	D.O. (mg/l)	PH	CONDUCTIVITY (μmhos/cm)	B.O.D. (mg/l)	NITRATENAN N+ NITRITENANN (mg/l)	FECAL COLIFORM (MPN/100ml)	TOTAL CO	year	CATEGORY
GOA	29.8	5.7	7.2	189	2	0.2	4953	8391	2014	alkaline
GOA	29.5	6.3	6.9	179	1.7	0.1	3243	5330	2014	acidic
GOA	29.7	5.8	6.9	64	3.8	0.5	5382	8443	2014	acidic
GOA	29.5	5.8	7.3	83	1.9	0.4	3428	5500	2014	alkaline
GOA	30	5.5	7.4	81	1.5	0.1	2853	4049	2014	alkaline
GOA	29.2	6.1	6.7	308	1.4	0.3	3355	5672	2014	acidic
GOA	29.6	6.4	6.7	414	1	0.2	6073	9423	2014	alkaline
GOA	30	6.4	7.6	305	2.2	0.1	3478	4990	2014	alkaline
GOA	30.1	6.3	7.6	77	2.3	0.1	2606	4301	2014	alkaline
GOA	27.8	7.1	7.1	176	1.2	0.1	4573	7817	2014	alkaline
GOA	27.9	6.7	6.4	93	1.4	0.1	2147	3433	2014	acidic
GOA	29.3	7.4	6.8	121	1.7	0.4	11633	18125	2014	acidic
GOA	29.2	6.9	7	620	1.1	0.1	3500	6300	2014	neutral
GOA	30	6	7.5	72	1.6	0.2	4995	9517	2014	alkaline
GOA	29	7.3	7	247	1.5	0.2	1095	2453	2014	neutral
GOA	29.1	7.3	7	188	1	0.1	1286	3048	2014	neutral
GOA	28.7	7	6.9	224	1.2	0.3	3896	6742	2014	acidic
GOA	28.7	7.3	6.7	144	1.5	0.1	1940	3052	2014	acidic
GOA	29.5	5.3	6.8	319	1.8	0.3	6458	10250	2014	acidic
GOA	29	6.3	6.4	79	1.6	1.4	7592	12842	2014	acidic
GOA	29.4	5.4	7.6	39	1.4	0.1	3176	6367	2014	alkaline
GOA	28.3	2.2	6.5	322	4.7	1.2	11210	14920	2014	acidic
GOA	30.1	5.2	7.1	192	2.6	0.3	5073	8925	2014	alkaline
GOA	30.3	5.6	7.5	282	1.8	0.1	3205	5082	2014	alkaline
GOA	30.5	5.5	7.4	275	1.5	0.1	4698	8625	2014	alkaline
GOA	29.1	7.3	6.7	55	1.4	0.1	2638	4003	2014	alkaline
GOA	30.1	6.5	7.5	415	2	0.1	864	1538	2014	alkaline
GOA	29.2	7.2	6.3	100	1.5	0.1	7942	13575	2014	acidic
MAHARASHTRA	25.1	6.6	7.8	95	4.9	0.2	16	36	2014	alkaline
MAHARASHTRA	29.6	6.9	7.9	99	5	0.4	15	34	2014	alkaline
MAHARASHTRA	27.4	6.8	7.7	85	5.2	0.3	11	23	2014	alkaline
MAHARASHTRA	27.8	6.7	7.8	80	4.9	0.3	12	29	2014	alkaline
MAHARASHTRA	30.6	5.1	7.3	3937	10.3	1.8	31	83	2014	alkaline
MAHARASHTRA	25	5.6	7.9	468	3.6	1.9	66	164	2014	alkaline
MAHARASHTRA	25	6.4	7.6	541	5.7	0.6	23	45	2014	alkaline

Fig. 2. India river water quality dataset

3.2 Pre-processing

Before implementing the water quality classification model, the dataset underwent a pre-processing stage that aims to improve the quality of the dataset. The dataset consists of total 1,992 instances but with many missing values. To deal with missing values, the entire rows are removed because most attributes are also missing such as station code, locations, state, temperature, pH, conductivity biochemical oxygen demand, nitratenan, fecal coliform, total coliform, year, and pH category [16].

After data cleaning, data selection is carried out by selecting the most effective attributes in a dataset. Only twelve attributes were selected to be used in this experiment, which is the attributes are selected and chosen based on previous research and focus on attributes that have the least missing values. The final number of instances used in the experiment is only 492 rows after data cleaning and data selection are performed.

3.3 Classification Algorithms

The classification algorithm used in this research is the tree-based approach, which is applying Random Forest and Random Tree. These algorithms are applied during the modelling stage in the Cross-Industry Standard Process for Data Mining (CRISP-DM) as deliberated as shown in Fig. 1.

3.3.1   Random Forest

Random Forest is a supervised classifier that combines various individual tree predictors whereby each tree is independent but with the same distribution for all trees in the forest depending on the value of a random vector sampled [17]. Random Forests use the best split between all variables, whereby each node is split [18, 19]. This makes the random forest highly accurate. A random forest classifier aggregates a family of classifiers of $h(x|\theta_1)$, $h(x|\theta_2)$, ... $h(x|\theta_k)$ where h is a classification tree and k is the number of trees chosen from a model random vector. This means each θ_k has been randomly chosen from the vector of parameters.

Let $D(x,y)$ denotes the training dataset, each classification tree in the ensemble tree (forest) is built using a different subset $D\theta_k(x,y)$. Thus, $h(x|\theta_k)$ is the kth classification tree which uses a subset of features $x\theta_k \subset x$ to build a classification model. The algorithm for each tree will operate like regular decision trees whereby the data is partitioned based on the value of the feature. When the data is fully partitioned, this indicates that the allowed depth has been reached. The final output y is obtained by aggregating the results as shown in Eq. 1:

$$y = argmax_{p \in \{h(x_1) \cdots h(x_k)\}} \left\{ \sum_{j=1}^{k} (I(h(x|\theta_j) = p)) \right\} \tag{1}$$

where I denotes the indicator function.

3.3.2   Random Tree

The random tree is a supervised classifier whereby the learning algorithm generates many individual learners. Next, it uses a bagging idea to build a random set of data that forms a decision tree. Bagging is basically assembling the individual trees to increase the stability and accuracy of the classification model. In the standard tree, every node is split using the best split among all variables. Random trees are able to address various classification issues of classification as well as regression [19, 20]. Random trees is a collection of tree predictors knows as forest. The random trees classifier takes the vector of the input feature, classifies it with each tree in the forest and produced the class label receiving the majority of votes. In the case of regression, the classifier response is the average of the responses over all the trees in the forest.

In machine learning, random trees are generally developed from a combination of two existing algorithms, which are single model trees and random forest idea. Model trees are decision trees where every single leaf has a linear model that is optimized for the local sub-trees as described from the leaves [15, 21, 24]. The ability to offer split selection makes the algorithm capable to induce reasonably balanced trees where a global setting for the ridge value works across all leaves, hence simplifying the process of optimization [26].

3.4 Evaluation Metrics

The performance of classification algorithms used in the experiments is measured using three evaluation metrics, which are accuracy, precision, and recall. The detailed description of the metrics is presented in the following equations.

- **Accuracy.** Accuracy is the percentage of the total number of samples correctly classified from the total number of samples [22, 23]. The formula to calculate the accuracy rate is shown in Eq. 2:

$$Accuracy\ (A) = \frac{(TP + TN)}{(TP + TN + FP + FN)} \qquad (2)$$

where TP, TN, FP, and FN represent as true positives, true negatives, false positives and false negatives, respectively.

- **Precision.** Precision is the percentage of correct samples predicted and calculated as in Eq. (3):

$$Precision\ (P) = \frac{TP}{(TP + FP)} \qquad (3)$$

where TP and FP represent as true positives and false positives respectively.

- **Recall.** Recall or Sensitivity additionally alludes as true positive (TP) rate, for example, the extent of positive tuples that are accurately recognized [25].

$$Recall\ (R) = \frac{TP}{(TP + FN)} \qquad (4)$$

where TP represents true positives and RN represents false negatives.

4 Experimental Results

The purpose of this experiments is to compare the performance of water quality model using the Random Forest and Random Tree algorithms via the WEKA data mining tool. The performance will be measured using three evaluation metrics, which are accuracy, precision, and recall. We used the split data method in the ratio of 70:30 for validation, whereby 70% from dataset was used for training and the balance 30% used in testing. The experimental results from two classification algorithms are recorded and illustrated in Table 1 and Fig. 3, respectively.

Based on Table 1, it is shown that in terms of accuracy performance, the Random Forest algorithm achieved higher accuracy than the Random Tree algorithm, which is 93.56% vs. 90.15%. In terms of precision, again, the performance Random Forest is higher than the Random Tree, which is 92.5% against 90.1%. Finally, the results for recall also show that Random Forest achieved a higher percentage than Random Tree, which is 93.6% vs. 90.2%.

Table 1. Comparison of classifier performance

Algorithm	Accuracy (%)	Precision (%)	Recall (%)
Random Forest	93.6	92.5	93.0
Random Tree	90.2	90.1	90.2

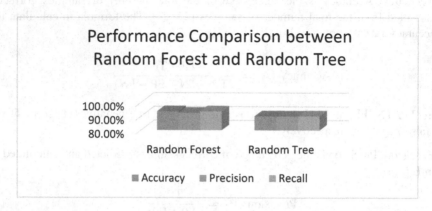

Fig. 3. Performance comparison between Random Forest and Random Tree

The experiments concluded that the performance of Random Forest is better than Random Tree in predicting water quality across all evaluation metrics; accuracy, precision, and recall. These results are supported by the literature such as in predicting water contaminants [28] and river pollution [29]. Random forests have been reported to be more accurate than a single random tree since the forest consists of multiple single trees from each training data [30]. More trees will result in a smoother decision boundary during training. In addition, the trees in the forests are generally unpruned (as opposed to single random forest), resulting in smaller feature space, hence higher classification accuracy.

5 Conclusions and Future Work

In conclusion, this paper proposed a classification model for water quality using a tree-based data mining approach, which is Random Forest and Random Trees. The result from this experiment is evaluated using split data in the ratio 70:30 and the result indicated that Random Forest performed better than the Random Tree Classifier. Other than the accuracy, the performance of both classification algorithms is also measured with precision and recall. In future research, we hope to explore more attributes along with other classification algorithms on the water quality dataset such as in [27]. Random forests, although highly accurate, is considered a black-box model, due to complexity in explaining the unpruned forests. It is hoped that the findings from this paper can be used to assist local government agencies to take care of the local environment.

Acknowledgement. This research is supported by Universiti Tun Hussein Onn Malaysia.

References

1. Heath, A.G.: Water Pollution and Fish Physiology. CRC Press, Boca Raton (2018)
2. Mekonnen, M.M., Hoekstra, A.Y.: Global anthropogenic phosphorus loads to freshwater and associated grey water footprints and water pollution levels: a high-resolution global study. Water Resour. Res. **54**(1), 345–358 (2018)
3. Mostafa, S.A., Ahmad, M.S., Firdaus, M.: A soft computing modeling to case-based reasoning implementation. Int. J. Comput. Appl. **47**(7), 14–21 (2012)
4. Dunham, M.H.: Data mining introductory and advanced topics. Alan R. Apt, United States of America (2003)
5. Gunasekaran, S.S., Mostafa, S.A., Ahmad, M.S.: Knowledge transfer model in collective intelligence theory. In: El-Alfy, E.-S.M., Thampi, S.M., Takagi, H., Piramuthu, S., Hanne, T. (eds.) Advances in Intelligent Informatics. AISC, vol. 320, pp. 481–491. Springer, Cham (2015). https://doi.org/10.1007/978-3-319-11218-3_43
6. Abdullah, M.: Analisis Regresi. Dewan Bahasa Dan Pustaka, Kuala Lumpur (1994)
7. Bird, K., Boopathy, R., Nathaniel, R., LaFleur, G.: Water pollution and observation of acquired antibiotic resistance in Bayou Lafourche, a major drinking water source in Southeast Louisiana, USA. Environ. Sci. Pollut. Res. 1–13 (2019)
8. Kasan, N.A.: Kualiti air sungai berdasarkan analisis kimia dan kepelbagaian alga (Doctoral dissertation, Universiti Teknologi Malaysia) (2006)
9. Najah, A., Elshafie, A., Karim, O.A., Jaffar, O.: Prediction of Johor River water quality parameters using ANN. Eur. J. Sci. Res. **28**(3), 422–435 (2009)
10. Mohammed, M.A., et al.: Decision support system for nasopharyngeal carcinoma discrimination from endoscopic images using artificial neural network. J. Supercomput. 1–19 (2018)
11. Mohammed, M.A., Ahmad, M.S., Mostafa, S.A.: Using genetic algorithm in implementing capacitated vehicle routing problem. In: 2012 International Conference on Computer & Information Science (ICCIS), vol. 1, pp. 257–262. IEEE (June 2012)
12. Arunkumar, N., Mohammed, M.A., Mostafa, S.A., Ibrahim, D.A., Rodrigues, J.J., de Albuquerque, V.H.C.: Fully automatic model-based segmentation and classification approach for MRI brain tumor using artificial neural networks. Concurr. Comput. Pract. Exp. e4962 (2018)
13. Wirth, R., Hipp, J.: CRISP-DM: towards a standard process model for data mining. In: Proceedings of the 4th International Conference on the Practical Applications of Knowledge Discovery and Data Mining, pp. 29–39. Citeseer (April 2000)
14. Kalmegh, S.: Analysis of weka data mining algorithm reptree, simple cart and randomtree for classification of indian news. Int. J. Innov. Sci. Eng. Technol. **2**(2), 438–446 (2015)
15. Khalfallah, J., Slama, J.B.H.: A comparative study of the various clustering algorithms in e-learning systems using WEKA tools. In: 2018 JCCO Joint International Conference on ICT in Education and Training, International Conference on Computing in Arabic, and International Conference on Geocomputing (JCCO: TICET-ICCA-GECO), pp. 1–7. IEEE (November 2018)
16. Liu, Y., Zheng, Y., Liang, Y., Liu, S., Rosenblum, D.S.: Urban water quality prediction based on multi-task multi-view learning (2016)
17. Kalmegh, S.R.: Comparative analysis of WEKA data mining algorithm randomforest, randomtree and ladtree for classification of indigenous news data. Int. J. Emerg. Technol. Adv. Eng. **5**(1), 507–517 (2015)
18. Singh, B., Sihag, P., Singh, K.: Modelling of impact of water quality on infiltration rate of soil by random forest regression. Model. Earth Syst. Environ. **3**(3), 999–1004 (2017)

19. Mostafa, S.A., et al.: Examining multiple feature evaluation and classification methods for improving the diagnosis of Parkinson's disease. Cogn. Syst. Res. **54**, 90–99 (2019)
20. Mostafa, S.A., Mustapha, A., Khaleefah, S.H., Ahmad, M.S., Mohammed, M.A.: Evaluating the performance of three classification methods in diagnosis of Parkinson's disease. In: Ghazali, R., Deris, M.M., Nawi, N.M., Abawajy, J.H. (eds.) SCDM 2018. AISC, vol. 700, pp. 43–52. Springer, Cham (2018). https://doi.org/10.1007/978-3-319-72550-5_5
21. Mostafa, S.A., Mustapha, A., Mohammed, M.A., Ahmad, M.S., Mahmoud, M.A.: A fuzzy logic control in adjustable autonomy of a multi-agent system for an automated elderly movement monitoring application. Int. J. Med. Inform. **112**, 173–184 (2018)
22. Khaleefah, S.H., Mostafa, S.A., Mustapha, A., Darman, R.: A general framework of multi-agent features extraction operators for deformed images identification. In: 2018 International Symposium on Agent, Multi-Agent Systems and Robotics (ISAMSR), pp. 1–5. IEEE (2018)
23. Mishra, A.: Metrics to evaluate your machine learning algorithm (2018). https://towardsdatascience.com/metrics-to-evaluate-your-machine-learning-algorithm-f10ba6e38234
24. Khalaf, B.A., Mostafa, S.A., Mustapha, A., Mohammed, M.A., Abduallah, W.M.: Comprehensive review of artificial intelligence and statistical approaches in distributed denial of service attack and defense methods. IEEE Access **7**, 51691–51713 (2019)
25. Sang, J.L., Keng, S.: A review of data mining techniques. Ind. Manag. Data Syst. **101**(1), 41–46 (2001)
26. Saxena, S.: Precision vs Recall. https://towardsdatascience.com/precision-vs-recall-386cf9f89488. Accessed 12 May 2018
27. Ding, Y.R., Cai, Y.J., Sun, P.D., Chen, B.: The use of combined neural networks and genetic algorithms for prediction of river water quality. J. Appl. Res. Technol. **12**(3), 493–499 (2014)
28. Lee, Y., Park, C., Lee, M.: Identification of a contaminant source location in a river system using random forest models. Water **10**(4), 391 (2018)
29. Tillman, F., Anning, D., Heilman, J., Buto, S., Miller, M.: Managing salinity in upper Colorado river basin streams: selecting catchments for sediment control efforts using watershed characteristics and Random Forests models. Water **10**(6), 676 (2018)
30. Pavlov, Y.L.: Random Forests. Walter de Gruyter GmbH & Co KG, Berlin (2019)

Multi View Face Detection in Cattle Using Infrared Thermography

Mohammed Jaddoa[1](✉) , Luciano Gonzalez[2] ,
Holly Cuthbertson[2] , and Adel Al-Jumaily[1]

[1] Faculty of Engineering and IT, University of Sydney Technology (UTS),
15 Broadway, Ultimo, NSW, Australia
Mohammed.A.Jaddoa@student.uts.edu.au,
adel.al-jumaily@uts.edu.au
[2] Faculty of Agriculture and Environment, University of Sydney,
Ultimo, Australia
{luciano.gonzalez,holly.cuthbertson}@sydney.edu.au

Abstract. Face detection in thermal imaging has been used widely in human for different purposes such as surveillance, obtaining physiological reading: respiratory and heart rate from face region via thermal imaging. Physiological reading via infrared thermal imaging used in emotion and stress detection as well as polygraph analysis. In animal as general and cattle in specific, face region localized manually in order to obtain temperature for eyes, nose and mouth, which used for stress, diseases and inflammation detection. In order to develop a future automated system for monitoring health conditions in cattle, it required to detect the face region automatically. Based on author knowledge, there is no research done regarding face detection in cattle using infrared thermal images. Unlike the human, cattle keep roaming, which lead to a change in the face and body orientation. The main objective of this paper is proposing a new method for Multi-view face detection in cattle with accuracy enhancement by using three classifiers and temperature thresholding. Classifiers are established by using Histogram Oriented Gradient (HOG) as features and Support vector machine (SVM) for classification. The results show that the proposed algorithm is performing well in term of Specificity, Recall and F-measure and detection rate compare to the currently used method in the literature.

Keywords: Infrared thermal · Face detection · Face detection in cattle · Multi view face detection

1 Introduction

Infrared thermography technology (IRT) is a non-invasive method that has been used to calculate and display temperature as an image. IRT can detect the variations in temperature and detect blood flow through determination the changes in body temperature [1, 2]. Several distinct features of infrared thermography make it the best choice for medical use. IRT is a fast method that visualizing temperature as an image in real-time without influencing local temperature. Also, it is non-invasive, non-contact approach

© Springer Nature Switzerland AG 2020
M. I. Khalaf et al. (Eds.): ACRIT 2019, CCIS 1174, pp. 223–236, 2020.
https://doi.org/10.1007/978-3-030-38752-5_18

and 100% side effect free. Thus, the clinical public in the US presented infrared thermography as a medical imaging tool can be used for diagnostics purpose [3, 4].

In the past decade, the enhancement in object detection and infrared thermal imaging have played a vital role in improving the medical sector. Using face detection lead to develop several automated systems for fever [5] and infection detection [6]. In addition, detecting face automatically used for obtaining body temperature, respiration rate and heart rate [7]. All of these applications of using infrared thermal imaging required to identify face region first as Area Of Interest (ROI) through applying a face detection algorithm. Many face detection algorithms developed by using machine learning algorithms, which include features extraction and automatic classification. These algorithms involve Viola and Jones (VJ), local binary patterns (LBPs), Histograms of Oriented Gradients (HOG), Deformable Parts Model (DPM), and Pixel Intensity Comparisons Organized in Decision Trees (PICO).

In the veterinary sector, Infrared thermal images used manually only for monitoring and evaluation of cattle's health for early detection of rising body temperature that is a sign of fever or local inflammation. As examples for veterinary application [8], IRT has successes in detection different disease such as mastitis in cattle, inflammation, and stress evaluation in cows, detect different diseases and infections, feed efficiency in cattle. For developing any future automated system, it required to detect face automatically in cattle.

In the current studies, two classifiers used in preparing face detection system in human: frontal face classifier or side face classifier. Frontal face detection in human required to collect images for human face in this position with a different orientation, and the same procedure applied with side face detection. Another limitation with current studies is false detection problem, which means detecting a face, but the face is not there. False detection leads to impact negatively on the accuracy of the face detector [9–11].

In animal for general and cattle in specific, it is not useful to use one or two classifiers because cattle are usually roaming in the field, and as result of this movement, animals face change in different angles and positions. For this reason, there are several variations in nose and eye shape in the frontal face position. In frontal face position, nose shape is different when cattle rise head compare to cattle when it's far from the camera. Also, it different when cattle put its head down, that hide nose with shown parts of eyes. However, the main contribution of this paper is developing an algorithm for multi-view face detection in cattle with enhancement the accuracy of detection rate. Multi-view face detection achieves through using three classifiers, which are established by using Histogram Oriented Gradient (HOG) as features and Support vector machine (SVM) for classification. Accuracy enhancement for face detector conducted through using temperature thresholding, which minimizes false detection significantly.

The structure of the paper is as the following: Related work presented in Sect. 2. The database is described in Sect. 3, followed by the proposed algorithm with its subsections in Sect. 4. The paper is concluded by a result discussion (Sect. 5) and a conclusion (Sect. 6).

2   Related Works

There is a lack of literature in developing face detection algorithm and use it in the infrared thermal images. While a massive number of studies proposed many face detection algorithms for visual spectrum image. The reason for this lack is all current methods are based on machine learning, which includes features extraction and automatic classification. Face detection based on machine learning requires manual annotation for face region of the massive number of images. This number of images is not available for infrared thermal spectrum [9]. In this section, the most well-known face detection methods in thermal spectrum are selected, which presented and discussed below.

First robust face detection method that presented by Viola and Jones (VJ) in [12]. It has ability to detect face in real time with limited computing power. Face detector using VJ trained using Haar features on set of face and non-face image. Afterwards, VJ detect face in input image through extracting Haar feature in cascading method from multi-scale for input image with applying sliding window. In each image scale and sliding windows, Haar features are extracted from sub image and compare with Haar features of trained VJ to find the possibility of matching. Further analysis performs by cascade when there is positive matching between extracted features and features of trained VJ. When matching is negative, sub image is rejected because it is not containing face. VJ algorithm detect face region in the input image when the sub image passes all cascade steps.

Cascade classifier used with local binary patterns (LBPs) instead of Haar features [13]. LBP features are required integral computations only, and LBP is more efficient than Haar features. Result reported that LBP features improve detection rate. LBP was proposed as features descriptor for texture in grey form. Each pixel in grey image compare with surrounding neighbouring pixels. Afterwards, binary string created after comparison made in gray image for centre pixel with neighbourhood pixels. Comparison that made binary string involve set 0 for each pixel in case this pixel has value less than centre pixel of neighbourhood pixels. Otherwise, pixel set to 1. Centre pixel will have value based on decimal representation of location for each value in binary string. LBP array created after applying this comparison for centre pixel and its surround pixels. Afterwards, histogram computed for LBP array, and normalized as pixel vectors. Pixels vectors used as data for training and testing via classification algorithm.

Histograms of Oriented Gradients (HOG) is features descriptor that presented as object detection algorithm [14]. Nowadays, it is one of widely used in object detection including face detection. HOG features are calculated through examining gradients intensity and edge direction of image. Gradients intensity and edge direction are represented as local histogram. HOG features are computed by analysing image gradients and grouping them into local histograms. Afterwards, gradient orientation converted as bins. Another grouping conducted to make cells as blocks. Final stage is normalization blocks to as histogram block, and use set of histogram blocks as descriptor. In order to use HOG for face detection, HOG features are calculated for training dataset, and this dataset include images contain face region and images not contain face region. Images with face region are called positive dataset, and images without face region called negative dataset. HOG features for both positive and negative converted as features vectors. Features vectors used to train classifier, which usually support vector machine (SVM). Afterwards, trained classifier will use to distinguish extracted HOG of future input image that contain face from one without fac.

The Deformable Parts Model (DPM) is presented by Felzenszwalb in [15]. This algorithm work based on using HOG and SVM in different strategy. Felzenszwalb and his colleagues proposed that each object has number of components such as face divided to eye, nose and mouth. Using HOG features for training with multiscale on each part of object. Training involve on root of object and parts of object. Afterwards, in detection many bounding box drawn around parts and root of object. Using non-maxima suppression technique to contain all bounding boxes to have one bounding box around object.

Pixel Intensity Comparisons Organized in Decision Trees (PICO) is new object detection approach presented by Nenad Markuš and his colleagues in [16]. PICO is modification of VJ method. The concept behind this method is scanning image in different scale and positions by using cascade of binary classifiers. Instead of Haar features, PICO method uses binary pixel intensity comparisons for object detection. Each binary classifier involves a group of decision trees with pixel intensity comparisons. Decision tree supported by GentleBoost. Every decision is made by comparison the intensity of two pixels from sub image. Object detection using decision tree is fast as result of removing features computation.

The recent study used VJ, LBPs and HOG for face detection in human in the frontal position without eyeglasses and the results have shown VJ accurate with average 95% compare to LBPs, and HOG. In this study, a dataset of 10,021 thermal infrared frontal face images adopted from two common databases: NIVE and I.Vi.T.E. For performance evaluation, True, False Positive Rate and ROC curve used to measure the performance of face detector [9]. In another recent study, comparison is made among VJ, LBP, HOG and DMP. The results were shown that VJ VJ, LBP, HOG and DMP are convergent in average of Precision, Recall, True Positive, False Positive. Database that used in that study include 2935 images [10].

According to our investigations in the previous work, most of the current face detection methods in human develop for frontal position, and little research done for multi-view face detection. In addition, there is no research done for face detection in cattle using infrared thermal spectrum. Therefore, multi-view face detection in cattle is crucial for any intelligent system, which infrared thermal has ability to extract temperature remotely. In this paper, HOG feature with SVM used due to HOG-SVM has ability to work with small database [17]. Also, Precision, Recall, F-measure, True and False positive used for performance evaluation.

3   Data Collection

The Infrared Thermography database was created by converting video with seq format to a sequence of grey images. The infrared thermal database includes 702 thermograms image show animal face in different position and orientation. Recording of IRT video imagery was done in a commercial abattoir in Arthursleigh farm. It is in Marulan town in the Southern Tablelands of New South Wales, Australia. The camera was setup at approximately 2 m from the target cattle as they moved through the race towards the knocking box. All cattle were in the shade under the roof during the recordings. And the camera was setup at approximately 45° angle from the head of the animal.

Duration of the video is two hours involve 300 cattle in different positions and orientation. There is not any kind of manipulation in the background. The images were acquired by using AGEMA 590 PAL, Therma Cam S65, A310, T335 with 320 × 240-pixel optical resolution of detectors. Preparing dataset start by extract frames from the Infrared Thermal video. After extracting 702 images from the video, extracted images divided into three groups each group will use to train the single classifier. In each group of images, using software for annotation face region manually.

4 The Proposed Methodology

The proposed method for face detection has the following components as illustrated in Fig. 1: pre-processing, image scanning, feature extraction, post-processing and end with place a bounding box around face. The output of each stage serves as inputs to the following stages. The proposed method for face detection starts by loading an infrared image in a grey format.

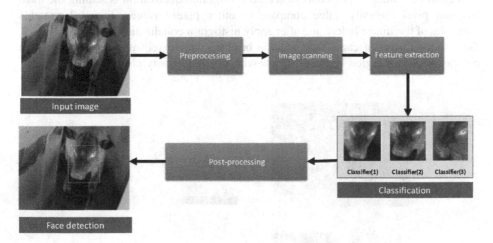

Fig. 1. Proposed face detection method includes pre-processing, image scanning, feature extraction, classification and post-processing.

Loaded infrared thermal image enhanced in two aspects: brightness and normalization. Pre-processed image used as input for image scanning stage. In this stage, the image scanned entirely by using windows in different scale and size. This stage is necessary to extract features from the region of image till find face as last outcome. In the feature extraction stage, Histograms of Oriented Gradients (HOG) used as features to distinguish a face from the background region. HOG worked based on the computational calculation of intensity gradient of an image presented by Dalal and Triggs

[14]. Currently, it is one of the most widely used methods for object detection. HOG is computed and converted as a feature vector and use feature vector for creating three face classifiers and use these classifiers in the classification stage. Three classifiers used to detect the face in a different orientation. Each classifier was created after training on the cattle face in a particular position. As shown in Fig. 1, the first classifier trained when cattle face in the frontal orientation shown a clear vision for eyes and nose. Second classifier trained when cattle face in frontal orientation but head down that show part of the nose with showing eyes. Last classifier when cattle show one eye and side of the nose.

All classifiers used Support vector machine (SVM) for training and testing. SVM is a well-known classification algorithm that used widely in literature for classification purpose. After classification, post-processing is applied to eliminate the undesired region and remain face region only. The last stage is necessary to reduce false detection, which improves face detection significantly.

4.1 Pre-processing

In this stage, all input image converted to grey format and apply normalization of pixels intensity by using histogram equalization. The aim of the histogram equalization step is to normalize image brightness and contrast by modifying pixels intensity by using histogram distribution. The concept behind histogram equalization is scaling the most frequent pixel intensity value compare to other pixels values. Figure 2 presents examples of the image before and after apply histogram equalization. As seen in Fig. 2, the eyes and nose of cattle face become brighter with pixel intensity reach 255. In contrast, the dark region becomes darker with pixels intensity close from 0.

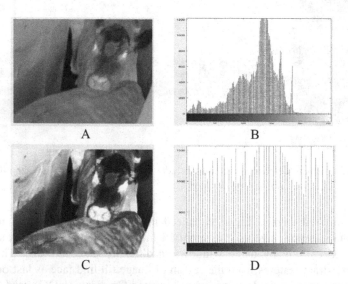

Fig. 2. Pre-processing stage using Histogram equalization: (A) Input image with grayscale, (B) histogram distribution for the input image, (C) Input image after applying histogram equalization, (D) Final image with noise elimination.

4.2 Image Scanning

The aim of this stage is scanning each image at various locations and scales. The goal of the scanning is to simplify a method to localize the face in an image, regardless of where in the image the face appears and how large/small it is. There are two sub-stages in image scanning: Image pyramids and Sliding windows.

4.2.1 Image Pyramids

Image pyramids are image representation on a different scale. Using an image pyramid enable us to find faces in images at different scales of an image. It starts from the original image in the bottom with original size (in terms of width and height). In each subsequent layer, the image is resized and optionally applied Gaussian blurring filter in each layer. The image is progressively resized until some stopping criterion is met, which normally a minimum size is being reached. In each resized image, a sliding window is applied searching about-face region.

4.2.2 Sliding Windows

Sliding windows combined with the Image pyramids, and this combination leads to find a face in images at various locations. A sliding window is a rectangular region with a fixed width and height that slide from left to right and top to bottom of each scale in the image pyramid. For each of these windows, we can take the window region, extract features from it, and apply an image classifier to determine if the window contains an object that interests us in this case, a face. Image pyramids and sliding windows, while simple, play a critical role in object detection and image classification.

Fig. 3. Image sliding windows with size 64 × 64 across image in different scale and position till find face region. (Color figure online)

As shown in Fig. 3, green rectangular represent sliding window with size 64 × 64 pixel. It slides in each image scale green rectangular slid from top to bottom with moving start from left to right side. In this case, if we had an image trained classifier, we could take each of these windows and classify the contents of the window till find face region.

4.3 Feature Extraction

This step is necessary for face detection by preparing features for classification stage. Histogram oriented gradient (HOG) used as feature for face detection. Linear Support Vector Machines used for classification.

Histogram Oriented Gradient (HOG) constructed with following parameters: pixels per cell = 4, cells per block = 2 and orientations = 9. In addition, Square root normalization is applied. These parameters work well during establish classifiers. Figure 4 illustrates the HOG feature for cattle face.

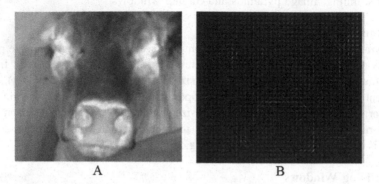

Fig. 4. HOG features for cattle face: (A) Input image with grayscale, (B) HOG for input image.

4.4   Classification

In the classification stage, SVM used for classification the HOG features. After HOG computed, HOG features converted to vectors and use these vectors in training and testing. Feature vector classifies to two classes. Due to these classes can be separated linearly, linear SVM used for classification. In this study, we are using three classifiers as a result of cattle face take various orientation and position as explained in the next section.

4.4.1   Training and Testing

Training involve separated dataset into three groups of infrared thermal images. Data set include manual annotation for face region of image. Each group of infrared thermal images divided into training and testing. The training set includes 80% of dataset and 20% for testing, and this means for overall dataset 560 images used in training and 140 images for testing. This dataset that includes face region classified to positive. Negative region refers to image without showing face. As can be seen in Fig. 5(A), training starts with using the annotated image. In this stage, we use image labeller app from Matlab for face region labelling. Afterwards, skimage library with python used for HOG extraction from face region (positive) and non-face region (negative). HOG features for both positive and negative image to convert to the list of vectors. List of vectors labelled to −1 and 1, where −1 means that the feature vector is not representative face region, and a value of 1 indicates the feature vector is representative face region. After that, vectors of HOG features saved as a separated file using h5py library. SVM using this file for training as shown in Fig. 5(A). This scenario applied in each group of images until creating three trained classifiers and all these classifiers saved as three separated files.

In testing, the scenario is different as shown in Fig. 5(B). It starts by image scanning by using image pyramids associated with sliding windows. HOG features extracted from each window and converted to the list of the feature vector. Feature vector tested by three classifiers to find out this vector belongs to which class. The bounding box is drawn around the face region after applying the post-processing stage as explained in the next section.

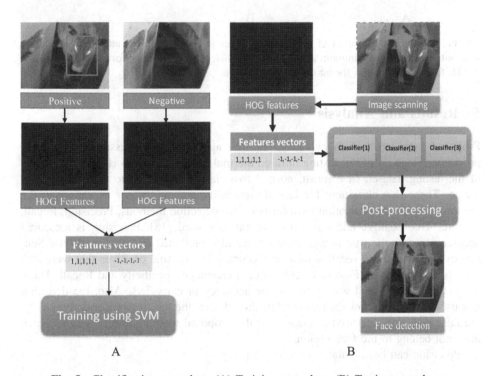

Fig. 5. Classification procedure: (A) Training procedure, (B) Testing procedure.

4.5 Post-processing

The last stage in face detection method is post-processing. This stage applied before drawing the bounding box around the face region. This stage is necessary for minimizing false detection and detect face region only. Normally, the eye region in the face has a temperature range of 30 to 38 C. This temperature range is obtained after checking the temperature value of the eye region for 300 subjects. As can be seen in Fig. 6, max temperature between 30 and 38, the mean temperature in range 24 to 34 and min temperature in range 20 to 30. In this stage, masking applied between candidature face region from the infrared thermal image and infrared thermal matrix in order to test temperature range. If the temperature range between 30 to 38 this mean candidate region could be facing. Otherwise, another region is scanned. This stage is necessary for minimizing false detection as illustrated in the result section.

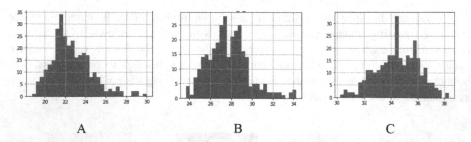

A   B   C

Fig. 6. Histogram distribution of temperature values for eye region in cattle: (A) Histogram distribution for mean of minimum temperature, (B) Histogram distribution for mean temperature, (C) Histogram distribution for maximum temperature.

5 Results and Analysis

Proposed face detection is evaluated through applying three classifiers with post-processing stage on 143 of testing infrared thermal images. Figure 6 is shown a sample of the testing dataset. In contrast, normal two classifiers applied to the same testing image. These two classifiers for face detection used in this paper as shown in the literature [9, 10]. In evaluation term for two face detection methods, Precision, Recall, F-score, True positive and False positive rate are used [18]. Precision is measured accuracy in case the true negatives that were also predicted as negative. While Sensitivity that also called recall is measure accuracy in case true positives that were also classified as positives. F-score calculates the percentage Specificity and Recall. These evaluation metrics used widely to test the accuracy of classifiers. Also, the detection rate used to measure how the proposed method detects the face region correctly. Lastly, the false detection rate used to measure if the proposed method detects region, which does not belong to the face region.

Precision can be calculated by using Eq. (1).

$$P = \frac{T_P}{T_P + F_P} \tag{1}$$

T_p where refers to true positive and F_P refer to false positive.

Recall can be computed by using Eq. (2).

$$P = \frac{T_P}{T_P + F_N} \tag{2}$$

T_p where refers to true positive and F_N refer to false positive.

F-score measures Precision and Recall by calculating the percentage between Recall and precision. A higher value of F-score refers to a better result in terms of accuracy. It can be computed with the mathematical Eq. (3).

$$F = 2 \times \frac{P \times R}{P+R} \qquad (3)$$

Lastly, the detection rate D_R of proposed face detection method is obtained by dividing the number of images F_D where face detected correctly by the total number of test images T_A as shown in Eq. (4).

$$D_R = \frac{F_D}{T_A} * 100\% \qquad (4)$$

Table 1. Face detection result.

Evaluation	Current method	Proposed method
Precision	0.98260	0.99502
Sensitivity	0.79021	0.91006
F-score	0.87596	0.95064
True positive rate	0.78	0.90
False positive rate	0.2	0.0

As shown in Table 1, the proposed method performs well compared to the used method in the literature. In precision and sensitivity, the proposed method has a percentage of 0.99 and 0.91 respectively compared to the currently used method. Also, the proposed method can detect face region correctly with the percentage of 0.90 compare to current method with the percentage of 0.78. However, the current method has false detection compare to the proposed method as shown in Fig. 7. As seen in Fig. 7, the current method can detect face correctly in 114 from 143 testing images. While the proposed method can detect face correctly in 128 from 143. Besides, the current method has false detection with number 3 means wrong to classify the region as a face while it belongs to the background or other parts from the animal body. In the proposed method, there is no face detection, which is performing well (Fig. 8).

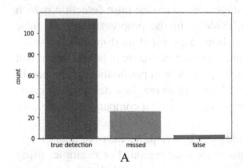
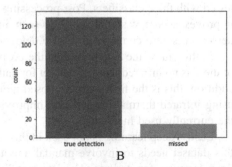

Fig. 7. Face detection rate: (A) Current method using two classifiers, (B) Proposed method using three classifiers.

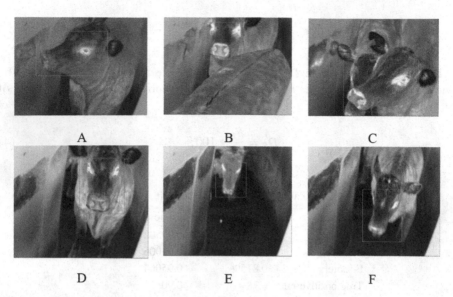

Fig. 8. Face detection with different positions: (A) Face region with side direction, (B) Frontal face with up nose, (C) Frontal face with aside nose, (D) Frontal face with clear nose and eyes, (E) Far frontal face with hidden nose, (F) Frontal face with down nose.

6 Discussion

According to the results, we can reach the following findings. As shown in Table 1, it is clearly shown that the proposed method better than the current method in term of Precision 0.99, Recall 0.91, F-score 0.95 with high True positive rate 0.90 and zero False-positive rate. Using three classifiers increase the performance of face detection as a result of the improve SVM generalization. SVM generalization enhanced because of splitting dataset as a group of sub dataset and each sub dataset used to train one classifier. In this study, author re-organize dataset in a way make similarity high with less difference, and this strategy makes the proposed method perform well compared to the currently used method in the literature. Also, each single infrared thermal image tested with three classifiers. Post-processing stage used to reduce false detection, which improves accuracy significantly as seen in Table 1. In the proposed method, false detection is zero compare to 3 false detection from the current used method.

In this study, the author applied the proposed method on his own dataset as a result of there is no infrared thermal dataset for cattle to provide it in public for researchers. In addition, this is the first study proposed method for multi-view face detection in cattle using infrared thermal images with improving accuracy, and a comparison made with the currently used method.

Lastly, deep learning is not used in this study due to it requires massive dataset, and this dataset needs to involve manual annotation for face region. For example, using deep learning for pedestrian's detection in railway using infrared thermal required manual annotation for a total of 30.129 [19]. Therefore, it is recommended to prepare enough dataset in order to obtain robust face detection.

7 Conclusion

This paper presents the details of the multi-view face detection in cattle. The main contribution of the proposed face detection in this study that differs from previous studies: it is the first study conducted for multi-view face detection in the indoor environment using infrared thermal images. In addition, this is the first face detection study using three classifiers, which are more powerful compared to the currently used method in the literature. Using eye region temperature to reducing false detection that also improves the accuracy of face detection significantly as explained in Sect. 4.5. According to the results of this study, the proposed method is effective with the following average 0.95064 and 0.90 for F-score and detection rate. This means that the proposed method is accurate with less error compared to currently used methods as explained in Table 1. Constructing face detection is useful for developing an intelligent system for extracting temperature from the eyes or mouth region. Eyes and mouth region used widely for identifying infection and disease in cattle [8]. In future work, it is intended to increase the number of images in order to use deep learning that could increase performance significantly.

References

1. Nääs, I.A., Garcia, R.G., Caldara, F.R.: Infrared thermal image for assessing animal health and welfare. JABB-Online Submiss. Syst. **2**, 66–72 (2014)
2. Roberto, J.V.B., de Souza, B., Furtado, D.A., Delfino, L.J.B., Marques, B.D.A.: Thermal gradients and physiological responses of goats in the Brazilian semi-arid using thermography infrared. J. Anim. Behav. Biometeorol. **2**, 11–19 (2014)
3. Faust, O., Acharya, U.R., Ng, E., Hong, T.J., Yu, W.: Application of infrared thermography in computer aided diagnosis. Infrared Phys. Technol. **66**, 160–175 (2014)
4. Adam, M., Ng, E.Y., Tan, J.H., Heng, M.L., Tong, J.W., Acharya, U.R.: Computer aided diagnosis of diabetic foot using infrared thermography: a review. Comput. Biol. Med. **91**, 326–336 (2017)
5. Somboonkaew, A., et al.: Mobile-platform for automatic fever screening system based on infrared forehead temperature. In: 2017 Opto-Electronics and Communications Conference (OECC) and Photonics Global Conference (PGC), pp. 1–4 (2017)
6. Wong, W.K., Ishak, N.I.N.B., Lim, H.S., Bin Md Desa, J.: An intelligent thermal imaging system adopting fuzzy-logic-based Viola Jones method in flu detection. In: Recent Advances in Applied Thermal Imaging for Industrial Applications, pp. 1–39. IGI Global (2017)
7. Sun, G., et al.: Remote sensing of multiple vital signs using a CMOS camera-equipped infrared thermography system and its clinical application in rapidly screening patients with suspected infectious diseases. Int. J. Infect. Dis. **55**, 113–117 (2017)
8. Rekant, S.I., Lyons, M.A., Pacheco, J.M., Arzt, J., Rodriguez, L.L.: Veterinary applications of infrared thermography. Am. J. Vet. Res. **77**, 98–107 (2016)
9. Basbrain, A.M., Gan, J.Q., Clark, A.: Accuracy enhancement of the Viola-Jones algorithm for thermal face detection. In: Huang, D.S., Hussain, A., Han, K., Gromiha, M. (eds.) ICIC 2017. LNCS (LNAI), vol. 10363, pp. 71–82. Springer, Cham (2017). https://doi.org/10.1007/978-3-319-63315-2_7

10. Kopaczka, M., Nestler, J., Merhof, D.: Face detection in thermal infrared images: a comparison of algorithm- and machine-learning-based approaches. In: Blanc-Talon, J., Penne, R., Philips, W., Popescu, D., Scheunders, P. (eds.) ACIVS 2017. LNCS, vol. 10617, pp. 518–529. Springer, Cham (2017). https://doi.org/10.1007/978-3-319-70353-4_44

11. Cruz-Albarran, I.A., Benitez-Rangel, J.P., Osornio-Rios, R.A., Morales-Hernandez, L.A.: Human emotions detection based on a smart-thermal system of thermographic images. Infrared Phys. Technol. **81**, 250–261 (2017)

12. Viola, P., Jones, M.J.: Robust real-time face detection. Int. J. Comput. Vis. **57**, 137–154 (2004)

13. Ojala, T., Pietikäinen, M., Mäenpää, T.: Multiresolution gray-scale and rotation invariant texture classification with local binary patterns. IEEE Trans. Pattern Anal. Mach. Intell. **24**, 971–987 (2002)

14. Dalal, N., Triggs, B.: Histograms of oriented gradients for human detection (2005)

15. Felzenszwalb, P.F., Girshick, R.B., McAllester, D., Ramanan, D.: Object detection with discriminatively trained part-based models. IEEE Trans. Pattern Anal. Mach. Intell. **32**, 1627–1645 (2009)

16. Markuš, N., Frljak, M., Pandžić, I.S., Ahlberg, J., Forchheimer, R.: Object detection with pixel intensity comparisons organized in decision trees. arXiv preprint arXiv:1305.4537 (2013)

17. Kopaczka, M., Schock, J., Nestler, J., Kielholz, K., Merhof, D.: A combined modular system for face detection, head pose estimation, face tracking and emotion recognition in thermal infrared images. In: 2018 IEEE International Conference on Imaging Systems and Techniques (IST), pp. 1–6 (2018)

18. Cho, S., Baek, N., Kim, M., Koo, J., Kim, J., Park, K.: Face detection in nighttime images using visible-light camera sensors with two-step faster region-based convolutional neural network. Sensors **18**, 2995 (2018)

19. Van Beeck, K., Van Engeland, K., Vennekens, J., Goedemé, T.: Abnormal behavior detection in LWIR surveillance of railway platforms. In: 2017 14th IEEE International Conference on Advanced Video and Signal Based Surveillance (AVSS), pp. 1–6 (2017)

Deep Learning for Face Expressions Detection: Enhanced Recurrent Neural Network with Long Short Term Memory

Wafaa Mahdi Salih[1]([⊠]) [iD], Ibraheem Nadher[2] [iD],
and Ahmed Tariq[1] [iD]

[1] Computer Science Department, University of Technology, Baghdad, Iraq
wafaa.m.salih@gmail.com, drahmaed_tark@yahoo.com
[2] Faculty of Basic Education, AL- Mustansiriya University, Baghdad, Iraq
Ibraheemnadher@uomustansiriyah.edu.iq

Abstract. In recent years, deep learning neural frameworks have been given significant attention in programming development, especially in machine learning, machine vision and artificial intelligence (AI). The ability to detect faces has inspired many researchers because a human face shows great dissimilarities in form and figure due to changes in position and expression in different situations. This research aims to produce a method of applying recurrent neural network (RNN) designs using long short-term memory (LSTM) to identify facial expressions. The proposed method involves an improved RNN that uses LSTM to increase the effectiveness of the feature extraction process using input sets which regenerate the input-data from the features. The accuracy and computing time of this technique were studied. With LSTM-RNNs, the results show that the design gives enhanced outcomes compared with other methods, including most image/video face detection methods. The efficiency evaluation of LSTM-RNNs in images and in video frame series shows that there are performance improvements of more than 5% compared with traditional neural networks.

Keywords: Deep learning · Images classification · Face expressions detection · Long short term memory (LSTM) · Recurrent neural network (RNN)

1 Introduction

Facial expressions are thought to have global meanings that have evolved over thousands of years. Recognition algorithms of facial expressions are an inspiring and challenging field of research, but most work has been concentrated on one method or one database [1]. In deep learning, facial expression recognition (FER) is an inspiring task with many uses in a large range of applications, including games, human-computer interactions and healthcare [2]. Therefore, research of facial expressions has garnered much attention during recent years [3].

Deep learning methods could be the solution that powers image classification. It offers the ability to make exact classifications in huge image datasets by training the algorithms with carefully chosen training data [4]. Deep learning can be useful in a number of applications, especially in the field of image analysis [3].

© Springer Nature Switzerland AG 2020
M. I. Khalaf et al. (Eds.): ACRIT 2019, CCIS 1174, pp. 237–247, 2020.
https://doi.org/10.1007/978-3-030-38752-5_19

When applied to learning data which is used for image classification, deep learning offers some advanced classification technologies which support control models containing a number of processing layers [5]. The algorithm is first trained with portions of known datasets before the network is tested using the remaining parts of the datasets. This process provides feature maps which result in highly accurate image classifications [4].

When limited by network arrangements and the absence of suitable datasets for training, networks are unable to accurately produce the required feature maps using dimensional reduction. This could be the result of network over-fitting. To mitigate this problem, appropriate neural network classifiers known as recurrent neural networks (RNNs) with original deep learning algorithms are used [6].

The classifiers are adjusted to produce accurate feature maps from the input dataset. Existing studies of deep learning use different algorithms and techniques for enhanced feature extraction and image classifications [7]. In previous techniques, RNNs were applied to images without temporal series. For accurate classifications of facial expression images, it is essential to analyse the proper set of input datasets with simple neural networks for algorithm training [8].

The purposes of this research are to decrease the processing time and increase the classification accuracy for the image classification of facial expressions. This paper aims to provide a highly exact features map and high classification accuracy by extracting representative features from the input datasets [9]. The input datasets are passed for depooling and deconvolution to extract the more complex image features with a high order structure. The known main expressions are sadness, disgust, anger, happiness, fear, and surprise, and the small differences between them create recognition difficulties [10].

The remaining sections of this paper are arranged as follows: Sect. 2 describes an overview of related work and Sect. 3 describes the RNN concept. Section 4 describes the LSTM-RNN Structure. Section 5 outlines the proposed model, and discusses the experiments and their results. Section 6 summarizes and concludes.

2   Related Work

Emotion recognition from facial images is a common problem in the field of computer vision and is the subject of much research. Algorithms for emotion recognition can be categorized into two types of methods: those based on image sequences and those based on still images.

Image sequence based methods have been used to increase recognition performance by extracting useful temporal features from the image sequence, which is generally better than still image based methods. Recently, RNNs have had great success in controlling sequential data, especially in speech recognition, natural language processing (NLP), action recognition and image treatment [11].

A method for recognizing micro expressions was presented by Verburg and Menkovski [2] using an RNN on optical flow features to code the temporal changes in specific face parts by extracting a histogram of oriented optical flow (HOOF) feature. An RNN spots small intervals that are likely to have interconnected facial micro-movements. The evaluated work was done on the SAMM dataset reduced by RNN training and by using leave one-subject out-cross validations. The results showed 1569 false positives with half of the associated micro-movements.

Sang et al. [3], proposed 3D-Inceptions ResNets networks (3DIRs), which extend the recognized 2D-Inceptions ResNets modules for processing image sequences. The additional dimensions result in a volume of features map and extract the spatial relationships among the sequence of frames. The proposed module is followed by long short-term memory (LSTM), which receives the temporal relationships and uses this information to categorize the sequence. This allows it to differentiate between different parts of facial components. The proposed method incorporates face landmarks, which are multiplied with the input tensors in the residuals module which is exchanged with the traditional residuals layer. The proposed architecture addresses both spatial and temporal features of the sequence and incorporates facial landmarks during training, helping the architecture to identify the significant face components in the features map which results in a more exact recognition rate. As an input, the LSTM takes the improved features map resulting from the 3DIR layers and extracts the temporal data from it. The proposed method ends with a fully connected layer connected with softmax activation functions.

Minaee and Abdolrashidi [4], proposed a deep learning approach based on convolutional networks, which are able to concentrate on the essential parts of faces. Their approach accomplishes major improvements over earlier models on various databases, including JAFFE, FERG, CK+ and FER2013 datasets. Using a visualization procedure, it is able to locate the main face areas for emotion detection based on the classifier's output. The experimental results showed that altered emotions require sensitivity to changed portions of the face.

Kahou et al. [5], produced a combination of video facial features to reach emotional recognition using RNNs for spatial-temporal evolution modelling. The work was done using double methods, on levels of decisions and features. The researchers found it difficult to draw conclusions from the results due to the enormous number of undefined cases and because an excessive number of training videos indicated a combination of two or more emotions.

Gu et al. [6], proposed RNNs for tracking and joints estimation of facial features in video images. The experimental results of the proposed method on head pose estimation and face landmark localization from video demonstrate that it outperforms frames-wise models and Bayesian filtering to create a huge-scale synthetic database for head pose estimations.

Jung et al. [7], adopted a deep learning network as a tool for feature extraction which is based on two diverse models. The first one extracts temporal features from an image sequence, while the second network extracts temporal geometric features from temporal face landmark points using the Oulu-CASIA and CK+ datasets. These networks are joined using an integration technique.

3 Recurrent Neural Network Concept

RNNs are a type of artificial neural network that add additional weights to the network to produce sequences within it in an effort to maintain internal states. The ability to add states to the neural network enables them to clearly learn sequence prediction problems, including problems with an order or with temporal components [11].

A better way to reflect this is that when the training sets contain examples with sets of inputs for the current training examples, this approach is termed conventional, for example, a traditional multi-layered perceptron [12]. When the training examples are improved with a set of input from the earlier examples, this is termed unconventional, for example, an RNN [9].

RNNs can learn temporal features by mapping input sequences to sequences of hidden states [13], and furthermore mapping the hidden state to an output sequence [14]. RNNs have shown encouraging performance on several tasks. Training on long term sequences is not an easy task, primarily due to vanishing and exploding gradient problems [15], but it could be resolved with a memory that can remember and forget earlier states [16]. LSTM [17] provides such a memory and can remember the data for long period of time. An LSTM unit has three gates:

(1) Inputs gate (i)
(2) Forget gate (f)
(3) Output gate (o)

4 LSTM-RNN Structure

LSTM blocks replace the hidden layers of a typical RNN. Each block holds three component gates (input-output-forget) for (write-read-reset) operations and holds one or more memory cells. The gate controls the activities of the cells [18].

If c_t is the input summation at two times t and $t - 1$, the input gate activations vector is calculated as:

$$i_t = \sigma\left(W_{yi}y_t + W_{hi}h_{t-1} + W_{si}s_{t-1} + b_i\right) \tag{1}$$

where σ represents sigmoid functions, W is the weights matrix, x_t is the input at time t, h_{t-1} is the hidden-state vector of the previous time, and b_i denotes the input bias vectors. In addition, the forget gate could be calculated as:

$$f_t = \sigma\left(W_{yf}y_t + W_{hf}h_{t-1} + W_{sf}s_{t-1} + b_f\right) \tag{2}$$

The memory cell value c_t is calculated as:

$$c_t = i_t tanh\left(W_{ys}y_t + W_{hs}h_{t-1} + b_s\right) + f_t \cdot s_{t-1} \tag{3}$$

The activations value of the output-gate is calculated as:

$$o_t = \sigma\left(W_{yo}y_t + W_{ho}h_{t-1} + W_{so}s_{t-1} + b_o\right) \tag{4}$$

Memory cell output is:

$$h_t = o_t \cdot tanh(c_t) \tag{5}$$

Using bidirectional RNN-LSTM structural design, the input image/frame is processed with two distinct hidden layers to acquire extra features [19, 20]; h_t^f, h_t^b are the forward and backward activation values of the hidden layer, and the output layer will be updated as follows:

$$y_t = W_{fz}h_t^f + W_{bz}h_t^b + b_y \quad (6)$$

where W_{fy} and W_{by} are the forward and backward weight matrices and b_y is the hidden bias-vectors [19].

LSTM was used to allocate the locations of expressions. LSTM provides more exact estimation points compared with normal neural networks [19].

5 The Proposed Model

In the first cascade stage, LSTM was used to collect the initial expression locations. A components-based search approach was used in the second stage, and in the third stage, an RNN was used to improve the results.

The key contributions of the proposed model are the following:

(1) Applying RNNs for facial expression detection for both videos and images.
(2) Evaluating RNN-LSTM performance and the robustness of its facial expression detection.

Proposed architecture is shown in Fig. 1.

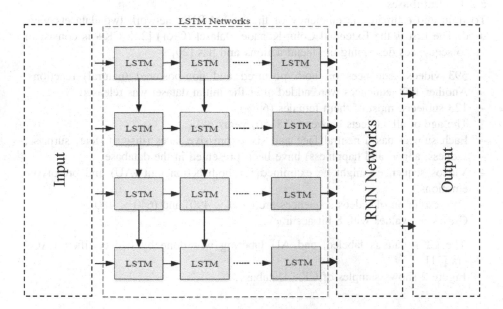

Fig. 1. LSTM-RNN architectures

5.1   RNN-LSTM Structure for Video and Image

One benefit of applying RNNs as a replacement for regular neural networks is that the noise/speech signal is fairly well interrelated with the future and previous signals.

RNNs are also useful for finding the landmarks of the face. In a video, facial expressions are clearly closely related to their future and previous shapes. The first network target is learning an approximation of facial expression points.

The LSTM inputs are sets of video frames, and its outputs are the coordinates of the equivalent expression points. There are k hidden layers weighted to build the RNN. A recursion function was used within the LSTM cells.

A linear activation function in the output layer is required to plot the 2D-coordinates of the learned features. For images, there are no time sequence patterns as there are for videos. A set of feature patterns should be constructed by the RNN, which first accepts the RGB colour channels independently by sharing the same weights. The hidden recurrent layer provides data on other colour spaces. LSTM is used to determine which data should be sent.

To increase network performance, some image-improving operators were used to get more network inputs from the same original image. The average of all the results was taken to allocate the primary positions of the facial features.

5.2   Experiments and Results

This section describes the results of experiments on video frame series and images databases for comparing and evaluating the LSTM-RNN network architecture.

5.2.1   Databases

To train and estimate the efficiency of the LSTM-RNN network two datasets were used. The first is the Extended Cohn-Kanade Dataset (CK+) [22], CK+ is consist of video sequences describing the facial actions and has [20]:

- 593 videos sequences on both postured and non-postured (natural) reactions. Another 107 sequences were added after the initial dataset was released.
- 123 subjects, most of them females (69%).
- The age of all subjects between (18–50) years old.
- Each subject has a neutral face and six expressive faces (disgust, fear, surprise, sadness, anger, and happiness) have been presented in the database.
- Videos sequences might be examined for both action unit (AU) and prototypic emotions.
- The resolution of videos sequences are (640 × 490) and (640 × 480).
- Gray scale values with 8-bit accuracy.

The CK+ data is labeled, and AU labeling was done by two certified FACS coders [21].

Figure 2 shows samples of CK+ Database.

Happy   Sad   Surprised   Disgusted   Angry   Fear   Neutral

Fig. 2. Examples of the CK+ dataset

The second dataset is Facial Expression Recognition 2013 dataset (FER2013), was created by Google images search with 184 emotion related keywords, and collected from 600 different search queries [22].

Form each query, image was collected form the first 1000 images, then and before grouping the image, it has to pass the post processing first, which involved image alignment and face region cropping. It contains [23]:

- 36,000 images.
- Gray scale images with 48 × 48 pixels (resized to 299 × 299). Since, larger sequences will get deeper networks and extract more abstract features.
- Thousand images from each class (only disgust with only 547 frames).
- Within each image, the face is approximately centered and occupies about the same amount of area.
- The images have some variant poses and the existence of external occlusions produced by hair, hand and eyeglasses.

Figure 3 shows examples of the FER2013 dataset.

Fig. 3. Examples of the FER2013 dataset

5.2.2 Experimental Analysis

The training of proposed model followed the second protocol first with 60% from FER2013 dataset, the model evaluated by 40% from the same dataset, the highest classification rates had been achieved with the happy face 77% and the lowest rates for angry face 62%.

Figure 4 and Table 1 show FER2013 dataset results.

Table 1. The Classification Rates Results of FER2013 dataset

	Angry	Disgust	Fear	Happy	Sad	Surprise
Angry	**0.62**	0.18	0.12	0.0	0.08	0.0
Disgust	0.13	0.75	0.07	0.0	0.05	0.0
Fear	0.18	0.04	0.68	0.0	0.10	0.0
Happy	0.0	0.0	0.0	**0.77**	0.0	0.23
Sad	0.07	0.03	0.13	0.0	0.76	0.01
Surprise	0.0	0.0	0.0	0.23	0.01	0.76

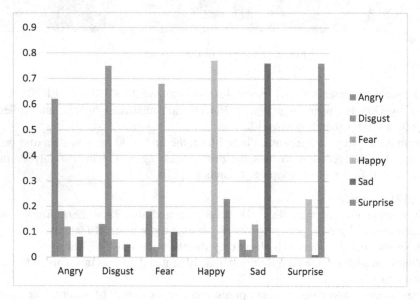

Fig. 4. The Classification Rates, Training and Evaluating FER2013 dataset

The training of proposed model with 60% from CK+ dataset, the model evaluated by 40% from the same dataset, the highest classification rates had been achieved with the happy face 96%. And it notices that there is a high confusions rate among the fear and sad expressions as well as the sad and angry expressions, the lowest rates for angry face 85%. Figure 5 and Table 2 show CK+ dataset results.

Table 2. The Classification Rates Results of CK+ dataset

	Angry	Disgust	Fear	Happy	Sad	Surprise
Angry	**0.85**	0.07	0.06	0.0	0.0	0.02
Disgust	0.06	0.86	0.06	0.0	0.02	0.0
Fear	0.07	0.0	0.88	0.0	0.05	0.0
Happy	0.0	0.0	0.0	**0.96**	0.0	0.04
Sad	0.0	0.05	0.0	0.0	0.93	0.02
Surprise	0.02	0.02	0.0	0.04	0.0	0.92

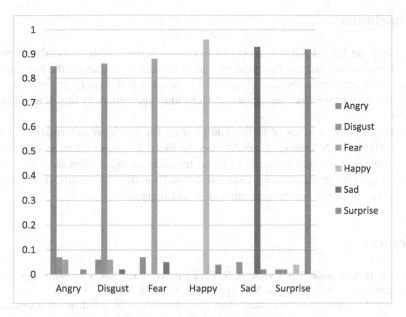

Fig. 5. The Classification Rates, Training and Evaluating on CK+ dataset.

The normalized root means square errors (NRMSE) and the test errors were used to measure the network performance. The space between the eyes was used for NRMSE normalizing.

The efficiency evaluation of LSTM-RNN in images and in video frame series shows that there are performance improvements by more than 5% compared with the feed-forward neural network (FNN) and the stack auto-encoders network (SAE). The result is shown in Table 3.

Table 3. The LSTM-RNN performance compared with traditional NNs.

Networks types	Layers	Weights	Success rates (NRMSE $\leq$ 0.1)	Success rates (NRMSE $\leq$ 0.2)
SAE	(1) 3901600	(2) 1450100	65.6%	93.9%
	(3) 400400	(4) 60668		
FNN	(1) 3901600	(2) 1450100	65.8%	93.89%
	(3) 400400	(4) 60668		
LSTM-RNN	(1) 23231210	(2) 7487400	72.3%	90%
	(3) 1773900	(4) 60668		

Faces in this dataset are labeled with any of the six important expressions as well as neutral. Compared with the other datasets, FER2013 has more different in the image, including faces obstruction frequently with hands, eyeglasses, incomplete faces, and low contrast images [24].

6 Conclusion

In this paper, an LSTM-RNN is proposed to extract several types of facial expressions for the detection of features. The network can simultaneously capture the presence and dynamics of partial and complete geometry and process still data. Experimental results on two datasets prove that the proposed technique succeeded in this state-of-the-art application.

For future work, a series of RNNs can be used for nonlinear deformation in facial imaging. The first RNN network would map the facial image with low resolution. The following networks would capture the facial modules as input from the first network outputs to give more exact facial expressions and modify the results. The proposed method gives inspiring results on both video and images.

References

1. Ahmed, H.A., Rashid, T.A., Sidiq, A.T.: Face behavior recognition through support vector machines. Int. J. Adv. Comput. Sci. Appl. **7**(1), 101–108 (2016)
2. Verburg, M., Menkovski, V.: Micro-expression detection in long videos using optical flow and recurrent neural networks. arXiv:1903.10765, vol. v1 (2019)
3. Sang, D.V., Van Dat, N., Thuan, D.P.: Facial expression recognition using deep convolutional neural networks. In: Proceedings of 2017 9th International Conference on Knowledge and Systems Engineering, KSE 2017, vol. 2017, pp. 130–135 (2017)
4. Minaee, S., Abdolrashidi, A.: Deep-Emotion: Facial Expression Recognition Using Attentional Convolutional Network (2019)
5. Ebrahimi Kahou, S., Michalski, V., Konda, K., Memisevic, R., Pal, C.: Recurrent neural networks for emotion recognition in video. In: Proceedings of the 2015 ACM on International Conference on Multimodal Interaction - ICMI 2015, pp. 467–474 (2015)
6. Gu, J., Yang, X., De Mello, S., Kautz, J.: Dynamic facial analysis: from Bayesian filtering to recurrent neural network. In: Proceedings - 30th IEEE Conference on Computer Vision and Pattern Recognition, CVPR 2017, vol. 2017, pp. 1531–1540 (2017)
7. Jung, H., Lee, S., Yim, J., Park, S., Kim, J.: Joint fine-tuning in deep neural networks for facial expression recognition. In: Proceedings of the IEEE International Conference on Computer Vision, vol. 2015, pp. 2983–2991 (2015)
8. Jeyaraj, P.R., Samuel Nadar, E.R.: Computer-assisted medical image classification for early diagnosis of oral cancer employing deep learning algorithm. J. Cancer Res. Clin. Oncol. **145**, 829–837 (2019)
9. Mohsen, H., El-Dahshan, E.S.A., El-Horbaty, E.S.M., Salem, A.B.M.: Classification using deep learning neural networks for brain tumors. Future Comput. Inform. J. **3**(1), 68–71 (2018)
10. Aubreville, M., et al.: Automatic classification of cancerous tissue in laserendomicroscopy images of the oral cavity using deep learning. Sci. Rep. **7**(1), 11979 (2017)
11. Antonio, V.A.A., Ono, N., Saito, A., Sato, T., Altaf-Ul-Amin, M., Kanaya, S.: Classification of lung adenocarcinoma transcriptome subtypes from pathological images using deep convolutional networks. Int. J. Comput. Assist. Radiol. Surg. **13**(12), 1905–1913 (2018)
12. Graves, A., Schmidhuber, J.: Offline handwriting recognition with multidimensional recurrent neural networks. In: NIPS (2009)

13. Bell, S., Zitnick, C.L., Bala, K., et al.: Inside-Outside Net: Detecting Objects in Context with Skip Pooling and Recurrent Neural Networks, arXiv preprint arXiv:1512.04143 (2015)
14. Graves, A., Mohamed, A., Hinton, G.: Speech recognition with deep recurrent neural networks. In: Proceedings of IEEE International Conference on Acoustics, Speech and Signal Processing, pp. 6645–6649 (2013)
15. Graves, A., Jaitly, N.: Towards end-to-end speech recognition with recurrent neural networks. In: Proceedings of International Conference on Machine Learning, pp. 1764–1772 (2014)
16. Mikolov, T., Karafiát, M., Burget, L., Cernocký, J., Khudanpur, S.: Recurrent neural network based language model. In: Proceedings of INTERSPEECH, vol. 2, pp. 1045–1048 (2010)
17. Sanin, A., Sanderson, C., Harandi, M.T., Lovell, B.C.: Spatiotemporal covariance descriptors for action and gesture recognition. In: IEEE Workshop on Applications of Computer Vision (2013)
18. Zhang, T., Zheng, W., Cui, Z., Zong, Y., Li, Y.: Spatial-temporal recurrent neural network for emotion recognition. IEEE Trans. Cybern. arXiv:1705.04515 (99), 1–9 (2018)
19. Yang et al.: FER using WMDNN based on double-channel facial images. IEEE Access 6, 4630–4640 (2016). [8]
20. Yao, A., Cai, D., Hu, P., Wang, S., Shan, L., Chen, Y.: HoloNet: towards robust emotion recognition in the wild (2016)
21. Khorrami, P., Paine, T.L., Brady, K., Dagli, C., Huang, T.S.: How deep neural networks can improve emotion recognition on video data. In: IEEE Conference on Image Processing (ICIP) (2016)
22. Jain, D.K., Kumar, R., Jain, N.: Decision-based spectral embedding approach for identifying facial behaviour on RGB-D images. In: Modi, N., Verma, P., Trivedi, B. (eds.) Proceedings of International Conference on Communication and Networks. AISC, vol. 508, pp. 677–687. Springer, Singapore (2017). https://doi.org/10.1007/978-981-10-2750-5_69
23. Jain, D.K., Zhang, Z., Huang, K.: Hybrid patch based diagonal pattern geometric appearance model for facial expression recognition. In: Zhang, Z., Huang, K. (eds.) IVS 2016. CCIS, vol. 664, pp. 107–113. Springer, Singapore (2016). https://doi.org/10.1007/978-981-10-3476-3_13
24. Chernykh, V., Sterling, G., Prihodko, P.: Emotion Recognition From Speech With Recurrent Neural Networks, arXiv:1701.08071v1 [cs.CL] (2017)

The Application of Artificial Intelligence Technology in Healthcare: A Systematic Review

Mohamed Alloghani[1,2(✉)] ⓘ, Dhiya Al-Jumeily[1] ⓘ,
Ahmed J. Aljaaf[1,3] ⓘ, Mohammed Khalaf[4] ⓘ, Jamila Mustafina[5] ⓘ,
and Sin Y. Tan[1] ⓘ

[1] Liverpool John Moores University, Liverpool L3 3AF, UK
phdmn2015@gmail.com, {D.Aljumeily,
A.J.Kaky}@ljmu.ac.uk, S.Y.Tan@2013.ljmu.ac.uk
[2] Abu Dhabi Health Services Company (SEHA), Abu Dhabi, UAE
mloghani@seha.ae
[3] Centre of Computer, University of Anbar, Ramadi, Iraq
a.j.aljaaf@uoanbar.edu.iq
[4] Department of Computer Science, Almaarif University College,
Ramadi, Anbar, Iraq
M.I.Khalaf@acritt.org.uk
[5] Kazan Federal University, Kazan, Russia
dnmustafina@kpfu.ru

Abstract. The proliferation of artificial intelligence and its continued development can be attributed to the pursuit of advanced machine learning techniques for handling big health data. Even though AI appears to be an independent system while considering algorithms and learning techniques, it, however, requires integration of different machine learning algorithms to enable it to handle different data structures. Notably, the number of articles addressing AI implementation from a medical research perspective are on the rise. Further, AI in medical research have machine learning component and as such relies on algorithms such as support vector machine, neural network, deep learning, and convolution neural networks. Of these algorithms, support vector machine is the most commonly used, and it has been applied in medical imaging, diagnosis and treatment of stroke as well as early detection of cancer and neurology conditions. As per the survey, AI results in higher accuracy of diagnosis and risk prediction compared to human approaches. Despite such success and promising future, AI faces regulatory and data related challenges.

Keywords: Artificial Intelligence · Deep learning · Machine learning · AI medical research

1 Overview of the Medical Artificial Intelligence Research

One of the emerging and fast-growing computing fields is artificial intelligence (AI), and the pursuit of deep learning algorithms with less energy overhead and computing resources seem to move machine learning towards AI. Despite the ongoing debate on

© Springer Nature Switzerland AG 2020
M. I. Khalaf et al. (Eds.): ACRIT 2019, CCIS 1174, pp. 248–261, 2020.
https://doi.org/10.1007/978-3-030-38752-5_20

AI replacing doctors, it is apparent that AI is at its research and development phase, and not unless an AI singularity occurs, it suffices to deduce that AI will not be replacing physical doctors any time soon [1]. However, AI can and will play a revolutionary role in assisting doctors to make clinical decisions as well as diagnosis and prognosis of different medical conditions. Hence, it is plausible that AI has the potential of replacing human judgment in certain functional medical areas such as radiology.

Even though developing and implementing such technologies seem to be in the realms of science fiction, the continued growth in healthcare data alongside the rapid development in big data analytics will continue to support prosperity in AI implementation in healthcare. In the context of big data and with the correct optimization algorithm, successful implementation of AI can unlock hidden clinical patterns within the big healthcare data. As of now, the chances are that some in Australia or China require emergency treatment with causes that another person experienced in Cuba. With pooled big data under the auspices of healthcare cloud platforms, AI will possible recommended successful treatments that had been previously administered and is so doing reduces the amount of time required for diagnosis [2]. Such would be a critical and an effective means of making decisions and administering treatments in cases that would otherwise result in mortality.

Given the importance and role of AI in healthcare and the future of medicine, it is imperative to survey and explore the current status of AI in healthcare while considering its applicability in the future. The exploration comes at a time that Industry 4.0 and its concepts are continuing to revolution many sectors. For instance, technologies such as wireless sensor networks leverage the Internet of Things (IoT) to collect data in real time while concurrently allowing doctors to monitor patients remotely [2]. Against the backdrop of such possibilities, it suffices to account for the research updates and status on the developments, implementation, and application of AI in the healthcare industry. Additionally, the survey explores the reasons for using AI in healthcare, the types of data that the AI systems require, the techniques and algorithms that AI systems require to generable actionable clinical results, and the diseases that AI are currently aiding in the processes of detection, diagnosis, and prognosis. This paper is structured in the following format. In Sect. 1, we discuss the overview of the medical Artificial Intelligence research along with motivation of study, data science in healthcare, AI components and domain areas of AI implementations. While Sect. 2 presents the proposed methodology. In Sect. 3, we discuss about the AI Application in Stroke. Early Detection and Diagnosis, Treatment and Outcome Prediction and Prognosis Evaluation. The conclusion work is presented in the last section.

1.1 Motivation

Critics and proponents alike asseverate that AI has innate clinical and productivity improvement influence. At its core, is the capability to unearth hidden patterns within large data and based on the patterns, the hospital can optimize its performance and improve its service delivery through optimization of existing resources, managing time and saving costs. Over the years, evidence-based practice has been debated, and health professionals encouraged to embrace to improve efficacy [1, 2]. Today, AI integrates primary data collected from patients with information retrieved from secondary sources such as electronic books and research notes within the shortest time possible and synthesize the information to provide information that the doctors can use to make decisions.

AI, being an advanced machine learning algorithm or being based on one, uses sophisticated learners to provide insight into the big healthcare data. AI, unlike conventional algorithms, has both learners and self-error correcting mechanisms for improving the accuracy of the outcome based on the feedback. Due to such feedback loops, a physician can engage an AI in an interactive research session with the system providing up-to-date medical information from authoritative sources [3]. Most importantly, AI systems are pertinent in reducing both diagnostic and therapeutic errors that are unavoidable in human practice hence a solution to the adage to err is to human. Furthermore, AI systems, can extract data and predict vulnerability among a population leading real-time inference making and health risk mitigation. It is also imperative to note that roles of AI in predictive medicine, especially from the perspective of genomics, are endless and promising because the human genome is the hallmark of big data and its application for predictive medicine will require smart systems [4]. However, it is critical to note that while deploying AI systems, automation should not be the objective and a full understanding of the AI system by the operators is necessary.

1.2 Healthcare Data

In data science and its applications, training the chosen algorithm is a critical step to ensuring that the predictive outcomes are reliable. In healthcare applications, AI algorithms require training using historical data that activities such as diagnosis, screening, treatments, and morbidities among others yield. The objective of training the algorithms is so that they identify and recognize similar groups and association between attributes that serve as features for predicting different health outcomes. While discussing healthcare data, it suffices to mention that such data are stored using electronic health records and such information management systems have become an essential part of hospitals and other medical caregivers.

The EHRs are contemporary versions of patient charts although they are real-time and patient-centred with the objective of making patient information available to authorized users. Even though debates about privacy and confidentiality of patient data continues, the underlying assumption is that access to EHRs is secure and with the right privileges, and as such it can be said to preserve confidentiality, integrity, and availability (CIA) triad of the patient data. A standard medical electronic record contains historical medical information, diagnosis results, and scans from radiology including medication (Fig. 1). Some other health data available for use with AI systems include medical notes that the doctors make, electronic records from the medical devices, genetic test results, and electrodiagnosis. However, most of the AI systems rely on these data types during diagnosis, and they have been used in different instances. For example, researchers have recommended AI for the analysis of images because of the amount of information that they contain. Besides images from radiology, physician

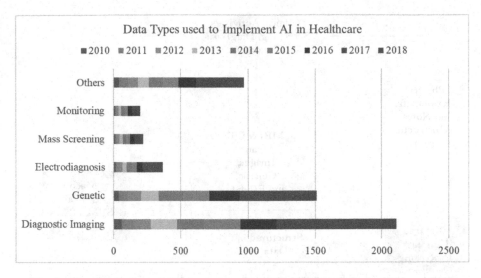

Fig. 1. The distribution of data types based on search articles between 2010 and 2018

notes alongside lab test results the other major sources of health data (Fig. 1). It is imperative to note that the two sources of health data are unstructured, hence present unique challenge to big data analytics.

Besides the electronic medical records (EMRs) sources, sensors are becoming an essential part of sourcing healthcare data. The taxonomy of such sensors is all-encompassing, but generally, they consist of physiological sensors, wearable activity sensors, human sensors, and contextual sensors. Physiological sensors record vital signs for both inpatient and outpatients and they include pervasive sensors embedded in smartphones such as iPhone and Samsung to monitor heart rate and other signals. Wearable activity sensors are also becoming common, and they measure attributes related to the activity of the user including all aspects of physical exercises.

1.3   Artificial Intelligence Devices

It is imperative to note that AI devices are either meant for machine learning or natural language processing. AI devices that aim to complete machine learning tasks analyse the structured data such as radiology images through clustering of patients into ideal groups or use of probability associated with the outcome of a given disease. However, natural language processing (NLP)-based AI platforms make deduction and inferences from unstructured data. Notably, NLP converts human language-based text to machine-readable text that machine learning algorithms can train, learn, and predict. It is similar to creating to corpus from text documents and using the corpus to create word cloud and conduct the sentimental analysis.

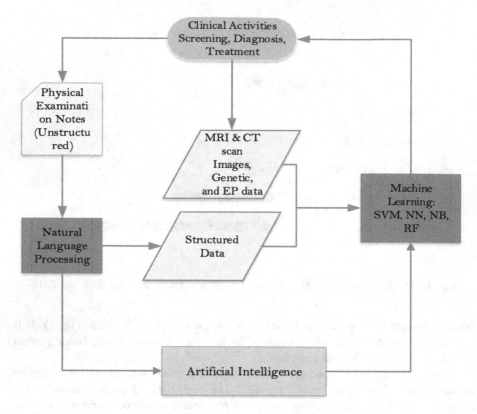

Fig. 2. The framework for generating, processing and analysis clinical data using a healthcare AI system

Given the two categories of AI devises and analytical approaches, Fig. 2 summarizes data flow in the ideal AI implementation scenario. From Fig. 2, the sources and sinks of data play a pivotal role in the outcome of the AI analysis process. The four distinct processes in Fig. 2 include data generation from clinical activities, data enrichment through NLP pre-processing, and data analysis using machine learning algorithms, and clinical decision making based on the results obtained from the models. However, it is important to commence and end the AI analytical process with clinical activity. That is, the decision made after implementing a machine learning algorithm must of relevance to an underlying clinical process other the AI system will not be serving its purpose.

1.4 Disease Focus

It suffices to deduce that imagery has made medical application of AI in disease diagnosis, treatment, and prediction possible. Of the many areas of applications, fields or diseases that require imagery for diagnosis have emerged to be the beneficiary of AI applications. In specific, cardiology, cancer and neurology have been the major beneficiaries. It is clear that poor prognosis has been one of the challenges associated with cancerous conditions, although AI can detect cancer at its early stages and help save patients before their conditions become terminal [5]. Through observations and simulation of similar conditions, it has been shown that AI can achieve a 95% accuracy in detecting mesothelioma, an accuracy rate than normal and standard cancer prognosis procedures cannot achieve. Some of the studies awaiting publications have shown that AI is 10% accurate in detecting melanoma compared to dermatologists, and higher levels of accuracies are attestations of the medical breakthroughs that will be possible because of artificial intelligence [5, 6]. Some other specific application of AI has been in the detection and treatment of breast cancer.

In neurology, AI can aid in detecting and treating seizure disorders, neurosurgical OT, and it has also emerged to be critical in upskilling neurosurgical procedures besides playing an essential part in neuro-oncology. According to Ganapathy, Abdul, and Nursetyo [7], brain tumour ablation is one of the procedures that can benefit from autonomous robotic surgery because the process involves perception and adaptation to dynamic changes within the operating environment. However, the authors acknowledge that the dynamism of the neurosurgical environment and knot tying remain the key challenges for autonomous robotic surgery. The system that authors discussed leverages AI algorithms to conduct such surgeries, and it is the fixation of the parameters of the algorithms that limit the performance of the AI-based robotic systems [8, 9]. Most importantly, AI is fast becoming essential for three-dimension simulations of ventriculostomy catheter and its possible movement through the brain parenchyma while attempting to access the ventricle [10]. Nonetheless, AI advances in the field of haptics have proven critical in improving the learning and surgical skills required for such advanced procedures.

Finally, as per Johnson et al. [11], application of AI in cardiology is promising, and the potential relies on machine learning algorithms to provide analytic tools for augmenting and extending the effectiveness of cardiologists in service delivery. Of the many reasons, the authors cite the introduction of data-rich technologies that will force cardiologist to interpret and operationalize patient data from several disparate biomedical fields as the overarching reason for pursuing AI in cardiology. It is paramount to note that patients tend to demand faster care, especially in more personalized environments and with such demands come to the responsibility of processing large volumes of data and providing an accurate assessment. The proliferation of smartphones equipped with sensors alongside wearable sensors that collect heart-based parameters will facilitate the development of AI for cardiology-related detection, prognosis, and treatment of conditions [12].

2 Methods

The articles used in the research were retrieved from ProQuest Central database, and the main key words used in the string search included a combination of the plausible AI algorithms and title of this article or a combination of the key words that the title addresses. A screenshot of the search string implemented in ProQuest Central database is as shown in the following figure.

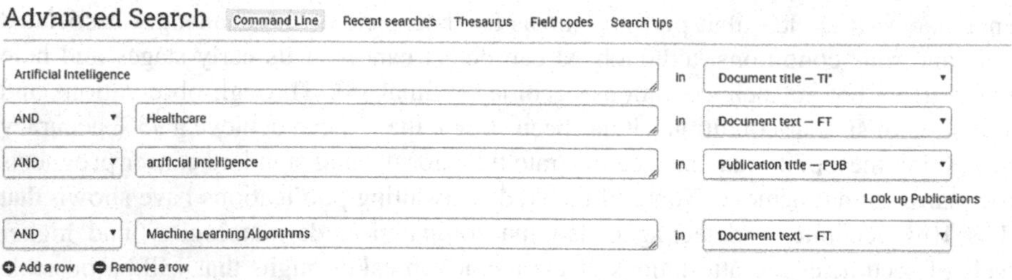

Advanced Search   Command Line   Recent searches   Thesaurus   Field codes   Search tips

Artificial Intelligence	in	Document title – TI* ▼
AND ▼ Healthcare	in	Document text – FT ▼
AND ▼ artificial intelligence	in	Publication title – PUB ▼

Look up Publications

| AND ▼   Machine Learning Algorithms | in | Document text – FT ▼ |

● Add a row   ● Remove a row

Fig. 3. Search string implemented in ProQuest Central database

The primary key search strings targeted the title of the document, full text as well as the publication. The publications were restricted to peer-reviewed and full-text documents that were published between 2010 and 2018.

As stated previously, the categories of AI devices depend on the analytic technique that the device implements and both ML and NLP emerged to be the common categories. However, from a more general perspective, the algorithms used in medical applications can either be classical ML, boosted deep learning, or NLP algorithms.

The systematic review process focused on the title, abstract, introduction, methods, results, discussions, and conclusion. The introduction section focused on rationale and objectives of the reviewed studies. The methods section focused on the eligibility of the study, the sources of the information, and selection and screening criteria of the study. The other key parameters for the evaluation of the study included the characteristics of the study, its limitations and conclusions. Some of the commonly used AI techniques are discussed as follows.

2.1   Classical Machine Learning

The classical ML techniques rely on techniques that extract hidden patient features or patterns from the data. The primary attributes that these algorithms require consists of patient demographics and occasionally health outcomes upon discharge. Some of the commonly used demographic data include age, gender, and ethnicity and these traits are considered attributes because of the proven vulnerabilities associated with each of the groups. For example, the elderly, especially those who 65 years and above are more vulnerable to illnesses, injuries, and diseases even with the least exposure levels [12]. However, while implementing classical ML algorithms, disease-specific data including symptoms, previous medication, and diagnostic results play an essential role in predicting the outcome of the patient. In most cases, outcomes serve as the predictand, and the recommendation to discharge relies on the doctor's evaluation and assessment of the condition of the patient before discharge. For example, a patient admitted with blood clot issues is dischargeable only after the required blood clotting levels are achieved and the profile of such a patient including the medication and other forms of care can use the server as the predictors of the outcome.

In a general sense, machine learning is either supervised or unsupervised depending on the objective of the analysis, although the learning can also be boosted or semi-supervised. From a general perspective, unsupervised learning involves the use of unstructured health data, and it is suitable for extracting features from the data [13]. Conversely, supervised learning involves the use of structured data as such has distinct target attribute that the other patient input features can model and explain. Predominantly, health outcome is the predictand while patient traits are the predictors. However, there have been cases where unsupervised learning is necessary to identify features necessary for supervised learning and as such cases are becoming common and are related under the auspices of semi-supervised learning. Semi-supervised learning is necessary when the available health data lacks an outcome variable because the unsupervised learning will recognize patterns and assign outcomes which then becomes an input in a supervised learning task.

Mostly, principal component analysis and clustering are considered unsupervised learning although clustering involves several algorithms. Some of the clustering algorithms include k-means, hierarchical clustering, DBSCAN, mixture models, and OPTICS algorithm [14]. It is critical to note that it is erroneous to refer to unsupervised learning as cluster analysis because the latter infers commonalities within the data and the latter infers labelling of the output variable. Nonetheless, from a classical ML stance, the clustering algorithms assign the classes or labels which then become the predictors for usage in the supervised learning phase.

Supervised learning, unlike unsupervised learning, requires a specification of a target variable (health outcome) and the predicting features that determine or explain the variation in the health outcome. Using these information, supervised learning requires all the attributes to return the best outcome from the training subset as a means of handling uncertainty and unexplained variability in the subsequent projections [13]. Based on the theoretical discourses for the two ML categories, it evident that supervised learning suit health care AI data analytics more than the unsupervised category because, for every health care, an outcome is mandatory. Some of the relevant classical ML techniques include regression, support vector machines (SVM), and decision trees algorithms [14]. Based on the search results, some of the commonly used supervised ML algorithms for learning images, genetic, and electrophysiological data are summarized in Fig. 3.

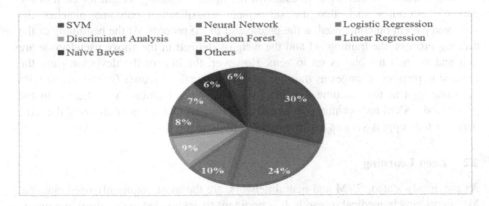

Fig. 4. The distribution of the commonly used algorithms in clinical AI research

According to Fig. 3, SVM and neural networks are the commonly used algorithms, and it suffices to explore these algorithms. SVM is a classifier, and it divided the target attribute into two classes that are represented by 1 or −1 [15]. The above premise assumes that input patient traits are linearly separable so that the optimal hyperplane assumes the linear form [1];

$$\alpha_i = \sum_{j=1}^{p} w_j X_{ij} + b_i \qquad (1)$$

Notably, w_j refers to the weighting factor placed j^{th} patient attribute in manifesting its importance and influence on the health outcome. Further, α_i is the decision criterion and if it great iser than one, then the patient belongs to group 1. Conversely, if it is less than one then, the patient belongs to the group −1. An example of a pseudocode that represent the implementation of the SVM algorithm is as shown below [16].

Algorithm 1: Support Vector Machine

INPUT

1. $T_{RAINING}S_{ET}$ $\{x_i, y_i, i = 1, 2, ..., l\}$
2. W_{EIGHTS} $\theta_i, i = 1, 2, ..., l$
3. B_{IAS} $\boldsymbol{b}$
4. $T_{RAINING}S_{ET}$ PARTITION INTO $S_{UPPORT}S_{ET}(\mathbf{S})$, $E_{RROR}S_{ET}(\mathbf{E})$, & $R_{EMAINING}S_{ET}$ $(\mathbf{R})$
5. $P_{ARAMETERS}$: ε, C K_{ERNERL} T_{YPE} & K_{ERNEL} $P_{ARAMETERS}$
6. R M_{ATRIX}
7. D_{RAW} N_{EW} S_{AMPLE} $C = (x_c, y_c)$

OUTPUT

1. N_{EW} $T_{RAINING}S_{ET}$ $\{x_i, y_i, i = 1, 2, ..., l + 1\}$
2. N_{EW} $C_{OEFFICIENTS}$ $\theta_i, i = 1, 2, ..., l + 1$
3. N_{EW} B_{IAS} $\boldsymbol{b}$
4. N_{EW} $T_{RAINING}S_{ET}$ $P_{ARTITION}$
5. N_{EW} R M_{ATRIX}

The objective of training is to establish the optimal training weight for each of the patient's attributes such that the subsequent classification outcome matches the observed patient outcome used as the predictand in the process. At the beginning of the training process, the training set and the weights defined in the above pseudocode are null and as such the bias is set to zero. However, the bias or the deviation from the optimal hyperplane changes as training proceeds, iterations search for the alphas with the same sign as the outcome variable for correct classification. As indicated in the pseudocode, SVM has optimization kernels and options that aid in minimizing the error between the support vectors and the optimal hyperplane.

2.2   Deep Learning

As previously stated, SVM and neural network are the most commonly used classical ML algorithms in medical research. It is pertinent to acknowledge that deep learning is a boost of the classical neural network algorithm. As such, deep learning is simple a

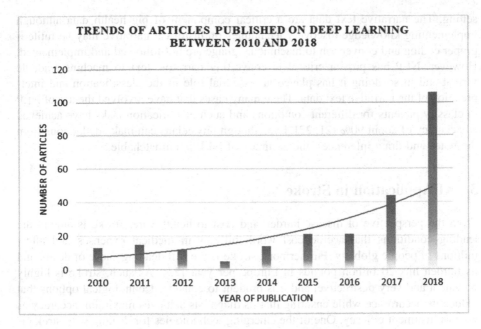

Fig. 5. The number of articles published on the deep learning

multi-layered neural network algorithm, and some of the modern computing techniques support development and implementation of deep learning with larger numbers of neural networks [8, 17, 18]. As per Fig. 4, the number of articles published on the application and implementation of deep learning algorithms in healthcare has been increasing exponentially.

The growth in the number of articles based on deep learning algorithms can be attributed to the increasing use of deep learning in diagnostic imagery, electrodiagnosis, clinical laboratory, and genetic diagnostics. It suffices to acknowledge that most of these applications reached their applicability and implementation phase in the last few years and the growth in the number of articles addressing deep learning application is an attestation to the trend (Fig. 5).

Notably, the most commonly used deep learning techniques include CNN, DNN, and RNN [19, 20]. However, convolution neural network algorithm tends to be popular compared to the others because of its ability to handle big dimension data without necessarily requiring implementation of any dimension reduction algorithm.

2.3 Natural Language Processing

One of the emerging and inevitable persistent challenge is processing and handling of the large volume of text data from medical notes and other points within the healthcare setting. The narrative text data are a critical component of big health data although implementing knowledge discovery techniques on historical narrative may be futile if proper coding and conversion to machine language are not followed and implemented. However, NLP has proven critical in converting narrative text to machine-readable format and in so doing it has played an essential role in the classification and interpretation of the narrative text data. There many cases that have involved the use of NLP to classify patients for different conditions and such classification tasks have achieved an accuracy of about 90% [21, 22]. Even though physicians can make deductions from the notes and draw inferences, the accuracy of NLP is unmatchable.

3   AI Application in Stroke

From the perspective of disease burden and cost to health care, stroke is among the leading conditions that accrue cost worth billions in medical expenses and affect millions of people globally. Furthermore, stroke is the fifth leading cause of death, and its burden hits 20 billion pounds in Europe per year [23]. As such, stroke is highly prevalent and very destructive, and it is prudent to consider technological options that reduce its occurrence while ensuring that its diagnosis achieves maximum accuracy as well as treatment efficacy. One of the emerging technologies for dealing with stroke is AI, and it aids in early detection and diagnosis, treatment and predictive analysis for the vulnerable populations.

3.1   Early Detection and Diagnosis

The primary cause of stroke among the reported 85% of cases is the existence of thrombus in cerebral infarction vessel [24]. However, due to poor techniques for early detection, only a few patients receive treatment in time, and current research efforts focus on early detection of the condition. Among other algorithms, principal component analysis and genetic fuzzy finite state have emerged to be some of the best techniques for detecting and diagnosing thrombus within the cerebral infarction. Several studies have established that data collected from wearable devices alongside SVM and Markov algorithms have attained 90.5% classification accuracy for the plausible pathological gaits for predicting the occurrence of stroke.

Some of the emerging datasets for early detection and diagnosis of stroke are neuroimages obtained from computerized tomography (CT) and magnetic resonance imaging (MRI) scans. ML algorithms such as SVM and CNN are suitable for classifying and identifying possible stroke cases based on endophenotype responses of motor disability that the patients are likely to exhibit before the stroke [25]. In some cases, Bayes classifier can be useful in classifying and identifying stroke lesions, and the results obtained from using such techniques are not comparable to those obtained by human experts. Further, patient CT scans are complex because the lesion of the thrombus is indistinguishable for carotid panel.

3.2 Treatment

Some of the emerging application of AI ML algorithms is in the field of predicting and analysing the response of the patient to administered treatment. As a basic principle, physicians have established a relationship between intravenous thrombolysis outcomes and survival rate following prognosis. In several cases, the images used as inputs in the SVM learner have shown better accuracy performance compared to traditional methods for analysing radiology results. However, it is also imperative to note that improving treatment outcomes will require the inclusion of meta-data and clinical trial data to provide an ideal background for exploring the effects of the treatment on the outcome [26, 27]. Besides relying on the relationship between intravenous thrombolysis and survival rate, AI and ML algorithms can also explore the appropriate dosage based on the traits of the patients.

3.3 Outcome Prediction and Prognosis Evaluation

Of importance is understanding and documenting the factors that affect both mortality and prognosis of stroke because that marks the beginning of using relying on improved predictive powers of the ML algorithms. Regardless of the input data deduced from patient traits and the performance of the used algorithm, it is critical and essential to understanding the factors that affect brain malformation and subsequent responses to treatment [28]. The evidence required to boost the understanding and improve the outcome of the modelling is available in the MRI and CT scan images. However, one of the emerging concerns is correcting bias between MRI, and CT scans from imbalance multiple datasets although, with appropriate techniques, different researchers have limited the effects and obtained improved classification results.

4 Discussion and Conclusion

Even though AI appears to be an independent system while considering algorithms and learning techniques, it, however, requires integration of different machine learning algorithms to enable it to handle different data structures. Despite focusing on specific data types, continued use of technologies and data collection using sensors will also exacerbate the need for AI in analysing and interpreting big data.

Furthermore, the emergence of AI systems such as IBM Watson and the capability of implementing such systems in the cloud will continue to revolutionize the application of AI in health data analytics. Notably, healthcare organizations are pursuing information systems that will make it easier to integrate AI and ML algorithms to support real-time data extraction, analysis, and interpretation. The proliferation of EHRs and other publicly available data has brought with its many privacy challenges. Further, current standards for implementing AI systems do not exist, and regulatory issues continue to derail any practical applications. Finally, most of the AI systems require training and consequent continuous of data although healthcare data are not sharable in real-time because of the necessary restrictions to ensure compliance with confidentiality, integrity and availability requirements.

References

1. Jiang, F., et al.: Artificial intelligence in healthcare: past, present and future. Stroke Vasc. Neurol. **2**(4), 230–243 (2017)
2. Hamet, P., Tremblay, J.: Artificial intelligence in medicine. Metabolism **69**, S36–S40 (2017)
3. Sikchi, S.S., Sikchi, S., Ali, M.S.: Artificial intelligence in medical diagnosis. Int. J. Appl. Eng. Res. **7**, 2012 (2012)
4. Amato, F., López, A., Peña-Méndez, E.M., Vaňhara, P., Hampl, A., Havel, J.: Artificial neural networks in medical diagnosis. J. Appl. Biomed. **11**, 47–58 (2013)
5. Hosny, A., Parmar, C., Quackenbush, J., Schwartz, L.H., Aerts, H.J.W.L.: Artificial intelligence in radiology. Nat. Rev. Cancer **18**, 500–510 (2018)
6. Jiang, J., Trundle, P., Ren, J.: Medical image analysis with artificial neural networks. Comput. Med. Imaging Graph. **34**, 617–631 (2010)
7. Ganapathy, K., Abdul, S.S., Nursetyo, A.A., et al.: Artificial intelligence in neurosciences: a clinician's perspective. Neurol. India **66**(4), 934 (2018)
8. Ravi, D., et al.: Deep learning for health informatics. IEEE J. Biomed. Health Inform. **21**, 4–21 (2017)
9. Pannu, A.: Artificial intelligence and its application in different areas. Int. J. Eng. Innov. Technol. **4**, 79–84 (2015)
10. Hashimoto, D.A., Rosman, G., Rus, D., Meireles, O.R.: Artificial intelligence in surgery. Ann. Surg. **268**, 70–76 (2018)
11. Johnson, K.W., et al.: Artificial intelligence in cardiology. J. Am. Coll. Cardiol. **71**(23), 2668–2679 (2018)
12. Jha, S., Topol, E.J.: Adapting to artificial intelligence: radiologists and pathologists as information specialists. JAMA – J. Am. Med. Assoc. **316**, 2353–2354 (2016)
13. Lu, H., Li, Y., Chen, M., Kim, H., Serikawa, S.: Brain intelligence: go beyond artificial intelligence. Mob. Netw. Appl. **23**, 368–375 (2018)
14. Miller, D.D., Brown, E.W.: Artificial intelligence in medical practice: the question to the answer? Am. J. Med. **131**, 129–133 (2018)
15. Giger, M.L.: Machine learning in medical imaging. J. Am. Coll. Radiol. **15**, 512–520 (2018)
16. Deepa, S.N., Aruna Devi, B.: A survey on artificial intelligence approaches for medical image classification. Indian J. Sci. Technol. **4**, 1583–1595 (2011)
17. Acampora, G., Cook, D.J., Rashidi, P., Vasilakos, A.V.: A survey on ambient intelligence in healthcare. Proc. IEEE **101**, 2470–2494 (2013)
18. Nemati, S., Holder, A., Razmi, F., Stanley, M.D., Clifford, G.D., Buchman, T.G.: An interpretable machine learning model for accurate prediction of sepsis in the ICU. Crit. Care Med. **46**, 547–553 (2017)
19. Liu, C., Sun, W., Chao, W., Che, W.: Convolution neural network for relation extraction. In: Motoda, H., Wu, Z., Cao, L., Zaiane, O., Yao, M., Wang, W. (eds.) ADMA 2013. LNCS (LNAI), vol. 8347, pp. 231–242. Springer, Heidelberg (2013). https://doi.org/10.1007/978-3-642-53917-6_21
20. Jin, K.H., McCann, M.T., Froustey, E., Unser, M.: Deep convolutional neural network for inverse problems in imaging. IEEE Trans. Image Process. **26**, 4509–4522 (2017)
21. Hengstler, M., Enkel, E., Duelli, S.: Applied artificial intelligence and trust-the case of autonomous vehicles and medical assistance devices. Technol. Forecast. Soc. Change **105**, 105–120 (2016)
22. Beam, A.L., Kohane, I.S.: Translating artificial intelligence into clinical care. JAMA – J. Am. Med. Assoc. **316**, 2368–2369 (2016)
23. Katan, M., Luft, A.: Global burden of stroke. Semin. Neurol. **38**, 208–211 (2018)

24. Bhatnagar, S., et al.: The Malicious Use of Artificial Intelligence: Forecasting, Prevention, and Mitigation Authors are listed in order of contribution Design Direction. CoRR (2018)
25. Pang, Y., Sun, M., Jiang, X., Li, X.: Convolution in convolution for network in network. IEEE Trans. Neural Netw. Learn. Syst. **29**, 1587–1597 (2018)
26. Davenport, T.H., Ronanki, R.: Artificial intelligence for the real world. Harv. Bus. Rev. **96**, 108–116 (2018)
27. Ibrahim, F., Thio, T.H.G., Faisal, T., Neuman, M.: The application of biomedical engineering techniques to the diagnosis and management of tropical diseases: a review. Sensors (Switzerland) **15**, 6947–6995 (2015)
28. Labovitz, D.L., Shafner, L., Reyes Gil, M., Virmani, D., Hanina, A.: Using artificial intelligence to reduce the risk of nonadherence in patients on anticoagulation therapy. Stroke **48**, 1416–1419 (2017)

Gain Scheduling Fuzzy PID Controller for Distributed Control Systems

Osama A. Awad[1]([⊠]) [iD] and Israa Laith[2] [iD]

[1] Systems Engineering Department, Information Engineering College,
Nahrain University, Baghdad, Iraq
usamaawad@coie-nahrain.edu.iq
[2] Networks Engineering Department, Information Engineering College,
Nahrain University, Baghdad, Iraq
israa@esraa.edu.iq

Abstract. The use of a communication network in the closed-loop control systems has many advantages such as remotely controlling equipment, low cost, easy to maintenance, efficient information transmission, etc. However, the Distributed or Networked Control Systems (NCS) has many drawbacks, such as network-induce end-to-end time delay and packet loss, which lead to a significant degradation in controller performance and may result in instability. Aiming at solving performance degradation in NCS, this paper propose to take the advantages and strength of the conventional Proportional-Integral-Derivative (PID), Fuzzy Logic (FL), and Gain Scheduling (GS) fundamentals to design a Fuzzy-PID like-Gain Scheduling (F-PID-GS) control technique, which has been proved to be effective in obtaining better performance. The TrueTime toolbox is used to establish the simulation model of the NCS. Ethernet as a communication network is simulated for different load conditions and random packet loss. The design approach is tested on a second-order stepper motor. The results obtained show the effectiveness of the proposed approach in improving the overall system performance.

Keywords: Fuzzy logic · Gain scheduling · Networked control system · Proportional-integral-derivative controller · TrueTime toolbox

1 Introduction

The traditional control system architecture is point-to-point control architecture, where the controller device is directly connected with the controlled system (plant). This control system scheme is no longer suitable to meet new requirements, such as modularity, decentralization of control, integrated diagnostics, quick and easy maintenance and low cost [1]. Networked Control System (NCS) is one type of distributed control system where the control loops are closed over a communication network [2]. NCS is closed loop control systems in which different devices (sensor, actuator, and controller) are connected by means of a shared communication network. NCS has become more and more common as the hardware devices for networks and network nodes have become cheaper. For many years now, general data networks are successfully applied

© Springer Nature Switzerland AG 2020
M. I. Khalaf et al. (Eds.): ACRIT 2019, CCIS 1174, pp. 262–270, 2020.
https://doi.org/10.1007/978-3-030-38752-5_21

in many industrial and military control applications [3]. The main reasons for using data networks for transmissions of control system signals (instead of using special control networks) are ease of installation, less system complexity by reducing system wiring, ease of system diagnosis and maintenance, and increased system agility [4]. NCS introduces the so-called "communication constraints" to the conventional control system, which includes the network-induced delay, packet dropout, and the synchronization issue. The delayed packets in NCS may be more harmful to system stability than packet loss [5, 6]. Besides the effect of the imperfect communication channel, which resulted in delayed control packets and degradation in the performance of overall control system, many other challenges must maintain a tradeoff between two important aspects for NCS: Quality of Service (QoS) of network and Quality of Performance (QoP) of control.

The well-known Proportional Integral Derivative (PID) controller is the most common way of using a feedback control system. PID controllers are commonly used, over 95% of the controllers in industrial applications are PID controller [7]. The Gain Scheduling (GS) concept can make the delay-independent controller, such as a PID controller, to be a delay-dependent controller by adjusting the controller parameters continuously based on the current time delay. When using GS, the time delay (the scheduling variable) values are first measured or estimated with different NCS conditions and discrete operating points, the time delay values arranged by partitioning it into certain groups, and then obtain the controller tunable gains for each group. The controller gains will be constant within each region or group.

The work in [8] proposes the use of Fuzzy Logic (FL) methodology within NCS instead of using the conventional control methodologies. The basic idea of using FL in control of systems is to use a machine on the fuzzy model for system control instead of a person, it is a computer numerical control method based on fuzzy set theory, fuzzy language variables and fuzzy reasoning. FL control belongs to a non-linear control and intelligent control, it is especially useful when the mathematical models of the controlled object are unknown or quite complex [9, 15]. The FL rules are established based on knowledge and human's experience.

The contributions of this paper are listed below:

- A new Fuzzy PID-like Gain Scheduling (F-PID-GS) controller is designed.
- The random variable delay is predicted to control signal.
- F-PID-GS controller has the capability to withstand against packet loss up to 20%.

The paper is structured as follows: in Sect. 2, the NCS platform has been introduced and explained. In Sect. 3, the fuzzy PID gain scheduling controller is presented and the structure is designed. The proposed controller has been simulated for diffenet network scenarios to control the speed of a a stepper motor via ethernet network in Sect. 4. Finally, Sect. 5 concludes the results and findings of the paper.

2 Related Work

The authors in [10] used TrueTime to investigate the plant response and to study the impacts of packets delay caused by the wireless sensor network (802.11b). The concept of packet priority was used to enhance the motor response. The experimental results show that the steady state time of the actuator is significantly raised by a wireless network, especially when the wireless channel is loaded. Moreover, they concluded that the sensor packets delay has more impact.

A study presented by [11] proposed a new Fuzzy-PID controller for Ethernet 802.3 Network Control System (NCS). The authors investigated the time delay of the conventional PID controller to design the new controller, which aims at handling the time delays in NCS. The aspects of fuzzy and gain scheduling control were utilized to measure the actual time delay in NCS. An NCS model was built to analyze the performance of the proposed controller. The experimental results show that Fuzzy-PID controller achieves impressive results with a time-varying delay.

The authors in [12] designed two controllers, which are the Sliding Mode and PID, to control the speed of a DC-motor over ZigBee network, which is an NCS-based communication network. Their study investigates the stability of the overall system by analyzing the performance for some boundaries of the problems that may occur in a specified wireless NCS. The authors used the TrueTime simulator under MATLAB to simulate various network scenarios for the two controllers by considering different ZigBee network parameters. The achieved results show that the data rate of the ZigBee network is significantly affecting the speed of the DC-motor, in which the performance of the Sliding Mode Control outperforms the performance of the PID controller in terms of the data rate change.

A work presented by [13] assessed the performance of ZigBee and Wi-Fi protocols in terms of power control scheme to help WSN planning. The work also analyzed the effect of interference in the network. The authors used the TrueTime simulation platform in their assessment. From using power control scheme, the experimental results show that Wi-Fi has high signal reach capabilities then ZigBee. Moreover, the authors observed that Wi-Fi has less effect of interference compared to ZigBee.

3 Networked Control System Platform

In order to test the designed F-PID-GS controller algorithm over a communication network, a complete NCS model should be designed. The effect of different communication network parameters and computation parameters on the control system performance could be further studied and analyzed. The used NCS platform is taken from our recent paper [14], which is built on using MATLAB and TrueTime toolbox [11]. Figure 1 shows the designed NCS model. As described in [14], the local side consists of a time-based sensor and an event-based actuator. Both sensor and actuator assumed to have a shared local memory and clock, and both connected with the plant directly by A/D and D/A input and output ports.

The remote side consists of an event-based controller connected with reference input via A/D input port and will be used to implement the designed controller algorithms. In this structure, there is no need for clock synchronization between controller and sensor nodes, which relief the network from additional packets needed for synchronization and that lead to better QoS of the network. Sensor and actuator are responsible for calculating the RTT value and send it to the controller node within the sensor packet.

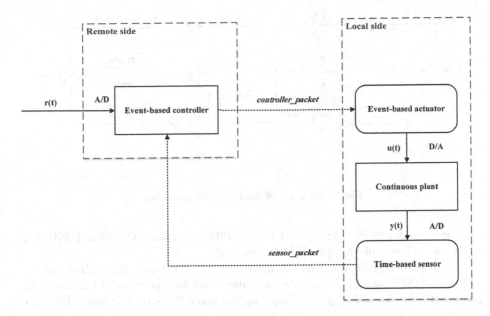

Fig. 1. The designed NCS model.

4   Fuzzy PID Gain Sceduling Controller

The proposed Fuzzy PID Gain Sceduling (F-PID-GS) controller consists of two main parts. The first part is used for adjusting the inputs and outputs of the second part by using scaling factors as multiplying gains. F-PID-GS controller is shown in Fig. 2, the first upper part will choose the appropriate scaling factors based on the time delay (RTT), and these scaling factors will be used in the second part.

The second part of the proposed controller is divided into three paths Feed forward, fuzzy PI control, and fuzzy PD control.

The scaling factors are used for mapping the inputs and the outputs values of the second part, this mapping means moving values between different sets but within their Universe of Discourse (UoD). The used scaling factors are: scaling factor of error (SFE), scaling factor of change of error (SFCE), scaling factor of the control signal (SFU), and scaling factor of change of control signal (SFCU).

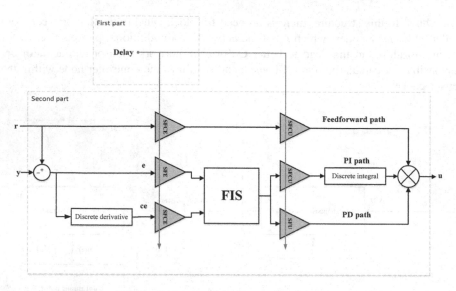

Fig. 2. Structure of the F-PID-GS controller.

The second part is a Fuzzy-PID like (F-PID) controller. The final F-PID is a nonlinear 2-Degree-of-Freedom (2-DoF) controller.

The important procedure is how to determine the FL gains (or the scaling factors): SFE, SFCE, SFU, and SFCU. They are obtained from the conventional PID controller parameters (K_p, K_i, and K_d). By comparing the expressions of PID and F-PID controllers, it is found that they are related by:

$$K_p = (\text{SFCU} \times \text{SFCE}) + (\text{SFU} \times \text{SFE}) \tag{1}$$

$$K_i = \text{SFCU} \times \text{SFE} \tag{2}$$

$$K_d = \text{SFU} \times \text{SFCE} \tag{3}$$

The designation of a fuzzy inference system consists of [12] input variables with triangular membership functions as shown in Figs. 3 and 4, and output variable with a singleton membership function as shown in Fig. 5. The fuzzy rule base for the demonstarted controller is summarized by Table 1.

5   Fuzzy PID Gain Scheduling Controller Evaluation

Ethernet network with 500 connected nodes and 10 Mbps data rate is used as the communication medium for the NCS. By applying different network traffic scenarios, as described in our previous work [11]. Controlling the speed of stepper motor as a plant case study, with the following transfer function is examined:

$$G(s) = \frac{1000}{s^2 + 3s} \qquad (4)$$

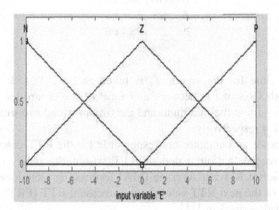

Fig. 3. The input membership function of error E.

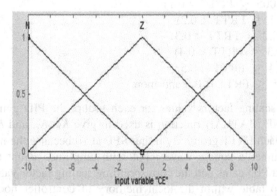

Fig. 4. The input membership function of change of error E.

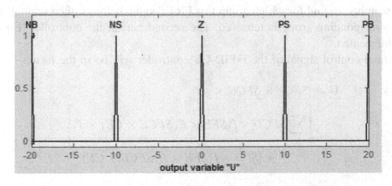

Fig. 5. Output membership function of output control signal U.

Table 1. Controller fuzzy rules

CE	E		
	N	Z	P
N	NB	NS	Z
Z	NS	Z	PS
P	Z	PS	PB

The sampling time for the sensor T_s is taken to be 0.05 s. It is chosen to be convenient for both QoS of the network and QoP of the controller. Throughout the simulation, it is found that the minimum and maximum round trip time RTT are equal to 5.615 ms, and 1 s respectively.

Because the sensor and actuator are responsible for the RTT calculation, the controller node will receive an old value of RTT within the received sensor packet. Therefore, a time series Moving Average (MA) forecasting technique will be used to give a predication of the next RTT value, or a Forecasted RTT (FRTT). The technique of using an MA is described in [11].

The FRTT values were divided equally into six groups:

1. Group one: $(0.005 \leq FRTT < 0.1)$
2. Group two: $(0.1 \leq FRTT < 0.2)$
3. Group three: $(0.2 \leq FRTT < 0.3)$
4. Group four: $(0.3 \leq FRTT < 0.4)$
5. Group five: $(0.4 \leq FRTT < 0.5)$
6. Group six: $(0.5 \leq FRTT < 0.6$ and more$)$

To obtain the scaling factors values for each group, the PID gains are calculated first. The PIDTUNE MATLAB function is used to give K_p, K_i, and K_d values for the median value for each FRTT group. By fixing SFE at 10 because the maximum error is equal to one (assumes a square wave input with amplitude equal to one). Table 2 shows the obtained PID gains and the corresponding scaling factor values. This table is stored as a lookup table within the local memory of controller node. The working procedure of F-PID-GS controller is as follow: when a sensor packet is received, the RTT value is examined and MA technique is applied to obtain the FRTT, the lookup table is searched to find for which group this FRTT value belongs, then scaling factors for the corresponding group is retrieved. The second part of the controller (F-PID) is then implemented.

The final control signal of the F-PID-GS controller will be in the form:

$$U = [SFCE \times SFCU \times r(t)]$$
$$+ \left[\sum_{t_k} SFCU \times f(SFE \times E, SFCE \times CE) \times T_s \right] \qquad (5)$$
$$+ [SFU \times f(SFE \times E, SFCE \times CE)]$$

Table 2. PID gains and corresponding scaling factors

FRTT	Parameter						
	K_p	K_i	K_d	SFE	SFCE	SFU	SFCU
0.05	19.62×10^{-3}	9.406×10^{-4}	5.172×10^{-3}	10	2.669	0.002	9.406×10^{-5}
0.15	5.712×10^{-3}	9.739×10^{-5}	1.514×10^{-3}	10	2.664	5.686×10^{-4}	9.739×10^{-6}
0.25	4.585×10^{-3}	6.048×10^{-5}	1.218×10^{-3}	10	2.666	4.569×10^{-4}	6.048×10^{-6}
0.35	3.768×10^{-3}	4.045×10^{-5}	1.068×10^{-3}	10	2.844	3.757×10^{-4}	4.046×10^{-6}
0.45	3.145×10^{-3}	2.858×10^{-5}	9.800×10^{-4}	10	3.124	3.137×10^{-4}	2.858×10^{-6}
0.55	2.746×10^{-3}	2.203×10^{-3}	9.605×10^{-4}	10	3.506	2.739×10^{-4}	2.203×10^{-6}

The response of the NCS with the F-PID-GS controller for 450 s simulation run is examined, along with control signal for unloaded Ethernet network from 0 to 150 s, medium loaded Ethernet network from 150 to 300 s and high loaded Ethernet network from 300 to 450 s. In order to check the robust stability and performance of the designed F-PID-GS controller, 10% random packet loss is applied to the communication network with the same previously obtained controller parameters. The NCS responses for these tests are shown in Fig. 6.

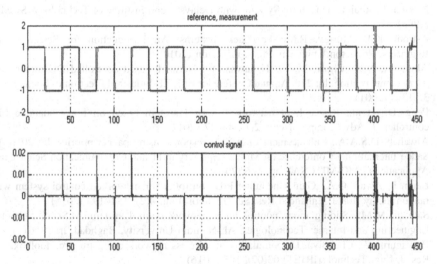

Fig. 6. The NCS response along with the control signal for different Ethernet network traffic and 10% packet loss probability using the F-PID-GS controller.

6 Conclusions

The time delay as the main issue of NCS is studied and analyzed for controlling the speed of a stepper motor system via an Ethernet network. The time delay was varied by changing the network traffic load. According to the estimated delay and the calculated actual network delay at each sample, the equivalent fuzzy control was developed based on the delay class and the best PID tuned parameters at each class was determined. The feasibility and effectiveness of the developed fuzzy PID gain scheduling control scheme had been proved. The proposed controller shows a good capability to withstand against packet loss up to 20%. The developed strategy outperforms the PID controller designed by previous work [11]. Using the same NCS model, an appropriate solution when a packet is lost will be our future work, as well as implement an F-PID-GS controller for a large-scale network.

References

1. Yang, T.C.: Networked control system: a brief survey. In: Proceedings of IEE on Control Theory and Applications, vol. 153, no. 4, pp. 403–412 (2006)
2. Chen, M.: Design and Implementation of a Networked Control System. Eastern Illinois University, United States (2005)
3. Wang, F.-Y., Liu, D.: Networked Control Systems Theory and Applications. Springer, UK (2008). https://doi.org/10.1007/978-1-84800-215-9
4. Zhang, W., Branicky, M.S., Phillips, S.M.: Stability of networked control systems. Control Syst. IEEE 21(1), 84–99 (2001)
5. Tipsuwan, Y., Chow, M.-Y.: Control methodologies in networked control systems. Control Eng. Practice 11(10), 1099–1111 (2003)
6. Nilsson, J.: Real-Time Control Systems with Delays. Lund Institute of Technology, Sweden (1998)
7. Aström, K.J., Murray, R.M.: Feedback Systems: An İntroduction for Scientists and Engineers. Princeton University Press, Princeton (2010)
8. Almutairi, N.B., Chow, M.-Y., Tipsuwan, Y.: Network-based controlled DC motor with fuzzy compensation. In: 27th Annual Conference of IEEE Industrial Electronics Society, vol. 3. IEEE (2001)
9. Peng, D., et al.: Research of networked control system based on fuzzy adaptive PID controller. J. Adv. Comput. Netw. 2(1), 44–47 (2014)
10. Alwahab, D.S.A.A.: Enhancement of WNCS response using packet priority. In: 2016 Al-Sadeq International Conference on Multidisciplinary in IT and Communication Science and Applications (AIC-MITCSA), pp. 1–6 (2016)
11. Laith, I., Awad, O.A.: Gain scheduling PID controller for networked control system with random delay. Int. J. Enhanced Res. Sci. Technol. Eng. 4(2), 184–193 (2015)
12. Salman, M.M.: Sliding mode control for a network control system. M.Sc in Networks Engineering and Internet Technologies, AL-Nahrain University, Baghdad, Iraq (2017)
13. Rajyaguru, V., Chotaliya, D.: Simulation of wireless network using truetime toolbox. Int. Res. J. Eng. Technol. (IRJET) 03(07), 1–5 (2016)
14. Cervin, A.: How does control timing affect performance analysis and simulation of timing using Jitterbug and TrueTime. IEEE Control Syst. Mag. 23(3), 16–30 (2003)
15. Awad, O.A., Maher, R.: Full parameterization process for singleton fuzzy logic controller: a computing algorithm. Int. J. Eng. Res. Technol. (IJERT) 3(6), 1057–1063 (2014)

Comparative Analysis for Arabic Sentiment Classification

Mohammed Abbas Algburi[(⊠)], Aida Mustapha[Ⓘ],
Salama A. Mostafa[Ⓘ], and Mohd. Zainuri Saringatb[Ⓘ]

Faculty of Computer Science and Information Technology,
Universiti Tun Hussein Onn Malaysia,
86400 Parit Raja, Batu Pahat, Johor, Malaysia
mu25ab@yahoo.com, {aidam, salama, zainuri}@uthm.edu.my

Abstract. Sentiment analysis categorizes human opinions, emotions and reactions extracted from text into positive or negative polarity. However, mining sentiments from the Arabic text is challenging due to the scarcity of Arabic datasets for training the context. To address this gap, this study builds an Arabic sentiment dataset sourced from tweets, product reviews, hotel reviews, movie reviews, product attraction, and restaurant reviews from different websites; manually labeled for training the sentiment analysis model. The dataset is then used in a comparative experiment with three machine learning algorithms, which are Support Vector Machine (SVM), Naïve Bayes (NB), and Decision Tree (DT) via a classification methodology. The best results for polarity prediction in sentiment analysis models was achieved by SVM with product attraction dataset, with the accuracy of 0.96, precision of 0.99, recall of 0.99, and F-measure of 0.98. This is followed by the average performance from NB and DT. It can be concluded that the ML classifiers need the right morphological features to enhance the classification accuracy when dealing with different words that play different roles in the sentence with the same letters.

Keywords: Sentiment analysis · Arabic language · Polarity · Tweets

1 Introduction

Because tweets are natural language texts in any language, research in languages other than English such as in Arabic poses a great challenge. Nowadays, the Arab World is playing an important role in the global economy and international politics, as well as grasping the attention of social and political researchers. Therefore, extracting sentiments from Arabic tweets is a beneficial process that aids politicians to predict the upcoming events according to the public comments and popular news. The Arabic language is used by over 313 million people residing mostly in the Middle East and North Africa [1] and is in the fifth rank of the widely written and spoken languages in the world, modern computational linguistic studies on the Arabic language is still limited. There is a shortage of minimal support and language resources for analyzing Arabic sentiments because of its richer morphological structure in comparison to English as an example [2]. Arabic is represented by many dialects such as Iraqi, Levantine, Moroccan

© Springer Nature Switzerland AG 2020
M. I. Khalaf et al. (Eds.): ACRIT 2019, CCIS 1174, pp. 271–285, 2020.
https://doi.org/10.1007/978-3-030-38752-5_22

and Egyptian, which makes it, requires special treatments, hence challenging. As a result, the field of Arabic NLP is attractive to researchers because of its resources scarcity and language complexity [3].

Because the Arabic language is complex in structure, performing Sentiment Analysis (SA) on Arabic tweets requires careful analysis on existing challenges arise in finding the best sentiment classification model specific for the Arabic language [4]. The first and foremost challenge is the number and limited size of datasets and Arabic corpora for SA. The corpora size has the significant role to effectively determine the accuracy of sentiment analysis and subjectivity, which poses an issue for research focusing the Arabic language. Datasets of the Arabic language are also very small in comparison to those of the English language. On top of that, such corpus is lacking in the Arabic dialects and only covers limited domains such as movie reviews [5] or news reviews [6]. Given a limited dataset, the number of Arabic lexicons available for SA is also limited. To date, there is very little sentiment lexicon for Dialect Arabic (DA) and most available lexicons for the Modern Standard Arabic (MSA) are very small in comparison to English lexicons. The effort to build the Arabic language lexicons has only started in recent years.

Next, Arabic tweets are sometimes written in Arabizi style, which is difficult to parse the Arabic language to extract the word features. This issue arises when social media users post their reviews in Latin characters (i.e. combined between English and Arabic characters), and this style of uploading posts by Latin symbols makes the recognition between English and Arabic so difficult. Finally, negation words in Arabic is another challenge. Negation means flipping the meaning of a given sentence from positive polarity to negative when using some words such as "لا" "no". For instance, the sentence "انا احب" (I like) is classified as positive whereas if a negation word comes in the previous sentence such as "انا لا احب" (I do not like) it changes the polarity to negative. Classifying the sentiment in such tweets is quite challenging.

To address the challenges in the scarcity of resources within the Arabic language context, this study investigates sentiment analysis using machine learning approach on Arabic texts. In specific, this study focuses on developing an Arabic sentiment analysis classification model using three machine learning algorithms, which are Support Vector Machine (SVM), Naïve Bayes (NB), and Decision Tree (DT). Next. this study compares the performance of Arabic sentiment classification models developed based on accuracy, precision, recall, and F-measure. The remainder of this paper is organized as follows. Section 2 presents related works in the area of Arabic sentiment classification. Section 3 presents the methodology. Section 4 presents and discusses the results. Finally, Sect. 5 concludes this paper.

2 Related Work

Many researchers worked sentiment analysis across many languages like Chinese [7], Arabic [8, 9], Turkish [10, 11] and English [12, 13]. However, sentiment analysis of the Arabic language is very few as compared to the English language. Rushdi-Salah et al. [4] built the Opinion Corpus for Arabic (OCA), which is considered the first corpus in the Arabic language. The dataset contains 500 movie reviews that were collected from various independent blogs. This dataset was used to study two classifiers, which were Naïve Bayes (NB) and Support Vector Machines (SVM) with term frequency-inverse document frequency (TF-IDF), term frequency (TF) and *n*-gram models. In this study the reviews were split into 250 positive reviews and 250 negative reviews. A trigram model of SVM classifier without stemming produced more than 90.6% accuracy while the same setting produced only 84% for NB. The research concluded that SVM is better than NB for the task and using TF or TF-IDF as weighting schemes produced no big effect.

Mountassir et al. [9] analyzed the Arabic sentiment for an unbalanced dataset by using supervised sentiment classification. Unbalanced dataset means there is a gap between the number of negative and positive reviews. The aim of this study was to evaluate the classifier performance tested with different sampling strategies in order to cater to the unbalanced dataset problem. Next, the effectiveness of the proposed methods was compared with the common random under-sampling strategy such as removing the features based on cluster, similarity, and distance. The research employed NB and SVM classifiers to test the dataset. The dataset was built from politics content that contains 1,082 comments about a political issue titled "Arab support for the Palestinian affair". The comments were sourced from Aljazeera's website and labelled manually (75.6% negative) and (24.4% positive). The highest accuracy for NB was 67% while the highest accuracy for SVM was 61%. The authors concluded that sensitivity of NB classifier was higher than sensitivity of SVM classifier towards dataset size.

A balanced and unbalanced dataset was examined by Nabil et al. [14] where a Large Arabic Books Review (LABR) dataset was developed. This is a large dataset with 63,257 instances made from reviews of 64 books in Arabic. The research divided the dataset into the unbalanced dataset and the balanced dataset (i.e. the number of reviews are equal in each three classes), and tested various popular machine learning classifiers such as the Bernoulli (BNB), Multinomial Naïve Bayes (MNB and SVM with different combinations of weighing models (TF-IDF, unigram, bigram, and trigram). MNB classifier was found to be the best classifier used in the research. However, this work only covered the book reviews domain, where the reviews have different overall polarity as compared to issues like politics.

El-Sahar and El-Beltagy [15] used a large dataset in different fields (hotels, products, films and restaurants) with over 33,000 comments. The authors proposed for building a semi-supervised sentiment lexicon as well as a multi-domain lexicon to be the dataset. In another work, Majeed et al. [6] created "AWATIF", which is a set of genre for Arabic self and sentiment Analysis. The sources of the genre were collected from discussion threads in seven web forums, Penn Arabic Treebank, and open topic on Wikipedia discussion. The dataset in this study contained sentences in Modern Standard Arabic (MSA) and this dataset is not used repeatedly in networking sites and social media.

Abdulla et al. [16] used supervised and unsupervised approaches to build a lexicon by manually annotating the corpus. The work used the same dataset (2,000 tweets) to compare various classifiers including the Decision Trees (DT), SVM, J-Nearest Neighbors (KNN) and NB with different stemming techniques methods, whether with root stemming, light stemming or no stemming applied at all. The best accuracy was from NB and SVM classifiers with light stemming technique. The study also found that the accuracy obtained was lower than the accuracy of the corpus-based approach.

Sentiment analysis of the Arabic language was conducted at the sentence level by Shoukry and Rafea [17]. The research used NB and SVM machine learning classifiers, where they trained 1,000 tweets on this classifier with some features (bigram and unigram). The results showed that the performance of NB classifier is lower than the SVM classifier and using bigram or unigram features did not contribute to any major difference in the results.

Farra et al. [18] collected the level of the sentence with the document level for text in the Arabic language, whereby the output of sentence-level classification is served as the input to document-level classification. In sentence-level, the authors applied the lexicon-based approach with the SVM classifier. The accuracy achieved was only around 89%. Figure 1 summarizes selected related work of sentiment analysis in Arabic language along with their dataset, model, and evaluation metrics.

3   Methodology

This study adopts the classification methodology for Arabic sentiment analysis. In general, a classification methodology consists of three main stages as shown in Fig. 1, which are pre-processing the dataset, extracting the features from the dataset, and training the model for the later classification task.

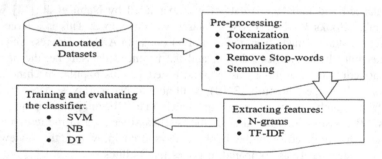

Fig. 1. Classification methodology for Arabic sentiment analysis.

Python programming language is used to build the sentiment analysis models since Python has a perfect ability to handle natural languages very well and more specifically strings. The language also supports Natural Language Processing (NLP) libraries as needed in this study.

3.1   Annotation of Dataset

The Arabic datasets used in developing the Arabic sentiment analysis models are sourced from Twitter using Twitter API (Application Programming Interface). The rest datasets were collected from different repositories but were unannotated, for example, Product Reviews and Product Attraction Reviews were gathered from the well-known "amazon.ae". Restaurant Reviews were collected from "qaym.com". Hotel Reviews were collected from "TripAdvisor.com". And finally, Movie Reviews were collected from "elcinema.com". This stage involves annotating the dataset as positive or negative sentiment and deletes some tweets and reviews that did not have sentiment.

The collected and annotated datasets include more than 36,000 sentences regarding tweets, product reviews, restaurant reviews, hotel reviews, and movie reviews. Features extraction for the sentiments from the text was carried out using various NLP libraries under Python platform. Meanwhile, the negation problem in the Arabic language was handled using the n-gram method.

3.2 Pre-processing

Pre-processing is applied after obtaining the data from the source in order to decrease errors, increase accuracy and remove noisy features. The operations that are carried out include tokenization, normalization (i.e. removing diacritics such as ́, ̣, ̃), stop-word removal, and stemming (i.e. removing Arabic prefixes and suffixes) using the Natural Language Toolkit (NLTK) from the Information Science Research Institute (ISRI).

Tokenization. Tokenization is the standard pre-processing step of many natural language processing tasks that can divide a sentence of written language into sequence words separated by white spaces to produce meaningful elements called tokens. It is also called segmentation especially Arabic processing field. There are a number of tokenization functions offered by Natural Language Toolkit (NLTK) libraries, for the purpose of dividing the sentences to words the researcher used word tokenize in this dissertation. NLTK platform deals with human language information by building Python programs and providing a package of libraries for the task of text processing such as stemming, tokenization and classification with an easy to use interface.

Normalization. Normalizing the data-set means to remove un-necessary symbols and letters from the dataset examples. It is necessary for the Arabic language since there are many diacritics in Arabic. Normalization replaces similar letters with only one of other letters and deletes the symbols from the sentences such as deleting diacritics or short vowels from the string such as (́, ̣, ̃) and deleting Tatweel (elongation) for example "جـــــيد" to "جيد" which means "good".

Stop-words Removal. Stop-words are usually referring to popular words in the language texts. These words are removed from dataset since the authors are the majority of the words and will reduce the presence of unique and important words. For obtaining a good accuracy and high, must remove the stop-words from the dataset. When removing stop-words, the sentence sentiment should not be affected. Arabic contains many stop words such as (هو,عن, حتى, لما, عليه,هذا, من).

Stemming. To stem a word means reducing it to its root. This will remove all suffixes and prefixes from the word, reduce the variations between words and reduce them to unified words. Stemming process minimize the effect of the shape and the pattern difference of the Arabic words. In addition, it decreases the required size of storing the words in indexes. Stemming works to collect all words that have some semantic relations and it shares the same origin in a mathematical way. Depending on the root or origin Arabic stemming algorithms are classified according to analysis level required [59]. This research used Python's NLTK ISRI (The Information Science Research Institute's) Arabic stemmer, which is non-root dictionary that depends on affix removal method.

A clear and unambiguous structure of a dataset is able to help the performance accuracy in the machine learning model. It also discovers inconsistent casing of letters, unnecessary punctuation, stop words and emoticons because the authors are noisy when be analyzed.

3.3   Feature Extraction

For the purpose of generating the feature vectors, two different feature extraction methods are used in the experiment, which is the language models unigram and bigram. The position of any term in the representation of a single dataset is significant since this term position detects and sometimes flips the phrase polarity. N-gram method is used to tackle the negation problem with the Arabic language because negation in Arabic is used to reverse the polarity of the word (i.e. "ما", "لم", "لا") as well as the location of these particles at the beginning of the sentence. For example, "هو لم يعجبه مشاهدة هذا الفلم" means "He did not love watching this film". The verb "love" is classified as a positive feeling but the word "did not" changed polarity of the sentence from positive to negative.

Next, the Term Frequency-Inverse Document Frequency (TF-IDF) is used to scale every feature (term, Unigram or Bigram) in the vector. The TF-IDF provides statistical information that measures the significance of a word in a dataset or a set of datasets. The value of the TF-IDF is incremented proportionally to the frequency count of a particular word particular in the dataset, and it is often repeated in the dataset. The TF-IDF score for a certain term is calculated by Eqs. 1 to 3.

$$TF(i,j) = \frac{F(i,j)}{N(j)} \tag{1}$$

where $N(i,j)$ represents the frequency of term i in the dataset j and $N(j)$ represents the total number of terms in the dataset j

$$IDF(i) = log\frac{N}{N(i)} \tag{2}$$

Where N represents the total number of datasets and $N(i)$ represents the total number of datasets contain the term i

$$TF - IDF(i,j) = TF(i,j) * IDF(i) \tag{3}$$

3.4   Algorithms

Experimentations are conducted on datasets of the current study by recruiting three machine learning classifiers, which are Support Vector Machines (SVM), Naïve Bayes (NB), and Decision Trees (DT). The literature has shown that these algorithms have proven to give high accuracy results [9, 17–33].

- **Support Vector Machines (SVM).** SVM is a type of supervised learning algorithm that works by defining a separating hyperplane or set of hyperplanes. The output of this algorithm is an optimal hyperplane that maximizes the separation distance between the two positive and negative hyperplanes used to categorize new examples when used with labeled training data. A perfect separation is when the hyperplane contains the largest distance to the closest training data points of any class, with the minimum magnitude of the vector $|w|$. The formula is shown in Eq. 4 where w is a weight vector, x is input vector, and b is the bias.

$$\min|w| = y_i(w \cdot x_i + b) \geq 1; \ i = 1; \ldots, N \tag{4}$$

- **Naïve Bayes (NB).** Naïve Bayes can be defined as a conditional probability model. And this algorithm is appropriate when inputs dimensions are high. The Naïve Bayes algorithm is used in medical diagnosis, spam filters and texts analysis. The Naïve Bayes algorithm is characterized independent, simple, useful for large datasets and easy used. The formula is shown in Eq. 5 where $p(C|x)$ is the posterior probability of the target class C, given the set of attributes x. Next, $p(C)$ is the prior probability of the class and $p(x|C)$ is the likelihood which is the probability of predictor given class.

$$p(C|x) = \frac{p(C)p(x|C)}{p(x)} \tag{5}$$

- **Decision Tree (DT).** Decision Tree (DT) is a supervised learning algorithm that is used to solve many classification and regression problems. The basis of its work is to construct a tree diagram that contains classification models and then divide the dataset into a smaller partial dataset and then develop the tree of decisions in gradual stages. The output of this algorithm is a tree, leaf nodes and the decision nodes. After then, using a given scale of information the tree is developed, where this needs to use the maximum extent of information when the two main leaves are equal in the number. In deciding which feature to split on at each step in building the tree, information gain is calculated as shown in Eq. 6 whereby J represents the classes and p are the items.

$$IG(p) = 1 - \sum_{i=1}^{J} p_i^2 \tag{6}$$

3.5 Evaluation Metrics

Next, the performance of these classification algorithms is measured based on the developed dataset. After training the model with some data, the testing process takes place with the remaining data. The evaluation metrics used in the experiments are accuracy, precision, recall, and F-measure as presented in the following equations.

- **Accuracy.** Accuracy is measured as the percentage of a total number of samples correctly classified by an algorithm divided by the total number of samples from the training data. The formula for calculating the accuracy is shown in Eq. 7.

$$\text{Accuracy (A)} = \frac{(\text{TP} + \text{TN})}{(\text{TP} + \text{TN} + \text{FP} + \text{FN})} \tag{7}$$

  where TP represents the count of true positives, TN represents the count of the true negatives, FN represents the count of false positives and FN represents the count of false negatives.

- **Precision.** Precision is the percentage of correct and calculated as in Eq. 8 based on the definition in Eq. 7.

$$\text{Precision (P)} = \frac{\text{TP}}{(\text{TP} + \text{FP})} \tag{8}$$

- **Recall.** Recall or Sensitivity is additionally alluded as true positive (TP) rate, for example, the extent of positive tuples that are accurately recognized as shown in Eq. 9. TP and FN follow the definition in Eq. 7.

$$\text{Recall (R)} = \frac{\text{TP}}{(\text{TP} + \text{FN})} \tag{9}$$

- **F-Measure:** F-Measure also called F-Score that measures the balance between the precision and the recall. The calculation for F-Measure as in Eq. 10.

$$F - \text{Measure} = \frac{2 * (\text{Recall} * \text{Precision})}{(\text{Recall} + \text{Precision})} \tag{10}$$

4 Results and Discussion

This section presents the distribution of negative and positive polarity among the samples as well as the performance of the three classifiers under study, which are Support Vector Machines (SVM), Naïve Bayes (NB), and Decision Trees (DT).

4.1 Analysis of Positive and Negative Polarity

Similar to software repositories that contain textual requirements and bug reports, social media datasets such as tweets and reviews are made of non-structured, textual content that is rich in semantic information. In this regards, mining techniques should treat text as software and address the results based on efficiency of their performance. Figure 2 shows the number of positive and negative polarity in sentences of each dataset.

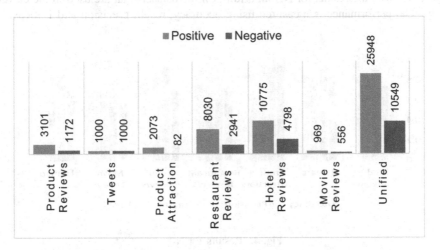

Fig. 2. The number of positive and negative samples.

4.2 Results for Support Vector Machines

Figure 3 shows results at the sentence level classification by applying SVM algorithm on the six datasets. The performance is measured using accuracy, precision, recall, and F-measure.

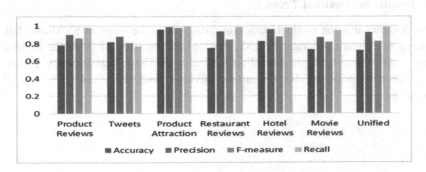

Fig. 3. Results for SVM.

The best results achieved by SVM was for product attraction dataset with an accuracy of 0.96, precision of 0.99, F-measure of 0.99 and recall of 0.99. The least accuracy was unified with 0.72, the least precision was the movie reviews dataset with 0.87, the least F-measure and recall were the tweets with 0.81 and 0.77 respectively.

4.3   Results for Naïve Bayes

Figure 4 shows the results for NB algorithm on the datasets that are used in the current study. The performance is measured using accuracy, recall, precision and F-measure.

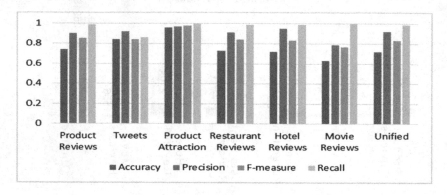

Fig. 4. Results for NB.

Similar to SVM, the best results achieved by NB are for product attraction dataset, the accuracy is 0.96, the precision is 0.97, the F-measure is 0.98 and the recall is 1.00. On the other hand, the least accuracy belongs to the movie review with 0.63, the least precision belongs to the movie reviews dataset with 0.79, the least F-measure also belongs to the movie reviews dataset with 0.77 and recall belongs to tweets with 0.86.

4.4   Results for Decision Trees

Figure 5 shows that the product attraction dataset is as the same as SVM and NB by obtaining the highest accuracy of 0.82, the highest precision of 0.88, the highest F-measure of 0.87 and the highest recall of 0.87 as well. The lowest accuracy, precision, F-measure and recall are for the movie reviews with 0.7, 0.74, 0.73 and 0.75 respectively.

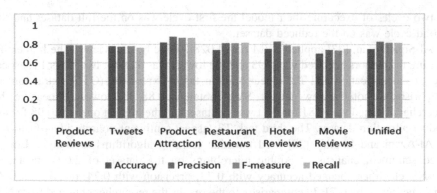

Fig. 5. Results for DT.

Table 1 shows a summary of the highest evaluation metrics obtains from the proposed model.

Table 1. Summary of the highest evaluation metrics.

Algorithm	Accuracy	Precision	Recall	F-Measure
SVM	0.96	0.99	0.99	0.99
NB	0.96	0.97	1.00	0.98
DT	0.82	0.88	0.87	0.87

4.5 Discussions

The results acquired in the experiments were found comparable with results from recent researches. For instance, the highest accuracy the researcher acquired when applied both SVM and NB was 0.96 and the highest of DT was 0.82 for the product attraction dataset. On the other hand, the lowest accuracy SVM obtained was 0.72 for the unified dataset, lowest accuracies NB and DT obtained were 0.63 and 0.7 respectively for the movie review dataset. In comparison, Elnagar et al. [25] acquired 0.91 as the highest accuracy with SVM (lower than the proposed work) on BRAD 2.0, which, claimed to be the largest Arabic book review (about 693,000), expressing dialectal and modern standard Arabic. Whereas 0.87 and 0.83 were the highest accuracy the authors obtained when applying NB (lower than the results of the current study) and DT (a bit higher than the results of the current study) respectively. The lowest accuracies acquired were 0.88 for the SVM classifier, 0.84 for the NB classifier and 0.82 for the DT classifier (all three higher than the results of the current study). The authors executed machine learning algorithms in two rounds, the first was with applying TF-IDF and the second was without.

Al-Radaideh and Al-Qudah [26] applied SVM, NB and DT on 4,800 Arabic tweets, the best accuracies the obtained were 0.65, 0.59 and 0.57, which are lower than the results from the proposed work. While the lowest were 0.6, 0.57 and 0.52, respectively, for two cycles of executing their model the first cycle was on the full dataset and the second cycle was on the reduced dataset.

Al-Smadi et al. [27] applied SVM on 24,028 Arabic hotel reviews. The highest F-measure the authors acquired was 0.93 and the lowest was 0.89 for two tasks T1: aspect category identification and T2: aspect opinion target expression (OTE) extraction. In comparison to hotel review dataset, SVM obtained 0.88, the lowest F-measure the researcher obtained was 0.81 for the tweets dataset and the highest one was 0.98 for the product attraction dataset. The third task T3: aspect sentiment polarity identification.

Al-Azani and El-Alfy [28] used machine learning algorithms to analyze Emoji-based sentiment analysis of Arabic microblogs on the dataset of 2,091 instances. The NB classifier obtained accuracy with 0.73, precision with 0.74, recall with 0.73 and F-measure with 0.71. In comparison to the results the researcher obtained from NB, the highest and lowest accuracy were 0.96 and 0.72, the highest and lowest precision were 0.97 and 0.79, the highest and lowest recall were 1.00 and 0.86 and the highest and lowest F-measure were 0.98 and 0.77. The DT classifier, on the other hand, acquired accuracy with 0.71, precision with 0.72, recall with 0.71 and F-measure with 0.69. In comparison to the results the researcher obtained from DT, the highest and lowest accuracy were 0.82 and 0.7, the highest and lowest precision were 0.88 and 0.74, the highest and lowest recall were 0.87 and 0.75 and the highest and lowest F-measure were 0.87 and 0.73. The authors stated that these results were abstained without applying feature selection process.

Elhag et al. [29] discussed and evaluated the NB and DT algorithms on a multi-data set for Dialect Arabic (DA), Modern Standard Arabic (MSA) and English are taken from Facebook and other platforms such as blogs. The highest accuracy the authors acquired from applying NB was 0.89 on MSA whereas the lowest was 0.5 on DA. In comparison to the results the researcher obtained from NB classifier, the highest accuracy was 0.96 and the lowest was 0.72. On the other hand, the highest accuracy the authors acquired from applying DT was 0.97 on MSA whereas the lowest was 0.54 on DA. In comparison to the results the researcher obtained from DT, the highest accuracy was 0.82 and the lowest was 0.7.

Alharbi and Khan [30] conducted a study to identify the comparative opinion in Arabic texts on YouTube comments using machine learning techniques. Their experiment comprised four runs for the NB classifier on two datasets: the original vs. the cleaned dataset. The highest accuracy the authors obtained was 0.81 (lower than the highest ratio in the current study) and lowest one was 0.8 (higher than the lowest ratio in current study). The highest precision was 0.74 (lower than the highest ratio in current study) and the lowest was 0.73 (lower than the lowest ratio in current study). The highest F-measure the authors obtained was 0.8 (lower than the highest ratio in current study) and lowest one was 0.78 (higher than the lowest ratio in current study). And finally the highest recall was 0.87 (lower than the highest ratio in current study) and the lowest was 0.84 (lower than the lowest ratio in current study).

[31] studied the impact of pre-processing and ensemble learning on about 40,000 sentences of tweets, movies, hotels, restaurants and products reviews. the authors executed their machine learning model twice: one to study the effect of n-grams and removing stop words and the other to study the effect of the stemming process. The highest accuracy SVM obtained was 0.88 (lower than the highest ratio in current study)

and lowest one was 0.8 (higher than the lowest ratio in current study), the highest precision was 0.89 (lower than the highest ratio in current study) and the lowest precision was 0.8 (lower than the lowest ratio in current study), the highest F-measure was 0.88 (lower than the highest ratio in current study) and the lowest F-measure was 0.8 (lower than the lowest ratio in current study), and finally the highest recall of SVM was 0.86 (lower than the highest ratio in current study) and lowest one was 0.81 (higher than the lowest ratio in current study). On the other hand, The highest accuracy NB obtained was 0.78 (lower than the highest ratio in current study) and lowest one was 0.52 (lower than the lowest ratio in current study), the highest precision was 0.8 (lower than the highest ratio in current study) and the lowest precision was 0.65 (lower than the lowest ratio in current study), the highest F-measure was 0.78 (lower than the highest ratio in current study) and the lowest F-measure was 0.65 (lower than the lowest ratio in current study), and finally the highest recall of NB was 0.76 (lower than the highest ratio in current study) and lowest one was 0.66 (lower than the lowest ratio in current study).

Alnawas and Arici [31] experimented sentiments analysis of Iraqi Arabic dialect by applying SVM, NB and DT on attraction, hotel, restaurant, movie, product and book reviews. The best precision of their SVM was 0.82 and the smallest was 0.77 (both lower than the results of the current study), the best F-measure was 0.78 and the smallest was 0.57 (both lower than the results of the current study) and the best recall was 0.79 and the smallest was 0.68 (both lower than the results of the current study). The best precision of their NB was 0.71 and the smallest was 0.64 (both lower than the results of the current study), the best F-measure was 0.65 and the smallest was 0.54 (both lower than the results of the current study) and the best recall was 0.66 and the smallest was 0.59 (both lower than the results of the current study). The best precision of their DT was 0.66 and the smallest was 0.85 (both lower than the results of the current study), the best F-measure was 0.65 and the smallest was 0.57 (both lower than the results of the current study) and the best recall was 0.65 and the smallest was 0.58 (both lower than the results of the current study).

5 Conclusion

This study was set to evaluate the performance of three Machine Learning (ML) algorithms; Support Vector Machine (SVM), Naïve Bayes (NB), and Decision Tree (DT) in classifying the sentiment polarity for a new Arabic sentiment dataset. The evaluation was carried out based on four evaluation metrics, which was accuracy, precision, recall, and F-measure. The obtained results showed that SVM and NB classifiers produced very high results while DT only achieved reasonable results. This is due to the complexities of some words that led to a weaker tree structure. From the observation, it can be concluded that the ML classifiers require a correct set of morphological features in order to help algorithm to classify different words that play different roles in the sentence with the same letters. This suggests that in general, a sentiment classifier should consider a robust feature extraction module that can cater to specific language such as the Arabic so the classifiers can perform better regardless the nature of the dataset.

Acknowledgments. This work is supported by Universiti Tun Hussein Onn Malaysia.

References

1. A macrolanguage of Saudi Arabia, ISO 639-3. https://www.ethnologue.com/language/ara. Accessed 21 Oct 2018
2. Alhumoud, S.O., Altuwaijri, M.I., Albuhairi, T.M., Alohaideb, W.M.: Survey on Arabic sentiment analysis in Twitter. Int. Sci. Index **9**(1), 364–368 (2015)
3. Alotaibi, S.S.: Sentiment analysis in the Arabic language using machine learning (Doctoral dissertation, Colorado State University. Libraries) (2015)
4. Al-Twairesh, N., Al-Khalifa, H., Al-Salman, A.: Subjectivity and sentiment analysis of Arabic: trends and challenges. In: 2014 IEEE/ACS 11th International Conference on Computer Systems and Applications (AICCSA), pp. 148–155. IEEE (2014)
5. Rushdi-Saleh, M., Martín-Valdivia, M.T., Ureña-López, L.A., Perea-Ortega, J.M.: OCA: opinion corpus for Arabic. J. Am. Soc. Inf. Sci. Technol. **62**(10), 2045–2054 (2011)
6. Abdul-Majeed, M., Diab, M.T.: AWATIF: a multi-genre corpus for modern standard arabic subjectivity and sentiment analysis. In: LREC, pp. 3907–3914 (2012)
7. Pan, L.: Sentiment analysis in Chinese. (Doctoral dissertation, Brandeis University) (2012)
8. Siddiqui, S., Monem, A.A., Shaalan, K.: Sentiment analysis in Arabic. In: Métais, E., Meziane, F., Saraee, M., Sugumaran, V., Vadera, S. (eds.) NLDB 2016. LNCS, vol. 9612, pp. 409–414. Springer, Cham (2016). https://doi.org/10.1007/978-3-319-41754-7_41
9. Mountassir, A., Benbrahim, H., Berrada, I.: Some methods to address the problem of unbalanced sentiment classification in an Arabic context. In: 2012 Colloquium in Information Science and Technology, pp. 43–48. IEEE (2012)
10. Akba, F., Uçan, A., Sezer, E., Sever, H.: Assessment of feature selection metrics for sentiment analyses: Turkish movie reviews. In: 8th European Conference on Data Mining (2014)
11. Kaya, M.: Sentiment analysis of Turkish political columns with transfer learning. (Doctoral dissertation, Middle East Technical University) (2013)
12. Daiyan, Md., Tiwari, S., Kumar, M., Alam, M.A.: A literature review on opinion mining and sentiment analysis. Int. J. Emerg. Technol. Adv. Eng. **5**(1), 262–280 (2015)
13. Kharde, V., Sonawane, P.: Sentiment analysis of Twitter data: a survey of techniques. arXiv preprint arXiv:1601.06971 (2016)
14. Nabil, M., Aly, M.A., Atiya, A.F.: LABR: A large scale Arabic book reviews dataset, CoRR, abs/1411.6718 (2014)
15. ElSahar, H., El-Beltagy, S.R.: Building large Arabic multi-domain resources for sentiment analysis. In: Gelbukh, A. (ed.) CICLing 2015. LNCS, vol. 9042, pp. 23–34. Springer, Cham (2015). https://doi.org/10.1007/978-3-319-18117-2_2
16. Abdulla, N.A., Ahmed, N.A., Shehab, M.A., Al-Ayyoub, M.: Arabic sentiment analysis: Lexicon-based and corpus-based. In: 2013 IEEE Jordan Conference on Applied Electrical Engineering and Computing Technologies (AEECT), pp. 1–6. IEEE (2013)
17. Shoukry, A., Rafea, A.: Sentence-level Arabic sentiment analysis. In: 2012 International Conference on Collaboration Technologies and Systems (CTS), pp. 546–550. IEEE (2012)
18. Farra, N., Challita, E., Assi, R.A., Hajj, H.: Sentence-level and document-level sentiment mining for Arabic texts. In: 2010 IEEE International Conference on Data Mining Workshops, pp. 1114–1119. IEEE (2010)

19. Neethu, M.S., Rajasree, R.: Sentiment analysis in Twitter using machine learning techniques. In: 2013 Fourth International Conference on Computing, Communications and Networking Technologies (ICCCNT), pp. 1–5. IEEE (2013)
20. Dhanalakshmi, V., Bino, D., Saravanan, A.M.: Opinion mining from student feedback data using supervised learning algorithms. In: 2016 3rd MEC International Conference on Big Data and Smart City (ICBDSC), pp. 1–5. IEEE (2016)
21. Altrabsheh, N., Gaber, M., Cocea, M.: SA-E: sentiment analysis for education. In: International Conference on Intelligent Decision Technologies, vol. 255, pp. 353–362 (2013)
22. Le, B., Nguyen, H.: Twitter sentiment analysis using machine learning techniques. In: Le Thi, H.A., Nguyen, N.T., Do, T.V. (eds.) Advanced Computational Methods for Knowledge Engineering. AISC, vol. 358, pp. 279–289. Springer, Cham (2015). https://doi.org/10.1007/978-3-319-17996-4_25
23. Zhang, L., Ghosh, R., Dekhil, M., Hsu, M., Liu, B.: Combining lexicon-based and learning-based methods for Twitter sentiment analysis. Technical report, HP Laboratories (2011)
24. Elnagar, A., Lulu, L., Einea, O.: An annotated huge dataset for standard and colloquial arabic reviews for subjective sentiment analysis. Procedia Comput. Sci. **142**, 182–189 (2018)
25. Appel, O., Chiclana, F., Carter, J., Fujita, H.: A hybrid approach to the sentiment analysis problem at the sentence level. Knowl.-Based Syst. **108**, 110–124 (2016)
26. Gautam, G., Yadav, D.: Sentiment analysis of Twitter data using machine learning approaches and semantic analysis. In: 2014 Seventh International Conference on Contemporary Computing (IC3), pp. 437–442. IEEE (2014)
27. Al-Smadi, M., Qawasmeh, O., Al-Ayyoub, M., Jararweh, Y., Gupta, B.: Deep Recurrent neural network vs. support vector machine for aspect-based sentiment analysis of Arabic hotels' reviews. J. Comput. Sci. **27**, 386–393 (2018)
28. Al-Azani, S., El-Alfy, E.S.M.: Emoji-based sentiment analysis of Arabic microblogs using machine learning. In: 2018 21st Saudi Computer Society National Computer Conference (NCC), pp. 1–6. IEEE, April 2018
29. Elhag, M.E.M., Shah, N.A.K., Balakrishnan, V., Abdelaziz, A.: Sentiment analysis algorithms: evaluation performance of the Arabic and English language. In: 2018 International Conference on Computer, Control, Electrical, and Electronics Engineering (ICCCEEE), pp. 1–5. IEEE, August 2018
30. Alharbi, F.R., Khan, M.B.: Identifying comparative opinions in Arabic text in social media using machine learning techniques. SN Appl. Sci. **1**(3), 213 (2019)
31. Alnawas, A., Arici, N.: Sentiment analysis of iraqi Arabic dialect on Facebook based on distributed representations of documents. ACM Trans. Asian Low-Resource Lang. Inf. Process. (TALLIP) **18**(3), 20 (2019)
32. Mohammed, M.A., Gunasekaran, S.S., Mostafa, S.A., Mustafa, A., Ghani, M.K.A.: Implementing an agent-based multi-natural language anti-spam model. In: 2018 International Symposium on Agent, Multi-Agent Systems and Robotics (ISAMSR), pp. 1–5. IEEE, August 2018
33. Mohammed, M.A., et al.: An anti-spam detection model for emails of multi-natural language. J. Southwest Jiaotong Univ. **54**(3) (2019)

Political Articles Categorization Based on Different Naïve Bayes Models

Dhafar Hamed Abd[1,2]([⊠]) [iD], Ahmed T. Sadiq[1]([⊠]) [iD],
and Ayad R. Abbas[1]([⊠]) [iD]

[1] Department of Computer Science, University of Technology, Baghdad, Iraq
Dhafar.dhafar@gmail.com, Drahmaed_tark@yahoo.com,
ayad_cs@yahoo.com
[2] Department of Computer Science, Al-Maarif University College, Alanbar, Iraq

Abstract. Sentiment analysis plays an important role in most of human activities and has a significant impact on our behaviours. With the development and use of web technology, there is a huge amount of data that represents users opinions in many areas such as politics and business. This paper applied Naïve Bayes (NB) to analyse the opinions by exploring categories from a text and classified it to the right class (Reform, Conservative and Revolutionary). It investigates the effect of using two feature extraction i.e. Term Frequency (TF) and Term Frequency-Inverse Document Frequency (TF-IDF) methods with Naïve Bayes classifiers (Gaussian, Multinomial, Complement and Bernoulli) on the accuracy of classifying Arabic articles. Precision, recall, F1-score and number of correct predict have been used to evaluate the performance of the applied classifiers. The results reveal that, using TF with TF-IDF improved the accuracy to 96.77%. The Complement was deemed the most suitable for our model.

Keywords: Naïve Bayes · Gaussian · Multinomial · Complement · Bernoulli · Political articles · Term Frequency · Term Frequency – Inverse Document Frequency · Sentiment analysis

1 Introduction

In the past few years, there has been an increase in the use of web resources like online review sites, social networking sites, personal blogs, etc., which have allowed the users to present or share their opinions, ideas and comments regarding different issues. It is important to collect and analyse these comments in actual situations. For instance, any customer wishes to know the opinions of other users before he buys a service or product. Similarly, a company wants to determine the customer's opinion and review to improve and adapt their product according to his requirements. In a political domain, a political party aims to predict the trends and orientation of the voters.

Since the 2000s, many researchers have used sentiment classification as a text classification tool, as there has been an increase in the number of subjective texts in social media, blogs, forums etc. [1]. A few researchers used different terms for the

© Springer Nature Switzerland AG 2020
M. I. Khalaf et al. (Eds.): ACRIT 2019, CCIS 1174, pp. 286–301, 2020.
https://doi.org/10.1007/978-3-030-38752-5_23

sentiment classification like subjectivity analysis, sentiment analysis, opinion mining, review mining, and opinion extraction [2].

Sentiment analysis plays a great role in many areas like education, e-commerce, and opinion polls [3]. The company determines the customer reviews and monitors the social media to determine the opinion regarding their services and products and take appropriate actions on time. A few researchers stated that the stock values and the sentiment analysis of the social media were correlated and the future stock price can be predicted using the sentiments from microblogs like Twitter [4].

The sentiment lexicon includes a few phrases and words that express negative or positive sentiments. However, using the sentiment lexicon for the sentiment classification is insufficient because of the opposite orientation of words in various domains. Further information regarding the issues related to the use of sentiment lexicon has been discussed by Liu [2]. Many machine-learning techniques are used for sentiment classification (called the corpus-based approach).

Studies stated that machine learning performed better than lexicon-based techniques, due to the flexibility using, easy handling of the parameter and high accuracy [5]. In the case of a machine learning-based process, the text is initially assessed as a bag of words, then, it is transformed into multiple features. Thereafter machine learning processes like the Naive Bayes (NB) are used for classification [1]. Sentiment analysis consists of three levels, document level, Sentence level and aspect level [2]. This study focus on document level, in order to determine categories and classify it in sentiment analysis.

NB is a supervised learning algorithm, which assumes that all features are independent and equally relevant. It is popularly used for document classification. Two common models are used for categorising the text without any generality, i.e., multinomial and multi-variate Bernoulli model. Even if the features were not independent, the NB algorithm is still effectively used for various machine learning issues. In comparison to many complicated machine learning algorithms, NB was seen to be a simple algorithm which was based on the probabilistic theory [5].

The reminder of this paper is organized as follows. Previous works will be discussed in Sect. 2. Section 3 illustrates the model architecture. The evaluation metric introduces in Sect. 4, followed by the presentation of our approach results in Sect. 5. Finally, Sect. 6 discuss our conclusions and future works.

2 Naive Bayes with Arabic Articles

Sentiment analysis (or opinion mining) refers to a type of text classification which extracts and determines the categories. We have determined the effect of stemming on the opinion classification of the Arabic texts. They tried to find the best representation of an Arabic text for sentiment classification. Earlier studies compared the Arabic texts for text classification [6, 7] or sentiment analysis [8].

Most of the studies that used sentiment analysis and opinion mining were carried out in the English language. Very few studies were conducted for the Arabic texts because of an absence of the free lexical resources and the complex nature of the automatic analysis in the Arabic language.

Duwairy [9] analysed various aspects which affected the classification performance (feature selection, text representation, and selection of a proper algorithm). We used two datasets: dataset 1 dealt with political issues and included 300 reviews while dataset 2 included OCA movie information [10]. For categorising the tasks, they used three algorithms (NB, SVM, and K-nearest neighbour). Results showed that the classification performance was based on the pre-processing method and the corpus used.

Irrespective of the method that has been used for Arabic Sentiment analysis, It is still important to rely on a reliable and confidential dataset for testing. In the past, very few datasets were available for Arabic Sentiment analysis. One of the earlier datasets included the Opinion Corpus for Arabic (OCA) dataset, published in 2011. Efforts needed for collecting, annotating and experimenting on the OCA dataset have been discussed earlier [6, 10]. This OCA dataset was a small dataset and was restricted to dialects (MSA), domains (movie reviews), and the polarity classes (either positive or negative) that it encompasses. Along with the OCA dataset, the AWATIF dataset [7] has also been used.

Mageed and Diab (2012) have discussed the effort needed for generating the data for the AWATIF, which considered the various aspects from the linguistics perspective and how the annotators' knowledge regarding these aspects affects their decision. Earlier studies have considered the aspects of the comments/reviews and authors. For instance, in a few studies [8, 11], the researchers collected the comments from the Yahoo!-Maktoob websites and analysed the domains of all comments, dialects used in these comments along with the gender of the person who wrote the comments, etc. Finally, the LABR dataset was developed in 2013, It was one of the biggest datasets used for the Arabic SA. In their study, [12] they collected numerous book reviews which were written in various Arabic dialects. This dataset was unique because the annotations used in the dataset were based on the authors who reviewed them (rather than relying on the external annotators). Thus, whenever a review was written, the author was requested to rank the book using a ranking scale, ranging between 1 and 5.

A study [13] described two approaches which conducted sentiment analysis in the tweets. The researchers compiled a novel dataset with 2000 tweets for research purposes. Here, the researchers compared 2 major approaches, i.e., the lexical and machine learning algorithms. The lexicon used in the study included 3479 words (1262 positive and 2217 negative). With regards to the machine learning process, the researchers used 4 classifiers (SVM, NB, KNN and DT).

3 Naïve Bayes Classification Algorithm

In this study, We used a model that was based on the conditional probability, described in Eq. (1).

$$P(c|d) = \frac{P(d|c)}{P(d)}, \; P(d) > 0$$

$$P(c|d) = \frac{P(d|c)P(c)}{P(d)}$$

(1)

where in d refers to the document that has to be classified, and c denotes the document class [14].

Practically, it was seen that $P(d)$ did not show a significant effect, hence, it was eliminated. We developed the Bays rule, as described in Eq. (2).

$$P(c|d) = p(d|c)P(c) \tag{2}$$

For every document, they calculated the features or words in the document [15], using the equation described below:

$$P(c|d) = P(x_1, x_2, x_3, \ldots, x_n|c)P(c) \tag{3-1}$$

$$P(x_1, x_2, x_3, \ldots, x_n|c) = P(x_1|c).p(x_2|c).p(x_3|c)\ldots P(x_n|c).p(c) \tag{3-2}$$

where; d = features from x_1 to x_n in the document. For calculating every word in a vector in the document, We used Eq. (3-2). In classification, the NB classifier combined the proposed model with the popular Maximum A Posteriori (MAP) decision rule. This rule selected the most probable hypothesis. The corresponding Bayes classifier refers to the function which assigned a label class, y = c, to Eq. (4) below.

$$y = P(c_k) \prod_{i=1}^{n} P(x_i|c_k) \tag{4}$$

where in y = final class noted for the test that was compared to the test label of the data. We used Eq. (4) for determining the maximum or minimum y based on the NB used. They also calculated the values for $P(c_k)$ and $P(x_i|c_k)$ using the two below-mentioned formulae as $P(c_k)$ was same for all NB types where in the value of $P(x_i|c_k)$ differed between the algorithms, based on the classifier used.

$$P(c_k) = \frac{documentP(c = c_k)}{N_{doc}} \tag{5}$$

$$P(x_i|c_k) = \frac{count(x_i|c_k)}{\sum_{x \in v} count(x|c_k)} \tag{6}$$

The major disadvantage of the NB was that if there is no occurrence of the class label and a specific attribute value, then, the frequency-based probability value would be 0. We used the Laplace smoothing technique by adding 1 for resolving this issue Eq. (7) below.

$$P(x_i|c_k) = \frac{count(x_i|c_k) + 1}{\sum_{x \in v} count(x|c_k) + 1} \tag{7}$$

Four types of NB have been used in this study, as described with the next sections [16].

3.1 Gaussian Naïve Bayes

In Gaussian NB classifier [17], the value of the numeric attributes were normally distributed. This distribution was represented with regards to the mean and standard deviation which will helps in computing the probability of the observed values using the estimates. The probability of the features was calculated as:

$$P(x_i|c) = \frac{1}{\sqrt{2\pi\sigma_c^2}} \exp\left(-\frac{(x_i - \mu_c)^2}{2\sigma_c^2}\right) \tag{8}$$

where μ = mean and σ = standard deviation. Equation (4) was used. The continuous data is handled by discretising the attribute values using the binning technique.

3.2 Multinomial Naïve Bayes

The multinomial NB classifier captured the word frequency of the information present in the documents. It was suited for discrete feature classification; since the multinomial distribution required the integer features [18].

$$P(x_i|c_k) = \frac{n!}{\prod_{i=1}^{|V|} x_i!} \prod_{i=1}^{|V|} P(x_i|c_k)^{x_i} \tag{9}$$

$$P(x_i|c_k) = \prod_{i=1}^{|V|} P(x_i|c_k)^{x_i}$$

where V = no. of features. In the model, normalization of $\frac{n!}{\prod_{i=1}^{|V|} x_i!}$ it was independent of class k [19]. Hence, $P(x_i|c_k)$ was calculated using Eq. (7) after adding the V parameter [18, 20]. Laplace equation was used for preventing the 0- frequency issue.

$$P(x_i|c_k) = \frac{count(x_i|c_k) + 1}{\left(\sum_{x\in v} count(x|c_k)\right) + |V|} \tag{10}$$

where V = the vocabulary in all classes of the training data set.

3.3 Complement Naïve Bayes

In the Complement Normal NB technique, instead of calculating the probability of the word that occurred in the class, the probability of its occurrence in other classes was determined [21]. Thus, the word-class dependencies $P(x_i|c_k')$ for other classes were estimated. We determined the minimum value of y and c_k' for the reverse class that was selected.

$$y = P(c_k) \prod_{i=1}^{n} \frac{1}{P(x_i|c_k')} \tag{11}$$

We look for a minimum value of y and c_k' the class of the reverse class we choose.

3.4   Bernoulli Naive Bayes Model

The Bernoulli NB classifier assumed that the features were binary and require only 2 values. The Bernoulli distribution equation was described below [22]:

$$P(x) = P^x(1-P)^{1-x} \tag{12}$$

Where x was the Bernoulli distribution, with a value ranging between 0 and 1. If it was 0, failure occurred while it was successful if it was 1. Based on the below equation, it was seen that [23]:

$$P(x=1) = P^1(1-P)^{1-1} = p$$
$$P(x=0) = P^0(1-P)^{1-0} = (1-p) \tag{13}$$

The likelihood of the word not occurring in the class document was $(1 - p(x_i|c))$ where x was a word in the document [24]. Thus, the below equation was:

$$P(x_i|c) = P(x_i|c)b_i + (1-b_i)(1-p(x_i|c)) \tag{14}$$

This product can be used for all the words. If the word, x_i was present in the document, then, $b_i = 1$ and the likelihood was $P(x_i|c)$. If the word x_i was absent, then $b_i = 0$ and the probability was $(1 - p(x_i|c))$. Thus, Eq. (4) was used to determine y. Table 1 shows the difference of the features with the previous studies.

Table 1. Comparison of the various types of Naïve Bayes

Deal	Gaussian	Multinomial	Complement	Bernoulli
Dataset	Continues	Occurrence Counts	Imbalanced data sets	Discrete
Document presentation	Numerical features	Word count	Word count	Binary
Decision rule: maximize or minimize	Maximize	Maximize	Minimize	Maximize
Concept	Gaussian Distribution	Multinomial distribution	Multinomial distribution	Bernoulli distribution
Zero effect	No	Yes	Yes	Yes
Document length	Big document	Longer document	Longer document	Best with short documents
Binarize	No	No	No	Yes

4   The Corpus

In this paper 206 corpus were used, the raw data collected from various sources like social networks, website blogs and newspapers. This dataset included 3 labels that covered topics like politics. Table 2 describes this dataset.

In Table 2 we tried to encode the Arabic labels to English to shorten the size of document name.

Table 2. Dataset used in the study.

Document number	Label of document	Encode label
80	Reform party	S
58	Conservative party	M
68	Revolutionary party	T

5 Evaluation Metric

In this section, the same validation method for determining the classifier percentages are used. This paper used dataset which had an approximately similar size and class distribution. For every fold, the classifier was trained with the help of the percentage value of that class. Table 2 presents the three classes used in the study.

According to the confusion matrix, several measurements could be used for examining the performance of the model [25, 26] with regards to the accuracy, which was determined and described in Table 3. The recall was used for determining the accuracy of every class known. Precision was also inaccurately classified using the equation below. This helped in calculating the F1 scores.

In Table 3, the accuracy is usually determined by using the confusion matrix. Here, the confusion matrix was dependent on the choice of the datasets. This study used the contingency table for improving performance and accuracy.

Table 3. Metric equations

Metric name	Equation
Accuracy	$\dfrac{TP + TN}{TP + TN + FP + FN}$
Recall	$\dfrac{TP}{TP + FN}$
Precision	$\dfrac{TP}{TP + FP}$
F1-score	$2 * \dfrac{Recall * Precesion}{Recall + Precesion}$

6 Proposed Approach

This study is attempted to determine the best representation of Arabic texts. We also investigated the effect of the feature extraction method on the classification performance (i.e., increasing, decreasing or maintaining the accuracy).

The methodology used for classifying the orientation of Arabic texts (i.e., text models, datasets or classifiers used, etc.). Three approaches were used for understanding the sentiment classification, machine learning processes, lexical and hybrid approaches that were derived after combining the earlier techniques. This study used the machine learning techniques which needed a labelled corpus for training and testing their classifier.

The NB classifier was a popular method that was used for classifying the texts. This algorithm was a probabilistic model which used the Bayes' theorem in the decision rule of the classifier. NB assumed that the value of a specific feature was not dependent on the values of other features, hence, it was called naïve. This algorithm estimated the posterior likelihood that the document belonged to another class and classified it to another class with the maximum posterior probability. Figure 1 showed the model for this study.

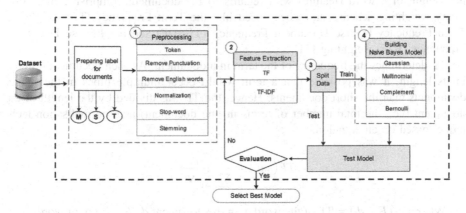

Fig. 1. Model used in the study.

6.1 Pre-processing

Each dataset have to be pre-processed in order to clean and prepare the text for further classification. The online texts generally contain a lot of noise and uninformative data like scripts, HTML tags or advertisements, which hinders the extraction of words. Furthermore, the presence of special Arabic characters or punctuation marks is also not accurately determined. Additionally, numerous words in the Arabic text show no effect on the orientation of the text. By keeping these words, the classification becomes more difficult as every word was treated as a single dimension. The classification process includes many steps.

Step 1 includes normalisation [27] which removes the diacritics from the words and converts the same word without any diacriticsas (ӧ,ӧ,ӧ,ǫ,ӧ,~,ӧ,ǫ,ӧ). This step removes all *harakat* from the Arabic language. Thereafter, the character (——) in the Arabic language, called (tatwill) was altered, for instance, (ﺔ——ﺳﻴﺎ,"politics") to (ﺳﻴﺎﺳﻪ,"politics"). Also, some alphabets are converted to other, where (ﺍ, ﺁ, ﺃ, ﺇ) became (ﺍ), (ﻯ) became (ﻱ); and (ﺉ,ﺅ) became (ﺀ) or (ﺓ) became (ﻩ). In the normalisation process, We removed 2 ≤ alphabetic words.

In step 2, the stop words function helps in the filtration and elimination of the unwanted Arabic words or tokens, by matching them with the list of stop words in

NLTK library. The final step is known as stemming. Stemming [28] was an important pre-processing step that was used for sentiment analysis and Natural Language Processing (NLP). The light stemmer removes the prefixes and the suffixes from all words. Stemming reduces every word to its stem form and decreases the size of the corpus data to a smaller dimensional space. Two major types: root stemming and light stemming are used for Arabic stemming [29], the Light stem was used in this study [30].

6.2   Feature Extraction

In the next step, the features were extracted from the documents. Here, We calculated the weight of a word (feature) with regards to the document comprising the word. Many weighting schemes have been used like the Term Frequency (TF) weighting, Term Frequency-Inverse Document Frequency (TF-IDF) and the Inverse Document Frequency (IDF) weighting [31].

TF determines the frequency of the term in a document. As each document differed in its length, it was possible that a term would occur multiple times in the longer documents than the short documents. Hence, the TF was divided by the length of the document (i.e., the total number of terms in one document) as a normalisation technique, based on an equation.

$$TF(t, d_i) = \frac{N_{t,i}}{\sum_{k=1}^{|T|} N_{k,i}} \qquad (15)$$

Wherein; $TF(t, d_i)$ = TF of the word, t, in the document d_i; $N_{t,i}$ = no. of words, t, in the document, d_i and $N_{k,i}$ = no. of all the words in the document, d_i.

TF-IDF is a popular technique that helped in classifying and retrieving information from the texts, it combined the two earlier methods of TD and IDF [32]. Mathematically, TFIDF was the product of the TF and IDF values. It also helped in determining the significance of the word in the text within the collection.

$$IDF = \log\left(\frac{N}{df}\right) \qquad (16)$$

where; N = no. of documents; df = no. of documents with the term. TF-IDF is very advanced and offers the best result since it detects the word in the same document or corpus. Thus, the TF-IDF was calculated using the below equation:

$$w(t, d_i) = TF(t, d_i) * IDF \qquad (17)$$

Where $w(t, d_i)$ = weight of the term, t, in the document, d_i.

This technique helped in decreasing the weight of all features appearing in numerous documents that were selected for feature selection for decreasing the vector size and then subjected to machine learning processes [33].

6.3 Split Data

Here, the data was split for training and testing purposes based on the percentage value used for splitting the document. For training, the splitting value was 70%, i.e., 144 documents, and for testing, it was 30%, i.e., 62 documents, as shown in Table 4.

Table 4. Split data for training and testing

Documents label	Training number documents	Testing number documents
S	55	25
M	43	15
T	46	22
Total	**144**	**62**

6.4 Building Naïve Bayes Model

In this study we developed a model for each NB type. The process includes building four models with the TF feature extraction. Every model was tested and the results were derived to select the best model with the feature extraction. Thereafter, we developed the TF-IDF model with four types of NB models, every model evaluated and then the results compared for TF and TF-IDF to determine the best model that could be used.

NB providing training sets of documents as attributes $(x_1, x_2, x_3,..., x_n)$ and the class for the documents $(y_1, y_2, y_3, ..., y_m)$ where $x_i \in inputfeatures$ and feature become as (x_n, y_m). Is described in Algorithm 1 [34].

Algorithm 1: Naïve Bayes

1 **Input:**
2 $T = \{(x_i, y_i) | x_i \in n, y_i \in m, \ i \in \{1,2,...,N\}\}$ – the set of N training samples and class;
3 $Z = \{z_i | \ z_i \in m, i \in \{1,2,...,t\}$
4
5 $\}$ – the set of t test samples;
6 **Initialization:**
7      $Y \leftarrow \emptyset$
8   Read the traning T
9   Calculate the parameter for predict class
9 **Computation:**
10 **for** $z_i \in Z$ **do**
11      $p_c \leftarrow$ calculate document class by equation 5;
12      $P_x \leftarrow$ calculate the likelihood for each class depend on model (Gaussian, Multinomial, Complement or Bernoulli);
13      $y \leftarrow$ the label predicted by applying p_c and p_x on z_i;
14      $Y \leftarrow Y \cup \{y;$
15 **Output:**
16 $Y = \{y_i | \ y_i \in m, i \in \{1,2,...,l\}\}$ - the set of predicted labels for the test samples in Z.

---

7 Results

The simulation results in this study applied machine learning algorithms. Various parameters have been used with NB, as shown in Table 5 and then the confusion matrix for determining accuracy is used. Two experiments are implemented in this work, the first one used TF with four NBs and the second one used TF-IDF. TF and TF-IDF is applied and derived 7602 features. The vector space included 206 documents and 7602 features.

Table 5. Parameters used for NB

Parameters	Value	Details
Alpha	1	Using Laplace for smoothing parameter
Fit prior	True	Whether to learn class prior probabilities
Class prior	None	Prior probabilities of the classes
Binarize	0	The threshold for binarizing of sample features used by Bernoulli
Norm	False	The second normalization of the weights is performed by complement
Var smoothing	1e − 9	Gaussian model in practice find, if the ratio of data variance between words is too small, it will cause numerical error. To address this problem, we artificially boost the variance

The confusion matrix was used for determining accuracy. The TF results for various NB techniques were noted. The experimental results are promising and showed that the proposed technique was better than other techniques. The evaluation results have been summarised below. The results also showed that complement was more accurate compared to other models. Table 6 presents the number of correct prediction values for all the NB models in TF.

Table 6. TF with different NBs.

NB	Label	Precision	Recall	F1-score	No. of correct predict	Avg accuracy
Multinomial	M	0.82	0.93	0.87	14	93.54%
	S	0.96	0.92	0.94	23	
	T	1	0.95	0.98	21	
Bernoulli	M	0.41	1	0.58	15	64.51%
	S	1	0.52	0.68	13	
	T	1	0.55	0.71	12	
Complement	M	0.93	0.93	0.93	14	**96.77%**
	S	0.96	0.96	0.96	24	
	T	1	1	1	22	
Gaussian	M	1	0.47	0.64	7	82.25%
	S	0.71	1	0.83	25	
	T	0.95	0.86	0.90	19	

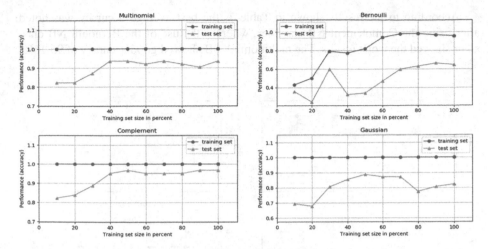

Fig. 2. Training and testing our model accuracy

Figure 2 presents the training and the testing curve. It can be seen that the Complement model was the best as the training and testing curves showed some space.

Figure 2 showed curve lines of training and testing. From the figure we can notice that when the two curves start a high-value and end with nearly the same value the accuracy achieve best accuracy.

Hence, algorithms (Multinomial, Complement and Gaussian) achieved excellent accuracy result at the training rather than Bernoulli which achieved the worst accuracy among them. All these cases were tested using TF case. When TF-IDF is applied on the machine learning techniques the results showed a relative change where we notice improvement for Multinomial and Gaussian model achieved less accuracy from 82.25% to 80.64% as described in Table 7 below.

Table 7. TF-IDF with different Naïve Bayes

NB	Label	Precision	Recall	F1-score	No. of correct predict	Avg accuracy
Multinomial	M	1	0.93	0.97	14	95.16%
	S	0.89	1	0.94	25	
	T	1	0.91	0.95	20	
Bernoulli	M	0.41	1	0.58	15	64.51%
	S	1	0.52	0.68	13	
	T	1	0.55	0.71	12	
Complement	M	0.93	0.93	0.93	14	**96.77%**
	S	0.96	0.96	0.96	24	
	T	1	1	1	22	
Gaussian	M	1	0.47	0.64	7	80.64%
	S	0.75	0.96	0.84	24	
	T	0.85	0.86	0.84	19	

According to the results shown in Table 7, the best average accuracy was noted after using the Complement NB classifier, whereas the use of the Bernoulli NB classifier showed the worst results. The multinomial NB showed good accuracy of 95.16%.

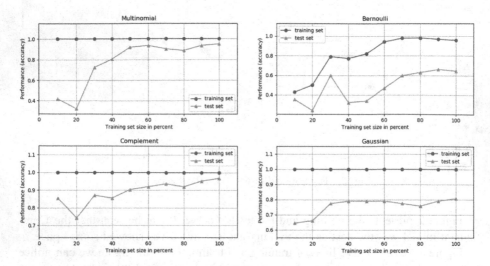

Fig. 3. Training and testing for improving our model accuracy.

Figure 3 described the relative changes occured after applying TF-IDF, we can observe that the algorithms (Multinominal, Complement) achieved better average accuracy than Gaussian and Bernoulli (Fig. 4).

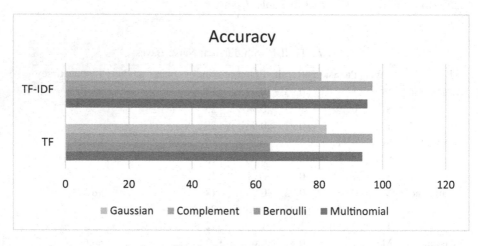

Fig. 4. Model accuracy rate

We used TF for extracting the features using four NB types. It was clear that the complement NB showed best results. The other technique used for extracting the data included the TF-IDF method, where the complement NB showed the best accuracy values. Bernoulli NB method showed the same value, irrespective of the method applied, whereas the multinomial NB showed a better value for TF-IDF than TF. Opposite results were noted, when the Gaussian NB was applied. Experimental results showed that the complement NB presented the best results when the TF-IDF method was applied.

8   Conclusion and Future Work

In this study, we focusing on analyzing the political Arabic texts with the help of four NB techniques. 206 articles collected from the newspapers, social networks and blogs for sentiment analysis. They carried out the sentiment analysis using the base paper method with the help of Naïve Bayes classifiers. four steps were used for sentiment analysis, i.e., pre-processing, feature extraction, split data and finally, classification. Here, We used four Naïve Bayes techniques for data classification. The complement Naïve Bayes classifier showed the maximal accuracy of $\approx 96.77\%$. As future works, we plan to extend this research by comparing the NB feature selection method tested in this paper with other feature selection techniques such as Information Gain, principle component analysis (PCA). Moreover, we intend to study other problems related to the opinion mining area, such as negation, sarcasm.

References

1. Xia, R., Zong, C., Li, S.: Ensemble of feature sets and classification algorithms for sentiment classification. Inf. Sci. **181**(6), 1138–1152 (2011)
2. Liu, B.: Sentiment analysis and opinion mining. Synth. Lect. Hum. Lang. Technol. **5**(1), 1–167 (2012)
3. Quan, C., Ren, F.: Unsupervised product feature extraction for feature-oriented opinion determination. Inf. Sci. **272**, 16–28 (2014)
4. Smailović, J., Grčar, M., Lavrač, N., Žnidaršič, M.: Stream-based active learning for sentiment analysis in the financial domain. Inf. Sci. **285**, 181–203 (2014)
5. Catal, C., Sevim, U., Diri, B.: Practical development of an Eclipse-based software fault prediction tool using Naive Bayes algorithm. Expert Syst. Appl. **38**(3), 2347–2353 (2011)
6. Rushdi-Saleh, M., Martín-Valdivia, M.T., Ureña-López, L.A., Perea-Ortega, J.M.: Bilingual experiments with an Arabic-English corpus for opinion mining. In: Proceedings of the International Conference Recent Advances in Natural Language Processing, pp. 740–745 (2011)
7. Abdul-Mageed, M., Diab, M.T.: AWATIF: a multi-genre corpus for modern standard Arabic subjectivity and sentiment analysis. In: LREC, vol. 515, pp. 3907–3914. Citeseer (2012)
8. Abdulla, N., Mohammed, S., Al-Ayyoub, M., Al-Kabi, M.: Automatic lexicon construction for Arabic sentiment analysis. In: 2014 International Conference on Future Internet of Things and Cloud, pp. 547–552. IEEE (2014)

9. Duwairi, R., El-Orfali, M.: A study of the effects of preprocessing strategies on sentiment analysis for Arabic text. J. Inf. Sci. **40**(4), 501–513 (2014)
10. Rushdi-Saleh, M., Martín-Valdivia, M.T., Ureña-López, L.A., Perea-Ortega, J.M.: OCA: opinion corpus for Arabic. J. Am. Soc. Inf. Sci. Technol. **62**(10), 2045–2054 (2011)
11. Abdulla, N.A., Al-Ayyoub, M., Al-Kabi, M.N.: An extended analytical study of arabic sentiments. Int. J. Big Data Intell. **1**(1–2), 103–113 (2014)
12. Aly, M., Atiya, A.: Labr: a large scale Arabic book reviews dataset. In: Proceedings of the 51st Annual Meeting of the Association for Computational Linguistics (Volume 2: Short Papers), vol. 2, pp. 494–498 (2013)
13. Abdulla, N.A., Ahmed, N.A., Shehab, M.A., Al-Ayyoub, M.: Arabic sentiment analysis: Lexicon-based and corpus-based. In: 2013 IEEE Jordan Conference on Applied Electrical Engineering and Computing Technologies (AEECT), pp. 1–6. IEEE (2013)
14. Zhang, D.: Bayesian classification. Fundamentals of Image Data Mining. TCS, pp. 161–178. Springer, Cham (2019). https://doi.org/10.1007/978-3-030-17989-2_7
15. Raschka, S.: Naive Bayes and text classification i-introduction and theory, arXiv preprint arXiv:1410.5329 (2014)
16. Geetha, S., Maniyosai, R.: An improved Naive Bayes classifier on imbalanced attributes. Int. J. Organ. Collect. Intell. (IJOCI) **9**(2), 1–15 (2019)
17. Xu, S.: Bayesian Naïve Bayes classifiers to text classification. J. Inf. Sci. **44**(1), 48–59 (2018)
18. McCallum, A., Nigam, K.: A comparison of event models for Naive Bayes text classification. In: AAAI-98 Workshop on Learning for Text Categorization, vol. 752, no. 1, pp. 41–48. Citeseer (1998)
19. Sharma, N., Singh, M.: Modifying Naive Bayes classifier for multinomial text classification. In: 2016 International Conference on Recent Advances and Innovations in Engineering (ICRAIE), pp. 1–7. IEEE (2016)
20. Rennie, J.D., Shih, L., Teevan, J., Karger, D.R.: Tackling the poor assumptions of Naive Bayes text classifiers. In: Proceedings of the 20th International Conference on Machine Learning (ICML 2003), pp. 616–623 (2003)
21. Anagaw, A., Chang, Y.-L.: A new complement naïve Bayesian approach for biomedical data classification. J. Ambient Intell. Hum. Comput. **10**, 3889–3897 (2018)
22. Chen, J., Huang, H., Tian, S., Qu, Y.: Feature selection for text classification with Naïve Bayes. Expert Syst. Appl. **36**(3), 5432–5435 (2009)
23. Tang, B., Kay, S., He, H.: Toward optimal feature selection in naive Bayes for text categorization. IEEE Trans. Knowl. Data Eng. **28**(9), 2508–2521 (2016)
24. Shimodaira, H.: Text classification using naive Bayes. Learn. Data Note **7**, 1–9 (2014)
25. Abd, D.H., Alwan, J.K., Ibrahim, M., Naeem, M.B.: The utilisation of machine learning approaches for medical data classification and personal care system management for sickle cell disease. In: Annual Conference on New Trends in Information & Communications Technology (2017)
26. Khalaf, M., et al.: Recurrent neural network architectures for analysing biomedical data sets. In: 2017 10th International Conference on Developments in eSystems Engineering (DeSE), pp. 232–237. IEEE (2017)
27. Oussous, A., Lahcen, A.A., Belfkih, S.: Impact of text pre-processing and ensemble learning on Arabic sentiment analysis. In: Proceedings of the 2nd International Conference on Networking, Information Systems & Security, p. 65. ACM (2019)
28. Mustafa, M., Eldeen, A.S., Bani-Ahmad, S., Elfaki, A.O.: A comparative survey on Arabic stemming: approaches and challenges. Intell. Inf. Manag. **9**(02), 39 (2017)

29. Abooraig, R., Al-Zu'bi, S., Kanan, T., Hawashin, B., Al Ayoub, M., Hmeidi, I.: Automatic categorization of Arabic articles based on their political orientation. Digit. Invest. **25**, 24–41 (2018)
30. Taghva, K., Elkhoury, R., Coombs, J.: Arabic stemming without a root dictionary. In: International Conference on Information Technology: Coding and Computing (ITCC 2005)-Volume II, vol. 1, pp. 152–157. IEEE (2005)
31. Abd, D.H., Sadiq, A.T., Abbas, A.R.: A New framework for Automatic Extraction Polarity and Target of Articles (2019)
32. Aggarwal, C.C., Zhai, C.: A survey of text classification algorithms. In: Aggarwal, C., Zhai C. (eds.) Mining Text Data, pp. 163–222. Springer, Heidelberg (2012). https://doi.org/10.1007/978-1-4614-3223-4_6
33. Alowaidi, S., Saleh, M., Abulnaja, O.: Semantic sentiment analysis of Arabic texts. Int. J. Adv. Comput. Sci. Appl. **8**(2), 256–262 (2017)
34. Khalaf, M., et al.: An application of using support vector machine based on classification technique for predicting medical data sets. In: Huang, D.S., Jo, K.H., Huang, Z.K. (eds.) ICIC 2019. LNCS, vol. 11644, pp. 580–591. Springer, Heidelberg (2019). https://doi.org/10.1007/978-3-030-26969-2_55

Single Runway Aircraft Landing Scheduling Using Simulated Annealing and Exact Timing Method

Abdulrahman Jassam[1] , Omar Salim Abdullah[1,2]([✉]) ,
Salwani Abdullah[2] , and Atheer Bassel[3]

[1] Faculty of Science, Diyala University, Baqubah, Diyala, Iraq
abidl974js@gmail.com, omarsalim@siswa.ukm.edu.my
[2] Faculty of Information Science and Technology,
National University of Malaysia, Bangi, Malaysia
salwani@ukm.edu.my
[3] Computer Center, University of Al-Anbar, Ramadi, Iraq
atheerbassel@yahoo.com

Abstract. One of the most challenging optimization problems in air traffic control is minimizing the deviation of aircraft arrival times from its target landing time. This can be achieved by efficiently allocating landing times and runways to the arriving aircraft. This problem is called the Aircraft Landing Problem (ALP). To address the ALP, this paper proposes a new approach which combines the Simulated Annealing (SA) algorithm with an exact timing method. The problem is solved in two stages: first, the optimal sequence is generated using the SA; in the second stage, the optimal landing time is determined using the exact timing method. The proposed approach is tested with 500 aircraft and a single runway using a well-known benchmark dataset from the scientific literature. The obtained results demonstrated the ability of the proposed approach to generate promising and competitive results.

Keywords: Aircraft Landing Problem · Exact timing method · Simulated Annealing

1 Introduction

Air transportation has become a cardinal aspect of human society in the last few decades. As such, the number of passengers traveling by air has increased significantly. This makes the scheduling of departure and landing operations in airports more complicated. For this reason, researchers in the field of scheduling optimization have invested much time and effort towards devising flexible and robust scheduling methods that can effectively schedule aircraft departure and landing times. The problem of generating the best schedule for aircraft seeking to land at the airport is called the Aircraft Landing Problem (ALP). ALP can be static (offline) or dynamic (online). In the former, the aircraft's information is available and there is no change in the problem environment during the time pass. In dynamic ALP, the information of the aircraft may change as time passes and aircraft may be added or removed from the schedule.

© Springer Nature Switzerland AG 2020
M. I. Khalaf et al. (Eds.): ACRIT 2019, CCIS 1174, pp. 302–311, 2020.
https://doi.org/10.1007/978-3-030-38752-5_24

Each aircraft is allotted a preferred landing time when it departs the source airport. This landing time may change at the destination airport whenever a number of aircraft seek to land at the same time. This change in landing time leads to a penalty cost which is proportional to the amount of deviation from the preferred landing time. In addition to the landing time, there exists a separation time (i.e., safety time) required between any pair of successive aircraft to avoid the occurrence of a clash when aircraft are landing. These factors make the ALP an NP-hard problem. As such, it is one of the most complicated optimization problems that require robust scheduling methods to generate the best scheduling times. In this regard, this paper proposes a new approach which combines the Simulated Annealing (SA) algorithm with an exact timing method to solve this ALP.

2 Related Works

Several optimization methods have been examined in the literature for solving the ALP. Researchers have considered both benchmark datasets and datasets collected from airports (called real-life datasets). The proposal in this paper is tested using OR-Library dataset which is the most popular dataset considered in the literature. In this section, we highlight a number of relevant researches works that have also studied the ALP using the OR-Library dataset.

In the year 2000, [1] introduced a mixed-integer zero-one formulation for solving the ALP in a scenario with 50 aircraft and 4 runways. They also presented a heuristic algorithm and showed all computational results. [2] introduced the scatter search and bionomic algorithms for solving the ALP in a scenario with multiple runways. They tested the proposed heuristic techniques on 500 aircraft and 5 runways. Along the same line, [3] proposed a hybrid of the Genetic Algorithm (GA) and Ant Colony (AC) algorithm for ALP. The authors treated the ALP as a job shop scheduling problem. They tested the proposed approach on 50 aircraft and 4 runways. Also, [4] introduced a hybrid of GA and Cellular Automation for ALP. The GA was used to improve the result obtained by Cellular Automation. The proposed approach was tested on 500 aircraft and a single runway.

On the same subject, [5] proposed a hybrid of Tabu Search (TS) algorithm and GA. The proposed algorithms were tested using 500 aircraft and 5 runways. [6] introduced Differential Evolution (DE) and a simple descent algorithm to solve multiple runway ALP. The simple descent algorithm was deployed to accelerate the performance of the differential evolution algorithm. The proposed hybrid algorithm was tested on 500 aircraft and 5 runways. Also, [7] proposed the use of Iterated Local Search (ILS) algorithm with multiple perturbation operators for multiple runway ALP. The multiple perturbation operators were used to modify the generated solutions. These operators assist ILS to escape from the local optimum solution. The proposed approach was tested on 500 aircraft and 5 runways. [8] introduced a hybrid Particle Swarm Optimization (PSO) algorithm to solve multiple runway ALP using 500 aircraft and 5 runways. The results were compared with two algorithms from the literature. A premiere effort by [9] proposed Harmony Search (HS) algorithm for multiple runway ALP using 500 aircraft and 5 runways.

3 Problem Description

ALP is a combinatorial optimization problem that requires the determination of optimal landing times while considering the number of runways and aircraft arrivals. Similar to [1], we define the ALP as follows:

- Each aircraft is strictly assigned to one runway.
- Not more than one aircraft should be assigned the same landing time on the same runway.
- Each aircraft should be assigned a landing time which has a predefined landing time window.
- The separation time between the aircraft that have been assigned to land on the same runway should be respected.

In ALP, there is a set of arrival aircraft. Each aircraft has its predetermined target landing time that must be within a specific time window. The time window begins with the earliest landing time and ends with the latest landing time. If an aircraft lands before or after its target landing time, a penalty is incurred. The objective of using these metaheuristic techniques is to minimize the total penalty incurred by advanced or delayed aircraft. This is achieved by generating an efficient solution that schedules landing times for given runways. Next, we describe the ALP formulation in this paper.

3.1 Notations and Meanings

n number of the arrival aircraft.
m number of runways.
s_{ij} separation time $(sij > 0)$ between aircraft i and j.
T_i preferred landing time (target time) of aircraft i.
E_i earliest landing time of aircraft i.
L_i latest landing time of aircraft i.
$C1_i$ incurred penalty per unit of time for the late landing of aircraft i.
$C2_i$ incurred penalty per unit of time for the early landing of aircraft i.

3.2 Decision Variables

x_i: assigned landing time of aircraft i $(i = 1, 2 \ldots n)$.
y_{ij}: equals 1 if aircraft i is assigned to land before aircraft j. Else, it equals 0.
y_{ir}: equals 1 if aircraft i is scheduled to land on a runway r $(r = 1, 2, \ldots m)$. Else, it takes 0.
a_i: tardiness of landing when an aircraft i scheduled to land after the target time, $ai = \max(0, x_i - T_i)$.
b_i: earliness of landing when an aircraft i is scheduled to land before the target time, $b_i = \max(0, T_i - x_i)$.

3.3 Objective Function

The objective of this work is to minimize the total deviation time from the target landing time. Therefore, the objective function is formulated as shown in Eq. (1).

$$\text{Min} f = \Sigma(a_i C1 + b_i C2) n_i = 1 \tag{1}$$

3.4 Constraints

1- Time window: to ensure that the assigned landing time is within the earliest and latest landing times,

$$E_i \leq x_i \leq L_i \qquad i = (1,..n) \tag{2}$$

2- Separation time: to ensure that there is at least s_{ij} time between the aircraft i and aircraft j,

$$(x_j - x_i) \geq s_{ij} \tag{3}$$

3- To ensure aircraft i lands before aircraft j or the reverse case,

$$y_{ij} + y_{ji} = 1 \qquad i, j = 1, 2 \ldots n \quad i \neq j \tag{4}$$

4 The Proposed Method

In this section, the proposed algorithm and the landing time generation procedures are explained.

4.1 Simulated Annealing Algorithm

Here, we describe the proposed SA algorithm used to solve the ALP for the scenario with multiple runways. SA is widely used to effectively solve diverse optimization problems in different domains. It is a single based solution metaheuristic inspired by the physical behavior of the annealing process. The annealing process is a phenomenon based on heating a metal and slowly cooling it to obtain a required crystalline structure [10]. SA represents the analogy between this thermodynamic phenomenon and the search for heuristic solutions for optimization problems. The algorithm begins with a heuristic solution and subsequently, iterations are performed to improve this solution. Better solutions are constantly accepted while unimproved solutions are only accepted under given conditions. The possibility of accepting non-improving changes depends on a parameter called "defined temperature" in SA literature. The defined temperature experiences a downturn during the implementation of the approach. A key feature of SA is that it provides a means to "escape" from the local optima by tolerating hill-climbing moves. As the temperature reduces and tends to *zero*, the "worsening" moves are accepted with lower frequency, and the solution tends to a local or probably global solution. For further details on simulated annealing, we refer readers to [11, 12].

4.2   Solution Framework

This subsection provides an exposition on how the ALP is solved using the proposed algorithm. The procedure is divided into three phases: the initial solution construction phase, the improvement phase and the evaluation as shown in Fig. 1.

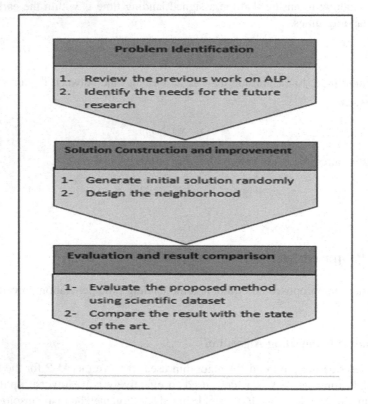

Fig. 1. Proposed solution model

The initial solution-phase begins by sorting the arrival aircraft according to their target landing times. It then assigns a landing time to each aircraft while respecting the separation time between each successive pair of aircraft. This procedure facilitates the assignment of a landing time to each aircraft considering two aircraft (current and previous) at each time. For the first aircraft, landing time is same as target landing time because no previous aircraft exists. For subsequent aircraft, it considers the separation time (for safety reasons) as required in aircraft scheduling design. After the first aircraft is assigned a landing time, the second aircraft is also assigned a landing time using the same procedure.

Algorithm 1: Simulated Annealing Algorithm

Input: Cooling schedule.
  $s = s0$; /*Generation of the initial solution*/
  $T = T_{max}$; /*Starting temperature*/
  Repeat
  Randomly generate a random neighbours';
  $\Delta f = f(s') - f(s)$; /*for minimization problem*/
    If $\Delta f \leq 0$
    Then $s = s'$ /*Accept the neighborsolution*/
    Else Accept s' with a probability $e - \Delta fT$
    $T = g(T)$; /*Temperature update*/
  Until Stopping criteria is satisfied /*e.g. $T < Tmin$ */
Output: Best solution found

Subsequently, the separation time between the current aircraft and the first (i.e., previous) aircraft is checked. If the target time of the current aircraft does not violate the separation time between the current and previous aircraft, the landing time will be the same as its target time. Otherwise, the landing time of the current aircraft will be equal to the target time of the previous aircraft plus the separation time between them.

This procedure is repeated until all the aircraft are assigned landing times and there are no more aircraft arrivals (as shown in Algorithm 2). The resulting solution is a sequence of aircraft timed to land with proper consideration of the separation time between each successive pair of aircraft.

Algorithm 2: Improvement Algorithm

Let n represent the number of arrival aircraft;
Let s_{ij} is the separation time between aircraft i and aircraft j where $i, j \in n$;
Let T_i represent the target landing time of aircraft i ($i = 1, 2 \dots n$);
Sort the aircraft n ascending according to their target landing time T;
  While ($n \neq 0$)do
    For each two aircraft a and b belonging to n
    If ($T_b \leq T_a + s_{ab}$)
      Then allocate landing time of aircraft $a = T_a$;
      Else landing time of aircraft $a = T_a + s_{ab}$;
    End for
  Check the validity of solution
  End While

4.3 Exact Timing Method

Timing generation is the second component of the ALP. This process entails the generation of the optimal landing time for the aircraft using the landing sequence generated. The timing generation method deployed in this paper starts by assigning the initial landing time as shown in Algorithm 2. Afterward, the aircraft with a penalty is assigned to a list. This shifts the landing times of the subsequent aircraft in the list to the left (i.e., it is minimized) by one unit of time (every time). Then, the solution is evaluated based on the objective function in Eq. (1). If the solution is optimized, the procedure will be repeated until no improvement is achieved.

4.4   Improvement of Solution

In the improvement phase, two neighborhood structures were incorporated to modify the current solution and accept the new solution based on the principle of SA. As mentioned in Sect. 4.2, the initial solution consists of a sequence of aircraft which have landed on the runway, with each aircraft having its allocated landing time. The first neighborhood modifies the landing time of the aircraft while respecting the time window and separation time constraints. However, this is not sufficient to get a highly efficient solution. The second neighborhood tests the swapping between two aircraft at a time randomly. This newly generated solution has a better objective value than the solution generated in the first neighborhood.

4.5   Experimental Study

To evaluate our proposed method, an experiment was carried out using a set of numerical datasets. The design of this experiment simulates the aircraft arrivals using an optimized schedule consisting of a sequence of the landing aircraft and the time window for each aircraft. We used the well-known OR-Library dataset, which consists of 13 instances, to verify the performance of the proposed algorithm. This data set [1], has been used in many research papers in the scientific literature. The file is publicly available on the OR-Library website in [http://people.brunel.ac.uk/~mastjjb/jeb/orlib/airlandinfo.html].

4.6   Results and Comparisons

This subsection reports the results of the proposed SA-based algorithm for the ALP with a single runway. The results for the experiments using the swap neighborhood and exact timing methods are also shown here. The ALP solved in this paper is based on the 13 instances of the benchmark data from [1]. In this case, we start with 10 aircraft and gradually increase it to 500 on a single runway. All the experiments were implemented using Java on a personal computer with 3.4 GHz Core i5 CPU having 4 GB memory.

As mentioned earlier, our main objective for solving ALP is to minimize the total penalty associated with deviation from the preferred landing time. Thus, the best solution is the solution with a closer value to the target time. The results obtained were compared with [2], which is the most popular work in literature. With regards to the solution's cost, the results obtained using the proposed methods are equal or very close to the results found in [2]. This is reported in Table 1. The gap between our result and the result in [2] is calculated based on Eq. (5).

$$Gap = (B - BKV)BKV * 100, \qquad (5)$$

where B represents the best result obtained by the proposed algorithms and the BKV is the best value obtained by other methods based on the comparison in literature. For the computational time, our results outperformed the results of the compared paper in all instances except in the case of instance 2 for SS.

Table 1. Computational results of SA compared with the state-of-the-art methods.

Instance name	BKV	SA	SS	BA	GAP
Airalnd1	700	700	4	60	**0.0**
Airalnd2	1.480	1.500	6	90	**0.01**
Airalnd3	820	820	8	99	**0.0**
Airalnd4	2.520	2.520	8	95	**0.0**
Airalnd5	3.100	3.100	9	100	**0.0**
Airalnd6	24.442	24.442	158	274	**0.0**
Airalnd7	1.550	1.550	195	79	**0.0**
Airalnd8	1.950	2025	42	287	**0.04**
Airalnd9	5.611	6333	119	554	**26.23**
Airalnd10	12.329	15150	227	925	**0.23**
Airalnd11	12.418	16.826	256	1417	**0.36**
Airalnd12	16.209	2.441	381	2011	**0.5**
Airland13	44.832	53.804	1237	5852	**0.2**

For better representation, the gap value between the algorithm in the comparison and the *BKV* represented in the Fig. 2. Where, the line with minimum value represent the better results which refers to our proposed algorithm.

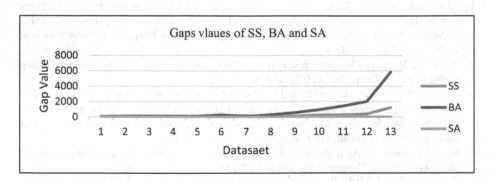

Fig. 2. Percentage gap comparison with SS and BA

5 Conclusion

In this paper, we tackled the ALP with a single runway using the simulated annealing algorithm. We investigated the impact of two different neighborhood structures with an exact timing method. The performance of the proposed algorithm was tested on 13 instances from the datasets of classical scientific literature. The computational results obtained show that the proposed algorithm can generate promising and competitive results when compared with another metaheuristic algorithm. In future work, we intend to hybridize the proposed algorithm and population-based metaheuristic algorithm.

References

1. Al-Betar, M.A., Khader, A.T.: A hybrid harmony search for university course timetabling. In: Proceedings of the 4th Multidisciplinary Conference on Scheduling: Theory and Applications (MISTA 2009), Dublin, Ireland, pp. 157–179 (2009)
2. Girish, B.S.: An efficient hybrid particle swarm optimization algorithm in a rolling horizon framework for the aircraft landing problem. Appl. Soft Comput. **44**, 200–221 (2016)
3. Beasley, J.E., Krishnamoorthy, M., Sharaiha, Y.M., Abramson, D.: Scheduling aircraft landings—the static case. Transp. Sci. **34**(2), 180–197 (2000)
4. Fesanghary, M., Mahdavi, M., Minary-Jolandan, M., Alizadeh, Y.: Hybridizing harmony search algorithm with sequential quadratic programming for engineering optimization problems. Comput. Methods Appl. Mech. Eng. **197**(33), 3080–3091 (2008)
5. Gao, K.Z., Suganthan, P.N., Pan, Q.K., Chua, T.J., Cai, T.X., Chong, C.S.: Discrete harmony search algorithm for flexible job shop scheduling problem with multiple objectives. J. Intell. Manuf. **27**(2), 363–374 (2016)
6. Geem, Z.W.: State-of-the-art in the structure of harmony search algorithm. In: Geem, Z.W. (ed.) Recent Advances in Harmony Search Algorithm. SCI, vol. 270, pp. 1–10. Springer, Heidelberg (2010). https://doi.org/10.1007/978-3-642-04317-8_1
7. Jaddi, N.S., Abdullah, S.: A cooperative-competitive master-slave global-best harmony search for ANN optimization and water-quality prediction. Appl. Soft Comput. **51**, 209–224 (2017)
8. Alia, O.M., Al-Betar, M.A., Mandava, R., Khader, A.T.: Data clustering using harmony search algorithm. In: Panigrahi, B.K., Suganthan, P.N., Das, S., Satapathy, S.C. (eds.) SEMCCO 2011. LNCS, vol. 7077, pp. 79–88. Springer, Heidelberg (2011). https://doi.org/10.1007/978-3-642-27242-4_10
9. Pinol, H., Beasley, J.E.: Scatter search and bionomic algorithms for the aircraft landing problem. Eur. J. Oper. Res. **171**(2), 439–462 (2006)
10. Sabar, N.R., Kendall, G.: An iterated local search with multiple perturbation operators and time varying perturbation strength for the aircraft landing problem. Omega **56**, 88–98 (2015)
11. Salehipour, A., Modarres, M., Naeni, L.M.: An efficient hybrid meta-heuristic for aircraft landing problem. Comput. Oper. Res. **40**(1), 207–213 (2013)
12. Sun, W., Chang, X.: An improved harmony search algorithm for power distribution network planning. J. Electr. Comput. Eng. **2015**, 5 (2015)
13. Turky, A.M., Abdullah, S.: A multi-population harmony search algorithm with external archive for dynamic optimization problems. Inf. Sci. **272**, 84–95 (2014)
14. Wang, G.G., Gandomi, A.H., Zhao, X., Chu, H.C.E.: Hybridizing harmony search algorithm with cuckoo search for global numerical optimization. Soft. Comput. **20**(1), 273–285 (2016)

15. Yuan, Y., Xu, H., Yang, J.: A hybrid harmony search algorithm for the flexible job shop scheduling problem. Appl. Soft Comput. **13**(7), 3259–3272 (2013)
16. Zeng, B., Dong, Y.: An improved harmony search based energy-efficient routing algorithm for wireless sensor networks. Appl. Soft Comput. **41**, 135–147 (2016)
17. Zheng, Y.J., Zhang, M.X., Zhang, B.: Biogeographic harmony search for emergency air transportation. Soft. Comput. **20**(3), 967–977 (2016)
18. Geem, Z.W., Kim, J.H., Loganathan, G.V.: A new heuristic optimization algorithm: harmony search. Simulation **76**(2), 60–68 (2001)

Towards Smart Meter Energy Analysis and Profiling to Support Low Carbon Emissions

Mutinta Mwansa[(✉)] , William Hurst , and Yuanyuan Shen

Department of Computer Science, Liverpool John Moores University,
Byrom Street, Liverpool L3 3AF, UK
M.Mwansa@2017.ljmu.ac.uk, {W.Hurst,Y.Shen}@ljmu.ac.uk

Abstract. Efforts of electrical utilities to respond to climate change require the development of increasingly sophisticated, integrated electrical grids referred to as the "smart grids". Much of the smart grid effort focuses on integration of renewable generation into the electricity grid and on increased monitoring and automation of electrical transmission functions. However, a key component of smart grid development is the introduction of the smart electrical meter for all residential electrical customers. Smart meter (SM) deployment is the corner stone of the smart grid. In addition to adding new functionality to support system reliability, SMs provide the technological means for utilities to institute new programs to allow their customers to better manage and reduce their electricity use and to support increased renewable generation to reduce greenhouse emissions from electricity use. As such, this paper presents our research towards the study of a smart home environment and how the data produced is used to profile energy usage in homes. The validity of the data is justified through analysis of the profiles generated while consumers use energy during off peak and peak periods. By learning, understanding and feeding patterns of home behaviour, it is possible to educate the consumer regarding their energy usage, helping them to reduce costs but also the emissions from their home.

Keywords: Carbon emissions · Smart meter · Behavioural profiling

1 Introduction

Smart meters incorporated with Internet communication Technology network and data management system make up the Advance Metering System (AMI), which are a core component of the smart grid. These systems communicate and work together via the internet Wi-Fi and play an important role in data capturing by recording load profiles and facilitating two way directional information flow. The extensive popularity of smart meters enables an expansive amount of fine granular information to be collected, and are therefore not only beneficial to utilities for just billing purposes. The information collected also gives us an insight into the electricity consumption behaviours and lifestyles of consumers. However, implementing massive energy saving techniques and educating our consumers on energy saving tips would be essential to enable us help reduce greenhouse emissions which become an important topic worldwide. Our aim is

M. I. Khalaf et al. (Eds.): ACRIT 2019, CCIS 1174, pp. 312–322, 2020.
https://doi.org/10.1007/978-3-030-38752-5_25

to increase energy efficiency, our first point in this project is to educate our consumers on the need to decrease their electricity consumption and may therefore need to make investments, e.g., buying more efficient appliances or choose to use energy at lower peak periods. Furthermore consumers will be required to change their living lifestyles, which may also involve changes of everyday behaviour and routines, e.g., using high energy consuming appliances like washing machine at a different time of the day when electricity tariff is at a lower peak period etc.

Utilities could introduce measures that would influence and help reduce electricity demand of households such as coming up with variable electricity tariffs and educating the consumer on them, smart metering to be installed in residential homes so as to enable the consumers to self-monitor their energy usage, smart appliances, and also a combination of all these elements put together [1]. The components described so far can further be incorporated in a smart home system of a home that would constantly monitor the usage consumption (smart metering) and plans the optimal use of devices like using certain devices when the load peak is lower (smart appliances) according to the electricity prices (variable tariffs).

To diminish this problem, in this paper a system platform that enables us to analyse and profile energy usage is proposed, this system is modelled in a way, which consists of various home appliances that communicate with the smart meter via a Wi-Fi network that collects the data of when each appliance is being used and hence analyses its behaviour. We tested and profiled some modern households and we present some results in this paper to demonstrate the effectiveness of our approach.

The remainder of the paper is organised as follows. Section 2 discusses the background research on smart meter data analysis Sect. 3 Subsequently looks at the research objectives and assumptions also included is the methodology and techniques used for profiling users. The paper is concluded in Sect. 5.

In particular, this paper focuses on the smart meter data that we can use to investigate the novel approaches for consumer profiling that would enable us to reduce greenhouse gas emissions and work towards combating climate change.

2   Background

In this section we discuss scenarios of energy efficiency that are key factors to help reduce greenhouse emissions. Linear regression has been used to extract meaningful values from the data collected and we thus use the data to extract different patterns knowing in mind that some additional factors have a significant influence on the overall energy consumption as weather and user behaviour lifestyles [1] Smart grids introduces a number of new opportunities for reducing the carbon footprint by employing residential energy management techniques [2]. Malekian et al., proposes an electrical consumption optimization algorithm (Smart-ECO algorithm) which has the capability to learn from historical patterns about the energy usage habits of residents in households [2]. Malekian also use regression analysis to analyse energy consumption correlated with the weather conditions [2].

Existing research done in the area of energy consumption has used different algorithms to analyse gathered collections of data which is collected by smart meters, Aurthor. S. Makonin et al., used single measurement disaggregation algorithm [3] Energy management techniques are based on the time of use rates, they encourage the users and educate them to run their appliances in off-peak hours and benefit from lower rates. At the moment, energy time of use rates are fixed, however dynamic rates are based on the time of use pricing, meaning the price will be determined and recorded at the particular time you use an appliance. Dynamic billing is one of the emerging areas of research in the energy sector. It is a demand-side response technique that can reduce peak load by charging consumers' different prices at different times according to the demand with dynamic billing [4], The changes in the price of electricity and variations in the emission rates becomes more challenging for consumers, because they really don't know the amount of gas that is being released and is harmful to the environment. In this case, energy management systems can help to decrease the energy bills and carbon footprints of the consumers in such a way that they are able to control, monitor and optimise the performance of the smart home system. Besides these opportunities, utilities can benefit from reduced residential peak loads because consumers can monitor and optimise their energy usage. The residential energy (RE) sector has become key to undertaking rapid emission reductions in a two-fold sense. Firstly, because the residential sector represents around 25% of energy consumption, and 17% of CO2 emissions, and therefore has direct significant effects on the environment [5]. For example, the recent study by Gertler et al. (2016) analyses the household decisions to acquire energy using assets in the presence of rising incomes. Public housing occupied approximately 60% of overall consumptions while private properties accounted for about 40%. Air-conditioners, water heaters and refrigerators account for around 76% of total energy consumption in a typical household [6] According to Balta-Ozkan et al. (2014), a smart home is equipped with connected devices, appliances and sensors that can communicate with each other, and can be controlled remotely by users. These functions provide consumers the flexibility of monitoring its electricity consumption and making lifestyle changes to save electricity [7]. Recently, various commercial energy management products have been deployed for residential use such as google power meter, which is a web service that allows consumers to view their energy consumption online on a daily basis [8]. This software is able to improve the energy efficiency of a house by measuring and profiling the power consumption of individual appliances inside the house, the consumer needs to be aware of how the system works and learn the readings to get full understanding of how to save energy. High Technological advances such as these, have made it increasingly possible to manage energy consumption and hence several online services to educate users have been introduced that can give a better understanding of energy in houses. Utility suppliers monitor these systems continuously and predict country-level energy requirements to reduce or eliminate power outages in future, and enables planning in advance energy demands more effectively. Estimates from the European commission find that households can reduce energy consumption by 20% from simple behavioural changes alone. This could include switching to energy efficiency appliances [9].

Behavioural change concerns the changing of general patterns of activity around a home, such as the way the occupants use their energy, devices or the time of day at which they use devices. However, it can also refer to the exchange of old appliances to newer more energy efficient ones; for example, replacing a washer to an energy saving model and replacing light bulbs to more efficient ones.

3   Methodology

The main objective of the proposed approach is to develop a model that can analyse the general energy consumption patterns in residential homes. The research aims to provide a holistic overview of the energy patterns rather than focusing on individual appliance detection, which would require sub-second sampling. The aim is to predict and construct detailed power profiles by assessing the cumulative energy consumption. However, to achieve this, smart meter energy samples are required. Therefore, the dataset used in this research is constructed through use of a simulation environment, in which a network of home appliances and smart meters is modelled. An overview of the home is presented in Fig. 1.

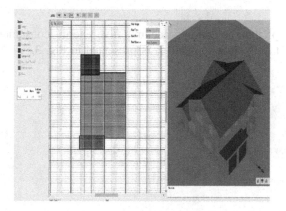

Fig. 1. Home simulation overview.

Due to its ability to construct realistic smart meter datasets, BeOpt Software is used as the chosen software for the data simulation. To set up the home, a list of common household appliances are simulated within the home. The user can conveniently specify simulation parameters and option such as simulation time and resolution, the number and configurations of smart sockets and the usage pattern and operating schedule of the appliances. The number and type of appliances present in the home are customised in Fig. 2 below. For more accurate prediction and analysis of energy consuming pattern, it is desirable to measure the energy consumption of individual appliances.

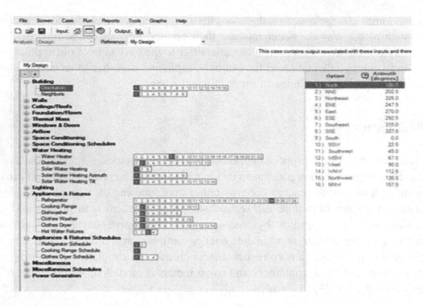

Fig. 2. Home simulation configuration.

An overview of the simulation's accumulative energy consumption, as well as detailed profiles of individual appliances, is presented in Fig. 3.

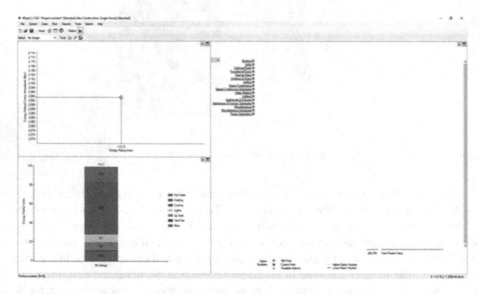

Fig. 3. Simulation data overview.

This data can then be categorised by season and type of day (e.g. weekend) and then averaged to create a load profile for a 'normal' customer. The load profiling method relies on load data being read regularly (daily). The research approach is to first define a baseline of performance by profiling households on the shape of their daily usage profiles. When data is collected at a high frequency every 30 min, this produces a large number of dimensions for the profiling exercise (i.e. the number of samples per day). Extracting meaningful values from the data collected is one of the key challenges in smart home technologies and so to extract the information about the household energy usage patterns we use linear regression analysis, which is the fastest method to analyse the consumption of data of residential buildings.

Table 1 presents a sample of the data generated by the simulation. The general supply of energy used on a daily basis (the energy consumed) is measured in kilo watts per hour (KWH) and can be described as what is used to bill the customer. Data is collected over a 30 min time interval period and the "energy delivered" in KWH. The customer key is the primary key used to identify the consumer while the End Date Time highlights the time and date of the acquired reading. Both the general supply and off peak supply are recorded based on the specified tariff.

Table 1. Smart meter data sample

User ID	Date/time	General supply (KWH)	Off peak (KWH)
1	01/01/2013 03:59	0.076	0.3
1	01/01/2013 04:29	0.051	0.12
1	01/01/2013 04:59	0.041	0.31
1	01/01/2013 05:29	0.041	0.36
1	01/01/2013 05:59	0.034	0.4

Figure 4 displays (a) the load profile for the user 1 simulated home and (b) displays the load profile for user 2 over a 24 h period. The y-axis displays the KWH energy reading for the half hourly time stamp which is defined on the x-axis.

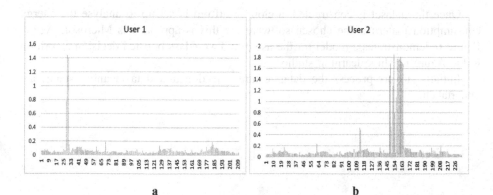

Fig. 4. Simulation data overview

Figure 5 displays the four homes energy usage trends over six months. An overview of the trends in the data, show that there are sharp peaks during the early hours of the day; indicating that the users of the household predominantly use energy during off peak times which is early mornings.

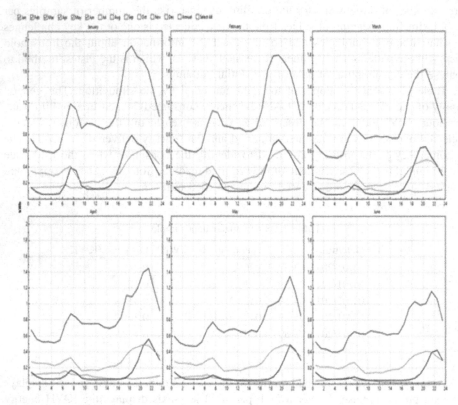

Fig. 5. Simulation data overview for six months

Once the dataset is constructed, a cloud platform is set up to analyse the energy consumption patterns. The chosen software for this is approach is Microsoft Azure. Figure 6 demonstrates a model for the use of a Two-Class boosted decision algorithm in the Azure machine learning studio.

Initially, to pre-process the data, feature selection and data cleaning stages are undertaken.

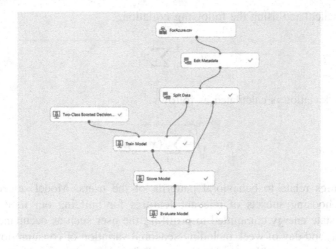

Fig. 6. Microsoft Azure two-class boosted decision algorithm

3.1 Feature Selection

Feature selection is the process of removing and isolating irrelevant and redundant features from a dataset and selecting key aspects of the dataset as a whole [10]. This would lead to a typically simpler prediction model like a regression function used in this research with smaller number of predictors. For this reason, an appropriate feature selection method is one of the key factors for a successful prediction. Figure 7 below, outlines our feature generation approach. The features used in this research are time series-based and are calculated in two-hour time blocks. Specifically, Max, Min, Mean and Standard Deviation as an initial test of the dataset.

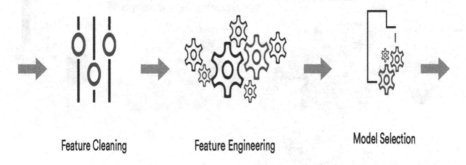

Feature Cleaning   Feature Engineering   Model Selection

Fig. 7. Data cleaning collection process

Mean is calculated using the following equation,

$$\mu = \frac{1}{m} \sum_{i=1}^{m} x_i \tag{1}$$

Standard deviation is calculated as follows,

$$\sigma = \sqrt{\frac{1}{m} \sum_{i=1}^{m} (x_i - \mu)^2}$$

The features relate to behavioral patterns of the users. Model selection output consists of choosing subsets of relevant features for building our model that will estimate the state energy committed to profiling the user such as occupancy patterns, hourly output, and day of week including seasonal variation of consumption. Figure 1 shows the high level machine learning portal. Below is our proposed system flow.

3.2 System Process Flow

Figure 8 illustrates the system process flow framework. These ICT solutions in the energy industry together with machine learning and algorithms are the go way to reducing carbon emissions related to households energy usage. Algorithms are implemented for certain purposes such as data processing, data cleansing, data transformation,

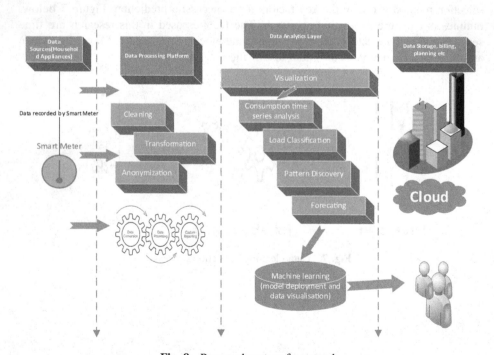

Fig. 8. Proposed system framework

data anonymization, processing and abnormal data detection. The data source column represents smart meter data collected from heterogeneous sources, in a home. The data processing platform and data analytics layer respectively are the data cleaning/ transformation sections. The data analytics layer consists of machine learning tool for data analytics and visualization. Lastly the data storage, publishing, and retrieval layer where the data is organized, stored, and used by the utility companies. The trained model can then be used to make predictions. Regression analysis is usually the best option and the fastest method to analyse the consumption data of in residential settings [11].

4   Results

This section is devoted to the analysis of energy for the two users as indicated in Fig. 4 above were we have used machine learning to get more accurate results using the two-class boosted algorithm. Below is the evaluation results with an AUC (area under curve) of about 70% result rate (Figs. 9 and 10).

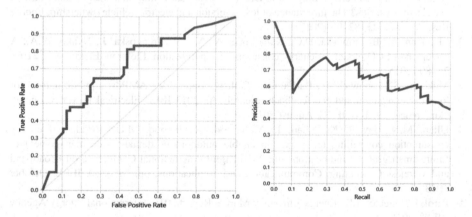

Fig. 9. ROC curves and precision-recall results

True Positive	False Negative	Accuracy	Precision	Threshold	AUC
31	17	0.695	0.674	0.5	0.714
False Positive	**True Negative**	**Recall**	**F1 Score**		
15	42	0.646	0.66		
Positive Label	**Negative Label**				
2	1				

Fig. 10. Evaluation results

5 Conclusion

The basis for this research was the energy consumption of two users in modern households in the UK. Large quantities of information about how customers use their energy is becoming available through the uptake of smart meters. We have described a two-class boosted algorithm on user 1 and user 2. In addition in order to get a more understanding phenomenon of the factors that influence energy consumption, we considered looking at the internal household factors, the main ones being the behavioural patterns of the members of the household. As we continue doing our research in future we would like to increase our AUC testing results to 100%. Lastly utilities can educate the consumers on these readings and anyone who is interested to reducing energy usage at home can benefit from this technique.

References

1. Nicolson, M., Huebner, G., Shipworth, D.: Are consumers willing to switch to smart time of use electricity tariffs? The importance of loss-aversion and electric vehicle ownership. Energy Res. Soc. Sci. **23**, 82–96 (2017)
2. Malekian, R., Bogatinoska, D.C., Karadimce, A., Ye, N., Trengoska, J., Nyako, W.A.: A novel smart ECO model for energy consumption optimization. Elektron. Elektrotech. **21**(6), 75–80 (2015)
3. Makonin, S., Popowich, F., Bartram, L., Gill, B., Bajić, I.V.: AMPds: a public dataset for load disaggregation and eco-feedback research. In: 2013 IEEE Electrical Power & Energy Conference, pp. 1–6. IEEE, August 2013
4. Ullah, M.N., Javaid, N., Khan, I., Mahmood, A., Farooq, M.U.: Residential energy consumption controlling techniques to enable autonomous demand side management in future smart grid communications. In: 2013 Eighth International Conference on Broadband and Wireless Computing, Communication and Applications, pp. 545–550. IEEE, October 2013
5. Birol, F., Director, I.E.: Energy Efficiency Market Report 2016. International Energy Agency (IEA) (2016)
6. Bhati, A., Hansen, M., Chan, C.M.: Energy conservation through smart homes in a smart city: a lesson for Singapore households. Energy Policy **104**, 230–239 (2017)
7. Karlstrøm, H., Ryghaug, M.: Public attitudes towards renewable energy technologies in Norway. The role of party preferences. Energy Policy **67**, 656–663 (2014)
8. Dutta, G., Mitra, K.: A literature review on dynamic pricing of electricity. J. Oper. Res. Soc. **68**(10), 1131–1145 (2017)
9. Jonker, R.T., Przydatek, P.B., Gunn, C.N., Teachman, M.E., Antoniou, C.A.: Revenue meter with power quality features. U.S. Patent 7,006,934. Power Measurement Ltd. (2006)
10. da Graça Carvalho, M.: EU energy and climate change strategy. Energy **40**(1), 19–22 (2012)
11. Kaboutari, A., et al.: An evaluation of feature selection methods for positive-unlabeled learning in text classification (2014)

Prediction of Compressive Strength of High-Performance Concrete: Hybrid Artificial Intelligence Technique

Mohammed Majeed Hameed [ID] and Mohamed Khalid AlOmar[(✉)] [ID]

Department of Civil Engineering, Al-Maaref University College, Ramadi, Iraq
mohmmag1@gmail.com, mohd.alomar@yahoo.com

Abstract. Compressive strength is the most important mechanical property of concrete due to its significant role in numerous design codes and standards. Precise and early estimation of compressive strength of concrete can reduce cost and save time. Many studies have demonstrated that the development of concrete strength is determined not only by the water-to-cement ratio, nevertheless, that is also affected by the content of other concrete parameters and ingredients. High-performance concrete (HPC) is considered an extremely complicated material and the modelling of its performance and behavior is extremely difficult. In this study, Multiple Linear Regression (MLR) and Artificial Neural Networks (ANN) approaches coupled with cross validation technique (CV) used to predict the compressive strength of (HPC). The result showed that ANN-CV model has a good agreement between experimental and predicted compressive strength of concrete values compared to MLR model. The performance of ANN-CV model in estimation compressive strength was very well and superior to MLR-CV model base on statistical criteria such as Correlation Coefficient (CC), Root Mean Square Error (RMSE) and Coefficient of Residual Mass (CRM). The outcomes of this study also revealed that proposed ANN-CV model preforms better than MLR-CV model with higher value of correlation and fewer error was noticed (CC = 0.965, RMSE = 4.736 (MPA), CRM = −0.019) compared to MLR-CV (CC = 0.789, RMSE = 8.288 (MPA), CRM = 0.008).

Keywords: Artificial Neural Networks · Multiple Linear Regression · Cross validation technique · Compressive strength · High-performance concrete

1 Introduction

Concrete was and still the most usable and reliable element in structural engineering. However, some structural elements need special combination and performance that ordinary concrete mixture cannot provide. Therefore, the high performance concrete HPC presented as a suitable replacement of ordinary concrete in some projects [1]. HPC has many advantages over the ordinary concrete in terms of durability, workability and most importantly the mechanical properties i.e compressive strength.

© Springer Nature Switzerland AG 2020
M. I. Khalaf et al. (Eds.): ACRIT 2019, CCIS 1174, pp. 323–335, 2020.
https://doi.org/10.1007/978-3-030-38752-5_26

Compressive strength considered as the most important property of concrete. The compressive strength is measured, for a sample, usually after 28 days soaked in water under laboratory environment [2]. Many parameters effect the compressive strength of concrete including; water cement ratio, aggregate size, age, compaction additives etc. The testing and evaluation of compressive strength can take a significant time especially for ongoing buildings and structure [3]. Prediction of compressive strength can afford a lot of time and effort, additionally, prediction can provide more security and confidence to engineers and contractors.

Recently, artificial neural network (ANN) has conquered many fields of research [4–7]. Concrete research has taken its shear from these privileges [8–11]. In this study, two predictive models applied to forecast compressive strength of high-performance concrete based on experimental data with different age of concrete samples. The first model was ANN combined with cross validation technique and the second model was Multiple Linear Regression (MLR) coupled with cross validation method. More than one thousand samples with various ages; 1, 3, 7, 14, 28, 90, 270 and 365 days used in this current study and introduced to both hybrid models. The performance of each model evaluated based on several statistical criteria in order to select the best forecasting and more reliable model.

2 Methodology

2.1 The Dataset

This study depended on high performance concert data attained from dozens of different sources collected by [12] and used to examine reliability and accuracy of the strength model. Modelling high performance concrete is difficult task due to the complexity of its components and minerals. Test samples were collected for concrete including cement, fly ash, superplasticizer and blast furnace slag. The samples were cast based on the mentioned materials in order to investigate the impact of these materials on high performance concrete compressive strength and presents the total data required for such assessment. Collected data consisted of 1030 samples and included many features such as blast furnace slag (kg in a m^3 mixture), superplasticizer (kg in a m^3 mixture), concrete containing cement (kg in a m^3 mixture), age (days), water (kg in a m^3 mixture), fly ash (kg in a m^3 mixture), coarse aggregate (kg in a m^3 mixture), fine aggregate (kg in a m^3 mixture), and concrete compressive strength (MPa, mega pascals). Some concrete samples were cast with the present of large size aggregates (more than 20 mm). Table 1 shows the details of the major concrete variables that used in this study. In the table $X_{max}, X_{min}, X_{max}, S_X, C_V, C_{sx}, C_c$ denote the maximum, minimum, stander deviation, coefficient of variation, skewness and coefficient of correlation with strength of concrete compressive.

Table 1. Statistical analysis of total compressive strength of concrete data

Component	X_{max}	X_{min}	X_{mean}	S_x	C_V	C_{SX}	C_C
Cement	540	102	281.17	104.46	0.37	0.51	0.498
Blast furnace slag	359.4	0	73.90	86.24	1.17	0.80	0.135
Fly Ash	200.1	0	54.19	63.97	1.18	0.54	−0.106
Water	247	121.75	181.57	21.35	0.12	0.07	−0.290
Superplasticizer	32.2	0	6.20	5.97	0.96	0.91	0.366
Coarse aggregate	1145	801	972.92	77.72	0.08	−0.04	−0.165
Fine aggregate	992.60	594.00	773.58	80.14	0.10	−0.25	−0.167
Concrete compressive strength	82.60	2.33	35.82	16.70	0.47	0.42	1

2.2 Multiple Linear Regressions

In this study, Multiple Linear Regressions (MLR) were employed to predict the compressive strength of concrete. MLR might be define as a multivariate statistical method utilize to find a relationship between dependent and independent variables. The regression equation can be expressed below

$$Y = \alpha_o + \alpha_1 X_1 + \alpha_2 X_2 + \ldots \alpha_j X_1 \tag{1a}$$

Where, Y represents the response variables; X_1, X_2, X_n are independent variables; and $\alpha_o, \alpha_1, \alpha_2 \ldots \alpha_j$ are the coefficient of regression which can be determined as below

$$e = \sum_{i=1}^{n} (Y - y_i)^2 \tag{1b}$$

$$\frac{\partial e}{\partial \alpha_o} = 0; \frac{\partial e}{\partial \alpha_1} = 0; \frac{\partial e}{\partial \alpha_2} = 0$$

Where e and y_i represent the error and current actual value of compressive concrete respectively.

2.3 Artificial Neural Networks (ANN)

Nowadays, ANN can be trained to solve several issues with high accuracy which are extremely hard for traditional methods. Neural networks system is consisted of simple components working in parallel. These components are inspired by biological nerves system. Basically, the concept of ANN is to try to mimic the function of human brain. Training ANN and updating weights that link elements is a major task for preforming specific function. Usually ANN system is trained and adjusted so that the specific input variables provide certain response output and this process can be shown in Fig. 1

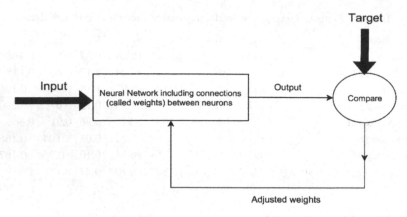

Fig. 1. Basic principle of artificial neural networks system

Herein, the ANN is trained and the weights between neurons have been adjusted in accordance with comparison of outputs and targets and these processes will continue until minimize the sum of square difference between actual and evaluated target values. Typically, ANN have been designed to execute complicated tasks in different sectors of applications, including, classification, regression pattern recognition and control systems.

Generally, multilayer perceptron neural network (MLPNN) and Radial Basis Neural Network (RBNN) are most famous types of neural network. In this study MLPNN which also known as feed forward neural network is employed to performer a regression task. MLPNN consists of three layers (input, hidden and output layers). Input layer introduce the data to the system. While the data are processed in hidden layer(s) and the last layer exhibits the result or the target of the system. Information and data pass from a layer to the next layer through weights and neurons. The main task of neurons in each layer are to connect the neurons in successive layer by a weight (w), that can be updated and tuned during training phase. All data set including values xi introduced to input layer (i) is transferred through the network system, the first hidden layer (j). Every hidden neuron obtains the weighted outputs (wijxij) from the neurons in the earlier layer. These are summed to create a net value, which is then converted to an output value upon the application of a transfer function [13, 14]. Based on typical neural network, the neurons of input layer are $X_o, X_1, X_2, \ldots X_n$; the hidden layer neurons are $h_o, h_1, h_2, \ldots h_n$ and the output layer neurons are $T_o, T_1, T_2, \ldots T_n$.

Each neuron contains multiple inputs and a single output. The sum of the inputs and their weights provides a summation operation that can be written as below

$$net = \Phi\left(b_i + \sum_{i=1}^{n} w_{ij}X_{ij}\right) \qquad (2)$$

Where, w_{ij} refers to established weight; X_{ij} input value b_{ij} bias for a specific layer; Φ activation function.

This study used hyperbolic tangent sigmoid activation function for hidden layer and linear transfer function for output layer that can be expressed below:

$$f(x) = \frac{2}{1+e^{-2x}} - 1 \tag{3}$$

$$f(x) = x \tag{4}$$

Backpropagation algorithm is commonly utilized to train ANN and update the weights and biases. Levenberg–Marquardt algorithm is adopted to train FFANN with a single hidden layer in this current study because it is less computationally cost and very fast convergence.

2.4   Cross-Validation Procedure for ANN and MLR Modules

Cross-validation is a modelling approach used to provide an indication of how well the model learn from the data during training phase, when it provides new and unknown data set to the proposed model for obtaining predictions in order to check and investigate the efficiency of the model prediction. One method to tackle this key issue is to not utilize the whole data during the training of the model. The beginning part of the data set is detained and used later to test the performance of model and the rest used in the learning model. In this study, different kind of lengths of the cross-validation data, set one–third and one fourth of the samples, were examined. Selection data set by using cross-validation approach for both phases training and testing is very significant and have an important impact on the performance of the models since it ensures that the data are divided and distributed efficiently [15].

Numerous approaches for carrying out the cross-validation method were employed in literature, nevertheless, the influence of these methods is similar with applying many iterations or rounds. Most famous methods related to cross–validation are (e.g. hold–out, k-fold and leave one-out). This study employed k-fold technique since it is easy and less computationally expensive compared with other methods. Fold technique could efficiently minimize the randomness of data set selection and calculate the precision and reliability of the forecast model scientifically [16].

The data set is split out into two phases, called training phase and testing phase without allocation of any specific choice of the partition. As illustrated in Fig. 2 the function approximate is trained to a function in accordance with training data set only and the function approximate is then utilizes to forecast of target values by introducing untrained data (testing set).

The input variables are scaled by using Eq. (5) in order to improve ANN model stability and performance [17, 18].

$$X_{new} = \frac{X_i - \mu}{\sigma} \tag{5}$$

Where X_i is the observed record, μ is the mean and σ is the standard deviation.

After scaling the input variables data were shuffled randomly and introduced to cross validation method to divide the data. Figure 3 showed the main process of model constitution.

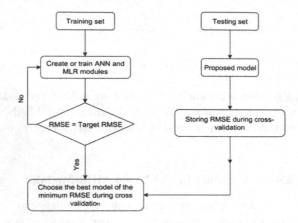

Fig. 2. Cross-validation procedure during the training of ANN and MLR modules.

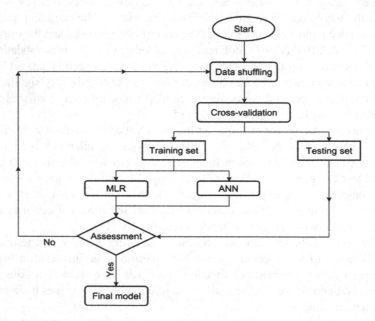

Fig. 3. Framework of the MLR and ANN models for the prediction of compressive strength of HPC.

2.5 Evaluating the Models

The performances of the models were assessed according to three statistical indexes which are Correlation of Coefficient (CC), Root Mean Square Error (RMSE) and Coefficient of Residual Mass (CRM)

$$cc = \frac{\sum_{i=1}^{n}(m - m^-)(p - p^-)}{\sqrt{\sum_{i=1}^{n}(m - m^-)^2 \sum_{i=1}^{n}(m - p^-)^2}} \tag{6}$$

Where n is the number of samples, m and p correspond to the measured and predicted data, while m^- refers to the mean value of measured data set.

$$RMSE = \sqrt{\frac{1}{n}\sum_{i=1}^{n}(m - p)^2} \tag{7}$$

$$CRM = \frac{\sum_{i=1}^{n}(m - p)}{\sum_{i=1}^{n}(m)} \tag{8}$$

3 Result and Discussion

This study investigates the capability of estimation the compressive strength of high performance concrete (HPC) using Multiple Linear Regression (MLR) and Artificial Intelligence (AI) models coupled with cross validation method. (ANN), considered a sort of AI, are employed in this study for carrying out forecasting task and trained by using backpropagation algorithm to modify the weights and biases. As there is no implicit method to determine the number of neurons inside the hidden layer(s) of ANN, this study used trial and error approach. These both models were evaluated using three statistical measures. Tables 2 and 3 present the statistical evaluation for both models during training and testing sets with 3-kfold and 4-kfold. In accordance with statistical measures such as RMSE, CC and CRM, the ANN model outperforms the MLR model in both cases, training phase and testing phase. Moreover, the correlation coefficient values indicate that the forecasted compressive strength values by using ANN combined with k-fold 4 (one of fourth length) correspond very well with experimental samples compared with MLR model. That variance in performance happened because the MLR didn't have the ability to extract the nonlinear relationship between variables and targets. However, the ANN model has the ability to adapt and find out much more informative features from data and mapping nonlinear relations. The highest values of CC and less values of RMSE lead to assign the employed ANN model coupled on cross validation approach to forecast the compressive strength of HPC. Additional assessment of forecasting models is shown in Figs. 4 and 5. It can be noticed that the proposed ANN model is reliable and has a good level of accuracy in the prediction of compressive strength of HPC and have a very good agreement the experimental values. Additionally, Figs. 6, 7, 8 and 9 illustrated the relationship between predicted values calculated by ANN and MLR models and actual values of compressive strength. With respect to ANN model, the points are scattered close to the line compared with MLR model and that indicate there is a robust relationship between forecasted values of compressive strength and the actual values.

In this study, lowest value of RMSE and highest value of CC was 4.736 (MPA) and 0.965 respectively. That indicate the proposed method preform very well compared with the study conducted by [12]. There are three main reasons behind that; first reason is, the current study employed Levenberg–Marquardt algorithm while the mentioned study used momentum algorithm. The second reason is, the effectiveness of using cross validation approach and the third one is because of using transfer function. Yeh employed sigmoid transfer function that activated the target of nodes between small ranged value (between 0 and 1) that could make the process of convergence becomes very slowly and difficult [12]. To overcome these issues, this study employed hyperbolic tangent sigmoid transfer function. This methodical activation function helps the algorithm to process the convergence and makes it fast and simple due to its wide range between −1 to 1. Moreover, Yeh ruled out some irregular experimental samples and preformed his study based on limited age of concrete while this current study used all samples with different ages.

Table 2. Assessment of ANN and MLR models cross validation (3 k-fold)

		Training phase			Testing phase		
Round	Model	RMSE (MPA)	CC	CRM	RMSE (MPA)	CC	CRM
1	ANN(8-3-1)	6.942	0.911	0.007	6.351	0.922	0.001
	MLR	10.454	0.784	0.514	10.273	0.780	0.001
2	ANN(8-5-1)	6.220	0.930	0.001	6.388	0.920	−0.016
	MLR	10.431	0.787	0.512	10.270	0.777	−0.016
3	ANN(8-10-1)	5.070	0.953	−0.005	5.890	0.939	−0.029
	MLR	10.652	0.769	0.511	9.822	0.810	−0.029
4	ANN(8-15-1)	5.310	0.948	0.0001	5.822	0.938	0.006
	MLR	10.455	0.778	0.491	10.225	0.799	0.006
5	ANN(8-20-1)	4.596	0.961	0.009	5.784	0.941	0.007
	MLR	10.105	0.791	0.521	10.926	0.768	0.007

Table 3. Assessment of ANN and MLR models with cross validation (4 k-fold)

		Training phase			Testing phase		
Round	Model	RMSE (MPA)	CC	CRM	RMSE (MPA)	CC	CRM
1	ANN(8-7-1)	4.823	0.955	0.001	5.067	0.959	−0.008
	MLR	10.271	0.799	0.679	10.738	0.731	−0.013
2	**ANN(8-14-1)**	**4.308**	**0.965**	**−0.007**	**4.736**	**0.965**	**−0.019**
	MLR	10.359	0.773	0.664	10.423	0.816	−0.019
3	ANN(8-15-1)	3.749	0.974	−0.010	4.876	0.962	−0.017
	MLR	10.344	0.787	0.679	10.450	0.774	−0.010
4	ANN(8-17-1)	4.018	0.969	0.003	4.884	0.962	−0.002
	MLR	10.309	0.796	0.667	10.562	0.749	−0.010
5	ANN(8-5-1)	4.362	0.921	0.004	5.530	0.930	0.007
	MLR	**9.914**	**0.783**	**0.667**	**8.288**	**0.789**	**0.008**

The bold numbers are selected to represent the best predictive model.

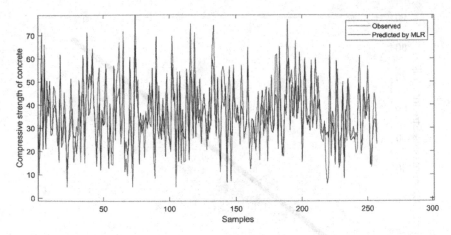

Fig. 4. The testing set of MLR model: actual values vs predicted values of concrete compressive strength.

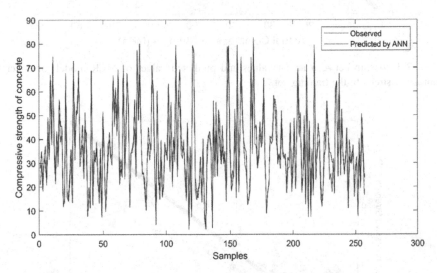

Fig. 5. The testing set of ANN model: actual values vs predicted values of concrete compressive strength.

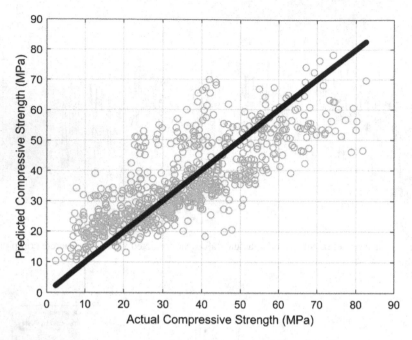

Fig. 6. Relationship between actual values and predicted values of MLR model for concrete compressive strength: the training set.

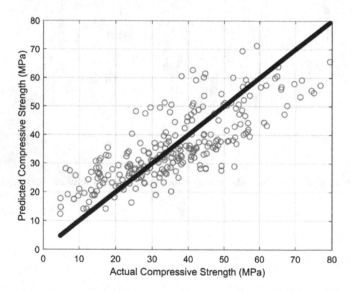

Fig. 7. Relationship between actual values and predicted values of MLR model for concrete compressive strength: the testing set.

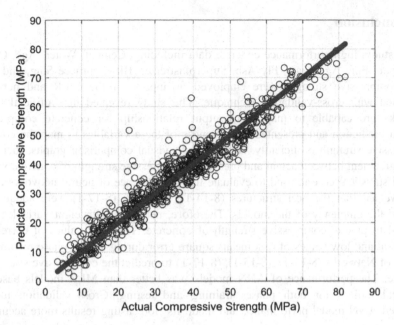

Fig. 8. Relationship between actual values and predicted values of ANN model for concrete compressive strength: the training set.

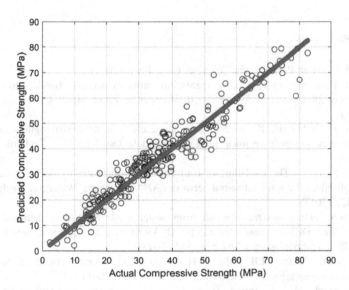

Fig. 9. Relationship between actual values and predicted values of ANN model for concrete compressive strength: the testing set.

4 Conclusion

In this study, high performance concrete data including, Cement, Water, Age, Coarse Aggregate, Fine Aggregate, Fly Ash, Superplasticizer, Blast Furnace Slag, and Concrete compressive strength were employed as inputs for the MLR and networks combined with cross-validation technique. The study revealed that artificial neural networks are capable to map input-output relationship for concrete compressive strength prediction and presented effectiveness of these variables to map the concrete compressive strength proficiently. According to visual comparison graphs, there was good agreement between actual and predicted compressive strength of concrete values. Several statistical criteria used to evaluate the performance of neural networks model and revealed that the best structures (8-14-1), (8-15-1), (8-17-1) were adequate to enhance the efficiency of the models. Therefore, networks with eight variables were required to predict compressive strength of concrete. The high values of correlation coefficient and low values of root means square error during testing phase recommend the use of Networks (8-14-1), (8-15-1), (8-17-1) to predict the compressive strength of concrete. The performance of ANN models was better than MLR models based on statistical indices for both phases training and testing. Cross–validation method enhanced ANN model performance and made its' forecasting results more accurate.

Acknowledgment. The authors express their thanks to Al Maaref University College for funding this research.

References

1. Aïtcin, P.-C.: High Performance Concrete. CRC Press (2011)
2. Khademi, F., et al.: Multiple linear regression, artificial neural network, and fuzzy logic prediction of 28 days compressive strength of concrete. Front. Struct. Civil Eng. **11**(1), 90–99 (2017)
3. Khademi, F., Behfarnia, K.: Evaluation of concrete compressive strength using artificial neural network and multiple linear regression models. Iran Univ. Sci. Technol. **6**(3), 423–432 (2016)
4. Fiyadh, S.S., et al.: The modelling of lead removal from water by deep eutectic solvents functionalized CNTs: artificial neural network (ANN) approach. Water Sci. Technol. **76**(9), 2413–2426 (2017)
5. Fiyadh, S.S., et al.: Arsenic removal from water using N, N-diethylethanolammonium chloride based DES-functionalized CNTs: (NARX) neural network approach. J. Water Supply: Res. Technol.-Aqua **67**(6), 531–542 (2018)
6. Shahin, M.A., Jaksa, M.B., Maier, H.R.: Artificial neural network applications in geotechnical engineering. Aust. Geomech. **36**(1), 49–62 (2001)
7. Cao, M., et al.: Neural network ensemble-based parameter sensitivity analysis in civil engineering systems. Neural Comput. Appl. **28**(7), 1583–1590 (2017)
8. Lee, S.-C.: Prediction of concrete strength using artificial neural networks. Eng. Struct. **25**(7), 849–857 (2003)

9. Atici, U.: Prediction of the strength of mineral admixture concrete using multivariable regression analysis and an artificial neural network. Expert Syst. Appl. **38**(8), 9609–9618 (2011)

10. Öztaş, A., et al.: Predicting the compressive strength and slump of high strength concrete using neural network. Const. Build. Mater. **20**(9), 769–775 (2006)

11. Hola, J., Schabowicz, K.: Methodology of neural identification of strength of concrete. ACI Mater. J. **102**(6), 459 (2005)

12. Yeh, I.-C.: Modeling of strength of high-performance concrete using artificial neural networks. Cem. Concr. Res. **28**(12), 1797–1808 (1998)

13. Hameed, M., et al.: Application of artificial intelligence (AI) techniques in water quality index prediction: a case study in tropical region, Malaysia. Neural Comput. Appl. **28**(S1), 893–905 (2016)

14. Imrie, C., Durucan, S., Korre, A.: River flow prediction using artificial neural networks: generalisation beyond the calibration range. J. Hydrol. **233**(1–4), 138–153 (2000)

15. Dawson, C.W., Wilby, R.: An artificial neural network approach to rainfall-runoff modelling. Hydrol. Sci. J. **43**(1), 47–66 (1998)

16. Zhang, M., et al.: Multiple mechanical properties prediction of hydraulic concrete in the form of combined damming by experimental data mining. Constr. Build. Mater. **207**, 661–671 (2019)

17. Yaseen, Z.M., et al.: RBFNN versus FFNN for daily river flow forecasting at Johor River, Malaysia. Neural Comput. Appl. **27**(6), 1533–1542 (2016)

18. Afan, H.A., et al.: ANN based sediment prediction model utilizing different input scenarios. Water Resour. Manag. **29**(4), 1231–1245 (2015)

Cancellable Face Biometrics Template Using AlexNet

Hiba Basim Alwan[1][✉] [iD] and Ku Ruhana Ku-Mahamud[2] [iD]

[1] Department of Computer Engineering, Al-Mansour University College,
10068 Al-Andalus Sq., Baghdad, Iraq
hiba.basim@muc.edu.iq
[2] School of Computing, Universiti Utara Malaysia,
06010 Sintok, Kedah, Malaysia
ruhana@uum.edu.my

Abstract. Biometric systems with traits like gesture, voice, fingerprint, palm print, handwritten signature, hand geometry, face, and iris have been utilized for authentication. Through these traits, face trait is considered as one of the strongest and an important biometric element. In this work, a presentation of a new cancellable algorithm of face image which is dependent on AlexNet and Winner-Takes-All (WTA) hash method has been proposed. AlexNet is a Convolutional Neural Networks (CNNs) that reached a state-of-the-art level of recognition precision compared to other conventional machine learning methods in terms of feature execution. WTA is used for similarity purposes, whereas random binary orthogonal matrices are applied to produce the projected features of vectors. Fundação Educacional Inaciana dataset and Georgia tech face dataset were used in evaluating the performance of the proposed algorithm. Experimental results illustrate the proposed algorithm has satisfactory execution performance in terms of Equal Error Rate. Thus the proposed algorithm can be used as an alternative method in security biometric implementation.

Keywords: Cancellable biometric · Feature selection · AlexNet · Hash function · Binary orthogonal matrix · Winner-Takes-All

1 Introduction

Biometric systems of human features have obtained significant recognition because of their implementations in pattern recognition. In such systems, individuals are said to be recognized based on several intrinsic features. A part of the body or an attitude by which individuals could be distinctively recognized is the biometric trait. Shape of the face, ocular region, autograph, fingerprint and palm print are several biometric traits.

Biometric traits are categorized as either behavioral or physiological. In behavioral trait, discrete forms could be noted from actions done by humans, for instance walking (gait) patterns, autograph, and manners of using a keyboard. Physiological trait refers to the physical appearance of a person determined by parts of the body like face, fingerprint, palm print, iris and lips [1, 2]. Both physiological and behavioral characteristics of human being are seen to be more valid to confirm any matching as compared to

M. I. Khalaf et al. (Eds.): ACRIT 2019, CCIS 1174, pp. 336–348, 2020.
https://doi.org/10.1007/978-3-030-38752-5_27

methods that rely on knowledge or token due to the fact that these characteristics are not possible to be imitated and are exclusive to individuals [2–5]. Approaches that are biometric based evade certain weak points of long established symbolic and information centered confirmation methods throughout substituting "something you possess" or "something you know" with "something you are" [2, 6].

Biometric confirmation is the authentication or the verification of an object or an individual so as to appear genuine. This involves several procedures which includes a comparison of the already existing query templates of the applicant with its biometric references. Along with the results of this analytical process, what is claimed will be verified as well as the system will state that individuals are either genuine or not [4]. Biometric has lately appeared as a distinctive means that performs a remarkable mission of an accurate recognition of individuals through those individuals' body features or even their behaviors [4]. Biometrics mechanization provides more than just a programmed identification process, but also saves the user from remembering information or having a particular emblem. Nevertheless, biometric confirmation has its drawback where both privacy and security will be lost when database of biometrics features are tempered [5]. However, due to its advantages, biometrics mechanization has driven an enormous amount of industrial profits and it is heading towards being an essential element to individual, cell phone, and governmental administration utilizations [2].

Cancelable biometric as well as cryptosystems are useful and hopeful systems to upgrade the protection. In contrast to secret code, biometric cannot be cancelled. Thus, outfitting security to the spared biometric pattern is incredibly basic [4]. Cancellable biometrics was initiated to pin point this matter through permitting the biometric pattern to be cancelled or reissued. In cancellable biometrics, biometric information is transformed through utilizing an efficient bending technique and matched in the transformed space. In the event that a cancellable biometric format is undermined, it tends to be supplanted alongside another pattern created utilizing another group of transformation parameters [5].

Biometrics can likewise be characterized like a dependable technique for automatic identification/verification of people dependent on their physiological and behavioral attributes. It has been utilized with the end goal of security recognizable identification/verification on the grounds that biometric information is non-transferable, extraordinary, and constantly convenient [7, 8].

Automated Biometrics Identification Systems (ABISs) have supplanted person specialist in-person recognition through making use of an automated methodology. ABIS comprises of dual stages: enrolment and identification. Figure 1 demonstrates a nonexclusive design of an ABIS framework [2].

The proposed algorithm in this paper is based on a methodology called Random Binary Orthogonal Matrices Projection to secure speech biometric portrayal [9]. Work in [9] has been recommended to look into other biometric modalities like face and fingerprint portrayal. Therefore, face biometric modalities has been the focus in this work. In addition to the suggestion in [9], a new cancellable image biometric template security has also been proposed because past image template security have several issues such as:

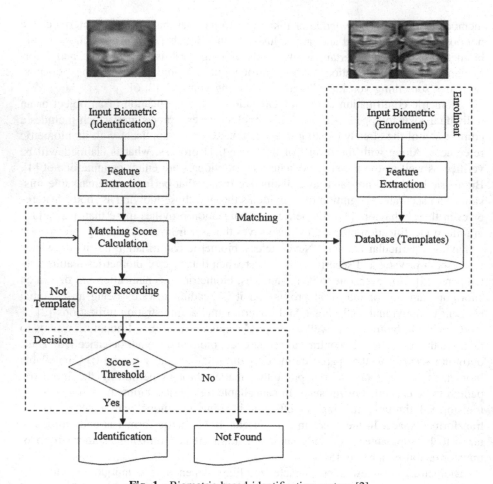

Fig. 1. Biometric-based identification system [2]

1. The vast majority of the image template security approaches were vulnerable against different attacks like attack via record multiplicity and stolen token because of the high connections between the templates made using the equivalent biometric aspect. In this way, the rival can acquire the first template through analysing the number of compromised patterns. Thus it is critical to guarantee that the made patterns are not subject to one another, satisfying the non-likability as well as revocability criteria.

2. The greater part of the image template security approaches when transform to biometric aspect starting with one space then onto the next space because of misfortune of the discriminative aspects. Accordingly, the intra class variety and in the long run might boost and cause to diminish the performance precision. In this way, the template protection approach must almost certainly keep the framework performance stable as much as possible and offer an adequate security insurance.

In this paper, a cancellable transform algorithm named AlexNet Cancellable Biometrics is proposed. The technique utilizes the outstanding image feature extraction technique labelled as AlexNet which is an element of the Convolution Neural Network (CNN) [10]. The algorithm is based on hashing strategy, which is Winner Takes-All (WTA) hashing strategy [11] which enable quick seek for similarity. The proposed algorithm integrates four (4) techniques which are AlexNet, non-invertible hashing function which is WTA, random binary orthogonal matrices, and permutated feature. According to the knowledge of the authors, these techniques have not been integrated before, particularly in the field of cancellable face biometric template.

The review on image template security is presented in Sect. 2 while Sect. 3 introduces some preliminaries of the proposed algorithm. The proposed algorithm is described in Sect. 4. Experimentation and results are shown in Sect. 5 while Sect. 6 exhibits the conclusion and recommendation.

2   Image Template Security

Many scholars have looked into cancellable fingerprint templates protection [6, 12–14]. The principal utilized for cancellable biometrics was first presented by [6]. The authors considered many non-invertible transforms, for example, Cartesian, polar, and functional transformation to develop numerous characters from a fingerprint template. The essential minutiae features are utilized in the template. Rather than putting away the original minutiae, the location and the orientations of minutiae that are put away are transformed irreversibly. The researchers can presume that a cancellable transform can be connected in the feature space. The error correction code-free key binding structure alongside cancellable transforms of minutiae depend on fingerprint biometrics was presented by [12]. The investigations were led on five datasets of the public and the researchers utilized VeriFinger 7 SDK to extract minutia. The researchers argue that the presented algorithm is powerful against many noteworthy security and protection breaches. The authors of [13] suggested another strategy to the design of alignment free cancellable fingerprint patterns. The researchers proposed a restricting minutia couple within the development of local structured minutia. The exploratory outcomes demonstrate that the new strategy performs positively among the current alignment-free cancellable fingerprint pattern. The author of [14] presented a novel indexing strategy which he named cancellable indexing to accelerate the Correlation-Invariant Random Filtering with no loss in its security in that the index which is transformed will release no data on the initial biometric feature. The researchers demonstrated that the transformed index releases no data about the initial index or the initial biometric feature.

Cancellable iris templates protection has been investigated by [15–17]. The research by [15] presented a new cancellable iris pattern creating method dependent over a random look-up table planning to secure the original IrisCodes. The trial results demonstrated that the given technique performs superior to the current methodologies in the wake of applying the transformation. Nevertheless, a setback of their methodology is that it needs four (4) images for iris for each individual to create alternative invariant pattern that can be caught on the initial period of enrolment. Moreover, the precision is influenced via the pre-processing stage as it cannot legitimately divide the iris district for low quality images. The authors of [16] presented a novel cancellable iris recognition framework. The researchers select iris feature to construct their framework and they adjust the current bio hashing to procedure and utilize dual tokens (for subject explicit and for subject free) bringing about two dimensions of security to put away patterns just as raw iris features. The examinations demonstrate that the proposed framework is better than the advanced methods for MMU1, UPOL, CASIA-v3, IITD, UBIRIS.v1 and CASIA-syn databases. The proposed framework additionally provides an equivalent dimension of security and wellbeing to all subjects or persons. The researchers proposed to structure another system for cancellable biometric framework which is dependent on subject's significance alongside his/her biometric traits. Another non-invertible transform that is dependent on cancellable iris framework was presented by [17] using "Indexing First-One" (IFO) hashing. IFO hashing is motivated from the min-hashing that basically utilized in content retrieval space. Broad and enhanced investigates CASIA-v3 iris benchmark database has been used to validate the performance and test results demonstrated that the IFO hashing fulfils revocability and diversity prerequisites.

Research on cancellable biometric on various biometric traits was performed by [18, 19]. The authors of [18] have presented a two-outcome score level fusion method for incorporating the scores derived from cancellable templates of various biometric traits. Test results demonstrate that the presented two-level cancellable score fusion enhances the general performance over uni-biometric framework fulfilling the prerequisite of assured authentication. The comparative investigation demonstrates that the presented fusion strategy outperformed the current methodologies. The work of [19] explores the effect of unequal feature fragment designations on the matching execution of multi-biometric frameworks. Through utilizing a fingerprint as well as face framework that employs feature level fusion, the researchers utilize an arbitrary projection depend on transformation and a percentage weight factor. The outcome of the experiment shows that ideal performance, accomplished with unmatched feature proportions, is superior to anything the execution got beside the usually utilized 50–50 feature ratio. The researchers of [20] present a safe and proficient template creation structure with a new irregular projection to biometric information, utilizing security keys taken from secret code. This is to produce intrinsically established, effective and revocable/renewable biometric patterns for verification of users. The researchers have assessed the performance of the system by using three freely accessible datasets of signature. The outcomes demonstrated that the presented structure does not essentially diminish the separating features of genuine and forget signatures. Cancellable multi-biometric trait is additionally another intriguing area and one of these intriguing pieces of work was presented by [21]. The researchers suggested a novel non-invertible cancellable biometric templates creation method utilizing Gaussian irregular vectors and one path of modulus hashing. Rather than utilizing the initial patterns, the presented framework utilizes its transformed adaptations for putting away and similar. The methodology was experimented on face and palm print biometric traits. A careful examination was held to break down the execution, non-invertibility and uniqueness of the suggested methodology which uncovers that the created patterns are non-invertible, simple for revoking, and convey great execution.

From the above literature, it can be seen that there is a lack in investigating face image template which encourages us to propose a cancellable image face biometric template.

3 Preliminaries

In this section, the theoretical background of how AlexNet functions is dealt with, and the way of how the Winner-Takes-All Hash search algorithm works are presented.

3.1 AlexNet

Convolutional neural networks (CNNs) are multiple-layered variations of artificial neural network (ANN) that can be used to classify images and observe patterns directly from images' pixel. The data is spread in a CNN through its many layers which permits it to extract features from the observed data at layers individually via means of performing digital filtering methods. CNN works on the foundation of two basic stages: convolution and subsampling [22]. CNNs have increased tremendous accomplishment in numerous applications when Alex Krizhevesky and his associates proposed in 2012 a more profound and more extensive CNN model contrasted with LeNet and won the most troublesome ImageNet challenge for visual object recognition named the ImageNet Large Scale Visual Recognition Challenge (ILSVRC) in 2012 with around 16.4% rate of errors. This CNN was called AlexNet [10].

AlexNet accomplished cutting edge recognition precision against all the conventional machine learning and computer vision methods. It was a critical leap forward in the field of machine learning and computer vision for visual recognition and classification undertakings and is the point in history where enthusiasm for deep learning expanded quickly [23–25]. AlexNet is a traditional deep CNN for image classification. Performance on feature extraction is great in AlexNet [26].

AlexNet consists of eight known layers with weights; five of which are convolutional and three fully connected [24, 25]. The new or unfamiliar characteristics of AlexNet are: Rectified Linear Unit (ReLU) nonlinearity, training on multiple graphical processing units, local response normalization, and overlapping pooling. The design of AlexNet is outlined in Fig. 2 [10].

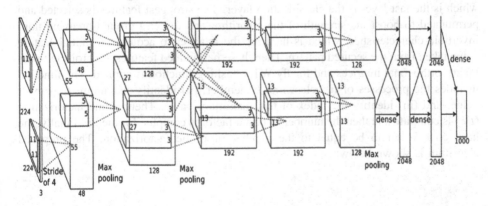

Fig. 2. AlexNet architecture [10].

The proposed algorithm has used AlexNet processes to extract features from input images.

3.2 Hashing Code

A standout amongst the most dominant hash functions that was actualized by Google in their image engine of searching is WTA. This method is use for quick similarity seek. Winner Takes All stores the index vector of the most extreme estimation of the biometric feature post performing irregular permutation. Different index vectors could be created by different permutation sequences [9, 11]. The hashing process of WTA can be seen in Fig. 3.

	f_1	f_2	f_3
Feature	0, 2, 4, 6, 8	1, 3, 5, 9, 7	1, 4, 6, 8, 2
Permutated Feature	4, 1, 2, 8, 6	3, 9, 1, 5, 7	8, 4, 2, 1, 6
Select First 3 Items	4, 1, 2	3, 9, 1	8, 4, 2
Index of Max Value	1	2	1
Hash Function	1, 2, 1		

Fig. 3. WTA example.

4 The Proposed AlexNet Cancelable Biometrics Algorithm

The proposed AlexNet Cancellable Biometrics algorithm can be summarized as follows: The images' features were extracted by using AlexNet. The standard AlexNet has been used which include eight weighted layers (five are convolutional and three are fully connected). The input layer which is the first layer need images of size $227 \times 227 \times 3$, where 227 is the size of images and 3 is the number of colors. AlexNet cannot work with grayscale or any other types of images. The output layer which is the last layer is the classification layer. The strongest features is selected and permutated to boost the strength of the algorithm and to get a ground-breaking non-invertible characteristics, which is hard for the attacker to acquire the initial feature value taken from the secured pattern. Then these permutated features are projected with binary orthogonal matrices and finally WTA hashing function is applied. The function includes the processes of (i) select first k member, (ii) identify maximum k member value, and (iii) identify the index of this maximum value. Then, prime factorization (*PF*) is compute and then the number of prime factor is compute for the PF. Finally, the hash code is set to be equal to the number of prime factorization. The proposed algorithm is shown below:

Algorithm 1: The Proposed AlexNet Cancellable Biometrics Algorithm

1. Read a set of image
2. Train AlexNet to extract and select suitable images' features
3. Permute the selected features
4. Create an orthogonal matrix
5. Overlap the permutated feature with the permutated orthogonal matrix
6. Select first k member
7. Identify the maximum value within the first k selected member
8. Identify the index of the maximum value within the first k selected member
9. Compute PF = (index of the maximum value within the first k selected member + 2) × random positive integer number
10. Find the number of prime factors for PF
11. Calculate hashed code = number of prime factorization

The proposed algorithm has numerous favorable circumstances in comparison with other algorithms. It is less complex with regard to computation time, and requires neither plaintext encryption nor brightness modification, or re-skewed as other algorithms such as hill cipher or region of interest algorithm. Hill cipher algorithm's fundamental disadvantage is that it encodes similar blocks of plaintext to similar cipher text block. Subsequently, it does not conceal features of image that uncover patterns in the plaintext. In addition, breaking it is possible with a compromised plaintext attack uncovering feeble protection by unfolding a linear equations system to find the decipher matrix. The extraction of region of interest pursued by brightness improvement method creates sensitivity to the feature of image displacement, skewed image, and poor brightening. Thus, recognizing the image's skew angle, rectifying the skewed image by depending on skewed angle, and improving the brightness should initially be performed before putting region of interest extracting method in play. This will prompt high calculation intricacy because of matrix duplication functions. There is no compelling reason to conceal image feature as needed in hill cipher in the proposed algorithm.

5 Experimental Results

Tests were performed on two datasets to look at the effectiveness of the suggested AlexNet cancellable biometrics algorithm.

The first dataset is Fundação Educacional Inaciana (FEI), a Brazilian face dataset which consists of a group of face images captured through June 2005 to March 2006 at the Artificial Intelligence Laboratory of FEI in Sao Bernardo do Campo, Sao Paulo, Brazil. For this dataset, a total of 200 people where each has 14 images taken giving a sum of 2800 pictures. Every single image is colored and captured besides a white homogenous surrounding in an upstanding frontal position with profile pivot of up to around 180 degrees. Scale may change about ten percent and the initial size of each picture is 640 × 480 pixels. All the participants are students and staff at FEI, with ages from 19 to 40 years. They varies in appearance, haircut, and decorates. Equivalent number of males and females has contributed to the collected images [27]. In directing the trials, the initial fifty subjects have been used so as to lessen calculation test time and the initial image of every individual was utilized as a basic template while the remaining 13 images of the subject were regarded as the investigation images utilized to process the False Rejection Rate (FRR). With respect to the calculation of False Acceptance Rate (FAR), the initial image of every client was chosen as the base template and every other image were considered as information inquiry.

The second dataset is Georgia Tech face which consists of 50 individuals' images in JPEG design. For every subject, 15 colored pictures were taken from 06/01/99 to 11/15/99 at the Centre for Signal and Image Processing at Georgia Institute of Technology. The greater part of the images was captured in two separate sessions to take the varieties in enlightenment conditions, gestures of face and appearance. The faces were caught at various scales and intentions. All images were taken at 640×480 pixels resolution. 150×150 pixels is the normal size of the faces in these pictures. Frontal as well as tilted faces, lighting conditions and scale beside various facial appearances are shown in the images. Each image is marked by hand to highlight the face's location in the image [28]. During the tests, the initial fifty people have been used so as to decrease the time of computation experiment and the initial image of every person was utilized as the basic template whereas the other 14 images of the person were taken as the query images used to process the FRR. In relation to the calculation of FAR, the user's primary image was chosen as the basic template and every other image were seen as input query.

The similarity score was calculated using Eq. 1 to indicate the availability of similarity or generally between the two feature vectors [9].

$$\text{Similarity score} = \text{Number of zeros/length of hash code} \qquad (1)$$

The technique for ascertaining the similarity value is as illustrated in Fig. 4 [9].

	Enrolled hashed code, S_x	5	9	2	3	6
Step 1	Query hashed code, $\acute{S}_x$	4	9	2	3	6
	$S_x - \acute{S}_x$	1	0	0	0	0
Step 2	Number of 0 = 4					
Step 3	Similarity score = number of 0/length of hashed code $4/5 = 0.8$					

Fig. 4. Computation of similarity score.

The similarity score determined by Eq. (1) is within the range of zero to one. Lower values indicate less similarity exists between feature vectors of both the template and query [18].

FAR as well as FRR are utilized as scales of the execution and the values are calculated according to suggestion in [29] as follows:

$$FAR = \text{No. of impostors that have been authentication} / \text{No. of impostor person} \quad (2)$$

$$FRR = \text{No. of persons that have been correctly authentication} / \text{No. of genuine person}$$
$$(3)$$

Ten hash function scores were used with various window sizes. The window size begins from 5 and ends at 50 with an increment of 5. Table 1 and Fig. 5 display the results of Equal Error Rate (EER). The Georgia Tech face dataset has a slight drop of EER as the window size increases. FEI face dataset displays an exceptionally enormous drop of EER as the window size increases. Big window measurement does not affect the EER. This leads to non-fulfilment when attempting to obtain zero in the chosen size of window.

Table 1. Effect of window size

Window size	Equal error rate (%)	
	FEI face dataset	Georgia tech face dataset
5	37.43%	1.68%
10	11.64%	1.64%
15	5.65%	1.64%
20	5.21%	1.64%
25	4.70%	1.63%
30	4.19%	1.60%
35	3.69%	1.60%
40	3.21%	1.53%
45	3.21%	1.53%
50	2.70%	0.99%

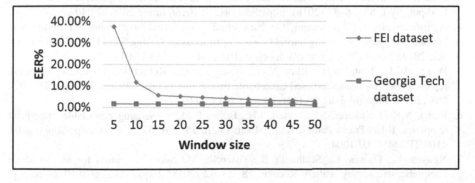

Fig. 5. Effect of window size.

AlexNet works only with color images and there is absence of typical experimental method for existing color face images template protection approaches. Thus comparison cannot be made with other techniques.

6   Conclusion

AlexNet algorithm which incorporates WTA hashing technique has been proposed to generate cancellable face biometrics template. Experimental results have have shown that the suggested algorithm can save the verification execution of EER = 2.70% and 0.99% for FEI and Georgia Tech face databases respectively. A user does not require to save the record of any self-assertive token or binary orthogonal matrix. The suggested algorithm has the advantage of velocity matching search technique from WTA and can display both the strength of non-invertible attributes combined with the non-invertible functions notwithstanding randomized user explicit produced token. Cancellable biometric frameworks likewise require to be demonstrated dependent on non-invertible effective functions. More research is needed in this field, particularly in (1) creating new feature extraction algorithm, (2) studying the effect of using different hash function, (3) investigating the revocability criteria of the proposed algorithm, (4) studying the robustness of the proposed algorithm during attacks and, (5) comparing the proposed algorithm with other state-of-art techniques related within this field.

Acknowledgements. The researchers thank the Malaysian Ministry of Higher Education for subsidizing this investigation under Fundamental Research Grant Scheme, S/O code 12490.

References

1. Das, S., et al.: Lip biometric template security framework using spatial steganography. Pattern Recogn. Lett. (2018). https://doi.org/10.1016/j.patrec.2018.06.026
2. Awad, A.I.: From classical methods to animal biometrics: a review on cattle identification and tracking. Comput. Electron. Agric. **123**, 423–435 (2016). https://doi.org/10.1016/j.compag.2016.03.014
3. Ali, Z., Hoossain, M.S., Muhammad, G., Ullah, I., Abachi, H., Alamri, A.: Edge-centric multimodal authentication system using encrypted biometric template. Future Gener. Comput. Syst. **85**, 76–87 (2018). https://doi.org/10.1016/j.future.2018.02.040
4. Amirthalingam, G., Radhamani, G.: New chaff point based fuzzy vault for multimodal biometric cryptosystem using particle swarm optimization. J. King Saud Univ.-Comput. Inf. Sci. **28**, 381–394 (2016). https://doi.org/10.1016/j.jksuci.2014.12.011
5. Wong, W.J., Teoh, A.B., Kho, Y.H., Wong, M.D.: Kernel PCA enabled bit-string representation for minutiae-based cancellable fingerprint template. Pattern Recogn. **51**, 197–208 (2016). https://doi.org/10.1016/j.patcog.2015.09.032
6. Ratha, N.K., Chikkerur, S., Connell, J.H., Bolle, R.M.: Generating cancelable fingerprint templates. IEEE Trans. Pattern Anal. Mach. Intell. **29**, 561–572 (2007). https://doi.org/10.1109/TPAMI.2007.1004
7. Nguyen, K., Fookes, C., Sridharan, S., Tistarelli, M.: Super resolution for biometrics: a comprehensive survey. Pattern Recogn. **78**, 23–42 (2018). https://doi.org/10.1016/j.patcog.2018.01.002

8. Sarier, N.D.: Multimodal biometric identity based encryption. Future Gener. Comput. Syst. **80**, 112–125 (2018). https://doi.org/10.1016/j.future.2017.09.078

9. Chee, K.-Y., Jin, Z., Cai, D., Li, M., Yap, W.-S., Lai, Y.-L.: Cancellable speech template via random binary orthogonal matrices projection hashing. Pattern Recogn. **76**, 273–287 (2018). https://doi.org/10.1016/j.patcog.2017.10.041

10. Krizhevsky, A., Sutskever, I., Hinton, G.E.: ImageNet classification with deep convolutional neural networks. In: 25th International Conference on Neural Information Processing Systems (NIPS 2012), pp. 1097–1105 (2012)

11. Yagnik, J., Strelow, D., Ross, D.A., Lin, R.-S.: The power of comparative reasoning. In: IEEE International Conference on Computer Vision, pp. 2431–2438. IEEE Press, New York (2011). https://doi.org/10.1109/iccv.2011.6126527

12. Jin, Z., Teoh, A.B., Goi, B.-M., Tay, Y.-H.: Biometric cryptosystems: a new biometric key binding and its implementation for fingerprint minutiae-based representation. Pattern Recogn. **56**, 50–62 (2016). https://doi.org/10.1016/j.patcog.2016.02.024

13. Wang, S., Yang, W., Hu, J.: Design of alignment-free cancelable fingerprint templates with zoned minutia pairs. Pattern Recogn. **66**, 295–301 (2017). https://doi.org/10.1016/j.patcog.2017.01.019

14. Murakami, T., Ohki, T., Takahashi, K.: Optimal sequential fusion for multibiometric cryptosystems. Inf. Fusion **32**, 93–108 (2016). https://doi.org/10.1016/j.inffus.2016.02.002

15. Dwivedi, R., Dey, S., Singh, R., Prasad, A.: A privacy-preserving cancelable iris generation schema using decimal encoding and look-up table mapping. Comput. Secur. **65**, 373–386 (2017). https://doi.org/10.1016/j.cose.2016.10.004

16. Umer, S., Dhara, B.C., Chandra, B.: A novel cancelable iris recognition system based on feature learning techniques. Inf. Sci. **406–407**, 102–118 (2017). https://doi.org/10.1016/j.ins.2017.04.026

17. Lai, Y.-L., et al.: Cancellable iris template generation based on indexing-first-one hashing. Pattern Recogn. **64**, 105–117 (2017). https://doi.org/10.1016/j.patcog.2016.10.035

18. Dwivedi, A., Kumar, S., Dwivedi, A., Singh, M.: Cancellable biometrics for security and privacy enforcement on semantic web. Int. J. Comput. Appl. **21**, 0975–8887 (2018). https://doi.org/10.5120/2535-3460

19. Yang, W., Wang, S., Zheng, G., Valli, C.: Impact of feature proportion on matching performance of multi-biometric system. ICT Express **5**, 37–40 (2018). https://doi.org/10.1016/j.icte.2018.03.001

20. Khan, S.H., Akbar, M.A., Shah-Zad, F., Farooq, M., Khan, Z.: Secure biometric template generation for multi-factor authentication. Pattern Recogn. **48**, 458–472 (2015). https://doi.org/10.1016/j.patcog.2014.08.024

21. Kaur, H., Khanna, P.: Gaussian random projection based non-invertible cancelable biometric templates. Comput. Sci. **54**, 661–670 (2015). https://doi.org/10.1016/j.procs.2015.06.077

22. Roy, S.S., Ahmed, M., Akhand, M.A.H.: Noisy image classification using hybrid deep learning methods. J. Inf. Commun. Technol. **17**, 233–269 (2018)

23. Alom, M.Z., et al.: The History Began from Alexnet: A Comprehensive Survey on Deep Learning Approaches. ArXivabs/1803.01164 (2018). n. pag

24. Suh, H.K., Ijsselmuiden, J., Hofstee, J.W., Henten, E.J.: Transfer learning for the classification of sugar beet and volunteer potato under field conditions. Biosyst. Eng. **174**, 50–65 (2018). https://doi.org/10.1016/j.biosystemseng.2018.06.017

25. Fu, Y., Aldrich, C.: Froth image analysis by use of transfer learning and convolutional neural networks. Miner. Eng. **115**, 68–78 (2018). https://doi.org/10.1016/j.mineng.2017.10.005

26. Bai, C., Huang, L., Pan, X., Zheng, J., Chen, S.: Optimization of deep convolutional neural network for large scale image retrieval. Neurocomputing **303**, 60–67 (2018). https://doi.org/10.1016/j.neucom.2018.04.034

27. Artificial Intelligence Laboratory of FEI. https://fei.edu.br/~cet/facedatabase.html
28. Centre for Signal and Image Processing. http://www.anefian.com/research/face_reco.htm
29. Cherifi, F., Hemery, B., Giot, R., Pasquet, M., Rosenberger, C.: Performance evaluation of behavioral biometric systems. In: Behavioral Biometrics for Human Identification: Intelligent Applications, IGI Global Disseminator of Knowledge, vol. 21 (2009). https://doi.org/10.4018/978-1-60566-725-6.ch003

Pattern of Diffusion Recognition in a Molecular Communication Model

Athraa Juhi Jani[✉]

Department of Computer Science, Al-Mustansiriyah University, Baghdad, Iraq
athraa.jj@gmail.com

Abstract. A nanomachine is the basic functional unit in nanotechnology that can perform simple tasks, like sensing and actuation. A set of nanomachines can perform more complex tasks through communicating and sharing information, and by that, they form a nanonetwork. Different communication techniques are proposed for information exchange among nanomachines. Molecular communication is one of these techniques, which is a bio-inspired communication mechanism. In this paper a time slotted model consist of n nanomachines in a bounded environment is considered. These nanomachines are communicate according to diffusion based molecular communication. Information molecules are encoded based on the variation in the concentration of molecules in the communication medium. Thus, the receiver nanomachine decode the sensed information molecules during a certain time slot as '1', if its concentration exceeds a certain threshold τ, and '0' otherwise. The main objective is to study the performance of diffusion based molecular communication model, the pattern of diffusion was explored, by inspecting how a receiver nanomachine could distinguish a message from one transmitter nanomachine at a distance d or two transmitter nanomachines at different distances. The information molecules were represented as 2-bits by using 2^2 different values with $2^2 - 1$ thresholds. In the implemented experiments the effects of distance, time, sensed molecular concentration and interference are considered.

Keywords: Nanonetworks · Nanomachines · Molecular communication · Diffusion · Performance analysis

1 Introduction

Nanotechnology can be defined as the science of engineering functional systems at an atomic and molecular scale, the prefix 'nano -' denotes a factor of 10^{-9} and means a billionth [1]. The rapid evolution in nanotechnology has provided appropriate development in miniaturization and fabrication of nanomachines with simple sensing, computation, data storing, and communication and action capability [2]. Further capabilities and applications can be enabled if multiple nanomachines communicate to perform collaborative and synchronous functions in a distributed manner to form a nanonetwork [3]. Molecular communication is considered a bio-inspired paradigm, in which molecules are transmitted, propagated and received between nanomachines [4].

© Springer Nature Switzerland AG 2020
M. I. Khalaf et al. (Eds.): ACRIT 2019, CCIS 1174, pp. 349–363, 2020.
https://doi.org/10.1007/978-3-030-38752-5_28

1.1 Related Work

In [5] an estimation of the achievable information rates is presented for a diffusion based molecular communication, and information is encoded as a set of distinct molecules. Through extending the framework and results in [6], the outcomes in [5] show large gains in the information rate, compared to the case where the emitted molecules are of the same type. In the literature, various studies have aimed to model the physical channel of the diffusion based molecular communication [7], governed by Fick's laws, in particular some research have explored the channel transfer function [8], while other research focused on channel capacity from information theoretical aspects [9–13]. The noise effects on channel capacity have been investigated in [14–16], concluding that diffusing a larger number of molecules increases the signal to noise ratio and could reduce the noise impact. The authors in [17] presented the design challenges and principles in diffusion based molecular communication, considering the propagation delay and channel distortion to be the main challenges. Synchronization between the transmitter nanomachine and receiver nanomachine is considered one of the challenges in molecular communication systems. Synchronization is important, as it can affect the error rate performance of the receiver nanomachine [18]. Mostly in literature related to molecular communication, authors assume that the system is synchronized; however, studying biological mechanisms brings opportunity to find different tools that can be used to overcome challenges. In biology, there is a mechanism known as *quorum sensing* [19, 20], in which bacteria can utilize to synchronize their behaviour, through the emission and sensing of a certain type of molecules called autoinducer. The authors in [19, 21] proposed *quorum sensing* as a tool to achieve synchronization among nanomachines in diffusion based molecular communication system.

In [22] performance analysis of the flow assisted diffusion channel molecular communication is investigated. The effect of flow velocity, interference of time slotted transmission and diffusion coefficient on average symbol error rate and achievable mutual information rate of the channel is derived.

The authors in [23] proposed an improved non-coherent signal detection scheme, aiming at addressing ISI and noise contamination. Through utilizing three non-coherent metrics to characterize transient features of received signals, and furthermore, designed an optimized combination scheme for more reliable signal detections.

In [24] the performance of molecular communication model has been studied, by presenting an algorithm to find the maximum distance that diffused molecules can reach, and an energy harvesting model for the nanonodes has been proposed. Then the pattern of diffusion issue has been explored, to find out how could nanonodes can distinguish the pattern of diffusion of one nanonode in a distance d_0 from it in the same network. Where the information molecules represented as two bytes: 00, 01, 10, 11. The diffusing nanonode would continue to diffuse unites of molecules through 8 time slots, each slot is of length t_0.

1.2 The Work in This Paper

The main objective is to study a diffusion based molecular communication model, through the analysis of diffusion propagation medium. Taking in consideration the parameters that impact communication in diffusion based systems. The pattern of diffusion has been explored, by inspecting how a receiver nanomachine could distinguish a message from one transmitter nanomachine at a distance d or two transmitter nanomachines at different distances. The information molecules were represented as 2-bits by using 2^2 different values with $2^2 - 1$ thresholds. taking into consideration the effects of the following parameters: distance, time, sensed molecular concentration, interference.

In the literature, the performance of the molecular propagation channel has been explored in [24–31]. Through the evaluation of their results, the factors that can affect the sensed molecular concentration at the receiver nanomachine are concluded. These factors have facilitate the model assumptions in this paper. Including the assumption that the estimation of the interference from previous diffused information molecules on the current diffused information molecules, depends on distance, time and sensed molecular concentration. The experiment results of diffusion pattern recognition show that:

- If the duration of symbol was relatively short, then the diffused symbols were not recognized correctly due to the short symbol duration. (Symbol duration is the time duration between two consequent transmissions). In this experiment the symbol duration was 0.02 ms.
- The receiver nanomachine was able to recognize the symbols correctly after increasing the symbol duration. The symbol duration increased to 3.2 ms.

Experiments with two different transmitter nanomachines at different distances from the receiver nanomachines diffusing information molecules. The experiment results to check how the receiver nanomachine can recognize the pattern of diffusion show that:

- The receiver nanomachine can recognize the diffused symbols correctly. However, it cannot distinguish whether symbol came from one nanomachine or another. Due to the overlapping in the values of the sensed molecular concentration which come from each nanomachine in this experiment. Where the reason of the overlapping in these values came from the close distance between the two transmitter nanomachines.
- Changing the distance of the two transmitter nanomachines from the receiver nanomachine can make the overlapping quite low.

In the case when one transmitter nanomachine is in a close distance from the receiver nanomachine, and the other nanomachine is in a far distance from the receiver nanomachine, the results show:

- The receiver nanomachine cannot recognize the diffused symbols correctly, because of the higher data rate of the sensed molecular concentration from the close transmitter nanomachine. Thus, the sensed molecular concentration from the far nanomachine is affected by the interference of molecules from the previous symbol duration,
- By increasing the symbol duration, the receiver nanomachine can recognize the diffused symbols correctly, distinguishing also if the symbol came from one nanomachine or another.

There are research which study the effects of Inter Symbol Interference on the channel capacity and the channel performance. However, we study the effects of the interference on recognizing the pattern of diffusion. Besides that, through experiments we study the effects of symbol duration, data rate, and distance on reducing the effects of the interference.

The paper is organized as follows. In Sect. 2 the model is described. The proposed pattern of diffusion algorithm, the factors that affect distinguishing the sensed molecular concentration, and the experiment results are demonstrated in Sect. 3. Finally, Sect. 5 presents the conclusions from the experiments results.

2 Model

Network Environment: A system of n nanomachines is considered, these nanomachines communicate according to diffusion based molecular communication. The environment of the communication might contain residual molecules from previous diffusion, and also contain molecules from other nanomachines (that are not among n) and these molecules can be considered as noise. In [32] the diffusion based communication system has showed that only the molecules last previous diffusion can affect the current diffusion. Nanomachines are assumed to have simple computational capability, and storage space for the needed computations.

Time Slots: The model is time slotted with length t; thus, a transmitter nanomachine can keep diffusing molecules during this t time slot, where $t = \frac{d^2}{D}$.

Information Molecule Encoding: The concentration of received molecules is considered to be the information molecules (though it is also called the transmitted symbol). Thus, a receiver nanomachine decode the received symbol as '1' in case the number of molecules sensde by the receiver nanomachine during t time slot is higher than a given threshold τ; if not, then the symbol is decoded as '0'. Generally nanomachines are assumed to sense at least $(\varepsilon + \mu)$ molecular concentration, where ε represents the residual molecular concentration and μ can represent the environmental noise. If the nanomachine sense molecular concentration that is higher than $(\varepsilon + \mu)$; i.e., τ, it can recognize that at least one nanomachine is diffusing molecules. In [33] modulation techniques have been explored, one of which is *Concentration Shift Keying*, where symbols (information molecules) can be represented as b bits through 2^b different values, and the levels of threshold can be $2^b - 1$.

Network Communication: The nanomachines n are assumed to communicate through diffusion; thus, once the molecules are released by a transmitter nanomachine into the propagation medium, these molecules shall be diffused freely according to the Brownian motion dynamics. The function of the molecular concentration at the receiver nodes in response to an impulse of information molecules (symbol) emission from the transmitter with Q molecules is of the form [34]:

$$Qh(t) = \int_0^T (Q \times \frac{1}{(4\pi Dt)} \times \exp(\frac{-d^2}{4Dt})) \tag{1}$$

where, t represents time and it is the integral variable and range from 0 to T, d denotes the distance between the receiver and the source, D is the diffusion coefficient, Q number of diffused molecules. Thus, the receiver nanomachine sense the accumulated molecular concentration diffused through the time slot t.

Pattern of Diffusion: Assuming that the information molecules (symbol) are represented as 2 bits with 2^2 different values and 2^2-1 thresholds, the aim is to check how a receiver nanomachine can distinguish a message transmitted from a transmitter nanomachine at distance d. A receiver nanomachine can sense the transmitted information molecules through the following expression, where [34] stated that the molecular concentration peak at a receiver nanomachine is obtained through:

$$Q(p) = Q\left(\frac{3}{2\pi}\right)^{3/2} \frac{1}{d^3} \tag{2}$$

where $Q(p)$ means the function to compute the peak of the diffused Q molecules.

From Eq. (2) the peak of molecular concentration at a receiver nanomachine is inversely proportional to the cube of the distance d, and it is not affected by the diffusion coefficient D of the medium. However, the time that it takes diffused molecules to reach their peak can be affected by D; thus a receiver nanomachine at distance d from a transmitter nanomachine can sense that then molecular concentration at d peaks at $t' = \frac{d^2}{6D}$, where t^0 here is computed from the derivative of Eq. (1) [25].

3 Pattern of Diffusion Recognition in Molecular Communication Model

This section examines how a nanomachine at distance d can recognize the information molecule (symbol) that a transmitter nanomachine has been diffusing. Where the information molecules (symbol) is represented as 2 bits with 2^2 different values and $2^2 - 1$ thresholds, i.e., the symbol is encoded according to the Quadruple Concentration Shift Keying(QCSK) [29, 33], as Fig. 1 shows.

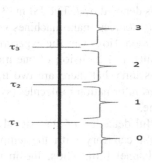

Fig. 1. QCSK technique for 2 bits per symbol [33]

Thus, the diffused symbol is represented as two bits in different forms: 00, 01, 10, and 11, and there are three different thresholds for the receiver nanomachine to distinguish the symbol. In order to give values to these thresholds, the transmitter nanomachine in this section is assumed to diffuse units of molecules throughout 8 time slots, each slot of length t; and the accumulated value of the diffused units throughout 8 t would encode a symbol either $s_0 = (00)$, $s_1 = (01)$, $s_2 = (10)$, and $s_3 = (11)$. To encode a symbol, a transmitter nanomachine diffuses either Q molecules to represent 1 or 0 molecules to represent 0, during each t of the 8 t. Here, it is assumed that symbols are represented as the following:

Symbol	Molecules No.	Diffused molecules in each t	thresholds
$s_0= 00$	n_0	1 0 0 0 0 0 0	τ_0
$s_1= 01$	n_1	1 1 1 0 0 0 0 0	τ_1
$s_2= 10$	n_2	1 1 1 1 1 0 0 0	τ_2
$s_3= 11$	n_3	1 1 1 1 1 1 1 1	τ_3

Fig. 2. Symbols representation through 8 time slot

In Fig. 2 the second column represents the 'Number of Molecules', while the third column represents' Molecules diffused through each t of 8 time slots'. Although s_0 means that no information molecules would be diffused, but to distinguish between no diffusing and diffusing 0, it is assumed that n_0 is diffused to represent s_0. The number of molecules, for example n_1 equals to $(1 \times Q) + (1 \times Q) + (1 \times Q) + (0 \times Q) + (0 \times Q) + (0 \times Q) + (0 \times Q) + (0 \times Q)$. The expression in Eq. (2) represents the peak of diffused information molecules, the values of thresholds can be computed through [34]:

$$\tau = X \times Q \left(\frac{3}{2\pi}\right)^{3/2} \frac{1}{d^3} + I \tag{3}$$

where X represents the diffused units in each time slot t^0, i.e., 0 or 1. The Inter Symbol Interference (ISI), which means the residue molecules from the previous symbol that can affect the current symbol is denoted by I. The ISI in [34] is assumed to come from a sufficient number of interfering sources (nanomachines which are diffusing), in a way that I follows a normal distribution. However, the experiments which have been carried out in this paper, study the pattern of diffusion of one transmitter nanomachine and a receiver nanomachine, then assume that there are two transmitter nanomachines and one receiver. Thus, the diffused information molecules (symbol) will be affected by ISI from at least one nanomachine.

ISI can affect the successful detection of the (signal) diffused molecular concentration [25]. The effects of ISI can vary with the temporal spreading properties of molecules in the diffusion channel [26]. Thus, the increased distance between the transmitter and receiver nanomachines, and/or the higher data rate (sensed molecular concentration) can cause increased effects of ISI [25]. The authors in [27] proposed a scheme to reduce the effects of the ISI, through reducing pulse-width of the transmitted information molecules, as the molecules encoding technique discussed in the paper is on-off keying (OOK). The authors in [28] proposed an enzyme-based scheme to reduce the effects of ISI, through diffusing enzymes which chemically interact with the ISI information molecules (from previous symbol) and form intermediate products; thus, in this way the information molecules from the previous symbol would not cause ISI in the current symbol. Symbol duration can be defined as the time duration between two consequent transmissions. Symbol duration t_s represents the required time to transmit a symbol (information molecule), can also affect ISI, and a longer symbol duration can help to reduce the ISI caused by the previous symbol [33].

In the experiments to check the pattern of diffusion in this section, the value of ISI was assumed to vary depending on the distance, data rate and symbol duration, in a way that ISI $\leq \log(\frac{d}{t_s} \times$ date rate).

The rest of this section includes an algorithm to distinguish the pattern of diffusion, followed by the results of different experiments based on the algorithm. In order for a receiver nanomachine to distinguish the pattern of information molecules diffused by a transmitter at distance d, it should compute τ_1, τ_2, $\tau3$ and $\tau4$, through Eq. (3) and follow the steps in Algorithm 1 [24].

In Algorithm 1 [24], it is assumed that each bit of the transmitter message is diffused during t time slot. For simplicity, the time needed for molecular concentration to reach its peak near the receiver nanomachine t^0 and symbol duration t_s are assumed to equal $(8 \times t)$. Recall that X represents the diffused units in each time slot. As there are 8 time slots, $X(i)$ represents the diffused unit at a specific t from the 8 time slots.

Different experiments have been carried out to distinguish the pattern diffusion at a receiver nanomachine following the steps in Algorithm 1 [24]:

Algorithm 1: Diffusion Pattern Recognition

   Input: Initial values of Equation 3 parameters

   Output: Recognize the Diffused Symbol

1 $t1 \leftarrow 0$;

2 $\tau \leftarrow 0$;

3 $i \leftarrow 1$;

4 **while** $i \leq 8$ **do**

5     $x \leftarrow X(i)$;

6   **while** $t1 \leq t$ **do**

7       $\tau = \tau + (x \times Q \frac{3}{2\pi}^{3/2} \frac{1}{d^3} + I)$;

8       $t1 = t1 + 0.01$;

9 **if** $(\tau > (\varepsilon + \mu))$ & $(\tau \leq \tau_1)$ **then**

10   Symbol is 00 ;

11 **else if** $(\tau > \tau_0)$ & $(\tau \leq \tau_1)$ **then**

12   Symbol is 01 ;

13 **else if** $(\tau > \tau_1)$ & $(\tau \leq \tau_2)$ **then**

14   Symbol is 10 ;

15 **else if** $(\tau > \tau_2)$ & $(\tau \leq \tau_3)$ **then**

16   Symbol is 11 ;

---

4 Experiment Results

4.1 Recognizing the Diffusion Pattern of One Nanomachine

The first experiment is to check how a receiver nanomachine can recognize the received information molecules. Taking in consideration the effects the time slot length and the inter symbol interference on the recognizing the received molecules correctly.

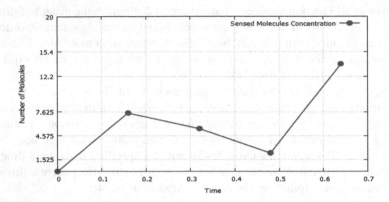

Fig. 3. Sensed symbols by receiver from transmitter at $d = 5$ and $t_s = 0.16$

Figure 3 represents an experiment where four symbols were diffused by a transmitter nanomachine at distance 5 from a receiver nanomachine. In the experiments, Q is assumed to equal 1000, and $(\varepsilon + \mu)$ is assumed to equal 0.25. The assumed time slot t to diffuse one bit of the 8bits symbol is 0.02 ms, and t0, ts = 0.16 ms. The ticked points at the y-axis in Fig. 3 represents the values of thresholds, where, $\tau_0 = 1.525$, $\tau_1 = 4.575$, $\tau_2 = 7.625$ and $\tau_3 = 12.2$. The x-axis represents the time required before the diffused symbol reaches to its peak at the receiver nanomachine. The y-axis represents the sensed molecular concentration (peak of the diffused symbol) at certain t0. Even though the receiver nanomachine can sense at least $(\varepsilon + \mu)$ in each time slot t, the figures which represent the experiments results have an initial value of the sensed molecules by the receiver that equals 0.

The four diffused symbols in Fig. 3 are: 10, 01, 00, 11. The effects of ISI during the first symbol duration is assumed to be quite low. Thus, it can be seen that the first diffused symbol sensed and distinguished correctly. However, the effects of ISI start from the second symbol; therefore, in Fig. 3, the sensed molecular concentration during the second, third, and fourth ts is higher than the actual diffused molecular concentration, and there is a chance of error in the process of distinguishing a symbol. Thus, symbols 01, 00, 11 have not distinguished correctly in Fig. 3. This can be due to the short symbol duration t_s.

In Fig. 4 the assumed time slot t to diffuse one bit of the 8bit symbol is 0.4 ms, and t^0, $t_s = 3.2$ ms. The diffused symbols in this figure are: 01, 11, 10, 00, 10, and the results show that the receiver nanomachine sensed and distinguished the correct symbols.

Thus, Fig. 4 shows that the diffused symbols were not recognized correctly due to the short symbol duration.

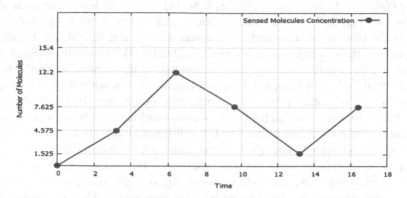

Fig. 4. Sensed symbols by receiver from transmitter at $d = 5$ and $t_s = 3.2$

Thus, the diffused symbols were not recognized correctly due to the short symbol duration in Fig. 3. However, The receiver nanomachine was able to recognize the symbols correctly after increasing the symbol duration in Fig. 4.

4.2 Recognizing the Diffusion Pattern of Two Nanomachines

In case there are two different transmitter nanomachines at different d from a receiver nanomachine. These two transmitter nanomachines are assumed to be synchronized. In a way that, one nanomachine starts diffusing at a certain symbol duration, and the second one waits, then at the next symbol duration the second nanomachine diffuses and so on. The receiver nanomachine is assumed to have 8 thresholds to recognize the diffused symbol and to distinguish from which transmitter nanomachine it has come.

Figure 5 shows the results of the sensed molecular concentration by a receiver nanomachine that was diffused from two transmitter nanomachines in d = 3, and 5.

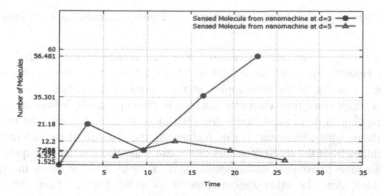

Fig. 5. Sensed symbols by receiver during $t_s = 3.2$ from transmitters at $d = 3$ and $d = 5$

The number of molecules diffused by each transmitter nanomachine is assumed to equal $Q = 1000$. The assumed time slot t to diffuse one bit of the 8bit symbol is 0.4 ms, and t^0, $t_s = 3.2$ ms. The threshold values of the transmitter nanomachine at $d = 3$ are: ($\tau_0 = 7.060$, $\tau_1 = 21.180$, $\tau_2 = 35.301$, $\tau_3 = 56.481$). The remaining thresholds are as described in Fig. 3. Thus, the ticks on the y-axis represent all 8 thresholds. The symbols diffused by the nanomachine at distance $d = 3$ are: 01, 00, 10, 11, and the symbols from the nanomachine at $d = 5$ are: 01, 11, 10, 00. The results in Fig. 5, seem to show that the receiver nanomachine can distinguish the symbols correctly, but, as some threshold values overlap, it is difficult for the receiver nanomachine to distinguish whether a symbol comes from one nanomachine or another. However, the figure differentiates between the symbols of each nanomachine (as the sensed molecular concentration of each nanomachine saved in a different array), but the receiver mainly just compares the sensed molecular concentration with the thresholds.

The experiment is repeated, but with different values of d, as Fig. 6 shows:

The overlapping of the threshold values in Fig. 6 might look quite low, but most values of one nanomachine are quite close to one threshold of the other nanomachine. The two transmitters are assumed to be at distances $d = 3$, and $d = 7$. The threshold values of $d = 7$ are: ($\tau_0 = 0.962$, $\tau_1 = 2.887$, $\tau_2 = 4.813$, $\tau_3 = 7.700$). The diffused symbols of the transmitter nanomachine at $d = 3$ are: 01, 00, 10, 11, and symbols of transmitter nanomachine at $d = 7$ are: 00, 10, 11, 01.

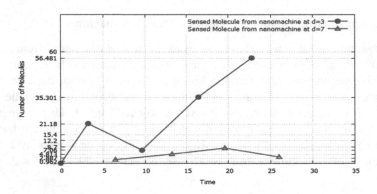

Fig. 6. Sensed symbols by receiver during $t_s = 3.2$ from transmitters at $d = 3$ and $d = 7$

Thus, in Fig. 5 the receiver nanomachine can recognize the diffused symbols correctly. However, it cannot distinguish whether symbol came from one nanomachine or another. It is due to the overlapping in the values of the sensed molecular concentration which come from each nanomachine in this experiment. Where the reason of the overlapping in these values came from the close distance between the two transmitter nanomachines. However, in Fig. 6 changing the distance of the two transmitter nanomachines from the receiver nanomachine can make the overlapping quite low.

In case one transmitter nanomachine is in a close distance from the receiver nanomachine. And the other nanomachine is in a far distance from the receiver nanomachine. This case is presented to avoid overlapping between thresholds values. Thus, different distances were selected in the next experiment.

Figure 7 shows the sensed molecular concentration by a receiver nanomachine, when two transmitter nanomachines at $d = 0.3$ and $d = 3$ diffuse information molecules.

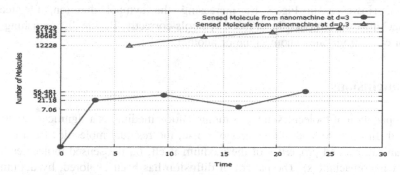

Fig. 7. Sensed symbols by receiver during $t_s = 3.2$ from transmitters at $d = 0.3$ and $d = 3$

In Fig. 7, the thresholds values of the sensed molecular concentration which come from the transmitter nanomachine at d = 0.3 are: ($\tau_0 = 12228$, $\tau_1 = 36685$, $\tau_2 = 61143$, $\tau_3 = 97829$), which shows a higher data rate at this distance. The symbols diffused by the nanomachine at d = 0.3 are: 00, 01, 10, 11. The symbols diffused by the nanomachine at d = 3 are: 01, 10, 00, 11. The diffused symbols from the nanomachine at d = 3 are affected by ISI. However, the diffused symbols from the nanomachine at d = 0.3 are not affected that much by ISI, as the range between its thresholds is high (for example, the difference between $\tau 0$ and $\tau 1$ is almost 24457). Besides this, the data rate of the diffused symbols from the nanomachine at d = 3 is quite low.

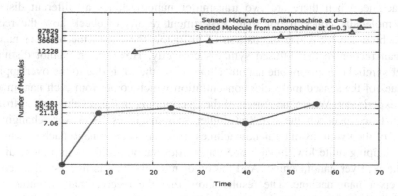

Fig. 8. Sensed symbols by receiver during $t_s = 8$ from transmitters at $d = 0.3$ and $d = 3$

In Fig. 8, the assumed time slot t to diffuse one bit of the 8bit symbol is 1 ms, and t^0, $t_s = 8$ ms. The diffused symbols from both nanomachine at $d = 0.3$ and 3, are the same diffused symbols in Fig. 7, as symbol duration increased the effects of ISI on the received symbols from the nanomachine at $d = 3$ is decreased in Fig. 8.

Thus, in Fig. 7 the receiver nanomachine cannot recognize the diffused symbols correctly. Due to the higher data rate of the sensed molecular concentration from the close transmitter nanomachine. Thus, the sensed molecular concentration from the far nanomachine is affected by the interference of molecules from the previous symbol duration. However, in Fig. 8 by increasing the symbol duration, the receiver nanomachine can recognize the diffused symbols correctly. Beside distinguishing if the symbol came from one nanomachine or another.

5   Conclusions

The propagation of molecules in the communication medium is a significant topic to be explored. In order to study the effects of noise, the residual molecules from previous communications and properties of the medium itself, on the sensed molecules by the receiver nanomachine(s). The pattern of diffusion has been explored, by defining the factors which can affect the sensed molecular concentration by the receiver, such as distance, interference, symbol duration and data rate. Experiment results showed the effects of increasing the symbol duration of diffused symbols on the sensed molecular concentration at the receiver nanomachine.

Two cases were considered in the experiment. The first case is how a receiver nanomachine can distinguish the pattern of diffusion of one transmitter nanomachine at distance d. The experiment results of diffusion pattern recognition show that the diffused symbols were not recognized correctly due to the short symbol duration. In this experiment the symbol duration was 0.02 ms. Then, the receiver nanomachine was able to recognize the symbols correctly after increasing the symbol duration. The symbol duration increased to be 3.2 ms.

The second case is related to recognizing the pattern of diffusion by the receiver nanomachine, when there are two transmitter nanomachines at different distances, diffuse molecular concentration. The experiment results to check how the receiver nanomachine can recognize the pattern of diffusion show that, the receiver nanomachine can recognize the diffused symbols correctly. However, it cannot distinguish whether symbol came from one nanomachine or another. It is due to the overlapping in the values of the sensed molecular concentration which come from each nanomachine in this experiment. Where the reason of the overlapping in these values came from the close distance between the two transmitter nanomachines. However, changing the distance of the two transmitter nanomachines from the receiver nanomachine can make the overlapping quite low. In case one transmitter nanomachine is in a close distance from the receiver nanomachine. And the other nanomachine is in a far distance from the receiver nanomachine. The results show that the receiver nanomachine cannot recognize the diffused symbols correctly. Due to the higher data rate of the sensed molecular concentration from the close transmitter nanomachine. Thus, the sensed molecular concentration from the far nanomachine is affected by the interference of molecules from the previous symbol duration. By increasing the symbol duration, the receiver nanomachine can recognize the diffused symbols correctly, beside distinguishing if the symbol came from one nanomachine or another.

As a future work, it is possible to think about exploring models of nanonetworks taking into consideration the drift of molecules in the medium. Research studies that address flow-based molecular communication are currently quite limited. The propagation medium in some of the nanonetworks applications can be in motion, as an example, nanomachines in bio-medical applications are placed in human blood. Thus, it is not feasible to assume that the propagation medium is always stable. In some cases, a drift velocity may be applied on purpose to increase a molecular communication systems low throughput. Thus, it would be good to study model of molecular communication with drift as well as channel capacity, noise effects and other related issues.

Acknowledgement. I would like to express my gratitude to Professor Dariusz R. Kowalski and Dr Alexei Lisitsa, who provided insight and expertise that greatly assisted the research.

References

1. ShahMohammadian, H.: System design for nano-network communications. Ph.D. thesis, University of Calgary (2013)
2. Akyildiz, I.F., Brunetti, F., Blázquez, C.: Nanonetworks: a new communication paradigm. Comput. Netw. 52(12), 2260–2279 (2008)
3. Roca Lacasa, N.: Modeling the molecular communication nanonetworks. Master's thesis, Universitat Polit`ecnica de Catalunya (2009)
4. Llatser, I., Cabellos-Aparicio, A., Pierobon, M., Alarcón, E.: Detection techniques for diffusion-based molecular communication. IEEE J. Sel. Areas Commun. **31**(12) 726–734 (2013)
5. Eckford, A.W.: Achievable information rates for molecular communication with distinct molecules. In: 2007 2nd Bio-Inspired Models of Network, Information and Computing Systems, Bionetics 2007, pp. 313–315. IEEE (2007)
6. Eckford, A.W.: Nanoscale communication with Brownian motion. In: 41st Annual Conference on Information Sciences and Systems 2007, CISS 2007, pp. 160–165. IEEE (2007)
7. Llatser, I., Alarcón, E., Pierobony, M.: Diffusion-based channel characterization in molecular nanonetworks. In: 2011 IEEE Conference on Computer Communications Workshops (INFOCOM WKSHPS), pp. 467–472. IEEE (2011)
8. Pierobon, M., Akyildiz, I.F.: A physical end-to-end model for molecular communication in nanonetworks. IEEE J. Sel. Areas Commun. **28**(4), 602–610 (2010)
9. Atakan, B., Akan, O.B.: On molecular multiple-access, broadcast, and relay channels in nanonetworks. In: Proceedings of the 3rd International Conference on BioInspired Models of Network, Information and Computing Systems, ICST (Institute for Computer Sciences, Social-Informatics and Telecommunications Engineering), vol. 16 (2008)
10. Pierobon, M., Akyildiz, I.F.: Information capacity of diffusion-based molecular communication in nanonetworks. In: 2011 Proceedings IEEE INFOCOM, pp. 506–510. IEEE (2011)
11. Arifler, D.: Capacity analysis of a diffusion-based short-range molecular nanocommunication channel. Comput. Netw. **55**(6), 1426–1434 (2011)
12. Nakano, T., Okaie, Y., Liu, J.Q.: Channel model and capacity analysis of molecular communication with Brownian motion. IEEE Commun. Lett. **16**(6), 797–800 (2012)

13. Liu, Q., Yang, K.: Channel capacity analysis of a diffusion-based molecular communication system with ligand receptors. Int. J. Commun. Syst. **28**(8), 1508–1520 (2015)
14. Moore, M.J., Suda, T., Oiwa, K.: Molecular communication: modeling noise effects on information rate. IEEE Trans. Nanobiosci. **8**(2), 169–180 (2009)
15. Pierobon, M., Akyildiz, I.F.: Capacity of a diffusion-based molecular communication system with channel memory and molecular noise. IEEE Trans. Inf. Theory **59**(2), 942–954 (2013)
16. Pierobon, M., Akyildiz, I.F.: Diffusion-based noise analysis for molecular communication in nanonetworks. IEEE Trans. Signal Process. **59**(6), 2532–2547 (2011)
17. Llatser, I., Cabellos-Aparicio, A., Alarcon, E.: Networking challenges and principles in diffusion-based molecular communication. IEEE Wirel. Commun. **19**(5), 36–41 (2012)
18. ShahMohammadian, H., Messier, G.G., Magierowski, S.: Optimum receiver for molecule shift keying modulation in diffusion-based molecular communication channels. Nano Commun. Netw. **3**(3), 183–195 (2012)
19. Abadal, S., Llatser, I., Alarcón, E., Cabellos-Aparicio, A.: Quorum sensing-enabled amplification for molecular nanonetworks. In: 2012 IEEE International Conference on Communications (ICC), pp. 6162–6166. IEEE (2012)
20. Jani, A.J.: Anti-quorum sensing nanonetwork. Indian J. Public Health Res. Dev. **9**(12), 1108–1114 (2018)
21. Abadal, S., Akyildiz, I.F.: Automata modeling of quorum sensing for nanocommunication networks. Nano Commun. Netw. **2**(1), 74–83 (2011)
22. Thakur, M.S., Bhatia, V.: Performance analysis of flow assisted diffusion based molecular communication for D-MoSK. In: 2018 IEEE 87th Vehicular Technology Conference (VTC Spring), pp. 1–6. IEEE (2018)
23. Liu, S., Wei, Z., Li, B., Guo, W., Zhao, C.: Metric combinations in non-coherent signal detection for molecular communication. Nano Commun. Netw. **20**, 1–10 (2019)
24. Juhi, A., Kowalski, D.R., Lisitsa, A.: Performance analysis of molecular communication model. In: 2016 IEEE 16th International Conference on Nanotechnology (IEEE-NANO), pp. 826–829, August 2016
25. Mahfuz, M.U., Makrakis, D., Mouftah, Hussein T.: Concentration-encoded molecular communication in nanonetworks. Part 1: fundamentals, issues, and challenges. In: Suzuki, J., Nakano, T., Moore, M.J. (eds.) Modeling, Methodologies and Tools for Molecular and Nano-scale Communications. MOST, vol. 9, pp. 3–34. Springer, Cham (2017). https://doi.org/10.1007/978-3-319-50688-3_1
26. Mahfuz, M.U., Makrakis, D., Mouftah, H.T.: Characterization of molecular communication channel for nanoscale networks. In: BIOSIGNALS, pp. 327–332 (2010)
27. Mahfuz, M.U., Makrakis, D., Mouftah, H.T.: Characterization of intersymbol interference in concentration-encoded unicast molecular communication. In: 2011 24th Canadian Conference on Electrical and Computer Engineering (CCECE), pp. 000164–000168. IEEE (2011)
28. Noel, A., Cheung, K.C., Schober, R.: Improving receiver performance of diffusive molecular communication with enzymes. IEEE Trans. Nanobiosci. **13**(1), 31–43 (2014)
29. Suzuki, J., Nakano, T., Moore, M.J.: Modeling, Methodologies and Tools for Molecular and Nano-scale Communications: Modeling, Methodologies and Tools (2017). https://doi.org/10.1007/978-3-319-50688-3
30. Wang, X., Wu, Z., Chen, J., Liu, B.: An increment detection algorithm to mitigate ISI for molecular communication based on drift diffusion. In: Proceedings of the 4th International Conference on Communication and Information Processing, pp. 234–238. ACM (2018)
31. Turan, M., Kuran, M.S,., Yilmaz, H.B., Demirkol, I., Tugcu, T.: Channel model of molecular communication via diffusion in a vessel-like environment considering a partially covering receiver. In: 2018 IEEE International Black Sea Conference on Communications and Networking (BlackSeaCom), pp. 1–5. IEEE (2018)

32. Kuran, M.S,., Yilmaz, H.B., Tugcu, T., Özerman, B.: Energy model for communication via diffusion in nanonetworks. Nano Commun. Netw. **1**(2), 86–95 (2010)
33. Kuran, M.S., Yilmaz, H.B., Tugcu, T., Akyildiz, I.F.: Modulation techniques for communication via diffusion in nanonetworks. In: 2011 IEEE International Conference on Communications (ICC), pp. 1–5. IEEE (2011)
34. Meng, L.S., Yeh, P.C., Chen, K.C., Akyildiz, I.F.: MIMO communications based on molecular diffusion. In: 2012 IEEE Global Communications Conference (GLOBECOM), pp. 5380–5385. IEEE (2012)

Computer Security and Cryptography

Querying Encrypted Data in Graph Databases

Nahla Aburawi[✉] ⓘ, Frans Coenen ⓘ, and Alexei Lisitsa ⓘ

Department of Computer Science, University of Liverpool,
Liverpool L69 3BX, UK
{nahla.aburawi, coenen, A.lisitsa}@liverpool.ac.uk

Abstract. Encryption is an effective way to protect sensitive data in a database from various attacks. Querying encrypted data, however, becomes a challenge. Either the data should be **decrypted** before the querying, leaving it vulnerable to server-side attacks, or one has to apply computationally expensive methods for querying encrypted data. In this paper, we present a flexible mechanism for the execution of queries over encrypted graph databases. Data privacy is protected at the server side, through the use of multi-layered encryption and encryption layer adjustment, conducted dynamically during the execution of queries. The proposed scheme reveals less information to the adversary than in the case of static adjustment done prior to execution. We report on the implementation of the scheme as applied to a subset of Cypher graph queries (graph traversal queries) directed at a Neo4j graph database. The experimental results show the efficiency of query execution for various types of query on encrypted graph data stores.

Keywords: Graph databases · Encryption adjustment · Data privacy · Security

1 Introduction

Database security is attracting considerable interest due to the importance of data that is routinely hosted in enterprise databases, the large amounts of found in organizations of all sizes, from large corporations to small businesses. The goal of database security involves protecting the database from unauthorised or accidental access to data, modification or destruction.

In order to protect data integrity and privacy, data encryption has been used, as an active protection mechanism. One of the most challenging and important aspect of data encryption is how to query the encrypted data. Starting from the influential work of Popa et al. [6] a lot of research has been conducted in the field of querying encrypted database, avoiding full data decryption. Using multi-layered encryption and appropriate encryption adjustment procedures is the key to finding the right balance between security and query execution performance.

In this paper, we present different mechanisms for adjusting encryption layers in the context of graph databases [7]. In order to provide a reasonable trade-off between data security protection and data processing efficiency CryptGraphDB [3] utilizes multi-layered encryption and encryption adjustment, inspired by the CryptDB system for relational DBs [6]. The graph query is translated into an encrypted form before processing. The encryption layers of the data are adjusted accordingly at the server side. Subsequently, the query is executed on a server and the encrypted results are sent back

© Springer Nature Switzerland AG 2020
M. I. Khalaf et al. (Eds.): ACRIT 2019, CCIS 1174, pp. 367–382, 2020.
https://doi.org/10.1007/978-3-030-38752-5_29

to a user where they are finally decrypted. In both, CryptDB and CryptGraphDB approaches various types of encryption are used, organized as encryption onion layers. Notice that in all mentioned works and in this paper only the variants of symmetric encryption as opposed to asymmetric (public key) encryption are used.

At the outermost layer, highly secure encryption schemes that leak virtually nothing about the data are typically used. Most common examples of such encryption schemes are random or randomized (RND) encryption schemes [4], meaning that the same plain text values are likely to be translated into different cipher texts under same encryption key. To make it possible to execute some queries over encrypted data that require, for example, equality checks, the encryption level should be adjusted to become a deterministic layer (DET). This allows for equality checking to be done, without revealing any more information. The DET layer can be easily provided by any deterministic symmetric encryption algorithm (e.g. DES or AES).

In this paper we elaborate a traversal-aware encryption adjustment mechanism for graph databases, first proposed in [2], report on its implementation for a subset of Cypher queries (traversal queries) and empirically evaluate its efficiency. The proposed mechanism reveals only the information required to execute the query. By using this approach, we can observe that not all property values in the graph are adjusted with respect to the DET layer, but only required values are adjusted, while the rest are still in the RND layer. One of the major drawbacks of the traditional way to search an encrypted database is to decrypt all the data to the DET layer, and then find the required records. Apart from representing a significant security risk, this traditional approach is resource intensive particularly when considering a large number of records. Our technique shows a clear advantage by dynamically adjusting encryption layers as query execution progresses. In this way, less information is revealed to any adversary watching the execution of the query on the encrypted store; while, as demonstrated in the paper, being reasonably efficient. The graph database system used to analyse the approach is Neo4j as developed by Neo Technology in 2007 [7, 8].

The remainder of this paper is organized as follows. The related work is outlined in Sect. 2. In Sect. 3 querying of encrypted graph DB, as proposed in [2, 3], is presented. Section 4 then explains the implementation of the proposed traversal-aware encryption adjustment and case studies. The experiments and analyses of the performance of the proposed approach is presented in Sect. 5. Some conclusions and some suggested areas for future work are presented in Sect. 6.

2   Related Work

One of the challenges of querying encrypted databases is revealing unnecessary data while performing the adjustment of the encryption layers. In a classical CryptDB paper [6], dealing with such an issue for JOIN queries for relational databases, the authors introduced a special JOIN-aware encryption mechanism. In [3] a CryptDB-like approach, referred to as CryptGraphDB, was proposed for graph databases and it was particularly noted that due to absence of a JOIN operator in the Cypher graph query language, there is no need in use of JOIN-aware encryption; however, the problem of unnecessarily revealing information after encryption layer adjustment continued to exist. To address this problem, in a position paper [2] a novel scheme of traversal-aware encryption adjustment for graph DBs was proposed and theoretically discussed, but no implementation, or empirical evaluation was reported. The work on structured encryption and controllable disclosure presented in [4] provided an interesting alternative to the methods developed in [2, 3, 7] and this paper. In particular [4] uses a different cryptographic scheme under which the whole (graph) data structure is encrypted, not only the data elements. The latter, unlike the approach we present in this paper, could make an implementation of the methods of [4] on the top of an existing graph DBMS challenging. The detailed comparison of both approaches is a topic of future research.

3 Querying of Encrypted Graph DB: Existing Approach

As noted above, there has been little work on querying encrypted graph databases. The only work that the authors are aware of is the work on Graph CryptDB presented in [3] and, the work on Traversal-Aware Encryption Adjustment presented in [2]. In both cases, the implementation was done with respect to Neo4j graph DBMS and Cypher as a query language. Each is discussed in further detail in the following two sub-sections.

3.1 Graph CryptDB

CryptGraphDB [3] works by executing Cypher queries over an encrypted graph database. By translating the query into an encrypted form, executing it over the encrypted data on the server without any decryption and sending the results back to the user where they can be decrypted. In this way data, privacy is protected at the server side. At the core of the Graph CryptDB are three ideas espoused by CryptDB [6]: (1) a Cypher-aware encryption strategy which maps Cypher queries to the encryption schemes; (2) Adjustable query-based encryption that lets CryptGraphDB adjust the encryption level of each data item based on the user query; and (3) Onion encryption to change data encryption levels in an efficient manner.

CryptGraphDB is composed of two parts: a trusted client-side frontend, and an untrusted DBMS server. The frontend keeps track of the database schema as seen by the application without encryption, and the current level of onion encryption exposed in the server for each data item. On the other hand, the server keeps track of the encrypted schema; the encrypted format of user data (the lowest level of encryption revealed to the server). It provides confidentiality for data content and for names of labels and properties; also, it does not hide the entire graph structure, the number of nodes, or the approximate size of data in bytes.

Processing a query Q in CryptGraphDB, as shown in Fig. 1, involves four steps:

1. The application issues a query that is rewritten by the proxy by anonymizing each label, node and relationship names; and encrypts each constant in the query with the most private encryption scheme (RND).
2. The proxy checks whether the DBMS needs to adjust the encryption level. If so, it sends an update query to adjust the encryption level.

3. The proxy sends the encrypted query to the DBMS server to be executed using a standard Cypher and returns the encrypted results.
4. The DBMS server returns the encrypted query result which are decrypted by the proxy and sent back to the application.

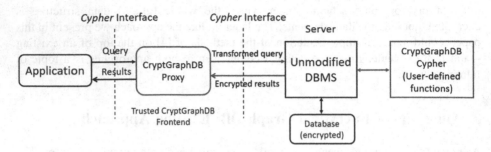

Fig. 1. The typical query flow in Graph CryptDB

In [3] the simple encryption adjustment method is proposed. Initially, each value in the graph is encrypted using RND, the outermost layer. At the second of the above steps checking by the proxy prior to query execution is done using simple syntactical criteria. In particular, if a value of some attribute may be required for the query in a plaintext form, or encrypted at DET level, the corresponding adjustments will be done across the whole data store. As was pointed out in [2] this may lead to unnecessary information leaks and therefore a more advanced Traversal-Aware Encryption Adjustment method for alleviating this issue was proposed in [2] as discussed in the following subsection.

An Example of Query Processing with Simple Encryption Adjustment
Given a query of the form:

```
MATCH (node:person)-[:knows]->( )
WHERE  node.name = {"Tom"}
RETURN node.age
```

In order to allow the equality check, this query needs to pass to the DET layer as detailed in Table 1.

Table 1. Data layout at the server where the application table on the left is created at the server from the table on the right.

Person

person

name	age	name at RND	age at RND	name at DET	age at DET
Tom	29	a4a895a87052	e6ba69bdf08c	UD82Pv8uGNi7	33TPfYgeYDKb
Smith	22	9d60b415e6e7	686097aa7a7a	j39IjDVyx/+	NMtqlsMp8Qaf

Step (1), Proxy sends to the DBMS: `UPDATE person SET name=DECRYPT` `RND(name)`, DBMS decrypts entire name property to `DET` layer:

`DECRYPT name, RND(a4a895a87052) = UD82Pv8uGNi7`. Next, Proxy updates its internal state to log that name is currently at layer DET in the DBMS.

Step (2), the proxy encrypts `"Tom"`, to the `DET` layer encryption value of `UD82Pv8uGNi7`, then, proxy generates query and sends it to DBMS:

```
MATCH (node:person)-[:knows]->( )
WHERE node.name = {""UD82Pv8uGNi7"}
RETURN node.age
```

Step (3), the proxy receives encrypted RND level result `e6ba69bdf08c` and decrypts it using: `DECRYPT age, DET(DECRYPT age, RND(e6ba69bd-f08c)) = 29`. Lastly, proxy sends decrypted result 29 to the application.

3.2 Traversal-Aware Encryption Adjustment

The idea of Traversal-Aware Encryption Adjustment (TAEA) is quite natural and simple. During the query execution, the paths starting with nodes with specific names values and progressing alongside specified relationships are traversed. The execution may perform additional checks of some properties of encountered nodes.

Therefore, the adjustment will not be everywhere, but just along the query execution path. The scheme of traversal-aware encryption adjustment is dynamic, and the encryption adjustment happens not before the query execution, but rather it gradually progresses alongside the execution.

The scheme follows the simple principles defined in [2]:

– Encryption adjustments and traversal query execution are interlaced;
– The adjustments happen in-between traversal steps;
– The adjustment is performed to enable one-step of traversal using all information accumulated to this step, in particular the set of nodes traversed so far.

By considering a simple case study in [2] (an execution of a simple query "on a paper") it was shown that indeed TAEA may reveal less information to a potential attacker as compared with simple adjustment. However, the study in [2] was only a proof-of-concept study.

4 Towards Implementation of TAEA

In this section, we describe an implementation of TAEA for a subset of the Cypher queries. We start with simple examples first. In general, an execution of a query with TAEA over an encrypted graph data store requires an execution of interlaced partial queries and encryption adjustment updates. While it is possible to compose these partial queries and updates using the WITH construct of Cypher, and thereby to execute all the sequence automatically (in one go), for simplicity, here we present the required sequence of separate queries and updates. The composition is discussed later in Subsect. 5.2.

Query with a Single Relationship. Consider a query Q consisting of one link and two search criteria:

```
MATCH (node1: label1)-[:Relationship]->(node2: label2)
WHERE   node1.propertyA   =   {value1}   AND
node2.propertyB = {value2} RETURN node2
```

The query Q, using the TAEA scheme, is processed, as follows:

1. Each value starts out encrypted with the most private encryption level where data is encrypted using the RND scheme.
2. To check the equality for the first part of the WHERE clause, node1.propertyA = value1, we need to lower the encryption of propertyA to level DET. The proxy issues this query to the server UPDATE Label1 SET propertyA = DECRYPT RND(propertyA), that use the DECRYPT RND UDFs, where DECRYPT RND is a user defined function implementing decryption which is discussed in Subsect. 4.1.
3. Executing the query Q_1 to allow the initial search node1.propertyA = encrypted value1 for nodes of Q to be executed. Here encrypted value1 is the encryption of value1, when the path required in the main query Q start as:

```
MATCH (node1:label1)-[:Relationship]->(node2:label2)
WHERE node1.propertyA = {encrypted value1}
RETURN node2 AS result
```

Where result is used as an alias for the result column name.
4. Lowering the encryption level of node2.propertyB for nodes that are reachable from the outgoing of Q_1 to DET layer.
5. Processing the second part of the query Q:

```
MATCH (node1:label1)-[:Relationship]->(result:label2)
WHERE result.property2 = {encrypted value2}
RETURN result
```

6. Finally, proxy decrypts the results from the server and returns them to the user.

Query with Multiple Relationships. In the case of having a query Q consisting of multiple statements and two search criteria, as follows:

```
MATCH(node1:label)-[Rel1]->(node2:label)-[Rel2]-
>(node3:label)
WHERE node1.propertyA={value1} AND node2.propertyB =
{value2} AND node3.propertyC = {value3}
RETURN node3
```

Processing a query Q of the above form under TEAE is as follows:

1. Each value in the graph is encrypted using the RND scheme.
2. According to the first part node1.propertyA = value1 of Q, we need to lower the encryption of propertyA to level DET. By using DECRYPT RND UDF: UPDATE Label SET propertyA = DECRYPT RND(propertyA).
3. As Q has multiple links, we start with the first part R1 which is (node1) - [Rel1]-> (node2), and execute the query Q1 to allow the initial search node1.propertyA=encrypt(value1) for nodes of Q to be executed. When the path required in the main query Q start as:

```
MATCH (node1:label)-[Rel1]->(node2:label)-[Rel2]-
>(node3:label)
WHERE node1.propertyA = {encrypt(value1)}
RETURN node2 AS result
```

Here, result is used as an alias for result column name of Q_1, while encrypt (value1) is the encryption of value1.

4. In order to implement the second part Q_2 of Q, we need to lower the encryption level of result.propertyB for nodes that have an incoming relationship with the result variable of Q_1 to the DET layer.
5. Processing the second part Q_2 of the query Q:

```
MATCH (result)<-[Rel2]-(node3:label)
WHERE node3.propertyB = {encrypted value2}
RETURN result
```

6. Finally, proxy decrypts the results and sends them back to the user.
   We now consider general case of the *simple traversal query* of the form:

```
MATCH(node1:label_1)-[:Relationship1]-
>...(node_i:label_i)-[:Relationship_i]->...(node_k:
label_k)
WHERE node_1.property_1={value1} AND ...
node_i.property_i = {value_i}... AND node_k.property_k
= {value_k}
RETURN node_k
```

The following is the process for resolving a query Q of the above form using the TEAE scheme:

1. Encrypt all values at RND layer.
2. Lowering the encryption of property-1 to level DET, by using decryptRND UDF: SET property-1 = decryptRND(property-1).

3. Execute Q_1 which is the first part of Q when the path required start as:

```
MATCH(node-1:label-1)-[:Relationship-1]->(nodei:label-i)
WHERE node-1.property-1 = {encrypt(value-1)}
RETURN node-i AS result
```

Here, `result` is used as an alias for the result column name of Q_1, while `encrypt (value-1)` is the encryption of `value-1`.

4. In order to execute the second part Q_2 of Q, we need to lower the encryption level of `result.property-i` for nodes that have an incoming relationship with result of Q_1 to the DET layer. Then, execute Q_2 as:

```
MATCH (result)<-[:Relationship-i]-(node-k:label-k)
WHERE result.property-i={encrypt(value-i)}
RETURN result-1
```

5. For $Q_{3,}$ lower the encryption of `property-k` for nodes that have an incoming relationship with `result_1` of Q_2 to DET, ...

6. Finally, proxy decrypts the results and sends them back to the user.

4.1   Implementation

We implemented a prototype system for evaluating the performance of traversal - aware encryption adjustment. To build this prototype, we utilized AES (Advanced Encryption Standard) algorithm [1]. For the RND layer we used AES in CBC mode with an initialization vector (IV) obtained as the hash of ID of the node to which encrypted data belong to. For DET layer we used AES in ECB mode. The security parameter of AES key encryption schemes is 128-bit.

We create a set of User-Defined Functions (UDFs) to be called directly from Cypher queries [8]. The functions *encryptDET*, *encryptRND*, *decryptRND*, and *decryptDET* implement encryption and decryption for the DET and RND layers, respectively. UDFs are written in Java, they are packaged in a Jar-file, deployed into the `$NEO4J_HOME/plugins`, and then can be called in the same way as any other Cypher function.

4.2   Case Studies

In this sub-section, we present several examples of the queries executed on a particular graph data store under different encryption adjustment policies using implemented UDFs for encryption and decryption. Suppose we have a graph database of `Person` and two properties of interest: `name` and `age`, and the relationships `KNOWS`; the scenario is illustrated in Fig. 2. Consider the Cypher query as follows:

```
MATCH (node1:person)-[:KNOWS]->(node2:person)
WHERE node1.name = "Tom" AND node2.age = "22"
RETURN node2
```

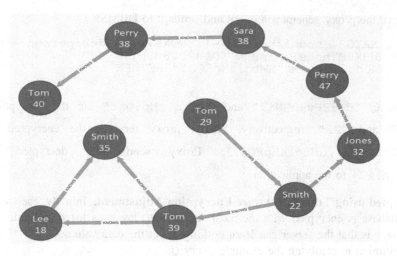

Fig. 2. Example data layout schema at the server of the graph database.

For this study, we considered the execution of the above query in three modes: (1) non-encrypted; (2) encrypted with simple adjustment; and (3) with traversal- aware encryption adjustment.

Non-encrypted. The search criteria WHERE clause has two parameters, starts with node1.name="Tom" when executed gives an output of three nodes Smith, 22}, {Smith, 35}, {Lee, 18} to be traversed (these are reached from the {Tom, 29} node in one step via the KNOWS relation). Next, execute the second part of the query node2.age="22". Lastly, get the {Smith, 22} node as the final result.

Encrypted with Simple Adjustment. Initially, each value in the graph is encrypted within the RND layer as the outermost layer, as follows:

```
MATCH (n)
SET n.name =
encryptRND((encryptDET(n.name)),ID(n)),
n.age=encryptRND ((encryptDET(n.age)),ID(n))
```

Where encryptRND and encryptDET are a user defined function implementing the encryption as mentioned in Subsect. 4.1. Resolution of the query requires the lowering of the encryption of name and age to level DET (as we need to check the equality). To do so, we need to update the data by using SET clauses:

```
MATCH (n)
SET n.name = decryptRND(n.name,ID(n)) AND
n.age=decryptRND(n.age,ID(n))
```

Next, the proxy generates a query and sends it to DBMS:

```
MATCH (node1:person)-[:KNOWS]->(node2:person)
WHERE node1.name = "UD82Pv8uGNi7" AND
node2.age = "NMtqlsMp8Qaf" RETURN node2
```

Where, `"UD82Pv8uGNi7"` and `"NMtqlsMp8Qaf"` are the encryption of `"Tom"` and `"22"`, respectively. Lastly, proxy receives the encrypted result `{j39IjDVyx/+,NMtqlsMp8Qaf}`. Proxy sends the decrypted result `{Smith,22}` to the application.

Encrypted using Traversal-Aware Encryption Adjustment. Initially, each value in the database is encrypted with the most secure RND layer, as listed in Table 2. The advantage is that the server can learn nothing about the data values.

Returning to resolving the example query Q:

```
MATCH (node1:person)-[:KNOWS]->(node2:person)
WHERE node1.name = "Tom" AND node2.age = "22"
RETURN node2
```

Subsequently, we need to remove the onion layer, as WHERE `node1.name="Tom"` requires lowering the encryption of name to level DET, the proxy issues the following query to the server UPDATE Label SET name = DECRYPT RND(name), that use the decryptRND UDFs, where decryptRND is a user defined function implementing decryption which is discussed in Subsect. 4.1.

Then we execute the query Q_1 that process the initial search for nodes where the path required resolving the original query Q may start:

```
MATCH (node1:person)-[:KNOWS]->(node2:person)
WHERE node1.name = "UD82Pv8uGNi7"
RETURN node2 AS output
```

Table 2. Plain text data, encryption at the RND layer and encryption at the DET layer (Ciphertexts shown are not full-length).

Name	Age	Name at RND	Age at RND	Name at DET	Age at DET
Tom	29	a4a895a87052	e6ba69bdf08c	UD82Pv8uGNi7	33TPfYgeYDKb
Smith	22	9d60b415e6e7	686097aa7a7a	j39IjDVyx/+	NMtqlsMp8Qaf
Tom	39	9b078f653478	21da9938c098	UD82Pv8uGNi7	Ss67Waxq2n+m
Lee	18	6cf77f7817b1	bcb86ac44437	RQpqwfEE8Kbm	fxEYkxe7g+P27L
Smith	35	e7a86cbc36ff	83e6b8ab0edc	j39IjDVyx/+	5K6xJRUEJ2s+
Perry	47	ca06d68f7c6b	c1051d53aae2	0nPCg1bAxh8R	oSLl00rhMbeZ
Tom	40	5f2041a58089	56c26c25e4d	UD82Pv8uGNi7	rXhFoilgAFoO

Here the output variable is used as an alias for the result column name of Q_1, and UD82Pv8uGNi7 is the encryption of Tom. As a result of the first stage of the query resolution, there are three nodes as the outgoing of the n.name = "UD82Pv8uGNi7" node.

Before processing the second part of the query Q, WHERE y.age = "22", we need to lower the encryption level of the age property of nodes in the output variable ONLY to the DET layer.

Then we execute the query, implementing the next step of Q execution:

```
MATCH (n: person)-[:KNOWS]->(output)
WHERE output.age = "NMtqlsMp8Qaf"
RETURN output
```

Lastly, Proxy receives the encrypted result of the above implementation {j39IjDVyx/+q, NMtqlsMp8Qaf}, decrypts the result and sends the decrypted result back {Smith, 22} to the application. This solution improves on previous methods by not decrypting all age properties at the DET layer, but only decrypting what the query resolution requires.

Bounded Traversal. In order to investigate how the traversal-aware adjustment works with a specific variable length path, we return to the database example that is presented in Fig. 2, a variable length path of between 1 and 3 relationships from node1 to node2 is considered below. For example, if we assume a query Q:

```
MATCH (node1)-[*1..3]->(node2)
WHERE node1.name = 'Smith' AND node2.age = '38'
RETURN node2
```

At the start point, all values are held in the RND layer. We then move values to the DET layer using the function UPDATE Label SET P = DECRYPT RND, where P corresponds to name. Thereafter, we perform the query Q_1 processing the initial search for nodes when the path required in the original query Q starts as:

```
MATCH (node1)-[*1..3]->(node2)
WHERE node1.name = "j39IjDVyx/+"
RETURN node2 AS output
```

Again, the output variable is used as an alias for the result column name of Q_1, j39IjDVyx/+, corresponds to the encryption of Smith. Further execution of Q_1 shows that there are six nodes as the outgoing of node1.name = "j39IjDVyx/+" condition. Before processing the second part of the query Q, Q, WHERE node2.age = "38", we need to lower the encryption level of the age property of nodes in the output variable to the DET layer.

Next we execute the query Q_2, implementing the next step of Q execution:

```
MATCH (node1)-[*1..3]->(output)
WHERE output.age = 'V01kYVwG13GU'
RETURN output
```

Where V01kYVwG13GU is the encryption of "38". Finally, Proxy receives the encrypted result of the above implementation {Z+NQr9J7iSRi,V01kYVwG13GU}, and sends the decrypted result {Sara,38} back to the application.

Unbounded Traversal. Now, we need to see the affect when the path length between nodes is unbounded; when the variable path length of any number of relationships from node1 to node2 is unlimited. With reference to the example graph in Fig. 2, assume the following query Q:

```
MATCH (node1)-[*]->(node2)
WHERE node1.name = 'Smith' AND node2.age = '38'
RETURN node2
```

To resolve the query the DET layer for name is required. We process the query Q_1 to allow the initial search for nodes to be executed, when the path required in the original query Q starts as:

```
MATCH (node1)-[*]->(node2)
WHERE node1.name = "j39IjDVyx/+"
RETURN node2 AS output
```

At this stage the output variable is used as an alias for the result column of Q_1,j39IjDVyx/+, corresponds to the encryption of Smith. Further execution of Q_1 indicates that there are seven nodes in output using the filter node1.name = "j39IjDVyx/+".

As soon as the lowering of the encryption level of the age property of the nodes in the output variable to the DET layer has been done, we can process the second part of the query Q, which is WHERE node2.age = "38". Next we execute Q_2, to implement the next step of Q:

```
MATCH (node1)-[*]->(output)
WHERE output.age = 'V01kYVwG13GU'
RETURN node2
```

Where V01kYVwG13GU is the encryption of "38". The Proxy receives the encrypted results from the previous implementation: {Z+NQr9J7iSRi,V01kYVwG13GU} and; and decrypts the results {OnPCg1bAxh8R,V01kYVwG13GU} and {Perry,38} and returns them to the user.

5   Experiments and Performance Analysis

In this section, we report on the results of experiments conducted to show the validity of the approach and estimate the performance.

5.1   Datasets

In order to study the traversal-aware encryption adjustment concept varieties of datasets have been used. A total of five Neo4j databases were constructed (Table 3). Each database consists of a number of nodes and edges, and each node has a different number of properties, as well as relationships. For the case study, we consider a particular graph database instance. In this example scenario, we have nodes with the label Person, and group of properties of interest: name, age, and gender. Graph datasets were created to contain approximately 10, 100, 500, 1000, and 10000 nodes to aid in assessing execution time of queries over non-encrypted data and encrypted data. The system used for testing ran on Windows, version 10. It has an Intel Core 2 Duo CPU running at 3.40 GHz and has 16 GB of RAM. The benchmarking program was the only application running when the results were created, but the machine was connected to the Internet and standard system processes were running.

5.2   Queries

To test the approach, we executed the queries $Q_1 - Q_5$ below over non-encrypted data and over encrypted data using traversal-aware encryption adjustment where applicable. We refer to encrypted versions of the queries as $Q'_1 - Q'_5$. This particular set of queries was selected to test some commonly used in graph databases queries.

Q1: Find All Orphan Nodes (No Incoming Edges and No Outgoing Edges)

```
MATCH (node)
WHERE not((node)-[ ]-())
RETURN node
```

Q2: Basic Relationships Matching

```
MATCH (node1)-[:KNOWS]->(node2)
WHERE node1.name = 'Tom' AND node2.age = '22'
RETURN node2.name, node2.age
```

Q3: Adding Relationship Length

```
MATCH (node1)-[:KNOWS]->(node2)-[:KNOWS]->(node3)
WHERE node1.name = 'Jones' AND node2.age = '47' AND
node3.gender = 'Female'
RETURN node3.name, node3.age, node3.gender
```

Q4: Variable Relationship Length

```
MATCH (node1)-[:KNOWS*1..3]->(node2)
WHERE node1.name = 'Jones' AND node2.age = '38'
RETURN node2.name, node2.age
```

Q5: Infinite Length and Length Limit

```
MATCH (node1)-[:KNOWS*]->(node2)
WHERE node1.name = 'Jones' AND node2.age = '38'
RETURN node2.name, node2.age
```

Notice that execution of each of $Q'_2 - Q'_5$, requires the execution of several queries/updates (unlike the single query execution of non-encrypted versions). In order to make a fair comparison we composed query/update parts of Q'_1 by using WITH clauses. Having WITH enabled the query parts to be chained together, passing the outputs from one to be used as starting points or criteria in the next. As in these queries the first condition is WHERE node1.name='value' we need to adjust the encryption level of name to the DET layer to allow equality checking. Take for example, Q'_2, as follows:

```
(1) MATCH (node1)-[:KNOWS]->(node2)
(2) WHERE node1.name=decryptRND(encryptRND
    (encryptDET('Tom'), ID(node1)),ID(node1))}
(3) SET node2.age= decryptRND(node2.age,ID(node2))
(4) with node2
(5) MATCH (node1:Person)-[:KNOWS]->(node2)
(6) WHERE node2.age = decryptRND
    (encryptRND(encryptDET('22'), ID(node2)),ID(node2))
(7) return decryptDET(node2.name), decryptDET(node2.age)
```

In step (1), we have a MATCH clause to determine the direction of the relationship and its depth. In step (2), as all values are held in the RND layer, we need to decrypt the name property within the DET layer, in order to allow the equality checking. In step (3), we lower the encryption of the age property for nodes in the previous step. In step (4), by using WITH we can pass the previous result so that it becomes the starting criteria to the next part of the query. In step (5) we determine the direction of the relationship. In step (6) we implement the second condition. In step (7) we return the result in plain text format.

5.3 Results

Each query was run over all five databases and execution times (in milliseconds) for non-encrypted data and encrypted data was collected, as presented in Table 3. The queries Q_1 and, to find orphan nodes, resulted in a similar result for both the non-encrypted and encrypted databases. Those nodes were iterated through, checking each node for the presence of edges. For the queries $Q_2 - Q_5$ the execution time was clearly faster, this was expected since the queries over non-encrypted databases do not require any encryption layer adjustment.

Table 3. Query results using different graph database sizes (milliseconds).

Database	No. of nodes	No. of relationships	Q1	Q2	Q3	Q4	Q5	Q'1	Q'2	Q'3	Q'4	Q'5
DB1	10	9	1	2	2	4	3	1	5	6	9	7
DB2	100	82	1	4	4	3	4	2	20	20	18	15
DB3	500	410	4	2	2	2	4	4	36	32	35	34
DB4	1000	820	4	2	2	2	4	4	63	61	58	55
DB5	10000	8200	4	2	2	2	4	15	555	504	505	655

From an overall perspective, the retrieval time for non-encrypted databases is small and roughly similar for all datasets. For the encrypted case, the execution time clearly grows with the size of the database but remains in a practically feasible range (under a second) for the largest considered dataset.

6 Conclusion

In this paper, we reported on the implementation and evaluation of traversal- aware encryption adjustment mechanism for querying encrypted data in graph databases. The method provides better security protection against server-side attacks while keeping good implement ability and reasonable performance of query execution.

Security. The considered case studies have shown the trade-off between simple and traversal-aware encryption adjustment policies. The simple policy requires less queries and updates to be followed, on the other hand, the traversal-aware policy provides better security, as it reveals less information to a possible server- side attacker. With the latter policy, as observed above not all age property values were adjusted to the DET layer, just those required to allow the query execution to progress.

Performance. We report on experiments and performance of the proposed schema in the Appendix. To evaluate the proposed mechanism a collection of five databases was **created**, the proposed approach was tested using five types of Cypher queries. The evaluation was conducted by doing experiments that measure the execution time for a set of queries directed at both non-encrypted data and encrypted data with different dataset sizes. Our results are encouraging, but still, need to be validated using larger data sets.

Implementability. Similar to the methods in [2, 3, 7] and unlike the methods in [4, 5] the proposed mechanism does not need to change the inner structure of the DBMS because it is implemented as a set of layers above the DBMS. In particular, the proposed approach is compatible with a concurrency control for multi-user DBMS, but related security aspects and performance evaluation in multi-user environment need to be addressed in future work.

References

1. Abdullah, A.M.: Advanced encryption standard (AES) algorithm to encrypt and decrypt data. In: Proceedings of the Cryptography and Network Security, pp. 1–12 (2017)
2. Aburawi, N., Coenen, F., Lisitsa, A.: Traversal-aware encryption adjustment for graph databases. In: Proceedings of the 7th International Conference on Data Science, Technology and Applications, Portugal, pp. 381–387 (2018)
3. Aburawi, N., Lisitsa, A., Coenen, F.: Querying encrypted graph databases. In: Proceedings of the 4th International Conference on Information Systems Security and Privacy, Portugal, pp. 447–451 (2018)
4. Chase, M., Kamara, S.: Structured encryption and controlled disclosure. In: Abe, M. (ed.) ASIACRYPT 2010. LNCS, vol. 6477, pp. 577–594. Springer, Heidelberg (2010). https://doi.org/10.1007/978-3-642-17373-8_33
5. Francis, N., et al.: Cypher: an evolving query language for property graphs. In: Proceedings of the 18th SIGMOD International Conference on Management of Data, USA, pp. 1433–1445 (2018)
6. Popa, R.A., Redfield, C.M.S., Zeldovich, N., Balakrishnan, H.: CryptDB: protecting confidentiality with encrypted query processing. In: Proceedings of the 23rd ACM Symposium on Operating Systems Principles, Portugal, pp. 85–100 (2011)
7. Robinson, I., Webber, J., Eifrem, E.: Graph Databases, 1st edn. OReilly Media Inc., Sebastopol (2013)
8. Neo4j, Inc. User Defined Procedures and Functions (2019). https://neo4j.com/developer/procedures-functions/. Accessed 18 Apr 2019

Secret Speech Hiding in Image Based on Quantization Level Modification

Shams N. Abd-Alwahab[1](✉) and Mousa K. Wali[2]

[1] Department of Computer Engineering, College of Technical Electrical Engineering, Middle Technical University, Baghdad, Iraq
shamsn328@gmail.com
[2] Department of Electronic Engineering, College of Technical Electrical Engineering, Middle Technical University, Baghdad, Iraq
musa.wali@mtu.edu.iq

Abstract. Data hiding is a form of steganography method that hides secret data in a cover medium like an image, audio or video. In this paper, a method of hiding speech data in a colored image is presented. The main method used in this proposal depends on the technique of quantization level modification with Discrete Wavelet Transform (DWT) to process the cover medium. The latter is used to extract from the RGB of colored images its three bands namely; Low-High (LH), High-Low (HL), and High-High (HH), to be used for embedding the data. As well as Discrete Cosine Transform (DCT) compression is used to compress the speech data by 40% ratio. The embedding method mainly depends upon Absolute Moment Block Truncation Coding (AMBTC) technique for manipulating the binary format of speech. In order to increase the complexity of this proposal, the cover image data is scrambled by using a permutation key that is generated by the Henon map. This proposal also can be utilized to hide any password needed to be extracted by the end-user. The experimental result shows that the average of mean square error (MSE) is 12.16186, peak signal to noise ratio (PSNR) is 33.34402, while the structural similarity (SSIM) is 0.97852.

Keywords: Discrete Wavelet Transform · Discrete Cosine Transform · Speech hiding · Henon map

1 Introduction

Speech is an essential way for humans to transmit information. The main goal of speech is to communicate. Speech may be defined as an audio track that is a response to one or more excitement signals [1]. The sheer volume of data transfer is extremely difficult in terms of transport and storage. One of the ways to convert human speech into an encoded manner that can be decoded to restore the original signal is through speech compression [2]. Compression is used to remove repetition between auxiliary cycles and adjacent sample. The main goal of speech compression is present the signal with fewer bits. Data must be reduced in such a way that there is an acceptable loss of quality [3].

© Springer Nature Switzerland AG 2020
M. I. Khalaf et al. (Eds.): ACRIT 2019, CCIS 1174, pp. 383–394, 2020.
https://doi.org/10.1007/978-3-030-38752-5_30

The explained purpose of hiding information is hiding confidential information by embedding it in various mediums called a transport company. This carrier may be video files, audio files, or images. This paper discusses modern methods in the steganography of image files. The main problems in the techniques of concealing information into the image are; ability to integrate, capacity for inclusion, and durability [4].

Overall, compression techniques are analyzed the information and discussed their advantages and disadvantages to determine the appropriateness of the method of hiding the data that will provide guidance. The image data can be hidden in the compressed area and/or the spatial domain as well. The technique of hiding data in the spatial domain works on adjusting pixel values of cover image in the spatial domain directly by embedding the data [5, 6]. Since images have richer redundancy in the spatial domain than that at the complex domain, therefore, the techniques of hiding information display considerably quality of the image and higher of payload in the spatial domain. Furthermore, after compressing an image, the frequency in the data will be decreased, so, the quality of hiding in compressed data (embedding ability) tends to be less.

The simple and efficient image compression technique among these lossy techniques is a Block Truncation Coding (BTC). Two quantization levels of a_i and b_i with a bitmap of B_i are applied through the compression code of an image block C_i by using an Absolute Moment Block Truncation Coding (AMBTC). The AMBTC is drawn attention to the search for data hiding because it requires a low cost of computational and provides a highly acceptable quality of the image [7]. This work presents an approach differs from other works in hiding in wavelet domain in high-frequency bands and keep the low frequency without modifying. From the other side, the embedding information has a specific mapping and all coded data will be scrambled. Discrete Cosine Transform (DCT) is a frequency conversion used for fixed and mobile video compression. This addresses the rapid implementation of DCT based on architectural transformations algorithm and frequency loss approach [8]. The Inverse Discrete Cosine Transform (IDCT) transforms an image into the spatial domain of the data representation that is most suitable for compression. IDCT-based decoding is the basis for current image and video compression standards [9]. Section 2 present the total steps of proposed method, in Sect. 2.1 present speech compression, in Sect. 2.2 present discrete wavelet transform, in Sect. 2.3 present Chaotic Function and Henon Map, in Sect. 2.4 present extraction proposed method, in Sect. 3 present excremental results, while Sect. 4 present conclusion.

2 Proposed Method

Hiding secret speech in an image is presented in this paper in which the DWT and AMBTC for an image have been used, while DCT compression is used for secret speech. The used image is divided into three bands; red, green, and blue (RGB) then each band is partitioned into equal size of blocks, for example (4 × 4). Each block will be represented by using three values (coding values) that are extracted depending on the mean pixel value as follows: b_i is average more than mean, a_i is average less than mean, and B_i is a bitmap of logical values of b_i equal to one and a_i equal to zero, as shown in Fig. 1. Two stages in the proposal are forward and backward for hiding and extraction, the forward stage is represented by inserting the secret speech into a covered image as confidential information as shown in Fig. 2. The compressed speech will be converted to binary form and every 16 bits will be reshaped into (4×4) to simulate the shape of bitmap (B_i) that replaced it in cover medium. The maximum size of embedding secret speech is depending on compressed speech size and should be equal or less than number of blocks multiplied by 16 (size of bitmap) multiplied by three if image is color image.

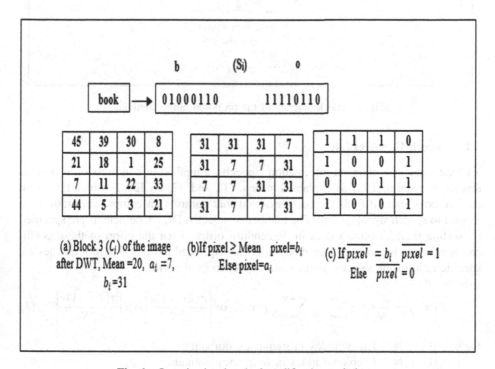

Fig. 1. Quantization level of modification technique.

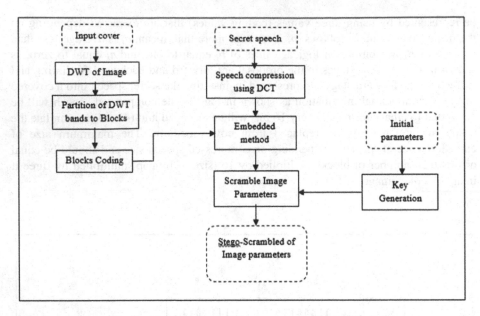

Fig. 2. Block diagram of the proposed hiding method.

2.1   Speech Compression

To reduce the size of secret information (speech), a method of compression is used in this work based on DCT as explained in Eqs. (1), and (2) for IDCT, which transform the vector of data. It finds the best threshold that controls on compression ratio with respect to speech signal quality. The number of selected DCT-Coefficients are specified by sorting their absolute values in descending order. Then the norm of these coefficients values is found in an increment order (as explained in Eq. (3) until it reaches the specific ratio of the selected norm with respect to total norm.

$$F(u,v) = \frac{2}{N}C(v)\sum_{x=0}^{N-1}\sum_{y=0}^{N-1}f(x,y)cos\left[\frac{\pi(2x+1)u}{2N}\right]cos\left[\frac{\pi(2y+1)v}{2N}\right] \quad (1)$$

for u = 0, ..., N − 1 (row index in frequency domain),

v = 0, ..., N − 1 (colomn index in frequency domain),

x is row index in spatial domain and y is colomn index in spatial domain where N = 8 and C(k) = $\{\frac{1}{\sqrt{2}}$ for k = 0 otherwise it is equal 1$\}$

$$f(x,y) = \frac{2}{N}C(v)C(v)\sum_{u=0}^{N-1}\sum_{v=0}^{N-1}F(u,v)cos\left[\frac{\pi(2x+1)u}{2N}\right]cos\left[\frac{\pi(2y+1)v}{2N}\right] \quad (2)$$

for u = 0, ..., N − 1, v = 0, ..., N − 1

$$norm = \|x\| = \sqrt{x_1^2 + \cdots + x_n^2} \tag{3}$$

where $x_{i:n}$ are DCT coefficient greater than threshold

2.2 Discrete Wavelet Transform (DWT)

DWT has the capability for analyzing a signal at both frequency and time domains. The joint time-frequency resolution obtained by DWT makes it the most suitable method for the extraction of details and approximations of the signals which cannot be obtained by FFT or STFT [10]. Wavelet Transform is a method to convert an array of (N) input samples of their decimal value to an array of wavelet coefficients of the N output. The coefficients of wavelets indicate the relationship between desired the function of wavelet while input signal samples. Thus, in order to obtain the entire coefficients of wavelet of the specified level ought to convert the wavelets gradually to retrieve a complete set of input samples. The wavelet will be testing the array with accurately which depends on its volume, and thus to retrieve a low high decision of the input array required for various wavelet size in each case. The general equation of the Mother Wavelet is defined in Eq. (4) [11].

$$\Psi_{b,a}(t) = \frac{1}{\sqrt{|b|}} \Psi\left[\frac{t-a}{b}\right] \quad a, \, b \in R, \, b \neq 0 \tag{4}$$

where a is the parameter wavelet (the location of the wavelet function), b is the wavelet scaling parameter that determines the size of the wavelets and R is the space of wavelets. In this research, each band of the color image is used as a grayscale image and can be used for hiding information. The image transforms into one level by Haar DWT as shown in Fig. 3 to produce four bands; High-High (HH), Low-High (LH), High-Low (HL), and Low-Low (LL), bands. The LL band includes the significant values of image information. Therefore, embedding can occur in any of the other bands.

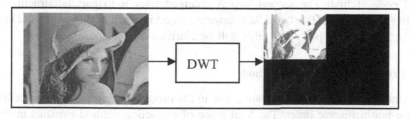

Fig. 3. Image Discrete Wavelet Transforms.

2.3   Chaotic Function and Henon Map

Chaotic maps are usually utilized in the investigation of dynamical frameworks [12]. At all, Chaotic maps produce fractals. In spite of the fact that a rehashed procedure may develop the fractal, a few fractals are considered as opposed sets to regarding maps that produce them [13]. This is on the grounds that there are numerous different iterative approaches to produce a similar fractal. Henon Map is an occurrence of a clamorous guide; it was presented by Michel Henon as a disentangled model of the Poincare area of the Lorenz demonstrate. For the traditional guide, a purpose from the plane will be approached either a lot of focuses recognized as the Henon odd attractor or separate to boundlessness. Henon Attractor is a fractured, smooth one-loader and cantor group in the other. Numerical evaluations yield a connection measurement of 1.25 ± 0.02 and Hausdorff measurement of 1.261 ± 0.003 for the attractor of the traditional guide. Confused qualities can be produced from applying conditions (5 and 6) which are iterated for n times to create the required components.

$$x(n+1) = 1 - a \times x(n)^2 + y(n) \qquad (5)$$

$$y(n+1) = b \times x(n) \qquad (6)$$

The qualities of the constants 'a = 1.76' and 'b = 0.1' were utilized to get an arbitrary succession [14]. The Henon Map is utilized for key age with beginning quality that produces genuine numbers in period (0, 1) to generate a real number, and these numbers are multiplied by power ten decimal number and modulated by 256 to keep the result in byte range (0, 255). These resultant numbers will be used for substitute the yield codded estimations of advances technique. For each block with size (m × m), compute the average pixel value in C_i, denoted as $\overline{C_i}$. The bitmap B_i can be developed and the lower quantization level a_i is gotten by adjusting the mean estimation of the pixel in C_i with qualities not exactly the incentive for C_i and the upper quantization level b_i is gotten by adjusting the mean estimation of the pixel in C_i with qualities not exactly the incentive for C_i. To disentangle the AMBTC trio (a_i, b_i, B_i), zero's qualities in B_i are decoded by a_i, and one's qualities in B_i are decoded by b_i, thus will translate picture $\widetilde{C_i}$. The way toward making secret content is by changing over into content to ASCII code at first. The second step is changed over it to parallel structure. The installing will cut from this two-fold arrangement and inserted in shrouded band in non-uniform length rely upon some edge will be clarified in implanting stage.

2.4   Proposed Extraction Method

The extraction method is a backward phase in the proposal using the same procedure in forward but in reverse order. The total stage of extraction method explains in Fig. 4. First, the same parameters of the Henon map are used to generate same sequences numbers for descrambling. The transmitted data will exclusive-OR with the generated key. The extracted data will use the bitmap of each block in AMBTC for reconstructing secret speech by reshaping every 16 bits into concatenated vector that will be changed to bytes (every 8 bits). The extracted values represent the sample value followed by its position and empty position will be replaced by zeros that quantized in DCT in forward before. This reconstructed vector will inverse transform using IDCT to produce secret speech that similar to original signal. Inverse DWT will be used to get the original image with minimal distortion.

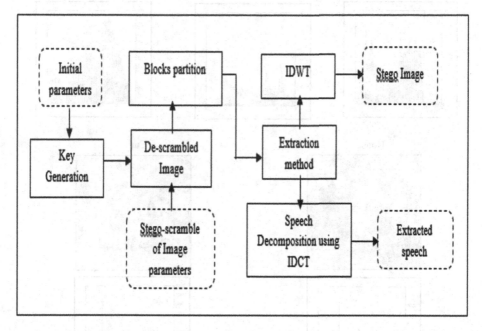

Fig. 4. Block diagram of the proposed extraction method.

3   Experimental Results

Experimental works are applied on selected images to test them before and after embedding with size of 512×512, Baboon, Lena, peppers, house, and car are used as test images. The size of the block is 4×4 used in AMBTC. The histogram of the original images and Stego-images are shown in Figs. 5 and 6 respectively.

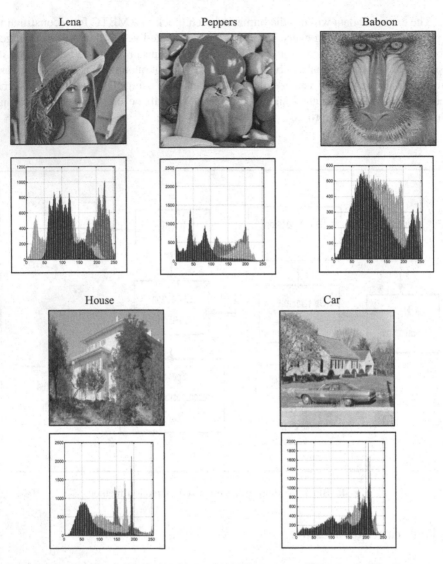

Fig. 5. The original tested images with histograms (before embedding).

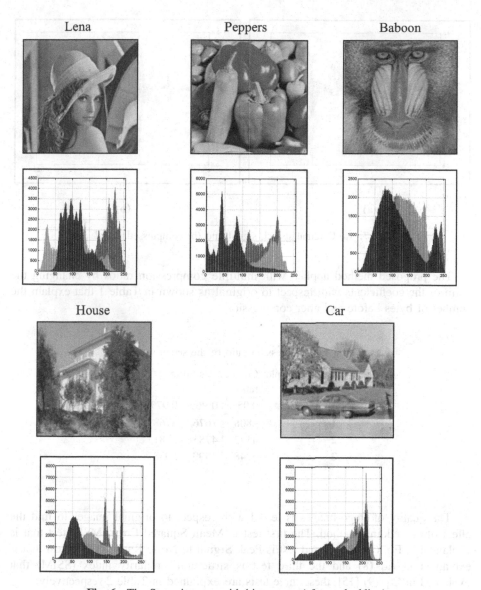

Fig. 6. The Stego-images with histograms (after embedding).

The DCT compression method is applied on secret speech with minimum distortion as shown in Fig. 7, and the total bytes of compression ratio is depending on the threshold value of total norm that used (as explained in Eq. (3)) such that 97% or 98%. The speech signal is represented by a high amount of data (bytes) with high redundancy, so, there is a need for reducing this data for hiding in image and keep signal with minimum distortion as possible.

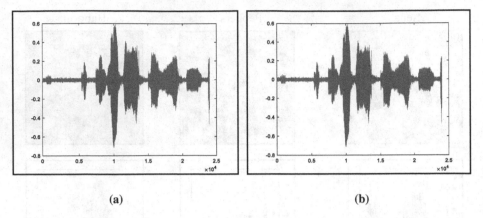

(a)   (b)

Fig. 7. (a) Original speech signal and (b) compressed signal.

The proposed method applied with multiple compression ratios by changing the norm of the coefficients with respect to original as shown in Table 1 that explain the number of bytes before and after compression.

Table 1. Compression ratio of the secret speech.

Speech sample	Coefficients norm ratio		
	0.95%	0.96%	0.97%
1	6808	7676	8768
2	4122	4785	5681
3	3248	3999	5038

The quality of stego-images is tested with respect to original images to find the effect of embedding method. The first test is Mean Squared Error (MSE) test that is explained in Eq. (7), the second test is Peak Signal to Noise Ratio (PSNR) test that is explained in Eq. (8) and the third test is structural similarity index (SSIM) that explained in Eq. (9) [15], these three tests are explained in Table 2 respectively.

$$MSE = \frac{1}{mn} \sum_{i=0}^{m-1} \sum_{j=0}^{m-1} [I(i,j) - K(i,j)]^2 \tag{7}$$

$$PSNR = 10 \cdot \left(\frac{MAX_I^2}{MSE} \right) \tag{8}$$

where, I is original image, K is distorted image,

and (m and n) is image dimensions

$$SSIM(x,y) = \frac{\left(2m_x m_y + c_1\right)\left(2\sigma_{xy} + c_2\right)}{\left(2m_x^2 + m_y^2 + c_1\right)\left(\sigma_x^2 + \sigma_y^2 + c_2\right)} \tag{9}$$

Where, m_x, and m_y are mean of orignal image and distorted image, σ_x, and σ_y are standard deviation of orignal image and distorted image, σ_{xy} coverance of two images, and c1, c2 are constant

Table 2. Quality measurement of tested images.

Image #	MSE	PSNR	SSIM
Lena	7.7262	34.8837	0.9915
Peppers	8.1462	34.6709	0.9913
Baboon	18.2149	31.4366	0.9598
House	12.4352	33.3401	0.9798
Car	14.2868	32.3888	0.9702

The experimental results of the proposed method present that the histogram of original and stego-images are kept with minimum distortion, and the speech signals that represent secret data are kept after compression that obtains accurate quality. Finally, the objective tests MSE, PSNR, and SSIM are in general accurate values.

4 Conclusion

Secret compressed speech hiding based on AMBTC with DWT of cover image is presented in this paper along scrambling the resulting image using Henon map to increase complexity. The reduction of distortion in the cover image is satisfied by using DWT where the embedding process is done in all DWT domains except the LL band. It is noticeable that the proposed method reduces the size of secret by compressing the speech using DCT and controls the compression ratio and the quality of reconstructed speech signal. The experiments present compression ratio about (23.206%) while attaining the need quality for reception. The proposed method improved both embedding capacity and image quality that the experiment resulted in keeping the MSE, PSNR, and SSIM quite as possible. Thus the proposed method may be utilized in applications that require authentication.

References

1. Chu, W.C.: Speech Coding Algorithms Foundation and Evolution of Standardized Coders. Wiley Interscience, London (2003)
2. Djebbar, F., Ayad, B., Meraim, K.A., Hamam, H.: Comparative study of digital audio steganography techniques. EURASIP J. Audio, Speech, and Music Process. 2–16 (2012)

3. Vatsa, S., Sahu, O.P.: Speech compression using discrete wavelet transform and discrete cosine transform. Int. J. Eng. Res. Technol. **1**, 1–6 (2012)
4. Hussain, A.J., Al-Fayadh, A., Radi, N.: Image compression techniques: a survey in lossless and lossy. Neurocomputing **300**, 45–69 (2018)
5. Kumar, R.R., Jayasudha, S., Pradeep, S.: Efficient and secure data hiding in encrypted images: a new approach using chaos. Inf. Secur. J.: Global Perpective **25**, 236–246 (2016)
6. Maheswari, S.U., Hemanth, D.J.: Performance enhanced image steganography systems using transforms and optimization techniques. Multimed. Tools Appl. **76**, 415–436 (2015)
7. Hong, W., Chen, T.S., Yin, Z., Luo, B., Ma, Y.: Data hiding in AMBTC images using quantization level modification and perturbation technique. Multimed. Tools Appl. **76**, 3761–3782 (2016)
8. El-Rahman, S.A.: A comparative analysis of image steganography based on DCT algorithm and steganography tool to hide nuclear reactors confidential information. Comput. Electr. Eng. **68**, 2–20 (2016)
9. James, J., Thomas, V.J.: Audio compression using DCT and DWT techniques. J. Inf. Eng. Appl. **4**, 119–124 (2014)
10. Hasan, T.S.: Image compression using discrete wavelet transform and discrete cosine transform. J. Appl. Sci. Res. **13**(3), 1–8 (2017)
11. Batra, R., Khatri, I.: Image compression & decompression using discrete wavelet transform approach. Int. J. Res. Appl. Sci. Eng. Technol. (IJRASET) **5**, 1755–1761 (2017)
12. Wang, D., Chang, C.-C., Liu, Y., Song, G., Liu, Y.: Digital image scrambling algorithm based on chaotic sequence and decomposition and recombination of pixel values. Int. J. Netw. Secur. **17**, 322–327 (2015)
13. Ye, G.: Image scrambling encryption algorithm of pixel bit based on chaos map. Pattern Recogn. Lett. **31**, 347–354 (2010)
14. Praveenkumar, P., Amirtharajan, R., Thenmozhi, K., Rayappan, J.B.B.: Triple chaotic image scrambling on RGB - a random image encryption approach. Secur. Commun. Netw. **8**, 3335–3345 (2015)
15. Ponomarenko, N., Leremeiev, O., Lukin, V., Egiazarian, K., Carli, M.: Modified image visual quality metrics for contrast change and mean shift accounting. In: International Conference the Experience of Designing and Application of CAD Systems in Microelectronics (CADSM), pp. 305–311 (2011)

A Secure Wireless Body Area Network for E-Health Application Using Blockchain

Mohammed Dakhel$^{(\boxtimes)}$ and Soukaena Hassan

Department of Computer Sciences, University of Technology, Baghdad, Iraq
0111812@student.uotechnology.edu.iq,
soukaena.hassan@yahoo.com

Abstract. The need to monitor the vital signals of the human body for the early diagnosis of diseases has led to the emergence of wireless body area networks (WBAN) for E-Health. One of the most important problems associated with this technology is to secure the user data over the internet and to keep it safe and inaccessible by unauthorized persons or manipulated by any person maintaining the privacy of the patient. In this paper, a system to secure patient data was proposed by employing the Blockchain technology to save user data and privacy, and cryptography algorithms were used to secure the data transmission channel between the patient and the E-health service provider. The results showed that the proposed system fulfilled the security objectives, namely confidentiality, integrity, authentication, and non-repudiation, in addition to protecting the privacy of the patient to maintain patient data from penetration.

Keywords: Blockchain · Security · Cryptography · Privacy · E-Health

1 Introduction

Wireless Body Area Network makes life easier and more convenient, especially for elderly people. Such technology has covered all human needs in various life fields. One of such technology is wireless sensor network (WSN). This technique is based on the collection of information from a range of sensors deployed at different environments to be examined and applied to serve the community in general or a specific sector such as a company, a government institution and a specific job. One of the most important techniques derived from the WSN is WBAN [1].

WBAN is concerned with networks consisting of several sensors spread on or planted within the human body. These sensors measure the vital health signals of the human body and then send them to the gateway device, which is a phone or a person digital assistant (PDA) owned by the user. The use of the WBAN to remotely monitor the patient's health is one of the factors that helps providing the patient sound opportunity to have a normal life and practice daily activities without the need of permanent medical accommodation or frequent visits to hospitals. It also reduces the

© Springer Nature Switzerland AG 2020
M. I. Khalaf et al. (Eds.): ACRIT 2019, CCIS 1174, pp. 395–408, 2020.
https://doi.org/10.1007/978-3-030-38752-5_31

costs of un-needed visits to the doctor or the hospital for further medical examinations or non-periodic of early detection of any chronic disease. The privacy of the patient, the confidentiality of the data and the medical record are the most important challenges in the WBAN [2].

This paper aims to address these problems by achieving integrity, confidentiality, authentication and non-repudiation. In this paper, a security system based on the blockchain technique to store patient data in impenetrable manner, and maintain the privacy of the patient was proposed. Also, hybrid encryption was used to encrypt and secure the data transfer channel between the patient and the service provider by using Advanced Encryption Standard algorithm (AES) with 128 key size, Rivest–Shamir–Adleman algorithm (RSA), and a hash function. Also to enable the patient to use an anonymous identity to avoid disclosure of the user real identity by anyone.

In an early study [3], it has been proposed SEKEBAN protocol that takes advantage of the physiological signals (electrocardiography (ECG)) of the patient to process the Key Exchange problem in WBAN. Generate of symmetric encryption keys and distribute the keys efficiently between the gateway device and sensors is the aim behind SEKEBAN to secure the transmission. In addition, it secures the connection between the sensors itself through the biometric data. Other work [4] has suggested a system to store the data in a trustworthy, secure, and distributed manner in WBAN. The author relies on three techniques combined to achieve authentication, dependability, and integrity. Which are: the digital signature, public-key cryptography, and the Redundant Residue Number System (RRNS) encoding. However, WBAN has received much attention where a previous work [5] has schemed a secure key generation and multi-layer authentication where in this study, the first layer was between the gateway device and the sensors in one-to-many authentication relationships and an algorithm to establish a group of keys. The second layer is between the gateway device and the medical center by utilizing Elliptic Curve Cryptography. Other work [6] has assumed that ensuring the integrity of the patient data stored on the cloud was the problem on which should addressed in WBAN and suggested to adopt auditing technique to achieve this point. Apparently, to secure the WBAN versus the brute force attack was suggested by previous work [7] by increasing the secret key power.

On the other hand, anonymous authentication protocol was proposed by recent work [8] to achieve patient data integrity and confidentiality based on a low-entropy password where random oracle model was used to prove the system security and client authentication was adopted on a password which was easy to remember while another protocol (cloud-aided) with a lightweight certificateless authentication was proposed by other work [9] where in this protocol, only the network manager can control the real identity of the user in the registration step but in the authentication step, he is unable to know this real identity. Also, a recent work [10] has proposed an encryption algorithm by utilizing hyper-chaotic Zhou system to ensure resistance against any attack in sense of long key and this system was used to create a chaotic key to be used in the encryption algorithm.

A protocol of key agreement was proposed to provide the privacy feature of sensor node anonymity and unlink-ability session based only on the components of symmetric cryptography where this protocol was designed to be an alternative method to the described key exchange ways in the IEEE 802.15.6 standard [11]. A framework was proposed to secure the data transmitted between the patient sink node and the base station. A hybrid algorithm for encryption the data was used: Elliptic Curve Cryptography algorithm and Advanced Encryption Standard algorithm. To generate a secret key in order to secure the communication channel between the base station and sink node, the Elliptic Curve Diffie-Hellman was used [12]. In another work, a certificateless signcryption as a novel protocol was proposed. The protocol aimed to achieve anonymity, authentication, confidentiality, non-repudiation, and integrity for WBAN. By utilizing the suggested signcryption, access control based on certificate less was presented too. Assessing the security of the protocol was done by using the random oracle model [13].

2 Basic Model

Four basic algorithms and techniques have been used in this paper which were RSA (Rivest–Shamir–Adleman), AES (Advanced Encryption Standard), Hash Function and Blochchain. The RSA algorithm is one of the most common algorithms among asymmetric key algorithms. It is a block cipher encryption algorithm. The message to be encrypted is transformed into several blocks of a certain size (n) and each block is encrypted individually. As is known in asymmetric key algorithms, the sender selects two keys, one public and the other private. It sends the public key to all the people who want to exchange information with them and keeps the private key to himself [14, 15].

AES is a block cipher encryption algorithm that uses a symmetric key. The block size is 128-bit, while the key size is 128, 192, or 256-bit. In the first step when AES is executed, the plaintext that is to be encrypted is transformed into blocks, each block is 16-byte (128-bit) size, and each character is represented in hexadecimal form. Then N of rounds is performed on each block depending on the size of the key used. With 128-bit key size, the number of rounds is 10, and 12 round with the 192-bit key size and 14 round with the 256-bit key size [16].

The hash function can be seen as a digital fingerprint of data. It is one of the most important cryptography algorithms due to its features which make it widely used. The advantage of a hash function is to achieve integrity by ensuring a way to determine whether the data to be protected is manipulated or not [17]. From a technical perspective, the hash function is a program that takes certain data and produces a random string of symbols with constant size referred to as the hash value or digest. No matter how the size of the input string is, the output has a fixed size, for example, whether the string size is 4-bit, 1024-bit or any size, the output is a fixed size, which is 128-bit, 256-bit or 512-bit depending on the type of the hash function used. The main features of the hash function are, it is case sensitive, one-way-function and collision resistance [18].

Nevertheless, many hash function algorithms have been developed over the years such as Message Digest series (MD1, MD2, MD3, MD4, and MD5) and Secure Hash Algorithm series (SHA-1, SHA-256, SHA-384, SHA-512, and SHA-224) in addition to other hash function series such as RIPEMD and HAVAL. In this work SHA-1 has been used [19–21].

Finally, the emergent of blockchain has been begun after a paper published by Satoshi Nakamoto 2008 [22]. The blockchain technology is founded by its creator in order to build a decentralized system that is cryptography-based that allow people exchange money over internet peer-to-peer without needed to a third party or intermediate such as banks or online money transfers companies. The most important characteristic of the blockchain is the dependence on the principle of mistrust and the use of the process of consensus or agreement by the participate parties to add the block to the chain to form the blockchain, which acts as a ledger in which all operations or transactions are stored as well as all parties involved in the network have a copy of this ledger [23, 24]. In this paper, the advantages of blockchain were taken in order to apply them on the WBAN.

The use of blockchain is not limited to cryptocurrency only, but it used in many applications and systems that needed a robust decentralized system such as smart contracts, data storage, transfer of values and assets. The reason behind the used of blockchain in this system is decentralization and consensus provided by the blockchain. There are several types of blockchain: public, private, and consensus [25, 26].

In the public blockchain, the data is publicly available and anyone can verify the transaction. While private and consensus blockchain provides more control and privacy [25–27].

3   System Design

In the proposed system, the blockchain technology and hybrid encryption were used to managed and secured WBAN. Basically, the system focused on protected the privacy of the patient by used the anonymous identity, stored the data in decentralized approach to prevent the control and manipulation by any of the participate parties using the shared ledger and consensus, secure transmitting the data between patient and doctor using cryptography, and performed mutual authentication to prevented any unauthorized access. Figure 1 shows the process of the proposed system.

To take the advantage of the E-health services the user sensing data was uploaded automatically once he logs in the system. E-health system provides to the user a medical service depending on the vital signs obtained from the sensors placed on/in his body such as blood pressure, ECG and other specific measurements. As miners or validators in blockchain networks, computer servers are distributed in certain hospitals or medical centers and referred as Validators (Vs).

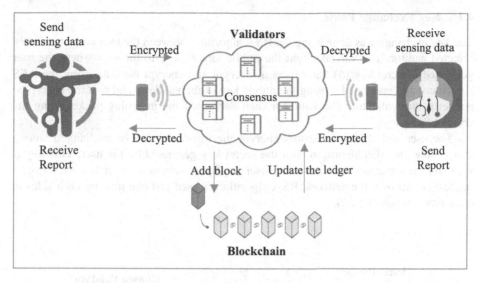

Fig. 1. The proposed system.

In the proposed system, consortium blockchain was used because of the need to participate anybody to the network but just well-known validators could valid the operation within the network. There is no use of the proof-of-work mechanism or any another one to choose the validator who adds the new block to the blockchain. Instead, one of the authenticated validators is random chosen to add the block because all validators are owned by the medical center and there is no need to make the validators compete among themselves to add the block because there is no reward given.

The system consists of several validators where each validator (V) is connected with all others in the network to form a group of validators (GoV) assuming that these validators are secured physically and connected with each other in a secure channel where each validator is a third trusted party (TTP).

This GoV has three basic roles. First, it stores the patient data in a secure manner and guarantees that such data never manipulated. Second, it validates the patient data and authenticated the patient/doctor identity. Finally, it generates new identities to the patient and doctor. In the doctor side or medical center, the doctor logs in to the system as the user does. The patient data and diagnostic doctor report are stored in decentralized ledger and each validator has a copy of this ledger.

4 System Implementation

However, the system was implemented using a number of laptops as Validators and two mobile devices, one representing the patient and the other the doctor. Python was used to write the code of validators and Java language under Android Studio environment to design the doctor and patient applications. Below explanation for the system implementation.

4.1   Key Exchange Phase

The key exchange was done using the RSA algorithm between the user and a randomly selected auditor. The validator sent the public key K_{pub_v} to the user where the user generated a secret key (S) (later used to decrypt and encrypt the data using the AES algorithm) and encrypted it using the public key of the validator and sent the encrypted packet to the validator. The validator then decrypted the incoming packet using the secret key K_{prv_v}.

The user and chosen validators encrypt the information to be exchanged among them using the AES algorithm with the secret key generated by the user. This key is valid for only one session, where the user randomly selects a secret key each time a request is sent over the network. RSA algorithm is used just one time by both sides in each new session (Fig. 2).

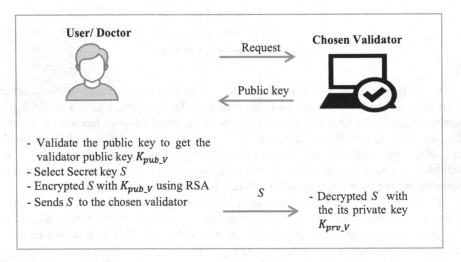

Fig. 2. Key exchange phase

4.2   Registration Phase

In this phase, both sides (user and validator) used AES-128 with the secret key S to encrypted and decrypted the data and exchanged it between them. Figure 3 shows the registration phase. The user sent an anonymous ID_{usr} to the validator who in turn generated a new user IDV_{usr} and sent the hash value of the IDV_{usr} to the user ($HIDV_{usr}$). The validator then broadcasted the hash value of the ID_{usr} (HID_{usr}) with the IDV_{usr} to all validators. In this way, the user has the ID_{usr} and ($HIDV_{usr}$), while the validator has HID_{usr} and IDV_{usr}. The idea of using this method for mutual authentication between the two parties. When the authentication is performed, the user sends the ID_{usr} that is received by any validator, which in turn hash it and looks for a match. The same is true for the validator, where the validator sends IDV_{usr} and the user hash it and compares it with the hash value he has.

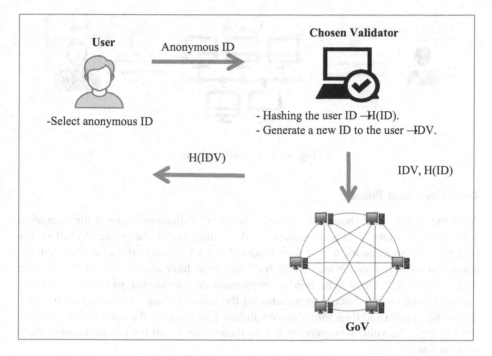

Fig. 3. Registration phase

4.3   Transmitting Phase

At this phase, the user sent the sensing data over the network. The validator received the data and verified the user's identity and the integrity of the data and re-sent it to the doctor, which in turn verifies the identity of the validator and the integrity of the data and resends a diagnostic report based on the data received. When the validator receives the data from the doctor, verify the data and the identity of the doctor and resend the data to the user. It is worth mentioning that both the doctor and the user use their secret key used with the AES, where the validator decrypts the user data using the user secret key and re-encrypts the data using the doctor secret key before sending it to the doctor and vice versa.

The system consists of three parties which are the user, the validators, and the doctor. Both the user and the doctor perform the same procedures for the key exchange session and the process of registration, receiving and sending data. The only difference is in identities (Fig. 4).

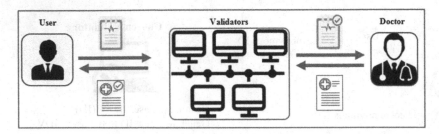

Fig. 4. Transmitting phase

4.4 Consensus Phase

After the transmitting phase has been completed, all validators declared the validation state of the operation. If a consensus on the validation of the packet by all or the majority of the validators, one of them randomly selected to added the new block to the chain that led to update the ledger which all validators have a copy of it. Otherwise, the packet is ignored. There is no need to implement the mechanism of proof-of-work or proof-of-stake or any other kind because all the validators are trustworthy as they are part of the system and their functions of validating and storing the data, so it there is no need to make the validators compete among themselves to get the reward because there is no reward.

4.5 Storage Phase (Add a New Block to the Blockchain)

The chosen validators after the consensus process add a new block to the blockchain. The new block is created containing: the hash value of the previous block, HID_{user}, ID_{Dr}, timestamp, sensing data, doctor report and the hash of the current block. All validators have an updated copy of the ledger to prevent any attempt to manipulate the blockchain. Each specific time period, the data in the blockchain is checked for each validator. Where each block is taken and hashing patient data contained in it and hashing the result with the hash value of the previous block and compare the result with the hash value of the current block. If it does not match, the blockchain of the validator where the hack was detected are updated by requesting a copy of the blockchain from the remaining validators. Figure 5 shows the system blockchain structure.

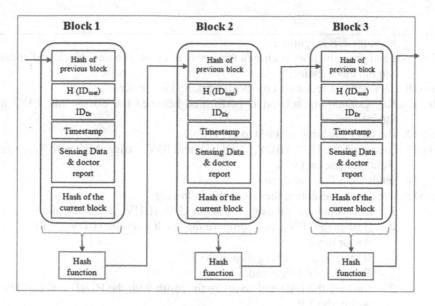

Fig. 5. The system blockchain structure

Algorithm 1 represents the proposed system to exchanging data among the involving parties.

Algorithm 1: Proposed Scheme Algorithm

Input: ID_{user}, ID_{Dr}, user sensing data (UsD), user secret key (S_{user}), doctor secret key (Dr_{user}). **Output**: doctor diagnosis's report (DR).

Step1: User hashes UsD to get the hash value of UsD (HUsD).
Step2: User encrypts ID_{user}, UsD and HUsD using AES with S_{user} to get user packet (UP).
Step3: Sends UP to the doctor over the network.
Step4: The chosen validator (CHV) in the network received the UP.
Step5: CHV broadcasts UP and S_{user} to all validators in the network.
Step6: Each validator is validating the UP as the following:
    1. Decrypted the UP using S_{user} to get ID_{user}, UsD and HUsD.
    2. Hashing the ID_{user} and looking for a matching within its database:
       If there is a matching then go to 3:
       Else: the UP is ignored.
    3. Hashing the UsD and compare the result with the HUsD that contain within the UP:
       If they are identical then go to step7:
       Else: the UP is ignored.
Step7: Each validator broadcasts a message to all validators to declare that the packet is valid.
Step8: If all validators or the majority are consensus that the UP is valid, then go to step9:

Else: the UP is ignored.

Step9: One of the validators is chosen randomly to create the new block and added it to the blockchain.

Step10: CHV sends a request to the doctor asking his services.

Step11: Key exchanging session is performed between the doctor and CHV to obtained S_{Dr}.

Step12: The CHV hashing the UsD to get HUsD.

Step13: Encrypted the UsD, $HIDV_{user}$, HUsD, and IDV_{Dr} using AES with S_{Dr} to get validator packet (VP).

Step14: Sends the VP to the doctor.

Step15: The doctor validating the VP as the following:
1. Decrypted the VP using S_{Dr} to get UsD, $HIDV_{user}$, HUsD, and IDV_{Dr}.
2. Hashes the IDV_{Dr} and compare the result with the $HIDV_{Dr}$ within doctor device:
   If there is a matching then go to 3:
   Else: the VP is ignored.
3. Hashing the UsD and compare the result with the HUsD that contain within the VP:
   If they are identical then go to step16:
   Else: the VP is ignored.

Step16: The doctor checks the UsD to return the diagnosis report (DR).

Step17: Decrypted his DR, the $HIDV_{user}$ sent by the validator, ID_{Dr} and HDR to get doctor packet (DP).

Step18: The doctor sends its DP to the CHV.

Step19: CHV received the DP and repeat the steps (5-9) to validate the DP (taking into consideration the different identities of the user and the doctor) and go to step20.

Step20: CHV encrypted the DR, HDR and IDV_{user} using S_{user} to get a validator packet (VP2).

Step21: The validator sends the VP2 to the user.

Step22: The user validating the VP2 as the following:
1. Decrypted the VP2 using S_{user} to get DR, HDR and IDV_{user}.
2. Hashing the IDV_{user} and compare the result with the $HIDV_{use}$ within his device:
   If there is a matching then go to 3:
   Else: the VP2 is ignored.
3. Hashing the DR and compare the result with the HRD that contain within the VP2:
   If they are identical then go to 4:
   Else: the VP is ignored.

Step23: The user adopts the DR.

5 Results and Discussion

In this section, the obtained results of the proposed system were reviewed by discussing them with some existing protocols to show how effective this system is in securing the data and with the traditional systems. In case of designing a security system, the system must provide needed security services as these services vary from one system to another according to the nature of the system. The proposed system in this paper is based on the provision of two important services. First is to maintain the privacy of the user while the second is to save data in a way that prevents the manipulation of any person to these data whatever the rights or privileges he has. Data confidentiality is not our concern because the data is a patient blood pressure, blood glucose level, heart rate, doctor report, etc. What is emphasizing thing is to preserve the patient privacy by hiding patient real identity avoiding the patient exhaustion by the attacker, and on the other hand to prevent the manipulation of data by any person to ensure the authenticity of data access to the doctor and the health of receipt of the diagnosis report by the patient.

Since we used the cryptography in the proposed system, it has provided us with several security services such as integrity, confidentiality, authentication and non-repudiation.

Integrity was ensured by using SHA-1, which gives the hash value of the data that is unique but not the same hash value from another data. Sending data with its hash value confirms integrity by comparing the hash value of the data within the received package with the hash value obtained by using SHA-1 with the data received.

Confidentiality was achieved by using the AES-128 algorithm, which encrypted data transferred between parties using the secret key. Confidentiality has been imposed by generating a secret key for each of the parties in each session to exchange of information between the parties.

Authentication was achieved by using RSA to exchange the secret key between user/doctor and validator side by side with the anonymous ID generated by the user, are work together to achieve authentication.

Non-repudiation was done by asymmetric cryptographic algorithms that often used with the hash function using the digital signature technique. In the proposed system, we have used the AES-128 algorithm with the anonymous identity created by the user to ensure the principle of non-repudiation. The secret key in which the data is encrypted and decrypted is generated by the user in addition to the anonymous user identity is generated by the user.

Since the proposed system is different from traditional systems, we have compared the proposed system with traditional systems in general, from several aspects such as confidentiality, availability, privacy, immutability, and centralization as shown in Table 1.

Based on the basic security services provided by each security system, the proposed system was compared with some of the related work mentioned in the Sect. 2. Table 2 showed the comparison between the proposed system and other related systems where P represent the proposal system and [12–21] represent the related works with which the proposed system is compared.

Table 1. Comparison between traditional systems and the proposed system

Security service	Traditional systems	Proposed system
Confidentiality	Encrypt data transferred between the parties involved in the system	Equivalent security level
Availability	The backup of databases must be done manually and periodically to ensure that the service is provided in case the system fails	All system validators have a copy of the database (blockchain), so the failure of any party to the system does not affect the operation of the system and is processed immediately
Privacy	The process of protection the privacy of the user identity is done by encryption, where the identity of the user is encrypted to ensure its privacy, and this method creates a relationship between the patient and his identity, leading to eventual patient tracking	The anonymous identity of the user gives him more privacy since there is no relationship between the patient and his data
Immutability	Any person who has the authority to modify the database can manipulate the data and modify it, in addition to that the occurrence of any accidental incident can lead to damage to the database in full	Even if the data is manipulated by anyone with authority, the system detects this manipulation and maintains the blockchain immediately. In addition, the existence of multiple versions of blockchain prevents the system from completely failing in the event of any accidental or natural accident
Controlling parties	The place where the server (health center or hospital) is fully controlled on all parties of the system	No party in the system has total control over the rest of the system, all parties have the same power in a fully decentralized system

Table 2. Comparison between the proposed system and other related systems.

Security services	[12]	[13]	[14]	[15]	[16]	[17]	[18]	[19]	[20]	[21]	P
Mutual authentication	×	×	×	√	×	√	√	×	√	√	√
Integrity	√	√	√	√	×	×	×	×	×	√	√
Confidentiality	√	√	√	√	√	×	√	√	√	√	√
Non-repudiation	×	√	×	√	×	×	√	×	×	√	√
Privacy	×	×	×	×	×	√	√	√	√	×	√

Table 2 showed that the proposed system has met all the security objectives other than the other protocols.

6 Conclusion

Securing patient data in WBAN is one of the most important problems of e-health applications. In this paper Blockchain technology and cryptography algorithms were used to secure the patient's data and maintain the privacy of his data as well as to store this data in a secure manner so that no one can tamper this data. The results showed that the proposed system could provide the confidentiality, integrity, mutual authentication, and non-repudiation between the patient side and doctor side and protection of patient privacy in addition to storing the data in a secure and protected way from manipulation by any person, whatever the rights or privileges it has. Future work will focus on working on encryption algorithms to make them lightweight as well as using machine learning techniques to help a doctor diagnose diseases.

References

1. Yuce, M., Khan, J.: Wireless Body Area Networks: Technology, Implementation, and Applications. Pan Stanford Publishing, Singapore (2012)
2. Thotahewa, K.M.S., Redouté, J.M., Yuce, M.R.: Ultra Wideband Wireless Body Area Networks. Springer International Publishing, Cham (2014). https://doi.org/10.1007/978-3-319-05287-8
3. Mana, M., et al.: SEKEBAN (secure and efficient key exchange for wireless body area network). Int. J. Adv. Sci. Technol. **12**(November), 45–60 (2009)
4. Faraj, S.T., Dawood, A.J., Salman, A.D.: Distributed data security and privacy in WBAN-related e-health systems. AL-Mansour J. **20**, 121–132 (2013)
5. Shen, J., Chang, S., Shen, J., Liu, Q., Sun, X.: A lightweight multi-layer authentication protocol for wireless body area networks. Future Gener. Comput. Syst. **78**(Part 3), 956–963 (2018)
6. He, D., Zeadally, S., Wu, L.: Certificateless public auditing scheme for cloud-assisted wireless body area networks. IEEE Syst. J. **12**(1), 64–73 (2018)
7. AL-Alak, S.M.K., Naser, M.A., Hussein, A.M.: Adaptive security protocol for wireless body area network. J. Kerbala Univ. **14**(2) 153–162 (2016). Scientific
8. Wei, F., Vijayakumar, P., Shen, J., Zhang, R., Li, L.: A provably secure password-based anonymous authentication scheme for wireless body area networks. Comput. Electr. Eng. **65**, 322–331 (2018)
9. Shen, J., Gui, Z., Ji, S., Shen, J., Tan, H., Tang, Y.: Cloud-aided lightweight certificateless authentication protocol with anonymity for wireless body area networks. J. Netw. Comput. Appl. **106**, 117–123 (2018)
10. Hasan, F.H.: Securing data in wireless body area network using hyper-chaotic Zhou system. Ibn Al-Haitham J. Pure Appl. Sci. **31**(1), 260–267 (2018)
11. Khan, H., Dowling, B., Martin, K.M.: Highly efficient privacy-preserving key agreement for wireless body area Networks. In: 2018 17th IEEE International Conference on Trust, Security and Privacy in Computing And Communications, 12th IEEE International Conference on Big Data Science and Engineering (TrustCom/BigDataSE), pp. 1064–1069. IEEE (2018)

12. Farooq, S., Prashar, D., Jyoti, K.: Hybrid encryption algorithm in wireless body area networks (WBAN). In: Singh, R., Choudhury, S., Gehlot, A. (eds.) Intelligent Communication, Control and Devices. AISC, vol. 624, pp. 401–410. Springer, Singapore (2018). https://doi.org/10.1007/978-981-10-5903-2_41
13. Li, F., Han, Y., Jin, C.: Cost-effective and anonymous access control for wireless body area networks. IEEE Syst. J. **12**(1), 747–758 (2018)
14. Ciampa, M.: Security + Guide to Network Security Fundamentals, 3rd edn. Cengage Learning, Boston (2009). Course Technology
15. Stallings, W.: Cryptography And Network Security: Principles and Practice, 5th edn. Pearson Education, Inc., London (2006). publishing as Prentice Hall, 2011
16. NIST. Secure Hash Standard, FIPS PUB 180-4 (2012)
17. Katz, J., Menezes, A.J., Van Oorschot, P.C., Vanstone, S.A.: Handbook of Applied Cryptography. CRC Press, Inc., Boca Raton (1996)
18. Rhee, M.Y.: Internet Security: Cryptographic Principles. Algorithms and Protocols. John Wiley, Hoboken (2003)
19. Stamp, M., Low, R.M.: Applied Cryptanalysis: Breaking Ciphers in the Real World. John Wiley, Hoboken (2007)
20. Indesteege, S.: Analysis and design of cryptographic hash functions (Doctoral dissertation, Ph.D. thesis (Katholieke Universiteit Leuven, Leuven, Belgium)) (2010)
21. Sobti, R., Geetha, G.: Cryptographic hash functions: a review. Int. J. Comput. Sci. Issues (IJCSI) **9**(2), 461 (2012)
22. Nakamoto, S.: Bitcoin: A Peer-to-Peer Electronic Cash System. https://bitcoin.org/bitcoin.pdf
23. Chuen, L.D.K., Linda, L.: Blockchain. Cryptocurrency and ICO. World Scientifc Publishing Co. Pte. Ltd., Singapore (2018)
24. Bambara, J., Allen, P.: Blockchain: A Practical Guide to Developing Business, Law, and Technology Solutions. McGraw-Hill Education, New York City (2018)
25. Bashir, I.: Mastering Blockchain: Distributed ledgers, decentralization and smart contracts explained. Packt Publishing Ltd., Birmingham (2017)
26. Sankar, L.S., Sindhu, M., Sethumadhavan, M.: Survey of consensus protocols on blockchain applications. In: 2017 4th International Conference on Advanced Computing and Communication Systems (ICACCS). IEEE (2017)
27. Drescher, D.: Blockchain Basics: A Non-Technical Introduction in 25 Steps (2017). Daniel Drescher

Anomaly-Based Intrusion Detection System Using One Dimensional and Two Dimensional Convolutions

Mohammed Hamid Abdulraheem$^{(\boxtimes)}$ (iD) and Najla Badie Ibraheem (iD)

Department of Computer Sciences, University of Mosul, Mosul, Iraq
{Mohammed.hamed,Najla.dabagh}@uomosul.edu.iq

Abstract. During the last years, unknown threats are increased against computer networks. For this reason, intrusion detection systems become imperative measures against these threats. Different types of machine learning models have been leveraged in anomaly-based IDS. Deep learning is an emerging discipline of machine learning. The applications of Deep learning showed good results in some fields, particularly in computer vision, natural language processing, image processing, and robots. In this research, we investigated in the intrusion detection using a deep Convolution Neural Network models. We developed four models: 1D convolution, 2D convolution, 1D&2D convolution sequentially integrated, and 1D&2D convolution parallel integrated. To train and test the models we used a state-of-the-art CICIDS2017 intrusion detection dataset. This dataset includes the latest threats and many features. The metrics used in evaluating the models, are F1-score, and Roc-Auc curve. The results were promising in detecting the attacks.

Keywords: Anomaly intrusion detection · Convolution neural network · Deep learning · CICIDS2017 · Cosine similarity

1 Introduction

Computer networks and the Internet become immanent for human life today. Many applications rely on the Internet, such as life-critical applications in healthcare and military, and excessive financial transactions exist over the Internet. This rapid growth of the Internet application has led to a significant increase in network traffic in recent years. With the Internet applications spread, the Internet attacks have multiplied, their techniques are diversified, and security systems to detect and prevent such attacks become necessary. An Intrusion Detection System (IDS) become indispensable component of the network security infrastructure. An anomaly-based IDS discover an attack by learning normal behavior and then report an alarm if there is any aberration from it. The power of the anomaly-based IDS is its ability to detect an unknown attack.

Improvements in IDS can be achieved by leveraging a recent advanced in machine learning, specifically deep learning. Deep learning belongs to a class of machine-learning methods, which employs successive layers of information-processing stages in a hierarchical way for pattern classification and feature or representation learning [1].

© Springer Nature Switzerland AG 2020
M. I. Khalaf et al. (Eds.): ACRIT 2019, CCIS 1174, pp. 409–423, 2020.
https://doi.org/10.1007/978-3-030-38752-5_32

The three important reasons for the adoption of deep learning are first highly improved parallel processing of hardware, particularly the general-purpose graphical processing units (GPUs), the second is the high increment of the size of data available for training, and third the recent advances in machine learning algorithms research. These advances make deep learning algorithms to effectively use complex, nonlinear functions, to automatically learn distributed and hierarchical features by effectively utilizing both labeled and unlabeled data [2].

The rest of this paper is organized as follows: Sect. 2 summarizes the related works. Section 3 presents the Convolutional Neural Network concepts. Section 4 outlines the steps of the research. Section 5 presents exploration and preprocessing of the CICIDS2017 dataset. Section 6 presents the design of Convolutional Neural Network models. Section 7 shows the evaluation of the results and discussion, and finally Sect. 8 shows the conclusions and future work.

2 Related Works

Few researchers have studied the application of deep convolutional in the field of IDS. Vinayakumar et al. [3] applied 3 models of 1D convolution neural network as a multiclass classifier. In addition, they combined each model with, Recurrent Neural Network (RNN), Long Short-Term Memory (LSTM), and Gated Recurrent Unit (GRU). The models are evaluated on KDDC up 99 dataset and models network traffic as time-series. The combination of RNN, GRU, and LSTM did not improve the result. Wang et al. [4] proposed a malware traffic classification model using Convolution Neural Network (CNN) architecture similar to LeNet-5. No hand-designed features extracted but took raw traffic directly and traffic data translated into images. They obtained an average accuracy of 99.41%, and created a traffic dataset USTC-TFC2016. in addition, they developed a data-preprocessing toolkit USTC-TK2016.

Li et al. [5] proposed a method of conversion of NSL-KDD dataset to an image without feature selection. In which, the classifier automatically learns the features from the image of NSL-KDD dataset. They used ResNet-50 and GoogLeNet as CNN methods for comparison. The result was that CNN performed better than most standard classifiers. For testing they used The NSL-KDD Test$^+$ and Test^{-21}. Yu et al. [6] proposed a network IDS model that depends on dilated convolutional Auto Encoders (AE), using a Contagio-CTU-UNB and the CTU-UNB dataset.

Liu et al. [7] established IDS Model based on LeNet-5 a CNN that is used in classifying handwritten numerals. They used 10% of KDD Cup 1999 data for training and testing. Compared with other IDS classifiers, intrusion detection model based on CNN has the highest detection rate and precision. Lin et al. [8] presented an intrusion detection model based on a CNN classifier. For enhancing the precision of model, the proposed approach modifies the LaNet-5 model. The proposed method improves the accuracy of intrusion detection for attacks classification by using enhanced behavior features from trained CNN.

Mohammadpour et al. [9] propose a CNN method to implement an effective Network IDS. They used a CNN as, binary classifier on NSL-KDD, a dataset for network intrusion. Chawla et al. [10] present anomaly based Host IDS based on RNN.

When using GRU rather than the normal LSTM networks, they obtain a set of comparable results with reduced training times, using Australian Defense Force Academy Linux (ADFA-LD) Dataset of system call traces. Ding et al. [11] propose an IDS model based on a CNN, utilizing entire NSL-KDD dataset. The results show that the performance of the IDS model outperforms the performance of models based on traditional machine learning models and modern deep learning models in multi-class classification.

Naseer et al. [12] developed an anomaly detection models based on various deep neural network models, including CNN, AE, and RNN. The NSL-KDD dataset is used for training, while the evaluation is done on two-tested sets NSL-KDD Test$^+$ and NSL-KDDTest^{21}. The result is promising to apply deep IDS models for real-world application. Wu et al. [13] propose a network IDS model using CNN. They used CNN to select traffic features from raw dataset automatically and solved the imbalanced dataset problem by setting the weight coefficient of the cost function for each class based on its numbers. They converted the raw traffic vector format into an image to reduce the calculation cost. The NSL-KDD dataset has been used to evaluate the performance of the proposed model. The results show that the accuracy, FAR and calculation cost of the proposed model performs better than traditional standard algorithms.

Liu [14] proposes a Network IDS based on the CNN model Lenet-5 using KDD99 dataset while training each of the data is transformed to image matrix as the inputs to the CNN. Xiao et al. [15] propose a network IDS model built on a 2D CNN-IDS using LeNet-5. They evaluated the model using a standard KDD-CUP99 dataset by converting the original traffic vector into an image.

The majority of the research above worked on old dataset, like KDD-CUP99 and its improved version NSL-KDD, by transferring traffic records into images through more than one transform. This may lead to lose some features in traffic. In addition, most of the research depends on available models crafted for images like LetNet5, ResNet50, and GoogLeNet. Those models may have a lot of parameters and more deep and complex layers that may lead to over fitting the data, and more training time, because those model crafted for images that have huge input pixels. In this research, we explored deep convolution neural network, 1D, 2D convolution, and combination of them in sequential and parallel fashion, as a multi-class classifier on a new IDS dataset CICIDS2017 without translating the traffic pattern to images.

3 Convolutional Neural Network

Most CNNs share basic properties. Typically, alternate one or more convolutional layers with one pooling layer can be seen in most of CNN's. Figure 1 shows a basic 2D convolutional network. The convolutional layers can detect features at every level of the receptive field size. The combined receptive field size of deeper layers is larger than the ones at the beginning of the CNN. This allows them to discover more complex features from larger input regions. The features discovered by the deepest layers are highly abstract. Usually, one or more fully connected layers are added after the last convolutional-pooling layers. The last fully-connected layer (output) will use the softmax activation function to estimate the class probabilities of the input.

The deeper convolutional layers in the network usually have more filters (i.e. higher volume depth), compared to the initial ones. A feature detector at the beginning of the network works on a small receptive field. It can only detect a bounded number of features, such as lines or edges, shared among all classes. Alternatively, a deeper layer would detect more complex and plentiful features [16].

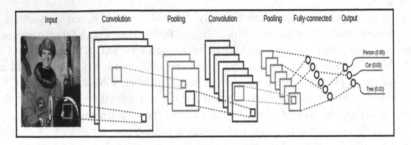

Fig. 1. A basic 2D convolutional network with convolutional and fully connected layers in blue and pooling layers in green [16]. (Color figure online)

The 1D convolutional layer extracts local 1D patch from a sequence. Such a 1D convolution layer will be able to discriminate local patterns in a sequence data. Because the same input kernel is applied on every patch, a pattern learned at a certain position in a sequence can later be distinguished at a different position. A 1D convolution layer take a three-dimension tensor as input. The input shape is samples, time step, and features. The output is a three-dimension tensor same as the input shape. The 1D convolution network consists of layers same as its 2D counterparts. Figure 2 shows a 1D convolution in which window size 3, the kernel cover all the features [17].

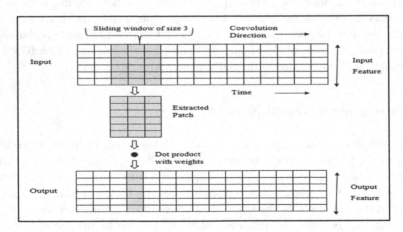

Fig. 2. 1D convolution operation [17].

4 Research Process Steps

The following list summarizes the process steps of the research:

- Downloads CICIDS2017 Dataset MachineLearningCSV.zip (8-csv files).
- Concatenate the 8 files in on dataset by (Pandas python library).
- Dataset analysis by (Pandas python library):
  - Remove records of null values from the dataset.
  - Remove features with zero values
- Balancing the dataset by (Imblearn balancing library):
  - down-sampling huge records of (BENIGN).
  - up-sampling small records of (Bot, Web AttackBrute Force, Web Attack-XSS, Infiltration, Web Attack-Sql Injection, and Heartbleed)
- Splitting the dataset into 70% tanning set, and 30% test set by (sklearn-train_test_split library).
- Normalize the dataset by Quantile transform.
- Design 4 convolutional models by (Keras_tenserflow python library):
  - 1Dconvolution, 2Dconvolution, 1D&2Dconvolution_sequantial, 1D&2Dconvolution_parallel.
- Training the models on the training set.
- Test the models on the testing set.
- Compute metrics for each model: accuracy, losses, F1-score, confusion matrix, Roc-Auc curve.
- Analysis and Compare the metrics results of the models.

5 Exploration and Preprocessing of the CICIDS2017 Dataset

The programming language and libraries used in the experiment are Programming Language: Python. Libraries used: python package for scientific computing (Numpy) [18], machine-learning library Scikit-learn [19], Python Data Analysis Library (Pandas) [20], Python Deep Learning library Keras with Tensor flow backend [21], and python dataset balancing library Imblearn [22].

5.1 Formation, Cleaning up and Balancing the Dataset

The machine-learning file of the CICIDS2017 dataset (MachineLearningCSV.zip) downloaded from [23]. The zipped file contains eight CSV files that represent the profile of the network traffic for five days, which includes normal and attack traffic for each day. To form a dataset that includes all attacks, we merged all 8 files into one dataset using the Pandas library, the dataset shape in terms of the number of records and number of features was as follows, 2830743 rows, 78 feature Columns, 1 label Column.

By viewing the details of the dataset, we detected 2867 records has null values. Machine learning algorithms do not accept null values. Since these values represent a small percentage of the number of records associated with each attack, so we removed those records from the dataset. The dataset shape becomes 2827876 rows, 78 feature Columns, 1 label Column.

The distribution of records by traffic type in the dataset is shown in Table 1. From column 2 in Table 1, it is clear that the dataset is imbalanced. The number of normal traffic records is very large compared to other records of attacks, and the existence of a few records of some types of attacks. To do some sort of balance, the normal traffic records (BENIGN) is down sampled to 250000 records, by using Random Under Sampler a python algorithm in Imblearn balancing library. In addition, to increase the sensitivity of the classifier to detect attacks with few records in multi-class classification problems, the numbers of records for the few attacks (Bot, Web Attack-Brute Force, Web Attack-XSS, Infiltration, Web Attack-Sql Injection and Heartbleed) are up sampled, in which the minimum number of records of any attack type is not less than 5000 records. The up sampling has conducted by using Adaptive Synthetic (ADASYN) algorithm in Imblearn balancing library. The semi-balanced data set becomes as shown in Table 1 column 3. The dataset shape becomes as follows: 832,373 rows, 78 feature columns, 1 label Column.

Table 1. The distribution of network traffic type before and after balancing the dataset.

Traffic class (type)	RecordCount before balancing	Record Count after balancing
BENIGN	2271320	250000
DoS Hulk	230124	230124
PortScan	158804	158804
DdoS	128025	128025
DoS GoldenEye	10293	10293
FTP-Patator	7935	7935
SSH-Patator	5897	5897
DoS slowloris	5796	5796
DoS Slowhttptest	5499	5499
Bot	1956	5000
Web Attack-Brute Force	1507	5000
Web Attack-XSS	652	5000
Infiltration	36	5000
Web Attack-Sql Injection	21	5000
Heartbleed	11	5000
Total	2827876	832,373

5.2   Features Analysis

The data set contains 78 features of numerical type, in addition to one feature representing the traffic category (label) of string type. By viewing some basic statistical details of those data set features, we detected 8 features of zero values they are:

BwdPSHFlags, BwdURGFlags, FwdAvgBytesPBulk, FwdAvgPacketsPBulk, FwdAvg BulkRate, BwdAvgBytesPBulk, BwdAvgPacketsPBulk, and BwdAvgBulkRate. Those features have no effect on discriminate any attack in the data set. Therefore, we removed from the dataset. The shape of the dataset becomes 832,373 rows, 70 feature Columns, 1 label Column.

5.3 Split and Normalize the Dataset

For the purpose of the training and evaluation of any classifier, the dataset must be split into a training set and a testing set. The classifier is trained on the training set and is evaluated on the testing set. We used the function train_test_split from Scikit-learn library for this purpose. Before splitting the dataset, the label column is pulled from the dataset in a separate list. The ratio of splitting 70% for the training set (x-train 70 features, y-train label), and 30% for the test set (x-test 70 features, y-test label). The labels (y-train and y-test) is of string type, it is translated into one-hot encoding, in which each unique string represented by a vector with 15 digits, one of them is 1 and the rest is 0.

The features values of the two datasets (x-train and x-test) must be normalized, in which all the features values will be consistent, thereby the classifier does not bias toward large values. There are several options for normalization. In this research, we choose the Quantile transform. This method transforms the features to follow a uniform or a normal distribution [24]. After that, the dataset becomes ready for training the classifier model.

6 Design of Convolution Neural Network Models

The deep convolution neural network models were implemented in Keras library and tensor flow as backend. The first model is 1D convolution, the structure of the model is shown in Fig. 3. In the model, the first layer is the input layer with 70 nodes equal to the number of input 70 features. The second layer is the reshape; it translates the input vector with length 70 to 10 *7 matrix to be input to the next layer. Followed by two of 1D-convolution layers with 16, and 32 filters respectively, the window size of the filters are 3. The activation function of those layers is Relu. Then max-pooling1D layer, to reduce the output size. The sixth layer is a flattened layer, it translates the 3D input to one dimension output, to be fed to the last classification dense layer with 15 nodes, according to 15 network traffic classes with a softmax activation function. The softmax function translates neural activation to probability for class prediction. The sum of the all 15-class probability is equal to one.

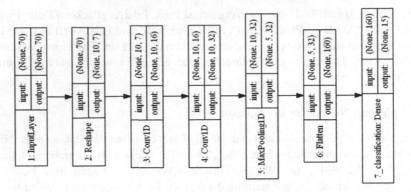

Fig. 3. 1D convolution model

The second model is 2D convolution as shown in Fig. 4. The first layer is the input layer with 70 nodes, the second layer is the reshape layer, and the 70 input is reshaped to 10*7*1 dimension that simulates an image to be fed to next layer. Followed by two of 2D convolution layers with 16 and 32 filters respectively, the size of the filters are 3 by 3, the activation function is Relu. Then maxpooling2D layer to reduce the output size, then flatten layer and finally the classification layer with 15 nodes as in the 1D convolution model.

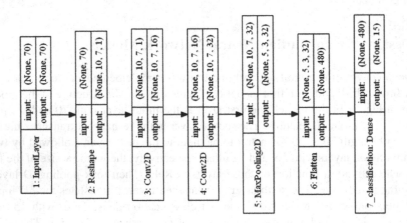

Fig. 4. 2D convolution model.

The third model is 2D&1D convolution sequentially as shown in Fig. 5. The model consists of 12 layers. It is a sequential bind of the 2D convolution and 1D convolution models (mentioned above) by layer 7.

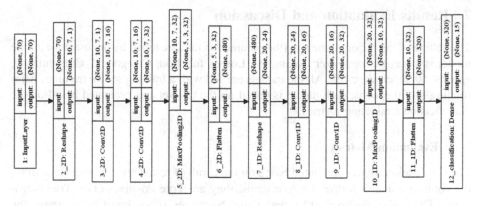

Fig. 5. 2D&1D convolution sequential model.

The fourth model is 2D&1D convolution in parallel as shown in Fig. 6. This model concatenates the two 1D and 2D convolution models (mentioned above) in parallel. The input is distributed in two branches, the first branch represents the 2D convolution model, and the second branch represents the 1D convolution model. Then the two branches merge at layer 7.

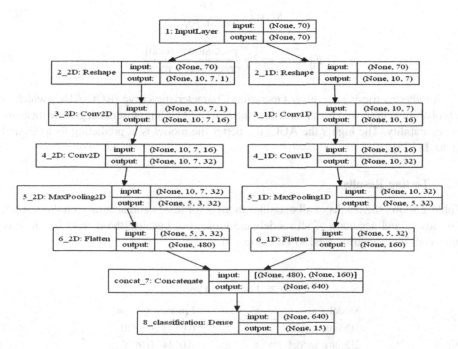

Fig. 6. 2D&1D convolution parallel model.

7 Results Evaluation and Discussion

The setting of the hyperparameters (the parameters that are tuned by the user) for all the model is same; the optimizer: Adam, the Losses function: Categorical_Crossentropy, epochs: 50, batch size: 128. All the models are fed with a training set for training. After running for 50 epochs, each model is tested on the test set and evaluated based on the classification evaluation metrics.

7.1 Evaluation Metrics

The Confutation Matrix computed based on the result of tested set, for binary classifier, the confusion matrix formed by four items; they are True Positives (TP), True Negatives (TN), False Positives (FP), and False Negatives (FN). From these items, the following metrics are computed: Accuracy, Precision, Recall, and F1-Score according to the Eqs. 1, 2, 3, 4 below [25]:

$$Accuracy = \frac{TP + TN}{TP + TN + FN + FP} \tag{1}$$

$$Precision = \frac{TP}{TP + FP} \tag{2}$$

$$Recall = \frac{TP}{TP + FN} \tag{3}$$

$$F1\ score = 2 * \frac{precision \cdot recall}{precision + recall} \tag{4}$$

Another metric is a Receiver Operating Characteristic curve (ROC-AUC) which is a probability curve, and the Area Under the Curve (AUC) represents degree or measure of separability. The higher the AUC, the better the model is at predicting 0s as 0s and 1s as 1s [25].

7.2 Testing Results

Table 2 shows the results of all classifier models for losses and accuracy on the test set. The losses and accuracy of all models are close, but because the dataset is not fully balanced, other metrics need to be compared.

Table 2. Losses and accuracy.

Model	Losses	Accuracy
1Dconv_model	0.0173	0.9920
2Dconv_model	0.0144	0.9936
2D&1Dconvo_sequential_model	0.0159	0.9932
2D&1Dconvo_parallel_model	0.0147	0.9936

F1-score considers good metric to evaluate the classifier model, its a function of precision and recall. The results of F1-score for all models are shown in the Fig. 7. All the models have a good result with all classes of the attacks, but for Web Attack-Brute Force and Web Attack-XSS, there is a difference in values between the models. The 1D convolution model gives moderate F1-score value for Web Attack-Brute Force but worse with Web Attack-XSS. For 2D convolution, and 2D&1D convolution sequential models give moderate F1-score value for Web Attack-XSS and worse F1-score for Web Attack-Brute Force. while 2D &1D convolution parallel model gives moderate F1-score values for the two attacks.

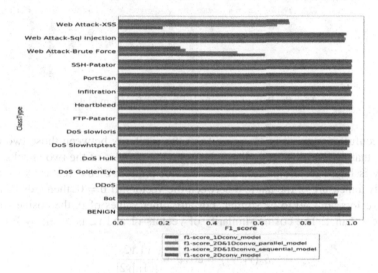

Fig. 7. F1-score for all models

To see further details about the fluctuation in values of Web Attack-Brute Force and Web Attack-XSS, we look at the confusion matrix. Figure 8 shows part of the confusion matrix for all the models, specific to Web Attack-Brute Force and Web Attack-XSS classes. There is confusion between those attacks in all models. In the 1D convolution model, the majority of the two attacks are classified as Web Attack-Brute Force. For 2D convolution model and 1D&2D convolution sequential models, the majority of the two attacks are classified as Web Attack-XSS. While the 1D&2D convolution parallel model, the classification of the two attacks approximately distributed between them.

True Label	BENIGN	Bot	DDoS	DoS GoldenEye	DoS Hulk	DoS Slowhttptest	DoS slowloris	FTP-Patator	Heartbleed	Infiltration	PortScan	SSH-Patator	Web Attack-Brute Force	Web Attack-Sql Injection	Web Attack-XSS	Model
Web Attack-Brute Force	8	0	0	0	0	0	0	0	0	0	0	0	1,244	79	33	1Dconv
Web Attack-Sql Injection	0	0	0	0	0	0	0	0	0	0	0	0	5	1,527	0	1Dconv
Web Attack-XSS	0	0	0	0	0	0	0	0	0	0	0	0	1,349	5	167	1Dconv
Web Attack-Brute Force	4	0	0	0	0	0	0	0	0	0	0	0	213	54	1,093	2Dconv
Web Attack-Sql Injection	0	0	0	0	0	0	0	0	0	0	0	0	15	1,517	0	2Dconv
Web Attack-XSS	0	0	0	0	0	0	0	0	0	0	0	0	12	4	1,505	2Dconv
Web Attack-Brute Force	10	0	0	0	0	0	0	0	0	0	0	0	239	29	1,086	1Dconv&2Dconv Serial
Web Attack-Sql Injection	0	0	0	1	0	0	0	0	0	0	0	0	62	1,469	0	1Dconv&2Dconv Serial
Web Attack-XSS	10	0	0	0	0	0	0	0	0	0	0	0	4	6	1,501	1Dconv&2Dconv Serial
Web Attack-Brute Force	7	0	0	0	2	0	0	0	0	0	0	0	598	61	696	1Dconv&2Dconv Parallel
Web Attack-Sql Injection	0	0	0	1	0	0	0	0	0	0	0	0	15	1,516	0	1Dconv&2Dconv Parallel
Web Attack-XSS	3	0	0	0	0	0	0	0	0	0	0	0	371	6	1,141	1Dconv&2Dconv Parallel

Predicted Label

Fig. 8. Part of a confusion matrix for all models.

The confusion at most is emerging from the similarity between those two attacks. To prove that, we use cosine similarity between the samples of the two attacks. Cosine similarity is based on the calculation of the dot product of the feature vectors. It is effectively a measure of the angle θ between the vectors: If $\theta = 0$, then $\cos(\theta)$ is 1 and the two vectors are said to be similar. For any other values of θ, the cosine similarity will be less than 1. The cosine similarity of vectors $v1$ and $v2$ is given by Eq. 5 [26].

$$S_c(v_1, v_2) = \cos \theta = \frac{v1.v2}{|v1|.|v2|} \tag{5}$$

Where the $|vi|$ corresponds to the usual Euclidean norm to measure the magnitude of the vector vi. Then we compute the cosine similarity between the samples of the two attacks. Figure 9 shows the mean of the cosine values for each instance of one attack compared to all instances of the other attack.

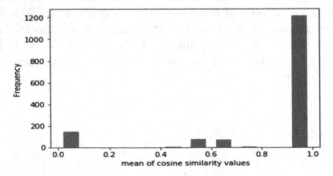

Fig. 9. The mean of the cosine similarity between Web Attack-Brute Force and Web Attack-XSS.

The figure indicates that the majority of the values are between 0.9–1.0 that means there is a high similarity between the samples of the two attacks.

To present another view for the results, we look at ROC-AUC curve of the models. For the purpose of comparison, we cut the parts related to class 12 (Web Attack-Brute Force) and class 14 (Web Attack-XSS) attacks from all ROC-AUC curve of the models, as shown in Fig. 10. We notice the behaviors of all models in a clearer way than confusion matrix mentioned above. We believe that the parallel model behaves more normal than other models because the model can discriminate between the little samples that dissimilar between the two attacks as mentioned in cosine similarity Fig. 9 above. The other models can discriminate one of the two attacks but do not discriminate the second attack.

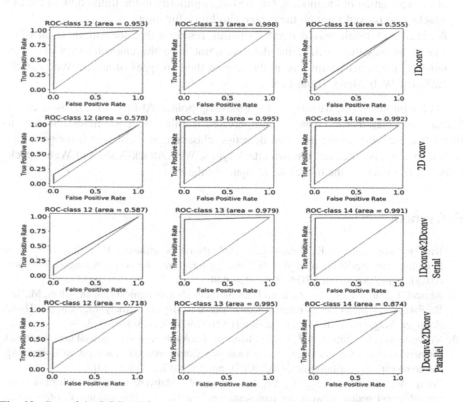

Fig. 10. Part of the ROC-AUC curve for class 12 (Web Attack-Brute Force) and class 14 (Web Attack-XSS) in all models.

8   Conclusions and Future Work

In this research, we investigated into a new intrusion dataset CICIDS2017 to evaluate an intrusion detection model based on convolutional deep learning. The analysis of the data set comprise of remove irrelevant values, semi balancing, split into training and test sets, and normalization. Then we designed 4 convolution models. We trained the models on the training set and checked them on tested set. To evaluates and compares the models, we computed the classification metrics that comprise of accuracy, losses, F1-score, confusion matrix, Roc-Auc curve. We conclude the following results:

- The results of the classification of the four models were close. 12 attacks were well-marked detection except the confusion between the Web Attack-XSS and Web Attack-Brute Force attacks.
- The 1D&2D in the parallel model is the more natural in distinction of the Web Attack-XSS and Web Attack-Brute Force attacks to a certain extent from the rest of the models.
- The confusion between the two above mentioned attacks in all models is not a lack of discrimination of the models, but the large similarity in the traffic flow of the two attacks that proved through the cosine similarity function.
- A significant result was derived from this research that the strongest classifier cannot be classified well if the data does not have the characteristics of distinguishing the items within it as in the case of the two types of attack: Web Attack-XSS and Web Attack-Brute Force.

As for future works, we suggest the following points. At first, we can use a cosine function as a classifier to create an unsupervised learning detection model. Second, to strengthen the work of the intrusion detection classifier, we will search for good features to distinguish between the two attack types, Web Attack-XSS, and Web Attack-Brute force, or merge them because of their similarity.

References

1. Kim, K., Aminanto, M.E., Tanuwidjaja, H.C.: Network Intrusion Detection using Deep Learning. SpringerBriefs on Cyber Security Systems and Networks. Springer, Singapore (2018). https://doi.org/10.1007/978-981-13-1444-5
2. Ahmad, J., Farman, H., Jan, Z.: Deep learning methods and applications. In: Khan, M., Jan, B., Farman, H. (eds.) Deep Learning: Convergence to Big Data Analytics. SCS, pp. 31–42. Springer, Singapore (2019). https://doi.org/10.1007/978-981-13-3459-7_3
3. Vinayakumar, R., Soman, K.P., Poornachandran, P.: Applying convolutional neural network for network intrusion detection. In: International Conference on Advances in Computing, Communications and Informatics (ICACCI), pp. 1222–1228. IEEE (2017)
4. Wang, W., Zhu, M., Zeng, X., Ye, X., Sheng, Y.: Malware traffic classification using convolutional neural network for representation learning. In: International Conference on Information Networking (ICOIN), pp. 712–717. IEEE (2017)
5. Li, Z., Qin, Z., Huang, K., Yang, X., Ye, S.: Intrusion detection using convolutional neural networks for representation learning. In: Liu, D., Xie, S., Li, Y., Zhao, D., El-Alfy, El-Sayed M. (eds.) ICONIP 2017. LNCS, vol. 10638, pp. 858–866. Springer, Cham (2017). https://doi.org/10.1007/978-3-319-70139-4_87
6. Yu, Y., Long, J., Cai, Z.: Network intrusion detection through stacking dilated convolutional autoencoders. Secur. Commun. Netw. 2017, 1–10 (2017)
7. Liu, Y., Liu, S., Zhao, X.: Intrusion Detection Algorithm Based on Convolutional Neural Network, DEStech Transactions on Engineering and Technology Research. ICETA (2018)

8. Lin, W.H., Lin, H.C., Wang, P., Wu, B.H., Tsai, J.Y.: Using convolutional neural networks to network intrusion detection for cyber threats. In: IEEE International Conference on Applied System Invention (ICASI), pp. 1107–1110. IEEE (2018)
9. Mohammadpour, L., Ling, T.C., Liew, C.S., Chong, C.Y.: A convolutional neural network for network intrusion detection system. Proc. Asia-Pac. Adv. Netw. **46**, 50–55 (2018)
10. Chawla, A., Lee, B., Fallon, S., Jacob, P.: Host based intrusion detection system with combined CNN/RNN model. In: Alzate, C., et al. (eds.) ECML PKDD 2018. LNCS (LNAI), vol. 11329, pp. 149–158. Springer, Cham (2019). https://doi.org/10.1007/978-3-030-13453-2_12
11. Ding, Y., Zhai, Y.: Intrusion detection system for NSL-KDD dataset using convolutional neural networks. In: Proceedings of the 2nd International Conference on Computer Science and Artificial Intelligence – CSAI 2018, pp. 81–85. ACM (2018)
12. Naseer, S., et al.: Enhanced network anomaly detection based on deep neural networks. IEEE Access **6**, 48231–48246 (2018)
13. Wu, K., Chen, Z., Li, W.: A novel intrusion detection model for a massive network using convolutional neural networks. IEEE Access **6**, 50850–50859 (2018)
14. Liu, P.: An Intrusion detection system based on convolutional neural network. In: Proceedings of the 11th International Conference on Computer and Automation Engineering, pp. 62–67. ACM (2019)
15. Xiao, Y., Xing, C., Zhang, T., Zhao, Z.: An intrusion detection model based on feature reduction and convolutional neural networks. IEEE Access **7**, 42210–42219 (2019)
16. Vasilev, I., Slater, D., Spacagna, G., Roelants, P., Zocca, V.: Python Deep Learning: Exploring Deep Learning Techniques and Neural Network Architectures with PyTorch. Keras and TensorFlow. Packt, Birmingham (2019)
17. Chollet, F.: Deep Learning with Python, 6th edn. Manning, New York (2017)
18. NumPy. https://www.numpy.org/
19. learn scikit-learn Machine Learning in Python. https://scikit-learn.org/stable/
20. Python Data Analysis Library. https://pandas.pydata.org/index.html
21. Keras: The Python Deep Learning Library. https://keras.io/
22. Lemaître, G., Nogueira, F., Aridas, C.K.: Imbalanced-learn: a Python toolbox to tackle the curse of imbalanced datasets in machine learning. J. Mach. Learn. Res. **18**(1), 559–563 (2017)
23. University of New Brunswick. https://www.unb.ca/cic/datasets/ids-2017.html
24. Sklearn.preprocessing.quantile_transform. https://scikitlearn.org/stable/modules/generated/sklearn.preprocessing.quantile_transform.html
25. Kelleher, J.D., Namee, B.M., D'Arcy, A.: Fundamentals of Machine Learning for Predictive Data Analytics: Algorithms, Worked Examples, and Case Studies. MIT Press, Cambridge (2015)
26. Rogel-Salazar, J.: Data Science and Analytics with Python. Chapman and Hall/CRC, Philadelphia (2018)

Design and Implementation of a Secure Mobile Banking System Based on Elliptic Curve Integrated Encryption Schema

Ahmad Salim[1](✉) [ID], Ali Makki Sagheer[2] [ID], and Linha Yaseen[1] [ID]

[1] Technical Institute of Anbar, Middle Technical University, Baghdad, Iraq
ahmadsalim@tia.mtu.edu.iq, eng.leena89@gmail.com
[2] Al-Qalam University College, Kirkuk, Iraq
prof.ali@alqalam.edu.iq

Abstract. Mobile banking relies on the Internet for transfer data between the customer's device and bank, thereby making financial data vulnerable to theft unauthorized people. As such, a secure system can be built to provides confidentiality, integrity and authentication. Also, most of the approved banking systems use security protocols to maintain the confidentiality of secret data, but most of these protocols suffer from problems at the handshake level (secret key exchange), thereby leading to the exposure of secret keys. In this study, a secure mobile banking system was designed. The proposed system was divided into three sections, namely, the sides in relation to the bank, the server, and the application, which was run on a mobile device. The model used the proposed Elliptic Curve Integrated Encryption Schema (ECIES) for the exchange of secret data between the client (the application on a smartphone) and the server. The ECIES that was offered used the Elliptic-curve Diffie–Hellman (ECDH) as the key agreement algorithm, the Advanced Encryption Standard (AES) in Galois/Counter Mode (GCM), i.e. the AES-GCM, as the encryption algorithm, and the MAC-384 as the Message Authentication Code (MAC) function, while the hash functions (SHA512 and SHA384) were utilized for the keys derivation process. Furthermore, the suggested system authenticated the user through a second password when a transaction was performed to send money.

Keywords: Mobile banking · Cryptography · Banking transactions · ECIES · AES-GCM

1 Introduction

Nowadays, information technology (IT) plays a major role in the life of a society [1]. The development of mobile devices connected to the Internet has helped to improve the reality of remote services, with many organizations and companies offering their services remotely to customers. Among these institutions, one of the most important is the bank, which today, is heavily dependent on modern technology to facilitate its banking transactions. However, this development is not free from threats, where applications that provide remote banking services are exposed to many malicious attacks that target the confidentiality and privacy of customer information. Currently, the smartphone

© Springer Nature Switzerland AG 2020
M. I. Khalaf et al. (Eds.): ACRIT 2019, CCIS 1174, pp. 424–438, 2020.
https://doi.org/10.1007/978-3-030-38752-5_33

stands out among the most essential innovative advancements. It has become an essential apparatus for individuals around the globe for correspondence and business applications [2]. A statistical study was conducted in 2015 to compare the number of mobile cellular subscriptions throughout the world in that year to the year 2000. The number of subscriptions in 2015 was 7 billion, while in 2000, it was 1 billion. The Internet share was 3.2 billion subscriptions, out of which 2 billion were from developing countries [3]. The number of smartphone users on the Internet increased from 1.2 billion in 2012 to 4.5 billion in 2018 [4]. The Internet is at the focus of this development as it is enabling companies and organizations to deliver online services [5].

Banks are one of the establishments that use IT in their tasks [1]. Online banking is an attractive way to conduct banking and business activities from anywhere and at any time [6]. Customers are more comfortable using online banking services than conventional banking as they are able to carry out their banking functions throughout the day from anywhere, saving them money and time, while also providing them with a better open market [5]. However, the biggest challenge to gaining customer confidence is the security aspect [7].

The term 'electronic financial transactions' refers to all of the activities or services provided by banks through the electronic network. The most important electronic banking services are the transfer of funds between accounts, the payment of bills, loan requests, payment of loan instalments, and the sending of money via e-mail at any time and regardless of the whereabouts of the customer. The definition of electronic banking differs among researchers because banking includes many kinds of services that are offered by banks to their clients and the several means by which they provide services such as through the use of mobile devices and computers [8]. Online financial services are operating under different threats such as the Man In The Middle (MITM) attacks, pharming (a cyber-attack aimed at redirecting website traffic to a phantom site chosen by the attacker), phishing and malware [6]. Many applications have been developed for mobile payments, and examples of such applications are Dwallo, LoopPay, Apple Pay, PayPass, PayPal, Google Wallet, and Square Financial [2].

Financial transaction applications face many security threats that target the integrity, confidentiality and privacy of the customer's information. Therefore, there is a need to find a secure way to exchange information between the client and the server. Most of the existing mobile applications use security protocols to send secret data to the server in a secure manner. However, these applications suffer from problems in terms of speed, specifically problems at the handshake level, to establish a secure connection between the client and the server. The ultimate aim of this paper was to design and build an application for secure financial transactions to help to address security threats that might expose the customer's secret information on the smartphone or during a transmission between the client and the server.

The reminder of this paper is organized as follows. Related works discusses in Sect. 2. Section 3 illustrates the cryptography methods used in this paper. The model architecture introduces in Sect. 4, followed by the alternative plan in Sect. 5. Section 6 shows our proposed security models. Section 7 shows the mobile devices used in system testing. Section 8 discuss the results and usability of the proposed system. Finally, conclude the paper.

2 Related Works

Many researches have been carried out in the area of electronic banking with the aim of improving the security of applications. In 2014, Marković et al. [9] proposed a model based on a service-oriented architecture (SOA) to build secure mobile applications. The model depends on the RSA (Rivest–Shamir–Adleman) as the public key infrastructure (PKI) algorithm, and the XML key management specification (XKMS) framework for authentication and data encryption. The proposed model is slow and expensive in a limited resource environment such as mobile devices. Kivisaari [10] designed an infrastructure across which banks can provide services to customers on mobile phones. The proposed infrastructure relies on a web service that connects the customer's device with the bank using secure protocols to address the threats that might be faced. The model relies on a hash-based message authentication code (HMAC) for authentication and to ensure the integrity of the messages between the server and the client.

Putra et al. [11] designed a secure mobile banking model to secure the data exchanged between the server and the client, especially during the authentication process. The schema works for authentication in multiple layers. It relies on a pair-based text authentication (PBTA) in the first step, where the username and password are entered by adopting a key pair for each party and exchanging the authentication data with the server. It then relies on a contactless smart card to process a one-time password that is sent to the recipient via an SMS message.

The research works mentioned suggested solutions to the problems of information confidentiality, authentication and data integrity. Nevertheless, the proposed methods suffer from several problems, the proposed method in [9] depend on RSA as a PKI to key distribution process, this makes the process very slow and unsuitable for devices with limited capabilities, in addition to the fact that it depends on HMAC as an one level to authenticate the communication parties this makes the system vulnerable. The researchers in related works aims to find a methods to authenticate the customer who is transferring the money, in [11] a one-time password is sent to the SIM card that is opened through the application only for the money transfer process, but this makes the process useless in the event of a physical attack such as stealing the phone. In [5] used CQ containing personal information that has been answered previously in order to verify the identity of the person used the application to transferring the money, but this gives the attacker an opportunity to stealing money by analyse the client's personality such as through social media sites.

In this paper, the ECIES schema was suggested relies on asymmetric encryption in the keys distribution without sending the secret key itself and then this key is used in the symmetric encryption process. Subsequently, exchange keys securely and at the same time encrypt the secret data in a secure and fast manner. In addition, the use of a second pass number helps to identify the person who is sending money from the application and prefer to use one of the biometric identification methods in the future to increase the security level.

3 Cryptography

Today, in addition to the sharing of secret information, cryptography encompasses user authentication protocols, techniques for generating and sharing secret keys, mechanisms to ensure integrity, and much more. Briefly, modern cryptography is primarily based on the study of mathematical techniques and their use to preserve and secure digital data against attacks. This is accomplished through mathematical-based algorithms that encrypt data to make it difficult for attackers to obtain the secret data [12]. The following sections explain the most important cryptography techniques employed in this paper.

3.1 Elliptic Curve Integrated Encryption Scheme (ECIES)

The Diffie-Hellman Integrated Encryption Scheme (DHIES), which is an improvement over the ElGamal encryption scheme, uses public key cryptography in addition to symmetric encryption algorithms, hash functions and MAC codes to obtain an integrated schema. The integration of these algorithms and functions in the DHIES technology provides a very strong security against chosen ciphertext attacks without the need to increase the key length [13, 14].

The DHIES relies on the same hint and blindness used in the ElGamal encryption scheme [15] between the blind and the secret message based on symmetric key algorithms in lieu of a modular multiplication. The use of elliptic curves in the production of the Elliptic Curve Integrated Encryption Scheme (ECIES) is widespread and attractive because it achieves the same level of security as the RSA or DLP-based algorithms, but with a smaller key size, thus making it the fastest and most reliable security technology. A committee of the Japanese government and other committees in Europe have confirmed this [16].

As is evident from its name, the DHIES is an integrated encryption system or scheme that relies on the following functions:

- Key Agreement (KA): This is a function that is applied to distribute the shared secret key between both parties of the connection.
- Key Derivation Function (KDF): The function or mechanism through which a set of encryption keys is generated, depending on the shared secret key.
- Encryption (ENC): Symmetric encryption algorithms that are commonly used.
- Message Authentication Code (MAC): A code that is used to validate and authenticate the message.
- Hash (HASH): It is used in several stages, mainly for KDF and MAC functions

Figure 1 illustrates the steps in the technique and how it is used for correspondence between two parties. The figure shows the role of each function in the ECIES technique.

3.2 Galois Counter Mode (GCM)

The GCM is a block cipher mode that provides data authentication in addition to data encryption. It uses one of the block cipher encryption algorithms in addition to a counter mode (CTR). The authentication process is done by using hash functions through a binary Galois field to authenticate the encrypted message [17]. The AES-GCM algorithm is a combination of the AES Counter Mode encryption and the Galois Hash authentication algorithm that produces an encrypted text as well as an authentication tag. The AES-GCM consists of three stages: Pre-processing (encryption, authentication); Processing Loop and Post Processing [18].

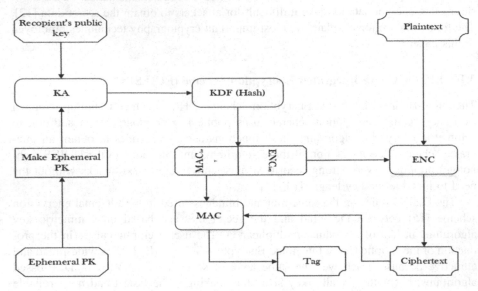

Fig. 1. ECIES model

4 Proposed Model

The system is a mobile application that enables users to transmit money to each other in a secure way at any time and from anywhere. The secure transmission process is done by encrypting the secret data that is transmitted from the user's device to the server or vice versa. In addition, the necessary measures are taken to protect the user's private data on the device, not only to protect money, but also to protect the customer. In a banking transaction, although the money is transferred from a bank account owned by a customer to someone else's bank account, the process does not take place directly but requires the control of a third party representing the bank. Therefore, the customer's remote access to his bank account to manage his money is considered as a service that is provided by the financial institution. Figure 2 explains the complete model of the proposed system.

Mobile Devices

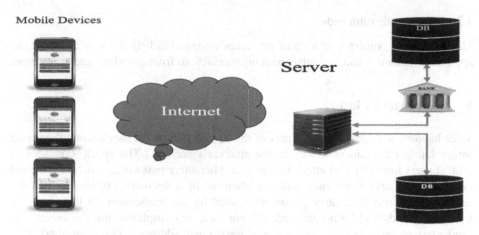

Fig. 2. The proposed system model

4.1   The Bank Side

Nowadays, many people own a bank account and manage their money remotely using smartphones, which are available to almost everyone. In the proposed system, in order for a customer to open a bank account, he/she is required to go to the bank and provide the following information: Active email address (or phone number), alternative email address (or phone number), primary password, alternative password as well as other personal information. The alternative email address and password are used if the customer is at risk. Correspondingly, the customer will receive a private number (or card number) from the bank that is used to confirm the customer's possession of the account during the registration process.

4.2   The Server Side

Most of the mobile applications in use today provide online services to clients, where these applications work according to the methods set for the client and the server. In the proposed application, a web service was built in order to connect clients with their bank accounts, hence, enabling clients to be in full control of the system. Messages sent from the client to the server typically take the form shown in Fig. 3, in which the message is represented in JSON or XML form. The web service contains a set of functions to perform the main activities.

Header: Identifier (Hash (email) and Hash (Device ID))	Body: Encrypted data

Fig. 3. Client's message structure

4.3   The Application Side

The application consisted of a set of interfaces designed to help the user to utilize the application smoothly and to conduct banking transactions from anywhere and at any time.

5   Alternative Plan

What happens if a thief comes to know of this application on the user's smartphone and forces him/her to transfer money to the attacker's account? The application tries to protect users from physical attack by using an alternative password, which is specified (with an alternative emergency address) when the bank account is opened. When the user is at risk, the alternative password is used for the transaction. In this way, the transfer of funds will be normal and will not raise any suspicion, but the server will send a hazard message to an emergency address (email address or phone number). This message will contain information about the user and the current location of the user (GPS). Figure 4 shows an example of a hazard message and the precise location of the user on Google Maps.

a   b

Fig. 4. a. Hazard message. b. User location on Google Maps

6   Security of the Proposed System

The security of the system is fully dependent on a hybrid cryptography method called ECIES. This method consists of a combination of symmetric and asymmetric cryptography. The application was based on elliptic curve cryptography (ECC) in the exchange of keys and digital signatures between parties through ECDH and ECDSA, using AES-GCM as the encryption algorithm.

As mentioned before, the integrated encryption schema uses several functions: key agreement (KA), key derivation function (KDF), encryption (ENC), hash (H) and message authentication code (MAC). In this model, ECDH was used as the KA function, SHA512 and SHA384 as the KDF, MAC-384 as the MAC function and AES-GCM as the encryption algorithm. Figure 5 illustrates the model that was proposed for encryption in this system. The same model is used for decryption, but in a reverse manner, where the recipient uses private key with the advertised sender key to generate secret keys and decrypt the received message. Initially, the KA is applied through a function called Hello-Server, where a set of sequential steps is applied. This process enables the client and the server to transmit secret data securely after exchanging public keys. Algorithm 1 shows the key exchange between the server and the client.

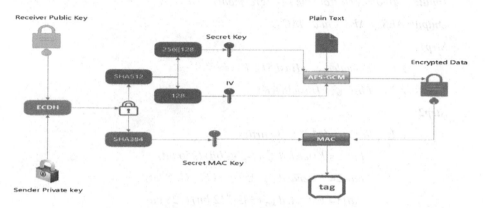

Fig. 5. The proposed ECIES model

Algorithm 1: KA Function

Goal: Exchange public keys between the client and the server

Input: Email, DeviceID and Client PuK (from client)

Output: Server_Client PuK (from server)

Step1: generate Client key pairs (PuK and PrK) in client device.

Step2: send message (Email, DeviceID and Client PuK) from client to server.

Step3: receive client message and keep it in new session (in server side).

Step4: generate Server_Client key pairs (for each client) and keep key pairs in a client session (in server side).

*Step5: **Return** Server_Client PuK from server to client to use these keys in Encryption process.*

(PuK = public key, and PrK = private key)

The KA algorithm is implemented when logging in or when the keys are changed between the server and the client periodically, where the server sends a changing message through which the client is returned to the login screen again. After obtaining the shared secret key between the two parties following the key agreement stage by using the ECDH algorithm, the next stage involves the derivation of the keys for the AES-GCM encryption algorithm and the key for the MAC function. The key derivation is explained by the following algorithm.

Algorithm 2: KD Function

Goal: generate AES secret key with IV and MAC secret key

Input: *Shared key (K from the key agreement)*

Output: *AES $_{key}$ AES $_{IV}$ and MAC $_{key}$*

Step1:

       1.1.   Extended $_{key}$ =Hash512(K)

       1.2.   MAC $_{key}$ =Hash384(K)

Step2:

       2.1. split Extended $_{key}$ to 3 parties

            Part1= Extended $_{key}$ (1-256 bit) (256 bit)

            Part2= Extended $_{key}$ (257-384 bit) (128 bit)

            Part3= Extended $_{key}$ (385-512 bit) (128 bit)

Step3:

       3.1. AES $_{key}$ = Part1

       3.2. AES $_{IV}$ = part2

Step4:

       Return(AES $_{key}$, AES $_{IV,}$ MAC $_{key}$)

6.1   Message Encryption/Decryption Model

In order to encrypt the message using AES-GCM, the keys to encrypt the message through it must first be provided. The keys required in this algorithm are the secret key (128 bit or 256 bit) and an initialization vector (128 bit). The keys that are derived through the KDF are used for the data encryption. Figure 6 illustrates the encryption process using AES with the GCM mode, in addition to using the MAC function for message authentication. The use of a GCM is allowed to obtain different ciphertexts for a set of the same plaintext encrypted by the same key.

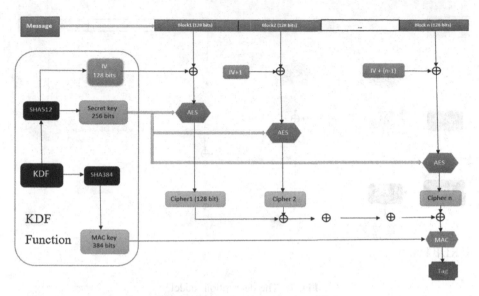

Fig. 6. Message encryption model

The AES uses three lengths of keys (128, 192, and 256 bits) and the number of rounds depends on the key length. If the key length is 128 bits, the number of rounds will be 10, but if the key length is 192 bits, the number of rounds will be 12, and 14 rounds are used if the key length is 256 bits. Each round takes a different key derived from the original key through a process called key expansion.

As mentioned previously, the shared secret key is generated by the ECDH in the key agreement process. The sender uses his private key and the recipient's public key to generate a shared key, while correspondingly, the recipient uses his private key with the sender's public key to obtain the shared secret key. Next, the recipient applies the same KDF function that was employed by the sender to decrypt the message. Figure 7 shows the proposed decryption model. As in the encryption process, the recipient uses the AES-GCM algorithm to decrypt the received message. During the decryption process, the AES algorithm works in reverse of the encryption process with the same number of rounds. Therefore, the keys obtained through the key extension process used in the encryption are now used in reverse for the decryption, meaning that the key used in the first round of encryption is now used in the last round of decryption.

As its name indicates, the MAC is a message authentication code, where, after calculating the tag (x) by the sender and sending it with the message, the receiver uses the received message in addition to the key obtained by the KDF in the MAC function to compute the tag (x') to verify the authentication and integrity of the message. Algorithm 3 shows the message authentication process.

After clarifying the mechanism by which the message is encrypted and decrypted, the role is now to clarify the method of sending the encrypted message. Algorithm 4 illustrates the message transmission process.

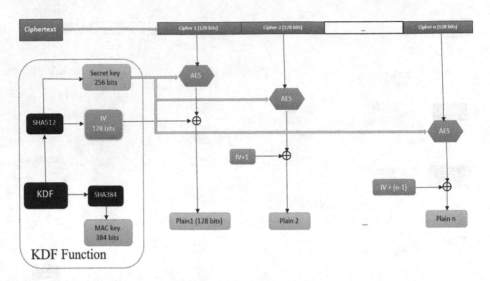

Fig. 7. The decryption model

Algorithm 3: Received Message Authentication

Goal: Authenticate the Received Message

Input: *ciphertext*

        MAC $_{key}$ ◀—— *key obtain by KDF process (384 bits)*

        tag ◀—— *received with the message*

Output: *True or False*

Step1:

    Blocks = Split the ciphertext to array of blocks (each block 128
bits)

    Nb = number of blocks

Step2:

    data = block(0)

    i =1

    Loop *(i < Nb)* **do**

        *data = data **Xor** block(i)*

        i = i+1

    End Loop

Step3:

    tag' = MAC_function(data, MAC $_{key}$)

Step4:

    If (tag = tag') **Then**

        ***Return**(True)*

    Else

        ***Return**(False)*

    End if

Algorithm 4: Message Transmission
Goal: *Transmit Secret Message*
Input: *client_message*
Client_Puk ◄── *client public key*
Client_Prk ◄── *client private key*
Server_Puk ◄── *server public key*
Output: *message acknowledgment from the server*
Step1:
PhoneID = get phone ID
Email = get sender email
Step2:
Header = hash(Email)+hash(PhoneID)
Message = (Header, client_message)
Enc_Msg=ECIES_Enc(Message, Client_Prk, Server_Puk)
Signature = ECDSA(Enc_Msg, Client_Prk)
Body=(Enc_Msg, Signature)
Final_Msg = {"header":Header , "body": Body}
Step3:
Akn = send_Msg_to_server(Final_Msg)
Step4:   *Return(Akn) from server*

7 Mobile Devices Used in Testing

Several devices were used to test the proposed system. These devices were based on the Android operating system and had different computational capabilities. The different types of devices and their computational capabilities are shown in Table 1.

Table 1. Mobile phone devices used in application experiments

Market name	Android version	CPU	RAM
Samsung Galaxy S3 Neo	4.3 Jelly Bean	1.2 GHz	1.5 GB
Huawei P8 Lite	5.0.2 Lollipop	1.2 GHz	2 GB
Huawei GX8	6.0 Marshmallow	4×1.5 GHz	3 GB
Sony Xperia Z2	6.0 Marshmallow	2.3 GHz	3 GB
Samsung Galaxy S8	7.0 Nougat	4×2.3 GHz	4 GB

8 Discussion on Usability

In order to determine the efficiency of this system, the computational overheads were calculated with regard to the use of the proposed (ECIES*) method. As illustrated, the ECIES consists of several functions (KG, KA and KDF). In this section, the effectiveness of the method is discussed in terms of the time required for each of the functions mentioned. Figure 8 presents the time required for each function according to the type of mobile device used, and compares these results with two popular open-source cryptographic libraries, OpenSSL version 1.1.0 and Nettle version 3.3. The Curve25519 was used in the proposed system.

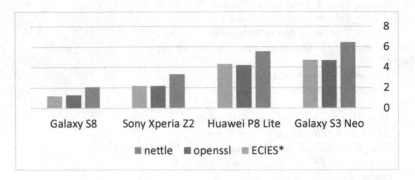

Fig. 8. Comparison of proposed ECIES* with related libraries (MS)

Consequently, the proposed method was good compared to the other libraries. Although the SHA512 was used for the shared secret key as a KDF function by splitting the result of hash into two keys (AES-GCM key, AES-GCM IV), and the SHA384 was used as the MAC key, the time required to perform these operations was acceptable compared to the other techniques used. Furthermore, the SHA512 is a one-way function, and taking parts of the SHA512 code keeps the original shared key secret even if the key used in the encryption process is detected by the attacker. The time required to perform the AES-GCM encryption and decryption is shown in Table 2. The results indicate that the time required to encrypt messages was very small, making the method suitable for use in limited-resource devices such as smartphones. Although the time taken with this algorithm was greater than the time required in the traditional AES, this algorithm was more secure because the encryption operations were more complex, where the use of a different IV produced two different ciphertexts for the same encrypted plaintext. This can be done by using the same key, and it was achieved by the presence of the IV, which was turned every time through the counter. Also, the modified AES-GCM algorithm can be used in the encryption process instead of the traditional AES-GCM to provide a more randomized ciphertext, and therefore, more security for the system [19].

Table 2. Performance time (MS) for secret message (AES-GCM)

Message size	Galaxy S3 Neo		Huawei P8 Lite		Sony Xperia Z2		Galaxy S8	
	Enc	Dec	Enc	Dec	Enc	Dec	Enc	Dec
512 Byte	4.24	4.29	3.85	3.79	3.26	3.31	2.22	2.28
1 KB	5.08	5.25	4.93	5.11	3.83	3.85	2.73	2.75
2 KB	6.93	6.06	5.96	6.07	5.22	5.36	4.78	4.84
3 KB	8.74	8.94	7.6	7.15	6.39	6.51	5.47	5.51

Bank services or the user authentication process in the suggested system are carried out entirely through server functions. In order for the application to be usable, the response time between the server and the client should be as fast as possible. Table 3 shows the time needed for a server to respond to a client through a Huawei GX8 smartphone and web service on a free Somee web hosting. The results were focused on the essential functions that would be relied on by customers to take advantage of the proposed application. The speed of the Internet during the testing process was 0.51 Mbps for downloading and 3.02 Mbps for uploading.

Table 3. Connection time between application and server

Server function	Time (S)
Hello Server	1.67
Sign In	1.40
Registration	1.86
New Transaction	1.91

9 Conclusion

In this paper, a secure mobile financial transaction system was designed. The proposed system was tested on many target devices. The most important conclusion obtained based on the results was that the proposed ECIES schema can be used to secure the data exchanged between the server and the client. The suggested schema depends on the ECDH as the key agreement algorithm, and uses the hash functions to generate three keys from the shared secret key. This method helps to resolve the handshake problem that occurs with traditional protocols. The AES-GCM encryption algorithm is used to encrypt the secret data and thus provides confidentiality. The proposed ECIES supports data integrity through the use of the MAC function and digital signature. Moreover, it preserves the privacy of the customer by keeping customer information out of the reach of hackers. In addition, it authenticates the client in the funds transmission process by using a second password. furthermore, the suggested system solves the problem of the transfer of funds under threat by using an alternative plan to protect the user as well as to protect the user's secret information in the application by putting in an option to force the user to enter fingerprint to access the application each time in case the device has a fingerprint sensor.

References

1. Nosrati, L.: A review of mobile banking security. In: IEEE Canadian Conference on Electrical and Computer Engineering (CCECE) (2016)
2. Pukkasenunk, P., Sukkasem, S.: An efficient of secure mobile phone application for multiple bill payments. In: 2016 30th International Conference on Advanced Information Networking and Applications Workshops (WAINA), pp. 487–492 (2016)
3. Sanou, B.: Facts & Figures 2015. ICT Facts & Figures (2015)

4. 10 of the hottest trends in consumer behaviour in 2015 (2015). http://www.manager.co.th/Weekly54/ViewNews.aspx?NewsID=9560000157612&TabID=3&
5. Khan, W.A., Saleem, Y., Shah, G.A., Farooq, A.: Modified mobile transaction authentication number system for 2-layer security. In: 2016 International Conference on Intelligent Systems Engineering (ICISE) (2016)
6. Mondal, P.C., Deb, R., Huda, M.N.: Transaction authorization from Know Your Customer (KYC) information in online banking. In: 2016 9th International Conference on Electrical and Computer Engineering (ICECE), pp. 523–526 (2016)
7. Singh, R.K., Pais, A.R.: Secure web based single sign-on (SSO) framework using identity-based encryption system. In: 2009 International Conference on Advances in Recent Technologies in Communication and Computing, ARTCom 2009, pp. 430–432 (2009)
8. Bairagi, A.K., Abdullah-Al-Nahid: A new approach of E-banking through the use of mobile, post-office and VPN in the perspective of Bangladesh. IJCIT 2(1), 36–41 (2011)
9. Markoviá, M., Đjorđjević, G.: Secure android application in SOA-based mobile government and mobile banking systems. In: Herrero, Á., et al. (eds.) International Joint Conference SOCO'13-CISIS'13-ICEUTE'13. AISC, vol. 239, pp. 589–599. Springer, Cham (2014). https://doi.org/10.1007/978-3-319-01854-6_60
10. Kivisaari, T., et al.: Providing Secure Web Services for Mobile Applications (2015)
11. Putra, D.S.K., Sadikin, M.A., Windarta, S.: S-Mbank: secure mobile banking authentication scheme using signcryption, pair based text authentication, and contactless smart card. In: 2017 15th International Conference on Quality in Research (QiR): International Symposium on Electrical and Computer Engineering, pp. 230–234 (2017)
12. Katz, J., Lindell, Y.: Introduction to Modern Cryptography. CRC Press, Boca Raton (2014)
13. Abdalla, M., Bellare, M., Rogaway, P.: DHAES: an encryption scheme based on the Diffie-Hellman problem. IACR Cryptol. ePrint Arch. **1999**, 7 (1999)
14. Abdalla, M., Bellare, M., Rogaway, P.: The oracle Diffie-Hellman assumptions and an analysis of DHIES. In: Cryptographers Track at the RSA Conference, pp. 143–158 (2001)
15. ElGamal, T.: A public key cryptosystem and a signature scheme based on discrete logarithms. IEEE Trans. Inf. Theory 31(4), 469–472 (1985)
16. Holden, J.: The Mathematics of Secrets: Cryptography from Caesar Ciphers to Digital Encryption. Princeton University Press, Princeton (2017)
17. McGrew, D., Viega, J.: The Galois/counter mode of operation (GCM). Submission to NIST Modes of Operation Process, vol. 20 (2004)
18. Jankowski, K., Laurent, P.: Packed AES-GCM algorithm suitable for AES/PCLMULQDQ instructions. IEEE Trans. Comput. 60(1), 135–138 (2011)
19. Bader, A.S., Sagheer, A.M.: Modification on AES-GCM to increment ciphertext randomness. Int. J. Math. Sci. Comput. (IJMSC) 4(4), 34–40 (2018). https://doi.org/10.5815/ijmsc.2018.04.03

Design a Compact Non-linear S-Box with Multiple-Affine Transformations

Omar A. Dawood[1](✉) , Mohammed Khalaf[2] ,
Falath M. Mohammed[3] , and Hussein K. Almulla[1]

[1] College of Computer Science & IT, University of Anbar, Ramadi 31001, Iraq
Omar-Abdulrahman@uoanbar.edu.iq,
the_lionofclub@yahoo.com,
hu_albasri@yahoo.co.uk
[2] Department of Computer Science, Al-Maarif University College,
Ramadi, Anbar 31001, Iraq
M.I.Khalaf@acritt.org.uk
[3] College of Education for Humanities Sciences, University of Anbar,
Ramadi, Anbar 31001, Iraq
falathm@yahoo.com

Abstract. The present paper introduces a new method of S-Box construction which work as a byte-oriented substitution scheme. The S-Box design considers the core part for the building most block cipher algorithms and play a major role in generating confusion property. Modern ciphers build with different types of S-Box of half-byte (nibble of 4-bit) or full-byte 8-bit as lookup tables with distinct mathematical Boolean functions (BFs). The proposed method generates the S-box based on multiplications of multiple different affine transforms with multiple distinct overlapped vectors of 8-bit to achieve high nonlinearity. The construction of S-box focused on use an irreducible polynomial of order eight over Galois Field GF (28). The proposed S-box quit similar to the S-box of Advance Encryption Standard (AES) but with more algebraic complexity and high non-linearity factor.

Keywords: S-box · Strict Avalanche Criterion (SAC) · Affine transform · Confusion property · Galois fields $GF(2^8)$ · Nonlinearity

1 Introduction

Numerous symmetric block ciphers are concentrated on the Shannon definition for the confusion and diffusion properties. Where the confusion is generated by the substitution process through complicating the correlation between the ciphering key and the ciphertext as complex as possible. Whilst the diffusion property distributes the statistical of plaintext along the resultant ciphertext [1]. The confusion and diffusion properties together increase the cipher complexity over the round transformation via recursive series of substitutions and permutations processes. The substitution means the alteration part of bits or word with other different part. Permutation process refers to the dissipate the sequence of bit regarding to specific arrangement [2].

© Springer Nature Switzerland AG 2020
M. I. Khalaf et al. (Eds.): ACRIT 2019, CCIS 1174, pp. 439–452, 2020.
https://doi.org/10.1007/978-3-030-38752-5_34

To make the plaintext are more sophisticate on the one hand non-consistency it is need to spread the plaintext along the statistics of structure. The construction of a new S-box is a necessary issue in designing any secure and robust cryptosystem. Since the design process may be different form cipher to cipher according to the design process. Some S-boxes are built randomly and other mathematically as a fixed lookup table or as a dynamic generation of on-fly method [3]. The designer must realize that the most important part in the algorithm design is the S-box that provide non-linearity. Also, the designer must aware that the S-box construction is not only random values or chaotic numbers. Thus, the design S-boxes can be considered as a mathematical built according to certain context likewise Boolean functions, affine functions, and non-linear equations. The block cipher algorithms based on the non-linearity notation to secure the round transformation [4]. This paper introduces a compact S-box that focused on algebraic design and shows how it achieves the resistance against the most well-known attacks. The present design based on several previous published algorithms that have had a significant impact in terms of internal mathematical design and construction steps which can be viewed in [5–7] respectively.

The proposed S-box contains three levels of affine layering and encapsulated Boolean polynomial with different non-linear equations XORed with multiple of distinct vectors that are responsible for confusion generation. The imposed vectors represent an effective impact on the implementation as well as the protection aspects.

This paper has discussed the general background of the substitution layer and the rest of paper is organized into following sections. Section 2 states the related works to the proposed S-box by other researchers. Section 3 introduces the mathematical preliminaries for S-box design and the basic adopted criteria for design strategy. Section 4 includes most popular approaches of S-box construction and the design methodologies. Section 5 applies the proposed S-box design and the main principles for algebraic construction. The security analysis and the investigated results can be shown in Sect. 6. Section 7 Includes the conclusions of this research.

2   Related Works

In this part some related works have been searched and reported by several researchers with modern methods that are so far related to the proposed method, which will be discussed in the section.

In 2016, Rodinko et al. [8], they have introduced a new method for generating S-box with high non-linearity based on appropriate selected criteria. The enhanced generation method reduces the consuming energy for the generated S-box through the generating process and gives a reasonable implementation. The improved method involves minimizing the time checking for the S-box selected criteria through design process.

In 2017, Alamsyah et al. [9], they have proposed a new cryptographic approach based on usage a different mathematical irreducible polynomial of $m(x) = x^8 + x^6 + x^5 + x + 1$ and a distinct constant vector of 8-bit with binary notation (00000001). The enhanced S-box has been evaluated by numerous effective tests via different security criteria likewise SAC, BIC nonlinearity and other criteria. The developed

S-box provides a good security level compared to other popular S-boxes according to the author's claim. The resultant tests stated that the developed S-box is bijective and balance Bolean function.

In 2017, Gomes and Moreno [10], They presented a compact S-box implementation for Twofish cipher by adopted Altera Quartus Cyclone board. The introduced labor characterized by less amount of logical circuit design compared with original design. The main objective behind the design notation is to extend the implementation to a large scope of applications with Field Programmable Gate Array (FPGA) technique. The author plans to adopt this work as a part of big project for customizing the utilization as alternation for the AES cipher.

In 2019, Zahid et al. [11], have been developed a new technique for construction a modern Substitutes-boxes based on Cubic Fractional Transformation (CFT). The strength of the intended S-box was evaluated and assessed by several significant criteria. The authors claimed that the present S-box achieves good results and can be used as a strong S-box for the most modern block cipher algorithms.

3   Mathematical Preliminaries

The present section explains the main notations and comprehensions for the cryptographic mathematical functions. The mathematical guide for the S-box design includes knowledge some Boolean functions with non-linear equations. The S-box is a critical part for the SPN structure since it is the only non-linear part in the algorithm's stages. A large number of S-Box design methods are available with different mathematical notations. Some of the popular methods depend on preprocessing approach for the construction the nonlinear layer. Other methods depend basically on affine transformations with multiplicative inverse. The S-box of AES cipher is considered as a benchmark S-box which inspirited by several posterior algorithms. The AES cipher was adopted a new mathematical idea that focuses on wide trail strategy where each part has it is own function independently [12]. Thus, the S-box construction comprises 8-bit multiplicative inverse under irreducible polynomial of order eight followed by 8*8 binary affine transform. The calculation of multiplicative inverse on $GF(2^8)$ which requires to be addressed in composite field. An isomorphic mapping function $f(x) = x*y$ with two sides-inverses that is bijective under the set of elements is required to represent the polynomial. The incoming entry polynomial is multiplied and computed under the multiplicative inverse, thereafter, the affine transform is computed and the resultant XORed with constant vector [13].

Let $S = ()$ a non-linear sub-byte transformation with $x \times y$ and the $f(i)$ is a Boolean function from x variables $x_1, x_2 \ldots x_n$. The affine with multiple equations acts as $S(x) = A(P(x))$ that mapping over the $GF(2^8)$ as an $x * y$ S-box of a non-linear mapping $GF(2)^n \psi \to \leftarrow GF(2)^n$. Let $w \in \{0, 1\}n \backslash \{\mathbf{0}\}$, $z \in \{0, 1\}m$. The XORed table entry of an S-box S corresponding to $(w * z)$ is $XOR(w, z) = \#\{x \in \{0, 1\}n :$ $S(x) \oplus S(x \oplus v1\} \oplus S(x \oplus v2) \oplus S(x \oplus v3\} = z\}$ where # is the cardinality in algebraic set with multiple affine. The input polynomial for the internal function is mixed with ciphering key to generate the sub-keys dependent S-boxes. Where each S-box involves p of 8-bit fixed permutation powered with multiple affine which ultimately

XORed with specific ciphering key. If the ciphering key with length of 128-bit the key dependent S-box will be as follows

$$y0 = s0(A0) = p1\,[p2[p3[A]\ XOR\,s0, 0]\ XOR\ s1,\ v0]$$
$$y1 = s1(A1) = p1\,[p2[p3[A]\ XOR\ s0, 1]\ XOR\ s1,\ v1]$$
$$y2 = s2(A2) = p1\,[p2[p3[A]\ XOR\,s0, 2]\ XOR\ s1,\ v2]$$
$$y3 = s3(A3) = p1\,[p2[p3[A]\ XOR\ s0, 3]\ XOR\ s1,\ v3]$$

The S-box construction is built according to different Boolean functions as a bent function that gives a high nonlinearity for the S-box. Suppose the bent function termed as $S : \{0, 1\}n \rightarrow \{0, 1\}^m$ where m for even number can be considered equal to one. From another perspective, it is simple to produce two functions g(x) and f(x) and proof these two functions are belong to the same class if $g(\overrightarrow{x}) = (f(Ax + b))$. In case with two S-boxes the Boolean function will be depicted as $S2(x) = B(S1(A(x) + a)) + b$. The opposite implementation for the multiple affine transform can be summarized by the following mathematical formula:

$$^{-1}y0 = s0(A0) = p1^{-1}[p2^{-1}[p3^{-1}[A]\ XOR\ s0,0]\ XOR\ s1,0]$$
$$^{-1}y1 = s1(A1) = p1^{-1}[p2^{-1}[p3^{-1}[A]\ XOR\ s0,1]\ XOR\ s1,1]$$
$$^{-1}y2 = s2(A2) = p1^{-1}[p2^{-1}[p3^{-1}[A]\ XOR\ s0,2]\ XOR\ s1,2]$$
$$^{-1}y3 = s3(A3) = p1^{-1}[p2^{-1}[p3^{-1}[A]\ XOR\ s0,3]\ XOR\ s1,3]$$

The cryptographic power of any S-box is critically assessment unless it was satisfying the important metrics of S-box design. The most important criteria for the design black box include the mathematical functions for the S-box built. Thus, good S-box must be met the essential metrics for the Boolean functions represented by: bijection, nonlinearity, bit independence criterion, strict avalanche effect, and linear and differential approximation probabilities [14].

1. **Bijection Criteria:** is a class of mathematical function that represents two sets where the element in one set is correspondence to the other element in other set as one-to-one relation. If the S-box n*n then the relation will be pair of related vectors one for input vector of n-bit into m-bit of the mirror in out vector.
2. **Strict-Avalanche Criterion:** is a desirable metric for the measuring the strength of S-box where small change in input vector propagate with a high change in output vector reach to half probability change. The design step will need function dependency on input vector with 50% to have a significant avalanche effect on output vector.
3. **Bit-Independence Criterion:** The Bit-independence concept depicts the immunity of coefficients correlation between the input and output streaming bits. It declares the extent to which outputs ith and jth string bits are affected and changed independently when any change in kth of input bits.
4. **Nonlinearity Criterion:** The non-linearity property states the strength of the mathematical function in S-box design against the differential cryptanalysis. It

prevents the S-box to be mapped linearly from input vector to the output vector. If the S-box is built with high nonlinearity it will ensure high resistance in a linear approximation for the bent function and the affine parameters. The nonlinearity is bounded as an immune procedure against linear cryptanalysis and enhanced the security margin for the cipher.

5. **Balance Criterion:** the balance metric is responsible for balance in Boolean vector where the Boolean function has an equal number of zeros and ones. The importance of balance criterion is to make the cipher hard in terms of attacks. The balance property is highly desired metric for the strong S-box, since it ensures that the bent function cannot be approximated by fixed operations [15, 16].

4 The S-Box Design Methodologies

The power of the cipher design influences by the measure of confusion that generated in the ciphertext. Thus, the strength of the cryptographic block cipher depends heavily on the nature of S-Box design and the type of generation approaches.

1. **Random S-box:** several researchers and designers investigated and searched for long times to design numerous methods for designing various S-boxes. A large number of these methods were random S-boxes generation. The random S-box produces an acceptable security level because it uses a diverse S-boxes per each key. Random S-box is a method that uses different techniques in generation process that withstanding against major of cryptanalysis attacks. Randomness principle give a high computational complexity and has no fixed points of reverse reconstruction steps. Thus, the random s-box is difficult to exploit from the internal structure since it depends on various S-boxes of derived-key for each round [17].

2. **Random with Testing S-box:** Random S-box exhibits a good alternative for the S-box generation process since it has no subject to the underlying pattern that can be exploited in cryptanalysis. The random with testing method depends on pre-selection of the entry input values which have been tested according to different criteria. The resultant of tested output data selects the data those with good features and discard those fail to pass the threshold of testing. Random with Testing S-box is very similar to the random S-box except it contains some pre-computational operations [18].

3. **Human-Base S-box:** S-box is generated by a manual method accompanied with simple mathematical operations this type of design is suitable only for small S-box. In case of large S-box this method would be lossless and uncompact [19].

4. **Mathematical-Base:** S-box is generated according to the mathematical base and algebraic structure. Many researchers have designed and discovered methods for building new benchmarks of strong S-Boxes and investigate their strength against some cryptanalysis attacks. such Strict Avalanche Criterion (SAC), Linear Probability (LP), as Non-linearity (NL), Differential Probability (DP), Bijection and bit Independence Criterion (BIC), and etc. [20].

5   The Proposed S-Box Design

The proposed S-box has been designed with multiple mathematical affine equations. It has put some additional conditions on the non-linear layer of a sub-byte stage that will enhance the avalanche and completeness comprehensions for the intended S-box. In addition, the imposed S-box is developed to fulfill the critical criteria of the best strong ciphers' structures.

5.1   Non-linear Substitution Transformation

The sub-byte layer will be the most discriminating part of the design strategy, as a result, its size and construction process significantly influence the whole algorithm. The S-Box construction contains three affine equations with their convenient vectors. The construction of the forward S-Box basically depends on the following steps, the first step by taking the multiplicative inverse of all tables' of 256 values according to the new irreducible polynomial. $m(x) = x^8 + x^5 + x^4 + x^3 + x^2 + x + 1$. The second step applying the first affine (F1) transform and the outcome XORed with the first constant vector (V1) represented by the value (87) in hex notation as shown in Eq. (1). After that repeated the process with second affine (F2) transform and the result XORed with the second constant vector (V2) that is represented by the value (2B) as stated in Eq. (2). Eventually, repeated the process with third affine (F3) transform and the outcome makes a bit-wise exclusive-OR with the third constant vector (V3) that represented by the value (3D) as stated in Eq. (3). as it explained in Table 2.

$$P \longrightarrow M\text{-}inverse(P) \bmod m(x) \text{ where } m(x) \text{ is an irreducible polynomial.}$$

- *The first affine equation (F1)*
- *The first Inv-affine equation (F1')*
- *The first vector (V1)*
- *The first Inv-vector (V1')*
- *The second affine equation (F2)*
- *The second Inv-affine equation (F2')*
- *The second vector (V2)*
- *The second Inv-vector (V2')*
- *The third affine equation (F3)*
- *The third Inv-affine equation (F3')*
- *The third vector (V3)*
- *The third Inv-vector (V3')*

Suppose (A), (X) and (M) are 1st, 2nd and 3rd forward Affine matrices respectively with (8*8) dimension and in another side (B), (Y) and (N) the inverse (Backward) affine matrices respectively. Let (C), (Z) and (S) forward XORed vectors and (CC), (ZZ), and (SS) can be considered as the corresponding backward vectors respectively to make the forward and backward compatible and the whole operations are reversible as stated in Table 1. All these interrelated matrices and the vectors values have been computed mathematically and inaccurately.

Table 1. Non-linear affine of transform matrices with their vectors

Polynomial arrays	Forward matrix	Backward matrix	XORed forward vector	XORed inverse of backward vector
Affine Matrix1	A	B	C	CC
Affine Matrix2	X	Y	Z	ZZ
Affine Matrix3	M	N	S	SS

$$\text{Ciphertext}\,(C) = (F3(F2(F1(P) \oplus V1) \oplus V2) \oplus V3)$$

Let (V) the entry vector which we want to encrypt it.

$A * B = I$

$X * Y = I$

$M * N = I$

Where (I) is an Identity matrix

Forward Operations: Where F1, F2, and F3 represent the three functions or levels of affine transform and P1, P2 and P3 refer to the initial entry for the plaintext in each layer of affine mapping equations respectively.

$$F1 = A * [V] \oplus C$$
$$= AV \oplus C$$
$$F2 = X * [P1] \oplus Z$$
$$= X * [AV \oplus C] \oplus Z$$
$$= XAV \oplus XC \oplus Z$$
$$F3 = M * P2 \oplus S$$
$$F3 = M * [XAV \oplus XC \oplus Z] \oplus S$$
$$= MXAV \oplus MXC \oplus MZ \oplus S$$

Ex. Let the Input vector $b = 13$

$$A * 13 \oplus C = B0$$
$$= B0 * X = EA \oplus Z = C1$$
$$= C1 * M = D5 \oplus S = E8$$

$$b' = \begin{bmatrix} b'_0 \\ b'_1 \\ b'_2 \\ b'_3 \\ b'_4 \\ b'_5 \\ b'_6 \\ b'_7 \end{bmatrix} = A \begin{bmatrix} 0 & 1 & 0 & 0 & 0 & 1 & 0 & 1 \\ 1 & 0 & 1 & 0 & 0 & 0 & 1 & 0 \\ 0 & 1 & 0 & 1 & 0 & 0 & 0 & 1 \\ 1 & 0 & 1 & 0 & 1 & 0 & 0 & 0 \\ 0 & 1 & 0 & 1 & 0 & 1 & 0 & 0 \\ 0 & 0 & 1 & 0 & 1 & 0 & 1 & 0 \\ 0 & 0 & 0 & 1 & 0 & 1 & 0 & 1 \\ 1 & 0 & 0 & 0 & 1 & 0 & 1 & 0 \end{bmatrix} * b \begin{bmatrix} b_0 \\ b_1 \\ b_2 \\ b_3 \\ b_4 \\ b_5 \\ b_6 \\ b_7 \end{bmatrix} \oplus C \begin{bmatrix} 1 \\ 1 \\ 1 \\ 0 \\ 0 \\ 0 \\ 0 \\ 1 \end{bmatrix} \qquad (1)$$

$$b'' = \begin{bmatrix} b''_0 \\ b''_1 \\ b''_2 \\ b''_3 \\ b''_4 \\ b''_5 \\ b''_6 \\ b''_7 \end{bmatrix} = X \begin{bmatrix} 1 & 0 & 0 & 1 & 1 & 1 & 1 & 0 \\ 0 & 1 & 0 & 0 & 1 & 1 & 1 & 1 \\ 1 & 0 & 1 & 0 & 0 & 1 & 1 & 1 \\ 1 & 1 & 0 & 1 & 0 & 0 & 1 & 1 \\ 1 & 1 & 1 & 0 & 1 & 0 & 0 & 1 \\ 1 & 1 & 1 & 1 & 0 & 1 & 0 & 0 \\ 0 & 1 & 1 & 1 & 1 & 0 & 1 & 0 \\ 0 & 0 & 1 & 1 & 1 & 1 & 0 & 1 \end{bmatrix} * b' \begin{bmatrix} b'_0 \\ b'_1 \\ b'_2 \\ b'_3 \\ b'_4 \\ b'_5 \\ b'_6 \\ b'_7 \end{bmatrix} \oplus Z \begin{bmatrix} 1 \\ 1 \\ 0 \\ 1 \\ 0 \\ 1 \\ 0 \\ 0 \end{bmatrix} \qquad (2)$$

$$b''' = \begin{bmatrix} b'''_0 \\ b'''_1 \\ b'''_2 \\ b'''_3 \\ b'''_4 \\ b'''_5 \\ b'''_6 \\ b'''_7 \end{bmatrix} = M \begin{bmatrix} 1 & 1 & 1 & 0 & 0 & 0 & 1 & 1 \\ 1 & 1 & 1 & 1 & 0 & 0 & 0 & 1 \\ 1 & 1 & 1 & 1 & 1 & 0 & 0 & 0 \\ 0 & 1 & 1 & 1 & 1 & 1 & 0 & 0 \\ 0 & 0 & 1 & 1 & 1 & 1 & 1 & 0 \\ 0 & 0 & 0 & 1 & 1 & 1 & 1 & 1 \\ 1 & 0 & 0 & 0 & 1 & 1 & 1 & 1 \\ 1 & 1 & 0 & 0 & 0 & 1 & 1 & 1 \end{bmatrix} * b'' \begin{bmatrix} b''_0 \\ b''_1 \\ b''_2 \\ b''_3 \\ b''_4 \\ b''_5 \\ b''_6 \\ b''_7 \end{bmatrix} \oplus S \begin{bmatrix} 1 \\ 0 \\ 1 \\ 1 \\ 1 \\ 1 \\ 0 \\ 0 \end{bmatrix} \qquad (3)$$

Table 2. Forward proposed S-box

	0	1	2	3	4	5	6	7	8	9	A	B	C	D	E	F
0	AD	4B	37	41	09	47	DB	B6	FF	A4	31	29	7F	14	C9	45
1	84	0A	C0	6E	E3	EE	06	74	2D	5D	71	55	76	2E	D9	8F
2	39	B3	7E	C4	1B	8B	A5	9D	63	03	0C	FD	78	B4	A8	23
3	04	E6	3C	81	C3	EC	38	87	40	54	85	A0	97	DF	BC	22
4	E7	99	A2	69	44	3F	19	7C	F6	4E	BE	05	A9	18	B5	6A
5	CA	8A	13	6B	94	F8	6C	7A	AE	FA	21	65	C6	DC	EA	6D
6	90	89	08	58	8C	75	52	DD	9A	42	E4	11	8E	0B	B8	FE
7	B2	28	51	F5	50	FB	C2	EB	59	4A	7D	79	25	62	83	80
8	61	49	B7	8D	2A	2F	26	E8	B0	4C	0D	F0	1E	E1	AC	91
9	E9	AA	5C	9F	CD	2B	F9	E2	AF	DE	77	BF	48	AB	A7	60
A	F7	32	D7	B1	F2	01	CE	A6	D8	33	07	72	4D	1C	46	E5
B	2C	9C	EF	D0	02	D4	20	30	F1	15	FC	B9	0E	88	24	16
C	DA	34	56	0F	96	5F	57	CF	3D	1D	C1	43	BB	F4	95	92
D	36	A1	5A	98	E0	73	1A	70	D5	35	17	BD	27	7B	ED	64
E	CB	12	6F	C8	3A	D6	68	82	53	93	86	D1	F3	5B	67	D2
F	3E	D3	5E	4F	C5	10	C7	66	00	1F	A3	CC	BA	9B	3B	9E

5.2   Non-linear Substitution Transformation

The inverse of the proposed S-box is constructed by applying the reverse steps of the forward procedure. Firstly, mapping the inverse of the third affine transform XORed with the corresponding Inv-vector that is represented by (73) in hex representation as it is shown in Eq. (4). Secondly mapping the inverse of the second affine transform XORed with the corresponding Inv-vector that represented by (F6) as shown in Eq. (5). Finally, mapped the first affine transform XORed with the corresponding Inv-vector that represented by (3C) as it is clarified in Eq. (6) and the outcome has taken by the multiplicative inverse according to the irreducible polynomial and consequently the backward or InvS-Box as shown in Table 3. The rational clue for the user more constant vectors is to increase the complexity of the S-box and make it difficult computationally, in addition, to eliminating any fixed point of tractable computation respectively. The following are the mathematical proof that represents the backward operations details and the underlined terms indicate either to a null operation or identity operation.

Backward Operation: where the (F1', F2' and F3') are the three inverse process or Functions

$$\text{Plaintext (P)} = (\text{F1}'(\text{F2}'(\text{F3}'(\text{P}) \oplus \text{V3}) \oplus \text{V2}) \oplus \text{V1})$$

$$\text{F3}' = \text{N} * [\text{MXAV} \oplus \text{MXC} \oplus \text{MZ} \oplus \text{S}] \oplus \text{SS}$$

$$= \underline{\text{NMXAV}} \oplus \underline{\text{NMXC}} \oplus \underline{\text{NMZ}} \oplus \underline{\text{NS}} \oplus \text{SS}$$

$$= \text{XAV} \oplus \text{XC} \oplus \text{Z} \oplus \textbf{Null}$$

$$\text{F2}' = \text{Y} * [\text{XAV} \oplus \text{XC} \oplus \text{Z}] \oplus \text{ZZ}$$

$$= \underline{\text{YXAV}} \oplus \underline{\text{YXC}} \oplus \underline{\text{YZ}} \oplus \underline{\text{ZZ}}$$

$$\text{A V} \oplus \text{C} \oplus = \textbf{Null}$$

$$\textbf{F1}' = \textbf{B} * [\textbf{AV} \oplus \textbf{C}] \oplus \textbf{CC}$$

$$\textbf{BAV} \oplus \underline{\textbf{BC}} \oplus \underline{\textbf{CC}}$$

$$= \textbf{V} \oplus \textbf{Null}$$

$$= \textbf{V} \rightarrow (\textbf{The Original Vector})$$

Let the Input Vector = E8

$$\textbf{N} * \textbf{E8} = \textbf{B2} \oplus \textbf{SS} = \textbf{C1}$$

$$= \textbf{C1} * \textbf{Y} = \textbf{46} \oplus \textbf{ZZ} = \textbf{B0}$$

$$= \textbf{B0} * \textbf{B} = \textbf{2F} \oplus \textbf{CC} = \textbf{13}$$

$$
b'' \begin{bmatrix} b_0'' \\ b_1'' \\ b_2'' \\ b_3'' \\ b_4'' \\ b_5'' \\ b_6'' \\ b_7'' \end{bmatrix} = N \begin{bmatrix} 1 & 0 & 0 & 1 & 0 & 1 & 0 & 0 \\ 0 & 1 & 0 & 0 & 1 & 0 & 1 & 0 \\ 0 & 0 & 1 & 0 & 0 & 1 & 0 & 1 \\ 1 & 0 & 0 & 1 & 0 & 0 & 1 & 0 \\ 0 & 1 & 0 & 0 & 1 & 0 & 0 & 1 \\ 1 & 0 & 1 & 0 & 0 & 1 & 0 & 0 \\ 0 & 1 & 0 & 1 & 0 & 0 & 1 & 0 \\ 0 & 0 & 1 & 0 & 1 & 0 & 0 & 1 \end{bmatrix} * b''' \begin{bmatrix} b_0''' \\ b_1''' \\ b_2''' \\ b_3''' \\ b_4''' \\ b_5''' \\ b_6''' \\ b_7''' \end{bmatrix} \oplus SS \begin{bmatrix} 1 \\ 1 \\ 0 \\ 0 \\ 1 \\ 1 \\ 1 \\ 0 \end{bmatrix} \quad (4)
$$

$$b' \begin{bmatrix} b'_0 \\ b'_1 \\ b'_2 \\ b'_3 \\ b'_4 \\ b'_5 \\ b'_6 \\ b'_7 \end{bmatrix} = Y \begin{bmatrix} 0 & 0 & 1 & 1 & 0 & 1 & 0 & 0 \\ 0 & 0 & 0 & 1 & 1 & 0 & 1 & 0 \\ 0 & 0 & 0 & 0 & 1 & 1 & 0 & 1 \\ 1 & 0 & 0 & 0 & 0 & 1 & 1 & 0 \\ 0 & 1 & 0 & 0 & 0 & 0 & 1 & 1 \\ 1 & 0 & 1 & 0 & 0 & 0 & 0 & 1 \\ 1 & 1 & 0 & 1 & 0 & 0 & 0 & 0 \\ 0 & 1 & 1 & 0 & 1 & 0 & 0 & 0 \end{bmatrix} * b'' \begin{bmatrix} b''_0 \\ b''_1 \\ b''_2 \\ b''_3 \\ b''_4 \\ b''_5 \\ b''_6 \\ b''_7 \end{bmatrix} \oplus ZZ \begin{bmatrix} 0 \\ 1 \\ 1 \\ 0 \\ 1 \\ 1 \\ 1 \\ 1 \end{bmatrix} \quad (5)$$

$$b \begin{bmatrix} b_0 \\ b_1 \\ b_2 \\ b_3 \\ b_4 \\ b_5 \\ b_6 \\ b_7 \end{bmatrix} = B \begin{bmatrix} 0 & 1 & 0 & 1 & 0 & 0 & 0 & 1 \\ 1 & 0 & 1 & 0 & 1 & 0 & 0 & 0 \\ 0 & 1 & 0 & 1 & 0 & 1 & 0 & 0 \\ 0 & 0 & 1 & 0 & 1 & 0 & 1 & 0 \\ 0 & 0 & 0 & 1 & 0 & 1 & 0 & 1 \\ 1 & 0 & 0 & 0 & 1 & 0 & 1 & 0 \\ 0 & 1 & 0 & 0 & 0 & 1 & 0 & 1 \\ 1 & 0 & 1 & 0 & 0 & 0 & 1 & 0 \end{bmatrix} * b' \begin{bmatrix} b'_0 \\ b'_1 \\ b'_2 \\ b'_3 \\ b'_4 \\ b'_5 \\ b'_6 \\ b'_7 \end{bmatrix} \oplus CC \begin{bmatrix} 0 \\ 0 \\ 1 \\ 1 \\ 1 \\ 1 \\ 0 \\ 0 \end{bmatrix} \quad (6)$$

Table 3. Backward proposed S-box

	0	1	2	3	4	5	6	7	8	9	A	B	C	D	E	F
0	F8	A5	B4	29	30	4B	16	AA	62	04	11	6D	2A	8A	BC	C3
1	F5	6B	E1	52	0D	B9	BF	DA	4D	46	D6	24	AD	C9	8C	F9
2	B6	5A	3F	2F	BE	7C	86	DC	71	0B	84	95	B0	18	1D	85
3	B7	0A	A1	A9	C1	D9	D0	02	36	20	E4	FE	32	C8	F0	45
4	38	03	69	CB	44	0F	AE	05	9C	81	79	01	89	AC	49	F3
5	74	72	66	E8	39	1B	C2	C6	63	78	D2	ED	92	19	F2	C5
6	9F	80	7D	28	DF	5B	F7	EE	E6	43	4F	53	56	5F	13	E2
7	D7	1A	AB	D5	17	65	1C	9A	2C	7B	57	DD	47	7A	22	0C
8	7F	33	E7	7E	10	3A	EA	37	BD	61	51	25	64	83	6C	1F
9	60	8F	CF	E9	54	CE	C4	3C	D3	41	68	FD	B1	27	FF	93
A	3B	D1	42	FA	09	26	A7	9E	2E	4C	91	9D	8E	00	58	98
B	88	A3	70	21	2D	4E	07	82	6E	BB	FC	CC	3E	DB	4A	9B
C	12	CA	76	34	23	F4	5C	F6	E3	0E	50	E0	FB	94	A6	C7
D	B3	EB	EF	F1	B5	D8	E5	A2	A8	1E	C0	06	5D	67	99	3D
E	D4	8D	97	14	6A	AF	31	40	87	90	5E	77	35	DE	15	B2
F	8B	B8	A4	EC	CD	73	48	A0	55	96	59	75	BA	2B	6F	08

6 Security Analysis and Experimental Results

In this section, the main themes will be discussed and the pros and cons of the proposed S-box will be diagnosed from the point of view of cryptography aspects. The proposed S-box characterized with an organized internal structure that tends to be balanced and non-sacrifice. The "balanced term means that the algorithm has an elegant step with the same execution time in encryption & decryption processes in opposite to the AES cipher that suffers from some delay in decryption with embedded devices. The modern design for the non-linear stage or S-box built does not need to construct with three tables in forward and the same in backward or to enlarge it with a big size on the account of memory and the hardware requirements. So the S-Box has been reduced to work only with one table in encryption and its inverse for decryption and supported by three correlated affine transforms to defeat the algebraic, interpolation and large range attacks.

We have experimented the construction of S-Box with all equations of the irreducible polynomial (30 equations of degree 8) see ref [21] and there have gotten thirty different of new S-box tables with their inverses. The designers aware to the idea that the design process with three affine is equal to that one affine in term of S-box design but in fact, the design of S-box with three affine gives a completely different of hex-values distribution map compared with single affine overall 30 irreducible equations. The enhanced S-box is designed to face and overcomes the linear and differential attacks as well as to consume the same execution time for encryption and decryption in order to eliminate the timing attacks and to combat the power analysis attack. The last part in the round transformation that plays an important role in security strength is the key-dependent S-box algorithm that is responsible for the sub-keys scheduling, which acts the nerve of the proposed model and should be kept secret. The Related-key attacks almost not effective (even if the $2^{99.5}$ chosen plaintext/cipher text value all the consideration about it still theoretical entirely and was not from evaluation criteria during the AES selection. The complexity of the brute force attack is appraised by 2^{k-1} encryptions. The attacker is unable to estimate or reconstruct the algebraic equations from the deduced information hence, each stage built separately and the algebraic attack becomes very hard.

The basic challenges of building steps for the proposed S-box till now, that it has the same as the AES structure where the encryption and decryption processes do not completely utilize the self-stages since the inverses of S-box and linear mapping have to be executed separately. The proposed S-box has been checked by several statistical analytical tests and exhibited accepted implications. Understanding the strength and weakness of any algorithm gives a good conception of the algorithm but the evaluation and assessment of algorithm construction are not easy. Since it includes the algebraic and statistical analysis and may be the hardware implementation. So many tools have been developed by companies and individual developers and released on the internet to use in measuring and evaluating the algorithms according to several important metrics. But each of these tools gave differentiate results from each other and none of them provides accurate measurements, thus; there are no uniformly standard criteria in evaluation and analysis.

The analysis and the assessment of the proposed S-box also comprise the algebraic characteristics for the internal structure between the suggested S-box and the AES S-box from several factors for each stage in the round transformation as it is shown in Table 4. The intended S-box showed great similarities in characteristics and qualities with S-box of AES cipher but with more complexity and non-linearity criteria.

- **The Algebraic Complexity:** is the study of the minimum number of operations sufficient to perform various computations. It can be seen that there are 9 for S-box and 253 nonzero coefficients involved in algebraic expression for the AES S-box coefficients, but with the triple affine the count of algebraic raise from 9 to 253 and the inverse S-box stays 255, which enhances the capability of the S-box so as to face algebraic attack and interpolation attack.

- **Non-linearity property:** refers to the weight of the lowest weight nonzero Hadamard coefficient that is equal to the nonlinearity. Therefore, the nonlinearity of the proposed S-box with the upper bound is 114. Thus. This factor tends to be solid to defeat the effectively linear cryptanalysis.
- **The Differential Uniformity:** is a mapping of values for every non-zero input difference and any output difference with the number of possible inputs that has a uniform upper bound. Therefore, there are only four values in uniform mapping form. It is clear that the proposed S-box is differential with 4 uniformity, which makes the differential cryptanalysis very hard.

Table 4. Algebraic comparison between the S-box of AES and the proposed S-box

Algebraic properties	Proposed S-box	AES cipher
Correlation immunity property	Zero	Zero
Algebraic degree property	Seven	Seven
Algebraic complexity property	252/255	9/255
Bijection property	Yes	Yes
Strict avalanche criteria (SAC)	1/2	1/2
Non-linearity property	113	112
Differential uniformity property	4	4
Power mapping property	By-Three affine	By-One affine
S-box dependency property	Yes	Yes
Key scheduling property	Yes	Yes

7   Conclusions

A new compact and adaptable S-box that based on a new design strategy with multiple affine transforms has been constructed. The essence of design lies in increasing the confusion of the algorithm and enhancing the key dependent S-box. The suggested S-box characterized by high non-linearity and maximize algebraic complexity to encounter the cryptanalytic attacks. The design scheme is to defeat the linear and differential attacks and to reinforce the security metric. The proposed S-box has been tested by different assessment tests according to various irreducible polynomials and it has been applied an accepted result. Finally, the proposed S-box can be adopted as a compact S-box for the modern block cipher algorithms with multi-security layers.

References

1. Dragomir, I.R., Lazăr, M.: Generating and testing the components of a block cipher. In: Proceedings of the 8th International Conference on Electronics, Computers and Artificial Intelligence, IEEE, ECAI 2016, pp. 1–4 (2017). https://doi.org/10.1109/ecai.2016.7861190
2. Lin, Z.: Diffusion and confusion of chaotic iteration based hash functions. In: International Conference on Embedded and Ubiquitous Computing (EUC) and 15th International

Symposium on Distributed Computing and Applications for Business Engineering (DCABES). IEEE, pp. 444–447 (2016)

3. Du, Z.Q., Xu, Q.J., Zhang, J., Li, M.: Design and analysis of dynamic S-box based on Feistel. In: Proceedings of 2015 IEEE Advanced Information Technology, Electronic and Automation Control Conference, IAEAC 2015, pp. 590–594. IEEE (2016). https://doi.org/10.1109/iaeac.2015.7428622

4. Agrawal, D.P., Wang, H., Dey, S., Ghosh, R.: A review of cryptographic properties of 4-bit S-boxes with generation and analysis of crypto secure S-boxes. In: Computer Cyber Security, pp. 527–555 (2019). https://doi.org/10.1201/9780429424878-20

5. Dawood, O.A., Rahma, A.M.S., Abdul Hossen, A.M.J.: The new block cipher design (Tigris Cipher). Int. J. Comput. Netw. Inf. Secur. 7(12), 10–18 (2015)

6. Dawood, O.A., Rahma, A.M.S., Abdul Hossen, A.M.J.: New symmetric cipher fast algorithm of revertible operations' queen (FAROQ) cipher. Int. J. Comput. Netw. Inf. Secur. 9, 29–36 (2017)

7. Dawood, O.A., Rahma, A.M.S., Mohssen, A., Hossen, J.A.: The euphrates cipher. IJCSI Int. J. Comput. Sci. 12(2), 154–160 (2015)

8. Rodinko, M., Oliynykov, R., Gorbenko, Y.: Optimization of the high nonlinear S-boxes generation method. In: Third International Scientific-Practical Conference Problems of Infocommunications Science and Technology (PIC S&T), vol. 70, pp. 93–105. in Tatra Mountains Mathematical Publications (2017)

9. Alamsyah Bejo, A., Adji, T.B.: AES S-box construction using different irreducible polynomial and constant 8-bit vector. In: 2017 IEEE Conference on Dependable and Secure Computing, pp. 366–369 (2017). https://doi.org/10.1109/desec.2017.8073857

10. Gomes, O.D.S.M., Moreno, R.L.: A compact S-box module for 128/192/256-bit symmetric cryptography hardware. In: Proceedings - 2016 9th International Conference on Developments in eSystems Engineering, DeSE 2016, pp. 94–97 (2017). https://doi.org/10.1109/dese.2016.17

11. Zahid, A.H., Arshad, M.J., Ahmad, M.: A novel construction of efficient substitution-boxes using cubic fractional transformation. Entropy 21, 245 (2019)

12. Dawood, O.A., Hammadi, O.I., Asman, T.K.: Developing a new secret symmetric algorithm for securing wireless applications. In: Proceedings - 2018 1st Annual International Conference on Information and Sciences, AiCIS 2018, pp. 152–157 (2019). https://doi.org/10.1109/aicis.2018.00038

13. Shreenivas Pai, N., Raghuram, S., Chennakrishna, M., Karthik, A.S.V.: Logic optimization of AES S-Box. In: International Conference on Automatic Control and Dynamic Optimization Techniques, ICACDOT 2016, pp. 1042–1046 (2017). https://doi.org/10.1109/icacdot.2016.7877745

14. Dawood, O.A., Sagheer, A.M., Al-Rawi, S.S.: Design large symmetric algorithm for securing big data. In: Proceedings - International Conference on Developments in eSystems Engineering, DeSE 2018-September, pp. 123–128 (2019)

15. Cui, L., Cao, Y.A.: New S-box structure named affine-power-affine. Int. J. Innov. Comput. Inf. Control 3, 751–759 (2007)

16. Lee, J., et al.: Avalanche and bit independence properties of photon-counting double random phase encoding in gyrator domain. Curr. Opt. Photon. 2(4), 368–377 (2018)

17. Lambi, D., Živkovi, M.: Comparison of random S-Box generation methods. Publications DE L'Institute Mathematique Nouvelle série 93(107), 109–115 (2013)

18. Mroczkowski, P.: Generating pseudorandom S-boxes – a method of improving the security of cryptosystems based on block ciphers. J. Telecommun. Inf. Technol. 2, 74–79 (2009)

19. Ivanov, G., Nikolov, N., Nikova, S.: Cryptographically strong s-boxes generated by modified immune algorithm. In: Pasalic, E., Knudsen, L.R. (eds.) BalkanCryptSec 2015.

LNCS, vol. 9540, pp. 31–42. Springer, Cham (2016). https://doi.org/10.1007/978-3-319-29172-7_3

20. Sagheer, A.M., Al-Rawi, S.S., Dawood, O.A.: Proposing of developed advance encryption standard. In: Proceedings - 4th International Conference on Developments in eSystems Engineering, DeSE 2011, pp. 197–202 (2011). https://doi.org/10.1109/dese.2011.74

21. Baylis, J., Lidl, R., Niederreiter, H.: Introduction to Finite Fields and Their Applications. Cambridge University Press, Cambridge (1988). Math. Gaz. 72, 335

Computer Network and Communication

A Comprehensive Study of the Environmental Effects on WiFi Received Signal Strength: Lab Scenario

Rawaa Akram Mohammed$^{(\boxtimes)}$ (iD), Aseel H. Al-Nakkash (iD),
and Omar Nameer Mohammed Salim (iD)

Department of Computer Engineering, Electrical Engineering Technical College,
Middle Technical University, Baghdad, Iraq
rereak444@gmail.com, omarnamer2005@gmail.com,
Aseel_Alnakkash@eetc.mtu.edu.iq

Abstract. The characteristics of indoor dense environment required accurate modeling. The multipath effects due to different obstacles with different materials and dimensions make the behavior of the propagated signal unpredictable. In this paper, a reliable ray tracing simulator is used for assessing the performance of WLAN based on the 802.11n dual-band system, was a real lab scenario is adopted as a complex indoor environment. The effects of different parameters are investigated. They are objects materials, object dimension, and frequency to address the effects of diffraction and reflection phenomena on the received power. Object materials are analyzed and this paper verifies that metal object, especially with large dimensions has significant effects on signal strength fluctuations due to their electrical properties. In addition, small object effects can be neglected at the cost of 4.86 dBm and 5.27 dBm losses at 2.4 GHz and 5 GHz respectively to reduce the simulation computational time. On the other side, the results show that the propagation signal is prone to more attenuation at a higher frequency due to path loss increasing.

Keywords: WiFi · Signal propagation · Indoor environment · Building material · SBR

1 Introduction

The performance of the wireless communication system is governed by many environmental factors in addition to the system parameters [1]. The need for accurate channel model characterization is an essential step in any application based on wireless communication [2]. The radio wave is prone to a number of reflections, diffraction, and scattering during propagation through different paths, which in turns causes signal attenuation and distortion [3]. The signal strength is related directly to the operation frequency, since the object may consider as smooth or rough surface based on the wavelength [4]. Frequency also determines the diffracted signal quality. Form the other side, object dialectical properties, size and the angle of incident rays determine the quality of reflected wave [5]. In addition to abovementioned, the quality of the signal is strongly influenced by the environment architecture (indoor or outdoor, Line of Sight

© Springer Nature Switzerland AG 2020
M. I. Khalaf et al. (Eds.): ACRIT 2019, CCIS 1174, pp. 455–464, 2020.
https://doi.org/10.1007/978-3-030-38752-5_35

(LOS) or Non-Line of Site (NLOS)…etc.) [6]. The indoor environment is considered as a complex one since it is consists of many details. The floor plan variations, building construction materials, besides different obstacle's dimensions and electrical properties result in unpredictable multipath effects [7]. This loss Known as path loss which is caused by effects of the signal propagation characteristics such as power absorption by obstacles during its collision [8]. In this work, a comprehensive study on the propagated signal quality is simulated and implemented for real case study materialized by a dense lab scenario. Many factors effects are investigated. They are; lab building material, lab furniture materials, and dimensions.

The organization of this paper is as follow Introduction - propagation model - Research Methodology - Simulation Results and Discussion – Conclusion.

2 Related Work

Accordingly, quantifying radio wave propagation in such an environment is a big challenge. Many researchers' efforts are employed to analyze the interaction between the radio waves and the propagation environment. Such interaction is considered as the key factor of many applications nowadays, such as localization aware system, planning optimization, and many others. Some of the researchers' work will be discussed next.

The author in [9] studied the correlation between the experimental and simulation results for dual-band 802.11n with 2×3 MIMO systems. The results in terms of received power and throughput were evaluated in LOS and NLOS environment that implemented in the 3rd-floor corridor. The simulation was performed using Wireless InSite program based on 3D SBR method. The results show that a higher throughput rate can be achieved in the LOS environment using 802.11n with a MIMO system, besides 3D SBR was proved to simulate the channel model precisely.

In [10] the author studied the indoor propagation module by comparing the measured received power system with the simulated received power using 3D SBR simulator. The indoor environment was tested in a corridor based on 1x2 MIMO WiFi system with two different routes and variable distance between the receiver and transmitter. The author found that LOS and the shortest distance between the transmitter and the receiver have the maximum signal strength while the materials of floor and walls decrease the signal strength.

A range of frequencies was depended in [11] to investigate the effect of this range on the performance of the WiFi system in an indoor environment. The author used 3D SBR method to simulate the LOS and NLOS characteristic at 26 GHz, 28 GHz, and 60 GHz. The performance was evaluated in terms of received power, Path Loss (PL) and delay spread. The author concluded that with high frequencies PL will increase, while the received power and delay spread is certainly degraded.

In [12] the author discussed the effect of object size and permittivity on the received power and Root Mean Square (RMS) of delay spread for both LOS and NLOS cases in an indoor environment. It was found that the RMS delay spread is higher in LOS environments than NLOS environments, in addition, it is affected by the object size and its position. The author interpreted that received power does not affect by a small object.

The channel model prediction of mm-Wave propagation was verified in [13]. The prediction was based on the ray tracing method to simulate the channel characteristics, then the simulation results were validated by conducting the measurements.

Assessing the indoor environment contribution on the propagated radio wave needs an intensive survey. All the above-mentioned works discuss this issue from one or two points of view. The influences of affecting factors such as; LOS and NLOS, frequency band, building material are investigated solely.

3 Propagation Model

In order to analyze the performance of the wireless communication system in an indoor environment, a suitable propagation model that must be determined. One of these propagation models is the deterministic models which is approved to be an efficient method to model the complex multipath scenarios [14]. Deterministic models are usually based either on Maxwell equations or geometrical approaches to simulate the indoor environment [15]. In this work, the ray tracing technique combined with the Uniform Theory of Diffraction (UTD) is adopted as the geometrical approach [16, 17]. This technique simulates the signal propagation as optical rays propagate from the transmitter to the receiver and take into account the signal interaction with the environment. The computing of this interaction based on reflection and refraction theorems, besides UTD, is being combined with the ray tracing to mitigate the field discontinuities. The number of rays and the objects (that are located in the area of interest) details such as size and material type is the main two factors that affect the computational time and accuracy [18]. Accordingly, an accurate decision must be taken to the tradeoff between these two factors when modeling the environment before conducting the simulation.

4 Research Methodology

Quantifying the field strength of the RF signal in an indoor environment is a hard task since it is considered as a complex model composed of large and small objects which affect directly the signal quality. In this paper, the main parameters that have noticeable effects on the WiFi signal strength are being investigated through simulation for indoor lab scenario as below:

4.1 Object Material

Different materials in the area of interest will have a different impact to the resultant reflected and refracted waves due to their different permittivity and conductivity. Accordingly, in this work, the effect of each material type is investigated with respect to free space (free space will be used in this work to address the non-furnished indoor environment). Then simulation complexity can be reduced and hence computational time by excluding the material that has minimal influence compared to the other materials.

The relative permittivity is also known as the dielectric constant which is inverted the material impact on the electric field which is dependent on the frequency. Relative permittivity is approximate estimation in most ray-tracing simulations. Therefore it fails to apply the real indoor environment. This leads to an incorrect simulation estimation. therefore the permittivity of the material of any object in the indoor environment is measured to simulate the radio signal propagation as much as possible at both frequencies 2.4 GHz and 5 GHz.

The permittivity of each metal can be clarified using the Eq. (1):

$$\varepsilon = \eta' - j\eta'' \tag{1}$$

Where η', η'' is the real part and imaginary parts of relative permittivity, respectively. For the conductivity, it describes the imaginary part of relative permittivity [19]. The conversion between them can be clarified in Eq. (2):

$$\varepsilon = \eta' - j\frac{\sigma}{\omega} \tag{2}$$

Furthermore, the can be obtained from the conductivity and frequency and based on Eq. (3) [19]:

$$\eta'' = 17.98\frac{\sigma}{f} \tag{3}$$

4.2   Object Dimensions

As explained in the previous section, each lab's object detail will have its own weight in determining the signal strength quality. In addition to the object material, the object dimensions may also affect the propagated signal. For instance, the effect of small conductor object can be less than big isolator object. Accordingly, the object dimensions are also investigated through this work to compare their effects. Due to this comparison, the object with the least significant effect can be excluded in order to speed up the computation run time. Hence, the indoor lab environment is considered either as light furnished (such as laptops, stools...etc.) or heavy furnished (like a metal cabinet, wood tables...etc.).

4.3   Frequency

The frequency is another factor that affects the signal strength and PL. in this study all the above-mentioned factors are simulated under two systems' frequencies (2.4 GHz and 5 GHz). The relationship between the frequency band and the signal strength is an inverse relationship. For all factors mentioned above, the quality of WiFi signal propagation in the lab environment is evaluated in terms of received power and the PL.

$$P_R = \sum_{i=1}^{N_p} P_i \tag{4}$$

P_i is the time averaged power in watts of the i-th path, N_p is the number of paths. P_i is given by [20]:

$$P_i = \frac{\lambda^2 \beta}{8\pi\eta_0} \left| E_{\theta,i} g_\theta(\theta_i, \phi_i) + E_{\phi,i} g_\phi(\theta_i, \phi_i) \right|^2 \tag{5}$$

$$\lambda = \frac{c}{f} \tag{6}$$

Where η_0 is the impedance of free space (377Ω), E_θ and E_ϕ are the theta and phi components of the electric field of the i-th path at the receiver point. θi and ϕi give the direction of arrival. The quantity β is the overlap of the frequency spectrum of the transmitted waveform and the spectrum of the frequency sensitivity of the receiver. λ is signal wavelength, c is light speed.

PL is increased as the frequency increased in the following [11]:

$$L_{Path}(dB) = P_T(dBm) - P_R(dBm) + G_{T,Max}(dBi) + G_{R,Max}(dBi) - L_S(dB) \tag{7}$$

$G_{T,Max}$ and $G_{R,Max}$ are the maximum gains of the transmitting and receiving antennas, respectively.

5 Simulation Results and Discussion

The simulation was performed using a 3D ray tracing method deployed by Wireless InSite software. A real case study is adopted, which is a computer lab space on the 2nd floor of "departments building" at "Electric Engineering Technical College". Lab dimensions are; the height is 3.2 m, the length is 17.5 m and the width 7 m. The lab is also including two small rooms as technicians' office and storage room. Many objects are contained within the lab space (metal cabinets, wood table, plastic stools, laptops… etc.). A dual-band (2.5 GHz, 5 GHz) access point is located at the technicians' office at the height of 1 m. From the receiver side, a set of (57) test points are organized as a route inside the lab room and are based to test the received power [12] has depicted in Fig. 1.

Fig. 1. A computer lab space.

In the lab scenario, the furniture includes metal cabinets, wood table, plastic stools, laptops… etc. with different sizes and distributions. In Fig. 2, it has been shown the furniture distribution in the lab environment and their size.

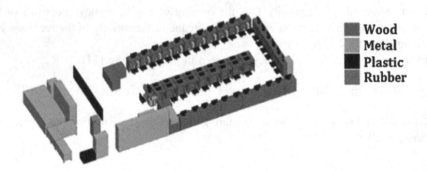

Fig. 2. Furniture distribution in the lab space

5.1   Object Material Effects

A Fig. 3 depicts the comparison of simulation results in terms of received power between 2.4 GHz and 5 GHz. Each material was isolated and simulated solely to quantify its effect on the propagated signal with respect to free space.

It is obvious that each material has a different amount of contribution due to different interactions with the propagated signal and the electrical properties of that material. For instance, metal is the significant contributor in signal strength fluctuations, since it represents a good conductor and hence good reflector that scatter the signal in many directions. The resultant received signal from such scattering waves could be either stronger or weaker than the case of free space. On the other hand, isolators such as; wood and plastic may also contribute the reduction in signal strength, where they represent an absorption surface which is also based on the object's thickness and the signal wavelength. Rubber seems to have the least contribution and almost behave like free space especially there only two rubber chairs that are located inside the lab.

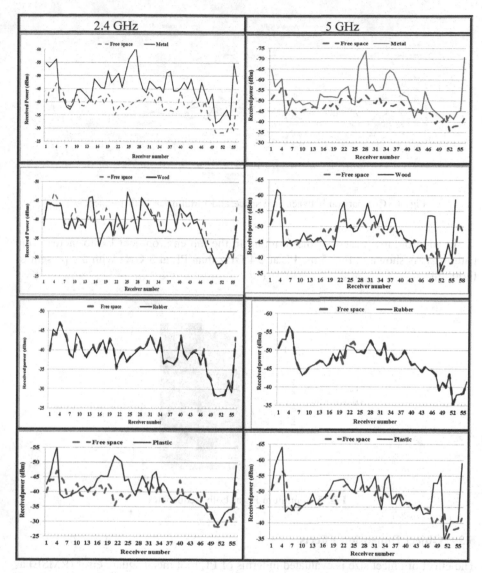

Fig. 3. Received power comparison between free space and different material in an indoor environment at 2.4 GHz and 5 GHz.

5.2   Furniture Effect

From the frequency point of view, increasing the frequency leads to signal strength reduction even in a free space environment. This can be noticed clearly in Fig. 4, where the effect of 2.4 GHz and 5 GHz on received power is being simulated in free space and furnished environment respectively.

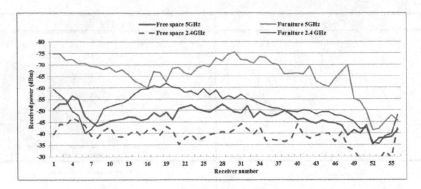

Fig. 4. Comparison between free space and furniture at both frequencies.

In addition, the present of the furniture in the lab environment led to increase the path loss. As shown in Fig. 5 the PL at 2.4 GHz than PL at 5 GHz with the present of furniture.

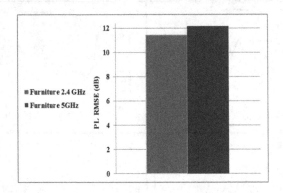

Fig. 5. Furniture PL at both frequencies.

5.3 Object Dimension Effects

The effect of object size is evaluated in terms of PL root mean square error (RMSE) as explained by Eq. (8) and depicted by Fig. 6. PL RMSE represents how these objects produce extra losses to signal propagation with respect to free space. It can be seen that 5 GHz frequency results in extra quality degradation due to PL increasing.

$$RMSE = \frac{1}{n}\sqrt{\sum_{i=1}^{n}(X_i^2 - Y_i^2)} \tag{8}$$

Where n is receivers number X_i is simulated PL at free space and Y_i is simulated PL for specific material at i-th receiver.

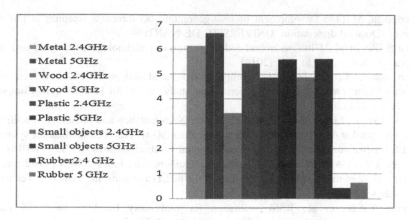

Fig. 6. RMSE PL with respect to free space.

6 Conclusion

In this paper, the effects of dense indoor environment on the propagated signal is investigated, where a lab scenario is adopted. The evaluation of such an environment is verified through simulation based on 3D ray tracing which is deployed by Wireless InSite software. It can be concluded from the simulation results that, metal object is the significant contributor in signal quality fluctuation due to its electrical ability of reflection and scattering. On the other side, wood, rubber, and plastic have fewer effects and hence these materials can be excluded to reduce the computational time-consuming. The simulation results show also that small object can be eliminated at the cost of 3.6 dB and 2.8 dB losses at 5 GHz and 2.4 GHz respectively. The effect of two band frequencies is also investigated, where more signal strength attenuation is noticed at higher frequency due to PL increasing.

Acknowledgements. The authors would like to thank Dr. Raed A. Abd-Alhmeed (School of Engineering and Informatics, University of Bradford, UK) for supporting this work. Also, the acknowledgment is extended to the computer lab. Staff.

References

1. Akram, M.R., Al-Nakkash, A.H., Salim, O.N.M.: A comparative study of indoor propagation models for IEEE 802.11n network. In: International Conference of Information and Communication Technology (2019)
2. Popovski, P., et al.: Wireless access for ultra-reliable low-latency communication: principles and building blocks. IEEE Netw. **32**(2), 16–23 (2018)
3. Guo, C., Liu, F., Chen, S., Feng, C., Zeng, Z.: Advances on exploiting polarization in wireless communications: channels, technologies, and applications. IEEE Commun. Surv. Tutor. **19**(1), 125–166 (2017)
4. Kurt, S., Tavli, B.: Path-loss modeling for wireless sensor networks: a review of models and comparative evaluations. IEEE Antennas Propag. Mag. **59**(1), 18–37 (2017)

5. Kodnoeih, M.R.D.: Development of next-generation 5G directive antennas at millimeter waves (Doctoral dissertation, UNIVERSITE DE NANTES) (2018)
6. Alarifi, A., et al.: Ultra wideband indoor positioning technologies: analysis and recent advances. Sensors **16**(5), 707 (2016)
7. Van Haute, T., et al.: Comparability of RF-based indoor localisation solutions in heterogeneous environments: an experimental study. Int. J. Ad Hoc Ubiquit. Comput. **23** (1–2), 92–114 (2016)
8. Li, S., Liu, Y., Lin, L., Sun, D., Yang, S., Sun, X.: Simulation and modeling of millimeter-wave channel at 60 GHz in indoor environment for 5G wireless communication system. In: IEEE International Conference on Computational Electromagnetics (ICCEM) (2018)
9. Dama, Y.A.S., Abd-Alhameed, R.A., Salazar-Quiñonez, F., Jones, S.M.R., Gardiner, J.G.: Indoor channel measurement and prediction for 802.11n system. In: Vehicular Technology Conference (2011)
10. Dama, Y.A.S., et al.: RSSI evaluation for multi-story building. In: 2015 Internet Technologies and Applications (ITA), pp. 414–416. IEEE, September 2015
11. Manan, W., Obeidat, H., Alabdullah, A., Abd-Alhameed, R., Hu, F.: Indoor to indoor and indoor to outdoor millimeter wave propagation channel simulations at 26 Ghz, 28 Ghz and 60 Ghz for 5G mobile networks. Int. J. Eng. Sci. 7, 8–18 (2018). https://doi.org/10.9790/1813-0703020818
12. Liu, Z.Y., Guo, L.X., Li, C.L., Wang, Q., Zhao, Z.W.: Sensitivity of power and RMS delay spread predictions of a 3D indoor ray tracing model. Opt. Express **24**(12), 13179–13193 (2016)
13. Hossain, F., Geok, T., Rahman, T., Hindia, M., Dimyati, K., Abdaziz, A.: Indoor millimeter-wave propagation prediction by measurement and ray tracing simulation at 38 GHz. Symmetry **10**(10), 464 (2018)
14. Azpilicueta Fernández de las Heras, L.: Characterization of wireless propagation in complex indoor environments. Alizadeh-Shabdiz, F., Jones, R.K., Morgan, E.J., Shean, M.G.: U.S. Patent No. 8,965,412. Washington, DC: U.S. Patent and Trademark Office (2015)
15. Steinmetzer, D., Classen, J., Hollick, M.: mmTrace: modeling millimeter-wave indoor propagation with image-based ray-tracing. In: 2016 IEEE Conference on Computer Communications Workshops (INFOCOM WKSHPS), pp. 429–434. IEEE, April 2016
16. Obeidat, H., et al.: Performance comparative study between vector and ECOLOCATION algorithms for indoor positioning. In: Internet Technologies and Applications (ITA), 2017, pp. 230–234. IEEE, September 2017
17. Xia, B., Lai, Z., Villemaud, G., Zhang, J.: Joint ray launching method for outdoor to indoor propagation prediction based on interpolation. In: 2015 9th European Conference on Antennas and Propagation (EuCAP), pp. 1–5. IEEE, May 2015
18. Depatla, S., Muralidharan, A., Mostofi, Y.: Occupancy estimation using only wifi power measurements. IEEE J. Sel. Areas Commun. **33**(7), 1381–1393 (2015). 7&2
19. Liao, Q.: Ray-tracing based analysis of channel characteristics and capacity improvement capabilities of spatial multiplexing and beam forming at 15 and 28 GHz. Master thesis, Department of Electrical and Information Technology, Lund University (2016)
20. REMCOM. (2018) Wireless insite 3D wireless predictionsoftware. https://www.remcom.com/. wireless-insite-em-propagation-software

Cooperative Spectrum Sensing Method Using Sub-band Decomposition with DCT for Cognitive Radio System

Muntasser S. Falih$^{(\boxtimes)}$ [iD] and Hikmat N. Abdullah [iD]

Department of Information and Communication Engineering,
Al-Nahrain University, Baghdad, Iraq
mntaser.faleh.1990@ieee.org,
hikmat.abdullah@coie-nahrain.edu.iq

Abstract. In this paper a new cooperative spectrum sensing method for cognitive radio systems is presented. The proposed method is based on a new soft decision rule at Fusion Centre (FC) for deciding the primary user (PU) signal presence using the received energy from each Cognitive User (CU) after performing a set of transformations. The sensing process can be summarized as follows: each CU collects the available spectrum and one-level Discrete Wavelet Transform (DWT) decomposition for the input spectrum is taken. After the decomposition, only the first lower frequencies (LL) and the last high frequencies (HH) bands of two-dimensional DWT are truncated. Then Discrete Cosine Transform (DCT) for the truncated sub-bands is computed. The energy of each sub-band with Average Ratio (AR) between LL and HH energies is calculated. Finally, only the energy in LL band and AR are sent to FC via reporting channel. At FC the received energies and ARs from all CUs are averaged. The proposed fusion rule is designed such that if the average energy falls below the half of predefined threshold, PU is declared to be absent. From other hand if the average energy equals or greater than threshold value and average AR is greater than 1, PU is declared to be present. Otherwise, it is declared to be absent. The simulation results in both AWGN and Rayleigh fading channels showed that the proposed method has improved detection probability especially at low SNR, reduced sensing time and reduced energy consumption as compared to censoring hard fusion rules available in the literature.

Keywords: Spectrum sensing · Cognitive radio · Cooperative spectrum sensing · Discrete wavelet transform · Discrete cosine transform

1 Introduction

Nowadays the massive usage of wireless devices such as smart phones and multi-media applications used for social media communication leads to acting congestion in available spectrum for example in ISM-band. Therefore, there must be a solution to this problem at least in technologies available before the advent of Fifth Generation (5G) of mobile wireless communication. Depending on the studies, provided by Frequency Commission Committee in US about 73% of the spectrum used in TV-band transmission is busy in

© Springer Nature Switzerland AG 2020
M. I. Khalaf et al. (Eds.): ACRIT 2019, CCIS 1174, pp. 465–475, 2020.
https://doi.org/10.1007/978-3-030-38752-5_36

fashion of time and spatial dimension. So, there must be a solution to seize these opportunities in busy spectrum to compensate the wireless frequency shortage. Dynamic Spectrum Allocation (DSA) is the solution form to utilize the spectrum scarcity and can be achieved in context of Cognitive Radio (CR). CR is the wireless agile technology used to optimize communication resources utilization by exploiting the spectrum opportunity of licensed users or Primary Users (PU) by the unlicensed users or Secondary Users (SU).

CR life cycle is represented by a number of operating steps. The basic step in CR life cycle is the Spectrum Sensing (SS) process, SS can be defined as the process of PU detection in specific channel to decide the channel status that either busy H_1 or ideal H_0. SS process should be accurate enough to avoid the harmful interference between PU and SU. There are a number of techniques associated with SS in CR system such as Match Filter (MF), Cyclosationary features detection (CS) and Energy Detection (ED) based sensing approach. In MF the detection mechanism is based on the correlation between input signal and MF impulse response. In MF sensing approach, the SU needs be aware of all features of the signal to be sensed. CS spectrum sensing approach is based on the idea of detecting the semi-period features of modulated signal that related to frequency and phase of sinusoidal carries. ED spectrum sensing approach senses the spectrum depending on the value of accumulated energy compared with predefined threshold; ED also called blind spectrum sensing [1, 2].

The reminder sections of this paper are structured as follow: In Sect. 2, we present the related works that associated to Cooperative spectrum sensing. Section 3 reviews the basic principles of spectrum sensing in both non-cooperative and cooperative forms. In Sect. 4 we illustrate the proposed spectrum sensing method with its flowcharts, while Sect. 5 shows the simulations testing of the proposed and its performance evaluation with respect to previous approaches. The conclusions that extracted from this work presented in last section.

2   Related Works

There are some efforts have been made to develop the cooperative spectrum sensing in CR. For example, in [3] the authors proposed soft decision CSS method based on DWT decomposition with traditional periodgram based DFT. The main drawback of this method is the transmission of all sensing samples via reporting channel that cause extra energy consumption and reducing the network throughput by increasing sensing time. In [4] the authors proposed a new CSS method based on DCT instead of DFT that used in traditional periodgram. However, the author didn't utilize de-noising property of DWT decomposing that can act to reduce sensing samples of collected energy. In [5] the authors proposed an efficient energy consumption detector using the traditional energy detector but with selective dropping in frequency domain samples for reducing the consumed energy of sensor node. The main disadvantaged of this method is that the spatially samples dropping defect influences the accuracy of detection probability. In [6] the authors suggested a new hard fusion rule in cooperative spectrum sensing based on traditional energy detection. This rule mixes censoring (OR) and (AND) fusion rules. This rule treats the problem of final decision-making but does not deal with utilizing an efficient procedure for PU signal identification using an appropriate time-frequency transform. In [7] the authors designed a two-stage compressed spectrum sensing approach using DWT and DCT. In this scheme the authors did not utilize the relative energy collected in different sub-bands that can be exploited for noise only signal recognition at low SNR values.

In this paper we present an efficient CSS method for CR system. This method combines the advantages of DWT and DCT in respect of spectrum samples reduction and PU signal from noise only signal recognition. The variation between decomposition sub-bands of DWT is utilized in an efficient manner to achieve this goal.

3 Spectrum Sensing Model

In CR system, the spectrum sensing is a necessary process and it is achieved in the beginning of CR life cycle. SS is used to detect the spectrum hole (white space) at specific frequency band. It based on binary hypothesis in which H_0 represents spectrum hole and H_1 represents the busy channel or PU presence. The following equation shows the detection hypothesis in noisy channel.

$$y(n) = \begin{cases} w(n) & ; H_0 \\ s(n) + w(n) & ; H_1 \end{cases} \tag{1}$$

where y(n) is the received sample, w(n) is the Additive White Gaussian Noise AWGN samples collected from the transmission channel, s(n) is the PU signal sample, H_0 and H_1 are null and power hypothesis respectively. In this the work, energy detector is the used model and the test statistics of the received sample is defined as follows:

$$T = \frac{1}{Ns} \sum_{n=1}^{Ns} |y(n)|^2 \tag{2}$$

where Ns is the total number of received samples. The distribution of T is chi-squared with 2Ns degrees of freedom [8]. Energy detection can be achieved either in time or in frequency domain. Frequency domain energy computation is better than time domain because it gives efficient resolution over wider bandwidth. The traditional frequency-domain energy computation called "preiodgram". The principle of periodgram is transforming the input samples y(n) into frequency domain using DFT then summing the squared values and finally averaging over samples length [9]. The final decision of energy detection depends on the collected energy compared with a pre-defined threshold value λ as in Eq. (3).

$$\begin{cases} H_1, & \frac{1}{Ns} \sum_{n=1}^{Ns} |DFT(y(n)|^2 \geq \lambda \\ H_0, & \text{otherwise} \end{cases} \tag{3}$$

where λ is the pre-defined threshold value. Figure 1 Shows the Conventional Energy Detector (CED) block diagram.

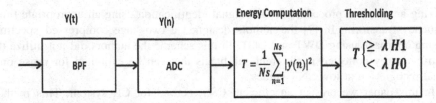

Fig. 1. Conventional energy detector block diagram.

The performance of ED is measured by Receiver Operating Characteristics (ROC) that is represented by Probability of Detection (P_D) and Probability of False Alarm (P_{FA}) at certain SNR and Ns values. P_D represents the correct detection when PU is present, P_{FA} represents false detection alarm that indicates the presence of PU but actually, it is not there. From [10] P_D and P_{FA} in AWGN are calculated in case of unity noise variance as in Eqs. (4) and (5) respectively.

$$P_D = P[T > \lambda|_{H_1}]Q\left(\frac{\lambda - Ns(1 + SNR)}{\sqrt{2Ns(1 + SNR)}}\right) \tag{4}$$

$$P_{FA} = P[T > \lambda|_{H_0}]Q\left(\frac{\lambda - Ns}{\sqrt{2Ns}}\right) \tag{5}$$

From Eq. (4) threshold value λ is calculated as in Eq. (6).

$$\lambda = \sqrt{2Ns}Q^{-1}(P_{FA}) + N_s \tag{6}$$

where Q is complementary Q-function (Marcum function).

3.1 Cooperative Spectrum Sensing

Because of hidden terminal problem, fading and shadowing in communication system can cause a wrong decision in PU detection. So, CSS is necessary to countermeasure this situation. CSS, briefly, cooperation topology among sensing nodes to achieved proof PU detection decision. In CSS there are two types of topologies: centralized and decentralized. In centralized scheme, there is a central node called Fusion Centre (FC) responsible on achieving final detection result. In decentralized scheme there is no FC and the final detection result is taken based on negotiation among sensing node as in mesh topology. Centralized sensing scheme is either hard decision or soft decision. Hard decision is the simple from of centralized CSS in which the sensing node sends the result after applying certain fusion rule for the measured results from CUs. In Hard decision, the well-known rules are OR and AND rules. In OR rule, the FC decides the PU presence if at least one sensing node detects the PU. In contrast, AND fusion rule declares the presence of PU when all sensing nodes detect the PU. Soft decision rules are more complicated than hard fusion rules. With soft fusion rules, the sensing node sends it measured energy to FC without any local decision. FC combines these energies and makes an appropriate soft fusion rules. There are two major combing rules in soft fusion, these are: Square Low Combination (SLC) and Maximum Ration Combination (MRC). The test statistics of each one are given ins Eqs. 7 and 8 respectively [11].

$$E_{SLC} = \sum_{i=1}^{Nu} E_i \tag{7}$$

$$E_{MRC} = \sum_{i=1}^{Nu} WiE_i \tag{8}$$

where Nu in number of cognitive users, Ei is the energy received from ith user and Wi is the weight coefficient of ith user.

4 The Proposed Method

In this paper we present a new cooperative spectrum sensing method for Cognitive Radio system. In this method a new approach for energy computation at CU side and soft fusion rules at FC side is introduced. The general layout of this method is depicted in Fig. 2.

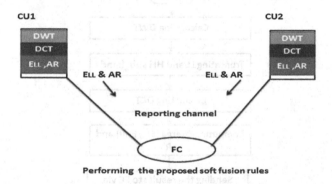

Fig. 2. Layout of the proposed method.

The sensing procedure for the proposed method has two parts. The first part is achieved at CU with following steps: the samples of the frequency channel to be sensed are collected and DWT using Daubechies wavelet [9, 12] is taken. LL and HH sub-bands of DWT are truncated only and other sub-bands are dropped to reduce processing time. After that, LL and HH sub-bands are DCT transformed using Eqs. (9) and (10) [13] and their energies E_{LL} (energy in LL sub-band) and E_{HH} (energy in HH sub-band) are calculated using Eqs. (11) and (12) respectively. Then the Average Ratio (AR) between E_{LL}, E_{HH} is computed using Eq. (13) for the use as measure about the presence of PU according the proposed decision rule which will be explained later.

Finally, E_{LL} and AR of each node are sent to FC via reporting channel. Figure 3 reveals the flowchart of spectrum sensing at CU side.

$$A[0] = \frac{1}{\sqrt{N}} \sum_{n=0}^{N-1} a[n], \quad M = 0 \tag{9}$$

$$A[M] = \frac{2}{N} \sum_{n=0}^{N-1} a[n]\cos(\frac{\pi K(2n+1)}{2N}), 1 \le M \le N-1 \tag{10}$$

$$E_{LL} = \frac{1}{N_{LL}} \sum_{n=1}^{N_{LL}} |DCT(LL(n))|^2 \tag{11}$$

$$E_{HH} = \frac{1}{N_{HH}} \sum_{n=1}^{N_{HH}} |DCT(HH(n))|^2 \tag{12}$$

$$AR = \frac{E_{LL}}{E_{HH}} \tag{13}$$

where N_{LL} and N_{HH} are number of samples in LL and HH sub-bands respectively. LL (n) and HH(n) are the signal samples in LL and HH sub-bands respectively.

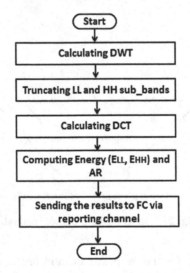

Fig. 3. The proposed cooperative sensing method flowchart at each CU

The second part is achieved at FC with following steps: averaging the values of E_{LL} and AR that are received from all CUs using Eqs. (14) and (15) respectively.

$$E_{AVG} = \frac{1}{N_u} \sum_{i=1}^{N_u} E_{LLi} \tag{14}$$

$$AR_{AVG} = \frac{1}{N_u} \sum_{i=1}^{N_u} AR_i \tag{15}$$

After that, applying the proposed fusion rule. The proposed fusion rule has three possible decisions according to E_{AVG} and AR_{AVG} values. At first, E_{AVG} is compared with halved threshold value $\lambda/2$, if it is lower that this value leads to white space decision H_0 and then reporting the CUs to activate sharing process. Otherwise, the second rule is triggered as follows: If and only if E_{AVG} greater or equal to λ and AR_{AVG} greater than 1, H_1 hypothesis is declared and the reporting activate CUs for sensing another channel, otherwise H_0 is declared. Figure 4 shows the proposed fusion rules in a flowchart form.

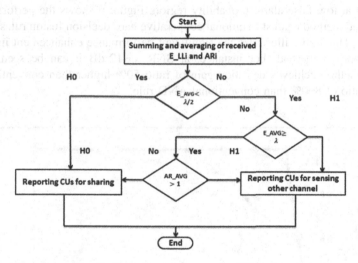

Fig. 4. Flowchart of the proposed FC rules.

5   Simulation Results

The proposed method is simulated using MATLAB m-files. The suggested scenario is cooperative centralized sensing topology for both AWGN and Rayleigh fading channels. Monte Carlo simulations are used and Receiver Operating Characteristics (ROC) are used for experiment statistical tests. The simulation parameters are presented in Table 1. The presented results show ROC of the proposed method at different SNR values, as well as for censoring methods to evaluate the performance.

Table 1. Simulation parameters

Parameter	Value
PU signal type	QPSK
Channel type	AWGN and Rayleigh fading
Monte Carlo trying	10^3
Number of samples N_s	1500
SNR range	-20 to 0 dB
Number of users	4

Figure 5 shows the ROC of the proposed method at SNR = -20, -15 and -10 dB. From this figure it can be seen that the proposed method achieves good detection probability at low false alarm probability region. Figure 6 shows the performance of the proposed method against traditional cooperative hard decision fusion rules methods in AWGN. This figure illustrates the significant performance enhancement introduced by the proposed method. For instance, at SNR = -12 dB it can be seen that the proposed method achieves detection gain of ratio 50% higher than conventional OR rule and ratio of 800% than conventional AND rule.

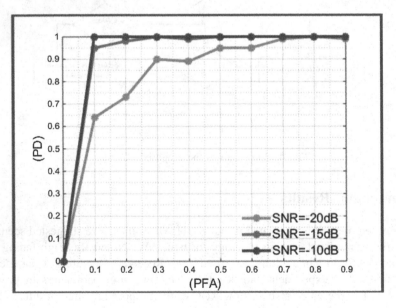

Fig. 5. ROC of the proposed method at different SNR values.

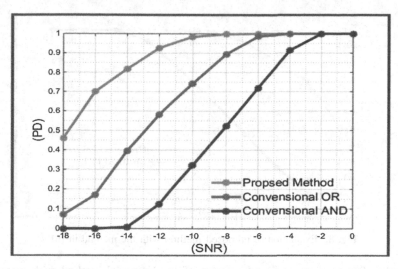

Fig. 6. Evaluation of proposed method with traditional hard fusion rules methods in AWGN

Another comparison is performed between proposed method and traditional hard fusion rules method in Rayleigh fading channel as shown in Fig. 7. From this figure, the high immunity of the proposed method against fading effect can be observed. For example, at SNR = −12 dB, the proposed method outperforms the traditional OR and AND fusion methods by ratios of 40% and 300% respectively.

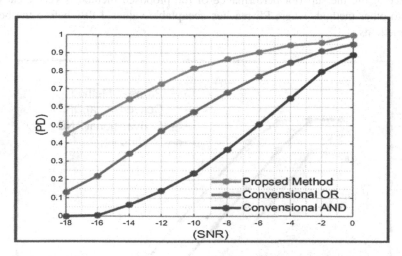

Fig. 7. Evaluation of proposed method with traditional hard fusion rules methods in Rayleigh fading channel

Figure 8 shows the performance of the proposed method versus the method in [6] in AWGN. From this figure it can be seen that the proposed method outperforms this method. For example, at SNR = −12 dB, the proposed method has detection probability with improvement factor of 52%.

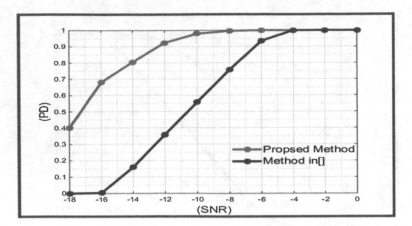

Fig. 8. Evaluation of proposed method with the method in [6].

Finally, Fig. 9 shows the performance of the proposed method with respect to traditional hard decision method and method in [6] in form of probability of error. Probability of error (P_E) includes the resultant form of miss detection and false alarm errors as shown in the following equation:

$$P_E = (1-P_D) + P_{FA} \tag{16}$$

Once again, the superior performance of the proposed method is very clear compared to other methods where PE reaches acceptable values 4 dBs before the best of other methods.

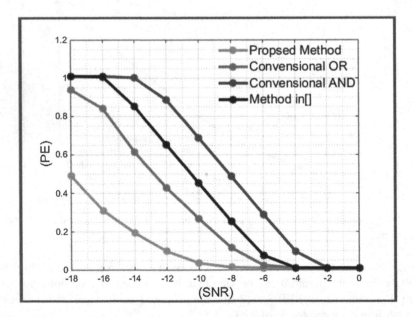

Fig. 9. Error probability evaluation of proposed method than traditional and method in [6]

6 Conclusions

In this paper, we presented a new cooperative soft fusion rules for CR spectrum sensing. This method utilizes the advantages of both DWT and DCT in noisy signal reduction. It uses the domain sub-band of DWT that contains most of PU user signal features. As well as utilizing the DWT recognition property between PU and noise only signal based the collected energies in low and high decomposition sub-bands. From the simulated results, it can be observed that the proposed method reached good detection probability at low SNR and reducing the sample number at CU sensing process by utilizing two-stage compressing using DWT and DCT which in turn reduces the number sensing samples to half of their values in classical sensing methods.

References

1. Falih, M.S., Abdullah, H.N.: Evaluation of different energy based spectrum sensing approaches in cognitive radio system: practical perspective. IJSR 6(12), 85–88 (2018)
2. Falih, M.S., Abdullah, H.N.: Double threshold with knowledge based decision spectrum sensing method. J. Adv. Res. Dyn. Control Syst. (13), 2169–2175 (2018)
3. Youssef, M.E., et al.: Efficient cooperative spectrum detection in cognitive radio systems using wavelet fusion. In: 2018 International Conference on Computing, Electronic and Electrical Engineering (ICE Cube), Quetta, Pakistan (2018)
4. Salman, E.H., et al.: A new cooperative spectrum sensing scheme based on discrete cosine transform. In: 2016 IEEE 3rd International Symposium on Telecommunication Technologies (ISTT), Kuala Lumpur, 28–30 November 2016
5. Abdullah, H.N., Abed, H.S.: Low energy consumption for cooperative and non-cooperative cognitive radio. Eng. Technol. J. 35 Part A(3), 222–228 (2017)
6. Abdullah, H.N., Baker, N.Sh.: Modified Hard Fusion Rule for Improving Throughput in Cognitive Radio Network. Int. J. Sci. Eng. Res. (IJSER) 5(9), 80–84 (2017). ISSN 2347-3878
7. Salman, E.H., et al.: LTE signal detection using two-stage cooperative compressive sensing system. In: Al-Mansour International Conference on New Trends in Computing, Communication, and Information Technology, NTCCIT (2018)
8. Farag, H.M., Ehab, M.: An efficient dynamic thresholds energy detection technique for cognitive radio spectrum sensing. In: International Conference on Computer Engineering, pp. 139–144 (2014)
9. Fragkiadakis, A.G., Tragos, E.Z., Askoxylakis, I.G.: A survey on security threats and detection techniques in cognitive radio networks. IEEE Commun. Surv. Tutor. 15, 428–445 (2013)
10. Song, J., Feng, Z., Zhang, P., Liu, Z.: Spectrum sensing in cognitive radios based on enhanced energy detector. IET Commun. 6(8), 805–809 (2012)
11. Wang, X., Jia, M., Guo, Q., Gu, X.: A soft decision rule for cooperative spectrum sensing in mobile cognitive radio networks. In: Globecom Workshops (GC Wkshps). IEEE, San Diego (2015)
12. Daubechies, I.: Ten lectures on wavelets. SIAM, New Delhi (1992)
13. Oppenheim, A.V., Schafer, R.W., Buck, J.R.: Discrete-Time Signal Processing, Edition 2. Prentice-hall, Englewood Cliffs (1989)

Performance Comparison of Multi-band Frequencies for Outdoor Communication

Karrar Shakir Muttair[1](✉) iD, Oras A. Shareef Al-Ani[2](✉) iD,
and Mahmood Farhan Mosleh[2](✉) iD

[1] Department of Computer Techniques Engineering,
Islamic University, Najaf, Iraq
karraralnomani123@gmail.com
[2] Department of Computer Techniques Engineering,
Middle Technique University, Baghdad, Iraq
oras.a.s.alani@gmail.com, drmahfa@yahoo.com

Abstract. A comparison between the performance of C-, S- and Millimeter Waves (mm-Waves) bands with different range of frequencies has been presented in this paper. To implement an outdoor communication network, which can satisfy the coverage requirement of signal propagation, an optimal design has been proposed using the Wireless InSite (WI) program. Comparison of measurements derived in the same outdoor environment but at different frequency bands including 28 and 73 GHz, which they related to 5G technique. The obtained results are compared according to other models with different bands including 2.4 GHz and 5 GHz for S- and C-bands, respectively. These ranges of frequencies are quite important for the development of channel models in a specific area. An algorithm has been formed in this work to calculate the probability of the best-received points. That means the points that achieved the highest received power, highest average signal quality (ASQ) and average received power (ARP) for each frequency. The obtained results of this model showed that S-band (2.4 GHz) produce the best results in term of delay spread, path loss, received power, ASQ and ARP as compared with other frequencies. We found that increased frequency leads to increasing in the signal losses and decreasing in the received signal strength (RSS), and thus an increase in the propagation paths. These effects have resulted from the reflections from the building, where there is gradually decreasing in the network performance. In addition, we found that mm-Waves frequencies cause successive losses in the paths.

Keywords: 5G · mm-Wave propagation · RSS · Outdoor coverage · Wireless InSite · Multi-scale algorithm

1 Introduction

With the rapid evolution and revolution in wireless telecommunication technology, the fourth-generation (4G) cellular system has undoubtedly become the higher version of wireless technology. The operation of this system is based on internet protocol that provides signals having significant characteristics. For example, 4G can provide signals with high-speed data transfer rates, less attenuation, and high quality faster multimedia

© Springer Nature Switzerland AG 2020
M. I. Khalaf et al. (Eds.): ACRIT 2019, CCIS 1174, pp. 476–487, 2020.
https://doi.org/10.1007/978-3-030-38752-5_37

streaming [1]. Furthermore, the 4G technology is being designed to provide channel capacity from 100 Mbps to 1 Gbps. Among various applications of a 4G network in the internal and the external environments, WiMAX (Worldwide Interoperability for Microwave Access) and LTE (Long-Term Evolution) represent the most attractive techniques that lead to developing the growth of 4G [2]. However, it is agreed that 4G cannot satisfy the requirement of growing demands for broadband data transmissions with high resolution. Therefore, it is widely expected that 5G can offer broadband network operate with fast speeds (>10 Gbps), very high bandwidth, and reliable connections that can cover large areas [3]. One of the significant challenges in a 5G wireless system is the design architecture of the network. Generally, a 5G network is consist of different tiers, transmit, receiver and radio access technologies (RATs) which are accessed by a non-precedent number of smart devices and heterogeneous wireless networks [4].

With increasing the demand for broadband wireless networks, which can service academy, industry, and various practical aspects, 5G wireless networks system is expected to provide much higher bits rate compare with other related techniques [5]. For example, one of the techniques that utilize the principle of the 5G network is based on sending radio signals to a high-frequency range (30–300 GHz). This frequency range is known as mm-Waves which are recently attracted by many researchers in the communication field. The aim of these researches is attempting to design a wireless network with significantly high speed that can be used in advanced communication applications. For example, the large-signal bandwidth is commonly used in radar, satellite and some military system with avoiding wireless traffic congestion [6, 7]. One of the significant advantages to using mm-Wave in these applications is transferring a wide range of data which require using high frequencies. This characteristic of the wave can be used television channels, computer data and other purposes [8]. However, the propagation of mm-Wave can suffer from successive losses as a result of the shortness of these waves. Furthermore, the propagation of these waves in media can cause multipath loss, including actual leakage problem, transmit power and interference among other users [9]. The technology that expected to solve this problem is called Massive MIMO antennas, in which each user has a specific channel to avoid the interference that may occur between users. By this way, improvement can happen in reliability and capacity of the signals [10]. Moreover, this technique can provide a higher total capacity for more synchronized of the users and the highest spectral efficiency than other available techniques [4].

Extensive works have been achieved to study channel and multipath propagation characteristics at different frequencies. For example, in [11], a communication network has been implemented for New York City. In that study, mm-Waves were used at the frequency 73 GHz using directional antennas. The receivers have been deployed in all area to cover the wireless signals for this city. The obtained results showed that there is a reasonable coverage overall the small area of the city, especially with using broadband waves. Another study [12] has been investigated for designing and implementing an external environment using the WI program. The purpose of that study was to tracing and stores the ray values generated by Geographic Information System (GIS) database. In addition, a program in the MATLAB has been executed to calculate the number of reflections when the ray has collided from the certain variable barrier. The latter is reflecting or absorbs the strength of the ray depending on the barrier material type.

On the other hand, a study has been achieved to design a simulation model for a university campus consisting of several floors by using the WI program. The frequencies that have been used in that study were 0.85 and 1.9 GHz for the transmitters that have been installed over another building and deployed of receiver's points inside the building in a university. The purpose of this design [13] was to coverage and receives signals from the outdoor to the indoor and follows the beam when entering the campus. Comparisons were performed between these two frequencies, showing that the frequency of 1.9 GHz was higher in attenuation than 0.85 GHz.

In this paper, the main objectives are to implement an outdoor wireless network capable of working effectively to cover the college area with the lowest cost. Consequently to provide communication service for faculty members, administrators, and students. In this work, we investigate the best implementation of the constructed network. The propagation of the signals and impediments has been tested through encounter the signals when transmitted from the transmitting antennas to the receiving points. Then, the best frequency is examined by forming and implementing a multi-scale algorithm using the MATLAB program. The obtained results have been visualized using Graphical User Interface (GUI), displaying the best frequency for the S-, C- and 5G mm-Wave frequency bands. The paper format in this study is structured as follows. The channel propagation characteristics have been presented in Sect. 2. In Sect. 3, presents a detailed explanation of the steps of modeling a multi-scale algorithm to compare frequencies to determine the best frequency for college coverage. Section 4 discusses the case study of this work. In Sect. 5, the result and discussion have been analyzed. Finally, Sect. 6 outlines the conclusion of this paper.

2   Channel Propagation Characteristics

There are several key parameters help measure the performance of wireless communications networks as shown in the following subsections.

2.1   Path Loss

Generally, path loss (PL) is the reduction in power density of an electromagnetic wave or signal as it propagates through the environment in which it is traveling in free space. It is substantial to specify the location of the transmitter, and also to determine the transmit power and sensitivity of the receiver. Several parameters affect the signal path when it is spread in free space such as reflections, absorption, and refractions. PL is affected by the number of propagation and the separation distance. The most commonly used definition of PL is presented in the following equation [14].

$$PL_{(dB)} = 20 log \left(\frac{4\pi d_0}{\lambda}\right) + 10\alpha log \left(\frac{d}{d_0}\right) \tag{1}$$

where d_0 is reference distance in free space, whereas d is the distance between transmitter station and each receiving point, λ is the wavelength and α is an exponent of the PL.

2.2 Received Power

Another important characteristic of channel propagation is the received power (P_R). It is the amount of decreasing in signal power during the transition of the signal from the transmitter to the receiver in the free space. The P_R can be calculated by [15]:

$$P_R(dBm) = 10log\left(\frac{P_t\lambda^2 G_t G_r}{16\pi^2 d^2}\right) + 30(dB) - L_s(dB) \tag{2}$$

where L_s is an additional loss that may pass through the network system. G_t and G_r are the transmitter gain and receiver gain respectively, and P_t is the transmitter power.

2.3 Delay Spread

In the fields of wireless communications, signal emanating by the transmitter can propagate in a different direction toward the receiver. In each path, delay spread (σ_τ) can be determined as the statistical measure of the variety of multi-paths related effect. Mathematically, it can be interpreted as the difference between the arrival time of the first multi-paths component to the arrival time of the last path.

$$\sigma_\tau = \sqrt{\frac{\sum_{i=1}^{N_P}(t_i - \bar{t})^2 P_i}{P_R}} \tag{3}$$

Where P_i is the time average power in watts, N_P is number of the paths, t_i is the time of arrival (TOA) for each path i^{th} and $\bar{t}$ is the mean time of arrival (MTOA), which they are given by the following equations [15].

$$t_i = \frac{L_i}{c} \tag{4}$$

Here, L_i is the path length of the total geometrical and c is the speed of light.

$$\bar{t} = \frac{\sum_{i=1}^{N_p} P_i t_i}{P_R} \tag{5}$$

3 Modelling Multi-scale Algorithm

In this work, we construct an algorithm based on a measure P_R that resulted from the simulated model. By this model, the best frequency among S-, C- and mm-Wave frequency bands has been recognized, which achieve the best coverage. The steps of this algorithm are summarized in the following:

Step 1: Measuring of the RSS value for 73 received points through the WI program for each S-band, C-band and 5G band frequencies.

Step 2: Saving the RSS values for all frequencies in the database.

Step 3: The ARP is calculated for each S-band, C-band and 5G band frequencies as given below.

$$ARP_{(i)} = \frac{\sum_{j=1}^{Nrp} P_{R(j)}}{Nrp} \tag{6}$$

where $P_{R(j)}$ is received power for each jth received point in each ith frequency and Nrp is the total number of the received points.

Step 4: The ASQ is calculated for each S-band, C-band and 5G band frequencies as described below [16].

$$ASQ_{(i)} = \frac{\sum_{j=1}^{Nrp} 2 * [P_{R(j)} + 100]}{Nrp} \ \% \tag{7}$$

Step 5: Comparison among the obtained values of ASQ and ARP values to determine the highest values that represent the best frequency.

Step 6: Displaying the results of comparison for each frequency via the GUI screen.

Step 7: If the comparisons in step 5 are equal in all the frequencies, a message is visualized, indicating that the values of ASQ and ARP are equal.

4   Case Study

We designed a simulation scene for the specific campus (Electrical Engineering Technical College in Baghdad), with the real case study. The real geometrical dimensions of the campus have been recorded and used in the simulation of this work. The campus consists of six main buildings which are the college deanship, the department of graduate studies, the internal student dormitory, engineering laboratories, scientific departments, and student club. These buildings are distributed on two and three floors. For example, the buildings of the college deanship, the scientific departments, the graduate studies department, and the student club are consisting of two floors. The height of each floor is 3.5 m that means the overall height of the buildings is 7 m. In contrast, the buildings of internal student dormitory and engineering laboratories are consists of three floors. Each floor has a height of 3.5 m (the overall is 12 m). In addition to that, there are secondary rooms and outer walls distributed over these buildings in the campus with height 3.5 and 2.8 m, respectively. Using the WI program, a simulation model for this case study of the campus has been designed as shown in Fig. 1.

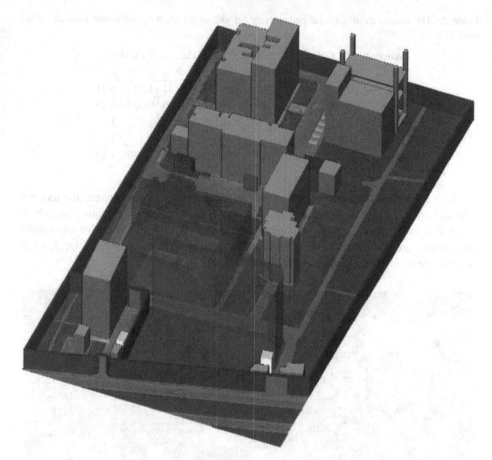

Fig. 1. Simulation scene structure designed using WI program.

It is worth to mention that the types of materials used in the construction of this scene play a vital role in the measurements of the study. The ceilings of the building in this campus have been built from the concrete, whereas bricks are used to build the walls. Dense foliage is used to represent the gardens. While metal and wood are used for indoor structures. The thickness for each material is listed in Table 1, white including the electrical characteristics (conductivity σ and the permittivity ε) for each with different frequencies are listed in Table 2 [17]. The bandwidth selected for our case study is 20 MHz for 2.4, 5, 28 and 73 GHz.

Table 1. Thickness for each material.

Materials	Thickness (m)
Ceiling from concrete	0.30
Wall from bricks	0.28
Metal	0.0625
Dense foliage	0.00035
Wood	0.045

Table 2. The conductivity (σ) and permittivity (ε) values for each material that utilized in this work [17].

Materials	2.4 GHz		5 GHz		28 GHz		73 GHz	
	σ	ε	σ	ε	σ	ε	σ	ε
Concrete	0.066	5.31	0.119	5.31	0.483	5.31	1.051	5.31
Brick	0.038	3.75	0.038	3.75	0.038	3.75	0.038	3.75
Metal	$1.0\,e^8$	1	$1.0\,e^8$	1	$1.0\,e^8$	1	$1.0\,e^8$	1
Foliage	0.1	1	0.1	1	0.1	1	0.1	1
Wood	0.012	1.99	0.026	1.99	0.167	1.99	0.467	1.99

We have installed the transmitter at the entrance of the college, whereas the receiver antennas are deployed over the college regions. 73 possible received points have been distributed at height 1.2 m as visualized in Fig. 2. The antennas used for transmitter and receiver are directional and omnidirectional respectively as shown in Fig. 3, while the characteristics these antennas are listed in Table 3.

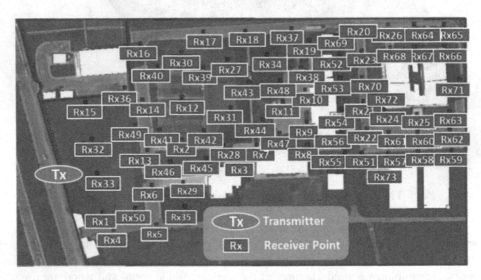

Fig. 2. The transmitter antenna and received points that installed in the college.

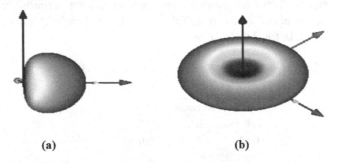

(a)   (b)

Fig. 3. The radiation pattern for (a) Directional and (b) Omnidirectional.

Table 3. Properties of the transmitter and receiver antennas.

Properties	(Transmitter Antenna)	(Receiver Antenna)
	Directional	Omnidirectional
Waveform	Sinusoid	Sinusoid
Polarization	Vertical	Vertical
Voltage standing wave ratio	1	1
Transmit power (dBm)	30	–
Temperatures (K)	293	293
Receiver threshold (dBm)	−90	−90
Electric field plane beam width	120°	360°
Antenna gain (dBi)	19	2

5   Results and Discussion

The case study that has been clarified above is simulated using WI software. Channel characterization is incorporated based on delay spread, path loss, received power and signal quality, for multi bands including C-, S-, and mm-Wave bands. Figure 4 shows the relation between delay spread and the separation distance. It is clear that for all range of frequencies, the delay spread is decreased with increasing distances between the transmitter and all distributed points of the receivers. The received signal is mostly affected by reflections, especially with Non-Line-of-Sight (NLOS) regions. This is because of the presence of the barriers that cause deterioration of received signals unexpectedly. Furthermore, the time delay is reduced with higher frequency (73 GHz) compare with S-band (2.4 GHz). As noted in Fig. 4, there is a fast decrease in the delay spread with increasing frequency along the distance. It is also noted that S-band frequency achieves the maximum delay spread as compare with C-band and 5G mm-Wave bands.

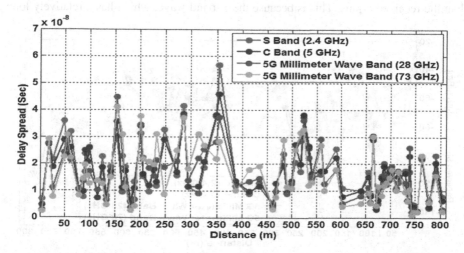

Fig. 4. Delay spread versus separation distance for different band frequencies.

The relation between path loss and separation distance for various frequencies are shown in Fig. 5. It is noticed that there is a raise in PL with increasing the separation distance and frequency. However, there is a rapid increase in the PL at high frequencies, due to the difficulty of the signal to reach large distances with high frequency (mm-Waves band). On the other word, the short wavelengths of the wave gradually increase the values of the path loss.

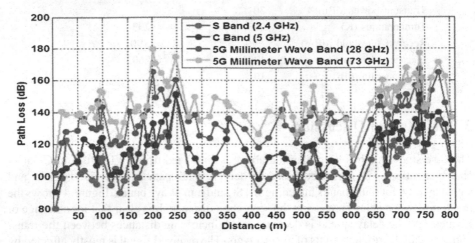

Fig. 5. Path loss versus separation distance for different band frequencies.

In term of the received power, the relation between the received power and separation distance for different frequencies is illustrated in Fig. 6. The obtained data in this figure include also studying the effect of changing the frequency change upon the received power. We find that increasing the distance and frequency leads to a decrease in the received power. This perhaps indicates that the S-band yields the highest power than the received points. This is because the S-band wave, which has a relatively long

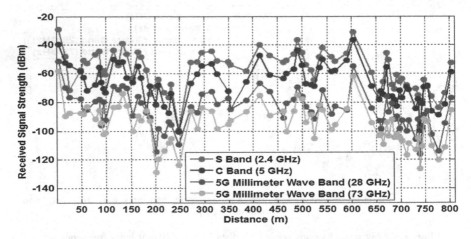

Fig. 6. Received power versus separation distance for a different band frequencies.

wavelength can penetrate the available barriers and obstacles throughout its transition. In contrast, the frequency of mm-Waves band causes multipath, leading to a decrease in the strength of received power.

The values of signal quality (SQ) for each band frequency are shown in Fig. 7. It can be noticed that the S-Band for (2.4 GHz) achieved better results with less losses as compared to the rest of the band frequencies. The range of the SQ in 2.4 GHz between 32.12 to 100% and this range is considered better than the rest of the band frequencies.

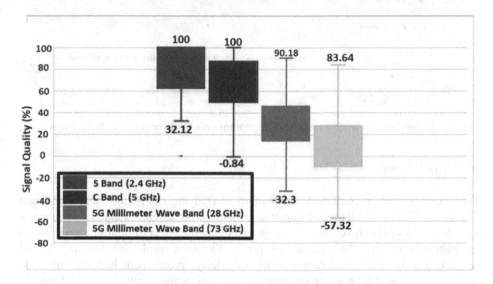

Fig. 7. The values of SQ for different band frequencies.

Figure 8 shows the GUI screen that has been created by applying the multi-scale algorithm using the MATLAB to conduct the comparison between the multi-band frequencies. The obtained results show that the S-band (2.4 GHz) is relatively better than other frequencies in term of the ASQ and ARP. In addition, the signal quality that reaches the receiving points is high and the coverage is also better than the rest of the frequencies.

Finally, for all the above figures, we find that 2.4 GHz for S-band frequency produces the best outcome regarding delay spread, path loss, received power, ASQ and ARP as compared to other frequencies. We know that increasing the frequency lead to an increase in the path losses, and thus decreasing in the RSS. Furthermore, raising the wave propagation of paths that resulted from reflections from walls, ceilings and other barriers in the college.

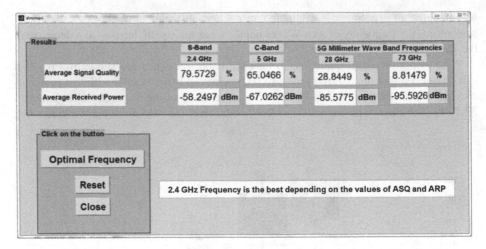

Fig. 8. Obtained results from a multi-scale algorithm on a GUI for different band frequencies.

6 Conclusions

This paper presents a combined contribution of studying the performance of S-band (2.4 GHz), C-band (5 GHz) and mm-Waves bands with different range of frequencies for (28 and 73 GHz). In addition, this paper studying the effect of building materials on the path direction and the transmission power. Obtained results indicate that S-band (2.4 GHz) produce the best results in term of delay spread, path loss, and received power as compared with other frequencies. As well as the results obtained from the multi-scale algorithm confirm that S-band (2.4 GHz) is better than the rest of the bands in terms of ASQ and ARP. The path losses increase with increasing frequency in particular with mm-Wave as an example of the short wavelength. In this wave band, it is noticed a reduction in the strength of the received power. The main reason behind this reduction is that the mm-Wave paths that carry the high frequencies cannot penetrate available barriers in the way of the transmitted signal. This causes also an increase in the path loss of the signal. In addition, we notice that the transmitted signals are greatly affected when they pass through walls especially that made from concrete, bricks, and wood. These effects can reduce the delay spread and the received power of the transition signals; whereas they cause an increase in the multipath, especially in the NLOS regions. Moreover, the mm-Waves propagation that caused multipath yield a gradual decrease in the performance of the designed network in the selected building. This is due to the fact the mm-Wave band cannot penetrate some barriers, and thus the multipath of the wave is increased. The data and models presented in this paper will allow for the development of the performance of the network. Simulation and practical models using Massive MIMO (multiple-input and multiple-output) antennas can be applied as future work to provide the user with a personal channel with less overlapping among users.

References

1. Samimi, M.K., Rappaport, T.S., MacCartney, G.R.: Probabilistic omnidirectional path loss models for millimeter-wave outdoor communications. IEEE Wireless Commun. Lett. **4**(4), 357–360 (2015)
2. Moustafa, N., Hu, J.: Security and Privacy in 4G/LTE Network. Springer, Heidelberg (2018)
3. Fettweis, G.P.: A 5G wireless communications vision. Microwave J. **55**(12), 24–36 (2012)
4. Wang, C.X., et al.: Cellular architecture and key technologies for 5G wireless communication networks. IEEE Commun. Mag. **52**(2), 122–130 (2014)
5. Osseiran, A., et al.: Scenarios for 5G mobile and wireless communications: the vision of the METIS project. IEEE Commun. Mag. **52**(5), 26–35 (2014)
6. Azar, Y., et al.: 28 GHz propagation measurements for outdoor cellular communications using steerable beam antennas in New York city. In: ICC, pp. 5143–5147 (2013)
7. Jungnickel, V., et al.: The role of small cells, coordinated multipoint, and massive MIMO in 5G. IEEE Commun. Mag. **52**(5), 44–51 (2014)
8. Molkdar, D.: Review on radio propagation into and within buildings. In: IEEE Proceedings Microwaves, Antennas and Propagation, vol. 138, no. 1, pp. 61–73. IET Digital Library (1991)
9. Rangan, S., Rappaport, T.S., Erkip, E.: Millimeter wave cellular wireless networks: Potentials and challenges (2014). arXiv preprint arXiv:1401.2560
10. Niu, Y., Li, Y., Jin, D., Su, L., Vasilakos, A.V.: A survey of millimeter wave communications (mmWave) for 5G: opportunities and challenges. Wireless Netw. **21**(8), 2657–2676 (2015)
11. MacCartney, G.R., Rappaport, T.S.: 73 GHz millimeter wave propagation measurements for outdoor urban mobile and backhaul communications in New York City. In: ICC, pp. 4862–4867 (2014)
12. Karim. A.H.: Radio resource management optimization for next-generation wireless networks. Electronic Thesis and Dissertation Repository (2016)
13. Jimenez, M.J.C., Arana, K., Arias, M.R.: Outdoor-to-indoor propagation mechanisms in multistorey building for 0.85 GHz and 1.9 GHz bands. In: 2017 IEEE 37th Central America and Panama Convention (CONCAPAN XXXVII), pp. 1–6. IEEE (2017)
14. Jain, R.: Channel models: a tutorial. In: WiMAX forum AATG, vol. 10 (2007)
15. State College Remcom Inc. S., 315 S. Allen St.: Wireless insite reference manual. IEEE Trans. Veh. Technol. **58**(1), 16801 (2012)
16. RSSI (dBm) relate to signal quality. https://www.speedguide.net/faq/how-does-rssi-dbm-relate-to-signal-quality-percent-439. Accessed 2 Jan (2019)
17. Oras, A.S., Karrar, S.M., Mahmood, F.M.: Outdoor transmitter localization using the multiscale algorithm. IJSSST **20**, 3.1–3.7 (2019)

Real World Application in Information Science and Technology

Analysis of the Publications on Ontology-Based Smart Grid Applications: A Bird's Eye View

Moamin A. Mahmoud[1]([⊠]) , Andino Maseleno[1]([⊠]) ,
Alicia Y. C. Tang[1]([⊠]) , Fung-Cheng Lim[2] ,
Hairoladenan Bin Kasim[2] , and Christine Yong[3]

[1] Insitute of Informatics and Computing Energy, Universiti Tenaga Nasional,
Kajang, Malaysia
{moamin, aliciat}@uniten.edu.my,
andimaseleno@gmail.com
[2] College of Computing and Informatics, Universiti Tenaga Nasional,
Kajang, Malaysia
{fclim, hairol}@uniten.edu.my
[3] Tenaga Nasional Berhad, Kuala Lumpur, Malaysia
christine@tnb.com.my

Abstract. Smart grid ontology is a field of research recently viewed from the field of smart grid research as well as from the field of ontology research. The integration between smart grid and ontology is expected to enable the sharing of ontology among applications and stakeholders. By using the same language, the common problems that occur during applications interoperability will be prevented and solved. This brief paper intended to help researchers get an overview of the current smart grid ontology research in the world and also to know the connection between smart grid ontology paper publications with research attention leading to smart grid ontology. To do so, we conduct a comprehensive survey on three databases which are IEEE Xplore, Springer, and Elsevier ScienceDirect. From the survey, we obtained the number of smart grid ontology research studies, their citations, and the country. From the number of papers and their citations, it can be known which country has an interest in smart grid ontology research. From the results of this review, it was found that countries in continental Europe are the most widely issued publication about smart grid ontology. Similarly, the papers that cite largely dominated by countries in continental Europe.

Keywords: Smart grid · Ontology · Interoperability · Systematic review

1 Introduction

Smart grid is a modern electric grid concept that has a high degree of flexibility, accessibility, and efficiency. In the smart grid network, there are digital sensors, smart meters, online monitoring, automation equipment and two-way communication system that allows between operators and consumers interact with each other so as to improve

© Springer Nature Switzerland AG 2020
M. I. Khalaf et al. (Eds.): ACRIT 2019, CCIS 1174, pp. 491–502, 2020.
https://doi.org/10.1007/978-3-030-38752-5_38

reliability in service compared with the existing power system. The smart grid is an integrated and interdisciplinary power grid technology concept that is still in development stage. Nevertheless, the development of smart grid should be anticipated from now on as it will become a model of modern electricity network that has very wide benefits. The smart grid system is one solution to alleviate the problems faced by the current power grid. The advantage is to reduce the amount of power needed because the electric utility knows the amount of electricity needed at a given time. Another advantage of smart grid is to reduce peak load by encouraging consumers to use less energy during peak hours.

Application of this technology can also be performed on the electrical system of major cities in the world, which has the most varied loads, ranging from households, commercial sectors, and industrial sectors. The increased load on the commercial and industrial sectors, as well as the high-reliability requirements of the power system and the freedom of choice of electric services, are also increasing in major cities, theoretically demonstrating that Smart Grid Technology applications deserve to be considered and applied.

2   Smart Grid Ontology Publication

In this paper review, we obtained papers from IEEE Xplore, SpringerLink, and ScienceDirect databases. In search of IEEE Xplore, we obtained papers from the journal and conference proceedings. For Springer, the paper that was taken which in the journal category because the Book Chapter and Conference Proceedings in Springer are often in one part, which makes it difficult for us and we think it is also difficult for many people to access it, it is rare that college willing to buy or subscribe to book chapter. For ScienceDirect, only papers in the category of journal that were taken. From the direct search results, in May 2018, by entering the keyword "Smart Grid" + "Ontology" in the search box obtained 105 papers from IEEE Xplore, 101 papers from SpringerLink, and 242 papers from ScienceDirect.

From this search result, it can be quickly seen that the incorporation of smart grid and ontology is something new. From the search results directly by entering the keyword, Smart Grid Ontology obtained search results 87 papers from IEEE Xplore, 3468 papers from SpringerLink, and 754 papers from ScienceDirect. Next from the search results by entering the keyword "Smart Grid Ontology" obtained 1 paper search results from IEEE Xplore, 1 paper SpringerLink, and 3 papers from ScienceDirect. Graphical display of search results by using the keyword is "Smart Grid" + "Ontology", Smart Grid Ontology, and "Smart Grid Ontology" can be seen in Fig. 1.

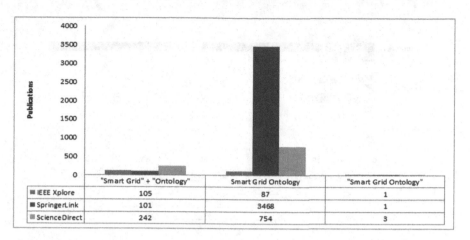

	"Smart Grid" + "Ontology"	Smart Grid Ontology	"Smart Grid Ontology"
▪ IEEE Xplore	105	87	1
▪ SpringerLink	101	3468	1
▪ ScienceDirect	242	754	3

Fig. 1. Number of publications retrieved from the keywords "Smart Grid" + "Ontology", Smart Grid Ontology, and "Smart Grid Ontology"

In Fig. 1 it can be seen that the more specific the keyword, the less the search result will be. The ranking of search results based on the number of papers obtained by entering the keywords "Smart Grid" + "Ontology", Smart Grid Ontology, and "Smart Grid Ontology" in 3 databases including IEEE Xplore, SpringerLink and ScienceDirect can be summarized as follows. In IEEE Xplore database, "Smart Grid" + "Ontology" > Smart Grid Ontology > "Smart Grid Ontology" with the value of 105 papers > 87 papers > 1 paper. In SpringerLink, "Smart Grid" + "Ontology" < Smart Grid Ontology > "Smart Grid Ontology" with the value of 101 papers < 3468 papers > 1 paper. In ScienceDirect, "Smart Grid" + "Ontology" < Smart Grid Ontology > "Smart Grid Ontology" with the value of 242 papers < 754 papers > 3 papers.

After searching by keyword, we then manually looked at the titles of the papers consisting of smart, grid, smart grid, ontology, and smart grid ontology. These search results are based on the Smart Grid Ontology keyword that was entered into the search box, we believe the results will be more if we use one of the keywords that have been common like Smart Grid keyword or Ontology keyword because these keywords have existed a long time and also many researchers who have generally researched the field. In the IEEE Xplore database, there were only 4 papers which in the title there are smart, grid and ontology [1–4], there were 26 papers with only the word smart grid, and there were 15 papers that have ontology on the title. In the SpringerLink database, there was no paper which in the title there is the word smart grid ontology, 4 papers which have only the word smart grid, and there were 114 papers which contain ontology word on the title. In the ScienceDirect database, there were only 2 papers in the title of smart grid ontology [5, 6], 27 papers have smart grid keywords in the title, and the same number of 27 papers have ontology keywords. Figure 2 shows a number of publications obtained from the titles of the papers consisting smart grid ontology, smart grid, and ontology.

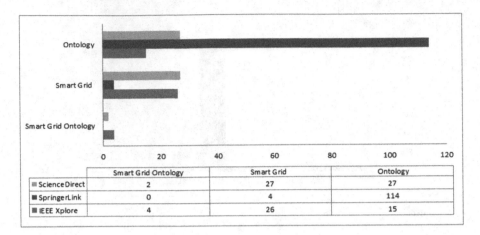

Fig. 2. Number of publications obtained from the titles of the papers consisting smart grid ontology, smart grid, and ontology.

For the distribution of researchers who write the smart grid ontology paper based on their country there are 8 countries that do this research mostly come from European countries that are Austria, United Kingdom, France, Turkey, Germany, Spain, Czech Republic and Portugal [1–6]. For distribution of origin country of author, 1 researcher for Austria, United Kingdom, France, Turkey, Czech Republic, and Portugal. Two researchers for Germany and Spain respectively. Figure 3 shows distribution by researchers' nationality for smart grid ontology paper.

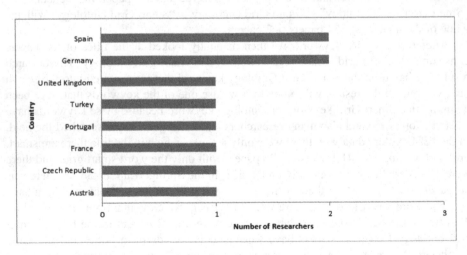

Fig. 3. Distribution by researchers' nationality for a smart grid ontology paper

Based on the smart grid ontology paper published year, in 2014 there were 2 papers, 1 paper whose authors from Turkey [1], and 1 paper whose authors from

Germany and Spain [2]. In 2015 there were 1 paper whose authors from 3 countries namely Spain, Czech Republic, and Portugal [6]. In 2016 there were 2 papers namely 1 paper whose authors from United Kingdom and France [3] and 1 paper whose authors from Austria [4]. In 2017 there was 1 paper whose authors from Germany [4]. Figure 4 shows distribution by year for smart grid ontology paper.

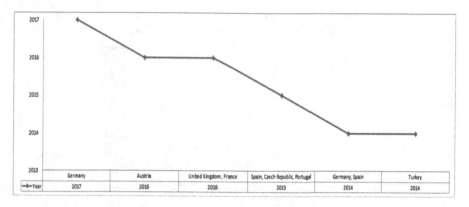

Fig. 4. Distribution by year for smart grid ontology paper

3 Citation Analysis

Based on the paper published that cite smart grid ontology paper, for smart grid ontology paper publication in 2014 whose authors from Turkey [1] has been cited by 3 papers [7–9], 1 paper whose authors from China [7], 1 paper whose authors from Brazil [8] and 1 paper whose authors from Portugal [9].

Smart grid ontology paper publication in 2014 whose authors from Germany and Spain [5] has been cited by 29 papers [5, 10–32], 15 papers whose authors from China, 1 paper whose authors from Germany and Sweden, 2 papers whose authors from Canada, 1 paper whose authors from Germany and Spain, 1 paper whose authors from Russia, 1 paper whose authors from China and Iran, 1 paper whose authors from France, 1 paper whose authors from Turkey, 1 paper whose authors from Morocco, 1 paper whose authors from Spain, 1 paper whose authors from India, 1 paper whose authors from Mexico and Spain, 1 paper whose authors from Portugal and Spain, and 1 paper whose authors from Germany and United Kingdom.

Smart grid ontology paper publication in 2015 whose authors from Spain, Czech Republic, and Portugal [6] has been cited by 5 papers [28, 33–36]), 2 papers whose authors from, 1 paper whose authors from Greece, and 1 paper whose authors from Turkey.

Smart grid ontology paper publication in 2016 whose authors from the United Kingdom and France [3] has been cited by 4 papers [37–40], 1 paper whose authors from Denmark, 1 paper whose authors from United Kingdom, 1 paper whose authors from Spain and Ireland, and 1 paper whose authors from Portugal and Spain.

Smart grid ontology paper publication in 2016 whose authors from Austria [41] has been cited by 6 papers [2, 14, 15, 32, 41, 42], 3 papers whose authors from Austria, 1 paper whose authors from United Kingdom, 1 paper whose authors from Germany, and 1 paper whose authors from Portugal and Spain. Figure 5 shows a number of citations for smart grid ontology paper.

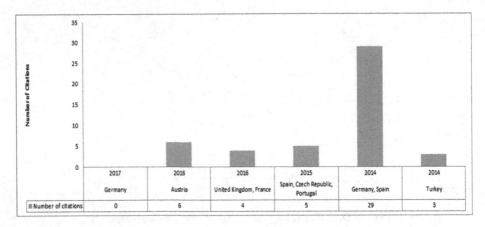

Fig. 5. Number of citations for a smart grid ontology paper

Based on the countries that cite smart grid ontology paper obtained 23 countries, namely Turkey, Germany, Spain, Czech Republic, Portugal, United Kingdom, France, Austria, China, Brazil, Russia, Canada, Iran, Mexico, India, Morocco, Philippines, Singapore, Italy, Greece, Denmark, Ireland, and Sweden. To get an idea of the relationship between the countries of citation, we drew a figure of the relationship between the state and the number of citations. Names of countries to be placed in nodes are numbered, i.e. 1 for Turkey, 2 for Germany, 3 for Spain, 4 for Czech Republic, 5 for Portugal, 6 for United Kingdom, 7 for France, 8 for Austria, 9 for China, 10 for Brazil, 11 for Russia, 12 for Canada, 13 for Iran, 14 for Mexico, 15 for India, 16 for Morocco, 17 for Philippines, 18 for Singapore, 19 for Italy, 20 for Greece, 21 for Denmark, 22 for Ireland, and 23 for Sweden. Figure 6 below shows a graph of the relationships between countries that cited the smart grid ontology paper and the number of papers that were cited.

Figure 6 above explains that the paper published in 2014 by authors from Turkey [1] received a total of 3 cites from China, Portugal, and Brazil. The paper which published by authors from Germany and Spain in 2014 [17], received a total of 29 cites, 15 papers from China, 1 paper from Germany and Sweden, 1 paper from Canada, 1 paper from Germany and Spain, 1 paper from Russia, 1 paper from China and Iran, 1 paper from France, 1 paper from Turkey, 1 paper from Morocco, 1 paper from Spain, 1

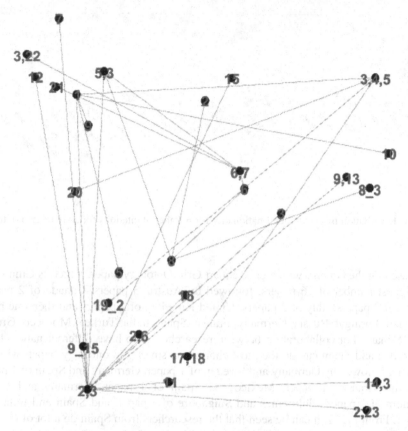

Fig. 6. Graph representation of the relationship between the countries and the number of citations.

paper from India, 1 paper from Mexico and Spain, 1 paper from Portugal and Spain, and 1 paper from Germany and United Kingdom. The paper published in 2015 by researchers from Spain, Czech, and Portugal [6] has been cited 5 times, 1 paper by researchers from Philippines and Singapore, 2 papers from Italy, 1 paper from Greece, and 1 paper from Turkey. The paper published in 2016 by researchers from the United Kingdom and France [3] received a citation 4 times, 1 paper from researchers from Denmark, 1 paper from United Kingdom, 1 paper from Spain and Ireland, and 1 paper from Portugal and Spain. The paper published in 2016 by researchers from Austria [41] obtained a total of 6 cites of 3 citations from their own countries, Austria, 1 paper from Portugal and Spain, 1 paper from United Kingdom, and 1 paper from Germany.

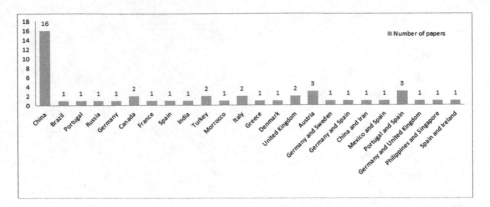

Fig. 7. Distribution by researchers' nationality for number of citations for a smart grid ontology paper

Based on the country which cited Smart Grid Ontology paper, which is China with the highest number of 16 papers, followed by Austria 3 papers, Canada of 2 papers, Turkey of 2 papers, Italy of 2 papers, United Kingdom of 2 papers and then one paper for Brazil, Portugal, Russia, Germany, France, Spain, India, Turkey, Morocco, Greece, and Denmark. For collaboration between researchers who have different nationalities, in Portugal and Spain can do the most citation on smart grid ontology paper, which is 3 papers, followed by Germany and Sweden of 1 paper, Germany and Spain of 1 paper, China and Iran of 1 paper, Mexico and Spain of 1 paper, Germany and United Kingdom of 1 paper, Philippines and Singapore of 1 paper, and Spain and Ireland of 1 paper. From Fig. 7, it can be seen that the researchers from Spain do a lot of research collaborations between countries that is with Mexico, Germany, Portugal, and Ireland.

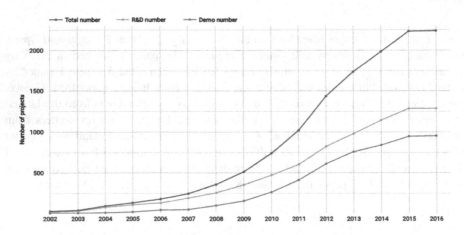

Fig. 8. Number of smart grid projects in Europe

Fig. 9. Smart grid project map: organisations and implementation site

From the review of papers which cited smart grid ontology paper, it is illustrated that some countries in Europe have shown their interest in the development of smart grid ontology, this is not surprising because of the rapid project of smart grid in European countries as shown in Figs. 8 and 9 [40]. The current publication of smart grid ontology comes from countries in Europe, including Turkey which is a country bordering between Europe and Asia.

4 Conclusion

This paper presents a bird's eye view of smart grid ontology publications. The results have been obtained by analyzing papers from IEEE Xplore, SpringerLink, and ScienceDirect databases in May 2018. Smart Grid is an electrical network that uses digital technology and other advanced technologies to monitor and manage the transportation of electricity from electricity generation sources to meet the changing needs of electricity from customers. There are several benefits of developing an ontology including to share a common understanding of the domain and the related information either among humans or among software agents, to separate domain knowledge from operational one, and to analyze domain knowledge. The number of papers that cited smart grid technology papers came from China, but overall it appears that papers originating from countries in continental Europe dominate citation for smart grid ontology paper. The rapid development of the smart grid and the emergence of research on smart grid ontology in Europe is expected to be followed by other hemispheres such as in Asia, USA, Australia, and Africa.

Acknowledgments. This work is sponsored by Tenaga Nasional Berhad (TNB) under TNB R&D Seeding Fund Scheme No. TC-RD-18-19. We also gratefully appreciate Universiti Tenaga Nasional & Uniten R&D for securing and managing the fund.

References

1. Dogdu, E., et al.: Ontology-centric data modelling and decision support in smart grid applications a distribution service operator perspective. In: 2014 IEEE International Conference on Intelligent Energy and Power Systems (IEPS), pp. 198–204. IEEE, June 2014
2. Schachinger, D., Kastner, W., Gaida, S.: Ontology-based abstraction layer for smart grid interaction in building energy management systems. In: 2016 IEEE International Energy Conference (ENERGYCON), pp. 1–6. IEEE, April 2016
3. Hippolyte, J.L., et al.: Ontology-based demand-side flexibility management in smart grids using a multi-agent system. In: 2016 IEEE International Smart Cities Conference (ISC2), pp. 1–7. IEEE, September 2016
4. Schumilin, A., Stucky, K.U., Sinn, F., Hagenmeyer, V.: Towards ontology-based network model management and data integration for smart grids. In: 2017 Workshop on Modeling and Simulation of Cyber-Physical Energy Systems (MSCPES), pp. 1–6. IEEE, April 2017
5. Santodomingo, R., Rohjans, S., Uslar, M., Rodriguez-Mondejar, J.A., Sanz-Bobi, M.A.: Ontology matching system for future energy smart grids. Eng. Appl. Artif. Intell. **32**, 242–257 (2014)
6. López, G., Custodio, V., Moreno, J.I., Sikora, M., Moura, P., Fernández, N.: Modeling smart grid neighborhoods with the ENERsip ontology. Comput. Ind. **70**, 168–182 (2015)
7. Daqing, X., Yinghua, H.: An adaptive data management model for smart grid. In: 2015 8th International Conference on Intelligent Computation Technology and Automation (ICICTA), pp. 126–129. IEEE, June 2015
8. Barriquello, C.H., Garcia, V.J., Schmitz, M., Bernardon, D.P., Fonini, J.S.: A decision support system for planning and operation of maintenance and customer services in electric power distribution systems. In: System Reliability. InTech (2017)
9. Santos, G., Pinto, T., Vale, Z.: Ontologies for the interoperability of heterogeneous multi-agent systems in the scope of power and energy systems. In: De la Prieta, F., et al. (eds.) PAAMS 2017. AISC, vol. 619, pp. 300–301. Springer, Cham (2018). https://doi.org/10.1007/978-3-319-61578-3_42
10. Gao, W., Farahani, M.R.: Generalization bounds and uniform bounds for multi-dividing ontology algorithms with convex ontology loss function. Comput. J. **60**(9), 1289–1299 (2017)
11. Gao, W., Zhu, L.: Gradient learning algorithms for ontology computing. Comput. Intell. Neurosci. **2014**, 24 (2014)
12. Gao, Y., Gao, W.: Ontology sparse vector learning based on accelerated first-order method. Open Cybern. Syst. J. **9**, 657–662 (2015)
13. Gao, W., Zhu, L., Wang, K.: Ranking based ontology scheming using eigenpair computation. J. Intell. Fuzzy Syst. **31**(4), 2411–2419 (2016)
14. Butzin, B., Golatowski, F., Timmermann, D.: A survey on information modeling and ontologies in building automation. In: IECON 2017-43rd Annual Conference of the IEEE Industrial Electronics Society, pp. 8615–8621. IEEE, October 2017
15. Zanabria, C., Tayyebi, A., Pröstl Andrén, F., Kathan, J., Strasser, T.: Engineering support for handling controller conflicts in energy storage systems applications. Energies **10**(10), 1595 (2017)
16. Hernández, O., Guinea, D., Santos, M.: Semantic sensors: a proposal from smart building to smart city model. In: Proceedings of the Mexican International Conference on Computer Science, 2nd. Workshop on Semantic Web and Linked Open Data, Oaxaca, Mexico, vol. 35, November 2014

17. Santodomingo, R., Uslar, M., Rodríguez-Mondéjar, J.A., Sanz-Bobi, M.A.: Rule-based data transformations in electricity smart grids. In: Bassiliades, N., Gottlob, G., Sadri, F., Paschke, A., Roman, D. (eds.) RuleML 2015. LNCS, vol. 9202, pp. 447–455. Springer, Cham (2015). https://doi.org/10.1007/978-3-319-21542-6_29
18. Essayeh, A., Abed, M.: Towards ontology matching based system through terminological, structural and semantic level. Proc. Comput. Sci. **60**, 403–412 (2015)
19. Gong, S., Gao, W.: Ontology Learning Algorithm via WMW Optimization Model. In: 2016 12th International Conference on Computational Intelligence and Security (CIS), pp. 431–434. IEEE, December 2016
20. Hamdaqa, M., Tahvildari, L.: Prison break: a generic schema matching solution to the cloud vendor lock-in problem. In: 2014 IEEE 8th International Symposium on the Maintenance and Evolution of Service-Oriented and Cloud-Based Systems (MESOCA), pp. 37–46. IEEE, September 2014
21. Lan, M.H., Xu, J., Gao, W.: Ontology feature extraction via vector learning algorithm and applied to similarity measuring and ontology mapping. IAENG Int. J. Comput. Sci. **43**(1), 10–19 (2016)
22. Lan, M., Xu, J., Gao, W.: Ontology similarity computation and ontology mapping using distance matrix learning approach. IAENG Int. J. Comput. Sci. **45**(1), 164–176 (2018)
23. Rosinger, M.: Visualisierung als Projektcockpit im Smart Grid Projekt DISCERN (2016). https://www.discern.eu/datas/Messen_Bewerten_und_Vergleichen_Visualisierung_als_Projektcockpit_im_Smart_Grid_Projekt_DISCERN_OTTI_2016.pdf
24. Wei, G.A.O., Jianzhang, W.U., Linli, Z.H.U.: Ontology similarity measuring and ontology mapping algorithms based on proximal technologies. Int. J. Simul.-Syst. Sci. Technol. **17**(43), 1–9 (2016)
25. Yan, L., Li, Y.J., Yang, X., Gao, W.: Gradient descent technology for sparse vector learning in ontology algorithms. J. Disc. Math. Sci. Crypt. **19**(3), 753–775 (2016)
26. Ravikumar, G., Khaparde, S.A.: A common information model oriented graph database framework for power systems. IEEE Trans. Power Syst. **32**(4), 2560–2569 (2017)
27. Zhu, L., Pan, Y., Farahani, M.R., Gao, W.: Magnitude preserving based ontology regularization algorithm. J. Intell. Fuzzy Syst. **33**(5), 3113–3122 (2017)
28. Küçük, D., Küçük, D.: OntoWind: An Improved and Extended Wind Energy Ontology (2018). arXiv preprint arXiv:1803.02808
29. Balabanov, M.S., Baboshkina, S.V., Hamitov, R.N.: Ecological aspects in energy saving policy at the stage of creation in Russia of intelligent power systems with an actively adaptive network. In: Proceedings of the Tomsk Polytechnic University, vol. 326 (2015)
30. Marsal-Llacuna, M.L.: The standards evolution: a pioneering meta-standard framework architecture as a novel self-conformity assessment and learning tool. Comput. Stan. Interfaces **55**, 106–115 (2018)
31. Mountasser, I., Ouhbi, B., Frikh, B.: Hybrid large-scale ontology matching strategy on big data environment. In: Proceedings of the 18th International Conference on Information Integration and Web-based Applications and Services, pp. 282–287. ACM, November 2016
32. Teixeira, B., Pinto, T., Silva, F., Santos, G., Praça, I., Vale, Z.: Multi-agent decision support tool to enable interoperability among heterogeneous energy systems. Appl. Sci. **8**(3), 328 (2018)
33. Ferrante, P., La Gennusa, M., Peri, G., Porretto, V., Sanseverino, E.R., Vaccaro, V.: On the architectural and energy classification of existing buildings: a case study of a district in the city of Palermo. In: 2016 IEEE 16th International Conference on Environment and Electrical Engineering (EEEIC), pp. 1–6. IEEE, June 2016

34. Guarino, F., Tumminia, G., Longo, S., Mistretta, M., Bilotta, R., Cellura, M.: Energy planning methodology of net-zero energy solar neighborhoods in the mediterranean basin. Sci. Technol. Built Environ. **22**(7), 928–938 (2016)
35. Karakosta, C., Flamos, A.: Managing climate policy information facilitating knowledge transfer to policy makers. Energies **9**(6), 454 (2016)
36. Tuballa, M.L., Abundo, M.L.: A review of the development of smart grid technologies. Renew. and Sustain. Energy Rev. **59**, 710–725 (2016)
37. Billanes, J.D., Ma, Z., Jørgensen, B.N.: Energy flexibility in the power system: challenges and opportunites in Philippines. J. Energy Power Eng. **11**, 597–604 (2017)
38. Cuenca, J., Larrinaga, F., Curry, E.: A unified semantic ontology for energy management applications. In: Joint Proceedings of the Web Stream Processing workshop (WSP 2017) and the 2nd International Workshop on Ontology Modularity, Contextuality, and Evolution (WOMoCoE 2017), pp. 86–97 (2017)
39. Reynolds, J., Rezgui, Y., Hippolyte, J.L.: Upscaling energy control from building to districts: Current limitations and future perspectives. Sustain. Cities Soc. **35**, 816–829 (2017)
40. Joint Research Center Smart Electricity Systems and Interoperability. http://ses.jrc.ec.europa.eu/. Accessed May 2018
41. Schachinger, D., Kastner, W.: Ontology-based generation of optimization problems for building energy management. In: 2017 22nd IEEE International Conference on Emerging Technologies and Factory Automation (ETFA), pp. 1–8. IEEE, September 2017
42. Albalushi, A., Khan, R., McLaughlin, K., Sezer, S.: Ontology-based approach for malicious behaviour detection in synchrophasor networks. In: Power & Energy Society General Meeting, 2017 IEEE, pp. 1–5. IEEE, July 2017

Integrating Fuzzy Logic Technique in Case-Based Reasoning for Improving the Inspection Quality of Software Requirements Specifications

Salama A. Mostafa[1]([✉]) [iD], Saraswathy Shamini Gunasekaran[2] [iD],
and Shihab Hamad Khaleefah[3] [iD]

[1] Faculty of Computer Science and Information Technology,
Universiti Tun Hussein Onn Malaysia, 86400 Parit Raja, Johor, Malaysia
salama@uthm.edu.my
[2] College of Computing and Informatics, Universiti Tenaga Nasional,
43000 Kajang, Selangor, Malaysia
sshamini@uniten.edu.my
[3] Faculty of Computer Science, Al Maarif University College,
31001 Anbar, Iraq
shi90hab@gmail.com

Abstract. The development success of software is essentially based on the quality of its Software Requirements Specifications (SRS). A requirement represents the main objective that needs to be accomplished, while a specification is a full description of this objective. The inspection of the Software Requirements Specification (iSRS) system is developed to ensure that the SRSs are of high quality. This paper presents the contribution of integrating a fuzzy logic technique in the Case Base Reasoning (CBR) as a reasoning framework in the iSRS system. The fuzzy logic technique provides a disambiguation mechanism within the Retrieve, Reuse, Revise, and Retain steps of the CBR cycle. Specifically, it is used as a similarity measurement technique in the matching process between the inspected SRS cases and the existing SRS cases in the CBR case base. It then classifies and labels the cases in the case base to no-match, partial-match and, complete-match cases. This classification improves the overall reasoning and inspection of the SRS quality by comparing the inspected case with the most similar cases of the case base.

Keywords: Software Requirements Specifications · Quality inspection · Similarity measurement technique · Case-based reasoning · Fuzzy logic

1 Introduction

Software is a complex configuration surrounded by many parameters that must be taken into consideration by the developers' team. These parameters include functional and non-functional requirements such as customer requirements, hardware requirements, quality requirements, market requirements, technology requirements feasibility

M. I. Khalaf et al. (Eds.): ACRIT 2019, CCIS 1174, pp. 503–513, 2020.
https://doi.org/10.1007/978-3-030-38752-5_39

requirements, and others [1]. The Software Requirements Specifications (SRS) is an itinerary of documenting a collection of specified, standardized, and organized information involving in a software project development processes it is meant to demonstrate future software complete view [2].

The Inspection of Software Requirements Specification (iSRS) system is based on the SRSQAS system that is proposed by [3]. It aims to enhance the effectiveness of the SRS success on software development and implementation by inspecting the SRS and evaluating its quality. The SRS inspection process entails measurements of eleven SRS Quality Inspection Metrics (QIM) including complete, consistent, correct and unambiguous. Each of the QIM is defined by a subset of nine interrelated Quality Inspection Indicators (QII) including continuances, directives, imperatives, and options. The QII closely looks and takes into account structure, syntax and semantics of the SRS. This QIM is originally proposed by Wilson et al. [2] and it is widely adopted by many researchers such as [3, 4] and [5].

Additionally, the iSRS applies a Quality Inspection Checklist (QIC) that consists of ten categories of 50 checklist questions. The QIC is collected from different sources including the work of [6–8]. Within the QIC, the questions are separated into several main categories that represent different aspects and perspectives of the SRS inspection process. Examples of these categories include "the alignment level to the business objectives", "the compliance level to the standards", "the coverage level to the needs of the stakeholders" and "the depth level to the details of the specification". Different types of techniques like the defect-based and scenario-based are applied in constructing the questions of the QIC.

Subsequently, Case-Based Reasoning (CBR) is used in the implementation of the iSRS to handle the SRS inspection process through the QIM and QIC measurements. The inspection entails referring to previously-stored SRS inspection cases (i.e. past experiences) that have been successfully completed [3, 9]. However, there are problems of complexity and uncertainty in the case base content that affects the overall CBR inspection performance, especially, the retrieving process. The complexity results from the difficulty of the SRS inspection and the variation between the SRS cases. The SRSs are not following a standard template or format and they belong to a wide range of applications. These issues affect the matching and reasoning processes of the CBR and the final outcomes. On the other hand, the uncertainty is presented partially in the indexing and retrieving, sparse coverage of the problem space by the existing cases, and in the description of the inspection. Moreover, it is presented in the semantics of abstract features (i.e., QIC and QII) used to index the cases, the evaluation of the similarity measures computed across these features, the determination of relevancy of the similar cases, and the modification of the rules used in the case adaptation phase.

The integration of fuzzy logic with CBR is found useful in memory organization, selection or retrieval, matching, similarity measures, adaptation, evaluation and forgetting [10]. The fuzzy logic has the capability of easily integrating with other techniques. It is proven to provide solutions to some of the addressed problems in this work. Subsequently, this paper proposes the integrating of fuzzy logic technique in the CBR of the iSRS system to improve the inspection accuracy result of SRSs.

2 Related Work

The related work covers software requirements inspection, CBR and fuzzy logic. Apparently, the combination of fuzzy logic and CBR is yet to be used in SRS inspection. The CBR alone has been used in several SRS inspection systems as in [3, 9].

John Yen and Tiao [11] propose a House of Quality (HOQ) framework in the requirements inspection. The main idea behind the HOQ framework is that software products should be designed to reflect clients' desires. Subsequently, this framework provides a platform in which all participants can communicate their thoughts about a product to identify the requirements and their interrelationships. In the HOQ framework, fuzzy logic is used to capture participants' imprecise requirements and revise them in such a way that reduces the ambiguous phrases and facilitates the interactions between the participants.

The work that is made by Karsak [12] propose a Quality Function Deployment (QFD) framework to improve software product. The QFD applies several client satisfaction parameters. It also considered additional development limitations parameters that are related to the software product cost, budget and technical difficulties. It considers several functions of an organization such as design engineering, marketing and manufacturing. The QFD utilizes fuzzy logic with multiple objective approaches in the inspection process. The fuzzy logic determines the fulfilment of the requirements during the design phase by using sets of linguistic variables. These variables represent and evaluate the inspection parameters.

Sen and Baracl [13] propose fuzzy Quality Function Deployment methodology named (QFD) in handling the requirements analysis. QFD is used to overcome problems that occur in the requirements analysis process by obtaining and translating the requirements into a set of detailed design specifications. It focuses mainly on handling the specifications of the non-functional requirements. Fuzzy QFD approach is deployed to determine which of the non-functional requirements reported by earlier studies are important to a company's software.

The work of Dhote [14] presents three categorize of requirements namely business requirements, user requirements and functional requirements that need to be evaluated during software project development phases. This work proposes a framework that utilizes fuzzy logic technique to handle the uncertainty or the ambiguity in the specifications of these requirements. The framework includes linguistic analysis and checklist approaches to determine the ambiguity level of the requirements. Finally, a traceability table is generated to specify the ambiguous requirements and the necessary revision.

Mat Jani and Mostafa [3] propose an SRS quality assurance and audit framework to determine whether the required standards and procedures of the SRS document are being carefully achieved. The framework adopts Wilson et al. [2] SRS evaluation criteria and utilizes a CBR reasoning technique to analyses the quality of the SRSs. The framework is implemented to SRS Quality Analysis system (SRSQAS) as an executable prototype. The users of the SRSQAS are project architects and SRS reviewers that online interaction with the system through a series of Q&S sessions and checklists to check quality and characteristics of the SRSs. The CBR reasoning is performed by referring to stored similar cases in the case base as a past experience.

Daramola et al. [9] propose a framework for managing implicit requirements (ImRs) based on semantic reasoning and by using CBR technique. The framework attempts to analyze and discover the ImRs in the SRSs. The ImRs are basic requirements within an organizational context that usually not explicitly expressed in the SRS and neglected by the software development team. They claim that the insufficiently addressed ImRs is one of the causes of project failure. The framework provides automated means for analyzing and discovering the ImRs. The CBR applies analogies to analyze the ImRs then reuse the stored ImRs in the case base as solutions to modify the SRSs.

3 The Proposed Framework

The SRS reflects stakeholders' needs in developing an application with a clear description of the provided services. Generating the requirements is based on the users' actual work in the application domain [11]. Requirements Engineering is the process of extracting, gathering, analysing, specifying, validating and maintaining requirements [15].

This paper presents the iSRS system reasoning framework that employs a fuzzy logic technique within the CBR cycle with the objectives of improving its reasoning and decision-making process of the iSRS system [17–21]. The main aim of the iSRS system is to ensure that the SRS meets the satisfaction level of the stakeholders and users and eases the developers work by inspecting the SRS quality of software projects [16].

The iSRS system provides an interface for users to enter the new SRS descriptions. The system operates a parser to generate features of the SRS description and built a new case. Then the CBR cycle of the iSRS system begins with matching the new SRS inspection case with the cases that are stored in the case base (i.e., past cases). Figure 1 exemplify the CBR cycle of the iSRS system.

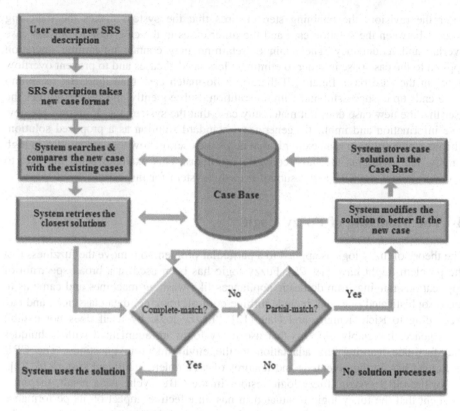

Fig. 1. The architecture of the CBR system.

Heuristic search is performed to find the relevant SRS cases to the new case. Based on Fig. 1, the search algorithm, the system classifies searched cases into three types: (i) complete-match in which the new case has a complete match with one case in the case base, (ii) partial-match in which there are some cases that partially matched with the new case and (iii) no-match in which there is no case matched with the new case [3, 18]. In the first type, if there is a complete-match, then the solution that the retrieved case has is directly used for the new case and the reasoning cycle has a successful retrieve operational state. More so, in the second type, if there is a partial-match then the cases that partially match the new case are revised to fit the new case. Here, the system performs two levels of matching: cases matching level and features matching level. These two matching levels are performed by the fuzzy logic in order to further explore the data of the cases and to find the patterns that most fit the new case. The outcome of the revision process is considered as a solution and the reasoning cycle of the CBR has a successful revise operational state. Furthermore, the new solution is retained in the case base as a possible solution or part of the solution(s) to future cases.

After the revision, the retaining step ensures that the system makes the matching process between the solution case and the other cases in the case base to prevent case overlap and redundancy. The retain or retaining may contain unlearning operation applied to the case base in order to eliminate less needed cases and to prevent overflow status in the case base. Finally, If there is a no-match case then the CBR reasoning cycle ends up unsuccessful and with no solution. Subsequently, the system notifies the user that the new case does not match any case that the system has. It ignores the new case information and implicitly generates a standard solution as a proposed solution. The no-match solution is an example that helps the user on how to write an SRS in high quality and highlights the most common problems. This example helps the user to manually revise the SRS and resubmit it to the system for inspection.

4 The Modeling of Fuzzy Logic

The theory of fuzzy logic is applied to a particular problem to remove the fuzziness that the problem might have [19, 20]. Fuzzy logic has been used in a broad spectrum of applications ranging from domestic appliances like washing machines and cameras to more sophisticated ones that include turbine control, tracking, data classifiers, and etc. According to Rich, Knight, and Nair [12], "Fuzzy logic by itself does not exhibit intelligence. Invariably, systems that use fuzzy logic are augmented with techniques that facilitate learning and adaptation to the environment in question." The CBR technique has all the potentials and features of a complete intelligent system [6, 21].

In the iSRS system, fuzzy logic resides in the CBR cycle. As a result, the environment that the fuzzy logic is situated in has an effective impact on its performance level. Moreover, by applying fuzzy set logic to the ideal CBR type, system cases can be more understandable and they become as configurations of attributes that appear in a different extent. Thus, the differences in cases kind and degree can also be easily studied and understood [13]. The following sub-sections illustrate how fuzzy logic is implemented in the CBR cycle.

4.1 The Fuzzy Logic in the CBR

In the Retrieve step, the system starts its cycle by checking the features that each case has to measure the similarity level between the existing cases and the problem case. In the proposed framework, fuzzy logic starts matching these cases using the obtained features in determining how much each case is close to the problem case. The cases are then classified into three groups: no-match, partial-match and complete-match cases as shown in Fig. 2. Adjusting the fuzziness of the matching features depends on some relations that are obtained from the CBR case base during heuristic Retrieve step. However, if there is a partial-match situation with the new case or problem case, the approach does another level of the matching process. Moreover, within the CBR cycle, matching processes to the Retain step is also required as illustrated in Fig. 2.

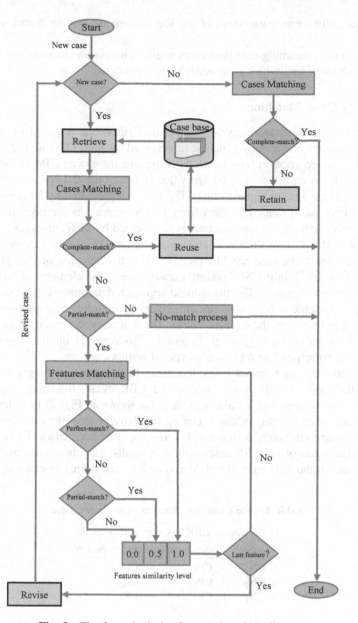

Fig. 2. The fuzzy logic implementation chart diagram.

In short, fuzzy logic in the CBR works on the following:

- Solving the fuzziness of cases matching in the Retrieve step (no-match, partial-match and complete-match).
- Solving the fuzziness of case features matching in the Retrieve step (no-match, partial-match and perfect-match).

- Enhancing the input parameters of the Revise step by finding features similarity levels.
- In Retain step, matching case base cases again (if necessary) to assist the unlearning process by deciding which case needs to be eliminated.

4.2 Fuzzy Cases Matching

The iSRS starts the reasoning cycle when a user enters the required information to inspect the quality of the SRS which is represented by both QIM and QIC sessions. The SRS quality description is extracted by inspecting the eleven QIM and the ten QIC items. The QIM is represented by 61 QII values (each of the QII has a range of values from 1 to 5, where 5 is the highest value). The QIC is represented by 50 questions (each of the questions has a range of values from 1 to 5, where 5 is the highest value).

Ultimately, each case in the case base is represented by 21 features (i.e. 11 items of the QIM and 10 items of the QIC), and each feature takes several elements and the overall elements in the case are 111 elements (i.e. 61 elements of the QIM and 50 elements of the QIC). In the SRS quality measurements, the elements of each case are weighted with a variable w. The fuzzy logic approach determines cases classifications according to dynamic w (i.e., w values are changing according to exploring processes that are held in retrieving the relevant cases). The w is assigned based on each element importance (w value is; $0 \leq w \leq 1$) and it also depends on the number of the elements that correspond to a particular type of features.

After retrieving the relevant cases, the fuzzy logic starts matching process of the cases in the case base. However, within the CBR cycle, matching processes are required in the Retrieve and Retain steps only (as shown in Fig. 2) in order to ensure efficient retrieval and storing of cases. During the Retrieve step, the cases are classified into three groups; no-match, partial-match and complete-match cases. Table 1 shows a sample of fuzzy sets of the CBR cases matching results. The approach classifies all the relevant cases in the case base to the three matching categories or classes.

Table 1. The cases classification of the fuzzy logic.

Fuzzy sets of CBR cases matching result		
no-match	*partial-match*	*complete-match*
1. CN_1	4. CP_1	7. CC_1
2. CN_2	5. CP_2	8. CC_2
3. CN_i	6. CP_j	9. CC_k

In Table 1, CN represents no-match cases; i represent no-match cases number; CP represents partial-match cases; j represents partial-match cases number; CC represents complete-match cases, and k represents complete-match cases number. The sum of i, j, and k are equal to the total number of relevant cases. The actual range of the no-match state starts from 0% until 10% matching level as shown in Fig. 3.

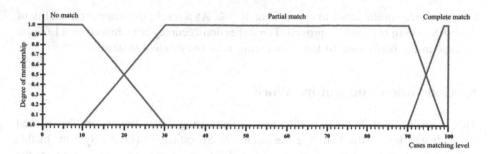

Fig. 3. The fuzzy cases matching.

From Fig. 3, cases matching falls under a fuzzy area shared with the partial-match state until 30% matching level. The actual partial-match range starts from 30% until 90% and it shares a fuzzy area with the complete-match state that starts from 90% and ends at 99%. The complete-match actual value is 100% case matching and it shares another 9.9% fuzzy area with partial-match case state.

The cases matching classifier is used to find the matching level of each case in order to find the solution case(s). If there is a complete-match state, the solution is directly used by the system and if the system does not find a complete-match case then, the highest-level matching case(s) are to be used to find some solutions.

Figure 4 is an example of how the system performs the similarity measurement to determine the relevant cases where each green scale area in the figure shows the matched elements in the relevant cases as compared with the new case.

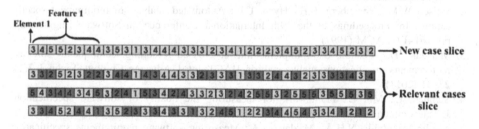

Fig. 4. An example of the fuzzy cases matching results.

Then, in the features matching process, each partial-match relevant case features are to be matched with the new case features independently to classify the features of each case to no-match, partial-match and perfect-match features as shown in Fig. 2.

The evaluation to the performance of the cases selection, retrieval and similarity measurement handled by the illustrated fuzzy logic approach, the iSRS system runs over 64 cases with the possibility of showing the three situations (no-match, partial-match and complete-match). The approach is able to filter out 40% of the irrelevant cases as the cases similarity level remains within the no-match range. The framework is able to reduce similar cases to approximately 5%. As a result, the inspection quality of the iSRS system is clearly improved. The inspection accuracy is increased by 11.6% on average in the performed 10 tests comparing with the original system.

5   Conclusion and Future Work

This paper has contributed to finding and implementing a new framework that is used in the Inspection of the Software Requirements Specification (iSRS) System. In this framework, both Case-Based Reasoning (CBR) and fuzzy logic are used in the inspection process. The CBR is used in reasoning the SRS quality by benefiting from experiences that are stored in its case base. Moreover, fuzzy logic makes the CBR and the overall system more effective by assisting in the classifications of the cases in the case base in finding the most similar cases that match the new given problem case. Hence, the accuracy of the Retrieve, Reuse, Revise and Retain steps within the CBR is increased. As part of future prospects, experiments with other techniques in refining iSRS performance are to be studied.

Acknowledgements. This project is partially supported by University Tenaga Nasional (UNI-TEN) under the UNIIG Grant Scheme No. J510050772.

References

1. Galin, D.: Software Quality Assurance: From Theory to Implementation. Pearson Education Limited, London (2004)
2. Wilson W.M., Rosenberg, L.H., Hyatt, L.E.: Automated analysis of requirement specifications. In: Proceedings of the 19th International Conference on Software Engineering, pp. 161–171. ACM (1997)
3. Mat Jani, H., Mostafa, S.A.: Implementing case-based reasoning technique to software requirements specifications quality analysis. IJACT: Int. J. Advance. Comput. Technol. **3**(1), 23–31 (2011)
4. Stephen, E., Mit, E.: Framework for measuring the quality of software specification. J. Telecommun. Electron. Comput. Eng. (JTEC) **9**(2–10), 79–84 (2017)
5. Nordin, A., Zaidi, N.H.A., Mazlan, N.A.: Measuring software requirements specification quality. J. Telecommun. Electron. Comput. Eng. (JTEC) **9**(3–5), 123–128 (2017)
6. Firesmith, D.G.: Specifying good requirements. J. Object Technol. **2**(4), 77–87. http://www.jot.fm/issues/issue_2003_07/column7/
7. Fitzgerald, B., Stol, K.J.: Continuous software engineering: a roadmap and agenda. J. Syst. Softw. **123**, 176–189 (2017)
8. Boegh, J.: A new standard for quality requirements. IEEE Softw. **25**(2), 57–63 (2008)
9. Daramola, O., Moser, T., Sindre, G., Biffl, S.: Managing implicit requirements using semantic case-based reasoning research preview. In: Regnell, B., Damian, D. (eds.) REFSQ 2012. LNCS, vol. 7195, pp. 172–178. Springer, Heidelberg (2012). https://doi.org/10.1007/978-3-642-28714-5_15
10. Bonissone P.P., Ramon L.M.: F4.3 Fuzzy Case-Based Reasoning Systems. Citeseer (2008). http://www.mendeley.com/research/f4-3-fuzzy-casebased-reasoning-systems/. Accessed 9 Aug 2011

11. John Yen, C.T., Tiao, W.A.: House of quality: a fuzzy logic-based requirements analysis. Elsevier, Eur. J. Oper. Res. **117**, 340–354 (1999)
12. Karsak, E.E.: Fuzzy multiple objective programming framework to prioritize design requirements in quality function deployment. Elsevier, Comput. Ind. Eng. **47**, 149–163 (2004)
13. Sen, C., Baracl, H.: Fuzzy quality function deployment based methodology for acquiring enterprise software selection requirements. Elsevier, Exp. Syst. Appl. **37**, 3415–3426 (2010)
14. Dhote, P.C.: Handling ambiguous data during requirements verification using fuzzy logic. Int. J. Comput. Sci. Commun. **2**(1), 105–107 (2011)
15. Asghar, S., Umar, M.: Requirement engineering challenges in development of software applications and selection of customer-off-the-shelf (COTS) components. Int. J. Softw. Eng. (IJSE) **1**(2) (2010)
16. Inayat, I., Salim, S.S., Marczak, S., Daneva, M., Shamshirband, S.: A systematic literature review on agile requirements engineering practices and challenges. Comput. Hum. Behav. **51**, 915–929 (2015)
17. Mostafa, S.A., Mustapha, A., Mohammed, M.A., Ahmad, M.S., Mahmoud, M.A.: A fuzzy logic control in adjustable autonomy of a multi-agent system for an automated elderly movement monitoring application. Int. J. Med. Inform. **112**, 173–184 (2018)
18. Mostafa, S.A., Ahmad, M.S., Firdaus, M.: A soft computing modeling to case-based reasoning implementation. Int. J. Comput. Appl. **47**(7), 14–21 (2012)
19. Ghani, M.K.A., Mohammed, M.A., Ibrahim, M.S., Mostafa, S.A., Ibrahim, D.A.: Implementing an efficient expert system for services center management by fuzzy logic controller. J. Theor. Appl. Inf. Technol. **95**(13) (2017)
20. Mostafa, S.A., Darman, R., Khaleefah, S.H., Mustapha, A., Abdullah, N., Hafit, H.: A general framework for formulating adjustable autonomy of multi-agent systems by fuzzy logic. In: Jezic, G., Chen-Burger, Y.-H.J., Howlett, R.J., Jain, L.C., Vlacic, L., Šperka, R. (eds.) KES-AMSTA-18 2018. SIST, vol. 96, pp. 23–33. Springer, Cham (2019). https://doi.org/10.1007/978-3-319-92031-3_3
21. Mohammed, M.A., et al.: Genetic case-based reasoning for improved mobile phone faults diagnosis. Comput. Electr. Eng. **71**, 212–222 (2018)

Author Index